G L E N C O E

Health

A Guide to Wellness

Second Edition

Mary Bronson Merki, Ph.D.
Don Merki, Ph.D.

GLENCOE

McGraw-Hill

New York, New York   Columbus, Ohio   Mission Hills, California   Peoria, Illinois

Illustrators
Barbara Barnett
Werner Eisen
Jeanne Koelling
Judy Morley
Betsy Paley
Phyllis Rockne
Charles Scogins
Gretchen Shields
Sally Shimizu
Diana Thewlis

Photographers
Sharon Beals
Victor Budnik
Garry Gay
Stephen McBrady
Nick Pavloff
Nita Winter

Contents

Part Three. You and the Environment

Health Handbook

Features

Health Update

Breakthroughs in Health Medicine

Health Careers

Drawings, Tables, Charts

Part One.   You and Your Health

U N I T

1

YOUR PERSONAL HEALTH AND FITNESS

Health and Wellness

Your body is a complex collection of parts that work together. How well these parts work depends greatly on the day-to-day care that you give your body. The physical, mental, and social choices that you make affect how healthy you will be.

After studying this chapter, you will be able to:
- define health and health education,
- define wellness,
- explain health and wellness in terms of a continuum,
- describe the characteristics of a high level of physical, mental, and social health,
- list the life-style factors that contribute to wellness,
- define fitness in relation to total health,
- summarize the benefits of exercise for physical, mental, and social health,
- identify ways to include more activity in one's daily life.

1. What Is Health Education?

This book focuses on you and the interrelationship of your level of health and the way you live. As you read through the book, you will gain a better understanding of the importance of good health. You will see that many factors, most of which are within your control, influence your health. Hopefully, you will apply what you learn to your own health by taking a more active role in caring for yourself.

Health Has Many Meanings

First, we must begin by defining the terms *health* and *health education*:

- **Health** is *the state of total physical, mental, and social well-being, not just freedom from sickness or ailments.*
- **Health education** is *the providing of health information in such a way that it influences people to take positive action about their health.*

Your health concerns everything about you. Health is **dynamic**, meaning that it is *always changing*. You experience different levels of health from day to day.

Your personal level of health affects how you look, feel, and act. It affects your attitudes and performance in work. It also affects how successful you are in your relationships with others. Do you ever evaluate your health on the basis of your ability to carry out your daily routine? Would you describe yourself as being in good health?

Your health stems not only from inherited factors, but from what you do to keep yourself healthy.

Many people associate only sickness and health, thinking that if they are not sick, they are healthy. One reason people tend to think of health in terms of physical well-being or illness is because the physical side of a person is the easiest aspect of health to see and to check on. You can tell by looking to see if a person is clean, is neatly dressed, or is sickly. You know when you have a cold, a fever, or a broken bone. However, being healthy means much more than not being sick. It means more than just being physically fit.

Wellness and Health

An important concept is now being used to describe good health. This concept is called *wellness,* and it considers health in broad terms. **Wellness** is *a way of living each day that includes choices and decisions based on healthy attitudes.* Wellness is dynamic because it is constantly changing.

Health and Wellness Continuum

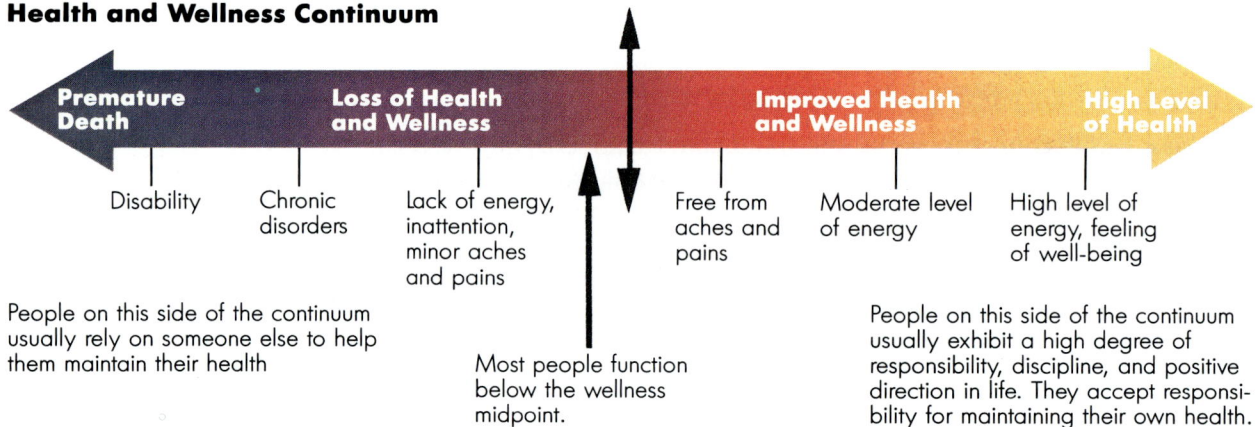

| Premature Death | Loss of Health and Wellness | Improved Health and Wellness | High Level of Health |

| Disability | Chronic disorders | Lack of energy, inattention, minor aches and pains | Free from aches and pains | Moderate level of energy | High level of energy, feeling of well-being |

People on this side of the continuum usually rely on someone else to help them maintain their health

Most people function below the wellness midpoint.

People on this side of the continuum usually exhibit a high degree of responsibility, discipline, and positive direction in life. They accept responsibility for maintaining their own health.

You can use the health continuum to assess your levels of physical, mental, and social health. Where are you on the continuum for each of them?

Study the Health and Wellness Continuum above. A **continuum** (kon-**tin**-you-um) is *a chart showing the progress of an activity, movement, or cycle.* It will help you to better understand the broader meaning of health.

The continuum illustrates that health is not an "either/or" condition, for it has many levels. Why do you think many people function below the wellness midpoint? What can you do to accept more responsibility for your health?

Aspects of Your Health

As you can see, you have much more to consider than physical well-being when you are discussing and evaluating your level of health. You must also consider the mental and social sides of your health. To obtain a complete picture of your health, you must take into consideration all sides of it.

■ **Physical health.** Physical health includes the care of your body and your body's ability to meet the demands of daily living.

- **Mental health.** This may be the hardest area of health to describe. The major focus of mental health is you, as a person, and your feelings about yourself. Perhaps the most important component of mental health is the ability to like and accept yourself. You must want to learn new information and skills, as well as to develop your thinking ability.

  Mental health includes being able to express your emotions in an acceptable, healthy way. Finally, your ability to face the problems and stresses of day-to-day living is an important part of mental health.
- **Social health.** Since we are all social beings, we need other people. People enrich our lives. Social health involves the way you get along with others, the ability to make friends and to keep them, being able to work and play in a cooperative way, and seeking and lending support when necessary.

Your Health Triangle

A direct relationship exists among physical, mental, and social health. For example, your physical health is changed by your level of mental health, just as your mental health is affected by your level of social health. Have you ever been very tired or hungry? How did that feeling affect the way you acted toward others? Did it affect how you did your work?

A Balanced Health Triangle

An Unbalanced Health Triangle

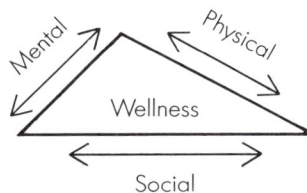

Equally paying attention to your physical, mental, and social development will help you to function at a high degree of wellness.

Consider these sides of your health in terms of an equilateral triangle. To achieve and maintain a high level of health, you must develop all three sides—physical, mental, and social. The sides do not develop at the same rate. However, it is easy to see how your health triangle can become unbalanced if you do not work to develop any one of the sides.

As you read further, you will learn ways to judge your level of health and ways to help improve each side of your health triangle.

CHECK YOURSELF

1. What is the relationship between health and wellness?
2. Explain what is meant by a health continuum.
3. Define physical, mental, and social health.
4. What is meant by the health triangle?

Caring for your health is primarily your responsibility. With that responsibility you have an opportunity to promote and maintain a high level of health. Let us look at some of the ways to do this.

Steps to Responsible Health

The **first step** in taking responsibility for your health is to *determine how much you know about your health*. This information is important in determining your own level of health.

The **second step** is to *obtain accurate information about how to stay healthy or improve your health*.

The **third step** is to *take action*. This can be done in three ways:

- Set some personal, realistic goals for yourself.
- Become actively involved in keeping yourself healthy.
- Develop a positive attitude toward healthy living. That is, make wellness a part of your life-style.

How are these boys functioning at a high degree of wellness—physically, mentally, and socially?

The exciting point to remember is that you are in control of all the steps to personal health. *You* can make changes and improve. *You* can work toward a high level of wellness.

What Is Your Level of Wellness?

On a separate sheet of paper, indicate each statement that is true for you. Count how many statements are true for you in each area and refer to the scoring directions below.

Physical Health 6 fair

- I seldom feel tired or run-down.
- I get at least 8 hours of sleep per night.
- I regularly use dental floss and a soft toothbrush.
- I do not use tobacco.
- I keep within 5 pounds of my ideal weight.
- I use stairs instead of escalators or elevators whenever possible.
- I do at least 20 minutes of aerobic exercise at least three times a week.
- I eat breakfast every day.
- I do not use alcohol or nonmedicinal drugs.
- I take at least 10 minutes each day to relax completely.
- I limit my dietary intake of refined sugar and salt.
- I eat a balanced diet that includes a variety of foods.

Mental Health 10 Good

- I ask for help when I need it.
- I am happy most of the time.
- Sometimes I like to be alone.
- I can name three things I do well.
- I feel okay about crying and allow myself to do so.
- I give others sincere compliments.
- I can accept compliments.
- I listen to and think about constructive criticism.

- I am able to say no to people without feeling guilty.
- I can be satisfied with my effort if I have done my best.
- I express my thoughts and feelings to others.
- I have at least one hobby or interest I pursue and enjoy.

Social Health 11 Good

- I meet people easily.
- I am comfortable entering into conversation with new acquaintances.
- I continue to participate in an activity even though I don't get my way in an argument.
- I have at least one or two close friends.
- When working in a group, I can accept other people's ideas and suggestions.
- I can say no to my friends if they are doing something I do not want to do.
- I can accept the differences in my friends and classmates.
- I usually have success making friends with females my age.
- I usually have success making friends with males my age.
- I am comfortable carrying on a conversation with an adult.
- If I have a problem with someone, I try to work it out.
- I avoid gossiping about people.

Scoring: The highest possible score for each area is 12. If your total score is 10 to 12, your level of health in that area is *very good*. A score of 7 to 9 is *good*, 4 to 6 is *fair*, and below 4 indicates a general area you may *need to be working on*.

LIFE MANAGEMENT SKILL

Self-Assessment

Being able to accurately assess yourself by identifying strengths and weaknesses is the first step to self-improvement. Self-assessment is a skill that must be practiced over and over. It is an ongoing process. Based on such assessments, a person can better set personal goals. Use the *Improving Yourself* box on this page to help you with this life management skill.

Remember that your level of health in each of the health triangle areas will vary from day to day. We have all experienced low days when nothing seemed to go right, just as we have all had days when things went very well. However, if your overall level of health is high, you will be better able to cope with those days that are low.

Health Promotion

Recent discoveries in medicine have helped to wipe out many of the diseases that killed people 30 years ago. Our life expectancy today is almost twice as long as it was for our ancestors at the turn of the century. Yet, the way we live today poses new threats to our health and our lives. Millions of people get sick, become disabled, or die each year because of the way they live. Many of these deaths could be prevented if people practiced a few simple health habits.

Life-Style Factors

After years of studying many groups of people, experts were able to identify seven behaviors, or habits, that seemed to make a difference in their lives. The people who practiced these habits regularly tended to be healthier and happier, and to live longer. Because these *factors are related to the way people live*, they are called **life-style factors**:

1. between 8 and 9 hours of sleep per night,
2. three meals a day at regular times,
3. no smoking,
4. daily breakfast,
5. moderate aerobic exercise daily, or at least three to four times a week,
6. minimum use of alcohol,
7. maintenance of recommended weight.

IMPROVING YOURSELF

Changing Your Behavior

Pick one of the seven life-style factors that you are not currently practicing daily:

- Set a goal for yourself to practice the health behavior at least four times in the next week.
- Write down at least two

benefits you could gain from practicing the behavior.
- Post your goal and your expected benefits in a visible place in your room. Check your program at the end of the week.

Practicing Basic Health Habits

What affects your decision to practice good health habits? The seven life-style habits may sound simple, but how many do you practice regularly? Why do you think people fail to practice these habits if they know their importance?

Practicing good health habits involves much more than just knowing what to do. Our attitudes about health have a major effect on how we take care of ourselves.

In order to practice good health habits, you must:

1. Believe that there is some benefit for you.
2. Believe that by not practicing good health habits, problems could develop.

Often, we tend to think, "That won't happen to me." As long as we have such an attitude, it is unlikely that we will change a health behavior. Yet 40% of young people between the ages of 11 and 18 are now estimated to have—already present—one or more of the risk factors associated with heart disease, factors that include overweight, high blood pressure, high blood cholesterol, cigarette smoking, or lack of exercise.

Present Behaviors and Your Future

Many of us think and live only in terms of today. We do not relate our present actions to how they will affect us in the future. But the habits you practice now are setting the stage for how healthy or unhealthy you will be in your adult life. At this point in life, it is probably hard for you to give much attention to your health. Teenagers generally tend to be strong and healthy. Their bodies can bounce back from illness. Teenagers don't always see immediate problems from poor health habits.

In order to be motivated to change health behaviors, you must see some personal benefits. In the remainder of this unit, you will learn some of the benefits of good physical health and fitness. You will also learn specific ways for starting a personal fitness program. In later units, you will learn the same things about your mental and social health.

CHECK YOURSELF

1. How do life-style factors affect one's health?
2. Why do people not practice good health habits, despite the conclusive evidence of their importance?
3. Write a summary statement for each of the three steps to responsible health, describing what someone with a high level of health would be doing.
4. Review the three steps to responsible health. Then relate each step to your present level of wellness. What improvements can you make? How can you make them?

3. What Does Total Fitness Mean?

As with the word *health,* many people think of fitness in terms of physical fitness. However, fitness is not limited to the physical. **Fit** or **fitness** means *one is ready.* Fit people are better equipped to handle what they are faced with on a day-to-day basis than are nonfit people.

Of course, physical fitness is a major part of this total fitness, but it is not the only part. Your level of total fitness affects all aspects of your health and life. It affects your physical, mental, and social health. Your level of fitness affects how you sleep, eat, and learn. If you are fit, you look well, you have energy, and you generally feel good about yourself. Maintaining a high level of fitness is a lifelong challenge. *Fitness is more than something you do; it is what you are.*

The Benefits of Being Fit

People who are fit are more at ease within themselves. They tend to be more confident and self-assured. They are physically, mentally, socially, and emotionally prepared for what lies ahead.

Being fit increases the chances of success in what you are doing. Having experienced success, you are more likely to take on new challenges with confidence. Success also enhances one's self-image.

By being fit and doing well, we tend to have more fun at what we are doing. Think of the things that you enjoy doing. Are they things that you do well? What role does fitness play in doing them?

Fitness in the Past

During the period when our country was growing and frontiers were being settled, fitness and exercise were a part of everyday life. In fact, being fit was necessary for survival during those days. Even in the nineteenth and early twentieth centuries, people had so much activity during their workday that they looked for ways to relax.

Then came the age of "labor-saving devices"—inventions that ranged from automobiles and dishwashers to electric shavers and hair dryers. Thousands of mechanical and electronic inventions made life so easy for many Americans that their lives, for the most part, became sedentary (**sed**-en-ter-ee). **Sedentary** living means *inactive* living, a way of life that is mostly spent sitting down.

Medical researchers and scientists have found that the sedentary way of life is not good for your health. In fact, it can actually be a health hazard. Studies conducted by the National Aeronautics and Space Administration (NASA) found that for every three days that a person is immobile, the person loses one-fifth of his or her remaining maximal muscle strength.

This NASA astronaut is checking his heart rate while exercising.

In addition, immobility negatively affects the circulatory, digestive, and nervous systems. These findings, along with the abundance of new information about disease prevention, have begun to change our attitudes toward fitness.

Fitness Today

Our country experienced a fitness boom during the 1970s that is still growing today. Jogging trails and walking and bicycle paths have been developed in neighborhoods all over the country. At almost any time of day, you can see people of all ages outside exercising. In fact, today, 70 million Americans make exercise a part of their regular schedule.

Aerobic exercise and dance classes, Jazzercise® and weight-training programs have become very popular. More and more people are participating in **lifetime sports,** such as tennis, swimming, and softball. These sports are *ones that can be enjoyed and participated in throughout life.*

As we become more used to labor-saving devices, exercise becomes less a part of our normal routine. For this reason, it is important to plan regular times for structured exercise. But there are many ways during the day to build more physical activity into your routine. Evaluate your own choices throughout the day. Do you choose the more active way to go about your life?

CHECK YOURSELF

1. What is the difference between physical fitness and total fitness?
2. What are three benefits of being fit?
3. What are the health implications of a sedentary life?
4. What are some indications that Americans are becoming more fitness-oriented?

We have looked at health as being total because it involves the physical, mental, and social sides of the individual. Exercise is the primary contributor to good physical fitness. It also contributes to mental and social health.

Exercise for the Body

Exercise contributes to the physical side of your health by building a strong, durable body. Exercise can also help to reduce the feeling of **chronic fatigue,** or *constant fatigue, stiffness, and lack of coordination*. It can help to improve your sense organ functions and motor responses. **Sense organ functions** refers to *your ability to use your senses to their optimal, or fullest, levels*.

IMPROVING YOURSELF

Exercising Throughout the Day

Do you

- Stand rather than sit whenever possible?
- Sit up rather than lie down whenever possible?
- Walk or ride a bike when possible, rather than ride in a car?
- Use stairs rather than an elevator or an escalator?
- Walk around (pace) rather than stand still?
- Use body power rather than a machine whenever possible?

These behaviors sound simple, but they all add up to an increase in physical activity. Be aware of times throughout your day that something more active could take the place of your normal routine.

Scoring: If you answered yes to *all* of the above, you are doing a good job of including activity in your day. If you answered yes to *three* or fewer, you may be too inactive.

Your Nervous System

Exercise contributes to the functioning of your nervous system by tuning it to a high level, allowing for more skillful body movements. Exercise can improve your **reaction time.** *You begin to respond more quickly to stimuli*. As exercise leads to a more finely tuned, efficient nervous system, your overall mental performance improves.

Your Respiratory System

With regular exercise, your respiratory system begins to work slower and more efficiently so that you take fewer but deeper breaths. Your **lung capacity,** *the amount of air that you can take in with a single breath,* increases. Less oxygen is needed for a given amount of work as your fitness level improves.

Your Circulatory System

Regular exercise is of great help to the heart. The heart is a muscle, and like any muscle, the more it is used, the stronger it gets. A strong heart can pump blood more efficiently than a weak one, so more work is done with less effort.

Exercise and Weight Control

One out of every three Americans is overweight. Sedentary living is as much to blame for this situation as is too much food.

Your Metabolism

Basal metabolism (**bay**-sul meh-**tab**-oh-liz-um) is *the absolute minimum amount of energy required to keep up the life process in your body.* We get our energy from food, and the energy value of food is measured in *units of heat* called **calories.** Your metabolic rate increases during exercise. This means that during exercise you burn up more calories than when you are at rest. Calories are the essential elements of weight control.

A Health Student Asks . . .

ON EXERCISE AND APPETITE

"Is it true that exercise can cut down a person's appetite? It seems like exercise would make a person hungrier since so much energy is used."

Yes, it is quite true that exercise slows the appetite. Some people still think that exercising will increase their appetite, leading to a possible gain in weight. Hunger occurs when the *blood sugar level* drops. If you maintain a regular exercise schedule, your blood sugar level will remain stable. This is because the muscles begin using more fat than sugar for their fuel.

The number of calories you burn depends on the nature of the activity. But did you know that the benefit of physical activity remains even after you stop exercising, especially if it is strenuous exercise? Your metabolic rate takes some time to return to normal, so during that time you are still burning more calories than normal. It has been shown that the *metabolic rate* is about 25% higher than the *resting rate* four hours after exercise.

Your Weight

Much has been written about dieting, weight reduction, obesity, and exercise. There is more about weight control in Chapter 9. However, here, suffice it to say that:

- If you take in fewer calories than you burn, you lose weight.
- If you take in more calories than you burn, you gain weight.

If you take in more calories than you can use, the excess is stored in the body as *fat*. One pound of fat is equal to about 3,500 calories.

Exercise is helpful in the prevention of obesity (o-**bee**-si-tee). **Obesity** is *the excessive amount of fat in the body.* This condition has been associated with heart disease and can be a problem among people in all age groups. Vigorous exercise can help reduce body fat and contribute to weight reduction.

Your Powers of Recuperation

Exercise can help the body's protection against disease by building resistance through improved fitness. A strong, toned body is capable of **recuperation** (re-**koo**-purr-ray-shun), or *restoring itself*, at a faster rate than a body that is overweight or in poor condition.

Exercise is one of the best active ways of keeping the mind, as well as the body, functioning at a high degree of wellness. Why is that so?

Exercise and Your Mental and Social Health

Some people in sedentary work for long periods of time find that an exercise break refreshes them and leads to more productive work time. Many people have found that after a long day of school and work, exercise gives them an energy boost. They are less fatigued during the evening hours. Feeling better has a positive effect on their overall attitude.

Mental Benefits

Exercise can be a healthy outlet for tension, anger, or frustrations. Exercise offers some people a form of relaxation. Vigorous exercise also produces chemicals in the body that act as natural antidepressants. Exercising can also help you to think more clearly because blood is carrying more oxygen to the brain. Many of these benefits from exercise are individual and are greatly affected by a person's mental attitude.

SPORTS MEDICINE

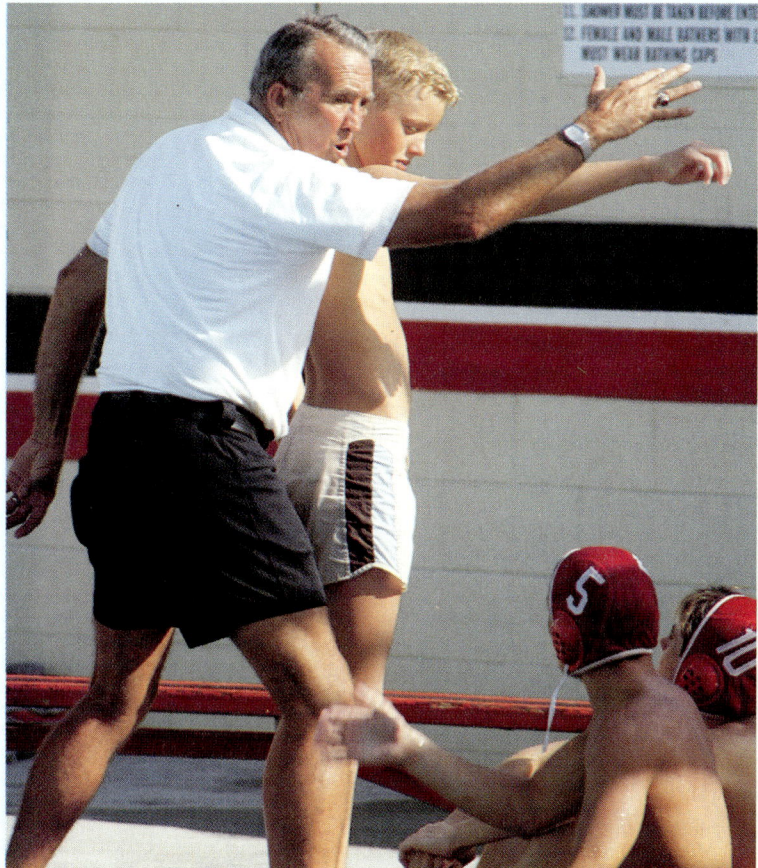

The tremendous sports and fitness boom in the United States has created a totally new area of study called sports medicine. **Sports medicine** is *the study of the scientific and medical aspects of exercise and athletics.* The knowledge gained from this study is used for the improvement and maintenance of the human body in physical work, exercise, and athletics, and for the prevention and treatment of disease and injuries related to exercise and athletics.

Specific areas of study are the relation of exercise to bodily health, sports psychology and sociology, exercise and athletics, athletic training, athletic medicine, adult fitness, and cardiorespiratory rehabilitation. These are all part of sports medicine.

Sports medicine is so new that few programs of study are listed under this title in colleges and universities. However, if you are interested in a career in this broad area or in one of the specific areas within sports medicine, contact the American College of Sports Medicine. This organization includes over 10,000 members, of which 40% are physicians. It is an organization representing many differ-

ent fields of study, but it is very concerned with the physical, mental, and social reactions of people involved in exercise.

The organization's office will be able to direct you toward the appropriate departments within colleges and

universities, where you may find more specific information on a career in sports medicine or a related area.

American College of Sports Medicine
1440 Monroe Street
Madison, WI 53706

Social Benefits

Some exercise programs can benefit the social side of your health. Through participation in organized exercise activities, you have an opportunity to meet new people. Many people find that exercising with a friend or in a group makes the workout more enjoyable. It can also help to motivate a person to continue with an exercise program.

Again, group and solo exercising are up to the individual. Some people enjoy being alone during a workout and see the ''alone time'' as an important benefit to exercising.

CHECK YOURSELF

1. What are three ways in which exercise contributes to your physical health?
2. What is the relationship of exercises to basal metabolism?
3. How does exercise contribute to your mental well-being?

CHAPTER 1   Review

CHAPTER SUMMARY

■ Health is the state of total physical, mental, and social well-being, not just freedom from sickness or ailments.

■ There is nothing you do during the day that is not in some way affected by your level of health (for example, studying for a test), or that does not affect your level of health (e.g., lack of sleep).

■ Wellness is a way of living each day that includes choices and decisions based on healthy attitudes and values.

■ You have a great deal of control over your personal level of wellness, and the daily choices you make affect your health now and in the future.

■ You can work to improve your health and to maintain a high level of fitness by practicing good health habits.

■ With the many labor-saving devices available today, you must make a more conscious effort to include activity in your life.

■ Your choices affect your total fitness, and a high level of overall fitness enables you to better meet the stresses of daily life.

■ Exercise is the major contributor to physical fitness, but it affects your total fitness as well.

■ There are physical, mental, and social health benefits to be had from regular exercise.

REVIEWING WHAT YOU LEARNED

1. Define health and health education.
2. Describe what is meant by *wellness*. How does wellness relate to fitness?
3. You are invited to speak to a fifth grade health class about the importance of good health. List the main points you would stress. How would you help the students to understand the importance of maintaining good health?
4. Explain what a health and wellness continuum is.
5. Define physical, mental, and social health.
6. Explain how physical, mental, and social health relate to one another.
7. Identify the seven basic life-style habits, and describe how they affect your level of health.
8. Summarize the benefits of exercise to one's level of total health.
9. Name three ways in which you can include more activity in your daily life.

CHAPTER VOCABULARY

health	life-style factors	lung capacity
health education	fit	basal metabolism
dynamic	fitness	calories
wellness	sedentary	obesity
continuum	lifetime sports	recuperation
physical health	chronic fatigue	sports medicine
mental health	sense organ functions	
social health	reaction time	

PUTTING VOCABULARY TO USE

On a separate piece of paper, write the following statements. Then supply the missing word or phrase from the chapter vocabulary list. You may use the words more than once.

1. Virtually everything you do in the course of a day affects your _____ in some way. Your _____ is _____, always changing. _____ is a way of living that includes healthy choices and decisions.
2. The level of health of your body is your _____ _____, while health related to your ability to get along with others is your _____ _____. Perhaps the hardest area of health to define is your _____ _____, which deals with your ability to express

emotions, to cope, and to like yourself.
3. As technology gives us more machines to do our work, our lives become more _____, which directly affects our level of _____. In order to maintain a high level of _____, you need to develop a regular _____ program.
4. Many benefits can be gained through a _____ program. As your _____ _____ increases during exercise, you burn more _____, which are the essential elements of weight control.
5. _____, which is a condition resulting from excess body fat, can be controlled through _____ _____.

APPLYING WHAT YOU LEARNED

1. Make a list of 10 things that you do almost every day. Next to each, write a statement indicating how a higher level of fitness would help you in each of the activities. Compare your list of statements with those of other class members.
2. Survey five people. Ask them what health personally means to them. Compare your findings with other members of your class. Do most people think of health in terms of prevention?
3. Make a list of all the labor-saving devices in your home. Find out what was used to accomplish the task before the invention of the labor-saving device. Write a report summarizing how our level of fitness has been affected by three such devices.
4. Find advertisements in magazines or newspapers for equipment that claims to increase physical fitness and well-being. Discuss the claims in class. Do the advertisements contradict one another? In what ways?

5. Write your own advertisement to promote wellness and physical fitness. Include at least five selling points.
6. For one day, keep a list of your activities and choices. Note all the ways in which you could add more activity to your normal day. Select at least two of these and make an effort to practice them for three days. Then evaluate your performance.
7. In your view, what invention during the Industrial Revolution of the 18th and 19th centuries had the greatest impact on the daily life and health of the people? Why?

FOCUS ON WELLNESS

Your level of health and wellness affects every aspect of your day-to-day life. Working to keep yourself fit reinforces in you and others the fact that your health is important to you. *Taking personal responsibility for my level of wellness means that I . . .*

Your Personal Fitness Program

Exercise can relieve stress, control weight, clear the
mind, and promote one's self-esteem. Exercise takes time
and discipline, but it is well worth it. It not only keeps you
in shape but may actually be a cure for some health problems.

After studying this chapter, you will be able to:
- explain the basic components of physical fitness,
- assess your personal level of fitness,
- describe steps to follow in starting a personal fitness program,
- identify parts of a workout, and describe why each part is important to overall fitness,
- distinguish among isometric, isotonic, and isokinetic exercises,
- describe benefits of aerobic exercise,
- describe the most common injuries that occur during exercise,
- explain ways to prevent injury during exercise.

Juan is the school's star soccer player. He moves up and down the field with speed and grace. Juan can outmaneuver almost any other player. Yet Juan cannot touch his toes or reach his hands to the ground.

Karen has competed on the balance beam since she was eight years old. Last year, she won the city title for her event. Yet when Karen is late for the bus, she gets completely out of breath after running half a block.

Jerry runs four miles every day. He also runs in 10K races all over the state. Yet Jerry cannot do 25 sit-ups or push-ups.

Would it surprise you to know that the physical fitness program of each of these students is lacking?

The Basic Components of Physical Fitness

Physical fitness can be defined as *the ability to carry out daily tasks easily and to have enough reserve energy to respond to unexpected demands placed upon you.* Physical fitness includes three basic components:

1. **Flexibility.** This is the range of movement of the joints.
2. **Muscle strength and endurance.** *Strength* refers to the greatest amount of work your muscles can do at a given time. *Endurance* refers to how well a group of muscles can keep performing over a period of time without causing undue fatigue.
3. **Heart and lung endurance.** This refers to the ability of the heart and lungs to deliver needed oxygen to the body during exercise, without causing undue stress, and then quickly return to a resting rate.

Assessing Flexibility

Flexibility is specific to each moving joint. For this reason, it is difficult to measure total body flexibility. However, the following test will give you a general measure of your level of fitness in this area. You should remember two important points when taking this flexibility test:

- *First*, do some light stretching to warm up your muscles. This will help prevent injury from too vigorous movement.
- *Second*, avoid quick, jerking movements. Your reach should be gradual and slow.

Now follow these directions to find your body flexibility:

- Sit on the floor with your legs straight in front of you. Your heels should touch a tape on the floor and be about five inches apart.

**L I F E
MANAGEMENT
S K I L L**

Beginning a Fitness Program

After reading this section, set goals for yourself and develop a plan that covers each of the points discussed in the diagram, "Steps to Begin a Fitness Program," page 22. All goals should begin with trying to improve your ratings *one* level.

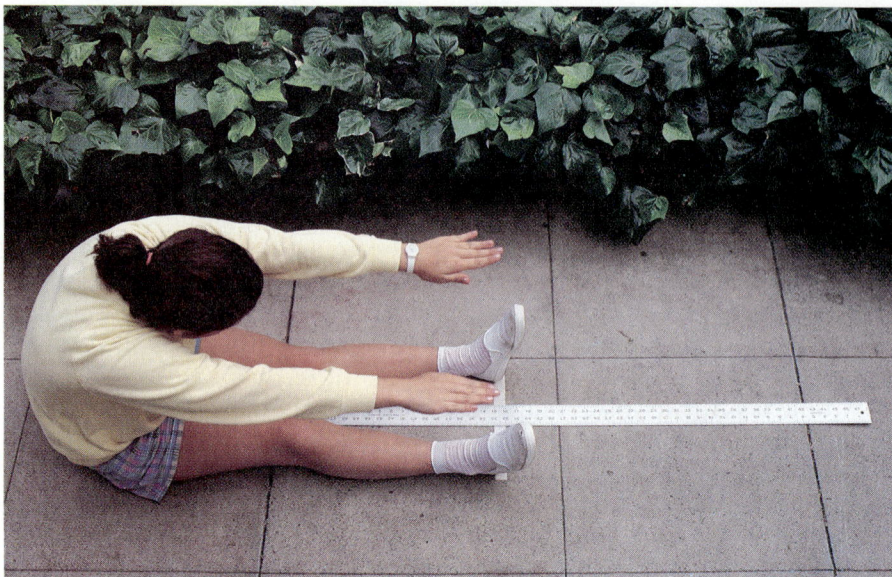

Body Flexibility

Scoring (in inches)

Male	Female	Rating
22 +	23 +	Excellent
17–21	20–23	Good
13–16	17–19	Average
9–12	14–16	Fair
8 or less	13 or less	Poor

- A yardstick is placed between the legs so it rests on the floor with the 36-inch end pointing away from your body. The 15-inch mark on the stick is to be even with your heels. (It is best to tape the yardstick in place so that it does not move.)
- Slowly reach with both hands as far forward as possible and hold this position.
- The score is the most distant point the fingertips reach on the yardstick in the best of three trials.

Assessing Muscle Strength and Endurance

Muscle strength and endurance has little to do with your height and weight. It has everything to do with how fit you are.

Leg Muscle Strength

Leg Muscle Strength

Scoring

Distance less than your own height—*poor*

Distance equal to your own height—*fair*

Distance between 2 and 4 inches (3 to 6 centimeters) more than your own height—*good*

Distance about 5.9 inches (8.75 centimeters) more than your own height—*excellent*

The standing broad jump measures your leg muscle strength:

- From a starting point, bend your knees and jump forward, landing with your weight on both feet.
- Measure your jump and compare your distance with your height.

Muscle Endurance

Test your muscle endurance with the one-minute sit-up test. You will need a stopwatch and a partner:

- Start by lying on your back with the knees slightly bent. Your partner should hold your ankles for support.

- With your hands behind your head, do as many sit-ups as you can in one minute.
- Return to full starting position with your back to the floor in between each sit-up.
- Be sure you do not hold your breath during the test. Breathe freely.
- Your partner should keep the time and your sit-up count.

Muscle Endurance

Scoring (number of situps in one minute)

Male	Female	
40 +	30 +	Excellent
33–39	24–29	Good
29–32	18–24	Average
21–28	11–17	Fair
Less than 21	Less than 11	Poor

Assessing Heart and Lung Endurance

This three-minute step test will test your heart and lung fitness:

- Using a locker sturdy bench, step up and down for three minutes.
- Fully extend each leg as you step. Step up with your right foot, then your left. Step down with your right foot first. Stepping should be continuous.
- Step at the rate of 24 steps per minute.
- Immediately after the three minutes, sit down and relax without talking.
- Find your pulse—either on your wrist or on the side of your neck—and count for one minute. This count gives you your **pulse recovery rate,** which is *the rate at which your heart beats following activity.*

Pulse Recovery Rate

Scoring (number of heartbeats)

70–80	Excellent
81–105	Good
106–119	Average
120–130	Fair
131 +	Poor

CHECK YOURSELF

1. Define physical fitness.
2. What two important points should you remember before taking a body flexibility test?
3. Define pulse recovery rate.

2. Beginning an Exercise Program

You have learned what exercise does for the body and its impact on your level of fitness. You have also had an opportunity to determine your level of physical fitness. Now you are ready to plan an exercise program to improve or maintain your fitness level.

Starting Out

There are many points to consider when planning an exercise program. The first and most important is to recognize that a personal exercise program may require some changes in your life. It will require a commitment on your part. Other points to remember are:

- Begin slowly with a plan.
- Set realistic personal goals.
- Be specific in what you want to accomplish.
- Reward yourself for your progress.
- Your exercise program should not become highly competitive, so try to avoid comparing yourself with others.
- Your goal should be for *personal* fitness, because your body system has its own unique needs and capabilities.

Steps to Begin a Fitness Program

Step 1 *Tune in to what you know.* Become aware of your own behaviors—how you spend your free time, how much physical activity you build into your day.

Step 2 *Set your own personal goals.* Be specific and realistic in what you want to accomplish. *Example:* I will begin a walking program by walking 1½ miles each evening before dinner. My goal is to be walking three miles by the end of the third week.

Step 3 *Alter your environment to reinforce what you are trying to do.* Be aware of and change situations that trigger the behaviors you want to change. Set up situations that will encourage you to participate in activities you want to do more often.

Step 4 *Take things one step at a time.* Practice new behaviors regularly. Do not attempt to make too many changes at one time. Give yourself at least three weeks to see improvment in any one area.

Step 5 *Be good to yourself.* Reward yourself for your progress. Positive feedback from within yourself is a strong force to keep going.

Step 6 *Commit yourself to long-term changes.* Change in fitness level takes time and effort. Fitness is not a fad.

Step 7 *Find and associate with people who believe in and practice what you are doing.* They provide encouragement and can reinforce what you are doing.

Look at the "Steps to Begin a Fitness Program" on page 22. It is an example of one kind of plan for developing a successful program for yourself. What do you think are the key elements in the steps that would encourage you to make a successful effort?

What Exercise Should You Do?

Choose exercises that are appropriate for the location in which you live. The available facilities and weather are important considerations. You also need to consider any physical problems or limitations you may have. Seek medical advice, especially if you have not been exercising at all or if you have any health problems.

As you consider what exercise to do, it is important to pick something you enjoy. It is unlikely that you will continue an exercise activity that you do not enjoy or cannot do very well. In addition, consider exercise that you already do during the day. You may walk briskly to and from classes, so you might want to pick an exercise that does not involve walking.

By developing a regular plan of exercise, you prepare yourself for dealing more effectively with the problems and challenges of daily living. You will look and feel better. As you begin to improve your level of fitness, you will find that the feelings of tiredness that may have been present in the past will gradually diminish.

Your body needs exercise just as it needs food. Planning for exercise in your daily routine is just as important to your body as meal planning.

By developing these exercise habits now, you will find that they will become part of your life as an adult. You will find yourself continuing to enjoy activities that others are not able to enjoy because you have chosen to take care of yourself. More than likely, you will live longer because people who take care of their bodies are less likely to develop poor health and disease.

When to Exercise

It is best to find a regular time during the day to exercise. This way exercise becomes a part of your routine. It is best not to exercise after eating. If you exercise on a full stomach, more blood will be diverted to the skeletal muscles, depriving the stomach of oxygen. This can cause stomach cramps or nausea.

CHECK YOURSELF

1. Explain what the three components of physical fitness are.
2. What should you consider in selecting exercises for your fitness program?
3. Why should you exercise on an empty stomach?

Every exercise program should begin with a warm-up and end with a cool down. There is very good reason for including both phases around the actual workout.

Warming Up

Warming up is *activity that stretches the muscles, preparing them for the exertion that is to come.* Hardworking muscles tend to shorten, making them easier to pull. Warming up helps to increase the elasticity of muscles and tendons. Stretching can help prevent strains and pulls.

Warm-ups also allow your pulse rate to increase gradually to its target rate (page 26). A sudden increase puts unnecessary strain on the heart and the blood vessels. Have you ever been to a sporting event and seen athletes run out and immediately start playing? Probably not, because their warm-ups are quite extensive.

Warm-ups should begin with some large muscle stretching. Stretches should be slow and smooth, not jerky. These exercises are good for improving flexibility. Research indicates that a good warm-up readies the joints for action by increasing the flow of the fluid that lubricates our joints.

You will find various basic warm-up exercises on pages HB2–HB4 of your *Health Handbook.*

Warming up and cooling down are "musts" for any successful daily exercise program.

The Cool Down

Just as your body needs to be readied for increased activity, it needs to be gradually returned to a less active state. During exercise, an increased amount of blood is pumped to the heart with the help of contractions of large leg muscles that pull against the veins. If the leg muscles relax suddenly, **pooling** may result. *The blood will collect in your extremities instead of getting back to the heart.* The heart is still pumping hard, but no blood is returning to it. Pooling can cause lightheadedness, even fainting.

When you are **cooling down,** you *gradually decrease activity.* Your muscles continue to assist in returning the blood until your pulse rate slows. During cool down, the muscles expel the *toxic* (poisonous) wastes produced by the exercising.

The Basic Cool-Down Technique

The *best* way to cool down is simply to slow down activity. Slower activity should be done for about five minutes, followed by five minutes of stretching. Cooling down adequately occurs when your heart rate is down to within 20 to 30 beats of your regular heart rate.

CHECK YOURSELF

1. Why is a warm-up an important part of your workout?
2. How does the warm-up contribute to physical fitness? How should warm-up exercise be done?
3. What are isometric, isotonic, and isokinetic exercises?

A Health Student Asks . . .

WEIGHT TRAINING

"What do I need to know to plan a weight-training program for myself? I have heard that weight training is a good way to tone muscles and lose weight, but I do not want to develop really big muscles."

Weight-training programs are designed to build muscle strength and endurance. Weight training is a good way to tone muscles. With a consistent weight-training program, you may lose inches as fat becomes muscle. You can expect to firm up your body. However, you may not lose weight. Muscle tissue weighs more than fat tissue.

There are three types of weight programs:

- **Isometric.** This type of exercise involves muscular contraction, but little or no movement of the body part that is stressed. You use muscle tension to build strength. Put the palms of your hands together in front of you and push. That is isometric. Pushing against a wall is another example.
- **Isotonic.** With this type of exercise, you develop strength by repeated movements using weights. Push-ups, pull-ups, and sit-ups are isotonic. Your body serves as the weight.
- **Isokinetic.** This type of exercise involves resistance by muscular effort that moves at a fixed speed, such as pushing and pulling against a hydraulic lever.

During exercise, muscle fibers become thicker and are able to do more work. Eventually, with the repeated same amount of exercise, the muscles reach a limit. For muscles to keep getting stronger, it is necessary that you gradually increase how *often*, how *hard*, or how *long* you use a particular muscle group.

Conditioning programs are reversible. A person in good physical condition can lose much strength and endurance in just two or three weeks of inactivity.

The *exercises that improve basic body movement and muscle strength* are referred to as **anaerobic.** They do not require the body to increase its use of oxygen. These exercises are centered on specific groups of muscles. Training with weights to build up a specific part of the body is an anaerobic exercise.

Brisk walking, jogging, swimming, cycling, and any *nonstop vigorous exercises* are **aerobic** activities. The body has a greater demand for oxygen, so that the muscles have the necessary energy to carry out the activity, and such exercise helps the lungs hold more air.

Aerobic exercises are rhythmic and sustained and use the large muscle groups, particularly those in the hips and legs. As these large muscles contract, they press against the blood vessels, sending increased amounts of blood to the heart. The heart becomes a stronger and more efficient pump.

Aerobics also help the heart to beat slower, while exercising and at rest. The slower the heart rate, the longer the heart muscles can rest between beats.

Aerobic exercise causes the arteries to enlarge and increases the number of capillaries that take blood to the muscles. It also increases the number of oxygen-carrying cells in the blood and improves the ability of the enzymes in your muscles to extract the oxygen from your blood.

Exercises that improve the condition of the heart and lungs must have three characteristics:

■ They must be *brisk,* in that they raise the heart rate and breathing rate.
■ They must be *continuous,* in that they can be done for 15 to 30 minutes without your stopping.
■ They must be *regular,* in that they should be repeated at least three times per week.

KEEPING FIT

How Much Exercise Do You Need?

To Improve Your Level of Fitness: Exercise within your target pulse range for a minimum of 15 minutes, three times a week. The preferred time is 20 to 30 minutes.

To Lose Weight and Body Fat: Exercise within your target pulse range for 30 minutes or longer, four times a week. See the *Health Handbook,* pages HB4–HB6, for information on exercising and loss of calories.

To Help Reduce Depression and Anxiety: Exercise within your target pulse range for 45 minutes to an hour at least three times a week.

Checking How Hard Your Body Is Working

How do you know if you are exercising at a brisk enough level to condition the heart and lungs? The best way to determine your exercise level is to monitor your pulse rate. On page 21, you learned how to check your pulse recovery rate. Now let's determine your **target pulse rate.** That is *the rate at which your heart must work for exercise to be aerobic.* Your target pulse rate is one of the most effective guides for determining how hard to exercise.

Before finding your target pulse rate, you must determine your maximum pulse rate. Simply subtract your age from 220. Your **maximum pulse rate** *is the most your heart should beat per minute.* It is dangerous to work your heart up to this rate.

Determining Your Exercise Level

Age	Maximum pulse rate	Target pulse rate
14	206	144–175
15	205	143–174
16	204	142–173
17	203	141–172
18	202	140–171

Your target pulse rate is a range within which you can and should work for the most benefit from your exercise. Multiply your maximum rate by 70% to get the lower rate. Multiply your maximum rate by 85% to get your upper rate. You now have a range of numbers within which to work. If you are 15 years old and your maximum pulse rate is 205, your target rate is between 143 and 174 beats per minute.

Planning an Aerobic Program

The charts on pages HB5–HB6 of your *Health Handbook* are sample programs for building up a fitness level. The length of time and calories burned are approximate. You will need to monitor your pulse rate to make sure you are working up to your target rate for at least 20 minutes.

Delayed-Onset Muscle Soreness (DOM)

In an aerobic exercise, it is especially important that you begin slowly and build up your endurance. Even if you are in good physical condition, this rule still holds true.

Strenuous, unaccustomed exercise may cause certain muscles to become painful. The pain will usually show up sometime after the exercise, so this condition is called **delayed-onset muscle soreness (DOM).**

DOM is not confined to aerobic or other exercises. It can be the result of any strenuous activity. If you do not get much exercise, even pushing the lawn mower or shoveling snow can bring on DOM.

Anyone starting out on a new exercise program should follow these simple rules:

1. Start your routine slowly, and build up gradually.
2. Do the exercise regularly. Do not try to make up time by cramming too much exercise into one session.
3. In your cooling down, stretch your limbs. Stretching seems to prevent a serious DOM attack.

LIFE MANAGEMENT SKILL

Determining and Maintaining Pulse Rate

Identify your target pulse rate. Find out what it takes to get your pulse in the target range. Run in place for two minutes and take your pulse. If it is not in the target range, continue for two more minutes until the pulse is in target range. Now look at *Keeping Fit* on page 26 to determine how long you must keep the pulse in the target range for specific health benefits. Determine activities you can do to achieve this aim.

The Value of Various Activities for the Heart and Lungs

Column A
High level of conditioning

Cross-country skiing
Uphill hiking
Ice hockey
Jogging
Jumping rope
Rowing
Running in place
Stationary cycling

Column B
Moderate level of conditioning

Bicycling
Downhill skiing
Basketball
Calisthenics
Field hockey
Handball
Racquetball
Soccer
Squash
Swimming
Tennis singles
Walking

Column C
Low level of conditioning

Baseball
Bowling
Football
Golf (on foot or by cart)
Softball
Volleyball

Column A
These exercises are naturally very vigorous. They need to be done at least 20 minutes, three times a week. They promote fitness and contribute to weight control.

Column B
These activities are moderately vigorous, but they can be excellent conditioners if done briskly for at least 30 minutes, three times a week. When done briskly, they offer benefits similar to those activities in column A.

Column C
These activities, though they may be vigorous, are usually not sustained long enough to provide conditioning benefits. They can improve coordination, flexibility, and muscle tone. But they must be combined with activities in column A or B to improve total fitness.

Circuit Training Courses

In order to have young people get used to a regular fitness program, **circuit training courses** are present on some high school campuses. These layouts resemble *obstacle courses that provide for a variety of exercise, utilizing simple equipment spaced around a designed course.*

Sometimes students have taken a leadership role in the construction of circuit courses with minimal expense. Pipes for bars and old telephone poles are the basic items. Details for the construction of such layouts can be secured from the President's Council on Physical Fitness and Sports.

Some circuit training course excercises are performed with the help of (1) the balance beam, (2) the situp bar, (3) the track field, (4) the chinup bar, (5) the step-up blocks, and (6) the gymnast's rings.

The President's Council was established in 1966 to honor young people who demonstrate exceptional physical achievement. The program is designed to:

- motivate young people to develop a high level of physical fitness,
- encourage good testing programs in schools and communities,
- stimulate improvement of health and physical education programs,
- provide more information on the fitness of America's young people.

If you are interested in achieving these awards and attempting to reach these high standards, you can write for information to the President's Council on Physical Fitness and Sports, 450 5th Street, N.W., Washington, DC 20001.

CHECK YOURSELF

1. What is the difference between anaerobic and aerobic exercise?
2. What are the benefits of aerobic exercise?
3. What is a target heart rate? How does it relate to your level of fitness?
4. Are there any justifications for engaging in physical activity that is *not* aerobic?
5. What is delayed-onset muscle soreness (DOM)?

With any movement activity, there is always a risk of accident or injury. There are many ways to prevent the more common injuries associated with exercise. The risk of injury during exercise increases when a person is not in good physical condition or has not sufficiently warmed up. To attempt activities beyond your level of ability also increases the risk of injury.

When the body is not prepared for the demands placed on it, injuries most often occur. Even when people are in good physical condition, there is risk of injury, solely because of the nature of the activity.

The more common injuries that occur from exercise are to the muscular and skeletal systems. This is because movement is fundamental to muscle and joint activity, as well as to exercise. Injury to these areas is often possible when you exercise too long or too hard.

Injuries to the Skeletal System

Sprains and dislocations are the most common injuries of the skeletal system. They involve joints and result from too much stress being placed on a joint. If you experience a sudden blow or twist or stretch, the tissues that join the bones can weaken, pull, or tear.

Bone fractures are less common but are usually more serious than sprains and dislocations. Fractures are discussed in Chapter 15.

Sprains

Have you ever stepped off a curb in the wrong way and twisted your ankle? Sprains can occur as easily as that!

A **sprain**, *a condition caused by a violent, sudden stretching of a joint or ligament*, may be accompanied by severe pain, swelling, and difficulty in moving. The swelling is caused by an increased amount of fluid entering the joint from surrounding membrane.

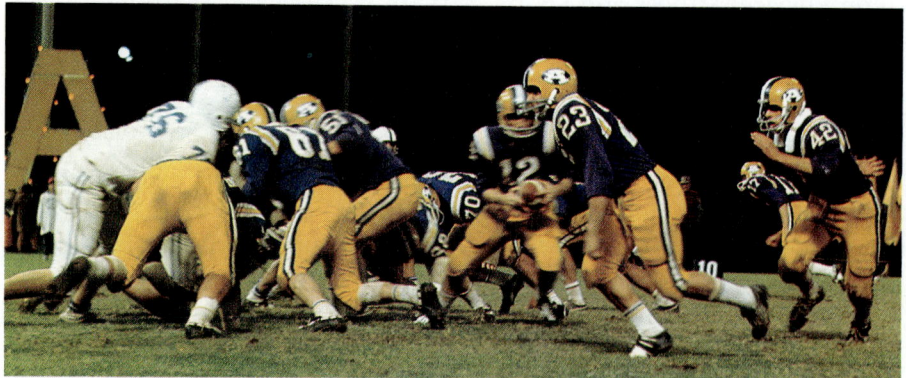

Injuries to the skeletal and muscular systems are not confined to close contact sports. We can receive such injuries while doing regular activities.

Apply cold packs or ice to the sprained area. Elevate the area, if possible, to help control swelling. Cold causes the blood vessels to become narrower, lessening the internal bleeding. Elevating the injured area increases the flow of blood in the veins that lead away from the injury.

Stress on a joint can result in **torn cartilage** (**kart**-uh-ledge) when *the strong connective tissue has been pulled out from the bone.* Surgery is usually required for this injury. Because it can be difficult to distinguish a sprain from a dislocation or a fracture (see Chapter 15), a health professional should check more serious sprains.

Dislocations

A dislocation (dis-low-**kay**-shun) is also a serious injury. A **dislocation** occurs when *the end of a bone is pushed out of its joint.* The ligaments holding the bones are severely stretched and may even be torn. Dislocations are usually quite painful. The joint must be set back into its normal position and held there while the surrounding tissue heals.

Never attempt to replace a dislocation yourself. Joints are surrounded by many tiny blood vessels and nerves. You risk further damage to them if you do not know what you are doing. Keep the injured area very still and seek medical attention right away.

Why does the player stretch before a pitch? What does it have to do with both physical and mental well-being?

Injuries to the Muscular System

Some of the most common injuries to muscles are *bruises, strains, tendinitis, pulled* and *torn muscles,* and a condition called *cramps.*

Bruises and Strains

A **bruise** is *an injury to tissues under the skin.* Bruises usually result from a blow to the muscle. The discoloration is a result of the capillaries breaking and oozing blood. If cold packs are applied immediately, swelling and discoloration will be reduced.

A muscle **strain** results when *muscles are overworked.* Have you ever participated in a strenuous activity you were not used to and then been sore the next day? You experienced muscle strain. Rest and heat to help the muscles relax are the best ways to treat muscle strains. You can prevent some strains by warming up properly and gradually building up your level of exertion. In other words, avoid going all out your first day of exercise.

Tendinitis and Pulled or Torn Muscles

Tendinitis (ten-**duh**-nite-us) occurs when *a tendon*—the connective tissue of the muscles and bones—*is stretched or torn.* The area becomes inflamed. A common example of tendinitis is *tennis elbow.* First, rest to decrease the inflammation and then medicines or physical therapy will help cure this injury.

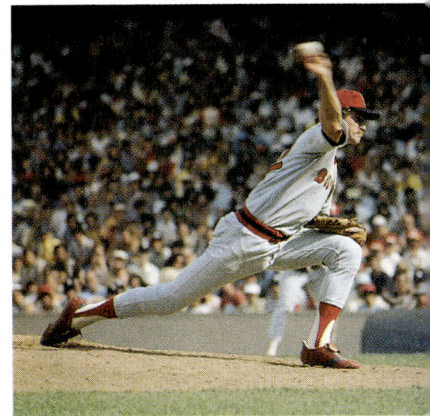

A Common Sports Injury

If someone told you that he or she had a contusion of the quadriceps femoris, what do you think the injury would be? If you guessed a *charley horse,* you are right! A charley horse results from a hard blow to the front of the thigh, which damages the muscle and surrounding tissue. Cold packs and rest are the best care for a charley horse.

This swimmer is correctly massaging a leg cramp.
If you get a muscle cramp in the water, try to get out immediately. If you cannot, knead it carefully and do not panic.

A pulled or torn muscle can cause severe pain and require you to cease your activity. In a **pulled** or **torn muscle,** *the large muscle is separated or torn from its point of attachment.* This can result in damage to the blood vessels that supply nourishment to that muscle. Immediate medical care may be necessary. Cold packs should be put on the muscle area right away.

As with other muscle injuries, lack of warm-up and overexertion of an unprepared muscle are the major causes of a pulled or torn muscle.

Muscle Cramps

Muscle cramps occur when *a muscle contracts tightly and will not relax.* Usually in a bundle of muscles, some fibers are contracting while others are relaxed. When a muscle cramp occurs, all fibers are contracting at the same time. This may be caused by temporary lack of food or oxygen to the muscle. Sometimes cramping occurs as a result of a person's losing large amounts of salt and water through perspiration. Tired, overworked muscles sometimes cramp. Muscles sometimes cramp during very strenuous exercise.

Massaging the muscle area with firm pressure can help a cramp. Moving the muscle or continuing to work it lightly can help to relieve the cramp. Heat can also help the muscle to relax. You can help to prevent cramps by warming up properly and by drinking enough fluids before and during exercise.

Cramps are especially dangerous if they occur while swimming. You could drown before being able to relieve a severe cramp. In such a situation, the most important point to remember is to remain calm and relaxed. Your body will float if you do not panic. It is best to take a deep breath, curl over, and knead the muscle.

Hernias

Hernias (**her**-ne-ahz), or *ruptures,* are weak areas in the muscle sheet supporting various organs in the abdomen. Part of an organ like the intestine may push through this weak area.

Hernias can be caused by lack of warm-up exercises, or by suddenly and improperly picking up heavy objects. Surgery is usually necessary to correct a hernia. For more information on hernias, see Chapter 17.

Weather-Related Risks

Both in hot and cold weather, certain risks and problems can occur. The major ones are *heat cramps, heat exhaustion, heatstroke,* and *frostbite.*

Heat Cramps

Heat cramps come about when *a person loses a large amount of body salt through perspiring and the muscles cramp up.* Massaging them and having the person drink small amounts of salt water every 15 to 20 minutes will usually relieve the condition.

Heat Exhaustion

Heat exhaustion usually results from exercise or overexertion in a hot, humid atmosphere. The *body becomes overheated with the loss of a large amount of water and salt*. The skin becomes pale and moist. A person may also experience dizziness, headache, shortness of breath, and nausea. The person should be moved to a cool place and kept lying down, with the head slightly lowered.

You can prevent heat exhaustion by drinking plenty of fluids before and during exercise. Activities on very hot, humid days should not be too prolonged or strenuous, especially if you are not accustomed to the weather.

Heatstroke

Heatstroke is a more serious condition. **Heatstroke** usually *follows prolonged exposure to direct sun rays, which leads to potassium or salt depletion*. It may also be caused by obesity or the inability of the body to **acclimatize** (ak-**clim**-uh-tize), or *adapt*, to a weather situation. The body loses its ability to rid itself of the heat that has built up. The body retains the heat, the person does not perspire, and body temperature can get as high as 108°. The person may collapse suddenly, have a rapid pulse, muscle twitching, and difficulty breathing. The skin will be dry and hot and the face will turn red.

If you are present when someone experiences heatstroke, call for an ambulance right away. Heatstroke is a life-threatening situation. Serious organ damage can result from such a high body temperature. Move the person to a cool place, loosen the clothing, and spray or sponge the person with cold water. Watch the person's breathing. It may be necessary to administer artificial respiration.

Frostbite

Frostbite occurs when there is prolonged exposure of a body part to a freezing or near-freezing temperature. With **frostbite,** the *tissue freezes*. The normal activity of the cells is slowed, even stopped. When circulation of the blood stops, cells begin to die.

Frostbite occurs most often to the chin, cheeks, nose, ears, fingers, and toes. Dressing warmly, covering all exposed skin—especially the head, face, fingers, and toes—and avoiding excessive exposure to cold and fatigue while exercising helps to prevent frostbite.

If frostbite does occur, the body should be warmed by applying blankets. The frostbitten body part should never be rubbed or exposed to intense heat. This causes further damage. The body must be gradually warmed. If frostbite is severe, the person should be kept quiet and watched for signs of shock or difficult breathing. Because of tissue damage, medical care should be sought.

KEEPING FIT

Body Temperatures

On hot days, body temperatures in excess of 106°F have been recorded in runners after marathons. Continuous exercise seems to produce high body temperatures, especially if the air temperature is high.

One of the major functions of the circulatory system is to transport the heat generated by the muscles to the surface of the body, where the evaporation process may occur. Drinking three to six ounces (85 to 170 grams) of water about every 15 minutes—depending on the level of activity and the heat of the day—helps the body's air-conditioning system.

PHYSICAL THERAPY

Physical therapy is one of the world's oldest healing arts. As early as 5,000 years ago, the Chinese used rubbing as a technique in healing the body. Modern physical therapy was first recognized in the United States during World War I. Physical therapists then were charged with the responsibility of developing physical reconstruction for lost limbs and in aiding in educational and vocational training programs as well.

Physical Therapist

Today, **physical therapists** have many more responsibilities. They work with children to overcome crippling birth defects and with stroke victims to restore movement and independent living. For postoperative patients, physical therapists are the link in the health-care team that speeds successful recovery for the patient.

Physical therapists work to help prevent and to treat athletic injuries. They teach special exercises and body mechanics to ease lower back pain, and plan treatment programs to reduce pain and to improve motion in arthritic joints.

More specifically, the physical therapist plans and administers programs for medically referred patients to restore function, relieve pain, and prevent disability following disease, injury, or loss of a body part. Therapists work in hospitals, rehabilitation centers, nursing homes, home health agencies, or in private practice. The physical therapist is a direct provider of health care.

To be a physical therapist, one needs a background in the basic sciences. All physical therapists have a bachelor's degree from a college or university. Upon graduation, physical therapists are licensed to practice their profession under state laws. These laws differ slightly from state to state.

Physical Therapy Assistant

The **physical therapy assistant** works directly with patients, giving the treatments that have been recommended by the supervising physical therapist.

A great variety of work is involved in being a physical therapy assistant—treating, training, and communicating with both children and adults.

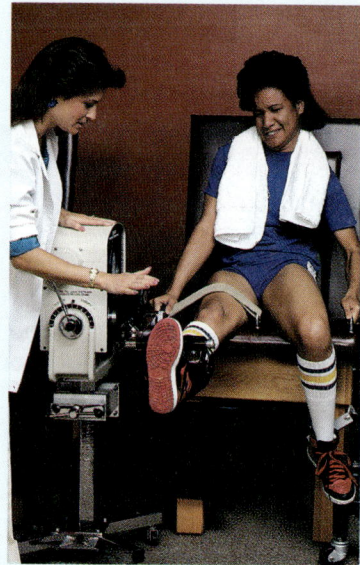

Training for the physical therapy assistant usually involves a two-year program of study after high school. Many physical therapy assistants go on to complete the four-year program for physical therapists.

For information on the physical therapist or physical therapy assistant program, contact the American Physical Therapy Association.

American Physical Therapy Association
1111 North Fairfax Street
Alexandria, VA 22314

Avoiding Risk and Injury During Exercise

What can you think of that would help you avoid being injured during exercise? Think back to your own experiences during exercise or to the experiences of others who you know have been injured.

Why do people get hurt? Here are some suggestions that may be helpful to you as you begin your own exercise program. If you think of your body as a very valuable resource, one that needs care and attention, then you will see that prevention is the best way to avoid injuries. See the 12 suggestions for a safe workout given on page HB4 of the *Health Handbook*.

CHECK YOURSELF

1. Make a list of (a) potential benefits and (b) potential risks from exercise.
2. Name two injuries to the muscles and to the joints that may occur when the body is not in condition or when there is not sufficient warm-up.
3. Contrast heatstroke and heat exhaustion.
4. What is frostbite?

CHAPTER 2   Review

CHAPTER SUMMARY

- To be successful, a personal exercise program needs to include activities that are enjoyable, as well as a set time each day to exercise.
- A workout must become a priority each day. Every workout should include a warm-up and a cool-down period.
- Exercise activities offer benefits in three general areas: muscle strength and endurance, heart and lung endurance, and body movement.
- To increase heart and lung fitness, exercise must be at the aerobic level.
- As with any moving activity, there is a risk of injury during exercise.
- Sprains and dislocations are the most common injuries to the skeletal system, specifically to joints.
- Bruises, strains, tendinitis, pulled or torn muscles, and cramps are the most common muscle injuries or conditions.
- Heat cramps, heat exhaustion, heatstroke, and frostbite are weather-related risks when exercising.
- Most injuries or conditions can often be prevented by taking adequate precautions, especially a good warm-up before exercising, and by using good equipment and proper techniques.

REVIEWING WHAT YOU LEARNED

1. Suppose you are asked to start a youth fitness program. Explain the steps you would follow and what you would include in the program?
2. Explain why warm-up and cool-down sessions are important parts of an exercise workout.
3. What are isometric, isotonic, and isokinetic exercises?
4. Your friend has decided to start exercising and is very enthusiastic about beginning. To get off to a good start, he is planning to run in a 10K race this weekend. Why might this not be a good idea?
5. What are two common injuries that occur during exercise?
6. Name two ways to prevent injury during exercise.
7. Why are cold packs applied to muscle injuries?
8. What is the difference between heatstroke and heat exhaustion? How can both be prevented?
9. What is the difference between a sprain and a strain?

physical fitness	isotonic	delayed-onset muscle	bruise	heat cramps
pulse recovery	isokinetic	soreness (DOM)	strain	heat exhaustion
rate	anaerobic	circuit training	tendinitis	heatstroke
warming up	aerobic	courses	pulled muscle	acclimatize
pooling	target pulse rate	sprain	torn muscle	frostbite
cooling down	maximum pulse	torn cartilage	muscle cramps	physical
isometric	rate	dislocation	hernia	therapist

PUTTING VOCABULARY TO USE

On a separate piece of paper, write the following statements. Then supply the missing word or phrase from the chapter vocabulary list.

1. _____ _____ stretches muscles, preparing them for exertion.
2. _____ _____ refers to your ability to carry out daily tasks easily, having enough reserve energy to respond to unexpected demands.
3. _____ _____ helps your body return gradually to a less active state.
4. _____ exercise involves any nonstop vigorous exercises.
5. _____ exercises are ones centered on specific groups of muscles.
6. The collection of blood in extremities, called _____, can cause lightheadedness, even fainting.
7. _____ _____ _____ _____ is brought about by strenuous, unaccustomed exercise.
8. _____ exercises involve muscular contraction, but little or no movement of the body part that is stressed.

9. The rate at which your heart beats following activity is called the _____ _____ _____.
10. _____ _____ _____ is the most your heart should beat per minute.

On a separate piece of paper, write the vocabulary term for each definition.

1. _____. Injury in which a bone is pushed out of its joint.
2. _____. Soreness resulting from an overworked muscle.
3. _____ _____. Separation of large muscle or tendon from its point of attachment.
4. _____ _____. A muscle contracts tightly and will not relax.
5. _____. Prolonged exposure to sun's rays, resulting in body's inability to release its heat.
6. _____. Tissues freeze as a result of prolonged exposure to extreme cold.
7. _____ _____. Exercise or overexertion in a hot, humid climate, resulting in loss of body salt and water.
8. _____. Injury to tissue under the skin, resulting from a blow to the muscle.

APPLYING WHAT YOU LEARNED

1. Call a spa or exercise studio in your community. Find out what preliminary work they do before prescribing an exercise program. What types of exercise programs do they recommend?
2. Interview a person who jogs regularly. What motivates him or her to work out? What benefits are realized?
3. Keep a record of your pulse rate during different physical activities. Which activity makes your heart work the hardest? Compare your pulse rate record with your classmates' records.

4. Some people start an exercise program only to give it up, claiming that exercise is boring or too hard or that they just do not have time. What suggestions can you give to help them?

FOCUS ON WELLNESS

Following some specific steps in planning your physical fitness program can help to ensure its success. Simple preventive behaviors also help to reduce your risks of injury. *The potential impact of a regular exercise program on my level of wellness includes . . .*

Healthy Skin, Hair, Nails, and Feet

Proper skin, hair, nail, and foot care not only helps to keep your body functioning, but it also helps to show you to best advantage. If you look your best, chances are that you will feel your best.

After studying this chapter, you will be able to:
- define the structure and function of the skin, hair, and nails,
- describe proper skin, hair, nail, and foot care,
- summarize the points of good posture,
- explain the relationship of skin, hair, feet, nails, and posture to total health.

Grooming involves *all the things you do in order to give yourself a pleasing, healthy outward appearance.* The way you take care of yourself gives others a message about what you think of yourself. But, even more important, your grooming, clothing, and appearance affect the way you feel and act. Whatever way you take care of yourself, you convey a message about how you value *you.*

Presenting Yourself as a Fit Person

The care of your skin, hair, and nails is a part of your grooming that directly affects your overall physical appearance. Also included are your neatness and the way you wear your clothes. This does not mean that you have to wear the most expensive jeans or the latest fashions. What is important is how your clothes fit and how appropriate they are for your activity.

Physical appearance includes how you stand, walk, and sit—your posture. How you carry yourself contributes to overall fitness.

Structure and Function of the Skin

Skin has a great effect on your appearance because much of it is visible. Your skin helps to do many things, including:

1. serving as a waterproof covering,
2. regulating body temperature,
3. acting as a barrier to germs.

The skin, the largest organ of the human body, is also a major sense organ, detecting pressure, pain, temperature, and texture.

Tactile Communication

Because the skin has many nerve endings, it can easily *respond to being touched,* or **stimulated tactilely.** Nerve endings that detect pain are the most numerous. *Pain* is a protective sensation for the body. It indicates overstimulation of any sensory nerve and the damage or potential damage to body tissue.

Pain can be classified into three general types:

- **Sharp pain.** When the skin is cut or jabbed with a sharp object, you react immediately. This pain is intense and easily *localized,* or pinpointed.
- **Burning pain.** This pain is slower to develop and lasts longer. It is also less accurately localized. Burning pain can be difficult to endure and often brings on cardiac and respiratory activity.

■ **Aching pain.** This pain develops when the body's internal organs are stimulated. The pain is persistent; that is, it continues without change. This pain is difficult to localize and often causes feelings of nausea.

Interpretation of pain takes place in the cerebrum of the brain. The cortex of the brain may also contain areas of pain identification, which aid in the localization of painful stimuli.

Parts of the Skin

The skin has two main layers, the epidermis and dermis.

The **epidermis** (ep-i-**dur**-mis) is *the outer layer of skin*, which is made up of dead cells that are constantly being rubbed off and replaced by new cells.

The **dermis** (**dur**-mis) is *the inner layer of skin*, which is made up of living cells.

Below the dermis is the subcutaneous (sub-kew-**tain**-nee-us) layer of skin. The **subcutaneous layer** is *made up of fatty tissue* and serves as the body's natural insulation against hot and cold. It also acts as an inner cushion to protect the body against injuries.

The Dermis   All of the vital structures of the skin, including nerves and blood vessels, are found in the dermis. The dermis contains oil glands that help to keep the hair and skin from cracking. The skin's **elasticity,** or *springy and flexible qualities,* is a result of protein fibers found in the dermis.

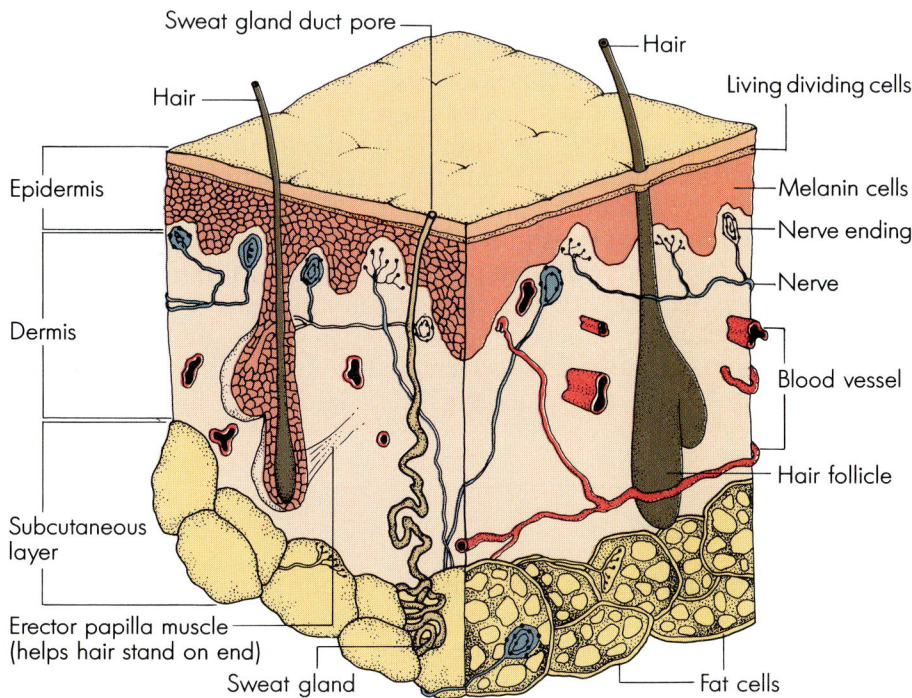

The skin is a waterproof shield, a regulator of body temperature, and a germ barrier.

Skin and Hair Facts

- The total surface area of an adult's skin is about 17 square feet. An area of skin about the size of a postage stamp contains over 100 sweat glands, 12 feet of nerves, hundreds of nerve endings, 10 hair follicles, 15 oil glands, and 3 feet of blood vessels.
- Skin heals so well that when a severely injured fingertip heals, even the fingerprint whorls return to their regular pattern.
- Attached to each hair on your skin is a tiny muscle. When you get cold or scared, the muscles contract, making the hairs stand up and pulling up the skin around the hairs. This is what causes goose bumps on the skin.
- Hair is as strong as aluminum. A single hair can hold a 3-ounce weight. If you made a thick rope out of strands of hair, it could lift a car.
- After being in water for a while, the skin on the soles of your feet and palms of your hands begins to wrinkle. This is because these areas do not have oil glands to prevent the skin of the soles from absorbing water.

Sweat glands are also found in the dermis. There are 2 to 3 million sweat glands in the body. When your body gets hot, the *tiny holes in the skin,* called **pores,** open up to release perspiration. **Perspiration** is *water and other waste products that are secreted from the sweat glands, which help to cool down the body.*

Many people think perspiration causes body odor. Perspiration itself does not cause an odor. Bacteria acting on the perspiration cause the odor. Sweat glands are more numerous under the arms, which is why body odor tends to be more of a problem under the arms. Thorough washing with soap and water on a daily basis slows bacterial growth and helps to control body odor. Deodorants and antiperspirants can help to mask the body odors or reduce the amount of perspiration. They cannot prevent odor or perspiration and are not substitutes for daily washing or bathing.

The dermis contains cells that produce melanin. **Melanin** (**mell**-lah-nin) is *a pigment that mainly gives skin its color.* It also gives color to the hair and the eyes. Melanin production increases when you are in the sun to protect the skin from sun damage. This increased production of melanin causes the skin to tan. *Freckles* are small spots of melanin.

Skin and the Sun

Understanding the sun's effects on the skin and knowing some protective steps to take can help you to better care for your skin. The sun does not have the same effect on everyone. Some people tan more easily than others. People with fair skin may never tan, but just burn.

SUN-BLOCKING AGENTS

"I work at a summer camp and am outside all day. There is no way to stay out of the sun, so I get a dark tan every summer. So many creams and lotions are advertised that I don't know what's the best protection for my skin. Do 'sunscreens' really block out the sun's harmful rays?"

You are right; there is a confusing array of suntan products. Knowing what the products are and what they do can help you to protect your skin.

Sun-blocking agents are *opaque* (light cannot pass through them) and *deflect* (bounce back) the ultraviolet rays. They may contain zinc oxide, titanium dioxide, or talc and are quite useful for areas that burn easily—the lips, earlobes, and nose.

Sunscreens absorb the stronger, midday rays that are the main cause of sunburn. These products are rated according to the degree of protection that they can give against ultraviolet light. The most effective sunscreens contain the chemical para-aminobenzoic acid (PABA) or benzophenone or both. Sunscreens do not prevent tanning or burning—they merely slow the whole suntanning process of the body.

Suntan lotions offer little or no protection against ultraviolet light and sunburn. They also do not promote tanning, as some companies advertise. These lotions contain oils that may speed up the sun's effect. Most products now, however, do contain a sunscreen. The sun protection factor (SPF) is identified by a number. The lowest number, 2, offers minimal protection. The highest number, 15, offers a complete sun block. Which one to use depends mostly on your type of skin. The fairer your skin, the higher the number you should choose for maximum protection. You should also consider where you live. You need a higher SPF in hot, humid climates, since damp, moist skin admits more ultraviolet rays. Also, the higher you are above sea level, the less the atmospheric filtering action on the sun's rays, so you need a higher SPF.

LIFE MANAGEMENT SKILL

Protecting the Skin

Use information in this section to respond to this student's problem:

Dear Abby,

I have a job lifeguarding in the summer. It requires spending eight hours a day in the sun. What can I do to protect my skin? Do I need to do anything special to protect my eyes or lips?

Signed,
Too Tanned

Ultraviolet Rays and the Skin   **Ultraviolet rays** are *light rays that come from the sun.* Two types of ultraviolet rays are important in considering the sun's effects on the human body. The *shorter rays,* most intense in the middle of the day, are the main cause of sunburn. The *longer rays,* in the morning and late afternoon, are less strong in terms of sunburn.

There is evidence now which indicates that the two types of rays can activate each other's harmful effects. If you got a moderate sunburn at noon and went out again in the late afternoon, you could get badly burned because your skin had been *sensitized,* or made receptive, to ultraviolet light.

Do not be fooled on a hazy or cloudy day. Up to 80% of ultraviolet rays can penetrate haze, light clouds, or fog. Ultraviolet rays can also be reflected upward from the ground, sand, and water. Snow is an excellent reflector, sending back more than 85% of the rays.

Do not judge how much sun you have gotten by how red you look while you are out in the sun. It takes about four hours after exposure for the full sunburn to show.

Other Effects of the Sun   Besides the effects of sunburn, exposure to the sun's ultraviolet rays can permanently destroy the elastic fibers that keep the skin tight. The sun causes the skin to age *prematurely,* that is, before its time. The layers of skin cells also thicken with repeated sun exposure. This gives the skin a hard, leathery texture.

Ultraviolet radiation also damages the *deoxyribonucleic acid* (dee-**och**-see-**rye**-bow-new-**clay**-ic **ass**-id) (*DNA*), the genetic material in skin cells. Accumulated DNA damage can result in the formation of cancerous cells. Excessive sun exposure is the primary cause of certain types of skin cancer.

The effects of the sun on your skin may not show up for years and cannot be stopped by any cosmetic ointments. These effects are *cumulative,* or increasing, and the damage is *irreversible,* or unrecallable. The healthiest behavior is prevention. Avoid overexposure to the sun's ultraviolet rays.

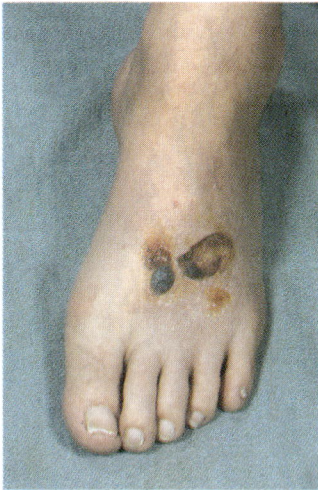

Overexposure to the sun can result in (left to right) *skin cancer, premature aging of the skin, and sunburn.*

Skin Problems

A number of common skin problems chiefly occur during the adolescent years. Among these is acne. Other skin problems happen throughout life.

Acne—The Most Common Skin Problem

Acne (**ak**-knee), which is *a clogging of the pores of the skin,* is the most common skin problem during adolescence. One reason that acne occurs during adolescence is the effect of the hormones the body secretes during that period.

Hormones (**hor**-monz) are *chemicals produced in the body that cause certain changes to take place.* In this case, hormones cause the oil glands to enlarge and to produce more sebum. **Sebum** (**see**-bum) is *an oil that makes the skin soft and pliable.* Too much sebum can make the skin oily, providing an ideal place for bacteria to grow. Since more oil glands are in the face than in other parts of the body, acne appears more on the face.

The oil secreted by the oil glands passes out through pores in the skin. Excess sebum can clog these pores and can cause the following acne conditions:

- A **whitehead** results when *oil gets trapped in a pore.*
- A **blackhead** develops if this *plug of oil becomes exposed to air, at which time it darkens.*
- A **pimple** is formed if *bacteria get into the clogged pore and inflame it.* The inflamed pimple develops a yellowish pus.

Controlling Acne   Picking or squeezing pimples can force the condition inward, possibly leaving the skin scarred. It is best to try other methods of control, even though, at this time, there is no cure for the condition. The most important practice is to wash your face with soap and water at least twice a day.

- Every morning and evening, wash with soap and water. If your face is very oily, wash it once more during the day.
- Pat your skin dry with a clean towel.
- Select creams and cosmetics carefully, if you use them at all, and avoid greasy preparations.
- Eat a well-balanced diet. Vitamin A helps to promote healthy skin. It is found in milk, egg yolks, liver, green and yellow vegetables, and yellow fruits.
- Get plenty of rest and exercise.
- Try not to pick at the infected area.

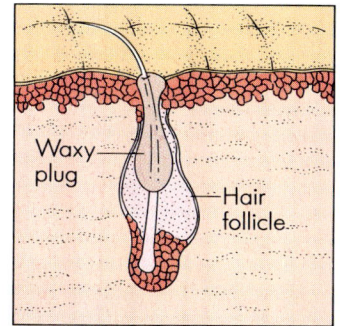

Whitehead

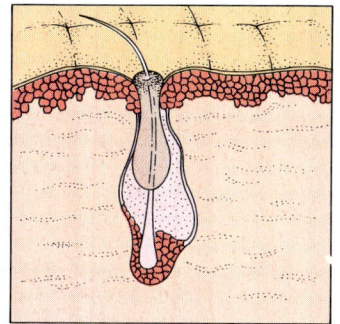

Blackhead

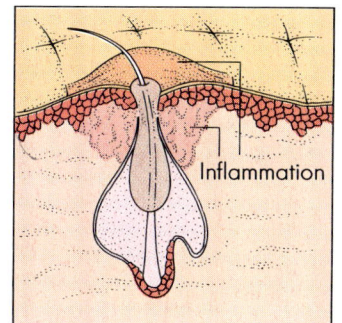

Pimple

Other Skin Conditions

Boils, warts, moles, skin irritations, cold sores, psoriasis, and vitiligo can occur at any time during or after adolescence.

- **Boils** are *skin infections that result in swelling, redness, and the formation of pus.* They are caused by bacteria and can destroy skin tissue. Boils can become seriously infected and should be treated by a doctor. Like acne, boils should not be squeezed. They are **infections,** which means that *the bacteria which cause them can spread and form other boils on the body.* The infection could spread to other parts of the body.

Chapter 3 Healthy Skin, Hair, Nails, and Feet   **43**

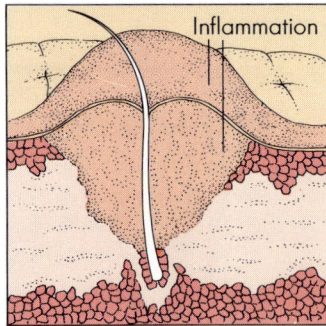
Boil

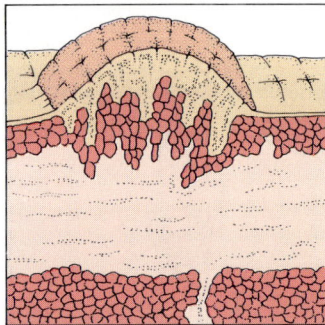
Wart

■ **Warts** are *small growths caused by a virus.* They usually appear as raised growths on the outer layer of the skin. Most warts are painless and harmless, but the virus that causes them can spread and form more warts. If that happens, or if there is any change in the size or color of a wart, see your doctor immediately. Color change may indicate a more serious problem like cancer.

■ **Moles** are *small, round, slightly thick places on the skin.* They may be black or brown and are present from birth. Moles are not dangerous, but if they start to change color, a doctor should be consulted immediately.

■ **Jock itch** is a common *skin irritation caused by fungi growing in the warm, moist areas of the body.* It is not confined to those who engage in sports. The disorder has symptoms of itching and redness. Jock itch mainly occurs in the groin area.

By washing and drying carefully, and by dusting with talcum or an antifungal powder, the condition will usually clear up. Avoid using ointments, because they can make the condition worse by holding in moisture. For jock itch, it is advisable to wear loose cotton clothing to allow proper ventilation.

Jock itch is highly **contagious,** that is, *it can be spread to others.* Use only your own soap and towels.

■ **Herpes simplex type I,** or the *cold sore,* is *a blister that forms on or around the lips.* A virus causes these cold sores. Do not confuse herpes simplex, type I, with herpes simplex, type II, which is a sexually transmitted disease. (See Chapter 30.) One must be careful, however, because the cold sore is *infectious,* that is, it can spread to other parts of the body.

■ **Psoriasis** (sur-**rye**-uh-sis) is an ailment in which *red patches appear on the skin, followed by the skin turning white and flaking off.* Psoriasis should be treated by a doctor and is usually lessened with the use of medicinal creams.

■ **Vitiligo** (vit-uh-**lee**-go) is probably caused by *an absence of melanin in certain patches of skin.* This skin turns whitish to pinkish. There is no cure for vitiligo, but it appears to be harmless. The affected area should be kept away from direct sunlight.

CHECK YOURSELF

1. What are the three major functions of the skin?
2. What are the differences among the epidermis, dermis, and subcutaneous layers of the skin?
3. How do ultraviolet rays affect the skin?
4. What is a whitehead? a blackhead? a pimple?
5. How can acne be controlled?
6. What main thing should a person be aware of concerning each of the following: (a) boils, (b) warts, (c) moles, (d) jock itch, (e) cold sores, (f) psoriasis, (g) vitiligo?

2. Hair and Nail Care

Humans have hair present on almost all skin surfaces of their bodies. You have between 100,000 and 200,000 hairs on your head! The roots of hair are made up of living cells and grow out of the inner layer of the skin, the dermis. A hair root grows out of a **follicle** (**fol**-i-kul), which is *a small pocket in the dermis that holds the root*.

Through the follicle, the root is supplied with blood and nerve tissue. As new hair cells are made, old hair cells are pushed up and out of the hair follicle and die. The hair visible on your head is made up of dead cells.

Hair normally grows at a rate of about 6 to 8 inches per year. Each hair on your head grows for about four years, rests a few months, and then falls out. You lose between 25 and 100 hairs a day.

Healthy Hair and Your Appearance

Your hair has a great impact on your appearance. Wearing a cut and a style that fits your features and type of hair is important. Proper hair care is also important.

Brushing your hair helps to keep dirt from building up and helps to evenly distribute the natural hair oils. These oils keep the hair soft and give it its shine. Overbrushing can cause hair to pull out or break off. A good brushing once a day is enough. Massaging the scalp along with brushing helps to increase circulation in the scalp.

Washing your hair regularly is necessary for healthy hair. It is best, if possible, to let your hair dry naturally. Try to avoid using blow dryers because the heat can damage your hair. This is especially important for females who use electric curlers or curling irons. The heat dries out your hair, causing the ends to break or split.

Hair Problems

Dandruff is one of the most common hair and scalp problems. It is caused by *the flaking of the outer layer of dead skin cells covering the skull*. It is noticeable on the head because the flakes of skin can cling to the hair. Regular, thorough washing of your hair can control ordinary dandruff.

Dandruff may become worse if the scalp is too dry. Sometimes what appears to be dandruff is actually a skin infection. If itching and scaling persist, you should check with a health professional.

Head lice are *insects that live in the hair and feed off the scalp*. They make the scalp itchy and uncomfortable and can cause infection. They can usually be killed by medicinal shampoos.

Ringworm is caused by *a fungus* (**fung**-us) *that lives off dead skin*. It appears as a whitish ring and so is called ringworm. The ailment can be treated. Head lice and ringworm can spread from one person to another. It is wise not to use other people's combs, brushes, or towels.

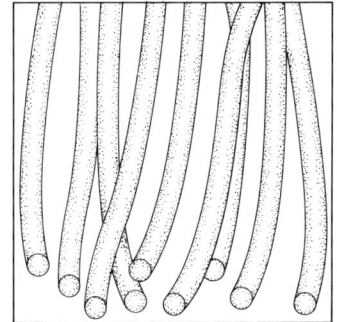

Round hairs (straight)

Flat hairs (curly)

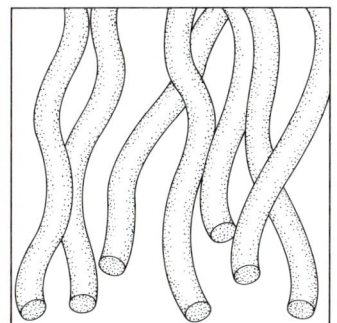

Oval hairs (wavy)

Hair is either straight, curly, or wavy.

Nail Care

Nail care is an important part of total fitness. It is a noticeable part of your overall grooming and makes a statement about how you care for yourself.

Keratin is the substance that makes nails hard.

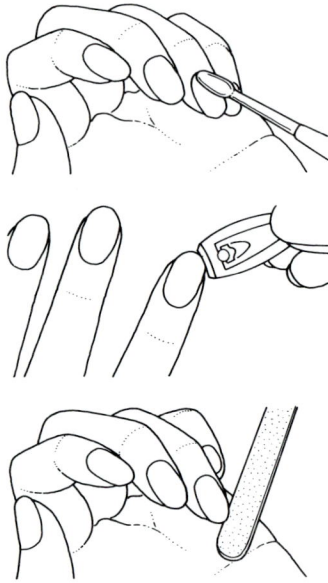

Soft keratin nail root   Hard keratin nail   Fat and connective tissue

Bone

Living cells

Dead skin cells

Use a cuticle stick, nail clippers, and emery board to care for your nails.

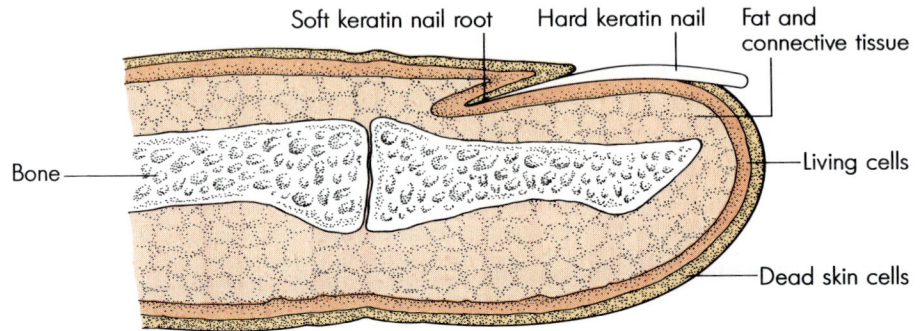

Like your hair, your toenails and fingernails are dead cells. Nails grow out of the skin's epidermis. Living cells extend from the root of the nail, below the epidermis, to just above the base of the nail. As living cells die and are replaced, they are pushed up, forming the rest of the nail. The nail is surrounded by the **cuticle** (**cute**-i-kul), *the nonliving epidermis surrounding the edges of your fingernails and toenails.* If you have ever lost a nail, you probably grew another one. New nails will grow as long as the root is still alive.

Nails and Your Appearance

Good nail care includes keeping nails clean and evenly trimmed. You should keep cuticles pushed back and clip **hangnails,** *slivers of cuticle that separate along the edges of the nail,* with a nail clipper. You should cut toenails straight across, leaving the nail just at or slightly above skin level. If cut too low, you increase your risk of skin infection.

Fingernails should be slightly rounded. Use a nail file or emery board to shape the nails. Always file in the same direction rather than use a sawing motion. Nail care is not difficult. It is an important part of your overall fitness.

Both skin and nails are made from cells, but nail cells have keratin (**kerr**-uh-tin) added to them. **Keratin** is *a transparent, proteinlike substance that makes nails hard.*

CHECK YOURSELF

1. What is the function of a follicle?
2. How can brushing the hair and massaging the scalp contribute to healthier hair?
3. What is involved in proper nail care?
4. What is (a) dandruff, (b) head lice, (c) ringworm?

3. Foot Care and Posture

Two of the most neglected areas in grooming are foot care and the development and maintenance of good posture.

Caring for Your Feet

Your feet should be kept clean because they perspire. It is also wise to wear shoes which fit you, which are comfortable, and that distribute body weight in a way that provides good posture. This simple rule will reduce many of the common foot problems that develop. Among these are *blisters, corns, bunions, calluses, ingrown toenails, and athlete's foot.*

Blisters are *baglike points on the skin, usually full of liquid.* They are mostly formed by the shoe rubbing against a toe. Blisters are painful and when they break should be cleaned carefully. Blisters can develop into corns.

Corns are *an overgrowth of the skin at some point on the foot.* They usually appear on the toes and are the result of a shoe being too tight and causing friction at a point where a toe rubs against the shoe. Corns can be painful, and if they thicken too much they must be cut by a foot specialist.

A **bunion** (**bun**-yun) is *a painful bony swelling in the first joint of the big toe.* It is caused by wearing tight or high-heeled shoes, which cramp the toes and cause them to bend in an abnormal way. The condition can usually be cured by wearing shoes that fit.

A **callus** (**kal**-us) is *a hard, thickened part of skin on the foot.* It is formed by the friction of the foot rubbing against the shoe and is frequently found on the heel or ball of the foot. Calluses are not harmful, but some people wear them off by using a pumice stone, a soft, porous volcanic stone. Calluses can also form on the palm of the hands and on the elbows.

One of the most important reasons for cutting your toenails is to avoid ingrown nails, especially in the big toe. But you must be careful. Do not cut the nail down too much because when growing back, it can push into the skin on either side of the toe. An **ingrown toenail** results when, with pressure bearing down on the foot, *the nail pushes into the skin and cuts it.* Trimming your toenails regularly and carefully will avoid the condition.

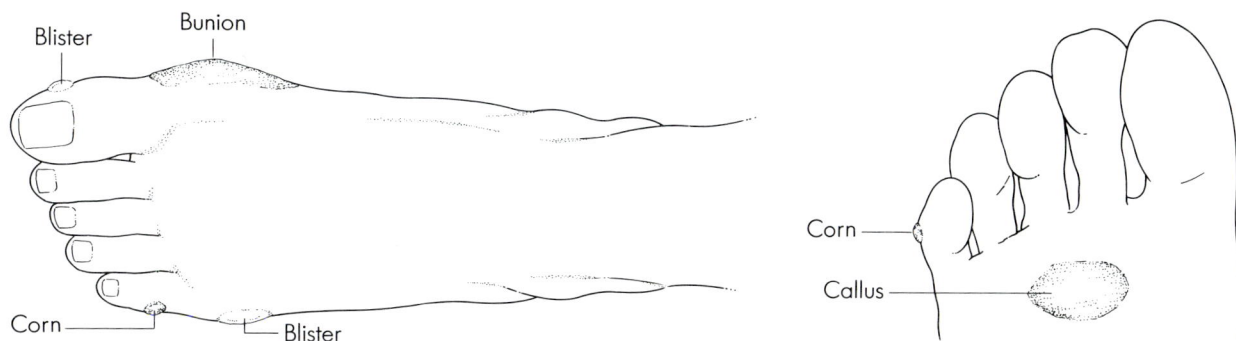

Athlete's foot is not directly caused by wearing shoes, but tight shoes can help it to spread. **Athlete's foot** is caused by *fungi growing in the warm, moist areas of the foot.* It produces redness and itching, and usually appears between the toes. Talcum or an antifungal powder will cure the ailment. It is wise to wear white or colorless socks while the athlete's foot is present.

Athlete's foot is very contagious. That is why it is important to wear sandals or another type of foot covering in locker rooms and showers.

Posture as a Part of Total Fitness

Perhaps no other single factor says more about you to other people than *the way you carry yourself*—your **posture.** Good posture is important for several reasons:

- Maintaining good posture helps you to move, stand, or sit with ease, without getting tired.
- Good posture makes it possible for your internal organs to function properly.
- Good posture helps your bones and muscles to develop properly.
- Good posture can help your clothes to fit properly and can enhance your figure or body build.

Check Your Standing Posture

Imagine that your body consists of three separate sections—the *head,* the *upper torso,* and the *lower torso.* These three areas are balanced on the balls of your feet. These points need to be in a single line, as shown in the drawing. In good standing posture, a straight vertical line could be drawn between the earlobe and the outer edge of the anklebone.

Check Your Sitting Posture

Good posture when sitting helps you to stay more alert and less fatigued over a long period of time. As in the case of standing posture, the head and shoulders should be balanced directly over the hips. Your feet should be flat on the floor and your back should be straight against the back of the chair.

Check Your Walking Posture

To ensure proper walking posture, balance the body over the balls of the feet. The shoulders should be held back in a comfortable position and the abdomen tucked in. Arms should hang freely at your sides. Let your upper leg lead the body.

To improve walking, practice walking a straight line. This helps to correct two common posture problems:

- *toeing out*—the tendency of the toes to turn out when walking,
- *walking with your feet too far apart.*

Postural Problems

High-heeled shoes can cause added postural problems. Your balance is thrown forward, changing your normal center of gravity, when you wear such shoes. This places excessive strain on the ankles and the arches of the feet.

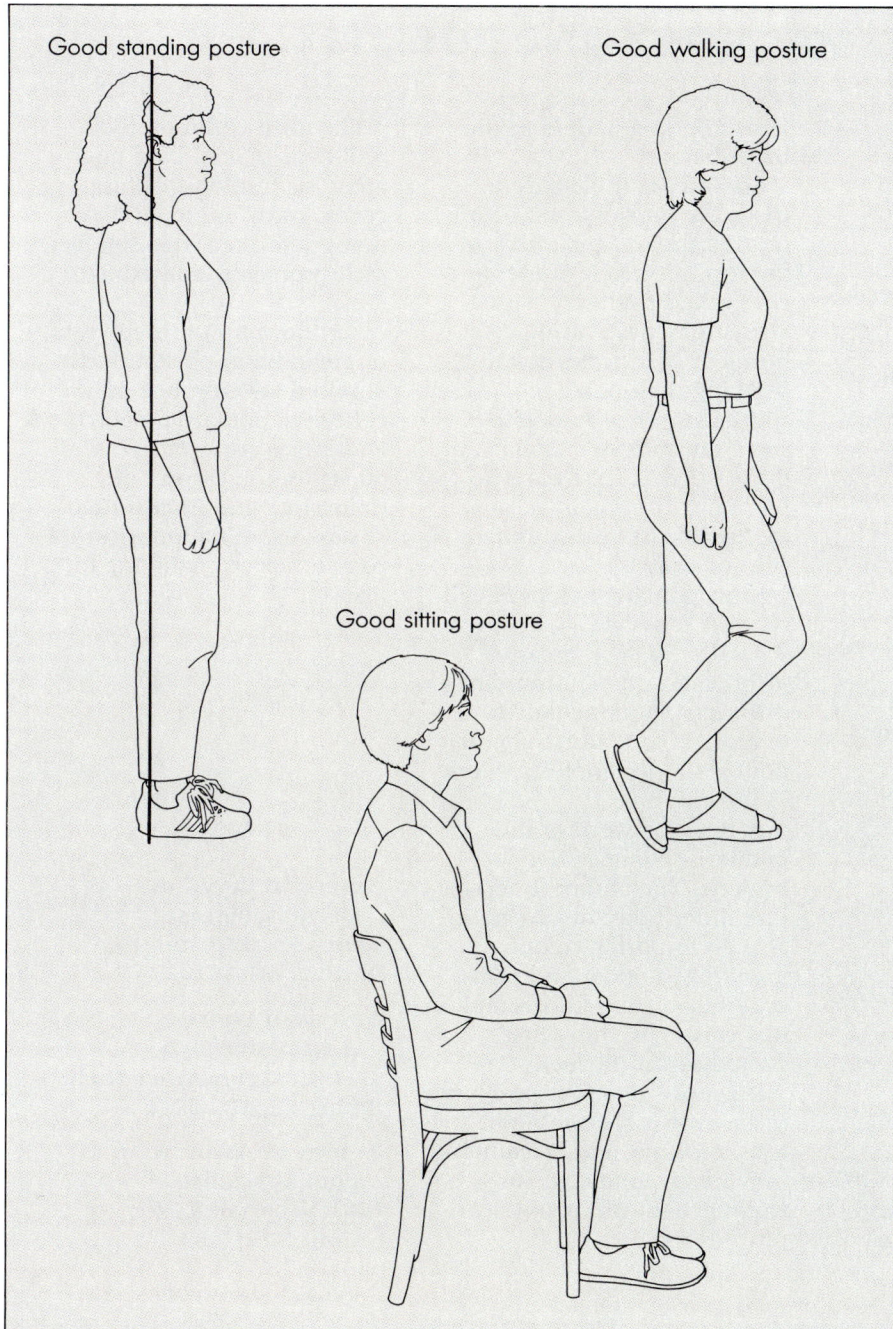

Good standing posture

Good walking posture

Good sitting posture

KEEPING FIT

Maintaining Good Standing Posture

An exercise to help you maintain good standing posture is to stand with your back to a wall or a door. Your head, buttocks, and heels should be touching the wall.

Stretch your hands out over your head along the wall. Then push off on your toes so that your heels are off the floor. This exercise will improve posture by helping you to gain more balance and by improving the muscle coordination needed for proper standing position.

DERMATOLOGY AND PODIATRY

Dermatologist

Dermatology (der-muh-**taul**-uh-jee) is *a branch of medicine dealing with the skin*, its structure and function, diseases and their treatment. The dermatologist is a specialist concerned with the care of healthy skin and its treatment when affected by disease. Some doctors may limit their practice to **dermatopathology** (der-muh-toe-puh-**thaul**-uh-jee)—*diseases* and *abnormalities* (outside of the normal) of the skin. The most common problem addressed by dermatologists is acne.

The American Board of Dermatology requires a doctor to have a three-year residency in dermatology, one-year internship, and six months of practice to be certified as a specialist. Most dermatologists have an office-based practice. For more information, write to the American Board of Dermatologists.

Podiatrist

Disorders of the feet are a major cause of disability today. Foot disorders are among the most widespread and neglected health prob-

lems affecting people in the United States.

Podiatrists (puh-**die**-uh-trists) are *doctors specializing in the care and treatment of the feet*, a branch of medicine called **podiatry.** Podiatrists may have an office at home or in a professional building with other specialists. They may also serve on staffs of hospitals, in the Armed Forces, government health programs, or on the faculty in health profession schools.

Most podiatrists provide all types of foot care, but some specialize in such areas as orthopedics (bone and joint disorders), podopediatrics (children's foot ailments), or podogeriatrics (foot disorders of the elderly).

A main concern of the podiatrist is preventive foot hygiene. The ability to recognize other body disorders is also an important requirement for the podiatrist. Disorders, such as arthritis and diabetes, may show first symptoms in the feet.

Diagnosis of a foot problem may involve X-rays, blood tests, or other tests. Treatment may involve medical, surgical, mechanical, or physical procedures.

The most common foot problems treated by a podiatrist are bunions, calluses, corns, warts, ingrown toenails, deformed toes, flat feet, arch problems, and athlete's foot.

A minimum of three years of prepodiatry education is required for entrance into a college of podiatric medicine. Podiatrists are licensed in all 50 states, the District of Columbia, and Puerto Rico. A state examination must be passed before qualifying for a license.

American Board of
  Dermatologists
Henry Ford Hospital
Detroit, MI 48202

American Podiatry
  Association
9312 Old Georgetown Road
Bethesda, MD 20814

American Association of
  Foot Specialists
1801 Vauxhall Road
Union, NJ 07083

Arches are *supporting bony structures that are shaped like an arc on the inside of the foot.* High, narrow heels make the ankles roll, which may cause injury or even permanent damage to the arches. If you have weak arches or poor posture, avoid wearing high heels. A lower heel on a comfortable-fitting shoe is best for your posture.

Even on healthy feet, it is best not to wear high heels. If they do not directly harm the feet, there is still the danger of tripping with them and hurting an ankle.

Flat feet, or **fallen arches,** come about when the longitudinal arch is so flat that all the underside of the foot touches the ground. It happens when the muscles, ligaments, and connective tissues that support the arch weaken, resulting in fallen arches.

See ''Avoiding Back Problems'' in the *Health Handbook*, page HB6.

CHECK YOURSELF

1. Name three common foot ailments and describe them.
2. Why is good posture important?
3. Describe how you would evaluate someone's posture.
4. What are arches? How do they affect posture?

CHAPTER 3 Review

CHAPTER SUMMARY

- Grooming involves all the things you do in order to give yourself a pleasing, healthy outward appearance.
- The skin is an important agent in regulating body temperature, in acting as a body covering, and in serving as a barrier to germs.
- The skin consists of the epidermis, dermis, and the subcutaneous layer.
- Sunlight can be very dangerous, so care must be taken to avoid sunburn.
- Acne is a common skin disorder of young people which can usually be controlled.
- Other skin conditions are boils, warts, moles, jock itch, cold sores, psoriasis, and vitiligo.
- Hair and nail care is essential to good grooming.
- Hair problems are dandruff, head lice, and ringworm.
- Foot care is important both in maintaining healthy feet and good posture.

- There are proper postures for standing, sitting, and walking.

REVIEWING WHAT YOU LEARNED

1. How is pain classified?
2. What structures are found in the epidermis?
3. What layer of skin is beneath the dermis?
4. What causes acne and dandruff?
5. What oil makes skin soft and pliable? What does an excessive amount of it cause?
6. How can you control acne?
7. Describe the two common skin irritations that are caused by fungi growing in the warm, moist areas of the body.
8. How should you take care of your hair and nails?
9. How should you take care of your skin and feet?
10. What are three common foot ailments? Describe them.

Skin	acne	**Feet**	**Hair**
stimulated tactily	hormones	blister	psoriasis
epidermis	sebum	corn	vitiligo
dermis	whitehead	bunion	follicle
subcutaneous layer	blackhead	callus	dandruff
elasticity	pimple	ingrown toenail	head lice
pores	boil	athlete's foot	ringworm
perspiration	wart	posture	
melanin	mole	fallen arches	**Nails**
sun-blocking agents	jock itch	flat feet	cuticle
ultraviolet rays	herpes simplex, type I	podiatrist	hangnail
sunscreens	dermatology	podiatry	keratin
suntan lotions	dermatopathology		

PUTTING VOCABULARY TO USE

On a separate piece of paper, write the following statements. Then supply the missing word or phrase from the chapter vocabulary list.

1. _____. Inner layer of skin made up of living cells.
2. _____. An oil that makes skin soft and pliable.
3. _____ _____. Skin irritation caused by fungi.
4. _____. A small pocket in the dermis.
5. _____. Hard, thickened part of skin on foot.
6. _____. Outer layer of skin made up of dead skin cells.
7. _____. Clogging of the pores of the skin during adolescence.
8. _____. Secreted from sweat glands to cool down the body.
9. _____. A small growth caused by a virus.
10. _____ _____ _____ _____. A cold sore.
11. _____. Bony swellings.
12. _____. Chemicals produced in the body that cause certain changes.
13. _____ _____. These can damage skin even on a hazy or foggy day.
14. _____. Pigment that mainly gives skin its color.
15. _____ _____. The underside of the foot touches the ground.

APPLYING WHAT YOU LEARNED

1. You have an opportunity to spend the weekend at the beach with a friend and his parents. You want to go but are afraid that you will get too much sun, as you usually do. If you decide to go, what protective measures should you take to keep from getting burned?
2. Write a paragraph about the dangers of the sun's ultraviolet rays and their effects on the human body.
3. What are some ways that you can improve your standing, sitting, and walking posture?
4. What are your favorite grooming activities? What are your least favorite ones? Why?

FOCUS ON WELLNESS

A person's physical appearance is directly related to the person's health. Care of a person's skin, hair, nails, feet, and posture tell a great deal about a person. *My health behaviors reflect my concern for my skin, hair, nails, feet, and posture because I . . .*

Healthy Teeth, Eyes, and Ears

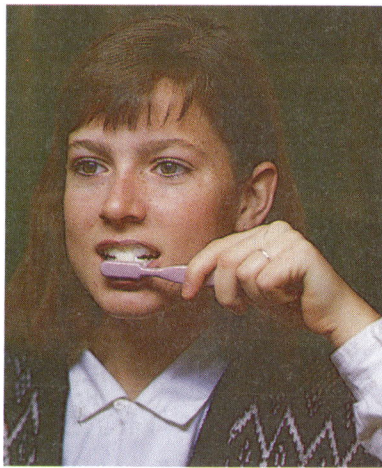

Sometimes we take our teeth, eyes, and ears for granted. But if we have a toothache, or an earache, or a speck of dust in our eye, we realize how important these body parts are in our daily lives.

After studying this chapter, you will be able to:

- describe the structure and function of the teeth and mouth,
- define peridontal disease—its causes and prevention,
- label the parts of the eye and ear,
- explain the processes of seeing and hearing,
- describe common vision and hearing problems,
- discuss mouth and teeth, ear and eye care.

Bitterness

Sour

Saltiness

Sweetness

Sour

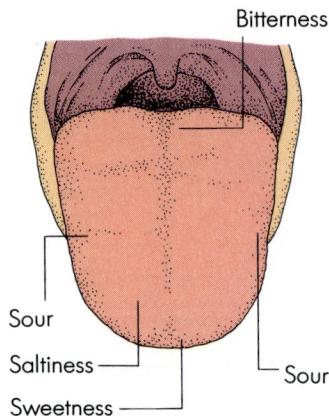

There are about 9,000 taste buds in the mouth. Most of them are on the tongue.

What do you think is the most common noncommunicable disease in the United States? If you guess tooth decay, you are right. About 98% of all Americans have or have had tooth decay. Yet it is one of the most preventable diseases. Before learning more about oral hygiene, let us first look at the structure and function of the teeth.

The mouth, tongue, and teeth make up a remarkably complex and vital body system. This system is responsible for evaluating, handling, breaking down, and swallowing food and liquids. It is amazingly versatile, being exposed to extremes in temperature and continuously being dried by air and moistened by saliva. More than 80 varieties of microorganisms live in your mouth.

Smell and Taste

Your sense of smell is located in the nose, while your sense of taste is located in the mouth.

Your Sense of Smell

There are several million **olfactory cells** (ohl-**fack**-te-ree **celz**), *receptors that detect smell*, embedded in the mucous membrane on the topside of each nasal cavity. From each of the millions of cells, 6 to 8 tiny sensory hairs project. Odors from molecules released in the air are picked up by the olfactory cells, which stimulate the sensory hairs, giving rise to an impulse, or message. The impulse travels to the brain, where the odor is interpreted.

Your Sense of Taste

In order for you to taste, a substance must be dissolved in saliva in the mouth. This solution then passes through openings in the **taste buds,** *sensitive areas on the tongue,* and stimulates sensory taste cells. This gives rise to impulses that travel to the brain through nerve fibers found at the base of each taste bud.

Receptors that sense taste are grouped in about 9,000 taste buds on the upper surface of the tongue, the palate, and the top of the throat. Taste buds for certain flavors are located on specific spots on the tongue.

When you eat, the flavors you sense are a result of smelling food, not tasting it. Have you ever had a bad head cold and not been able to taste the real flavor of a food? With nasal congestion, an increase in mucous secretions covers the olfactory nerve endings in the nasal cavity. You then are not able to detect the odor of the food. (For more information on your sense of taste, see Chapter 19 on the digestive system.)

The Structure and Function of the Teeth

Within the mouth, the teeth are the most vital structures and perhaps the single most noticeable contributor to health and to the appearance of the mouth and face. Your teeth not only allow you to chew food but also form the shape and structure of your mouth.

The Periodontium

The area immediately around the teeth is called the **periodontium** (per-ee-oh-**don**-tee-um). It is made up of the gums, periodontal ligament, and the jawbone. Together these structures support the teeth.

The Tooth

The tooth itself is divided into two major parts: the **root**, which is *inside the gum*, and the **crown**, which is *the visible part of the tooth*.

The **pulp** is *the very sensitive, living tissue inside the tooth*. The pulp is entirely enclosed by the hard inner walls of the tooth in *the root canal*.

A **toothache** is experienced *when the pulp becomes inflamed because of cavities or a disease*. The pain results from pressure because the inflamed pulp cannot expand within the inflexible walls of the tooth.

The pulp is surrounded by a material called **dentin**. The dentin is covered in the root area of the tooth by a substance called **cementum**. The crown of the tooth is covered with a hard material called **enamel**.

Enamel is the hardest material in the body. It is the second hardest naturally occurring substance in nature, diamonds being the hardest. However, it is this hard substance, the enamel, which can be the victim of tooth decay.

Proper care of the teeth should be one of the top priorities in personal grooming.

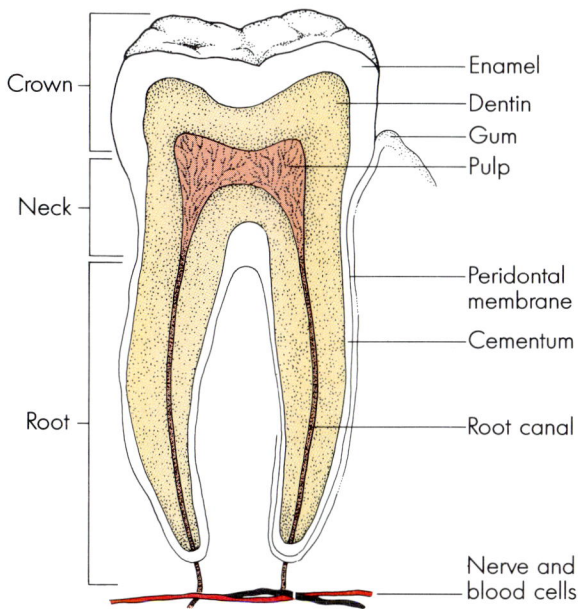

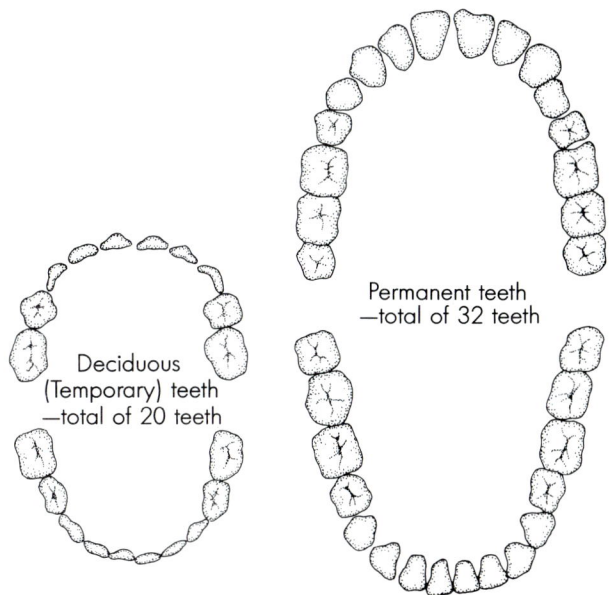

Crown
Neck
Root

Enamel
Dentin
Gum
Pulp
Peridontal membrane
Cementum
Root canal
Nerve and blood cells

Deciduous (Temporary) teeth —total of 20 teeth

Permanent teeth —total of 32 teeth

Periodontal Disease

Susan has bad breath. Larry's gums often bleed when he brushes his teeth. Michelle's front teeth have begun to spread. All three of these people have periodontal disease—a problem that could ultimately lead to the loss of all of their teeth.

More than 20 million Americans have already lost their teeth. But this does not have to happen to Susan, Larry, Michelle, or you. Periodontal disease, the most common cause of tooth loss, is almost entirely preventable. The choice is yours. If you spend 10 to 15 minutes a day cleaning your teeth and avoid foods high in sugar, you will probably be able to keep your teeth for your entire life.

By the age of 15, four out of every five Americans have the beginnings of periodontal disease. In the early stages, the disease can be stopped. To stop this process requires preventive oral hygiene and periodic visits to a dentist.

Tooth decay can be largely controlled by proper tooth care.

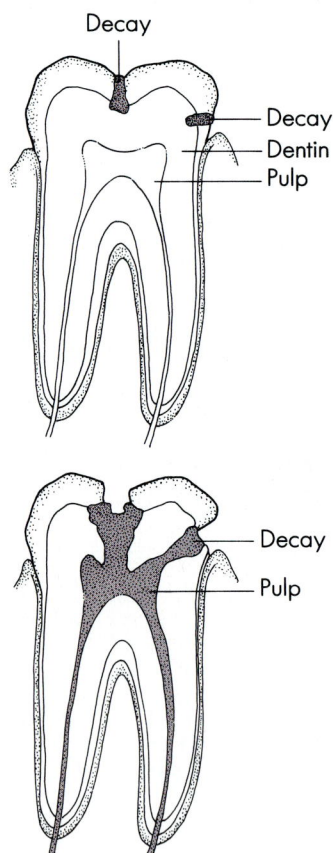

Decay

Decay
Dentin
Pulp

Decay
Pulp

Understanding the Decay Process

Periodontal disease (per-ee-oh-**don**-tal **dis-ease**) is primarily *the result of the destructive action of bacteria in your mouth.* Bacteria form plaque (**plack**). **Plaque** is *a sticky, colorless film that acts on sugar to form acids that destroy tooth enamel and irritate gums.*

Unless plaque is removed once every 24 to 36 hours, it can harden into tartar (**tar**-ter). **Tartar**, or *calculus*, as it is sometimes called, is *a very hard substance that irritates the underlying bone as well as the surrounding gums of your teeth.*

Decay begins as the plaque eats into the enamel, and the decaying process spreads to the dentin. Your tooth will become more sensitive as the decay reaches the pulp. You will experience a toothache when the decay reaches the pulp and exposes the nerve. If it is not treated, the bacterial infection can spread.

A tooth becomes abscessed when decay progresses to the stage of pus collecting in, and tissue becoming inflamed around, the bone sockets of a tooth. An **abscessed,** or *badly decayed*, **tooth** in the upper jaw can spread infection into the sinuses.

Your Diet and Dental Plaque

Your diet is a major contributor to the presence of plaque on the teeth. Frequent consumption of sugary foods promotes the formation of plaque. If you eat sweets, it is better to consume them at one time before you do your daily brushing and flossing.

If you do not eat sweets, you still have to be concerned with plaque removal. Plaque is continually forming. It will form even if you eat nothing at all, so daily plaque removal is essential.

William Morton and Anesthesia

Imagine sitting in the dentist's chair and having a tooth drilled or pulled without *anesthesia* (ann-es-**theez**-e-ah)—pain killer. That is what most people had to go through until some 140 years ago.

In 1842, Doctor Crawford Long used ether to numb his patient's senses before removing a tumor. Although this was the first recorded use of anesthesia in surgery, Long did not publish his work for four years, and then it was too late for him to receive credit. Doctor William Morton was the first to publicize its use.

William Morton had devised a new form of dental plate, but it required pulling all remaining teeth before fitting. Morton teamed up with a chemist, Charles Jackson, to develop a painless way of extracting teeth. In 1846, Morton successfully pulled a tooth while his patient was under the effects of ether. Morton, in collaboration with Jackson, patented the process, and Morton publicized his work. His success eventually made the use of anesthesia an essential addition to all forms of surgery.

The attention and fame that accompanied the discovery of anesthesia proved to be very controversial. Crawford Long tried to gain the recognition he thought he deserved, and Jackson began a lifetime battle to claim credit for the discovery of ether. Morton gave up his dental practice and devoted his life to the controversy.

Great Britain awarded a large sum of money to Morton for his discovery, but when Jackson raised a vocal protest the money was withdrawn. When the French Academy of Medicine presented a monetary award to both Morton and Jackson, Morton refused it. For three consecutive years, the U.S. Congress defeated a bill which proposed offering Morton a $100,000 award for his discovery. Morton died in poverty in 1868. In 1920, he was elected to the Hall of Fame for Great Americans.

Doctor Morton is shown holding a bottle of ether while another doctor operates on a sleeping patient.

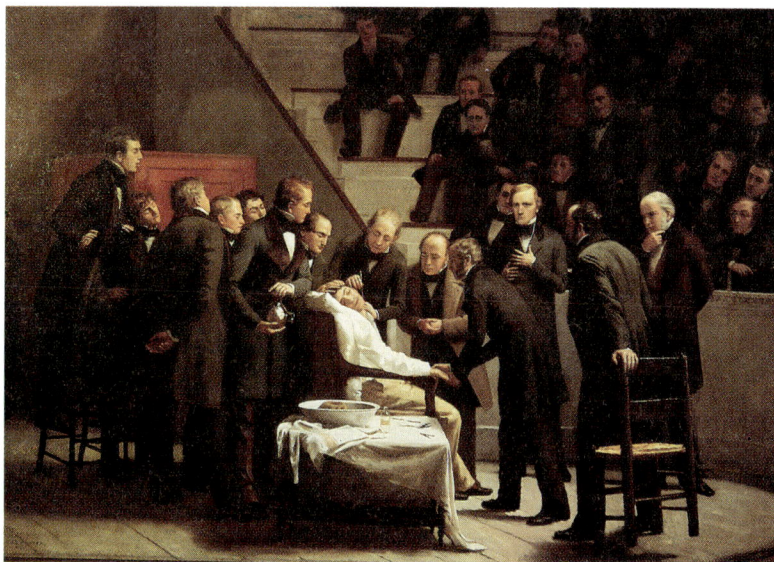

Other Mouth and Tooth Disorders

- **Halitosis** (hal-a-**toe**-sis) is *bad breath*, a condition that can be caused by such things as decayed teeth, eating certain foods, indigestion, and mouth infections. Mouthwashes and mints may temporarily cover up the odor. However, they do not cure it. Good oral hygiene can control halitosis. If halitosis is caused by tooth decay or other infections, the only way to cure it is to treat the underlying cause of the problem.

- **Malocclusion** (mal-uh-**klue**-shun) is a condition in which *the teeth of the upper and lower jaws do not properly align*. It is often hereditary. If the teeth are too large for the jaw to accommodate them, or if a person has an extra tooth, the teeth are pushed out of alignment.

  Other factors that might cause malocclusion are thumb sucking or tooth loss. Malocclusion can lead to decay and disease. It can also affect a person's speech and chewing. If malocclusion is severe, a person's appearance and self-esteem can be negatively affected.

  Orthodontics (or-tho-**don**-tics) is *the specialty of dentistry that corrects malocclusion*. Braces help to align the teeth.

Gum Disorders

- **Gingivitis** (jin-juh-**vite**-us) is *a disorder in which the gums become red and swollen and bleed easily*. The inflammation may be caused by dental plaque, misaligned teeth, or deposits of decaying food. A dentist must determine the cause of the inflammation in order to treat gingivitis.
- **Pyorrhea** (**pie**-or-ree-ah), or *periodontitis*, is *an inflammation of the membrane that covers the bony sockets of the teeth*. Gums that bleed easily, loose teeth, or persistent bad breath can all be signs of pyorrhea.

HEALTH UPDATE   HEALTH UPDATE   HEALTH UPDATE

Dental Terms

If your dentist says that you need a certain type of dental work, he may use one of these terms to describe it:

Bleaching—the painting of a chemical bleaching agent on stained or discolored teeth to lighten them.

Bonding—using a tooth-colored plastic on stained or damaged teeth to change color or shape.

Bridge—one or more artificial teeth fixed in the mouth by attachments to neighboring teeth.

Crown—also called a *cap*; an artificial cover for a decayed or damaged tooth.

Dentures—artificial teeth.

Filling—material, usually composed of a mixture of metals, or plastic or gold, used to fill a cavity.

Gingival (**jin**-juh-val) **surgery**—the removal of the infected part of the gum tissues in patients with peridontal (gum) disease.

Implant—an artificial tooth with metal roots that are surgically lodged in the jawbone or gums.

Inlay—a metal or porcelain filling from a mold of the tooth cavity and cemented in the tooth.

Laminate veneer (**lam**-i-nate ve-**neer**)—a thin, tooth-colored plastic or porcelain shell bonded to the tooth to hide stains, chips, or other imperfections.

Orthodontics (or-tho-**don**-tiks)—the use of braces or other devices to correct the position of teeth.

Root canal therapy—the cleaning out and filling of the innermost part (pulp) of a tooth that has been damaged or is severely decayed.

Sealant—a plastic coating applied to decay-prone surfaces of the back teeth to protect them from cavities.

Proper Tooth Care

Plaque is soft. You can easily scrub it off the surfaces of your teeth with a soft-bristled toothbrush. The plaque that forms between the teeth and just under the gum line really is the potential problem. This can only be removed by proper brushing and flossing. **Flossing** is *cleaning between the teeth with a special string.*

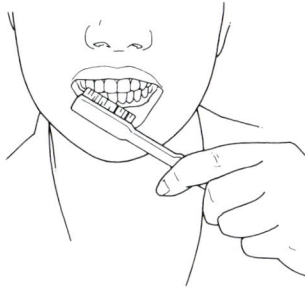

Proper Brushing of the Teeth

- Use a soft brush with rounded-end bristles and a flat brushing surface.
- Hold the brush sideways against teeth with the bristles at a 45° angle facing into the gum. (This allows bristles to get just under the gums to loosen plaque.)
- Wiggle the brush with short, back and forth strokes (do not scrub).

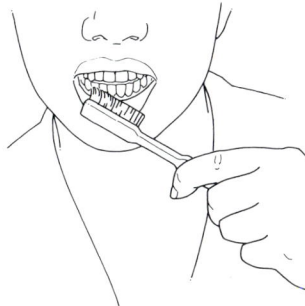

- Wiggle the brush on just two teeth at a time, and then move to the next two teeth. Brush both the cheek and tongue sides of all of your teeth.
- Brush the tongue to remove plaque and to reduce problems with halitosis.

Proper Flossing of the Teeth

- Floss the teeth, preferably with unwaxed dental floss, for more abrasive action.
- Work the floss between teeth, using a gentle sawing motion.
- Curve the floss into a C shape around the tooth, sliding it into the space between the gum and the tooth.
- Move the floss up and down, scraping against the side of the tooth.
- Curve the floss around the following tooth and repeat.
- Floss between all of your teeth.
- Rinse your mouth thoroughly.

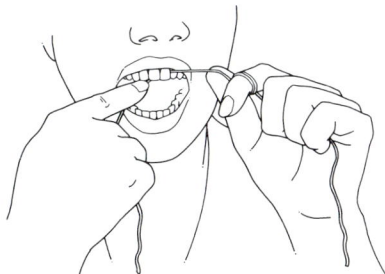

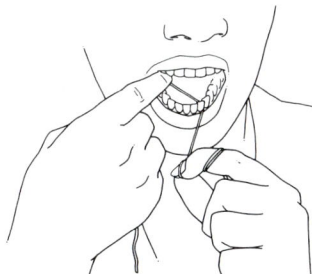

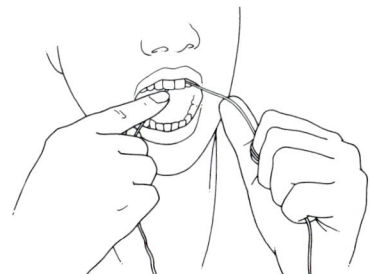

CHECK YOURSELF

1. Draw a tooth and label its parts.
2. What is periodontal disease?
3. Describe the process of tooth decay.
4. What is halitosis? How can it be controlled?

The eyes have over a million electrical connections and are responsible for about 80% of the knowledge you acquire. They can distinguish nearly 8 million differences in color! Of the special sense organs, the eyes provide the greatest knowledge of the environment. But individuals who do not have full use of sight often have developed their other senses to a much higher degree.

KEEPING FIT

What Does Preventive Eye Care Involve?

Check yourself with the following list. Do you promote healthy eye care by engaging in the following activities?

- Read in a well-lighted room.
- Watch TV in a well-lighted room, avoiding long periods of viewing.
- Have your eyes examined at least once every two years.
- Get a checkup once a year if you wear glasses or contact lenses.
- If you have corrective lenses, you wear them.
- When reading or studying for long periods of time, rest your eyes periodically by looking at a distant object.
- Avoid exposing your eyes to direct sun or bright glare.
- Have an eye test for glaucoma performed once a year if you are over 40 years.
- Do not use eye washes unless recommended by a doctor.
- Keep all sharp objects away from the eyes.
- Wear safety glasses or goggles when doing work or playing sports that could cause an eye injury.
- Avoid rubbing your eyes.

The Eyes' Built-In Protection

The eyes are situated in orbits protected by the bony sockets of the skull. These bones serve as protection for the eyes.

The general area around the eyes consists of the *lacrimal glands*, the *eyebrows* and *eyelids*, the *conjunctiva*, and the *eyelashes*.

- The **lacrimal gland** (**lak**-ree-mul **gland**), located above each eye, *is responsible for producing tears*. Tears are made up mostly of water and a small amount of salt and mucus. The salt gives the tears an antiseptic effect, which helps them to fight germs. Tears keep the eyeballs moist and help to keep foreign objects out of the eyes.

  Tears reach the surface of the eye through tiny ducts. Some of the tears evaporate from the eye's surface. Tears that do not evaporate are drained into the nasal cavity by two tear ducts located at the inner corner of the eye. These ducts open into larger ducts that run down the nose. When the production of tears increases, the tear ducts are not able to carry away the extra quantity, and tears flow over the lower lid.

- **Eyebrows** are *growths of hair that protect the eyes from foreign particles, perspiration, and direct rays of light*.

- **Eyelids** are *folds of skin that protect the eye by covering its surface*. The eyelids are controlled by an automatic reflex action that causes you to blink to protect the eyes. Your eyes are closed a total of about 30 minutes a day because of blinking!

- **Conjunctiva** (con-junk-**tee**-vah) is *a protective mucous membrane attached to the inner surface of the eyelids that continues over the outer surface of the eyeball*. Several different conditions, including lack of sleep, can irritate this membrane, causing the inflammation known as *conjunctivitis*.

- **Eyelashes** line the outer edge of the eyelids and *help to keep foreign particles out of the eyes*. The eyelashes receive a lubricating secretion from oil glands. The oily secretion prevents the eyelids from sticking together. If one of these glands becomes infected, a *sty*, or an inflamed swelling of the eyelid, may develop.

The Structure of the Eye

The **eyeball** is about 1 inch (2.5 cm) in diameter. The eyeball is slightly longer than it is wide. This is because of the bulge caused by the *cornea*, or the window of the eye.

The Eyeball Wall

The wall of the eyeball is made up of three layers: the *sclera*, the *choroid* (middle layer), and the *retina*.

The eye is a very flexible organ, but it needs proper care.

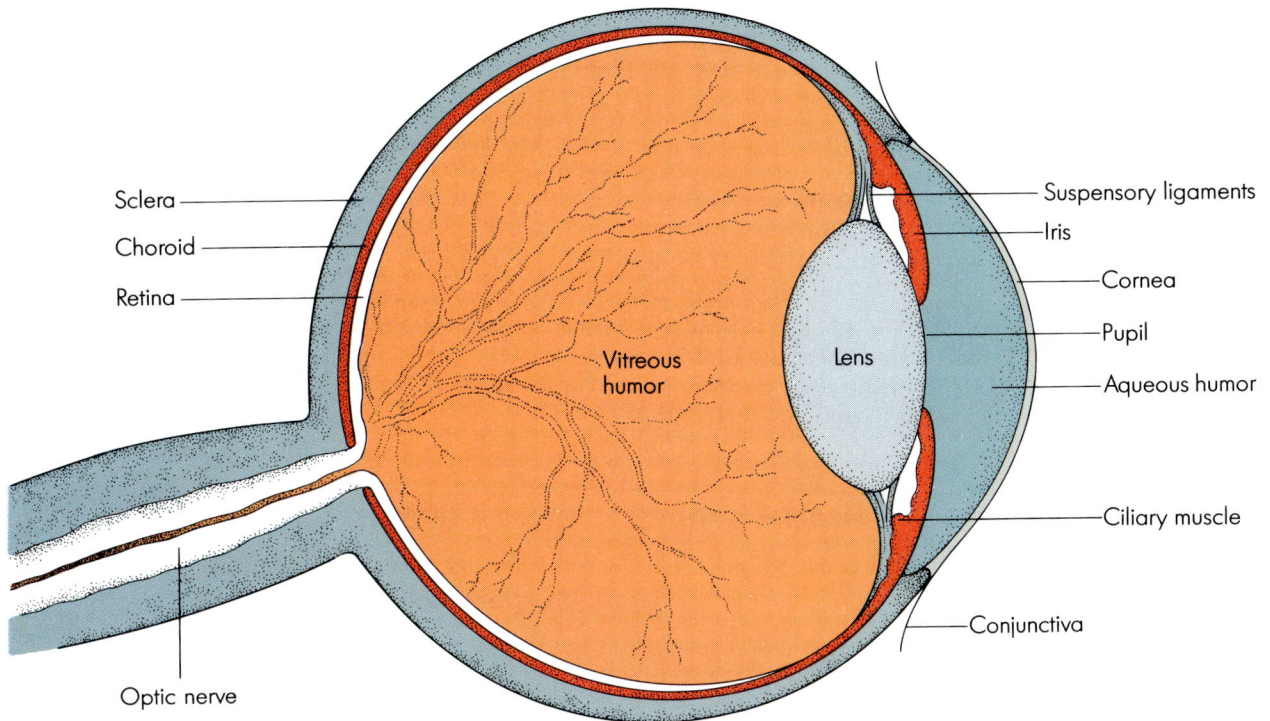

Sclera — Choroid — Retina — Vitreous humor — Lens — Optic nerve — Suspensory ligaments — Iris — Cornea — Pupil — Aqueous humor — Ciliary muscle — Conjunctiva

The Sclera   The **sclera** (**sklay**-ra) is *a white, tough membrane that helps the eye to keep its spherical shape.* This is the white part of your eye, and it helps to protect the eye's delicate inner structure. In the front part of the eye, the sclera forms the colorless, transparent **cornea** (**korn**-ee-ah), which is like *a round clear dish supplied with many free nerve endings.* Thus, it is extremely sensitive to particles that come in contact with its surface.

The Choroid   *The middle layer of the eyeball wall,* the **choroid** (**kor**-roid), contains:

- *the iris*, seen from the outside as the color of the eye,
- the *suspensory ligaments*, which blend with and hold the lens,
- the *ciliary muscles*, to which muscle fibers are attached.

The iris (**eye**-ris) is situated at the front of the eye. *Iris* is a Greek word meaning "rainbow." The **iris** *gives the eye its color* and is located in front of the lens. The *black circle in the center of the iris* is the **pupil**, which actually is a round hole, through which light passes.

Two sets of muscles in the iris change the size of the pupil, thus controlling the amount of light that enters the eye.

In dim light, one set of muscles, controlled by the sympathetic nervous system (see Chapter 14), pulls away from the iris, making it *larger*. This is called **dilation** (die-**lay**-shun).

In bright light, the other set of muscles, controlled by the parasympathetic system (see Chapter 14), makes the pupil *smaller*. This is called **contraction**.

Behind the pupil is the lens, held by the **suspensory ligaments.** These ligaments, in turn, are connected to the ciliary muscles. The **lens** *forms on the retina an image of what is before it.* The lens is curved and the ciliary muscles help to change its shape as the eye focuses on an object.

The *cavity between the cornea and the lens is filled with a watery fluid* called the **aqueous humor** (**ak**-kwee-us **hu**-mer). The words come from Latin. *Aqueous* means "water," and *humor* means "fluid." The aqueous humor is continuously formed and drained off.

The **vitreous humor** (**vit**-ree-us **hu**-mer), a thicker fluid, *is found behind the lens and keeps the eyeball firm. Vitreous* means "glasslike."

There are no blood vessels in the sclera, cornea, lens, aqueous humor, or vitreous humor. The choroid, the middle layer, contains the blood vessels that nourish the eyes.

HEALTH UPDATE   HEALTH UPDATE   HEALTH UPDATE

Laser Surgery for the Eyes

Doctors at the National Eye Institute have found that laser-beam treatment can be a significant factor in preventing **senile macular** (**mack**-u-lur) **degeneration,** a major cause of blindness in the elderly. *Blood vessels behind the retina enlarge, leak, and bleed. This forms scar tissue and eventually destroys vision.* The disease affects more than 10 million Americans over the age of 50.

In this technique, doctors use an argon lasar to sear and seal abnormal blood vessels that form in the eyes.

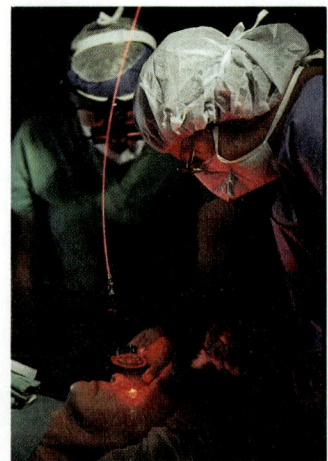

The Retina

The **retina** (**reh**-tin-uh) *makes up the third layer of the eyeball wall*. It contains the nerve cells and the processes responsible for vision. The retina contains millions of receptors that are classified as one of two kinds—rods or cones. Rods and cones, bearing names that describe their appearance, are light-sensitive receptors.

Rods   The rods are cylindrical, *register light and darkness*, and are used in dim light. They contain a photosensitive chemical called *visual purple*, making it possible to see in dim light. Light breaks down this visual purple so that when you go from a light room to a dark room you cannot see at first. As the rods re-form the visual purple, you begin to see objects in shades of black, white, and gray. *People who do not have enough visual purple* experience **night blindness**.

Rods lie toward the edge of the retina. An estimated 125 million rods are in a retina.

Cones   The cones are cone-shaped and are situated with their pointed end nearer the choroid layer. **Cones** *give you vision in bright light and are able to detect differences in color.* About 7 million cones are in a retina, concentrated in its back part.

Some people have *a deficiency in perceiving colors*, which is called **color blindness**. Almost all color blindness is mild. Color-blind people have trouble seeing shades of red or green. It is rare that a person has complete color blindness—a condition in which the person sees only shades of black, white, and gray. The picture on the right illustrates how color blindness is tested.

If you can see the number in the circle of dots your vision is normal. If you cannot see the number, you have red/green color blindness.

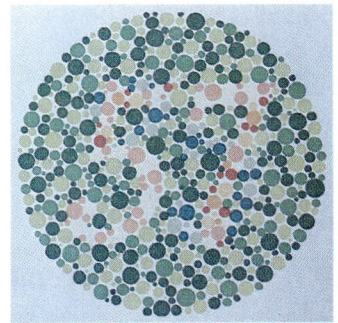

The Optic Nerve

At the back of the eye is *a large nerve cable that connects the eye with the brain*. This is known as the **optic nerve**. At the point where this optic nerve connects with the eye, the nerve spreads out to form a thin inner layer of the eyeball.

The *point where the optic nerve enters the eye* is called the **blind spot**. There are no cones or rods in this area, so vision in this spot is not possible. The presence of a blind spot can be demonstrated with the following test: Close your left eye and stare at the square below with your right eye. Bring the page closer to your eye. At a distance of nine inches, the circle will disappear from view. You can repeat the test by gazing at the circle with your left eye and closing your right eye.

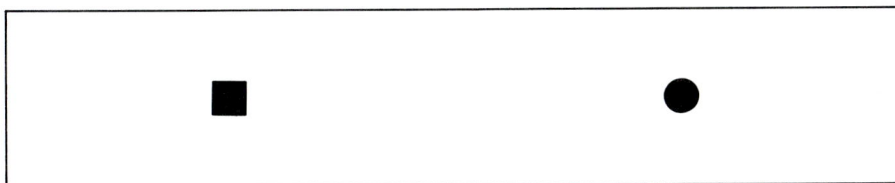

Use this illustration to demonstrate the presence of a blind spot.

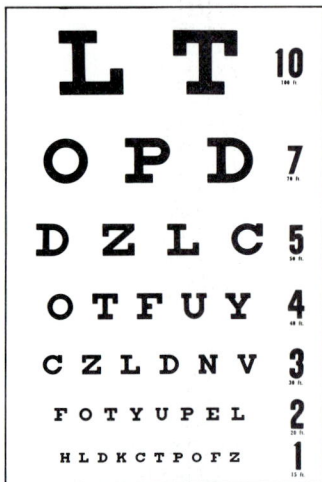

L T | 10
O P D | 7
D Z L C | 5
O T F U Y | 4
C Z L D N V | 3
F O T Y U P E L | 2
H L D K C T P O F Z | 1

Eye charts have been used in eye examinations for over 100 years.

The top picture shows a cataract being removed. The bottom picture shows a child with crossed eyes.

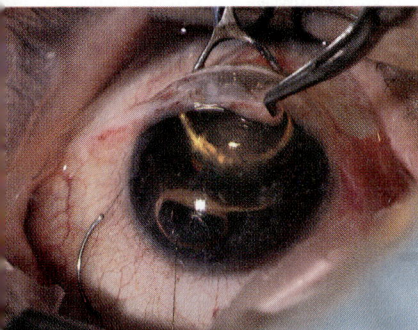

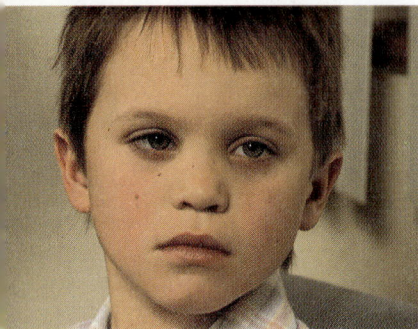

Your Vision

As the light rays pass through the cornea and aqueous humor, the image is magnified. The light rays then penetrate the lens, which adjusts to focus the light on the retina. This adjustment is called **accommodation**. *The lens bulges to accommodate near objects and flattens to accommodate faraway objects.*

The light-sensitive retina sends impulses from the optic nerve to the occipital lobe of the brain. The brain interprets the light rays as an image.

In normal vision, a sharp, wide-angle image is produced, despite varying conditions. If you stand 20 feet from the eye chart and can read the top eight lines, you have 20/20 vision. If you can read at 20 feet what a person with normal vision can read at 40 feet you have 20/40 vision. A person who has less than 20/200 vision and who cannot see the "L" at the top of the chart is legally blind.

Problems with Vision

- **Nearsightedness (myopia)** (my-**oh**-pee-ah). This is a condition in which *the light rays are focused in front of the retina.* You can see clearly when things are close, but distant objects are blurred. Concave corrective lenses in eyeglasses make the rays focus farther back.
- **Farsightedness (hyperopia)** (high-per-**oh**-pee-ah). This condition occurs when *the light rays are focused behind the retina.* You can see distant objects clearly, but material close-up is blurred. This condition is corrected by convex lenses in eyeglasses.
- **Astigmatism** (a-**stig**-muh-tizm) means "without point." This condition occurs when *the curvature of the lens is uneven.* Light rays focus at different points, causing the image to be distant. This condition is corrected with specially ground lenses for eyeglasses.
- **Cataract** (kat-**er**-act). This is *a clouded lens* that causes blurring or hazy vision and problems with night vision. The clouded lens may be surgically removed and vision restored with corrective glasses. A cataract is the most important single cause of blindness among adults.
- **Crossed eyes (strabismus)** (stra-**biz**-mus). This might occur when the eye muscles of both eyes do not work together, *causing one or both eyes to turn inward or outward.* The person may then see two images because the brain, even though it can interpret the images, cannot fuse the input from each eye.
- **Glaucoma** (glaw-**koh**-mah). This condition is caused by fluid pressures increasing in the eyeball, either because too much aqueous humor is produced or because it cannot drain off well. Glaucoma may cause damage to the optic nerve and blindness. It usually develops slowly and painlessly. Glaucoma can be diagnosed during an eye examination. If glaucoma is detected early, it can be treated with medication or surgery.
- **Sties (styz)**. A sty is an eye infection caused by bacteria. It lodges in the glands of the eyelids.

- **Epidemic conjunctivitis** (kuhn-junk-tuh-**vite**-us). This is an eye infection that affects the sclera and causes reddening. It is sometimes called *pinkeye*.
- **Detached retina.** The separation of the retina from underlying tissue causes a detached retina. It can be treated and corrected with laser surgery.
- **Amblyopia** (am-blee-**oh**-pee-ah) ("lazy eye"). This is a major cause of partial vision loss in children. It is a condition of reduced or dim vision in an eye that otherwise appears to be normal. Over 500,000 Americans suffer some degree of amblyopia that could have been prevented. Prevention depends on early diagnosis.

Wellness and Eye Care

Often, we take our sight for granted. Yet reports from the National Society to Prevent Blindness indicate that we could do much more to protect and promote healthy eyes. Did you know that:

- among people between the ages of 6 and 17, 12 million, or 1 in every 4, have vision problems?
- each year 54,000 young people between the ages of 6 and 17 suffer some degree of vision loss?
- each year 150,000 students suffer eye injuries?
- an estimated 71,000 people under the age of 15 are treated in hospital emergency rooms for product-related eye injuries (baseballs, cigarettes, pencils, metal pieces, and glass are the most hazardous products)?
- two-thirds of eye injuries occur during play or sports?
- 90% of eye injuries could have been prevented?

For more information on first aid for eye injuries, see page HB28 of your *Health Handbook*.

For more information on first aid for eye injuries, see page HB28 of your *Health Handbook*.

KEEPING FIT

Test for Astigmatism

If positive, the spokes of the wheel are not straight or look gray. If the spokes of the wheel are all of the same intensity, the person does not have astigmatism.

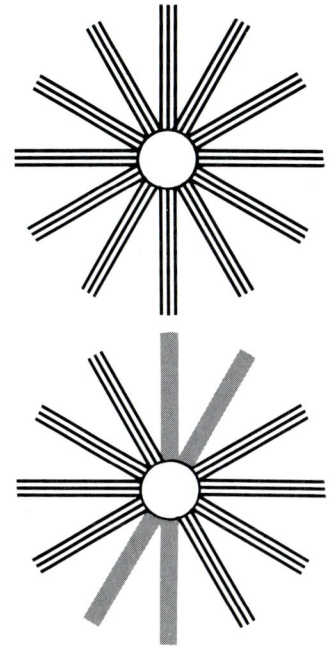

CHECK YOURSELF

1. How do lacrimal glands protect the eyes?
2. Describe the main functions of the three layers of the eyeball.
3. How does the eye receive its nourishment?
4. Explain the role of the rods and cones in vision.
5. Define myopia, hyperopia, cataract, astigmatism, and glaucoma.
6. What is a detached retina?
7. When do most eye injuries in young people occur? What is one way to prevent them?
8. What are three procedures that you can follow to keep your eyes healthy?

Julie, a tenth grader, spends two afternoons a week teaching sign language to deaf children. Julie lost her hearing as a young child, but she has not let that slow her down. Julie not only commmunciates through sign language, but she can also read lips.

Julie is among thousands of people who are deaf. Disorders of the ear may result in our loss of hearing, as well as affect our sense of balance. Birth defects, injuries, and diseases are the three causes of hearing loss. Before learning how these causes affect hearing, let's learn how the complicated process of hearing takes place.

Sign language is easy to learn and use.

The Parts of the Ear

The ear extends deep into the skull and has three main parts: the *outer ear*, the *middle ear*, and the *inner ear*.

The Outer Ear

The outer ear consists of a fleshy curved part that is attached to each side of the head and is called the **auricle** (**or**-ree-kul). Composed of fatty tissue and cartilage, the cuplike shape of the auricle *collects sound waves and directs them into the ear.*

Looking directly into the ear, you can see the **external auditory canal.** It is *a passageway about 1 inch (2.5 cm) long, the outer part lined with fine hairs and tiny wax-producing glands.* The wax and tiny hairs protect the ear by keeping out foreign substances. The inner two-thirds of the auditory canal is surrounded by the *temporal bone,* the hardest bone in the body. The auditory canal leads to the *eardrum,* which is a thin sheet of tissue about ¼ inch (0.625 cm) across. It separates the middle ear from the outer ear.

Proper ear care includes trying to avoid loud, sustained noise.

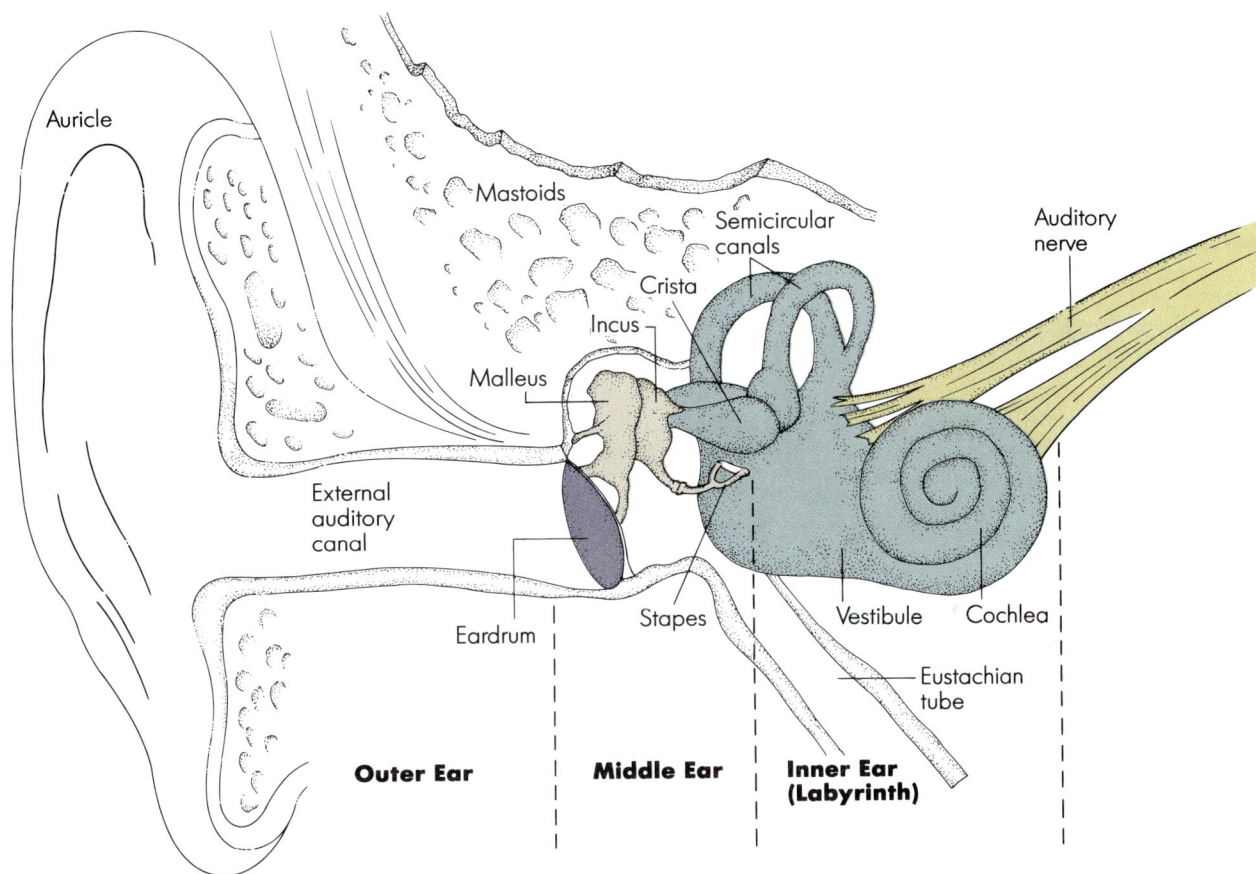

Auricle

Mastoids

Semicircular canals

Crista

Incus

Malleus

External auditory canal

Eardrum

Stapes

Auditory nerve

Vestibule

Cochlea

Eustachian tube

Outer Ear

Middle Ear

Inner Ear (Labyrinth)

The Middle Ear

Behind the eardrum are *three small bones* called the **ossicles** (**ah**-see-kulz), which *are linked together and connect the eardrum with the inner ear:*

- The **malleus** (**mal**-ee-us) ("hammer" in Latin) is the first bone. It is attached to the eardrum and is the largest of the three bones.
- The **incus** (**ing**-kuz) ("anvil" in Latin) is the middle bone. It connects the malleus and the innermost bone, the stapes.
- The **stapes** (**stay**-peez) ("stirrup" in Latin) is stirrup-shaped and attaches to the inner ear. It is the smallest bone in the body. The ends of the stapes are attached by ligaments to a membrane called the *oval window,* which leads to the inner ear.

Two other parts of the head connect to the middle ear. Although they are not actually a part of it, they can affect your hearing:

- The **mastoid** (**mass**-toid) **process** is a series of small, air-filled spaces in the bones that lie behind the middle ear. These spaces connect with the middle ear.
- The **Eustachian** (you-**stay**-she-un) **tube** is about 1.5 inches (3.8 cm) long and connects the nasal cavity in the back of the throat with the middle ear.

Have you ever experienced your ears popping as you rode in an elevator? That was your Eustachian tube opening to let air pass between your throat and middle ear. It opens when you swallow, blow your nose, or yawn, thus equalizing the pressure on either side of the eardrum. If the Eustachian tube did not open, the eardrum would rupture with a sudden change in pressure like the one which occurs when riding an elevator.

The Inner Ear

The inner ear, also called the **labyrinth** (**lab**-uh-rinth), consists of three delicate parts: the *vestibule*, the *semicircular canals*, and the *cochlea*:

- The **vestibule**, which forms the central part of the inner ear, *contains the utricle and saccule*. These tiny baglike structures are lined with hair cells. These hair cells are specialized sense cells with tiny,

IMPROVING YOURSELF

Care of the Ears

The ears are a delicate instrument that must be carefully maintained. It is important to clean them regularly and to protect them against weather, especially the cold.

Cleaning the outer ears should always be done with a cotton swab. The soft head of the swab can take out dirt and ear wax, but do not push the swab into the ear. Never use pencils or other sharp items to clean ears.

Sometimes, through vibrations or ear wax, the inside of the ear may feel ticklish. Gently use your thumb to wiggle the outer ear passage. Do not use swabs or sharp instruments to stop the tickling.

Cold weather, drafts, and sudden changes of temperature can prepare the way for ear infections. These infections can be very painful. Use ear muffs or a hat that covers the ears in the cold weather. This will prevent infection in the inner ear and frostbite of the earlobes. If there are bad drafts, you may want to put a cotton ball in the outer ear passage to stop wind from entering the inner ear.

hairlike projections. They play an important role in the hearing process.

- The **semicircular canals** consist of *three canals set at right angles to one another.* Each contains a fluid-filled duct that widens at one end to form a pouch. This pouch contains hair cells attached to nerve fibers. The ducts of the semicircular canals connect with the utricle, which is connected, also by a duct, to the saccule. The three semicircular canals are responsible for your sense of balance.
- The **cochlea** (**koh**-klee-ah) resembles a snail shell. It is *made up of three fluid-filled ducts.* Within one of these ducts is the *basilar membrane,* which consists of over 15,000 hair cells. These hair cells make up the *organ of Corti,* which contains our hearing receptors.

Also in the inner ear is the auditory (**aw-dee**-tor-ree) nerve. Fibers from the **auditory nerve** extend to each hair cell in the organ of Corti and to the hair cells of the saccule, utricle, and semicircular canals.

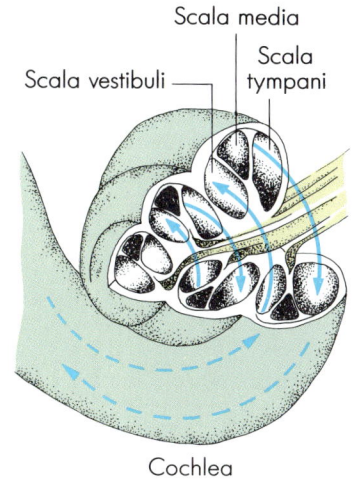

Scala media
Scala vestibuli
Scala tympani
Cochlea

The cochlea consists of three twisting pipe-like ducts.

The Path of Sound Waves

In order to hear, **sound waves,** which are *vibrations in the air caused by anything that moves,* must reach the organ of Corti. Sound waves enter the external auditory canal through the auricle, causing the eardrum to vibrate. These vibrations are carried across the middle ear by the malleus, incus, and stapes to the oval window, the opening between the middle and inner ear. Sound vibrations cause the stapes to move like a plunger in and out of the oval window, thus causing fluid in the cochlea to move.

What happens when sound waves reach the cochlea? Within the cochlea are about 24,000 tiny fibers that are set into motion by the sound waves. These fibers cause a vibration in the hair cells of the organ of Corti. The vibration of the hair cells stimulates the nerves attached to them. These

Some people's sense of hearing is keener because of hereditary factors.

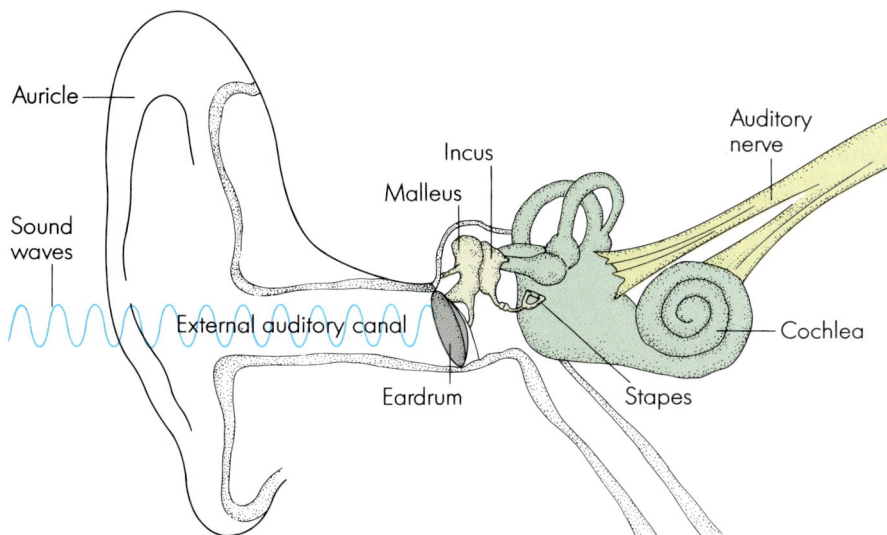

Auricle
Sound waves
External auditory canal
Eardrum
Malleus
Incus
Stapes
Auditory nerve
Cochlea

nerves send messages through the auditory nerve to the temporal lobe, which is the center of hearing in the brain. It is here that sounds are classified and interpreted.

Hearing with Your Ears

Binaural (by-**naw**-ral) **hearing** is *the ability to determine the direction a sound comes from by being able to hear it with both ears.* A sound coming from the right is slightly louder in the right ear. It also reaches your right ear a fraction of a second sooner than it reaches your left ear. Your brain, picking up on this difference in time and loudness, determines the direction from which the sound comes.

Your Sense of Balance

Do you think of balance when you are identifying your senses? How does your body maintain its balance? Your brain receives information from various sense organs about your body's balance. Your eyes and certain pressure-sensitive cells in your arms and legs send messages to your brain about changes in body positions. However, it is the semicircular canals that provide much of the brain's information about balance.

The Crista

Movement of your head causes the fluid in the semicircular canals to move in a certain direction. At one end of each canal is an organ called a **crista** (**kris**-tah). Each crista consists of tiny hairs covered by a dome-shaped, jellylike mass called the **cupule** (**kup**-pule). Nerves connect the crista to the brain.

Movements of the head cause fluid to press against a crista, bending the tiny, sensitive hairs. Nerve endings send a message to the brain about these bent hairs. The brain sends a message back, directing the muscles to make the necessary adjustments to maintain balance.

The semicircular canals also enable you to recognize the direction in which your body is moving, even with your eyes closed. One of the canals

The body's balance is controlled by the semicircular canals of the inner ear.

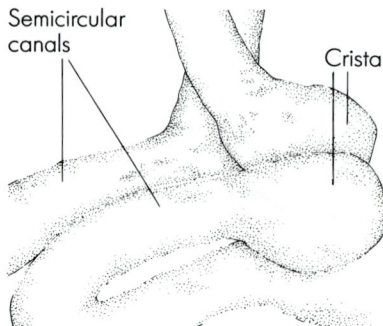

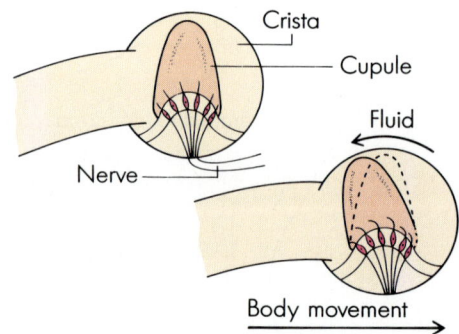

is horizontal, and the other two are vertical. When the head or body moves up or down, forward or backward, or from side to side, the fluid in the canals moves, affecting the delicate hairs in the crista. Again, the nerve endings are stimulated, sending an impulse to the brain.

Disorders of the Ear

Deafness is defined as *the loss of ability to hear, which may be partial or complete.* Causes of deafness include birth defects, injury, and diseases.

When the hearing problem is associated with the outer or middle ear, transmission deafness occurs. **Transmission deafness** means that *sound waves are prevented from reaching the eardrum or that sound waves are not being transmitted to the cochlea.* A buildup of wax or some other form of blockage can prevent sound waves from reaching the eardrum. Middle ear infections or diseases involving the ossicles can result in this type of deafness.

Otosclerosis (ot-o-scle-**row**-sis) is *a hereditary disease that is a common cause of partial deafness.* Otosclerosis occurs when, *because of an overgrowth of bone, the ossicles lose their ability to move, so the sound waves never reach the inner ear.* Otosclerosis is usually *progressive,* meaning that its severity increases with time. Surgical procedures can help to restore hearing.

IMPROVING YOURSELF

Sensory Deafness

Very loud noises that leave your ears ringing can cause permanent damage through accumulative hearing loss. It is usually not noticeable until one reaches the age of 40 or 50.

Sensory deafness is *hearing loss caused by excessive noise over a long time.* Such noise affects the sensitive sensory hair cells in the inner ear. Unfortunately, this type of deafness cannot be corrected. Its cause is all around us—noise. Constant exposure to 85 decibels or above can cause permanent damage to hearing. This type of deafness is gradual. At first, only the high-frequency sounds are lost. Gradually, the nerve cells that transmit lower tones become damaged, and a person cannot hear voices. Whether the sound is rock music or a motorcycle, the damage is caused by the *volume* of the sound, not the quality.

The prevention of sensory deafness is simple. The first step is to turn down the volume on the stereo, television, radio, or electric guitar to below 65 decibels. (60 decibels is about what ordinary conversation is.) If you work with an object that causes noise of 85 decibels or more—such as a lawn mower, motorcycle, vacuum cleaner, factory machinery, trucks, or planes—wear hearing protection. For more information on sensory deafness and noise pollution, see Chapter 32.

When hearing loss is associated with the inner ear, **sensory**, or **nerve, deafness** occurs. This means *there is damage to the cochlea, auditory nerve, and/or part of the brain.* Nerve deafness can result from continued exposure to high-intensity noise and from tumors.

Some drugs can damage the hair cells in the cochlea or the auditory nerve, causing a hearing loss. Certain drugs taken by a woman during pregnancy can prevent the normal development of the baby's cochlea.

Have you ever experienced *a ringing noise in your ears*? This common condition is called **tinnitus** (**tin**-neh-tus), and it can be irritating. It can be caused by several conditions, including a buildup of ear wax, fluid in the middle ear, change in pressure in the inner ear, or an ear infection. Tinnitus itself is not an ear disease. It is usually a symptom of some other problem. Once that problem is identified and corrected, the tinnitus goes away.

Testing Your Hearing

There are several tests for auditory function. One test that determines if sound waves are being transmitted through the ear is called the **Weber test.** The handle of a vibrating tuning fork is placed in the middle of the forehead. If the defect is in the middle or outer ear, the sound will still be heard in the deaf ear. This is because the sound waves are conducted to the inner ear through the bones.

An instrument called an **audiometer** (aw-dee-**om**-eh-ter) is used to test for hearing acuteness and pitch discrimination. The audiometer produces sounds of variable pitch and intensity. The person being tested signals when he or she hears the sounds.

Sound is the result of vibrations. *Pitch,* or *frequency,* refers to the number of vibrations per second. Frequency is expressed in hertz (Hz). One hertz equals one cycle per second. *Intensity* refers to **loudness or softness of sound.** It is measured in **decibels** (**des**-uh-belz) (dB). Individuals with normal hearing hear pitches from 50 to 25,000 Hz and hear intensities from 0 to 120 dB.

CHECK YOURSELF

1. What is the function of the auditory canal?
2. How is the ear protected?
3. Describe what makes up the labyrinth of the ear.
4. How should the ears be cleaned?
5. Explain how sound waves travel through the ear.
6. What is binaural hearing?
7. How does the body maintain its balance?
8. What is the difference between transmission and sensory deafness?

HEALTH

CAREER

DENTAL, EYE, AND EAR SPECIALISTS

Dentistry

Almost all dental schools offer a four-year program leading to a doctoral degree in dentistry. Beyond that, between 10% and 15% go to specialty schools in orthodontics, endodontics, oral pathology, oral surgery, pedodontics, periodontics, and dental public health.

There are many professional opportunities for dentists. Most dentists prefer private practice—either as solo practitioners or in a group. Besides private practice, dentists also have career opportunities in governmental health agencies, dental equipment manufacturing companies, pharmaceutical firms, health insurance companies, dental associations, and dental clinics.

Ophthalmology

Even though the **ophthalmologist** (op-thal-**mull**-uh-**jist**) *specializes in disorders and diseases of the eye*, most specialists in this area practice a combination of medicine and surgery, ranging from lens prescriptions and standard medical treatment to the most delicate and precise surgical manipulations.

There are many subspecialties in the field of ophthal-

mology. These include cornea and external diseases, glaucoma, neuro-ophthalmology, ophthalmic pathology, ophthalmic plastic surgery, pediatric ophthalmology, and vitreoretinal diseases.

When ophthalmologists complete their training, they are specialists in all aspects of eye care and are licensed to practice medicine and surgery in the prevention, diagnosis, and management of eye diseases and disorders.

Other experts in eye treatment are the:

- **optometrist**, one who examines people's eyes to diagnose vision problems and to detect signs of disease and other abnormal conditions. When necessary, optometrists prescribe lenses and other treatment.
- **optician**, one who is specially trained to fill eyeglass prescriptions. Opticians grind lenses and fit eyeglasses.

Otolaryngology

The **otolaryngologist** (otto-lar-an-**jol**-o-gist), also known as an ear, nose, and throat (ENT) specialist, is concerned with the structure, function, and diseases of the ear, nose, and throat. Some specialists are

known as otologists only, particularly if they are surgeons and specialize in mastoid operations or limit their practice to hearing defects. Others may choose to specialize in caring for the nose (rhinologist) or throat (larynologist).

ENT specialists examine affected organs using audiometers, prisms, nasoscopes, and fluoroscopes. They may perform tests to determine the extent of hearing or speech loss from illness or injury.

The otolaryngologist performs diagnostic and surgical procedures which may include reconstruction of the nose, ears, jaw, or facial area.

American Dental Association
211 East Chicago Avenue
Chicago, IL 60611

American Academy of Ophthalmology
655 Beach Street
San Francisco, CA 94109

American Optometric Association
243 North Lindbergh Boulevard
St. Louis, MO 63141

American Board of Otolaryngology
1301 East Ann Street
Ann Arbor, MI 48104

CHAPTER 4 Review

CHAPTER SUMMARY

- Perhaps one of the most noticeable parts of your appearance is your smile—your teeth and mouth.
- Good, regular oral hygiene is necessary for healthy, clean teeth.
- Oral hygiene is also an important factor in preventing periodontal disease.
- Your senses of smell, taste, sight, and hearing are very closely related to your nervous system.
- The highly specialized organs associated with these senses connect with sensory nerves, which carry impulses to the brain.
- The organs of these senses are the most delicate in the body.
- Each organ serves as a protector and has specific built-in protection.
- Many specific problems in vision and hearing can be corrected if they are detected in time.
- Almost all problems resulting from injury to the eyes and ears can be prevented.
- Good health care, including eye and ear examinations, is essential for protecting the sense organs.

REVIEWING WHAT YOU LEARNED

1. How can you protect and maintain your teeth?
2. Explain the process of tooth decay.
3. List four structures that help to protect the eye, and tell what each does.
4. How do farsightedness and nearsightedness differ?
5. Trace the path of a sound wave from the outside environment to its interpretation in the brain.
6. What does a score of 20/60 mean on an eye test?
7. What is the relationship between your sense of hearing and your sense of balance?
8. What can you do to care for your (a) eyes and (b) ears?

CHAPTER VOCABULARY

Teeth and Mouth
olfactory cells
taste buds
periodontium
root
crown
pulp
toothache
dentin
cementum
enamel
periodontal disease
plaque
tartar
abscessed tooth
halitosis
malocclusion
orthodontics
gingivitis
pyorrhea
flossing
dentistry

Eyes
lacrimal gland
eyebrow
eyelids
conjunctiva
eyelashes
eyeball
sclera
cornea
choroid
iris
pupil
dilation
contraction
suspensory ligaments
lens
aqueous humor
vitreous humor
retina
rods
night blindness
cones

color blindness
optic nerve
blind spot
accommodation
nearsightedness
farsightedness
astigmatism
cataract
crossed eyes
senile macular degeneration
glaucoma
sties
epidemic conjunctivitis
detached retina
amblyopia
ophthalmologist
optometrist
optician

Ears
sound waves
binaural hearing
crista
cupule

deafness
transmission deafness
otosclerosis
sensory deafness
tinnitus
audiometer
decibel
otolaryngologist

Outer Ear
auricle
external auditory canal

Middle Ear
ossicles
malleus
incus
stapes
mastoid process
Eustachian tube

Inner Ear
vestibule
semicircular canals
cochlea
auditory nerve

PUTTING VOCABULARY TO USE

On a separate piece of paper, write the following statements. Then supply the missing word or phrase from the chapter vocabulary list.

Teeth and Mouth

1. _____. An inflammation of the gums
2. _____. Supporting structures of the teeth
3. _____. Bad breath
4. _____. A very hard substance that irritates underlying bones and gum
5. _____. The very sensitive living tissue inside the tooth
6. _____. Types of cells that detect smell
7. _____. The material that surrounds the pulp
8. _____. A major part of the tooth, located inside the gum
9. _____. Hardest material in the body
10. _____. Sticky film that forms on teeth

The Eyes

1. _____. Outer layer of the eye that helps the eye to keep its spherical shape.
2. _____. Colorless, transparent front part of the eye, supplied with many free nerve endings.
3. _____ _____. Cavity between the cornea and the lens, filled with watery fluid.
4. _____. Location of nerve cells and processes responsible for vision.
5. _____ _____. Gland responsible for producing tears.
6. _____. Middle layer of the wall of the eyeball.
7. _____ _____. Thick fluid behind the lens that keeps the eyeball firm.
8. _____. Light rays focus at different points.
9. _____. Increased pressure in the eye.
10. _____. Light rays focus in front of the retina.

The Ears

1. _____. The three small bones in the middle ear.
2. _____. The outer part of the ear.
3. _____. Attaches to the inner ear and is the smallest bone in the body.
4. _____. Largest of the three middle ear bones; attached to the eardrum.
5. _____. The inner ear.
6. _____. Resembles a snail shell and is made of three fluid-filled ducts.
7. _____. Bone of the middle ear that connects two other small bones.
8. _____ _____. Series of small air-filled spaces in the bones that lie behind the middle ear.
9. _____ _____. Vibrations in the air.
10. _____. Cause of partial deafness.

APPLYING WHAT YOU LEARNED

1. If your Eustachian tube is blocked and you are planning to travel by airplane, what problems might you encounter?
2. Research the Braille alphabet or sign language. How were they developed?
3. Make a report on the use of fluoride to prevent tooth decay. Is it added to the water in your community? If so, has the rate of tooth decay changed since the introduction of fluoride?
4. Identify three ads for oral hygiene. What do the ads claim? Are they factual? Make up your own ad using only factual information. Share it with the class.
5. Interview someone who is blind or has limited vision, or visit a center for the blind. What special problems do blind people have? How have their other senses accommodated for their lack of vision?

FOCUS ON WELLNESS

The body's senses allow us to function fully in our environment. They are very closely related to learning. *My health behaviors reflect care for my senses because I . . .*

U N I T

2

GETTING ALONG WITH YOURSELF AND OTHERS

Wellness and Mental Health

How would you describe someone who is mentally healthy? Like physical health, mental health is often thought of in terms of the absence of mental illness. However, there is much more to mental health than not being mentally ill. There are many people who are not mentally ill, but who do not have good mental health.

After studying this chapter, you will be able to:
- describe the characteristics of good mental health,
- explain how self-concept develops,
- relate mental health to one's self-concept,
- describe Maslow's theory of needs,
- explain how an expression of emotions affects one's mental and physical health,
- describe a basic method for solving problems.

Think of the term *wellness* again—this time in relation to mental health. You experience varying levels of mental health at different times, and many factors influence each level of your mental health. Just as in the case of physical health, you can work to maintain a high level of mental health.

Your Mental Health

It is difficult to identify specific standards for evaluating a person's mental health. However, some general characteristics of good mental health exist. By looking at these characteristics, you can get an idea of what it means to be mentally healthy. You also can begin to determine your personal level of mental health. Keep in mind, however, that no one has all of these characteristics all of the time. You will find a chart on page 80 to help you.

The National Association for Mental Health describes a person with good **mental health** as one who:

■ *feels comfortable about himself or herself,*
■ *feels right about other people,*
■ *is able to meet the demands of life.*

What Influences Your Level of Mental Health?

Can you think of the one factor that all the characteristics listed on page 80 have in common? Somehow, they all relate to or are affected by a person's self-concept. Your **self-concept** is *the sum total of how you view yourself.* It is your unique set of perceptions, ideas, and attitudes about yourself.

How is your self-concept formed? From the moment you were born, you began to receive and accumulate messages about yourself. You learned how to get attention, what made you comfortable, what satisfied your hunger. You heard, "She's the cutest baby," or "No! No! Bad! Don't touch!" All of these experiences went together to form the beginnings of your self-concept.

By the time you reached school age, your self-concept was fairly well formed. Your adjustment to, and success in, school was largely determined by your beliefs and attitudes about yourself. Many studies have shown that self-concept is closely related to success in school.

Positive and Negative Influences on Self-Concept

You probably can see that other people have a significant impact on your self-concept. Can you remember events that occurred throughout

Determining Mental Health

Make up your own "Rate Your Mental Health" inventory. Compare the characteristics given in this list with those you compiled.

IMPROVING YOURSELF

Rate Your Mental Health

Let us look at some characteristics that describe a mentally healthy person. On a separate sheet of paper, indicate whether the statement describes you and how you feel or act *most of the time.*

1. *Feeling Comfortable about Myself*
   - ■ I can express my thoughts and feelings.
   - ■ I can express my emotions and am not overcome or immobilized by them.
   - ■ I can cope with both disappointment and success.
   - ■ I recognize personal shortcomings.
   - ■ I can laugh at myself.
   - ■ I am optimistic.
   - ■ I am generally cheerful and active.
   - ■ I know my limits as well as my abilities.
   - ■ I live by a set of standards and know what is important to me.
   - ■ I like who I am.

2. *Feeling Right about Other People*
   - ■ I enjoy spending some time alone.
   - ■ I get along well with others.
   - ■ I can interact with people and work with a group.
   - ■ I continue to participate when I do not get my way.
   - ■ I do not try to dominate.
   - ■ I can accept differences in other people.
   - ■ I feel I am a part of a group.

- ■ I am interested in and enjoy being with others.
- ■ I have several satisfying personal relationships.

3. *Meeting the Demands of Life*
   - ■ I face my problems rather than avoid them.
   - ■ I can ask for help when it is needed.
   - ■ I do not make excuses for my actions.
   - ■ I set realistic personal goals and have a plan for working toward them.
   - ■ I give my best effort in whatever I do.
   - ■ I can cope with change.
   - ■ I see challenges and experiences as opportunities for growth.

Scoring: The highest possible score is 24. A score of between 18 and 24 is *good,* 10 to 17 *fair,* 9 to 0 *poor.* Note that there is not a perfect score of 26, the number of entries above. Your level of mental health varies. Most of us have some areas that need work.

Look at the statements you did not check. Can you make some generalizations about an area in which you need improvement? Make a plan for working on that area. Set a goal for yourself. You are likely to see the benefits quickly.

elementary school? Was there always one student who was the first to be selected on a team and one who was the last? one who seemed to always be late or in trouble? one who was smart or seemed to catch on fast?

People tend to put labels on others for their behavior. Have you ever heard, "She's the smartest girl in the class," or "He's a born athlete," or "There's no task she can't handle"?

On the other hand, have you heard comments like, "He's always late," or "She's the class clown," or "He's so clumsy"? Not only do these negative kinds of remarks hurt one's self-concept, but they also reinforce the behavior.

If a boy hears over and over that he is always late or clumsy, chances are he will begin to conform to those comments. People then begin to expect such behavior from him. A cycle is developed that is hard to break. It becomes difficult for him to change.

People with good self-concepts grow up to be basically happy and positive.

The Importance of Self-Concept

Your self-concept is probably the single most important factor influencing what you do and how you do it. Your self-concept is directly related to your general level of wellness. How you feel physically, as well as how you take care of yourself—*your health habits*—are all affected by your self-concept.

Improving Self-Concept

We are constantly trying to protect or improve our self-concept. If your self-concept is high, you tend to see new experiences as challenging. If your self-concept is low, you are more likely to see new experiences as threatening—as sources for potential failure.

Think of some of the things you say and do during a school day. Look at the examples below. What would you say about each person's self-concept?

- "No sense in studying. I'm too dumb in math to pass anyway."
- "I didn't win the race, but I did my best and had a good time."
- "I'm not going to try out for the team, because I won't make it."

People with good self-concepts generally like who they are and what they do. They are basically happy and positive people. They can bounce back from defeats or losses. People with good self-concepts are likely to take good care of their health. Their appearance also reflects their feelings about themselves.

What kind of messages do you give yourself? For one day, jot down the internal messages you tell yourself. Are they generally positive?

Steps to Take People can change their self-concepts in either direction. Those with good self-concepts can, over a period of time, have enough negative experiences to lessen their self-concepts. Likewise, people with poor

self-concepts can find enough positive experiences to improve their self-concepts. But change is slow, and self-concept results from many years of experiences. Here are three steps to take in improving your self-concept:

1. *Recognize the messages you are presently giving yourself.* Catch yourself when the message is negative, and restate it in a positive way.
2. *Ask people to whom you are close for assistance and support.* This is critical because what those close to you think and say about you affects your self-concept.
3. *Concentrate on the things you do well.* Learn from your successes and gradually build more opportunities to be successful. Success builds confidence. Positive reinforcement from within and from others helps to build self-concept. On the other hand, negative comments break down self-concept.

CHECK YOURSELF

1. How is mental health similar to physical health?
2. Define self-concept and describe how it is formed.
3. How does one's self-concept relate to one's overall health—physical, mental, and social?
4. How can one change a self-concept?

2. Factors That Influence How You Act

Your self-concept is directly related to your level of mental health and influences your behavior. What other factors affect your behavior? As human beings, we have basic needs. Our behavior reflects an attempt to meet those needs.

A Hierarchy of Needs

Abraham Maslow, an American psychologist, presented human needs in the form of a pyramid. His idea is that we all have basic needs, but some are more basic than others. Consequently, there is a **hierarchy (higher-arc-key) of needs.** The *most basic needs come first. We must meet these needs before we even become aware of the other needs.*

Physical Needs

The most basic human needs are our physical needs—hunger and thirst, sleep, etc. The next level of needs is our need to feel secure and safe, to be free from danger.

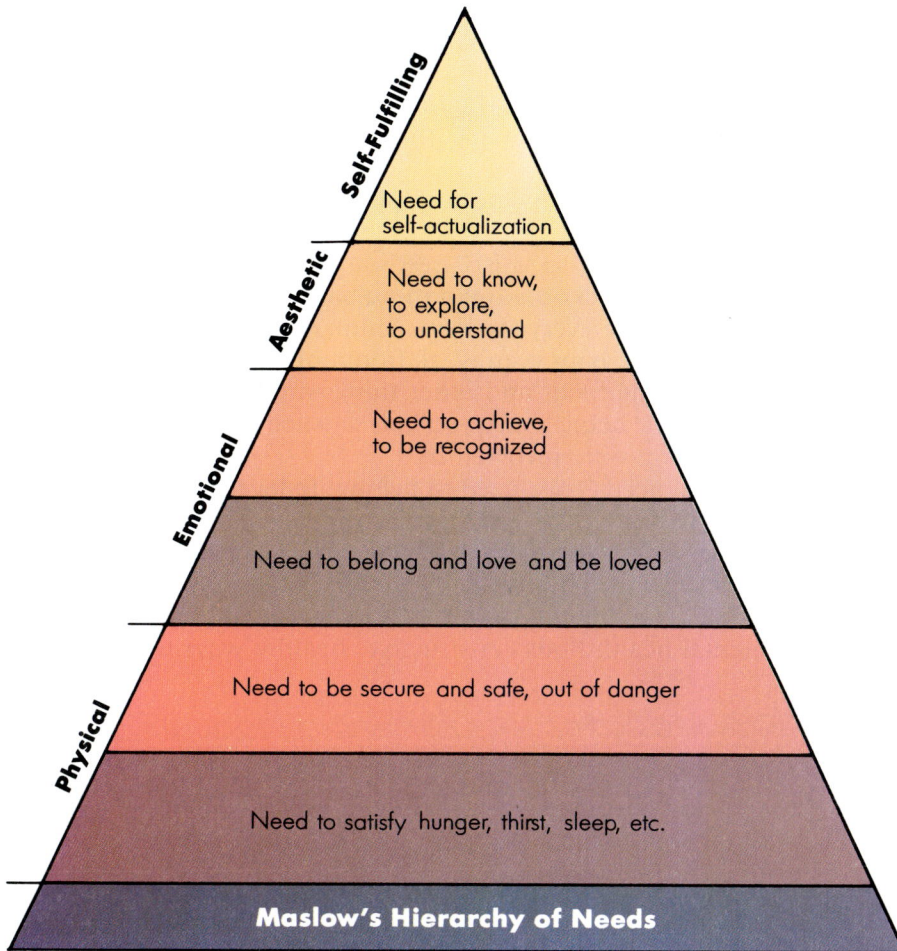

Maslow's Hierarchy of Needs

- Self-Fulfilling
  - Need for self-actualization
- Aesthetic
  - Need to know, to explore, to understand
- Emotional
  - Need to achieve, to be recognized
  - Need to belong and love and be loved
- Physical
  - Need to be secure and safe, out of danger
  - Need to satisfy hunger, thirst, sleep, etc.

If the first level of physical needs is not satisfied, we have little awareness of our other needs. Our behavior is aimed entirely at satisfying our hunger or thirst. Once these needs are met, we move to the next level and begin to satisfy our needs for security. It is not until these needs are met that we address our emotional needs.

Emotional Needs

The needs that are related to our emotions have a great impact on self-concept. We each have a need for love and belonging. Human beings are social beings; that is, they need other people. We need to feel like we belong to, and are a valued member of, a group. We each have a need to love and to be loved.

Another emotional need that all human beings have is feeling that they have personal value or worth. We have a need to achieve—to have ourselves and others recognize that we are competent at something. This is such a strong need that some people will seek negative attention just to be recognized.

We all need friends to grow as people, and our friends need us, too.

Think of the child who is constantly being fussed at for misbehaving. That child has probably learned that one sure way to get attention is to act up. How do you think this child might act as an adolescent or as an adult in order to meet the need to be recognized?

All of us need to feel worthwhile, that we have made a contribution. We must have something that we can do well, and we need recognition from others. It is important to find healthy, positive ways to meet these needs of recognition.

While we are working to satisfy needs at the third and fourth levels, we may drop down a level or two if a more basic need ceases to be met. This is easy to see in our everyday lives. Think of a time when you were exceedingly hungry, perhaps even weak from hunger. Your behavior was directed toward getting food, and other things around you became less important for the time being. Once you had satisfied that need, you could get back to what you were involved in.

The emotional needs—the need to belong, to love and be loved, and the need to feel worthwhile—are strong motivating forces behind our behavior. After we meet our physical needs, most of our behavior is an attempt to meet the basic emotional needs. We all have these basic needs. However, we each differ in the way we go about satisfying them. A person with good mental health finds constructive, healthy ways to meet these needs.

Aesthetic Needs

Maslow's hierarchy includes some higher needs—the desire to know and to understand aesthetic needs. Aesthetic needs include our appreciation of beauty in its many forms. They also include our need for order and balance in our lives.

Practicing any art form can bring rhythm, order, and beauty into our lives.

Self-Fulfilling Needs

Finally, it is Maslow's theory that we each have a need *to reach or strive for our full potential as a person,* that is, **self-actualization** (self-act-chew-uhl-uh-**za**-shun). This is often a lifelong process—not something a person one day arrives at. Each of us is continually striving to satisfy this need.

According to Maslow, in order to feel fulfilled, people need (1) to do what they are capable of doing, but (2) to do it as well as they are capable of doing. By challenging ourselves, Maslow theorized that we find a greater sense of fulfillment in life.

Personality and Mental Health

"She has a great personality."
"He has no personality at all."

Have you heard people described in this way? In these examples, the reference was not so much to personality, but to qualities or characteristics someone liked or did not like in the person.

Everyone has a personality. It is the sum total of you—you cannot separate yourself from your personality. Your **personality** encompasses *all of your traits, attitudes, feelings, behaviors, and habits.* It includes your *strengths, weaknesses, likes, and dislikes.* All of these go together to make up the person that you are, the person that others see.

Three main factors influence the development of your personality: *heredity, environment,* and *personal behavior.* To some extent, these factors work to influence your personality throughout life.

Personality and Heredity

Heredity is the first influence on your personality. You inherit some basic traits from your parents and past relations. The most obvious traits are your physical traits—hair and eye color, shape of the nose and ears, and body size. You also inherit basic intellectual abilities. What you do with these abilities determines how well they develop.

Personality and Environment

The second factor influencing the development of your personality is your environment. Your environment includes all of your surroundings—your family, where you grew up, all of your experiences. Compare the environment in which you have grown up with a friend's. How have your experiences affected your personality?

Friends, neighborhood, and family all contribute to forming our personalities when we are young.

Personality and Personal Behavior

The third factor affecting your personality is the one you have most control over—your behavior. The way you choose to act within your environment and with your inherited abilities has a very important impact on who you are.

Many factors affect how you act. You have already read how your basic human needs affect your behavior. Perhaps one of the most important factors in how you act is your values. **Values** are *guides for how you live—what is important to you*. You develop and learn your values primarily from your family. Your religion, school, and friends also influence your values.

How do values affect your behavior? Your actions are reflections of what is important to you. For example, if you have a high value for good health—that is, good health is really important to you—you will practice good health habits. You will actively work to take care of yourself and will choose behaviors that promote health. It is unlikely that you will take risks that threaten your health.

CHECK YOURSELF

1. Explain how our basic needs form a hierarchy.
2. How do our basic needs affect our behavior?
3. How do our basic emotional needs relate to self-concept?
4. Define personality, and describe how it develops.

3. Understanding Emotions

How do you feel right now? Are you in a good mood? Your *feelings,* or **emotions,** affect your thinking, your relationships with people around you, your behavior, and even your success or failure at accomplishing a given task. Your emotions have an obvious impact on you and your mental health. This is why you should spend some time learning more about them.

Mixed Emotions

Suzie is in the ninth grade. Most of the time she is happy. She works hard in school, has several good friends, and earns extra money with her part-time job. Lately, Suzie has been worried but she does not know what is wrong. It seems like one minute she is happy and knows just what she wants for herself. The next minute she is upset or angry, and for no good reason. Suzie feels confused. She has never had these mixed emotions before.

Suzie is experiencing what most young people do as they go through adolescence. This time of *rapid growth and change is caused by body chemicals* called **hormones.** Besides physical changes, hormones also cause emotional changes. You will read more about the effects of these hormones in Chapter 16. For now, it is important that you know that emotions are normal. Emotions themselves are neither healthy nor unhealthy. How you express your emotions, however, can be healthy or unhealthy.

Emotions Are Normal

Emotions are part of human existence. All people, young and old, have them. Emotions allow people to be all that they can be. They protect us from danger and help us to accomplish tasks and to reach goals.

You have probably studied about emotions before. However, learning about your emotions is quite different from doing something about them when they are building up inside of you. Because our deepest feelings are quite difficult to identify, we often cover them up or describe them as something different.

Have you ever said, "I'm furious with you," or "I hate you," when what you really meant was, "I'm so hurt that I do not know what to do"? Have you ever said, "I hate this class; it's dumb," when you really meant, "I am afraid I won't do well," or "I'm scared people won't like me"?

Knowing what you are really feeling is important because then you can better express your emotions and deal with them. Because different events and situations bring on different feelings from each of us, no one else can know for sure how you feel if you do not talk about your feelings. To be able to talk about your feelings, you first must know what they are.

IMPROVING YOURSELF

The Meaning Behind a Response

How many times have you said, "I'm bored"? Bored is a commonly used word, especially among young people. When you say that you are bored, what do you really mean?

- "There's nothing to do that's fun."
- "I'm lonesome."
- "I don't know how to be a part of what's going on."

- "No one asked me to the dance."
- "I have too much homework and don't know where to start."

If you focus in on the real meaning behind your response, you will be in a better position to do something about it. What remedy or remedies would you give for each of the above statements?

Recognizing Your Feelings

Recognizing your feelings and handling them effectively are two of the most important skills a person can learn. Perhaps one of the most critical aspects of good mental health is learning to recognize and express feelings in a healthy manner. The key word here is that this expression of feeling is *learned.*

In growing up, you have probably learned various ways of expressing your emotions. We learn from observing others, from our environment, and from our own experiences. Suppose, as a young child, you were repeatedly told that crying was a sign of weakness. Do you think that now you would be likely to express an emotion of sadness by crying? How have you learned to express joy and excitement?

Fear—A Protective Emotion

Everyone has fears. If we did not, we probably would not have survived this long. Fear can be a safeguard, a protection from danger. As with all emotions, fear produces a physical reaction in your body.

When you experience fear, your sympathetic nervous system (see Chapter 14) responds to prepare your body for necessary action. Your heart beats faster and sends an increased supply of blood to your muscles. Your body is readied to protect itself from danger. When something is done to deal with the situation causing fear, your body returns to its normal state.

What are some fears you learned as a child? Before you were old enough to reason and to recognize potential danger, someone probably instilled some fears in you to protect you. What did your parents or other adults tell you about playing in the street or with matches, or about accepting candy from strangers?

Fear can help us to become cautious in dangerous situations.

Major Fears

A team of researchers asked 3,000 Americans, "What are you most afraid of?" They received the following replies:

1. Speaking before a group	41%	
2. Heights	32%	
3. Insects and bugs	22%	
4. Financial problems	22%	
5. Deep water	22%	
6. Sickness	19%	
7. Death	19%	
8. Flying	18%	
9. Loneliness	14%	
10. Dogs	11%	
11. Driving/riding in a car	9%	
12. Darkness	8%	
13. Elevators	8%	
14. Escalators	5%	

Other fears that we learn about are not helpful. Rather, they can be destructive. Unrealistic fears, fears that immobilize us and interfere with positive living, are not healthy.

How might a person have learned any one of these fears as he or she was growing up? In certain situations, could these fears have been helpful?

Phobias   A *persistent fear* is called a **phobia** (**foe**-bee-ah). A person who has a phobia may be unable to carry out daily activities. The phobia disrupts normal routine. To avoid whatever he or she fears, the person's behavior becomes extreme. Oftentimes, the fear makes no sense, for it is not a realistic fear. For example, a person with a fear of strangers may follow basic safety behaviors when he or she is out in public. A person with a phobia for strangers may never go out in public.

Several programs can help people with phobias. They all start from the same point: the person must first recognize that he or she has a phobia, or a fear that could develop into a phobia.

Fear of flying (ariaphobia), animals (zoophobia), and fear of heights (acrophobia) are the most common phobias. Perhaps you have heard of some others:

- bibliophobia—fear of books
- brontophobia—fear of thunder
- claustrophobia—fear of closed spaces
- hydrophobia—fear of water
- murophobia—fear of mice
- pyrophobia—fear of fire

Anger

Emotions are neither positive nor negative. They are feelings that everyone has. The way that emotions are expressed differs from person to person, and they can be either healthy or unhealthy, positive or negative. Often,

Acrophobia—fear of heights—is sometimes caused by poor eyesight.

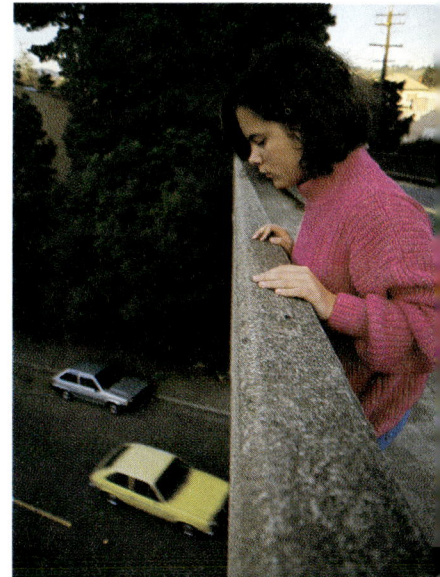

anger is thought of as a negative emotion. Perhaps this is because anger is often expressed in negative or violent ways. But anger is a normal emotion that everyone experiences from time to time. Learning how to express anger in healthy ways is a sign of good mental health—of emotional maturity. This can be a difficult thing to learn, for it is a skill that takes practice.

Think of some ways you have seen anger expressed. Perhaps you've seen a child throw a temper tantrum or someone kick a wall or take a swing at someone else. Some people let their anger build up, without saying or doing anything, until they explode and lash out at anyone who happens to be around.

Expressing Anger   How can you express anger in a constructive way? As in the case of other emotions, you must first recognize your feelings and, if possible, identify the source of the feelings. Sometimes there is nothing you can do about what is causing the anger, but you can find ways to cope with the anger so it does not build up.

Here are some suggestions:

- Channel your energies into productive work or recreational activity.
- Get away by yourself and let off steam—running or hitting a punching bag can be a good way to deal with anger.
- You have probably heard of the "count-to-ten-slowly" rule. Take a deep breath, then slowly exhale to the count of 10. Repeat, if necessary. This exercise can help you regain composure, relax you, and reduce the possibility of your acting on impulse.

What do you gain from trying to express feelings like anger? First, you have identified the emotion and expressed it. It is over, so you do not carry the feeling around with you—wasting energy by seething over it. Chances are that you feel better. The "knot" in the stomach that is usually present in emotions like anger subsides.

Productive work and recreational activities are two ways to channel our energies.

Talking It Over

When anger involves another person, you should talk about it. Express your feelings, describing what you perceive as being a problem.

When you are angry with another person, follow these Talking It Over guidelines. They may make it easier for you to discuss your feelings:

1. Start all of your statements with the word *I*.
2. Tell what has happened and how you feel.
3. Try not to use the word *you*. By using the word *I*, you are taking responsibility for how you feel rather than blaming someone else. Usually when people are blamed or accused of something, they try to defend themselves. When you use *I*, other people have no need to be defensive and are more likely to talk out the problem.
4. Tell the other person how your anger involves him or her.
5. List what measures you think will reduce your anger and how the other person can help you.

Following these steps does not ensure that you will solve the problem. The other person may choose not to talk about the problem. You have no control over how the other person responds or reacts. But you have expressed your feelings in a healthy, constructive manner, and you will feel better for doing it.

**L I F E
MANAGEMENT
S K I L L**

Communication

In small groups, make up a situation and have each member of the group take turns talking it over. The group members can interact. One member of the group can record responses for future reference.

The most important gain is that you are more likely to carry on healthy relationships with people you are close to. How is this so? Getting angry with someone is normal and is a likely possibility if you spend much time with that person. You clear the air if you express the emotion. If you bury it or ignore it, you will carry it around with you.

In time, the angry feeling may lessen, even go away. It goes away from your conscious awareness. But if you have not dealt with it, your anger may not go completely away, and eventually it may begin to affect how you act toward or feel about the other person. This can be unhealthy for you and the relationship.

Emotions Affect Your Physical Health

Strong emotions like anger cause physical changes to take place in your body. Your heart beats faster, you may perspire, your muscles tense, your stomach tightens. If you do not do something to deal with the emotions, the body does not relax. It stays in this state of tension. Over a period of time, fatigue can set in and physical illnesses may even develop.

Strong emotions, like anger, can produce tension. It is best to work them off in some physical way.

It is unhealthy to keep feelings inside, for you put an additional strain on your body. In addition, you are not learning constructive ways to deal with emotions.

If negative patterns are developing, they may follow you throughout your adult life. The longer you practice them, the harder they are to change. So try some different ways of expressing your feelings. Learn new, healthy ways to deal with emotions. Try out some of the suggestions you have read about in this section.

CHECK YOURSELF

1. What does the statement "emotions are neither positive nor negative" mean? If that statement is true, why are certain emotions like fear and anger often considered to be negative or unhealthy?
2. What are the benefits of expressing your feelings?
3. How do emotions affect your overall level of health?
4. What steps are involved in expressing emotions in a healthy way?

4. Problem-Solving

A person with good mental health faces problems and works on solving or adjusting to them. Everyone has problems—some small, others major. You may have no control over some of your problems because they are a result of other people or events. What you do have control over is how you respond to or cope with your problems.

Making Decisions

Problem-solving involves *making decisions*. (This procedure is also called **decision-making**.) Of course, not all the decisions you make are because of a problem. Stop for a minute and think of the decisions you have made since you got up this morning. How many of them related to, or in some way affected, your level of health?

If you think in terms of total health, you are likely to find that a great many of your decisions in some way influence some aspect of your health. You make many of these decisions with little thought. However, regardless of how large or small your problem is, the choice you are making is problem-solving, a skill that you can learn and then practice.

Problem-Solving Steps

Problem-solving involves making a decision, so let us look at the process involved in solving a problem. Note the word *process*. **Process** implies that some *procedures or steps are involved in developing a skill.*

1. **Clearly identify the problem.** This sounds easy; however, it is not only the most important step, but it can also be a difficult one. Be sure that you have a grasp on the real problem and that it is well-defined.

2. **Identify all of your possible choices.** Picture what the situation would look like if the problem were solved. What choices do you have? Try to think of as many as possible. Ask for input from your parents, other adults you can talk to, or others that the problem may involve.

3. **Consider and evaluate the consequences of each choice.** One way to identify the consequences is to ask yourself, "What will happen if I . . . ?" Again, you may want to seek input from others. The objective is to examine all parts of the problem and the possible solutions. Will the alternative you

**L I F E
M A N A G E M E N T
S K I L L**

Problem-Solving

In groups, think up a situation that needs to be resolved. Each group can use the problem-solving steps to reach a solution. All the groups can then discuss how each reached a solution.

HEALTH UPDATE   HEALTH UPDATE   HEALTH UPDATE

Mental Illness Statistics

According to the National Institute of Mental Health, one American in ten suffers from some form of mental or emotional illness at some time.

More patients are in hospital beds for mental disorders than for any other illness.

Stress has been estimated to cost approximately $10 to $20 billion a year, including lost workdays, injuries, and early stress-related deaths.

Since 1960, there has been a 40% increase in mental illness patients admitted for treatment in hospitals.

are considering solve your problem or just temporarily ease it? How will other people important to you be affected?

4. **Select the best choice and act.** This means that you know and accept the consequences of your actions.

5. **Evaluate the results of your choice.** Did your actions solve the problem or create a new problem? What did you learn?

Of course, you probably will not use such a detailed process for every problem with which you are faced. However, you might find it easier to practice your skills on easier problems. Then, when faced with more difficult decisions, you will be better prepared.

Your Choice

One of the most important points to remember in this process is that *you are the one responsible for your choice.* If you have examined the consequences before deciding, you should not have a list of excuses when someone asks you about your actions. "I did not know you would be mad," "She made me," "Everyone else went" are excuses and examples of not taking responsibility for your choice.

IMPROVING YOURSELF

Goal-Setting

As you read this chapter, you had several opportunities to evaluate your skills and your level of mental health. Perhaps you have identified some specific skill or area you want to improve. How do you go about making changes?

In Chapter 2, we gave procedures for beginning a fitness program. You can use similar steps for making any kind of change. You have already taken the first step by identifying something you want to change. Now you need to set a goal for yourself and make a plan for reaching your goal.

Much like problem-solving, goal-setting is a skill. It involves a process that gives you some direction within which to work.

1. **Decide on one thing on which you want to work.** Make your goal realistic, something you can attain.

2. **List what you will do to reach your goal.** Identify others who can help you and support your efforts.

3. **Give yourself an identified period of time to reach your goal.** Build in several checkpoints to evaluate how you are doing.

4. **State a reward for yourself for achieving your goal.**

LIFE MANAGEMENT SKILL

Setting Goals

Determine two goals you wish to reach this week. Use the goal-setting model to plan how you will reach each one. Assess your progress every morning. If you find that you need more time to reach a goal, adjust your plan. Be realistic, but do not take more time just to avoid reaching the goal.

PSYCHOLOGIST

Psychology (sigh-kah-**lah**-gee), one of the most popular majors in college, deals with the study of the mind and human behavior. It is a stimulating and diverse field of study. Through various levels of education, **psychologists** have a multitude of career choices.

The field of psychology offers a tremendous opportunity for creativity and specialization. Standard positions for a psychologist include clinical work and family or personal counseling, education, social research, industrial or corporate work, and many types of experimental research.

All types of psychology deal with human behavior. Human beings are very complex, and the study of their behavior is fascinating and challenging. Because of the nature of the field, a psychologist is in the position to help people, directly or indirectly. This is one aspect that makes a career in psychology so gratifying.

There are several alternatives in the professional education of psychologists. A bachelor's degree is essential, and almost all psychologists continue in school to pursue a master's or doctoral degree. Many schools offer a Ph.D. (Doctor of Philosophy) in psychology and some now offer a Psy.D. (Doctor of Psychology). Almost all psychologists also serve an internship for clinical experience. The amount and type of educational experience you need is largely determined by what you wish to do.

Earnings, hours, and working conditions in psychology vary tremendously. The rewards of the job come from the positive contributions you make in the classroom, the workplace, the clinic, or in society. It is this positive ability to make a difference that makes psychology one of the most popular of all the helping professions.

For more information, contact the American Psychological Association.

American Psychological Association
1200 17th Street, N.W.
Washington, DC 20036

This does not mean you will always make the best choice. Everyone makes mistakes, and we learn from our mistakes. However, part of being mentally healthy is learning to be responsible for your mistakes, learning from them, and then going on from there.

As you read this book, you will find many places to apply this problem-solving process. Remember, problem-solving is a skill that, once learned, you must practice.

Asking for Help

Not all problems can be solved. Part of being mentally healthy is knowing when to ask for help and then seeking help. In this book, you will learn about the different kinds of help available to people who have problems. But you also have people around you who can help—your family, a school counselor, or a friend. Sometimes it helps just to talk about your feelings. The other person may do nothing but listen. The important thing is that you let someone know you need assistance.

CHECK YOURSELF

1. Why are problem-solving, decision-making, and goal-setting referred to as skills?
2. How can following a *process* to solve a problem or make a change be helpful?
3. Give an example of how you might apply the steps to problem-solving in everyday life.
4. Give an example of goal-setting (a) in school, and (b) in your home.

CHAPTER 5 Review

CHAPTER SUMMARY

- Mental health means much more than not being mentally ill. Mental health is concerned with how you view yourself, how you function in society and get along with people around you, how you express yourself, and how you cope with and handle day-to-day ups and downs.
- There are varying levels of mental health. Your day-to-day experiences affect your level of mental health. You can work actively to maintain a high level of mental health. When you do, your outlook will become more positive.

- A person's self-concept has a great impact on his or her mental health. Your self-concept directly affects all aspects of your daily life and reflects how successful you are in your various endeavors.
- Improving one's self-concept and maintaining a good self-concept is a continuous process.
- Two very important skills related to good mental health are the ability to recognize and to express emotions and the ability to work out problems.
- Once you identify areas that you want to work on, you can set personal goals for improvement.

mental health   values   process
self-concept   emotions   psychology
hierarchy of needs   hormones   psychologist
self-actualization   phobia
personality   problem-solving

PUTTING VOCABULARY TO USE

On a separate piece of paper, write the following statements. Then supply the missing word or phrase from the chapter vocabulary list.

1. _____. What is important to you.
2. _____. A total of all that you are.
3. _____-_____. One's total picture of self.
4. _____ _____ _____. Its most basic level has to do with survival.
5. _____-_____. A necessary skill in facing the challenges of everyday life.
6. _____. Our feelings.
7. _____-_____. The need for self-fulfillment.
8. _____. A persistent fear that affects daily activities.

REVIEWING WHAT YOU LEARNED

1. Identify the characteristics below that are signs of good mental health. Add three more of your own.

   - easygoing attitudes,
   - lack of self-respect,
   - ability to accept disappointment,
   - fear of new ideas or experiences,
   - rejection of responsibility,
   - talks nicely to self,
   - satisfying and lasting relationships,
   - realistic goals.

2. Give three examples of what goes into forming one's personality.
3. Identify three statements that people with positive self-concepts would make about themselves.
4. What makes a phobia different from an ordinary fear?
5. Why is the expression of emotions an important part of mental health?

APPLYING WHAT YOU LEARNED

1. Phil does not have an effective method for dealing with problems. What kinds of additional problems is Phil likely to experience without such a skill?
2. You have been asked by a middle school student to describe a mentally healthy high school student. What would you say?

3. You are supposed to be in two different places at the same time, having promised two different friends that you would do something with each one of them. You forgot the first promise when you agreed to the other. Apply the correct problem-solving techniques to deal with this situation.
4. Give an example of a situation in which a person would have two different levels of needs present but then would make a choice to meet the more basic need.
5. Make a list of 10 events that took place in your day. Evaluate each according to how it affected your self-concept.
6. Ask five people you know to tell you three things that they do well. Write a report summarizing their responses.
7. Compare the scientific method to the decision-making process.

FOCUS ON WELLNESS

What people say about themselves is often a good indication of how they feel about themselves. *I can demonstrate a positive self-concept by making the following statements about myself . . .*

Managing Stress in Your Life

A two-ton truck falls suddenly on a man, pinning his
leg under it. His 15-year-old son runs to his aid and lifts up
the back of the truck so that his father can crawl out.
How is this possible? It is the result of the body's response
to a stress situation.

After studying this chapter, you will be able to:
- distinguish between stress and distress,
- identify stressors in daily life,
- explain the relationship of change to stress,
- relate excess stress to disease,
- list skills in managing time,
- describe ways to cope with and manage stress.

Stress is *the body's general response to any situation.* This simply means that anytime something or someone appears before us, or we hear or feel something, the body responds. The sound of a fire engine, the smell of freshly baked pastry, the hissing of a snake all cause the body to respond in some way. That response is different for different people and may even be different for the same person from time to time.

Stress and Distress

Stress is usually referred to in a negative sense. "I was under too much stress." This is more appropriately termed **distress**—*negative stress.* What is the difference? Not all stress is bad. Actually a certain amount of stress is necessary for life. If the body were not under some stress, it would cease to function. As a matter of fact, experts say that moderate amounts of stress improve productivity. What excites you, stimulates you, and challenges you certainly produces stress.

If some stress is vital, when does stress, or distress, become unhealthy? The answer to this question will vary from person to person. As you become aware of the distress in your daily life, you can better control it. Learning to manage and to cope with the stress in your life is an important part of staying healthy.

Factors Influencing Stress

Many reasons are given for the great variation in how well and how long people can hold up under stress. Some break down very quickly, while others endure for seemingly endless periods of time. What factors can you identify that might be responsible for this difference in the responses to stress? How might a person's life-style or attitude toward wellness affect his or her ability to hold up under stress?

The variation in the impact of stress on a person is related to the person's age, social status, income, stage or place in life, cultural background, and previous experience.

Your response to stress also varies, depending on how much control you think you have over the given situation. If you feel you are helpless, the stress can be overwhelming.

What Is a Stressor?

Before looking at the problems related to stress, let us examine the relationship between stress and stressors. Imagine a bell sounding. Each time the bell sounds, you clench your fist. The sounding of the bell is known

KEEPING FIT

Stress Quiz

On a separate sheet of paper, answer *true* or *false* to each of the following statements. You will find the correct answer to each statement at the end of the chapter.

1. Stress is important for living.
2. Stress is all mental.
3. Teenagers do not suffer from stress.
4. If there are physical effects from stress, the individual cannot tell what is happening.
5. People who are competitive do experience high levels of stress.
6. Change is a major producer of stress.
7. It is better to keep things to yourself when you are under extreme stress.
8. *Stress* means the same thing as *distress.*
9. A healthy life-style is an effective way to manage stress.
10. Healthy people avoid stress.

Preparing for a test or an athletic event can produce as much stress as buying and selling on the stock market.

as a stressor. A **stressor** is *something that initiates a stress response.* Stressors can be people, objects, places, or events. Think of some stressors you face during your day.

The clenching of your fist each time that the bell rings is your response to that stressor. In this case, it is *voluntary;* that is, you have conscious control over it. You can notice the tension in your fist as you clench it.

This action differs from a true stress response in two ways: (1) it is voluntary, and (2) you are conscious of it.

The stress response that takes place inside your body is *involuntary,* activated by the autonomic nervous system (see Chapter 14). Many times we are completely unaware of the changes that occur.

Have you ever been unable to sleep the night before a big event? Have you ever had knots in your stomach before a big game or presentation? Has your throat ever become dry when you were being confronted with a problem? All of these reactions were involuntary.

How the body responds to a stressor depends largely on how the individual perceives the stressor. What is stressful for one person may be a source of relaxation for another. Obviously, many factors determine whether or not you perceive a situation to be stressful.

CHECK YOURSELF

1. Define stress.
2. How can stress be good?
3. Describe how you have reacted to a stressor.

Think of three of the most memorable events in your life. Do you remember the emotions you experienced with each event? You may not have thought of the event as being stressful, but as a general rule, the more memorable an event, the more stress you are likely to experience. The first step in reducing stress is to become aware of the sources of stress in your life, especially your daily life.

The Life-Event Scale on page 102 can help you to determine the amount of stress you have experienced in the last year. Notice that each event reflects some change in life. *Change* produces stress. By being aware of this fact, you are better able to manage stress from day to day.

The Body's Response to Stress

The physical changes associated with stress are initiated by the *hypothalamus* (high-poe-**thal**-uh-muss), a nerve center in the brain, and a part of the endocrine system. We will study the nervous system in Chapter 14 and the endocrine system in Chapter 16, but here is some information on how parts of these systems influence reactions to stress.

When the hypothalamus is excited by a stressor, a complex series of changes takes place in the body. The result is a change in the functioning of almost every part of the body.

The hypothalamus activates the autonomic nerves of the autonomic nervous system, controlling involuntary actions, which, in turn, activate the pituitary gland. The *pituitary* (puh-**too**-it-err-ee) *gland* secretes a substance that stimulates the adrenal glands. The *adrenal* (uh-**dree**-nul) *glands* produce and secrete a *substance that prepares a person for a "fight or flight" response.* This substance is called **adrenaline** (uh-**dren**-uhl-en). Adrenaline is known as the "emergency" hormone.

Because of adrenaline, the heart speeds up its activity, providing more blood for the brain and muscles. Breathing becomes faster and deeper, providing more oxygen. Saliva and mucus dry up, increasing the size of the air passages to the lungs. Throat muscles may contract, making swallowing difficult. Perspiration increases, helping to cool the body. Muscles tense and tighten to prepare the body for action. The pupils dilate, making the eyes able to see more in the environment. Other body functions like digestion are suspended to conserve energy.

All of these changes take place when we are faced with something we perceive to be a stressor. Once the stressor has been dealt with, the body returns to normal. However, in cases where the stressor is prolonged or not dealt with, the body continues to work at this level. After a period of time, the body becomes exhausted. The system begins to break down. We become more susceptible to illness and accidents. We cannot think clearly, and want to flee the problem.

KEEPING FIT

Being Aware of Tension

Each joint in the body is surrounded by muscles that allow it to move. Muscles function by contracting and expanding. In everything we do, muscles are constantly tensing and relaxing.

Without a certain amount of muscle tension, we could not stand, move, or even breathe. However, when a muscle is not in use, it should be relaxed. If it remains contracted, excess tension results, using up energy that should be available for normal activity and, thus, causing fatigue.

Tension causes pain and even cramping. It causes backaches and headaches, restricts movement, and reduces blood circulation. Be aware of tension, especially in the neck and shoulders.

Adolescent Life-Change Event Scale

Rank	Event	Points
1.	A parent dying	98
2.	Brother or sister dying	95
3.	Close friend dying	92
4.	Parents getting divorced or separated	86
5.	Failing one or more subjects in school	86
6.	Being arrested by the police	85
7.	Flunking a grade in school	84
8.	Family member having trouble with alcohol	79
9.	Getting into drugs or alcohol	77
10.	Losing a favorite pet	77
11.	Parent or relative in your family getting very sick	77
12.	Losing a job	74
13.	Breaking up with a girlfriend or boyfriend	74
14.	Quitting school	73
15.	A close girlfriend getting pregnant	69
16.	Parent losing a job	69
17.	Getting very sick or badly hurt	64
18.	Hassling with parents	64
19.	Trouble with teacher or principal	63
20.	Having problems with acne, weight, height	63
21.	Attending a new school	57
22.	Moving to a new home	51
23.	Change in physical appearance (braces, eyeglasses)	47
24.	Hassling with a brother or sister	46
25.	Starting menstrual periods (for girls)	45
26.	Having someone new move in with your family (grandparent, adopted brother or sister, or other)	35
27.	Starting a job	34
28.	Mother getting pregnant	31
29.	Starting to date	31
30.	Making new friends	27
31.	Brother or sister getting married	26

Scoring. Add the points for each event that you have experienced over the past year. Of those people with over 300 points during a year, 80% will get sick. With a point total of between 150 and 299, people have a 50% chance of getting sick, and people with less than a 150-point total have a 30% chance of getting sick.

The important point is that you can significantly decrease your chances of serious illness by decreasing the amount of stress in your life. You can control much of the change that occurs.

In addition, by anticipating changes and planning for them, you better prepare yourself to handle stress.

L I F E MANAGEMENT S K I L L

Analyzing Your Situation

Look at the list of 31 events. Break them into three categories: (1) those I can control, (2) those I may be able to control, and (3) those I cannot control. Which events are within your control to avoid on a day-by-day basis? Which ones must you work on to avoid?

Fatigue—It Isn't All Physical

One of the most common complaints doctors hear from their patients is that of **fatigue**—*a tired feeling that lowers your level of activity.* Fatigue affects all levels of your health—physical, mental, and social. It interferes with work, school, and recreation.

Physical Fatigue

You have probably experienced one type of fatigue—**physical fatigue,** which is *fatigue of the body in general.* During exercise, the body produces waste products in the form of lactic acid from the muscles and carbon dioxide from all of the body's cells. A buildup of wastes in the muscle can produce soreness. When these wastes reach a certain level in the blood, the brain receives a message, and your activity level drops.

The best solution to physical fatigue is rest. If rest does not revive you, you might need to look for another cause of your fatigue.

Pathological Fatigue

A second kind of fatigue is **pathological** (path-oh-**lah**-jah-kal) **fatigue,** which is *fatigue brought on by the overworking of the body's defense mechanisms for fighting disease.* When a disease does develop, your body becomes overworked trying to fight the disease and, at the same time, trying to keep you going. The result is fatigue.

The common cold, the flu, and anemia are all examples of illnesses brought on by pathological fatigue. Being overweight and having a poor diet are also causes of pathological fatigue. This type of fatigue is the body's way of warning you that it is not well and that you need a rest.

Psychological Fatigue

The third and most common type of fatigue is **psychological fatigue,** which is *brought on by mental reactions.* Almost everyone experiences this type of fatigue. Think of a time you may have experienced psychological fatigue. What were some of the events going on in your life? Depression, boredom, worry—about schoolwork, home, dates, how you look, and being liked— can cause fatigue. Stress—too much to do, conflicts—also can cause it.

Lack of exercise means that your body does not circulate oxygen fast enough, which can also be a factor in psychological fatigue.

Unlike the answer to the other two types of fatigue, rest is *not* the answer to psychological fatigue. *Activity is*—do something! If fatigue continues, take a closer look at the source of it. Is there a problem you need to address? Perhaps you need to set a goal for changing a certain behavior. Perhaps you just need to talk to someone. Try to find out what is at the root of your fatigue. That is the first step toward eliminating it.

Remember, fatigue is the body warning you that something is wrong. You risk further health problems by merely covering up the symptoms. Do not self-medicate with vitamins or an over-the-counter stimulant.

Physical fatigue can build up to a point where the body cannot take any more effort.

Situations Causing Social Anxiety

The following situations are reported to cause the most anxiety when working or socializing with other people.

Situation	Anxiety Stress
■ At a party with strangers	74%
■ Giving a speech	70%
■ Being asked personal questions in public	65%
■ Meeting a date's parents	59%

Situation	Anxiety Stress
■ The first day on a new job	59%
■ Being the victim of a practical joke	56%
■ Talking with someone in authority	53%
■ Having a job interview	46%
■ Being at a formal dinner party	44%
■ Being out on a blind date	42%

If you are not sure what kind of fatigue you are experiencing, examine what you were doing before you got tired. How were you feeling? Strong, negative feelings can cause fatigue! Are you worrying about something that is in your near future?

The Effects of Stress on Wellness

It is easy to look at stress in purely physical terms. The body's physical response to stress can be felt and seen. In recent years, however, the stress response has been associated with situations involving mental health. Social or personal situations causing anxiety, frustration, or tension trigger the stress response and can lead to the development of physical ailments. The term **psychosomatic** (sigh-koh-so-**mat**-tick), meaning *mind-body*, is used to describe such illnesses.

A number of diseases, including heart disease, high blood pressure, asthma, ulcers, colitis, and migraine headaches, are thought to be related in some way to stress. In some cases, stress seems to be a contributing factor in all of these diseases. But it is hard to identify stress as *the* major factor, since so many other factors can be involved.

One point is certain. There is increasing evidence that emotions cause physical reactions which, over time, may be damaging to the body.

Stress has more than just a physical effect on the body. It can also affect you mentally and socially. Stress has been linked to accidents and injuries. People under stress take more senseless risks and are more likely to be careless.

Coping with Stress

Although it is true that some stress is good, even motivating, your body cannot distinguish between positive and negative sources of stress. The body's response is the same. This means your body is dependent upon *you* to identify and manage the stress in your life. You can do this by following these guidelines:

- Identify your own sources of stress, and examine your methods of coping.
- Make conscious choices that help to control the amount of stress you experience.
- Develop and use coping and relaxation techniques to diffuse the tension that builds up excess stress.
- Practice good health habits daily.

What is the relationship between health, fitness, and the ability to cope? Research continues to show that people who eat properly, get plenty of sleep, and exercise regularly are better able to cope with daily stress. When the unexpected does occur, the healthy body is capable of responding appropriately and efficiently.

CHECK YOURSELF

1. What effect has a life-change event had on you?
2. What involuntary actions take place in your body when you are in a stressful situation?
3. What are the three types of fatigue?
4. What is meant by psychosomatic illness? What is its relationship to stress?

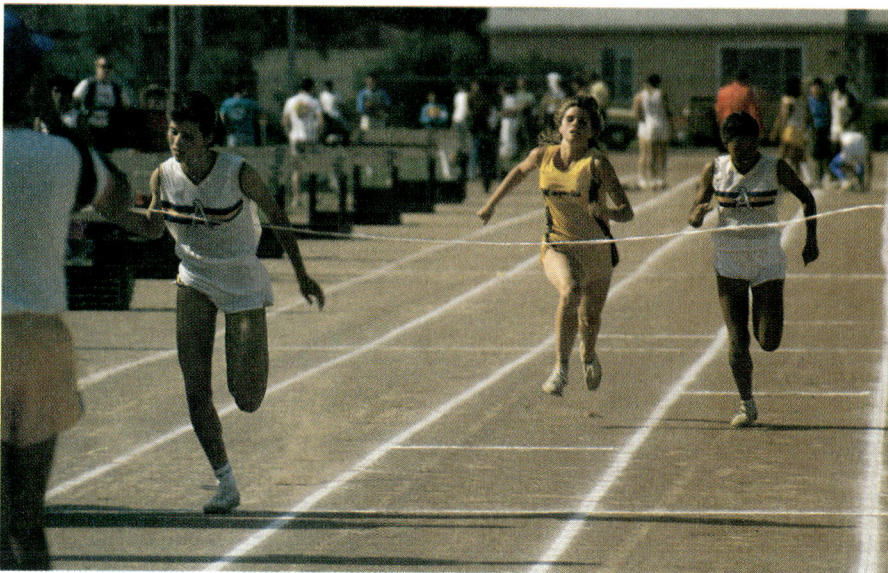

When the body is healthy, it can respond to most situations appropriately and efficiently.

Are you aware of your own needs, your anxieties, your motivations, your goals? The better you know yourself, the better able you are to identify and manage stress-producing behaviors and your typical responses to stress.

Types A and B Personalities

Several years ago, two doctors developed a theory on personalities that are more prone to stress. Have you ever heard someone described as a type A or type B personality? Doctors Friedman and Roseman have described the two personality types primarily on the basis of behavior patterns.

These types have nothing to do with intelligence, ambition, or success. Nor is one necessarily better than the other. Type A personalities seem to be more competitive, rushed, and time-oriented. Type B personalities appear to be more flexible and less rushed. While not wholly accurate, the theory is still a useful model. By being aware of your behavior patterns, you can manage stress and better adapt to stress-producing situations.

Also keep in mind that type A personalities can change their behavior patterns if they work on them. Even some drugs can help to change type A to type B personalities. Three German researchers have found that *beta blockers*—drugs that decrease heart activity and that are used to treat high blood pressure—can actually change a type A personality to a more relaxed and less stress-prone type B personality.

Take the test on page 107 to find out which personality type you might lean toward.

You can make time work for you by improving your time-management skills.

Time—Friend or Foe?

In any discussion of stress, we must consider time. Time is a major factor in stress management. People who manage their time well are better able to control stress in their lives, as long as they look at time as an ally and not as an opponent. How do you look at time? What are your **time-management skills**—*your effective ways of arranging your time*? Check yourself on the following behaviors.

- Are you always rushing?
- Do you continually bounce back and forth between unpleasant alternatives?
- Do you have trouble finding things?
- Do you find yourself tired from hours of nonproductive activity?
- Do you find insufficient time for rest or personal relationships?
- Do you regularly miss deadlines?

Personalities and Stress

Look at the behaviors below and decide if they describe you.

1. I become impatient when events move slowly. *Yes*
2. I set deadlines and schedules for myself. *Yes*
3. I feel guilty when I relax and do nothing. *Yes*
4. I speak, eat, and move at a quick pace. *Yes*
5. I am achievement-oriented. *Yes*
6. I have a strong need for success. *Yes*
7. I hurry the ends of sentences—or do not speak them at all. *Yes*
8. I try to do two or more things at once. *Yes*
9. I am number-oriented (like to count my accomplishments and possessions). *Yes*
10. I have aggressive or hostile feelings, especially toward competitive people. *Yes*

Scoring. If 6 to 10 of these statements describe you, you may be prone to the type A personality. There is a tendency to be competitive, impatient, and time-oriented, so you may want to identify ways to relax during your day. If few of these statements describe you, you may be prone to the type B personality. On the other hand, people fluctuate, depending on the situation.

The important thing to remember is to identify and be aware of how you are responding. Ask yourself if your response is a healthy one.

■ Are you overwhelmed by demands and details?
■ Do you find yourself doing several tasks at a time?
■ Do you have trouble deciding what to do next?

If you answered yes to six or more of these questions, you may need to work on managing your time better.

The Key to Time Management

Some people have difficulty managing their lives because they do not have good time-management skills. Part of this problem occurs because of a person's inability to say "No" to others. Saying "Yes" to virtually anything that is proposed to you says that you have not established your **priorities,** that is, *what is important to you.*

Maybe several things are important, but there are certain times to do certain tasks. Knowing when to do the tasks that must be done, and knowing when to say "No," is an important way of showing that we can manage our lives.

Sometimes we are afraid to say "No" because it might offend, or perhaps we are afraid of what the other person will do if we say "No."

LIFE MANAGEMENT SKILL

Managing Time

Give common statements (phrases) using the word "time." Put them on a sheet of paper (e.g., time out, on time, time flies when you're having fun, time is up, etc.). Ask, "Does time rule you or do you rule time? Why? Why not?"

In either case, we have to keep our primary objectives in mind and act on them. If we respond with a polite "No," the other person will probably react favorably.

CHECK YOURSELF

1. How does a type A personality differ from a type B personality?
2. How does time management relate to stress?
3. What is the key to time management?

4. Managing Stress

Six major ways to manage stress are planning, thinking ahead, laughing, rechanneling your energy, learning to relax, and calling on your support groups.

Planning

Laughing relieves stress and helps you to look at things with a fresh viewpoint.

Planning is a major key to managing stress effectively. *People who handle stress plan* well, yet they know that even with the best plans, other things can happen to change those plans. By recognizing that changes can and often do occur, especially when other people are involved, people are better able to deal with the changes, disappointments, frustrations, delays, or whatever might take place.

Thinking Ahead

You further manage stress by being realistic about your plans and your expectations. Anticipate the unexpected. Sometimes this simply means *thinking ahead.* Rather than concentrating on and living from moment to moment, think ahead enough to know what you might expect.

Of course, as in the case of each of these strategies, great variation exists. Some people spend so much time planning and anticipating what might happen that they do not enjoy the actual activity. This can be as stressful a situation as not planning at all. You have to decide what works for you.

Laughing

Another effective way to deal with stress is to *laugh.* There is the story of the little boy on his bicycle who went over a bump on the sidewalk and took a tumble. He got up, brushed himself off, and then burst out laughing.

A man passing by, who saw no fun in the scraped knee and elbow, asked, "What's so funny? Why are you laughing?" The boy replied, "Mr., I'm laughing so I won't cry." Laughter can be a relief when things have gone wrong. By laughing, you accept the reality that you are human and realize that sometimes unfortunate things happen.

By laughing, you release the stress that builds up when things go wrong. This does not mean that you do not care about what happened. It simply means that you have chosen a healthy way to deal with the stress of that particular situation.

Rechanneling Your Energy

Transferring or rechanneling your energy (which is actually the build-up of adrenaline) is another way to manage stress. If you find a situation is causing you to become tense, you might transfer your energy to some other activity—wash a car, take a walk, clean your room, just take a break.

If you cannot physically get away from the situation, give your mind a break. Let it wander for a few minutes. Daydreaming can be an excellent stress reducer.

Of course, we are assuming that you would know and use appropriate times to relax. Daydreaming when you are supposed to be taking notes in class can be a source of more stress. So can test taking. See the *Health Handbook*, page HB9, for directions on preparing for a test.

Learning to Relax

By learning to relax, you learn to counteract the body's reactions to stress and learn to control stress. One effective way of relieving stress is physical exercise. It burns pent-up energy and clears the mind. Choose exercise you enjoy and do it in a peaceful environment. Choose a setting that prevents more stress from developing.

A simple technique for reducing stress is the progressive relaxation technique. See the *Health* Handbook, page HB8, for information on it.

Calling on Your Support Group

A support group can help greatly in managing stress. What does a support group mean? Support means "to hold up." There are times when things get very difficult for us, and our energy and strength are worn down. On such occasions it is important for you to have a *support system* and to use it.

The supportive people in your life may include family, friends, a church person, teachers, employers, or other relatives. A strong support group would include several of these people. This puts less pressure on any one person. It also reduces the problem of depending on one person for some assistance and that person's possibly not being available at the time needed.

KEEPING FIT

Laughing

Laughing is an effective way to keep your body fit. When you laugh, your chest, thorax, and abdominal muscles, as well as your diaphragm, heart, lungs, and possibly your liver contract. A good belly laugh can make your blood pressure soar and can increase your heartbeat. Laughing also pumps adrenaline into the system.

After a good laugh, all systems return to normal or even a little below normal, resulting in less stress, hypertension, and muscle-tension headaches, as well as in an all-around good feeling.

HEALTH

CAREER

REHABILITATION COUNSELOR

Rehabilitation is often a long and stressful process, involving many types of specialists. People need help in recovering as fully as possible from illnesses, accidents, and handicaps. Handicaps may be mental, physical, emotional, or a combination of two or three of them.

The **rehabilitation counselor** is a very important professional who helps clients resume a more normal life-style. These counselors perform three main functions:

- They talk with clients about handicaps, limitations, and strengths.
- They help clients learn the necessary skills to manage with the handicap. These skills may include personal-care skills, coping methods, and occupational skills.
- Finally, rehabilitation counselors help clients find employment or further occupational training.

Since rehabilitation counseling is a multi-faceted job, the educational background is diverse. Most counselors obtain a master's degree from a school that the Council on Rehabilitation Education has accredited. A doctorate is also available for students wishing to advance. Internships in counseling are extremely helpful for anyone entering this field.

State and federal agencies offering rehabilitation programs for the disabled are the largest employers of rehabilitation counselors. A counselor may also work for a hospital, an insurance company, a special school, or a corporation, or he or she may have a private practice. Pay rates, work hours, and working environments vary accordingly.

A successful rehabilitation counselor displays confidence and a positive attitude toward the client. The counselor must instill motivation and self-esteem in a client. The counselor must be ready to deal with the numerous and varied psychological reactions a person may have to his or her handicap, and help the client work through any difficulties. A rehabilitation counselor must also work with people in the community to help them accept the disabled person into the workplace and into society. For more information, contact the National Rehabilitation Counseling Association.

Rehabilitation Counseling Association
Cary Building B-110
101 South Whiting Street
Alexandria, VA 22304

Building a strong support group is perhaps one of the most important strategies for managing stress and for overall wellness.

You may not be able to manage or control some stressors. However, you can control the effect you allow them to have on you. Sometimes just talking about a problem can help to reduce stress. Developing supportive relationships and maintaining a few close friendships are very helpful in coping with stress.

Support groups help us to compare experiences, receive advice, and manage stress.

CHECK YOURSELF

1. List three strategies for managing stress, and describe them.
2. How can exercise help you to manage stress?
3. What is a support system?

CHAPTER 6   Review

CHAPTER SUMMARY

■ Not all stress is bad—a certain amount of stress is necessary for life.
■ Stress involves both a physical and a psychological response to any stimulus that appears before the individual.
■ Anything that causes a stress response is known as a stressor.
■ The effect of a stressor on a person is highly individualized. Much depends on how the individual perceives the stressor.
■ When a person encounters a stressor, the brain activates the autonomic nervous system and the endocrine system. The result is a "fight or flight" response, in which the body is prepared for action one way or another.

■ An individual can use stress positively to work for himself or herself in accomplishing tasks. However, too much stress has been linked directly with disease, accidents, and injuries.
■ There are many different ways to handle stress; some are more effective than others.
■ Some stress-management efforts are so ineffective that they themselves may be sources of additional stress to the individual.
■ By managing stress effectively, one contributes to total health. On the other hand, poor stress management can affect a person physically, mentally, and socially.

stress	fatigue	psychosomatic
distress	physical fatigue	time-management skills
stressor	pathological fatigue	priorities
adrenaline	psychological fatigue	rehabilitation counselor

PUTTING VOCABULARY TO USE

On a separate piece of paper, write the following statements. Then supply the missing word or phrase from the chapter vocabulary list.

1. _____. Something that initiates a stress response.
2. _____. Mind and body.
3. _____. Prepares a person for a "flight or fight" response.
4. _____. Body's response to any situation.
5. _____. A tired feeling.
6. _____ _____ _____. Effective ways of managing time.
7. _____. Negative stress.
8. _____. What is important to you.

REVIEWING WHAT YOU LEARNED

1. In what ways is stress necessary for life?
2. What physical changes take place in the body when one encounters a stressor?
3. Give three specific examples of when your body might produce a stress response.
4. When does stress become distress?
5. What is the relationship of stress to (a) change and (b) disease?
6. Explain how the management of time is related to one's stress level. Give some real-life examples.

APPLYING WHAT YOU LEARNED

1. What jobs do you think would be high stress and low stress? Explain your answer.
2. Interview two adults and two working teenagers to determine what aspects of their jobs they find most stressful. Summarize your findings, comparing the two groups.
3. What suggestions might you give to a type A personality to become more like a type B personality?
4. Keep a daily diary. Then sit down and make a list of the most important priorities to you. Check to see how much of your day you are spending on the most important things in your life.

5. Imagine that you asked a friend to go to a movie, and the friend said "No." Would you feel that the friendship was lost or that the person didn't like you anymore? Probably not. Ask yourself how you would feel if you were asked but really didn't want to go. Would you feel comfortable refusing? Were there different feelings when your places are reversed? Draw some conclusions.
6. Make a pie graph, using no fewer than two and no more than five divisions, illustrating the percentages of time you spend on your daily activities.

FOCUS ON WELLNESS

Stress will be with each of us as long as we live. We have choices as to whether we manage stress or let it manage us. *I will manage my stress more effectively by . . .*

Answers to *Keeping Fit: Stress Quiz* on page 99

1. True		6. True
2. False		7. False
3. False		8. False
4. False		9. True
5. True		10. False

Mental Disorders and Mental Health

You face many different situations each day, all of which have an impact on your level of mental health. Your ability to recognize and cope with problems is a major factor in your level of mental health.

As you read about different problems, keep in mind that almost everyone faces problems from time to time. If you do not handle the problems well, they tend to grow and can lead to more serious mental health situations.

After studying this chapter, you will be able to:
- define organic and functional mental disorders,
- define the three categories of functional mental disorders,
- describe signs of suicidal behavior and ways to help prevent suicide,
- explain what is meant by alienation and its effect on one's wellness,
- list mental and behavioral signs and symptoms which indicate that one might need professional help,
- contrast the various types of care providers for mental health,
- list various therapies that mental health professionals can practice.

Perhaps no other area of health is less understood than that of mental illness. What constitutes **mental illness?** It is *a mental disorder, a disease, or a disturbance that prevents a person from leading a happy, healthy life.*

Mental illness carries a stigma (**stig**-mah) in our society. A **stigma** means *a blot on one's good name.* Mental health professionals are working to help people better understand mental illness and thus to lessen some of the negative attitudes that exist toward it.

Types of Mental Disorders

The term **mental disorders** is used to describe *the broad range of mental health problems.* There are two general classifications of mental disorders: organic and functional.

When the *disorder is caused by a physical illness or injury that affects the brain,* it is called an **organic disorder.** Brain tumors, alcoholism, infections, syphilis, and stroke are some potential causes of organic disorders.

A **functional disorder** *results from one of many psychological causes, in which no brain damage is involved.* These disorders are much more of an internal nature, resulting from such conditions as stress, emotional conflict, or poor coping skills. The three main categories of functional disorders are *neurosis, psychosis,* and *personality disorders.*

Neurosis

We have all, at one time or another, experienced anxiety or fear. A **neurosis** (new-**row**-sis) is *a disorder in which the anxiety or fear prevents a person from functioning effectively in day-to-day living.* The neurotic is not able to cope with life's problems. However, the neurotic does not lose touch with reality, as one does in the case of psychosis (see page 116). Most of the time, neurotics continue to function within their environment, although poorly.

Neurosis can disturb the body and can cause an increased heart rate, irregular breathing, increased sweating, and muscular tension. Psychologically, it may produce a feeling of powerlessness and **paranoia** (par-uh-**noy**-uh)—*an all-absorbing apprehension that interferes with carrying on normal activity.* This anxiety is different from fear, which is a realistic reaction to a true danger or threat. However, the phobias discussed in Chapter 5 are examples of neuroses. The fear becomes unrealistic and immobilizing.

Hypochondria (high-poe-**kon**-dree-ah)—*a preoccupation with the body and with fear of presumed diseases*—is another example of neurotic behavior. **Anorexia** (an-or-**reck**-see-ah)—*the loss of appetite, especially when it is prolonged*—can also be classified as a neurosis. It is especially characteristic of female teenagers who have a fear of becoming overweight.

Depression   Depression is a disorder that is usually classified under neurosis. **Depression** is *a condition characterized by sadness, anxiety, insomnia, and withdrawal.* It can interfere with the individual's ability to carry on daily activities. Of course, we have all experienced degrees of depression.

Depression ranges from a mild feeling of sadness to intense suicidal despair. It can be so severe that a person's reality becomes distorted, at which point depression is classified as a psychosis.

Any kind of emotional loss can cause depression. Unmet emotional needs and loneliness can also lead to feelings of depression. A healthy individual recognizes the feelings as a normal response to an event and looks for constructive ways to cope with feelings. It is when the person cannot cope with the feelings and is unable to get back into the swing of things that depression becomes a problem.

Suicide   Severe depression can lead to attempted **suicide,** the *taking of one's life.* The depressed person sees no way out of what seems to be an intolerable situation. Suicide is the tenth leading cause of death among all ages and the second or third leading cause of death among teenagers, depending upon the year (accidents are first; homicides are either second or third). About 25,000 suicides occur every year. For each suicide completion, an estimated 8 to 10 attempted suicides occur.

Why do young people attempt to kill themselves? Authorities on the subject have identified several contributing factors. One is a greater sense of social turmoil. Competition and pressure to succeed in an increasingly complex social environment can become overwhelming.

The loss of a love relationship, however, is most often the event that leads to a suicide attempt. Other kinds of losses, such as loss of health or loss of status because of academic or social failure, can also make a young person vulnerable to suicide.

Many suicides can be prevented if help is found when warning signs appear. Group support is one of the best preventive measures.

About 95% of those who attempt suicide really do not want to die. They are making a plea for help. The lists below identify signs of potential suicides and suggest ways to help.

■ *Warning signs of suicide can be verbal.* Listen for:

1. *Direct statements,* like "I want to die," "I don't want to live anymore."
2. *Indirect statements,* like "I want to go to sleep and never wake up," "They'll be sorry when I'm gone," and "Soon this pain will be over."

■ *Warning signs of suicide can be reflected in a person's behavior.* Look for:

1. Depression, lack of energy
2. An increase or decrease in sleeping patterns
3. An increase or decrease in appetite
4. Withdrawal from usual social activities
5. Loss of interest in hobbies, sports, job, or school
6. A good student's drop in grades or a poor student's new concern about grades
7. Giving away possessions
8. Increased risk-taking, e.g., driving a car recklessly
9. Frequent accidents
10. Personality changes—withdrawal, apathy, moodiness
11. Previous suicide attempts (80% of those who commit suicide have attempted suicide before)

■ *Warning signs of suicide can also stem from situations:*

1. Experience of a loss (death, divorce, breakup of a relationship)
2. Difficulty communicating with parents
3. Problems with school or employment
4. Drugs and alcohol
5. Trouble with the law
6. No significant other person in life. (This is a critical factor, for a person who feels no one is interested in him or her has little reason to keep on trying.)

Psychosis

A **psychotic** (sigh-**kah**-tick) is *an individual whose perception of reality is so distorted that he or she is unable to function properly in the environment.* The person's ability to think, communicate, or remember is usually seriously impaired. Psychosis is a much more severe mental disorder than neurosis. The individual needs professional help immediately. Psychotics are potentially dangerous to themselves and to others.

Schizophrenia   A variety of types and causes of psychosis exist. The most common psychosis is **schizophrenia** (skit-zoe-**free**-nee-ah), a mental disorder meaning *"split mind."* It affects about 1 to 2% of the population

A Health Student Asks . . .

POTENTIAL SUICIDES

"I have read a lot about the signs of a potential suicide, but I have seen very little information on what to do to help someone who may be suicidal. Are there guidelines for helping someone who is in this condition?"

There most certainly are such guidelines. Here are some suggestions for ways to handle—*and ways not to handle*—potential suicides.

1. Believe and trust your suspicions that the person may be self-destructive.
2. Ask if the person is thinking about suicide.
3. Be direct; talk openly and freely.
4. Allow the person to express his or her feelings.
5. Be willing to listen. This affirms a person's feelings.
6. Don't give advice. Express what you think, but do not be judgmental.
7. Don't dare the person to do it.
8. Don't act shocked.
9. Don't allow yourself to be sworn to secrecy.
10. Talk with your parents about getting help for the person. There are agencies specializing in crisis intervention and suicide prevention. Many communities have suicide crisis centers or a suicide hotline. Look in your local directory for services available in your community.

and appears most frequently among people between the ages of 15 and 35. Schizophrenics are severely disturbed. They exhibit abnormal emotional responses or, in some cases, no emotional response at all. They may respond inappropriately in some situations. The schizophrenic withdraws, often losing a sense of time and space.

Much research is still being carried out to better understand schizophrenia. Some doctors believe its causes stem from a physical disorder. Others think it is genetic in nature. Presently, with proper treatment, many schizophrenics can recover.

Personality Disorders

A variety of conditions are described as personality disorders. Unlike neurosis and psychosis, in personality disorders no apparent, distinct signs and symptoms appear. The individual continues to function, often effectively, in his or her environment. A person who has a **personality disorder** *may respond inappropriately in certain situations or may interfere with others' interactions.*

One common personality disorder is termed the *antisocial personality,* characterized by a person's being in constant conflict with society. The individual may display behavior that is cruel, uncaring, irresponsible, and impulsive. Knowing right from wrong, the antisocial personality often does not care and is, therefore, usually in trouble with the law.

Dysorganization

Another way to look at mental disorders and how they may develop and progress is by using a continuum. Dr. Karl Menninger, one of the leaders in the field of psychiatry, developed such a continuum of mental health and mental illness.

The mentally healthy person is at one end of the continuum and the mentally ill person is at the other end. Within the continuum are various *levels of progressive mental illness,* or stages of **dysorganization** (dis-org-uh-nuh-**zay**-shun). Dr. Menninger identifies five levels of dysorganization. These five levels, the highest being the most serious, describe the progression of mental illness.

Of course, in a continuum, people move back and forth. At any point on the first three levels, an individual could identify coping strategies or deal with the stress or seek help. It is when a person does nothing that the more serious mental disorders develop. Dr. Menninger's continuum is one of a number of theories that illustrates a progression in mental illness.

Dysorganization Continuum

Level One Experiences more tension, fear, anxiety, and anger than usual. Is easily irritated, may have trouble sleeping, is restless, may have psychosomatic illnesses. Symptoms here are caused by stress. According to Dr. Menninger, everyone experiences this level at one time or another.

Level Two A person has difficulty coping with stress or who experiences long-term stress may move into this level. At this level, a person is described as being neurotic.

Level Three Continuing stress becomes too much. The person may become very aggressive, finding it hard to keep control. At this level, it is possible that a person could harm himself or herself or others and needs professional help.

Level Four At this level, a person is described as being psychotic. Psychosis is a serious mental disorder. Some people become very depressed; others suffer from delusions. Sometimes the psychotic must be hospitalized.

Level Five The most extreme level of dysorganization is level five. The person gives up. Hospitalization may be necessary. Psychological treatment is necessary.

CHECK YOURSELF

1. What is the difference between the two general classifications of mental disorders?
2. Why is suicide a major problem among young people?
3. How does psychosis differ from neurosis?
4. How does Dr. Menninger explain mental illness?

2. Facing Problems and Conflicts

At various times, we all use **defense mechanisms,** which are *strategies used to cope with stressful situations.* They can provide temporary relief from anxiety and help us cope with problems. To a certain degree, using defense mechanisms is helpful to our emotional health. However, too much dependence on them tends to take the place of reality and other stress-management techniques. This dependence could be a sign of potential problems in coping with day-to-day living.

Common Defense Mechanisms

The following are common defense mechanisms:

- **Denial.** *Refusal to accept reality.* Carol's pet dog has died. It was Carol's friend since she was a small child. Carol refuses to accept that this has happened. She refuses to talk about it and continues to act like her dog is alive.
- **Escape, or fantasy.** *Running away from a problem through daydreaming, books, even excessive sleep.* (A world is created as a person would like it to be, not as it is.) Jim has failed to make the basketball team. He imagines that he is suffering from some hidden physical problem. When the others find out about his problem, they will view his effort to make the basketball team as a success, rather than as a failure.
- **Rationalization.** *An attempt to justify one's actions with an excuse rather than admitting to one's failure or mistake.* Yolanda justifies flunking her math test because she was absent the day it was scheduled and did not know what to study.
- **Projection.** *An attempt to protect one's self-concept by blaming unpleasant feelings or inappropriate actions on others.* Getting poor grades and blaming it on the teacher's not liking you is an example of evading personal responsibility.
- **Repression.** *Blocking out thoughts about unpleasant things or experiences— forgetting on purpose.* Repression is actually an unconscious method of escaping something unpleasant. You may have chores to do this weekend while your parents are away. You simply don't think about any of your responsibilities so that you can enjoy your weekend of fun with friends.
- **Identification.** *Acting like or modeling one's behavior after a person he or she likes.* It is a form of hero worship. However, it can take another form. People who have had a similar achievement or experience may identify with one another, sharing in something they all have in common. Juan has a favorite character on a television police program. He dresses, talks, and walks like this person.

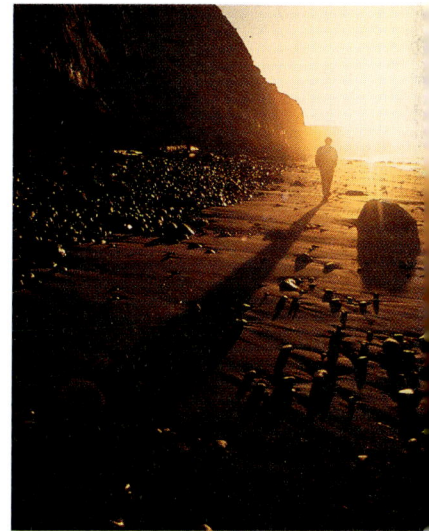

Defense mechanisms are useful, but we must not become dependent on them.

- **Displacement.** *Expressing feelings toward someone or something not associated with the source of the feelings.* Suzanna is upset because she did not get picked for the team. When her sister greets her at home, Suzanna gives her a shove, says "Leave me alone," and slams the door to her room.
- **Regression.** *Retreating to an earlier time that seems less threatening and requires less responsibility.* Paul is having trouble in high school adjusting to the new challenges, more students, and a strange atmosphere. He goes back and visits his old teachers and principal in junior high school, and entertains the idea that it would be nice to stay there.
- **Compensation.** *An attempt to make up for something you do not have, or did not receive.* Paul is not very good at basketball, but he is a first-rate swimmer.
- **Sublimation.** *Transforming unacceptable behaviors into acceptable ones.* It can involve redirecting specific behaviors. Jack is always fighting with people. He joins the wrestling team.

Conflicts and Stress in Our Lives

What is conflict? People at every age experience conflict. Perhaps no age-group experiences more conflict than that of adolescence. Conflict may be understood in two ways.

Interpersonal Conflict

Interpersonal conflict usually results from lack of communication or an attempt to meet different strong needs.

First of all, *a disagreement or an argument with another person* can be considered a conflict. We call it an **interpersonal conflict** because it happens between two or more people. A misunderstanding between two friends,

a parent and a teenager, a student and a teacher, or a brother and a sister can result in conflict. These are common and occur in every human relationship.

Conflict occurs in these situations for many different reasons. Some of the most common reasons include lack of communication between two people, or the attempt to meet different strong needs. Sometimes one person brings a specific purpose to the conflict—perhaps to win or to dominate. Conflict occurs when one person is defending, while the other is attacking or thought to be attacking.

Sometimes a conflict results when one person already has an impression of what the other person is like. The person bases his or her impression on some previous experience, making a judgment about the other person that may or may not be accurate.

There are times when individuals themselves are not confident, and they perceive any topic that is brought up as a threat to them. Thus, they become very anxious, and this can cause conflict.

Practicing the communication skills described in Chapter 5 can be very effective in resolving interpersonal conflict.

Intrapersonal Conflict

A second type of conflict is **intrapersonal conflict,** meaning *"conflict within a person."* Perhaps you have to make a decision. Your choices are very difficult, and you are torn about making a decision. This is an intrapersonal conflict. Use of the problem-solving steps described in Chapter 5 can be very effective in resolving the intrapersonal conflict.

Handling Conflict

Conflict is not all bad. It can have some constructive results, depending on how a person handles it. Here are some ways that conflict can be constructive:

1. Conflicts can make people more aware of problems that they need to resolve.
2. Conflicts can help individuals begin to know themselves better and to know what annoys them.
3. Conflicts encourage change, keeping individuals from getting into ruts and from maintaining old habits when they need to review and change.
4. Conflicts can usually reduce the small irritations in relationships. They serve to clear the air.
5. Conflicts can make life more interesting by causing a person to look more deeply into an issue, particularly from a new perspective.
6. Conflicts can help to deepen and improve a relationship, strengthening each person's belief that the bond between the individuals is stronger than any issue causing conflict.

Alienation and Loneliness

Two other common factors occasionally enter our lives. They can either deter us from solving problems or cause problems. We call these factors *alienation* and *loneliness*.

Alienation

There are times when we each feel distant from those around us. Sometimes the group pushes us away, while at other times we push the group away. In both cases the result is alienation (a-lee-en-**na**-shun). What does that word mean to you? **Alienation** means "withdrawing, diverting, estrangement." Basically it is *a feeling of being cut off from others, whether voluntarily or involuntarily.*

Alienation may be a particular concern during adolescence because of some of the changes and uncertainties that are part of this period. During this time, young people begin to define their independence—to seek their own identity. In doing so, there is a tendency to alienate others. Because of the confusion associated with the rapid changes during this period, many may not realize or understand how their actions alienate others.

A problem associated with alienation is the feeling of being all alone and not understood. These feelings can make the period of growth and adjustment during adolescence more difficult. People begin to look for acceptance and recognition in other—sometimes unhealthy—ways.

Loneliness

Alienation can lead to loneliness. We need, however, to distinguish between being *lonely* and *being alone*. We all need time alone—a time to get away from it all, to reflect, rest, and refuel. **Loneliness**—*feeling like you have no one to turn to*—is unhealthy.

People who are lonely feel like strangers in a strange world. Others seem not to care for or to understand them. This often happens to older people who are out of the mainstream of activity. These feelings can be painful. However, they are not limited to adults. Young people can have these same feelings. You may think of someone who is lonely as being physically alone. This is not always so. People can be in a crowd and feel lonely.

Alienation and loneliness can be reduced by meeting people and reacting with them.

Frustration and Violence

Two other common factors can deter us from solving our problems. These factors are *frustration* and *violence*.

Frustration

Frustration is defined as *keeping someone from doing or achieving something; baffling the efforts, hopes, or desires.* At one time or another, we have all

experienced frustration. What events led you to feeling frustrated? What did you do about it?

Frustration should be looked at as a temporary problem which will pass when other approaches to the problem are found.

Oftentimes our source of frustration is not within our control. For this reason, it is important to learn to tolerate the frustration until it passes. It is not healthy to waste energy becoming tense and upset over situations that you cannot control. This may be difficult, but try to channel those energies into more productive activity.

Violence

Violence is *the exerting of physical force with the intent of damage or inflicting harm.* Violence is perhaps the most destructive and negative acting out of stress. Violence is contrary to good mental health on many fronts. Can you think of some? Certainly, one of the most obvious is the lack of respect that a violent person shows for another person.

In the discussion of conflict, we mentioned that conflict can help the relationship if it helps the people to see the value of their relationship. Violence as a way to resolve conflict would make it very difficult to maintain a quality relationship. Violence is often an indication of the inability to handle aggression, frustration, and hostility.

CHECK YOURSELF

1. What are defense mechanisms? When do they become unhealthy?
2. How can conflict be constructive?
3. What is alienation? How can it affect one's mental health?
4. Why is violence destructive and negative?

The Menningers and Mental Illness

Mental illness has been a problem that has been feared by people for thousands of years. Ancient people thought that mental illness was caused by evil spirits. Ceremonies were held to drive these spirits out of the body. Sometimes, a hole was cut in the victim's head in an attempt to let out the evil spirit.

The Greeks believed mental illness was a punishment from their gods. The Greek doctor, Hippocrates, thought that it was caused by an imbalance of body fluids.

In Europe, during the 1500s, people with mental illness were believed to be witches. Many were burned to death, while others were imprisoned. Later, *asylums*, or institutions for the mentally ill, were built, but were often just jails for people. Efforts began in the early 1800s to seriously improve conditions. In 1883, a German psychiatrist developed a system of diagnosing and classifying mental disorders.

The famous Austrian psychologist Sigmund Freud (1856–1939) introduced several new approaches to mental illness. They would later become the basis for what is now called *psychotherapy*. Freud suggested that forces in the unconscious mind had a strong influence on a person's personality and behavior. He also suggested that certain personality problems during early childhood may affect the development of the unconscious mind.

In 1925, Charles Menninger, along with two of his sons, Karl and William, established the Menninger Clinic in Topeka, Kansas. These physicians were pioneers in promoting the treatment of mental disorders in a community clinic setting. They crusaded for the improvement of hospital facilities for psychiatric care and for more personalized treatment toward mental patients. Their writings did much to influence the public's attitudes toward mental illness.

Dr. Charles Menninger's belief in group practice—where a patient has available the services of several kinds of specialists—led to the establishment of the clinic. Today, the Menninger Foundation is one of the world's leading psychiatric centers. At the Foundation, mentally ill patients are treated, psychiatrists are trained, and research is conducted. The Menninger Clinic's School of Psychiatry is one of the world's major training centers for psychiatrists. The Menninger Clinic now encompasses two hospitals—one for adults and one for children—departments of neurology, neurosurgery and internal medicine, and outpatient and aftercare programs.

Left to right: *Doctors C.F., Karl, and William Menninger.*

As you have read in this chapter, many different types of problems are related to mental disorders. Within those types, the severity of the problems also vary greatly. It is hard to identify specific symptoms with certain mental problems, as is often common with other diseases, such as the common cold or measles.

Signs of Mental Health Problems

However, by being aware of and recognizing early warning signs, you are able to get help for yourself or offer help to someone else. Any of the following feelings or behaviors that persist over a period of days or weeks, and begin to interfere with other aspects of daily living, could be a sign that something is wrong:

- *Sadness* over a specific event, or for no reason,
- *Hopelessness*—the sense that your life is out of control,
- *Violent or erratic shifts in your moods,*
- *Inability to concentrate or to make decisions,*
- *Fear and anger* because "the world" is against you,
- *Trouble getting along* with those around you,
- *Severe sleep disturbances*—nightmares, insomnia,
- *Compulsive self-destructive behavior*—overeating, drinking, drug abuse,
- *Frequent physical ailments,* for which no medical cause can be found.

Of course, no one symptom means a person has a mental disorder. However, any one of them may be an indication that stress in your life is building up and is something you need to look at closely, before more serious problems develop.

Health-Care Services for Mental Health

Most people are not skilled in handling problems associated with mental and emotional health. Many times a friend may offer "emotional first aid," that is, support and a "listening ear," which may prevent more serious damage from taking place. However, this emotional first aid does not take the place of the aid that a mental health professional can give.

The principal health-care providers for mental health are psychiatrists, psychiatric social workers, clinical psychologists, neurologists, and occupational therapists. These individuals may work in or outside a hospital setting.

Also outside the hospital setting, help is available through marriage and family counselors, rehabilitation counselors, and pastoral counselors. All of these professionals differ from one another.

Psychiatrist

A **psychiatrist** *deals with mental, emotional, and behavioral disorders of the mind.* This person has completed four years of medical school and one year of internship and has passed a state licensing exam. Although this is all that is legally required, many psychiatrists have also spent several years as resident physicians in an institution that treats mental illness. Because psychiatrists are physicians, they can prescribe drugs.

After two years of additional experience following their residency, psychiatrists may take the examination of the Board of Psychiatry and Neurology of the American Medical Association, leading to board certification. In the United States, the Board certified about one-half of the 30,000 psychiatrists practicing in 1980.

The psychiatrist uses many **therapies,** or *treatment techniques.* Among them are:

- **Psychoanalysis.** A one-to-one analysis of a patient's past life, particularly his or her early life, to ascertain the early roots of a mental problem.
- **Psychotherapy.** Discussions by patient and psychiatrist, which are aimed at bringing out the problem, an understanding of it, and a possible solution.
- **Drug Therapy.** The use of drugs to reduce a mental disorder or to prepare for the above two treatments.
- **Electroconvulsive Therapy.** Electric shock given to a patient under anesthetic, usually on a side of the brain. This treatment can sometimes help severely depressed patients.
- **Group Therapy.** Meeting with other people with similar problems. These people pool their experiences and learn from one another, with the doctor as a guide.

Health care services for mental health is one of the most important medical developments in the 20th century.

Neurologist

A **neurologist** (new-**rahl**-uh-jist) is *a physician who specializes in organic disorders of the brain and nervous system.* This person has a degree in medicine, postgraduate training (and experience in this field), certification as a specialist, and a state license permitting practice. Neurologists usually have received some training in psychiatry. Those who specialize in surgery are called *neurosurgeons* or *neural surgeons.*

Consultation with and testing by a neurologist may be required for patients whose mental symptoms are suspected of being caused by an organic disease.

Clinical Psychologist

The **clinical psychologist** is *a psychologist who specializes in the study of abnormal human behavior in a clinical setting.* The person may have any one of several degrees: master of arts, master of science, doctor of philosophy in psychology, doctor of psychology, or doctor of education.

State law usually governs the title "psychologist." It requires that the person have a doctoral degree, at least two years of supervised experience at a psychiatric hospital or clinic, and the passing of an examination.

Since 1975, a *National Register of Health Science Providers in Psychology* has existed. It lists all of the psychologists licensed or certified in their respective states. To be listed in this registry, the psychologist must have a doctorate in psychology and two years of supervised experience in some type of mental health service. In 1981, about 25,000 psychologists were practicing in the United States. About one-fourth of these were women.

The clinical psychologist can practice psychotherapy, group therapy, and individual counseling, in addition to testing for specific mental disorders.

Educational Counselor

An **educational counselor** or **school counselor** is *a person who generally works with young people, helping them in personal or educational matters.* Counselors usually have a master's degree in counseling. They generally have special training in psychologic testing, as well as in counseling youngsters in a school or college setting. Some counselors address themselves to students' personal problems; others confine themselves to dealing with learning problems or assisting students in educational and vocational choices.

Pastoral Counselors

Informally, the clergy—ministers, priests, and rabbis—have been mental health practitioners for hundreds of years. A **pastoral counselor** *helps people within the context of mental and social problems.*

Today, many members of the clergy receive formal education in counseling as part of their training. Those who are particularly interested in this aspect of their ministry usually take additional training.

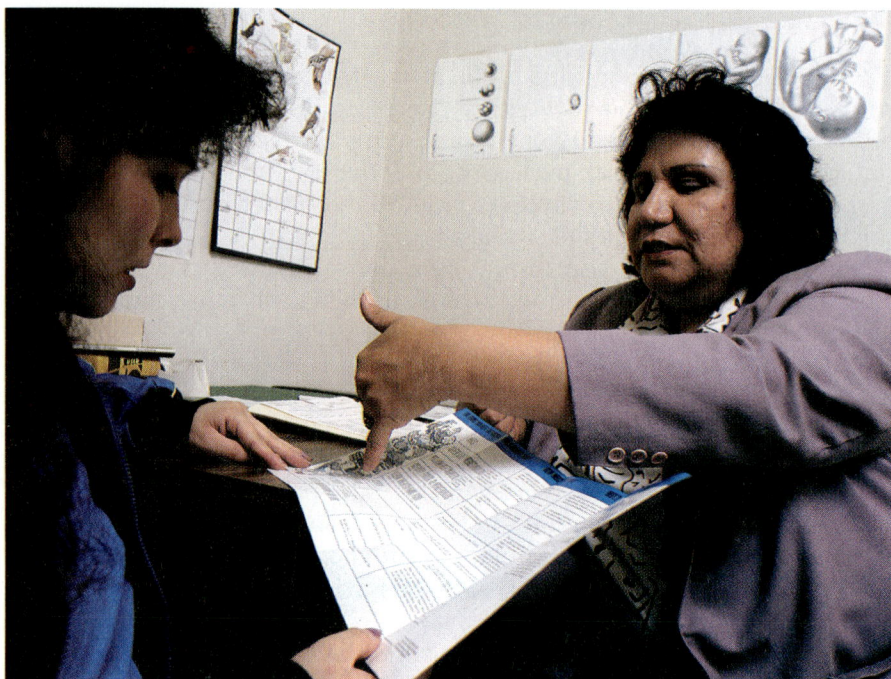

Social workers help to bring stability, support, and assistance to the people with whom they are dealing.

The American Association of Pastoral Counselors is a professional organization that has set standards for training and certification of individuals and institutions in the field of pastoral counseling.

Social Worker

A **social worker** is *a person who provides a link between the medical service center and the client and his or her family.* The social worker has completed four years of college and two years of postgraduate study in a school of social work. A psychiatric or clinical social worker is one who has concentrated on psychiatric casework, doing fieldwork in a mental hospital, mental health clinic, or family service agency that provides guidance, counseling, and treatment for clients with emotional problems.

A psychiatric social worker in a hospital maintains contact between patients and their families, serves as part of a treatment team (along with the psychiatrist, psychologist, nurses, and aides), helps the families understand and adjust to problems created by hospitalization, and supervises the rehabilitation of patients after they are released.

Occupational Therapist

The **occupational therapist** *evaluates a person's abilities in the light of his or her emotional or physical handicap.* This person usually works in a psychiatric hospital or general hospital, conducting programs that involve work, recreation, and creative activities. An occupational therapist has completed a four-year college program with specialization in occupational therapy.

A SOCIAL WORKER

While there are many types of social workers, all share one common goal. They provide services designed to help people lead more fulfilling lives. Such help is needed by those in all walks of life, including children, parents, the aged, the partially and totally disabled, the blind, and the poverty-stricken.

Social workers respond to other people in a positive manner. Their job is to bring stability, support, and assistance to the clients with whom they work. The social workers' overriding concern is the individual's well-being.

A social worker usually works for a tax-supported agency or for a voluntary agency. The social worker's task is to help communities provide maximum equality of opportunity for all of its citizens:

■ to help those in need to learn to cope more

effectively with their problems,
■ to help strengthen and improve the institutional systems that are responsible for educating people so that fewer failures occur in our rapidly changing society.

Social workers are needed wherever there are people who need help. Social workers tend to travel considerably, visiting people in their homes and going to various centers and facilities in the community. A hospital, a public school system, the court, or an agency for juvenile delinquents may employ social workers. Social workers can also work in a service outlet for the handicapped, in a psychiatric hospital or clinic, or in homes for the aged.

A career in social work offers considerable fulfillment from knowing that you are

helping human beings in need. This is the chief motivation for those who choose this career, although the pay is good and there is usually rapid advancement.

To be a social worker requires four years of college with a major in social work. Usually a person needs to do graduate work if he or she is going to move ahead in this career choice. Most major universities offer degrees in social work. You can obtain information about social work by writing to the registrar's office at the university or college of your choice. If you are not familiar with any one school in particular, ask your academic counselor or advisor for help.

Behavioral Therapist

The **behavioral therapist** *works with patients to help them change their habits.* This technique is called **behavioral therapy.** This approach has become popular with people who want to give up smoking or drinking. The behavioral therapist also works with people who have phobias and other unreasonable fears.

The behavioral therapist has completed a four year college program, with further specialization in behavioral therapy.

CHECK YOURSELF

1. Name four signs of mental health problems.
2. What is a psychiatrist?
3. What is a neurologist?
4. What is a clinical psychologist?
5. Name three therapies that a psychiatrist can employ. Describe them.
6. With what type of counselor are you most familiar? How does he or she help you?

CHAPTER 7   Review

CHAPTER SUMMARY

- Mental problems are quite common at all levels of our society.
- All of us, at some time or other, suffer from some type of mental letdown, such as depression, frustration, anxiety, or loneliness.
- Most of us have the resources within ourselves to bounce back from such difficulties, but sometimes we need the help of others. Even then, that might not be enough. We may have a reason to seek professional help.
- Suicide has become an increasing problem in the United States among all age-groups. Suicide is the third leading cause of death among teenagers. Depression is often the feeling that accompanies suicide. You can observe danger signs and take seriously any threats. Help is available in most communities to prevent suicide.
- We use a variety of defense mechanisms to protect our self-esteem. However, overuse of these mechanisms is not healthy.
- Conflict is a common problem that affects our emotions and our mental health. There are many ways to handle conflict. Some are more effective than others.
- Violence is another phenomenon that touches many lives in our society today. Violence is usually an expression of aggression, frustration, and hostility. Because of the strong impact of violence, the people who suffer from the violence need help, as well as those who resort to violence to solve problems.

- The mental health field has many different types of specialists, such as psychiatrists, psychologists, social workers, and counselors, to assist people in need.
- Some therapies that certain specialists practice are psychoanalysis, psychotherapy, drug therapy, electroconvulsive therapy, group therapy, individual counseling, occupational therapy, and behavioral therapy.

REVIEWING WHAT YOU LEARNED

1. Which classification of mental disorders has the most to do with learned behavior? Explain your answer.
2. What are three categories of functional mental disorders. Define them.
3. What makes the depression that a potential suicide victim feels different from that which most people experience at some point in everyday life?
4. Justify the use of defense mechanisms as a way of maintaining mental health and preventing mental disorders.
5. What is alienation, and what is its effect on one's wellness?
6. What basic skills and characteristics do all mental health professionals share in common?
7. Name five therapies that some mental health professionals can practice. Which type of professional can carry on each of the therapies?

mental illness	personality disorder	compensation	group therapy
stigma	dysorganization	interpersonal conflict	neurologist
mental disorders	defense mechanisms	intrapersonal conflict	clinical psychologist
organic disorder	denial	alienation	social worker
functional disorder	escape	loneliness	occupational therapist
neurosis	fantasy	frustration	occupational therapy
paranoia	rationalization	violence	behavioral therapist
hypochondria	projection	psychiatrist	behavioral therapy
anorexia	repression	therapies	educational counselor
depression	identification	psychoanalysis	school counselor
suicide	displacement	psychotherapy	pastoral counselor
psychotic	regression	drug therapy	
schizophrenia	sublimation	electroconvulsive therapy	

PUTTING VOCABULARY TO USE

On a separate piece of paper, write the following statements. Then supply the missing word or phrase from the chapter vocabulary list.

1. _____ _____. It is a disturbance that keeps a person from leading a happy, healthy life.
2. _____ and _____. There are two major types of mental disorders.
3. _____. This type of functional disorder is usually caused by fear or anxiety.
4. _____. A physician who deals specifically in mental and emotional disorders.
5. _____. When an individual withdraws from the people around him or the group rejects him.
6. _____. Something that might prevent you from getting a job, a promotion or acceptance in a social group.
7. _____. A special type of neurosis an individual feels that he or she is suffering from a number of ailments.
8. _____. A psychotic mental disorder.
9. _____. Mentally retreating into an earlier time that seems less threatening.
10. _____. The ultimate example of depression.
11. _____. Specializes in organic disorders of the brain and nervous system.
12. _____. Comes about by keeping someone from doing or achieving something.

APPLYING WHAT YOU LEARNED

1. Now that you have studied this chapter, what would you tell a friend who has talked about suicide on previous occasions?
2. At what point would you say the use of defense mechanisms becomes a problem and an unhealthy way to deal with life?
3. Choose any three defense mechanisms that you would use yourself. Give specific examples of how you would state each one.
4. Sometimes people will say they are lonely in a crowd of people. How can this be true?
5. What does Dr. Menninger mean by dysorganization?
6. What might indicate that a person needs the help of a health-care professional in mental health?

FOCUS ON WELLNESS

Mental illness affects one out of five people in the United States at some time in their lives. *I can prevent mental illness in my life by . . .*

U N I T

3

NUTRITION AND YOUR HEALTH

CHAPTER 8
You Are What You Eat

CHAPTER 9
Weight Control, Special Foods, and Special Diets

You Are What You Eat

"I'm on a diet."
"That's full of calories."
"I'm really in a pickle!"
"She brings home the bacon."
"He's a ham."
"That car is a lemon."

**Food is more than just something we eat. It is a part of
our conversation, a major part of our daily lives.**

After studying this chapter, you will be able to:
- describe external factors that influence eating behavior,
- evaluate the influence of advertising on one's food choices,
- define each of the six main classes of nutrients,
- describe the role of each class of nutrient in maintaining good health,
- identify food sources for each nutrient,
- define cholesterol and explain its relationship to overall health,
- name the five food groups,
- explain the meaning of RDA and how its information is helpful,
- point out the useful information found on food labels,
- make wise consumer choices in purchasing food.

1. Why Is Good Nutrition So Important?

Perhaps more than any other single substance, food in some way affects almost everything we do. It affects how we look, feel, and act. It affects how we grow, and it even affects our abilities—how well we function each day. Eating the correct amounts and kinds of food gives us energy and stamina for active schedules. Food provides for our growth and maintenance of a healthy body and helps to keep us mentally alert.

Food in Our Daily Lives

One might assume that we would know or would want to know as much as possible about something so important as proper nutrition. Obviously, we all want to look and feel good and do well. If good food choices aid appearance, health, and performance, then it seems reasonable that what and how we eat be important in everyday living. While all of these points seem logical, it remains true that six out of the ten leading causes of death in the United States are linked directly to our diet.

Think about what you have eaten today. Would you describe your food choices as healthy? Good **nutrition**—*eating the proper food for growth and development*—is especially important during adolescence.

Nutrition and Adolescence

Next to the first years of life, adolescence is the fastest period of growth that a person experiences. The growth during adolescence is a result of hormonal changes in the body. During the active growth period, the body uses more energy, making nutrition an even more important factor.

Yet the period of adolescence has traditionally been the years of poorest nutrition and eating habits. Why do you think this is true?

As you read about various foods and their effects on the body and health, evaluate your own eating habits. Identify which food choices you have control over, what changes you can make, and how some different choices could affect your appearance, your self-image, and your performance.

Why Do You Eat?

The body has a physical need for food. Food is necessary for survival. When your stomach is empty, the muscular walls contract, stimulating nerve endings. The nerve endings signal the brain that the body's food supply needs replenishing. The brain relays a message of "hunger," telling you

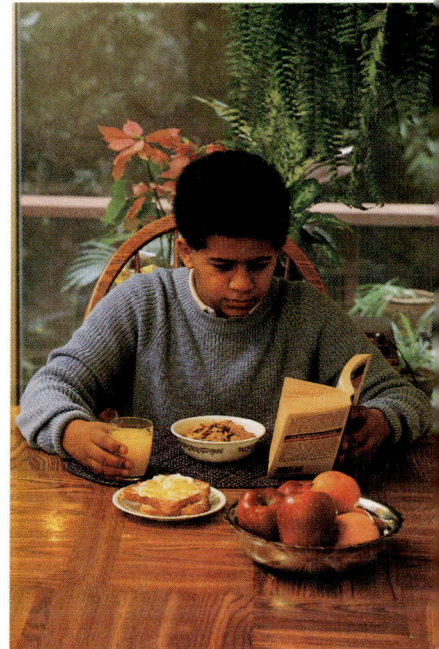

Good nutrition during adolescence is a vital link to healthy physical and mental development.

What you eat affects your levels of physical, mental, and social well-being.

to eat. With food in your stomach, the walls of the stomach are stretched and the nerve endings are no longer stimulated. You have satisfied your physical need for food.

But why do people eat when they are not hungry? Or why do people feel hungry when they smell fresh apple pie, even though they have just eaten?

Many factors control and stimulate your **appetite**, in this case, *your desire to eat*. Appetite is related to your eating habits, which form the basis for how and why you eat.

Influences on Your Eating Habits

Your early childhood experiences greatly influenced your eating habits. What you ate as a child, what you liked or did not like, when you ate your meals, can influence your current habits and preferences.

Family customs, ethnic background, economics, geography and climate, availability of certain foods, and convenience also have an impact on food choices.

Personal preferences based on taste, texture, color, and smell strongly influence what you choose to eat. How do your friends affect your food choices?

Advertising's Influence on Food Choices

An estimated 96% of American homes have at least one television set. On the average, the television set is on more than six hours per day. Television watching is particularly high until the age of 12, when it begins to drop off. What does television have to do with your nutritional choices?

One poll found that the American public receives most of its information from television advertising, followed by newspapers, magazines, and then television documentaries.

What is important is that many people often believe what they see and hear. Many people think that what is said on television is true. Over $550 million dollars is spent on advertising to young people alone, and more than 50% of this advertising is on food products. The chart on this page will show you what kinds of foods are advertised. Its figures are approximate.

Does it appear that advertising promotes wellness through good nutrition? With so much attention given to the convenience foods and high sugar foods, you can see that it is often difficult to know *what* to eat. By being aware of this advertising and its impact on your food selection, you take an important step toward making informed food choices.

Food Advertising on TV

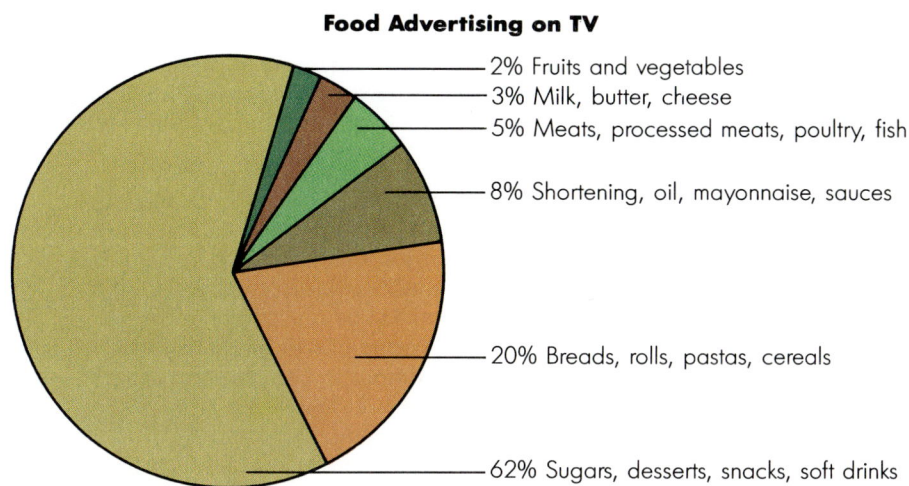

- 2% Fruits and vegetables
- 3% Milk, butter, cheese
- 5% Meats, processed meats, poultry, fish
- 8% Shortening, oil, mayonnaise, sauces
- 20% Breads, rolls, pastas, cereals
- 62% Sugars, desserts, snacks, soft drinks

What Are Nutrients?

With such an abundance of nutrition information, some of it accurate and some of it not, how is one to know what to buy and eat?

First, you must have an accurate base of nutrition information. This simply means knowing about your basic nutrients, what they do, and what foods are good nutrient sources. With this knowledge, then, you can evaluate advertisements and read labels to receive additional help in making wise food choices.

Nutrients themselves are *chemical substances obtained from food during digestion*. Those *nutrients that your body either cannot make itself or cannot make in sufficient amounts* are called **essential nutrients**. Your body is dependent on your diet to receive these nutrients.

Scientists have identified about 50 nutrients that your body needs. These 50 nutrients can be grouped into six main classes: carbohydrates, fats, protein, vitamins, minerals, and water. As you will see, no one food provides the body with all the nutrients it needs.

Are You Nutritionally Wise?

Perhaps no other area of health has more misleading and inaccurate information than the field of nutrition. Food fads, fad diets, diet pills, and supplements are a multimillion dollar business.

Below are a few of the more common statements about different topics on nutrition. Before continuing your reading, take this short quiz. On a separate sheet of paper, indicate if you think each statement is *true* or *false*.

1. Honey has fewer calories than sugar.
2. Gelatin is one of the best sources of protein and will strengthen the fingernails.
3. Only children need the nutrients in milk.
4. Healthy, active young people require concentrated sources of sugar, found in candy bars and other sweets, in their diets each day.
5. A reducing diet should not include bread or potatoes.
6. Large doses of vitamin C will cure the common cold.

7. The best source of energy for an athlete is protein.
8. Foods grown in organically fertilized soil are more nutritious than those foods grown in chemically fertilized soil.
9. Unlike whole-grain products, white bread and white flour have absolutely no nutritional value.
10. An increase in physical activity is then usually followed by an appropriate increase in appetite.

Scoring: Answers to the quiz begin on page 158 of this text. How did you do? A score of 8 to 10 correct means *good*—you have not been misled by inaccurate information. A score of 6 to 7 is *fair*, so be cautious to be sure you have accurate information. A score of 5 or less is *poor*, so be careful, for your food choices and diet may be suffering because of your lack of accurate information.

CHECK YOURSELF

1. What is the relationship between your nutrition and your general level of health?
2. Why is good nutrition especially important during adolescence?
3. What factors influence your choice of what you eat and how much to eat?
4. What impact does advertising have on one's nutritional choices?
5. What are nutrients?
6. Name the six main classes of nutrients.

2. Carbohydrates

Carbohydrates (kar-bow-**high**-drates) are *the starches and sugars that come mainly from plant food and give your body much of the energy it needs each day.* Carbohydrates have long been considered to be fattening foods that one avoids when dieting. However, this is not the case. *Starchy foods*—potatoes, breads, pasta—are called **complex carbohydrates** and, ounce for ounce, have the same number of calories as proteins and fewer calories than fats.

How can this be true? A 5-ounce potato provides about 110 calories, whereas a 5-ounce steak has about 550 calories. This is because the steak has more fat than protein in it, and fat is our most calorie-laden nutrient.

Complex carbohydrates, besides being essential for good health, can actually be helpful for the dieter. In addition to being a good source of energy, the complex carbohydrates give you a full, satisfied feeling, take longer to digest, add fiber to the diet, and contain other nutrients. This is in contrast to the **simple carbohydrates** like *sugars*, which provide energy but are also higher in calories and often leave the dieter still feeling hungry.

Complex carbohydrates– potatoes, pasta, and bread– are much more important to eat than the simple carbohydrates which we get from sugar and sugar products.

Glycogen and Glucose

Carbohydrates are chemical compounds made up of carbon, hydrogen, and oxygen. When carbohydrates are broken down into simple chemicals, the liver converts these chemicals into **glycogen** (**gly**-koh-jin), or *starch*, which can be stored in the cells and used as the body needs energy. The breakdown of carbohydrates also produces *blood sugar* called **glucose** (**glue**-kose). Glucose circulates throughout the body, providing a ready source of fuel for cells.

When you eat large amounts of carbohydrates but you do not get enough physical activity to use this energy, it is stored in the body as *fat*. This is why inactive people, especially those whose diets are high in sugar and starch, gain weight.

Carbohydrates and Dieting

Since the early 1900s, Americans have cut back on their consumption of carbohydrates, with the decrease being greatest for the complex carbohydrates. On the other hand, a steady increase has occurred in the intake of refined sugars, usually found in foods that are high in calories and low in nutrients.

In 1977, after analyzing the American diet, the U.S. Senate Select Committee on Nutrition and Human Needs recommended a sizable increase

---

HEALTH UPDATE   **HEALTH UPDATE**   **HEALTH UPDATE**

Guide to Complex Carbohydrates

Potatoes. Baked, steamed, or boiled potatoes are very high in nutrients. However, one pat of butter or margarine increases the calorie content of a medium-sized potato by a third. Deep-frying destroys some vitamins and adds significantly to the calorie count.

Flour. Grains consist of three parts: the starchy *endosperm* containing nutrients, particularly protein; the vitamin-rich *germ;* and the *bran*, the protective outer coat that provides undigestible roughage for humans. In the United States, the milling techniques used to produce white flour remove the bran and germ, leaving mostly the starch behind.

Bread. If you are eating white bread, be sure it is *enriched*, that is, has nutrients added. Your best buy is whole-grain bread or 100% whole-wheat bread.

Cereals. Your most nutritious choice is the whole-grain cereals. Look for cereals that are not sugarcoated. Some cereals are made up of at least 90% sugar.

Rice. Brown rice contains nearly all of the nutrients in the original rice grain. Polishing removes the brown coat and the germ that contains most of the B vitamins and minerals, but it renders the protein in the grain more digestible. Instant and minute rices are least nutritious.

Legumes and seeds. Dried peas and beans, seeds, and nuts are rich sources of protein, vitamins, and minerals. Seeds and nuts contain considerable amounts of fat, which increase their calorie count. Although most of them are not high in starch, these carbohydrate foods are vital sources of vitamins and minerals and excellent sources of fiber. Many contain small but significant amounts of protein as well. Their fiber and water content add satisfying bulk and volume to the diet. These foods are also natural sources of simple carbohydrates.

in our consumption of carbohydrates—particularly the complex starches and naturally occurring sugars in fruits and vegetables. The Committee suggested that these foods be at least 48% of our daily calorie intake.

Sugar: How Much Do You Eat?

The average American consumes 120 pounds (54 kg) of sugar each year, nearly one-third of a pound a day. Three-fourths of this sugar is invisible in foods and beverages prepared outside the home. *Invisible* means that we normally do not associate sugar's being in the food. The average American is so accustomed to sweet food that manufacturers add sugar to many foods just to make them appealing. The same is true of salt.

The consumption of soft drinks in the United States has more than doubled since 1960. The average person consumes over 20 pounds of sugar per year in soft drinks alone. One 12-ounce (340 g) cola contains 9 teaspoons (45 ml) of sugar, water, caffeine, carbonation, and no other nutrients!

Like starch, sugar is a carbohydrate and when found in different products is called by different names:

- *sucrose* (table sugar refined from sugarcane and beets),
- *lactose* (milk sugar),
- *fructose* (fruit sugar),
- *glucose* (blood sugar),
- *dextrose* (another fruit sugar),
- *maltose* (a starch sugar),
- *galactose* (a part of milk sugar).

Check the labels of prepared foods for the list of ingredients. Soups, cereals, salad dressings, ketchup, peanut butter, and baby foods all include sugar, or corn syrup, as a main ingredient.

The body needs sugar that is obtained from carbohydrates found naturally in fruits, vegetables, and breads. Refined, or processed, sugar provides energy, but no protein, fat, vitamins, or fiber.

Because it requires little or no digestion, sugar enters the bloodstream quickly, causing a rapid elevation of the blood sugar level. This is one reason why people thought sugar was a quick energy source. However, the "quick lift" is short-lived and is often followed by a very low, sluggish feeling, since the body does not receive any other nutrients.

CHECK YOURSELF

1. What are carbohydrates?
2. What is the difference between simple and complex carbohydrates?
3. What is glycogen?
4. What is glucose?
5. Why are glycogen and glucose important for us?
6. What is the difference between sugar found naturally in fruits, vegetables, and breads, and refined sugar?

Louis Pasteur and Pasteurization

The famous French scientist, Louis Pasteur (1822-1895), though honored by doctors for his contribution to medicine, was not a physician. He was a chemist who had planned on making the study of crystals his life work. However, he was called upon for help in solving scientific problems facing French industries. His research took him away from crystals, but led him to some of the most significant discoveries relating to the cause and prevention of certain diseases.

Most of us have heard of pasteurization. You probably think of Pasteur's work with milk when you hear the term. However, his first discoveries involved work with the French wine industry. France was exporting less and less wine because much of it was spoiling and turning sour. Pasteur began to study this problem.

Pasteur discovered that disease-causing bacteria were often present in the wine. His task was to find a way to kill the unwanted germs. First, Pasteur used various chemicals. They killed the microbes, but left an unpleasant taste in the wine. Finally, he tried heating the wine. After many trials, he discovered that if wine was kept at 130°F (55°C) for several minutes, all disease-causing microbes were killed. This heating procedure became known as *pasteurization*. Pasteur then demonstrated how milk and other food products could also be made germ-free and preserved by this method.

The theory of pasteurization was not readily accepted. But, today, over 100 years later, Pasteur's name is better known throughout the world than any other scientist who ever lived. The word "pasteurized" appears on millions of milk containers daily.

3. Fats

Fat is part of the structure of your body's cells. Stored body fat provides insulation and protects your vital body organs by forming a cushion around them. Fat is the highest source of stored energy. With 9 calories to the gram, the average American has the equivalent of 141,000 calories stored in fat.

Fats, or **lipids**, are *nutrients that supply food energy in compact form*. Fats supply more than two-thirds as much energy as carbohydrates or proteins.

What Is Cholesterol?

You have undoubtedly heard much discussion about cholesterol. What relationship does cholesterol have to fats?

Cholesterol (koh-**les**-tuh-rall) is *a fatty, waxlike substance which is an essential part of the membrane of each cell in the human body*. The body uses cholesterol in its production of certain hormones, vitamin D, and the protective sheath around nerve fibers. The liver uses cholesterol to make bile acids that aid in the digestive process.

All of the body's cells can make cholesterol, but most of it is produced in the liver at the rate of about 1,000 milligrams (0.032 oz) a day.

The Lipoproteins

Cholesterol is transported from the liver to all of the body's cells through the bloodstream. The **lipoproteins** (lie-poe-**pro**-teens), *special molecules that carry the cholesterol*, are of three types:

- high-density lipoprotein (HDL),
- low-density lipoprotein (LDL),
- very low-density lipoprotein (VLDL).

If you have ever had a blood sample taken for analysis, the laboratory probably showed one figure for HDL, another figure for LDL, and one for VLDL combined.

High levels of LDL- and VLDL-cholesterol have been linked to certain health problems, one of which is *arteriosclerosis* (are-tear-ee-oh-skleh-**row**-sis). This develops when fatty deposits containing cholesterol collect on the inner walls of blood vessels, narrowing the passageway for the blood.

Imagine LDL- and VLDL-cholesterol as being similar to marshmallows—bulky and slow to move. On the other hand, HDL-cholesterol might be compared to lead pellets rolling through the vessels. They move quickly and, therefore, do not attach to the vessel walls.

You can increase your level of HDL-cholesterol by eating fresh fruit and by lowering your intake of animal fats, eggs, and cheese.

The Structure of Fats

Fats are made up of substances called fatty acids, which are attached to *an alcohol molecule* called **glycerol** (**gliss**-uh-roll). Simple fats are classified according to the number of fatty acid molecules attached to a molecule of glycerol.

Have you seen the term *triglycerides* on food labels? A **triglyceride** (try-**gliss**-uh-ride) has *three fatty acids attached to one glycerol molecule*. A **monoglyceride** (mon-oh-**gliss**-uh-ride) has *one fatty acid*, and a **diglyceride** (die-**gliss**-uh-ride) has *two*. About 98% of the fats in foods, as well as the most common fat in your body, are triglycerides.

Essential Fatty Acids

The term **essential fatty acids** is used to describe *certain fatty acids necessary for growth and body maintenance*. They are the building blocks for mem-

How Much Cholesterol Is in the Food You Eat?

Food	Amount	Cholesterol (mg)
Liver (beef)	3 oz	375
Frankfurter	2 oz	112
Lean veal	3 oz	84
Lean beef	3 oz	77
Eggs	1 large	252
Chicken without skin	3 oz	77
Sardines	3 oz	119
Tuna, canned	3 oz	55
Butter	1 tbsp	35
Whole milk	1 cup	34
Hard cheese	1 oz	24–28
Cottage cheese (4% fat)	½ cup	24
Cottage cheese (1% fat)	½ cup	12
Ice cream	½ cup	27
Corn bread	1 oz	58
Lemon meringue pie	⅛ slice of 9-inch pie	98
Plain muffin	1	21
Egg noodles	1 cup	50

When analyzing your own diet, be sure to check your serving sizes. Notice that the figure for beef is based on three ounces (8 g) of meat. A small steak at a restaurant is usually six ounces (17 g). In addition, foods that are made only from plant sources, such as peanut butter, beans, vegetable margarines, fruits, grains, and vegetables, contain no cholesterol. For some suggestions on low cholesterol snacks, see the *Health Handbook*, page HB14.

branes that form the border of every cell in your body. Fatty acids are also a main part of the membranes of the retina (a part of the eye) and synapses (the point where a connection is made between two nerve cells). The body cannot make these essential fatty acids, so you must include them in your diet.

Excellent sources of the essential fatty acids are corn oil, soybean oil, and peanut oil. These oils contain unsaturated fatty acids. You have probably heard the terms *saturated, unsaturated,* and *polyunsaturated fats.* To understand what these terms mean, it is helpful to understand the structure of fats.

Most fats consist of one molecule of glycerol and three molecules of fatty acids. In turn, each fatty acid is a long chain of carbon molecules. Hydrogen atoms are attached to the carbon molecules.

- A **saturated** (**satch**-uh-rate-ed) **fatty acid** *has as many hydrogen atoms as possible attached to its carbon chain.* The word *saturated* means "full." There is no more room on the carbon molecule for more hydrogen atoms.
- **Unsaturated fats** *have carbon molecules that each hold only one hydrogen atom,* although there is room on the molecule for more hydrogen.
- **Monounsaturated fats** are those in which *the fatty acid molecule has room for two more hydrogen atoms.*
- **Polyunsaturated fat** is one in which *the fatty acid has room for four or more additional hydrogen atoms.*

More people are shopping for margarine and vegetable and fish oils, instead of animal fats, butter, and shortenings.

High consumption of saturated fats—butter, animal fat, shortening—has been linked to health problems, especially in relation to heart disease.

Fatty Acids to Use   Most liquid fats, such as vegetable oils and fish oils, are poly- or monounsaturated. How do these different fats affect your health? Polyunsaturated or monounsaturated fats tend to help lower the amount of cholesterol carried in the blood by aiding in the excretion of cholesterol in solid waste.

Most saturated fats tend to raise blood cholesterol, particularly VDL- and VLDL-cholesterol. In fact, ounce for ounce, saturated fats are two times as effective in raising blood cholesterol as polyunsaturated fats are in lowering it.

Refer to page HB10 of your *Health Handbook* for more information on types of fats and their contents and how to read labels dealing with fats in food.

Hidden Fats in the Food You Eat

Visible fats—butter, margarine, the layer of fat on meat—account for about 40% of the fat in our diets. Where are the remaining 60%? They are present in food as invisible fat—marbled through meat, in egg yolks, hard cheese, cream cheese, whole-grain cereals, nuts, seeds, cream soups, ice cream, and chocolate.

Look at the list of ingredients on factory-prepared products such as baked goods, processed meats, instant meals, whipped toppings, and granolas. You will see that fat is a major ingredient in a wide variety of foods.

Do you eat meals very often at restaurants? Perhaps you intentionally lower your fat by leaving the butter off your roll or eating your baked potato without sour cream. But are you aware of the hidden fat in the soups, salad dressings, gravy, and sauces? Check how the food is prepared. You greatly increase your fat intake if the food is fried or broiled in butter.

LIFE MANAGEMENT SKILL

Maintaining Health

Contact the American Heart Association for more information on reducing cholesterol and fat intake. Evaluate your own diet. What changes can you make?

IMPROVING YOURSELF

Lowering Fat Intake

You can lower your fat intake by following some of the suggestions below. In addition, read the list of ingredients on foods.

What to Avoid	What You Can Substitute
Heavily marbled meat	Flank steak and sirloin tips
All processed meats	Lean boiled ham, sliced turkey
Fried foods	Broiled or grilled meat, fish, and poultry
Tuna canned in oil	Tuna canned in water
Sour cream, sweet cream	Low-fat milk, yogurt, buttermilk
Hard cheeses, cream cheese	Cottage cheese, ricotta cheese, mozzarella cheese made from part skim milk, Parmesan cheese
Ice cream	Ice milk, frozen yogurt
Flour pastry pie crust	Graham cracker pie crust
Cookies with chocolate cream filling or nuts	Ginger snaps, vanilla wafers
Biscuits, muffins, butter rolls	Hard rolls, pita bread, English muffins
Soda crackers, saltines	Matzos, bread sticks
Cream soups	Clear soup prepared with vegetables and rice
Popcorn with butter	Popcorn without butter

What foods have hidden—and not so hidden—fats in this meal? What would you eliminate?

CHECK YOURSELF

1. What are fats?
2. What is cholesterol?
3. Why is HDL-cholesterol better for us than LDL- or VLDL-cholesterol?
4. What are essential fatty acids?
5. Why are polyunsaturated fats the best fats for us to use?

4. Protein and Vitamins

Protein and vitamins are two of the six main classes of nutrients. Protein is the second most abundant substance in your body; water is the first. On the other hand, vitamins are found in extremely small amounts in our bodies. The reason for the varying amounts of these substances centers around what they do for the body.

Protein in Your Food

Protein is a vital part of every cell. Muscle, bone, cartilage, skin, blood, and lymph all contain protein. Since cells are continuously being replaced, protein is needed throughout life.

Thus, **protein (pro**-teen) is *a nutrient that helps build and maintain all body tissues*. It is essential for growth. Protein also forms an important part of hormones, body fluids, and enzymes. **Enzymes (en**-zimes) are *substances that promote or initiate the chemical reactions in your body*.

Protein is an important part of your red and white blood cells and antibodies. Protein is also a source of energy. However, it is a less efficient source of energy than fats and carbohydrates. In fact, if your body does not get an adequate number of calories from the fat and carbohydrates in your diet, it is forced to use protein for energy, instead of for building and repairing body tissues.

Proteins are made up of chains of building blocks called amino acids. **Amino** (ah-**mee**-no) **acids** are *molecules that contain nitrogen*. There are 22 different amino acids, and your body is able to make all but eight of them. These eight are referred to as **essential amino acids**, which *your diet must supply in order for the body to be able to make the hundreds of different proteins it needs*.

How Much Protein Do You Need?

The amount of protein your body needs is determined mainly by your age and body size:

- If you are between the ages of 11 and 14, multiply 0.45 times your ideal body weight, measured in pounds.
- If you are between 15 and 18, multiply 0.39 times your ideal body weight, measured in pounds.

The final figure gives you the recommended daily grams of protein your body needs. The chart on page 150 will help you to select your daily protein allowances.

The average American eats two to four times the recommended amounts of protein. The body does not need the extra protein, and it simply becomes a source of calories. There are four calories per gram of protein.

Nutritionists recommend that about 10% to 15% of your daily caloric intake be protein. (Fats should be no more than 30% and preferably between 10% and 20%. Carbohydrates should be 55% to 60%.)

They further recommend that a maximum of one-third of your protein come from animal sources and the rest from vegetables. However, in the United States, 60% to 80% of the protein eaten is animal protein. Based on what you have read thus far, why might this present a health problem?

Getting the Most Out of Protein

Most *animal foods*, such as fish, meat, eggs, milk, and poultry, *contain all eight essential amino acids* and are called **complete protein foods**. *Plant foods*, such as grains, seeds, peas, and beans, *contain some, but not all of the eight essential amino acids*. They are called **incomplete protein foods**.

However, plant foods are good sources of complete proteins when you eat them with protein foods or with certain other plant foods.

Complete protein foods (left) contain all eight essential amino acids that we need. Incomplete protein foods (right) contain some, but not all of them.

The following are examples of plant food combinations:

- Tortilla and beans
- Peanut butter and whole-wheat bread
- Rice and beans
- Yams and beans
- Macaroni and cheese

The nutrients that foods provide besides protein vary greatly. It is helpful that you know what else is in the food you eat so that you can make healthier choices. You can see from the examples in the chart on page 150 that some protein sources are high in fat calories while others are high in carbohydrate calories.

Vitamins

Vitamins are *substances containing compounds necessary for growth and the maintenance of life.* They work in conjunction with enzymes to promote an increase in the rate of reactions of chemical changes that take place in your body.

Vitamins generally are classified into two main groups: the water-soluble vitamins (C and B complex) and the fat-soluble vitamins (A, D, E, and K).

Water-Soluble Vitamins

Water-soluble vitamins *dissolve in water.* This is important to know because these vitamins are found mainly in fruits and vegetables. If you cook these vegetables in large amounts of water and then drain off the water after cooking, you have lost much of the vitamin benefits.

Choosing the Best Protein Source

| Food | Percentage of Calories | | |
	Protein	Fat	Carbohydrates
T-bone steak	17	82	—
Cheddar cheese	25	73	2
Chicken with skin	44	53	—
without skin (white meat)	76	18	—
Eggs	32	63	—
Whole milk	22	46	30
Skim milk	40	2	57
Cottage cheese, creamed	51	35	11
Macaroni	14	3	81
Tuna, in oil	34	64	—
in water	88	6	—
Potato, baked	11	1	90
Oatmeal	15	16	70
Kidney beans	25	5	70

Also, after cooking food a long period of time, it loses much of its vitamin content through evaporation. Water-soluble vitamins are continuously being washed out of the body through urine and sweat. Thus, people need to consume them daily in adequate amounts.

See the *Health Handbook*, page HB11, for more information on water-soluble vitamins.

Fat-Soluble Vitamins

Fat-soluble vitamins are generally *found in meat and oils and are less apt to be lost through cooking*, as compared to the water-soluble vitamins. They are absorbed through the intestines with the aid of bile from the liver.

The fat-soluble vitamins can accumulate and are stored in the body's fatty tissue. Excess buildup of fat-soluble vitamins, especially A and D, can have a dangerous toxic effect. Deficiencies related to these vitamins are slower to materialize.

See the *Health Handbook*, page HB12, for more information on fat-soluble vitamins.

Why We Need Vitamins

Unlike carbohydrates, fats, and protein, vitamins are not a source of energy. They are important, however, in the conversion of food into useful energy in the body.

Why do we need vitamins if we get all of our calories from fat, protein, and carbohydrates? Vitamins assist in the body's processing of these other nutrients. If you were to live totally on these three nutrients, you would eventually get sick and die. Vitamins are chemicals that your body needs for very specific work.

There is much inaccurate and confusing information about vitamins. In general, since people need vitamins in very small amounts, eating a well-balanced diet provides all of the vitamins that people need. Taking vitamin pills may supplement the diet, but they should not take the place of eating nutritious foods.

CHECK YOURSELF

1. What is protein?
2. What are essential amino acids?
3. What is the difference between complete and incomplete protein foods? Give some examples.
4. What is a vitamin?
5. Name some water-soluble vitamins.
6. Name some fat-soluble vitamins.

5. Minerals and Water

Carbohydrates, fats, protein, and vitamins are **organic** (or-**gan**-ick) substances, that is, they *come from a living source*. Minerals and water are, on the other hand, **inorganic**, that is, *not composed of living substances*. The body needs a combination of both organic substances and inorganic substances in order to live and develop.

Minerals

Minerals are *inorganic substances formed in the earth that have special chemical and physical properties. Vitamins and minerals* are often called **micronutrients** (**my**-kro-new-tri-ents), in relation to the other nutrients, because *we do not need a great deal of them*. However, just as in the case of vitamins, minerals are an essential part of our diet.

The micronutrients iron, vitamins A, B1, B2, and C are frequently low in a teenager's diet. Examine your own diet, and if there are deficiencies, identify which foods you could add to your diet to supply the needed nutrients.

The chart on page HB13 of your *Health Handbook* will give you detailed information on the minerals that the body needs in order to function and develop.

LIFE MANAGEMENT SKILL

Nutrition and Calcium

Calcium is a mineral that helps build and renew bones and teeth. It is needed throughout life. Teenagers should consume four servings from the Milk and Milk Products Food Group (see page 153) to build strong bones and teeth early in life. See page 274 for a description of a major bone disease that is partially caused from a lack of calcium, especially early in life.

Water

Water has no calories, but next to air it is the most important substance for maintaining life. Water allows each cell in the body to do its work, aiding in some of the major chemical reactions that take place in the cells. In fact, much of your body is made up of water. Your blood is 83% water, your muscles, 75%, your brain, 74%, your bones, 25%, your body fat 20 to 35%.

Water carries nutrients, hormones, disease-fighting cells, antibodies, and waste products to and from body organs, primarily through your bloodstream. Water lubricates your joints and mucous membranes. It also enables you to digest and absorb food. Water helps to transport the body cells' wastes to the kidneys and large intestines and then aids in the removal of these wastes from the body.

Without water, your body could not cool itself to prevent the buildup of internal heat, which can be lethal.

Fiber in Your Diet

Fiber is *the nondigestible part of wheat and roughage found in fruits and vegetables* like apples, carrots, and celery. Fiber is not found in animal cells. The secretions of the stomach or small intestine do not affect fiber, and it passes through these organs undigested. Fiber does not have any nutritive value, but it is important in providing the bulk needed to move food through the digestive tract.

Although the evidence is not yet conclusive, in societies where more fiber is consumed, cancer of the colon is rare. When compared to the American population, countries that have high-fiber diets have significantly lower incidents of colon cancer.

When the diet is high in fiber, the body's solid waste passes through the colon more rapidly. It is thought that when there is little fiber in the diet, the colon's contents remain longer and bacteria thrive. This may eventually lead to the development of cancer cells.

The average American eats about 0.035 to 0.11 ounces (1 to 3 g) of fiber daily. Some nutrition experts recommend that our daily fiber intake should be at least 0.21 to 0.35 ounces (6 to 10 g).

Caffeine

Some people drink soft drinks, tea and coffee for their fluids intake. While these are fluids, they also contain a mild stimulant called caffeine.

Caffeine is a chemical found in certain plants. **Caffeine** is *an alkaloid, a chemical whose structure is closely akin to the structure of poisons*. The small amount taken in a cup of coffee or tea acts as a mild stimulant that perks up a person by increasing the pulse rate. It also causes increased urination.

However, users can abuse caffeine and can become dependent on it. Drinking excessive amounts of coffee or tea, and colas, can cause insomnia and irritability. Because caffeine is an alkaloid, people who have heart or stomach problems should not use products that contain it.

We should eat foods that contain fiber in order to ensure proper digestion and elimination.

*Consuming to[...]
cola, and tea c[...]
people to becom[...]
on caffeine.*

CHECK YOURSELF

1. What are minerals in our diet?
2. Name two reasons why water is so important in our diet.
3. What is fiber in our diet?
4. Why is fiber so important to good nutrition?
5. How can caffeine be harmful to health?

6. Daily Nutrients

To help in the selection of foods that supply a balanced diet, foods are classified into four basic food groups. They are grouped according to the nutrients they supply. By eating the recommended daily servings from each group, you can be sure you are getting a well-balanced diet. Many foods are in each group, which gives you a variety of choices.

The Food Groups

In the lists below, you will see that each food group has certain **leader nutrients**. This is a way to identify *key nutrients that the food group supplies*.

The Milk and Milk Products Group. The leader nutrients found in this group are protein, calcium, and riboflavin. Teenagers need four servings from this group daily, adults two servings. An eight-ounce (226.4 g) glass of milk, one ounce (28.3 g) of cheese, or a cup (0.24 l) of yogurt is one serving from this group.

The Meat, Fish, Poultry, Eggs, and Beans Group. The leader nutrients found in this group are protein, iron, niacin, and thiamine. Teenagers and adults need two servings daily. Three ounces (84.9 g) of beef, two eggs, or 1.5 cups (0.35 l) of lentils is one serving from this group.

Upper left: *Milk and Milk Products Group;* Upper right: *Meat, Fish, Poultry, Eggs, and Beans Group;* Lower left: *Fruits and Vegetables Group;* Lower right: *Breads and Cereals Group*

The Fruits and Vegetables Group. The leader nutrients in this group are vitamins A and C. Teenagers and adults need four servings daily. One serving equals one apple or one ear of corn or one-half cup of carrots.

The Breads and Cereals Group. The leader nutrients in this group are starch, iron, thiamine, and niacin. Teenagers and adults need four servings daily. One serving equals one slice of bread or one tortilla or three-fourths of a cup of cereal.

The "Other" Group. A fifth group of foods is called "Other" or "Extra" foods. These foods are high in fats or sugars, so they are also high in calories. Some have little or no other nutritious value. Others provide some nutrients, but because of their high caloric content, they generally are not a good food choice. Candy bars and soft drinks can be eaten or drunk occasionally, if one's personal caloric requirements allow, and if they do not take the place of more nutritious foods.

Making Wise Food Choices— Read the Label

Once you know the basic information about good nutrition, how can you use it to make healthy food choices? Certain information is required on the labels of all food products. By checking the labels, you can find out exactly what you are eating.

All food packages should list *serving sizes, number of servings per container,* and *number of calories per serving*. Nutrients are also listed.

The consumer should read the list of ingredients also found on the label. They appear in the order of weight, from the most to the least. This means that when sugar is listed first, more sugar is in the product than any other substance. Some labels also provide information about sodium, cholesterol, and unsaturated fat.

The RDA—A Helpful Guide

A group of scientists and diet specialists who serve on the Food and Nutrition Board of the National Research Council, the National Academy of Sciences, determine the dietary standards of the United States. Their book, *Recommended Dietary Allowances*, outlines the amount of proteins, calories, vitamins, and minerals we should have daily.

Recommended Dietary Allowances, often referred to as RDA, was first published in 1943, to serve as *a guide for planning balanced meals* for the Armed Forces during World War II. Each new edition, published around every five years, reflects the latest information about food and the body's need for certain nutrients.

Which bottle of hand lotion is the better buy? Why?

Based on the RDA guide, the Food and Drug Administration developed the U.S. RDA. It gives the amount of each nutrient that almost all people in the United States need. These amounts provide the legal standards for labeling food. The U.S. RDA provides helpful information about the nutrients in a food product. Manufacturer's labels list the percentages of U.S. RDA for protein, vitamin A, vitamin C, thiamine, riboflavin, niacin, calcium, and minerals, if the manufacturer chooses. But if a manufacturer adds vitamins or minerals to the product, these also must be listed.

The U.S. RDA is a general guide. Your personal nutrient requirements vary on the basis of your age, sex, body size, health, and activity.

Other Consumer Helps

In addition to the RDA guide, unit pricing and open dating help you to select foods wisely.

Unit pricing shows a person *how much different sizes of the same product cost per unit*. Suppose that you wanted to buy a can of Jiffy Beans. One size—8 ounces—is 88¢. The unit price per ounce is, therefore, 11¢. A 12-ounce can of the same brand of beans is $1.04. The unit price is approximately 8.7¢. You would save a little over 2¢ an ounce if you bought the larger can. Instead of going through this mental arithmetic, all you have to do is look at the unit price labels found on the shelves. Unit pricing can also help you to compare the prices of different brands.

These containers cannot be sold after the dates printed on them.

There is one point to consider when using unit pricing in purchasing foods. While you may get a better price on purchasing the larger size, do you need the extra ounces?

Open dating provides *a date on a product in order to tell you the date when it should be removed from the shelves, or the deadline on when it should be used, or when it was packaged*. For instance, a date on milk usually means that it cannot be sold after that date; but, if properly refrigerated at home, it can be used by the consumer six to eight days after that date.

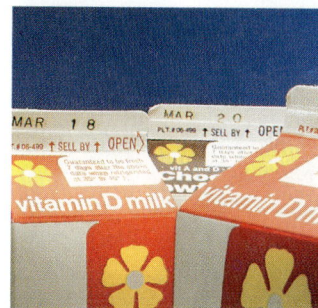

Is Your Diet Nutritious?

Even though proper nutrition cannot prevent your getting certain diseases, it can reduce your risk of getting them. Medical evidence indicates that the long-term effects of an improper diet can increase one's risk of developing heart disease, cancer, diabetes, and arteriosclerosis.

Is it surprising to you that the average American diet is not nutritionally adequate? The 1977 report of the U.S. Senate Select Committee on Nutrition and Human Needs, entitled "Dietary Goals for the United States," included the following goals and recommendations for the American diet:

Reducing Salt in Your Diet

How can you reduce your salt intake? Here are three easy ways:

- Remove the salt shaker from your eating area.
- If you are preparing foods, use other seasonings.
- Limit the intake of foods with a high salt content, such as canned foods, condiments, cured meats, and salted snacks.

Goals	Recommendations
1. Reduce overall fat consumption to 30% of caloric intake.	Decrease consumption of meat and increase poultry and fish. Substitute nonfat milk for whole milk.
2. Reduce saturated-fat consumption to account for about 10% of caloric intake; and balance that with polyunsaturated and monounsaturated fats, which should account for about 10% of caloric intake each.	Decrease consumption of foods high in fat, and partially substitute polyunsaturated fat for saturated fat.
3. Reduce cholesterol consumption to about 0.0096 ounces (300 mg) a day.	Decrease consumption of butterfat, eggs, and other high-cholesterol sources.
4. Increase carbohydrate consumption to account for 55% to 60% of caloric intake.	Increase consumption of fruits, vegetables, and whole grains.
5. Reduce sugar consumption to about 10% of caloric intake.	Decrease consumption of sugar and foods high in sugar content.
6. Reduce salt consumption to approximately 0.17 ounces (5 g) a day.	Decrease consumption of salts and foods high in salt content.

The chart on page 157 compares our current diet with these recommended changes.

The body needs much less salt than the average American consumes daily.

A Word About Salt

How much salt do you consume every day? Do you put salt on your food before tasting it? Consuming too much salt can be hazardous to your health. How much is too much? The recommended daily allowance is 0.11 to 0.28 ounces (3 to 8 g). Five grams is a teaspoonful. The average American consumes two to three times this amount.

Our taste for salt is acquired. We actually do not need to add salt to our diet to meet the body's need for sodium. However, many people do not realize just how much salt they take in daily. The average American consumes two to five teaspoons of salt a day, 15 pounds (6,804 g) of salt a year.

Next to sugar, salt is the greatest food additive. Look at the list of ingredients on a food label. Salt is in almost every processed food product.

The Average American's Diet

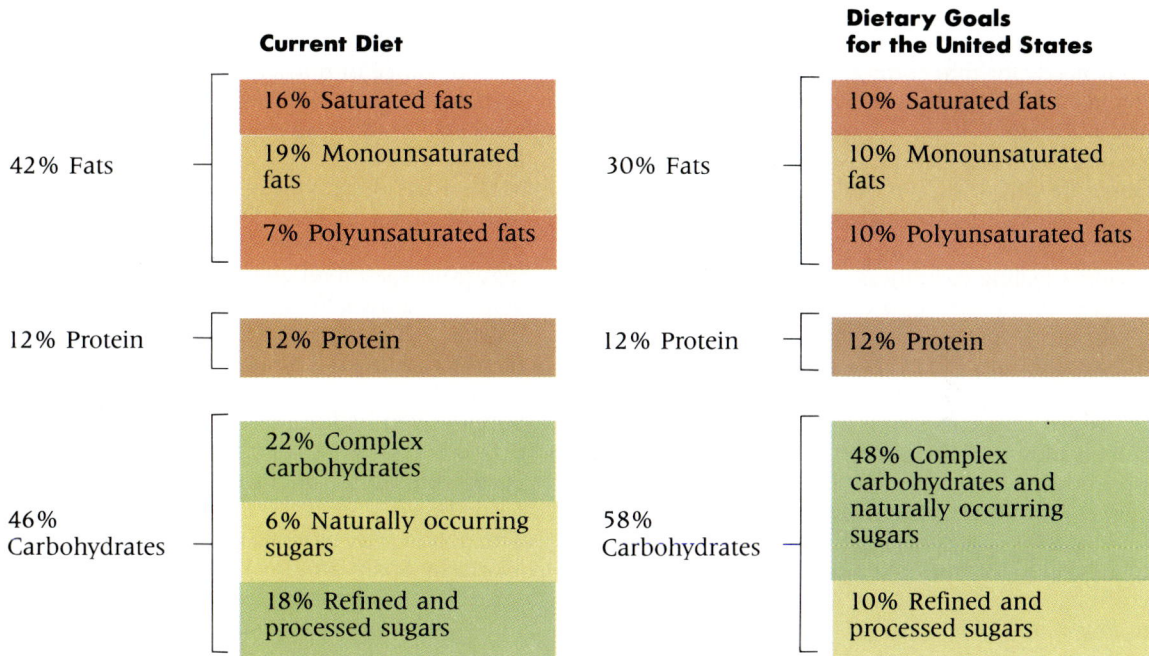

	Current Diet		Dietary Goals for the United States
42% Fats	16% Saturated fats	30% Fats	10% Saturated fats
	19% Monounsaturated fats		10% Monounsaturated fats
	7% Polyunsaturated fats		10% Polyunsaturated fats
12% Protein	12% Protein	12% Protein	12% Protein
46% Carbohydrates	22% Complex carbohydrates	58% Carbohydrates	48% Complex carbohydrates and naturally occurring sugars
	6% Naturally occurring sugars		
	18% Refined and processed sugars		10% Refined and processed sugars

(Percents refer to percent of calories.)

Salt provides minerals that are essential to health and life. It is composed of sodium and chloride, which help to maintain the balance of water and electrolytes inside and outside the cells. The body needs only small amounts of salt. Sodium chloride (table salt) provides more than enough sodium for most people.

Excessive sodium draws water from the cells, and diets high in salt have been linked to hypertension (high blood pressure). Salt causes the body to retain fluid, producing an increase in volume of blood, thus elevating the pressure within the blood vessels.

CHECK YOURSELF

1. What are leader nutrients? How do they assist you in selecting a balanced diet?
2. How can the U.S. RDA guide help you make better food choices?
3. What information must be included on food labels?
4. What is unit pricing?
5. What is open dating?
6. What are some of the dangers of eating too much salt?

CHAPTER 8   Review

CHAPTER SUMMARY

- Your body depends on you to provide nutrients that it needs for functioning. Carbohydrates, fats, proteins, vitamins, minerals, and water are the six basic nutrients.
- The body's primary and most efficient sources of energy are carbohydrates and fats.
- The complex carbohydrates, starches, are a more nutritious food choice than simple sugars. Starches provide a feeling of fullness, take longer to digest, add fiber to the diet, and contain other nutrients.
- Polyunsaturated fats are a better food choice than the saturated fats found in animal food sources.
- To help consumers ensure that they are getting all the needed nutrients, foods are grouped according to the leader nutrients. There are five food groups.
- The consumer receives assistance in selecting and eating a balanced diet by reading food labels.
- The U.S. RDA (*Recommended Dietary Allowances*) provides a guide for nutrients needed daily.
- Percentages of RDA that the food product supplies are found on the label of the product.

REVIEWING WHAT YOU LEARNED

1. Make a list of the factors that influence food choices. Next to each factor, write a statement describing how it affects one's eating behavior.
2. Make a chart of the six nutrients. Include what each one does for the body, a good food source for each, and the effects of a deficiency in each one.
3. Why is it advisable to limit one's intake of simple sugars, saturated fats, and salt? What might one do to make such dietary changes?
4. What is cholesterol and how might it affect our overall health?
5. Name the five food groups.
6. Why is a variety of foods in the diet important?
7. Why is it recommended that we limit our intake of simple carbohydrates?
8. What useful information is found on food labels?
9. Name three wise consumer choices that you can make purchasing food.

APPLYING WHAT YOU LEARNED

1. Select one of the foods identified in the chapter as a good source of nutrients and write your own advertisement for it. Be sure to include reasons why someone would want to buy this food over a less healthy food.
2. Make a list of everything you have eaten for the past 24 hours. In chart form, evaluate your diet based on the RDA and recommended daily servings from each food group.
3. Why is it especially important for adolescents to have a well-balanced diet? Why do you think that teenagers generally do not make nutritious food choices?
4. Suppose you had to present a nutrition lesson to fifth graders. What would you include? What could you say to convince them to make good food choices?
5. The potato was brought to Europe from the New World by Spain around 1750. By 1830, it was a staple in the diet of most peasants in Europe. Find out what impact the potato had on the Agricultural Revolution. What nutritional advantages did the potato provide?

FOCUS ON WELLNESS

Your level of nutrition directly and strongly influences your overall level of health and wellness. *I take responsibility for my wellness by making food choices that . . .*

ANSWERS TO NUTRITION QUIZ, PAGE 138

A brief explanation appears with each answer.

1. **False.** Honey is a supersaturated solution. It has 65 calories a tablespoon. Sugar has 40 calories a tablespoon.
2. **False.** Gelatin is actually a lower-quality protein than most animal sources of protein. It is not any better for fingernails than any other protein.
3. **False.** The major nutrients in milk are calcium, protein, and riboflavin. All people need these nutrients in varying amounts.

nutrition	lipids	monounsaturated fats	organic
appetite	cholesterol	polyunsaturated fats	inorganic
nutrients	lipoproteins	protein	minerals
essential nutrients	glycerol	enzymes	micronutrients
carbohydrates	triglyceride	essential amino acids	fiber
complex carbohydrates	monoglyceride	complete protein foods	leader nutrients
simple carbodydrates	diglyceride	incomplete protein foods	Recommended Dietary
glycogen	essential fatty acids	vitamins	Allowances (RDA)
glucose	saturated fatty acid	water-soluble vitamins	unit pricing
fats	unsaturated fats	fat-soluble vitamins	open dating

PUTTING VOCABULARY TO USE

On a separate piece of paper, write the following statements. Then supply the missing word or phrase from the chapter vocabulary list.

1. _____. Fatty substance found in all animal tissue.
2. _____ _____. Molecules that contain nitrogen.
3. _____. Organic compounds that work with enzymes to promote chemical changes.
4. _____. Inorganic substances formed in the earth, which have special chemical and physical properties.
5. _____. Chemical compounds that, when broken down during digestion, are converted to glycogen.
6. _____ _____ _____. A general guide to the amounts of nutrients needed daily.

7. _____. Special molecules that carry cholesterol through the bloodstream.
8. _____. A term used to describe vitamins and minerals, which are only needed in small amounts by the body.
9. _____ _____. Fatty acid with as many hydrogen atoms as it can hold.
10. _____. The second most abundant substance in your body; a vital part of every cell.
11. _____ _____. Fatty acid that has room for four or more hydrogen atoms.
12. _____. The nondigestible part of certain foods that aids in moving food through the digestive tract.
13. _____. Chemical substances obtained from food during digestion.
14. _____. Refers to three fatty acids attached to one glycerol molecule.

4. **False.** Concentrated sweets are not required in the diet. Fats, carbohydrates, or proteins can provide energy (calorie) needs.
5. **False.** An average slice of bread contains about 70 calories, or about the same number of calories as an apple. A medium-sized potato contains 90 calories. No one food is fattening. It is the total amount of food eaten daily that counts, along with the amount of energy you use.
6. **False.** Vitamin C helps to resist infection, but large doses beyond recommended amounts will not help. Because vitamin C is a water-soluble vitamin, the body eliminates what it does not need or use.
7. **False.** The carbohydrate is the most efficient source of fuel or energy. Excess protein intake can deprive the athlete of more efficient fuel and can induce dehydration, loss of appetite, and diarrhea.
8. **False.** Organic and chemical fertilizers produce crops of equal quality and are equally safe.
9. **False.** Enriched white flour, and bread made from it, has been enriched with the major nutrients lost in the milling process. Whole-grain products may contain more trace minerals, but the major nutrients are at the same level as those in white bread made from enriched flour.
10. **False.** Exercise tends to suppress the appetite rather than increase it.

Weight Control, Special Foods, and Special Diets

"Lose ten pounds in two days!"
"Eat whatever you want and lose a pound a day!"

Our society is obsessed with getting thin quickly and staying that way. Knowing how to diet wisely and to maintain a healthy weight for yourself is more important than any crash diet program.

After studying this chapter, you will be able to:
- define overweight and obesity,
- identify the impact of obesity on overall health,
- explain the relationship of weight control to eating behaviors,
- define eating disorders,
- discuss the major problems of successful weight control,
- discuss special problems relating to athletics and dieting,
- recall seven guidelines to follow in maintaining a healthy diet.

Weight control means *attaining as near to your ideal weight as possible and then staying at it*. **Ideal weight** is the *weight that is best for your height and body size*. (See page 165.)

More and more research is being conducted on nutrition and the consequences of being overweight and underweight. So, we have come to see that there are more benefits to health by maintaining one's ideal weight than by being overweight or underweight.

Obesity—A Serious Health Problem

Would you describe yourself as obese (oh-**beece**)? Probably not. When most people think of obesity, they think of an overweight person. However, although obese people are overweight, the two conditions are not the same. **Overweight** means that *a person weighs more than the desirable weight for his or her age and size*. Many well-developed athletes are overweight because of their muscular development, but they are not obese.

To be **obese** means that *there is an excess of fat, or adipose tissue, in the body*. **Adipose** (**add**-ee-pose) **tissue** is *a type of connective tissue in which many of its cells are filled with fat*. The body needs adipose tissue, but serious problems can develop if excess fat accumulates.

Hazards of Obesity

Obesity is one of the most common and serious nutritional and health problems for adult Americans. It is also a major problem among teenagers. There are about 10 million obese adolescents in the United States. Obesity in adolescence is more than a nutritional and health problem. It also can become a serious psychological and social problem. If obese teenagers do not lose weight and practice weight control, there is a strong possibility that they will continue to have this problem in adulthood.

There are many hazards in being obese. The additional weight adds strain to the body frame and the circulatory system. By eating more food, it is likely that the person will take in more fat, salt, sugar, and cholesterol, all related to different types of health problems. In addition, the obese person is often inactive, leading to an additional risk of heart disease. Other diseases related to obesity include high blood pressure, diabetes, appendicitis, hernia, gallbladder and liver ailments, arthritis, and hardening of the arteries.

Determining a Person's Percentage of Body Fat

There are different ways to determine when a person is obese. Hydrostatic (high-dro-**stat**-ick) weighing is perhaps the best way to determine the percentage of body fat in an individual. In **hydrostatic weigh-**

Obesity is a major health problem for millions of Americans.

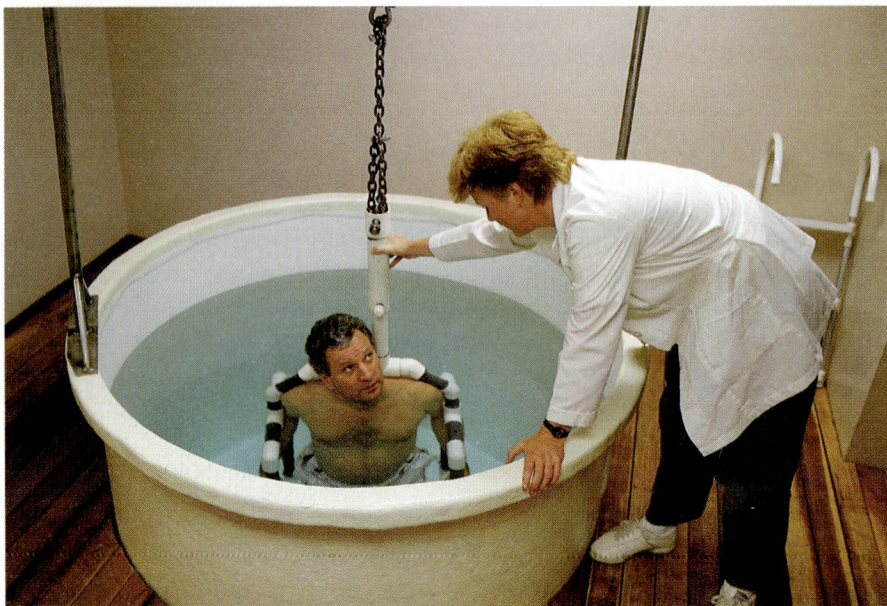

Hydrostatic weighing is the most accurate way of determining the amount of body fat.

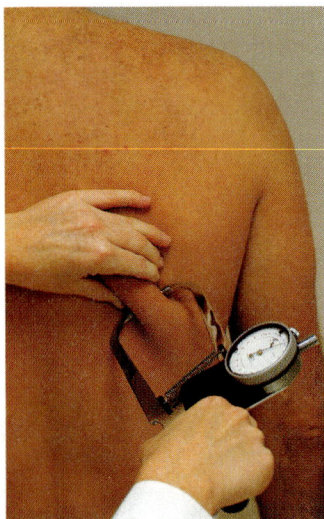

A caliper may also be used to determine body fat.

ing, the person is placed in a large tank of water. With the help of measurement instruments and the amount of water displaced in the tank, scientists can get a very accurate idea of how much fat is in the body. This is an expensive procedure and is not available to most people.

A second way to determine the percentage of body fat is by using a **caliper** (**kal**-uh-purr), *a device that measures the thickness of the skin.* A caliper looks like a handcuff and is about the same size as one. The most frequently measured areas are at the triceps muscle at the back of the upper arm (midway between the shoulder bone and the elbow) and the subscapular region just below the shoulder blade.

To determine roughly whether you are obese, try the *pinch test.* It is similar to using the caliper. Pinch a fold of skin on the back of your upper arm or at your hipbone just below your waist. If the fold is more than one-inch thick, you may have too much body fat.

Weight Reduction

If "fad diets" work as easily as they claim to do, why do we need so many of them? Why do new ones keep appearing on the market daily? The answer is because fad diets are often so extreme that they are hard to stick to. The idea of "going on" a diet implies that a person will also be "going off" another diet.

Perhaps no other area of health receives more attention or is more lucrative than weight control. People want quick, easy methods for losing weight. This helps to explain the multitudes of fad diets and gimmicks being sold today, all guaranteed to help you lose weight quickly and effortlessly.

You may think that if they are guaranteed, they must work. Look closely at the directions that accompany any diet pill or quick weight-loss advertisement. They are likely to include a statement about following a diet program of reduced calories. It is the reduction of calorie intake that results in weight-loss, not the miracle pill or powder.

Successful Dieting

How many people do you know who have gone on a diet? How many lost weight only to regain it shortly after they went off the diet? Actually, only 5% to 10% of all dieters keep off the weight they lose. Why?

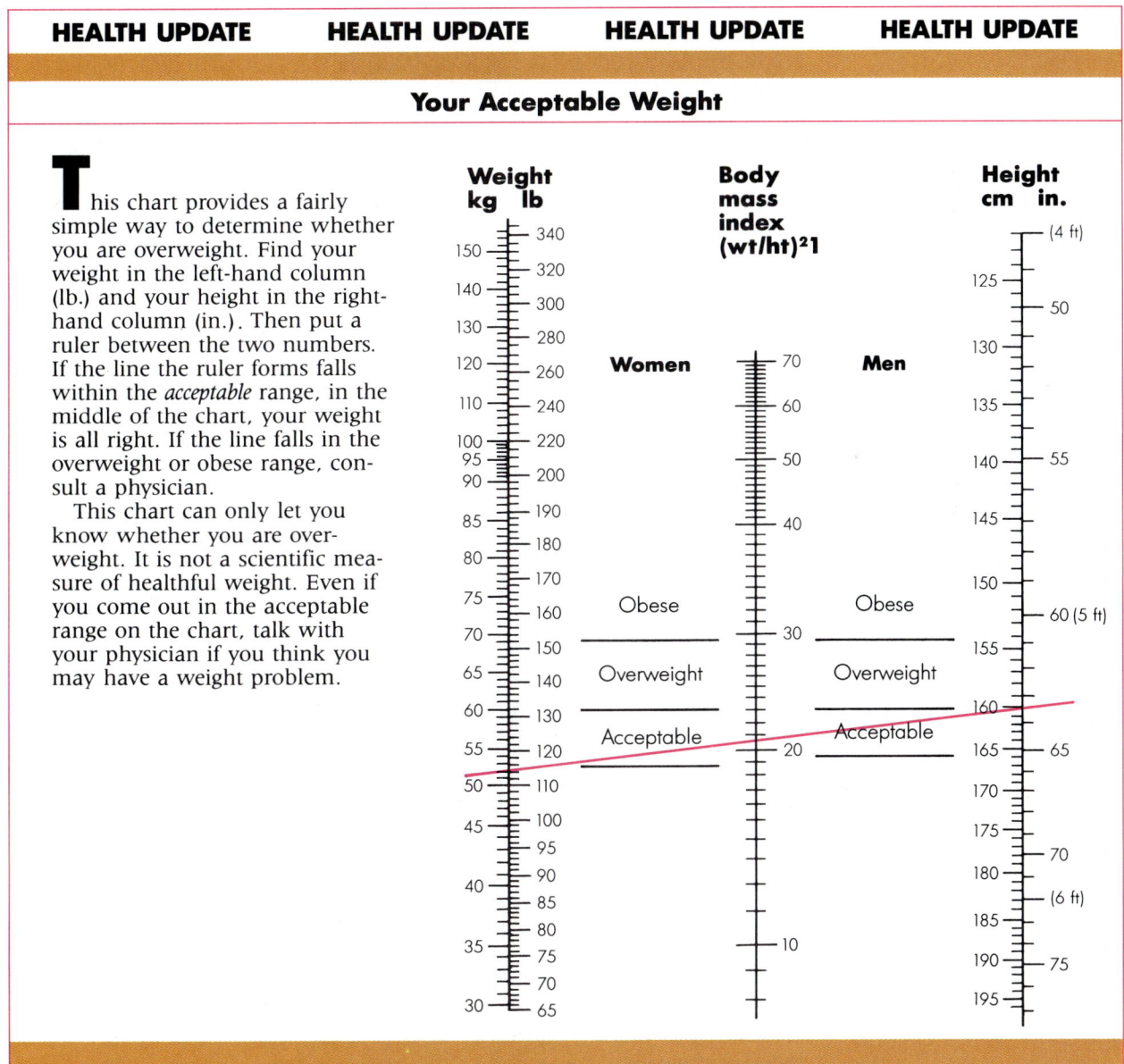

HEALTH UPDATE   HEALTH UPDATE   HEALTH UPDATE   HEALTH UPDATE

Your Acceptable Weight

This chart provides a fairly simple way to determine whether you are overweight. Find your weight in the left-hand column (lb.) and your height in the right-hand column (in.). Then put a ruler between the two numbers. If the line the ruler forms falls within the *acceptable* range, in the middle of the chart, your weight is all right. If the line falls in the overweight or obese range, consult a physician.

This chart can only let you know whether you are overweight. It is not a scientific measure of healthful weight. Even if you come out in the acceptable range on the chart, talk with your physician if you think you may have a weight problem.

Weight kg lb	Body mass index $(wt/ht)^2$ 1	Height cm in.

Women / **Men**

Obese — Overweight — Acceptable

There are only two basic methods for losing weight: (1) change your eating habits, and/or (2) change your activity habits. This may sound simple, but let us look at why so many people have problems with these methods.

What does "change your eating habits" mean? It is different from just going on a diet. Usually dieting is temporary and involves major cutting of two important groups of food—fats and carbohydrates. Changing your eating habits means a permanent change in behavior. It means planning and choosing proper amounts of a variety of foods. It implies that weight maintenance is a day-to-day effort rather than a short, crash course of quick weight loss.

One pound of fat is equal to 3,500 calories. This means that when you consume 3,500 calories above what your body uses, you gain one pound. For example, if your body requires 2,000 calories for all of its activities during a day, you would need to eat 2,000 calories for your weight to stay the same. But if you eat 2,100 calories a day, you will gain one pound in a little more than a month. If you continued this pattern, in a year you would be carrying an extra 10 to 12 pounds. Remember, it took a year to add those pounds, so it is unlikely that they will come off and stay off in a three-week diet period.

Exercise Is Important

You can increase the effectiveness of your weight-control efforts by increasing your daily activity. Exercise does more than just help you lose weight—it helps to tone your body. Exercise replaces fat with an increase of lean body tissue. Lean body tissue is your body's bone, organ, and muscle tissue. When you diet without exercising, you lose lean body tissue as well as fat.

Two doctors studied a group of 25 volunteers, all of whom were 20 to 40 pounds overweight. The volunteers were divided into groups:

- One group did not change its physical activity, but reduced caloric intake by 500 calories.
- A second group increased physical activity to burn 250 extra calories a day and reduced caloric intake by 250 calories.
- A third group did not alter caloric intake, but increased physical activity to burn 500 extra calories a day.

What do you think the results were at the end of 16 weeks? All three groups had lost weight. But the second and third groups lost significantly more *fat* and less muscle tissue.

Achieving Your Ideal Weight

Many people have written books on dieting. Magazines constantly advertise newly discovered weight-loss plans. And yet, as we have seen, there is exactly one healthy, sure way to lose weight. *You must use up more calories than you consume.*

Exercise must be part of any weight-control program.

Recommended Weight for Females and Males

Adapted from Metropolitan Life Insurance chart on weight of males and females.

Female Hgt.	Small Frame	Medium Frame	Large Frame	Male Hgt.	Small Frame	Medium Frame	Large Frame
4′ 8″	88– 94	92–103	100–115	5′ 0″	101–109	107–117	115–130
9	90– 97	94–106	102–118	1	104–112	110–121	118–133
10	92–100	97–109	105–121	2	107–115	113–125	121–136
11	95–103	100–112	108–124	3	110–118	116–128	124–140
5′ 0″	98–106	103–115	111–127	4	113–121	119–131	127–144
1	101–109	106–118	114–130	5	116–125	122–135	130–148
2	104–112	109–122	117–134	6	120–129	126–139	134–153
3	107–115	112–126	121–138	7	124–133	130–144	139–158
4	110–119	116–131	125–142	8	128–137	134–148	143–162
5	114–123	120–135	129–146	9	132–142	138–152	147–166
6	118–127	124–139	133–150	10	136–146	142–157	151–171
7	122–131	128–143	137–154	11	140–150	146–162	156–176
8	126–136	132–147	141–157	6′ 0″	144–154	150–167	160–181
9	130–140	136–151	145–164	1	148–158	154–172	165–186
10	134–144	140–155	149–169	2	152–162	159–177	170–191
11	138–148	144–159	153–174	3	156–167	164–182	174–196
6′ 0″	142–152	149–163	157–179	4	160–171	169–187	178–201

This is not always easy to do, but you can devise a plan for yourself:

- Set reasonable, attainable goals.
- Stick to the amount of calories you are to consume every day. Record *everything* you put in your mouth.
- Keep a diary of what you eat and when you eat it, so you become more aware of your eating patterns.

Getting Started

The following steps will help you start losing weight:

1. *Determine your ideal weight.* Decide whether your body size would be considered small, average, or large. Check the chart on this page. Your estimated recommended weight should not change as you grow older.

2. *Determine the number of calories you can eat daily and still not gain weight.* A moderately active person needs about 15 calories per pound to maintain his or her weight. You need more if you participate in regular, strenuous physical activity, and less if you do not. By multiplying your weight by 15, you get the number of calories you can eat daily to maintain your present weight.

3. *If you are above your ideal weight, figure out how many calories you must cut from your diet to lose weight and reach your ideal weight.* About 3,500 calories are in each pound of stored fat. To lose one pound a week, which is a very reasonable, realistic goal, consume 500 fewer calories each day. (Subtract 500 from the calories needed to maintain your present weight.)

A weight-loss program will usually be successful if you want to lose weight.

Balancing a Diet

Keep a 3-day eating journal. Use the following format: *Day/Time, Feelings, Place Eaten, Time Taken to Eat, Immediate Effects, Later Effects*. Draw conclusions about your eating habits from the data collected.

IMPROVING YOURSELF

Things to Do While Dieting

When you actually start your diet, try these:

1. Make exercise a part of your daily routine, especially when you are hungry. Make sure that your exercise is fun. See the suggested exercise programs and calorie expenditures in Chapter 2.
2. Make your meal last at least 20 minutes. Take small bites, putting your utensils down between bites.
3. Do something else when you are tempted to eat, even if it means getting out of the house.
4. Use nonfood rewards when you do something that is worth a reward.
5. Never buy foods when you are hungry. If you shop when you are hungry, you may be tempted to make poor food choices.
6. Wait five minutes before taking second helpings.
7. Try to avoid eating while standing, while alone, or while eating foods that you can gulp quickly.
8. Have a plan to follow when you are bored, particularly in the evening when you are home.
9. Recognize that plateaus are part of a diet, and look for others' support during those periods. **Plateaus** are *periods of time when you do not see yourself losing weight,* even though you are on your diet. They vary in time from person to person and pass.
10. If you slip on your diet, do not concentrate on what went wrong. Instead, focus on all of the progress you have made. Be positive. Recognize that slipping back is natural and happens to a great number of people.

4. *Determine how many weeks it will take you to lose your desired number of pounds and mark that date on your calendar.*
5. *Determine and put in writing what you will reward yourself with for achieving your goal.*

Underweight—A Health Risk

With so much attention directed to the problem of being overweight, we often ignore the problem of being **underweight**, or weighing below normal or average weight. However, being too thin is also a health risk. Being extremely thin can actually shorten a person's life span.

A person can inherit thinness. Certain body types do not have the normal amount of fat cells. Being too thin also can result from psychological problems. You will read about these problems on page 170.

Check the ideal weight chart on page 165. If you are 15% below the ideal weight for your height and body size, you may be too thin.

Healthy Ways to Gain Weight

Here are four suggestions for gaining weight:

- Increase your calorie intake, especially with foods high in complex carbohydrates—potatoes, rice, pasta, and bread.
- Eat between-meal snacks, but do so two to three hours before meals, so you do not lose your appetite.
- Drink plenty of water, but cut down on soda pop drinks. Because they are carbonated, they may make you feel full.
- Follow a personal exercise program. This point is important because the weight you want to gain should be in firm muscle tissue. Remember, you must increase your caloric intake substantially, since you will be burning more calories.

CHECK YOURSELF

1. What is the difference between being obese and being overweight?
2. What health problems are associated with obesity?
3. What roles does exercise play in weight reduction?
4. What are the only methods of successfully losing weight?

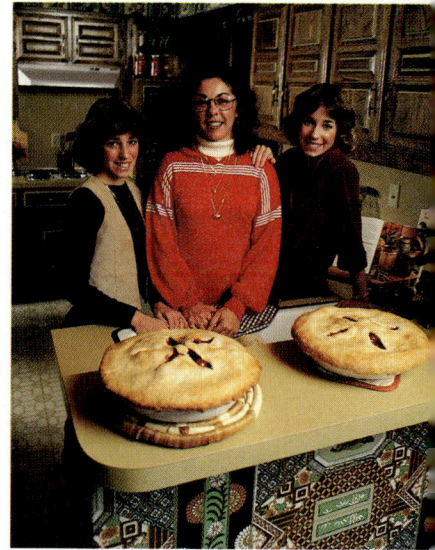

Because of inherited characteristics, some people, like this mother and her daughters, remain thin no matter how much they eat.

2. Healthy Eating Patterns

Whether you are dieting or not, there is more to weight control than exercising and watching your calories. You need to foster healthy eating patterns. You need to pay attention to *what* you eat and *when* you eat.

Break the Fast

The best time to begin a daily healthy eating pattern is at breakfast. After 10 to 12 hours of not eating, your body needs fuel to get going. But did you know that people who eat breakfast have several advantages over those who do not?

Nearly 7,000 people were studied over a period of 10 years and doctors concluded that eating a nutritious breakfast was associated with better physical and mental performance. Those who ate breakfast were more productive during the late morning hours. They also had a faster reaction time and experienced less muscle fatigue than those who skipped breakfast.

What does eating breakfast have to do with weight control? The calories you consume at breakfast are usually used during the morning activities. This is in contrast to the calories you take in at an evening meal, when you are usually less active. In addition, you are less likely to look for a quick snack later in the morning if you have eaten breakfast.

Experiment with different foods for breakfast. Be careful, however, not to consume foods high in sugar, since the energy they provide is burned up quickly. Select complex carbohydrates.

Snacks Can Be Healthy

Remember that one of the main purposes of food is to provide energy for the body. The energy is needed to perform whatever you have to do during the day. You may need snacks to provide more energy between meals. This is especially true if you are burning up a great deal of energy between meals.

What and how you eat at mealtime has much to do with the frequency of your snacks. If you do not eat properly, you will not have much energy. As you have already studied, foods differ greatly in the amount of energy they provide. They also differ in how quickly the body uses that energy. Foods high in sugar provide short-term energy, along with a quick drop in energy level, which usually means more snacking. If your meals consist of foods high in sugar, you may need more frequent snacks.

Remember to have snacks well in advance of the next meal so that your appetite is not spoiled. Snacking can be an important supplement to meals, but you should never use it as a substitute for meals.

Healthy snacks are easy to prepare and are not costly.

Some Suggestions for Nutritious Snacks

- *To add protein to your diet:* Try hard-boiled eggs, pieces of cheese, chunks of tuna, slices of leftover roast or steak.

- *To add vitamin C to your diet:* Try strawberries, other berries, melon, tomatoes, citrus fruits, raw pineapple, nectarines.

- *To add vitamin A to your diet:* Eat carrot sticks, raw broccoli, green pepper rings, dark green vegetables. Try cottage cheese

and crushed pineapple; tuna and mayonnaise; yellow fruits and vegetables.

- *To add calcium to your diet:* Try any dairy products, frozen yogurt, cheese chunks, custard, cottage cheese, or fruit.

- *To add B vitamins and minerals to your diet:* Use whole-grain or enriched breads and cereal, dairy products, or nuts. Raisins are also good.

L I F E M A N A G E M E N T S K I L L

Snacking

Make a list of your favorite snacks. Where does each fit into the five categories given here? What type of snacks should you retain and/or give up? What replacements should you add?

Weight Control and Fast Foods

According to a recent survey, one-third of this nation's adult population eat out every day. Of that one-third, 28% eat at fast-food establishments.

In general, fast foods contain too many calories, too much fat and sugar, too little fiber, and too few vitamins. Almost all fast foods are high in protein, but few Americans are deficient in protein.

This is not to say that all fast foods are bad. Just be sure your selections fit into a well-balanced diet and watch the calorie content.

When you select fast foods, try to get something from each of the four basic food groups. Try to limit the selections from the "other" group, since such foods are low in nutrients and high in calories. A hamburger (*meat*) with onions, lettuce, and tomato (*vegetables*) on a roll (*bread*), and without ketchup, pickles, and mayonnaise (*other*) is a healthy lunch, especially if you are drinking a glass of *milk* with it. See the *Health Handbook*, page HB15 for information on fast foods and the basic food groups.

Nutrient Density

The concept of nutrient density may help you to make better food choices for maintaining or controlling your weight. **Nutrient density** refers to *how nutritious food is relative to the number of calories it contains.* A tablespoon of sugar, for example, has 40 calories, while a tablespoon of green beans has 2 calories. Green beans, however, are a high nutrient density food. That is, they contain large amounts of nutrients and a comparatively small num-

Eating High Nutrient Density Foods

From the lists on the right, make your own list of foods that you eat regularly (i.e., daily, 2 to 3 times a week). How can you improve your daily intake?

ber of calories. Sugar is a low density food. It is said to have "empty calories."

Some other examples of high nutrient density foods include:

carrots	cashews	chicken
sweet potatoes	peanuts	tuna
spinach	almonds	dried fruit
broccoli	peanut butter	pumpkin seeds
strawberries	fortified cereal	whole-grain bread
green peppers	cottage cheese	whole-grain flour
oranges	Cheddar cheese	eggs
peaches	milk	brown rice
sunflower seeds	enriched macaroni	dried peas and beans

Eating Disorders—A Serious Health Threat

We have become a society obsessed with thinness and quick, easy weight loss. The average high-fashion female model is about 5 feet 8 inches tall and weighs less than 110 pounds. Do you think this model presents an accurate picture of beauty or of a typical female figure? No, of course not, but many people compare themselves to that type of model. And rarely do they compare favorably.

Anorexia Nervosa

This obsession with thinness along with some psychological pressures and problems are the main causes of anorexia nervosa. *Anorexia* (an-uh-**rex**-ee-uh) means "without appetite"; *nervosa* (ner-**voh**-suh) means "of nervous origin." Almost all anorexics are female, predominately adolescent and young adult. However, the eating disorder is now being found among many males, too.

Anorexia nervosa is *a behavior involving the irrational fear of becoming overweight and results in severe weight loss from self-starvation.*

Anorexia nervosa is as much a psychological disorder as a physiological one. It relates directly to the individual's self-concept and coping abilities. Outside pressures, high expectations, the need to achieve, and the need for attention can all lead to the development of this disorder.

Bulimia

A second type of eating disorder is **bulimia** (buh-**lim**-ee-uh), *an episodic pattern of binge eating that involves rapid consumption of a large quantity of food in a relatively short period of time.* Self-induced vomiting, laxative abuse, and/or severely restrictive diets are employed after an episode to restore a sense of control and to relieve panic about the possibility of weight gain.

The desire to become thin, more attractive, and more physically perfect can be overwhelming, until vomiting becomes a daily activity and an all-consuming preference. Associated with this behavior may be the notion that if the perfect figure is attained, everything in life will be fine.

Is bulimia a disease? Bulimia and vomiting both are symptoms that

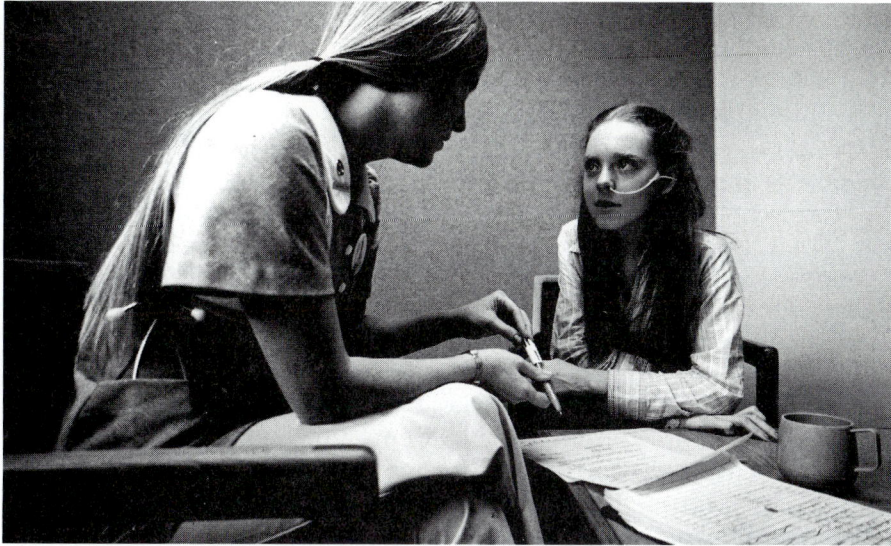

Counseling and medical assistance can successfully overcome anorexia nervosa and bulimia.

occur in a great variety of conditions. They are not diseases. Both are behaviors that occur within a range of severity and frequency. The point at which overeating becomes bulimia or when vomiting becomes abnormal is difficult to pinpoint. These symptoms may occur separately or in combination. The behaviors not only are unhealthy but can lead to serious health problems. They should in no way be considered a diet or a form of dieting.

Frequent episodes of overeating will lead to overweight and eventual obesity. By fasting, vomiting, and purging, weight control may result, but weight loss and protein-calorie malnutrition also are likely. Even if the weight remains within a reasonable range, vomiting and using laxatives can lead to serious medical complications, such as dehydration. Hypokalemia (a low level of potassium in the blood) is the most serious of the complications and can lead to cardiovascular and kidney failure.

In addition, regular use of laxatives can result in the body's inability to function normally. Extensive dental enamel erosion is a result of chronic vomiting. The development of vitamin and mineral deficiencies is possible, depending on the diet and the extent of vomiting and purging.

Because bulimia and anorexia are psychological in nature, the individual usually needs to seek the help of a qualified counselor. Both disorders are life-threatening situations. Prolonged starvation can shrink the brain and change the size of the heart.

CHECK YOURSELF

1. Why is breakfast so important?
2. How can snacks be a healthy part of your diet?
3. What is meant by nutrient density?
4. What is so dangerous about anorexia nervosa?
5. What is so dangerous about bulimia?

■ *Do athletes need extra vitamins?* Vitamins do not give energy. Some vitamins help to *release* energy from carbohydrates, fats, and proteins. Most people can get enough vitamins through a balanced diet.

Athletic activity does not significantly alter the body's need for protein, vitamins, or minerals. Physical activity *does* affect the need for calories, or food energy.

■ *Does carbohydrate loading work?* Many athletes involved in endurance activities have tried **carbohydrate loading**, or *glycogen packing*. This practice *increases the amount of glycogen in the muscles.*

Six days prior to the athletic event, athletes do strenuous exercises to empty the muscles of glycogen. Then for three days they eat a high-protein, high-fat diet. This is followed by three days of a high-carbohydrate diet.

The idea behind this practice is that all muscles require energy to move. They get this energy from carbohydrates, which are stored in the muscles and in the liver as *glycogen*. Glycogen is a readily available source of energy, but it is stored in limited amounts for a limited amount of time.

A Swedish scientist found that if athletes depleted their stores of muscle glycogen through strenuous exercise and then ate a diet of high carbohydrates and did not exercise, they could increase the muscle glycogen stores to substantially lengthen their endurance time.

This process is still under study. A person should not try it without close supervision. Researchers in Canada studied the process and found that the diet produced a decrease, instead of an increase, in aerobic performance—that is, the oxygen-burning capacity of the body that helps in endurance sports.

The best diet for athletes is a balanced one.

Food Additives

Food **additives** (**ad**-uh-tives) are *substances added directly to food or substances that come in contact with food sometime before they reach the consumer.* Food additives may be:

1. **Nutrient supplements**, which are in the form of vitamins and minerals,
2. **Flavoring agents**, which are added to some foods to make them taste better,
3. **Preservatives**, which are added to foods to keep them fresh and keep them from spoiling,
4. **Emulsifiers**, which are added to change the volume of some food products,
5. **Stabilizers and thickeners**, which are added to change the texture of some food,
6. **Alkaline and acid agents**, which are used to control the amount of alkaline and acid in soft drinks, bakery products, and desserts.

Most additives are used for artificial coloring and flavoring. One of the major problems with food additives is that most of them do not have to appear on labels, so a consumer often doesn't have a choice about buying food with or without additives. Additives, for the most part, would not be necessary, if consumers wanted to take extra time in preparing foods.

This diet can have serious side effects—even for athletes in top physical condition.

■ *Should athletes eat a high-protein meal before their game or event?* Extra protein can actually be a hindrance. You have heard of athletes who eat a big steak before competition. The body takes what it needs for immediate use in building and repairing body proteins.

The body does not store protein. The liver and kidneys break down the rest of the protein. This process requires energy, makes the liver and kidneys work harder, and uses extra water in the body, which can cause dehydration.

High-protein foods are also high in fat. Fat moves out of the stomach very slowly, which means the stomach will not be emptied by exercising.

■ *What should an athlete eat before competition?* The athlete should eat *at least* three hours before competition to allow the stomach to digest the food. The athlete's meal should be easy to digest, should keep him or her free from hunger pangs while competing, and should include at least three glasses of liquid.

■ *Does a candy bar or honey provide quick energy?* Concentrated sugars are not recommended before an athletic event. Sugar is absorbed very quickly in the body. A person is likely to feel a very quick lift and then a quick letdown.

A Final Word on a Healthful Diet

Dieting, maintaining weight control, and staying healthy can sometimes become very confusing. The National Dietary Guidelines of the U.S. Department of Agriculture provide seven guidelines that underpin the principles of a sound diet for a healthy person.

1. Eat a variety of foods.
2. Maintain desirable weight.
3. Avoid too much fat, saturated fat, and cholesterol.
4. Eat foods adequate in starch and fiber.
5. Avoid too much sugar.
6. Avoid too much sodium.
7. If a person drinks alcoholic beverages, he or she should do so in moderation.

CHECK YOURSELF

1. What is carbodydrate loading?
2. Why are high-sugar snacks not recommended for athletes?
3. From the material found in this chapter and the *Health Handbook*, page HB18, describe a healthful precompetition meal.

CHAPTER 9   Review

CHAPTER SUMMARY

- Obesity has serious health risks, including heart disease.
- Obesity and problems with overweight can be controlled. However, a person must begin by becoming aware of eating patterns, deciding what changes to make, setting a goal, and making a plan for reaching the goal. It is important that the goal be realistic.
- Because so many Americans lead inactive lives, yet have diets high in fats and carbohydrates, obesity is a prevalent health problem.
- Despite the millions of dollars worth of gimmicks and fad diets for weight loss, there is just one simple rule to follow for healthy weight control: *Consume fewer calories than you use.*
- With the extreme emphasis on being thin in our society today, problems are arising with eating disorders, particularly among adolescent females. These disorders present serious health risks and often require professional help to remedy.
- We have all heard about athletes' dietary needs in order to attain quick energy and better endurance. The athlete needs to follow a well-balanced diet, making sure to get enough calories, since the athlete is using more calories.

REVIEWING WHAT YOU LEARNED

1. Make one list of the reasons why obesity is a problem for many young people. Make a second list of reasons why some young people do not have a problem with their weight. Draw some conclusions about each group.
2. Distinguish between overweight and obese. How could one be overweight and not be obese? What are the dangers of both conditions?
3. Summarize the reasons why your eating behavior can affect your weight-control effort.
4. Does an athlete's diet necessarily have to differ from a nonathlete's diet? Explain your answer.
5. What factors should you consider when eating fast foods to ensure a healthful diet?
6. Name and define two eating disorders.

weight control
ideal weight
overweight
obese
adipose tissue
hydrostatic weighing

caliper
plateaus
underweight
additives
nutrient supplements
flavoring agents

preservatives
emulsifiers
stabilizers
thickeners
alkaline agents
acid agents

nutrient density
anorexia nervosa
bulimia
carbodydrate loading

PUTTING VOCABULARY TO USE

On a separate piece of paper, write the following statements. Then supply the missing word or phrase from the chapter vocabulary list.

1. _____. An excess of fat in the body.
2. _____ _____. The best way to determine the percentage of body fat.
3. _____. Weighing more than the desirable weight for your age and size.
4. _____. The device used in measuring the thickness of the skin.
5. _____. Substances added to food before it reaches the consumer.
6. _____. Substances added to food to change the volume of the product.
7. _____. Substances that change the way the food feels, that is, the texture of the food.

8. _____. Substances added to food to keep it fresh and prevent it from spoiling.
9. _____ _____. Substances added to food to make it taste better.
10. _____ _____. Disorder characterized by an obsession to be thin; more common in females.
11. _____. Eating large amounts of food in a short period of time, followed by self-induced vomiting.
12. _____ _____. Term used to describe values of food on the basis of caloric and nutrient content.
13. _____ _____. Eating large amounts of starches and proteins on days leading up to competition.

APPLYING WHAT YOU LEARNED

1. Study one diet that is available to the public today. What questions would you ask yourself in determining whether this diet would or would not be a healthy approach to weight control?
2. Besides an overindulgence in food, what other negative life-style practices can you list that are often brought about by being obese?
3. Suppose that you had to give a short talk to a group of fifth graders on the advantages of eating a good breakfast. What would you tell them in a two-minute presentation?
4. Make an advertisement for a weight-loss program that follows the two basic principles of losing weight. What gimmicks could you use to promote your method of weight loss?
5. Find three advertisements in magazines or newspapers that claim quick weight loss or an easy way to a "beautiful body." Investigate them for accuracy.

6. Call a fitness center in your area and ask about the kinds of programs it has for body building and weight loss. What kind of education do the programs include? What type of health professionals does the center have on its staff?
7. Select a weight reduction ad from the newspaper. Write a one-page descriptive paper on how you think an early settler in the United States might have responded to such an ad.
8. List the seven dieting guidelines in the order in which you need to work on them. Hang your list in your room.

FOCUS ON WELLNESS

Eating patterns and food selection directly affect weight control. Weight affects appearance and all levels of health. *I work to control or maintain my weight and to promote my overall level of health by . . .*

UNIT

4

DRUGS IN OUR SOCIETY— BENEFITS AND DANGERS

Drugs as Medicines

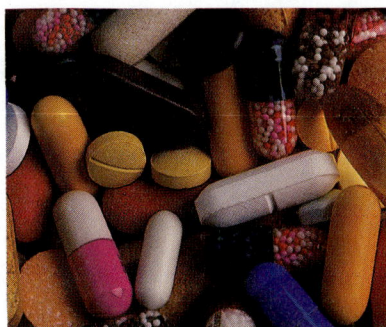

In this century, drugs have significantly changed the health of Americans. Drug discoveries since 1900 account for people being able to live longer and to lead healthier, fuller lives.

At this point, you do not have to contend with the fear of being crippled with polio, being quarantined with tuberculosis, or dying of pneumonia. The discoveries of new drugs are responsible for eliminating the suffering that many people had to endure in the past.

After studying this chapter, you will be able to:
- define drug and medicine,
- outline the major classifications of drugs,
- explain what happens to a drug in the body,
- explain the role of the Food and Drug Administration,
- tell the differences between regulations regarding prescription and over-the-counter drugs,
- describe the proper use of, and effects of, analgesics, antacids, and antihistamines,
- explain why the effects of drugs are unique to each individual.

1. Drugs and Medicines

A **drug** is *any substance, other than food, that when taken into the body alters the structure or function of the body in some way.* **Medicine** is *a kind of drug that is taken into or applied to the body to prevent or cure a disease or disabling condition.* Medicine is intended to be helpful. However, if a person does not use medicine cautiously and properly, any medicine can be harmful.

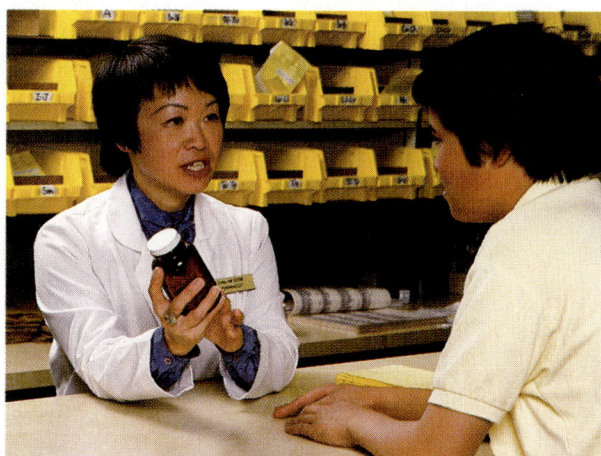

Your task in promoting and protecting your wellness is to be well-informed about drugs, to recognize their potential risks, and to use them only as needed. Even then, you must use drugs with caution.

This may not be as easy as it sounds. We live in a time of "quick cures." A pill or lotion remedy exists for every conceivable ache or pain. Advertisements repeatedly tell us which pill to take for what symptoms. We are also barraged with a tremendous amount of misinformation about some of the more common drugs. How is one to know what product is accurate and what is just an advertising gimmick?

Your best protection is to become knowledgeable about drugs in general, different types of drugs, their effects on the body, and their proper use. With this information, you are better able to make healthful decisions about drugs.

Classification of Drugs

Drugs are generally grouped according to their primary, beneficial effect on the body. The most widely used drugs fall into four classifications:

1. those that fight disease-producing organisms;
2. those that prevent disease;
3. those that affect the heart and blood vessels;
4. those that affect the nervous system.

If a person does not use medicine cautiously and properly, any medicine can be harmful.

Drugs That Fight Disease-Producing Organisms

Two kinds of drugs either kill or help the body to kill disease-producing organisms. One is antibiotics: the main kinds being the penicillins and the tetracyclines. The second kind is the sulfa drugs. An **antibiotic** (ant-uh-by-**ot**-ik) is a *drug that microscopic living organisms produce*. They work to destroy harmful disease-producing organisms in the body.

The **penicillins** (pen-uh-**sill**-lens) are *antibiotics that kill a wide variety of bacteria*. They are the most effective and well known of the antibiotics. In fact, when penicillin was first used, it was known as the "wonder drug," because it killed bacteria causing strep throat, pneumonia, and rheumatic fever.

Tetracyclines (tet-rah-**sigh**-kleens) are *antibiotics, less effective than penicillins, which are used to treat infection*. They are not as effective as the penicillins because they only slow down growth and multiplication, but do not kill the organisms. They can be especially helpful, however, to someone who is allergic to penicillin.

Another type of antibiotic, **topical antibiotics**, is *used to treat minor cuts, burns, and abrasions*. A panel of Food and Drug Administration experts, examining the safety and the effectiveness of these antibiotics, concluded that they were neither safe nor effective as antibiotics. But they are good skin-wound protectants. That is, they provide a protective, physical barrier to skin wounds.

Sulfa (**sull**-fah) **drugs** are *a large family of germ killers that are made from certain chemical substances*.

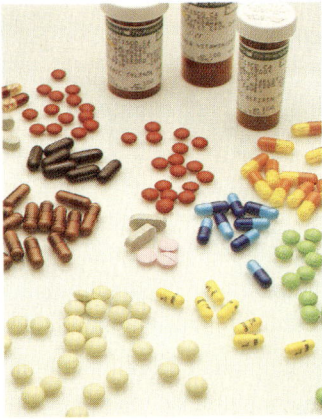

Medicine in capsule and pill form comes in different colors and shapes so that medical people can recognize the various kinds.

Drugs That Prevent Disease

Vaccines and antisera are the two main types of disease-prevention drugs. **Vaccines** (vak-**seens**) *cause the body to develop antibodies to fight the disease-causing germs*, thus making the body immune to the disease. An **antibody** (**ant**-e-bod-ee) is *a protein substance in the blood that acts against poisons or the bacteria producing them*. You will read more about vaccines in Chapter 29 on infectious diseases.

Antisera (singular form: antiserum) are blood fluids that contain *antibodies and act more quickly than vaccines*. They are given to a person who has not been vaccinated, but who has been exposed to an infectious disease. *Globulins* (**glob**-you-lins), blood proteins that contain antibodies, are also in this group. They are used to fight diseases such as measles, mumps, and hepatitis.

Drugs That Affect the Heart and Blood Vessels

There are five main kinds of cardiovascular drugs:

1. One group of drugs is known as digitalis (dij-uh-**tah**-lis). **Digitalis** *works to increase the force of contractions in the heart*. It also cuts down the number of heartbeats and controls irregular heartbeats.

2. A second group is known as diuretics (die-yur-**ret**-icks). **Diuretics** *help to relieve the body of water and sodium.* This is particularly important after heart failure.

3. The third group, **vasodilators** (**vah**-so-die-**late**-ors), *dilate (enlarge) the veins and arteries to increase blood and oxygen flow.* When there is a decreased blood supply in the arteries because of a spasm, a blood clot, or a buildup of cholesterol, vasodilators are very useful.

4. The fourth group, **antiarrhythmics** (anti-uh-ah-**rith**-micks), are *drugs given in cases of arrythmia, which is any disturbance in the rate, or rhythm, of the heart.*

5. The fifth group is the **preventive agents**. They work to *prevent such conditions as high blood pressure, blood clots, and the development of fatty deposits in the blood vessels in people who are prone to them.*

IMPROVING YOURSELF

Using Medicine Cautiously

Do you practice wellness in relation to using medicines? On a separate sheet of paper, indicate whether each statement describes you *most of the time, some of the time,* or *never.* Then check your score.

1. I try at least one healthful way to relieve physical discomfort before taking a medicine.
2. I use over-the-counter drugs only when necessary.
3. I use only one kind of medicine at a time, unless otherwise instructed.
4. If I am not sure about a medicine, I ask my parent, physician, or pharmacist.
5. I ask my doctor for information about a drug that is being prescribed for me.
6. I read all the enclosed information and follow the directions carefully when taking all medicines.
7. I never take someone else's prescription medicine.
8. I do not drink alcoholic beverages when taking medicine.
9. I continue taking prescription medicine for the prescribed time, even though I feel better.
10. If the doctor takes me off a medicine, I properly and safely dispose of what is left in the bottle.

Scoring. Give yourself 4 points for each statement that describes you *most of the time,* 1 point for *some of the time,* and 0 for *never.*

25 to 40: *Very good*—keep it up, your behavior concerning medicine is very healthy.

10 to 24: *Good*—you exercise some caution with medicine.

9 and below: *Be careful*—you may be taking some unnecessary and dangerous risks with medicine.

LIFE MANAGEMENT SKILL

Using Medicines

Examine this self-inventory to assess your use of medicines. Select two statements to which you answered *some of the time* or *never.* Identify ways to improve these behaviors.

Drugs That Affect the Nervous System

Perhaps the most widely used and—without question—the most abused drugs are those that affect the nervous system. Do you have any idea why this group of drugs are the most widely abused? Unlike the other groups, these drugs alter moods and feelings.

There are six major groupings of drugs that alter the nervous system in some way:

1. **Analgesics** (an-al-**jeez**-icks)—which are designed *to relieve or stop pain;*
2. **Antidepressants** (ant-ee-dee-**press**-ents)—which work to *relieve emotional depression;*
3. **Stimulants** (**stim**-you-lunts)—which work to *prevent sleep, reduce distractibility in hyperactive children, and suppress appetite;*
4. **Hypnotics** (hip-**naht**-icks)—which *give relief to moderate or mild anxiety or tension, and also aid in sleep;*
5. **Barbiturates** (bar-**bich**-u-ruts) (depressants)—which *are used for many of the same reasons as hypnotics, but also are used to prevent various types of seizures;*
6. **Tranquilizers** (**tran**-quill-lize-ers)—which are used *to relieve anxiety or tension;* also to relieve insomnia due to anxiety and tension.

The hallucinogens (hal-**loos**-in-ah-jins), a seventh group, require special identification. **Hallucinogens** are *drugs which alter consciousness.* Unlike those drugs in the other six groups, they have no generally accepted medical use in this country and are, therefore, illegal drugs.

What Happens to a Drug in the Body?

The effect of a drug in the body depends on several factors, one being the type of drug that the person takes. Another factor is the method by which the person takes the drug.

If the person swallows the drug, it goes into the stomach, much like food. Many drugs dissolve in the stomach, even before they pass into the intestines. As they dissolve, they pass through the walls of the stomach or the intestines and are carried directly to the bloodstream and then to the liver.

The liver processes all food and chemicals so that the body can either use them or eliminate them. If some of the chemicals consumed are **toxic**, or *poisonous*, to the body, the liver converts them into less toxic substances.

If food is in the stomach, the absorption of the drug is slowed. Sometimes the instructions on prescription drugs will state that the drugs should be taken at mealtime. Studies of these particular drugs indicate that this is the best procedure for the fullest absorption of these drugs with the least irritation to the gastrointestinal tract.

When a drug is taken **intravenously** (en-tra-**vee**-nus-lee) (*in the veins*) or **intramuscularly** (en-tra-**mus**-cue-lar-lee) (*in the muscles*) by injection, the drug goes immediately into the bloodstream and then on to the liver. Naturally, the effects of taking drugs in this way are much more immediate than if taken by swallowing.

The Body's Reaction to Drugs

Each person's body chemistry is different. This means that drugs will have different reactions on different people. Some people experience *side effects*, or reactions, to certain drugs. They may even be allergic to a drug. In some cases, the allergic reaction might be so severe that it causes serious illness, even death.

The Doctor's Judgment

Many conditions influence the doctor's choice of a drug or the dosage for a patient. For example, a forthcoming surgery, diabetes, epilepsy, glaucoma, heart disease, high blood pressure, and ulcers will all require some alteration in the type and amount of drug that the physician prescribes. So will people who have alcohol problems, pregnant women, women nursing an infant, a child, or a person over 60 years old.

Drug Interaction

Extensive research is done on drugs before they are made available to the public. Based on this research, scientists can predict side effects that might be expected with specific drugs.

However, these reactions can be quite different when drugs are combined, that is, *when two or more different drugs are taken at the same time*. It is difficult to predict **drug interaction**. Drug interaction can cause one or both drugs to have stronger effects on the body than if each one is taken in isolation. For this reason, people should not mix drugs. Before taking more than one kind of drug, people should seek their doctor's or pharmacist's advice.

Drug Tolerance and Dependence

Certain drugs cause the body to develop a **tolerance**, meaning that *the body becomes used to the drug's effect*. The body then requires larger doses to produce an effect. You will be reading more in Chapter 13 about drugs that cause a tolerance.

The body can also develop a **dependence** on certain drugs. *The user develops a need for the drug all the time*. There are two types of dependence, also called **addiction**—physical and psychological.

In *physical dependence*, the body develops a need for the drug. If the person does not take the drug, he or she experiences **withdrawal** symptoms, which are *negative, unpleasant physical or mental reactions*. Withdrawal can be a combination of mild nervousness, insomnia, severe nausea, vomiting, trembling, and cramps. These symptoms gradually ease and disappear after a period off the drug. Withdrawal from certain strong drugs may require medical supervision.

In *psychological dependence*, the person has become mentally dependent on the drug. He or she thinks the drug is needed to feel good. The drug provides the user some form of an escape from reality. It may be used to relax, sleep, or get energy. Soon the user is unable to relax, sleep, or feel energetic without the drug. The drug becomes a crutch.

CHECK YOURSELF

1. What are the four major groupings of drugs? On what are the groupings based?
2. What does it mean to take drugs *intravenously* and *intramuscularly*?
3. What is a drug interaction?
4. Explain what is meant by building a "tolerance" to a drug.
5. What is the difference between physical and psychological dependency on drugs?

2. Consumer Protection and Drugs

At all times in our history, there have been medicines sold on the market that did people little or no good. Since some of these medicines were actually harmful, people turned to the federal government for protection.

Two great factors are now regulating the use of drugs and medicines: the Food and Drug Administration and the increasing consumer awareness of what is available on the market.

Government Control

The consumer is now protected by and can receive accurate information about legal drugs from the Food and Drug Administration (FDA).

In the United States, the Food and Drug Administration must approve a drug before it can be made available to the public. All drugs must meet specific FDA regulations.

The FDA requires that a drug manufacturer supply information about the chemical composition, the intended use, the effects, and the possible side effects of the drug. Drugs are tested on animals first and then with different experimental groups of people.

Since the FDA requires information about the long-term effects of a drug, it takes about five years for a company to meet all of the FDA requirements. The FDA decides which drugs require a doctor's prescription. The FDA also decides when a drug is *safe to use without a doctor's supervision*, that is, to be sold as an **over-the-counter (OTC) drug**.

The Food and Drug Administration also controls all of the advertising for **prescription drugs**, *ones given with a doctor's order.* You do not see advertisements for prescription drugs on television or in the popular magazines. In what kind of magazines do you think you would find advertisements for prescription drugs?

Prescription drugs are advertised in medical journals, not in magazines that the general public reads. The reason is simple. The consumer does not decide which prescription medicine to buy. Advertisements for prescription drugs are most generally found in doctors' journals and magazines because doctors make the decisions about particular prescription drugs to use.

Laws also govern the advertising of OTC drugs. Advertisements cannot make or imply results that the drug cannot provide.

"Safe and Effective When Used as Directed"

When the FDA approves a drug, it is saying that the drug is a safe and effective one. *Safe* means that when used as directed the drug will not be harmful. *Effective* means there is a reasonable chance that the drug will do what it is supposed to do if it is used as directed. The safety and effectiveness of any drug are dependent on the consumer's using it *only as directed*.

The consumer receives assistance in using the medicine properly. The FDA requires that drug companies put certain information on all drug labels. The OTC drug labels include more information than do prescription drug labels. This is because OTC drugs are self-prescribed and self-administered. The OTC preparations are not as strong, have less potential for harm, and their method of usage is safer for self-administration than are methods for prescription drugs. However, as in the case of any medication, any OTC drug has a potential of being harmful—making a person sicker—if it is not used as intended.

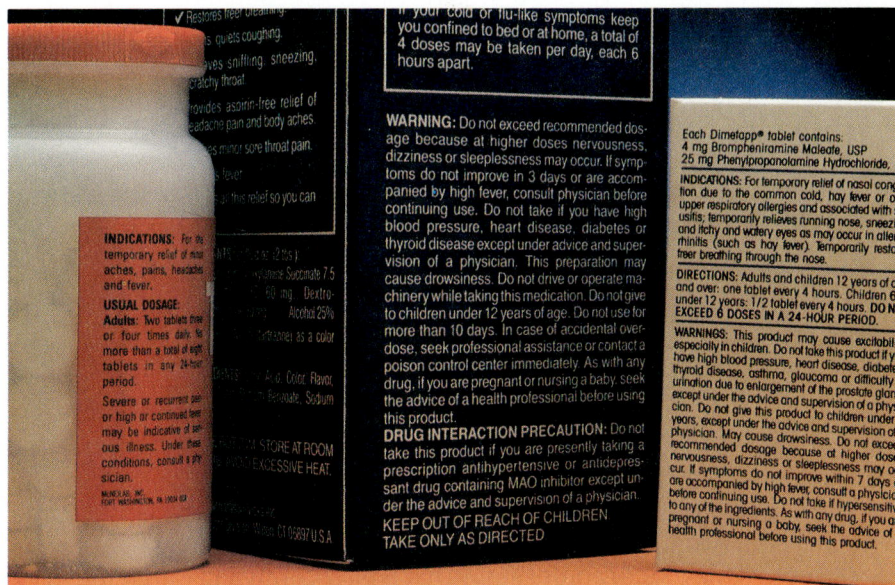

Read all the labels on an OTC medicine. They contain helpful information about ingredients and usage.

Information on an OTC Drug Label

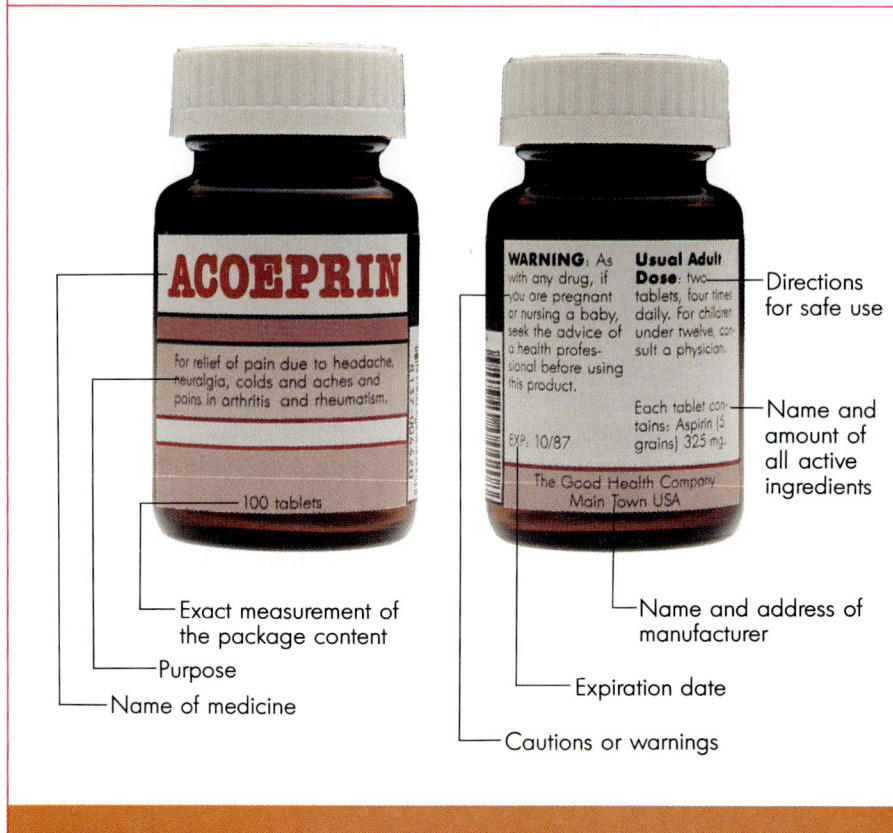

ACOEPRIN

for relief of pain due to headache, neuralgia, colds and aches and pains in arthritis and rheumatism.

100 tablets

WARNING: As with any drug, if you are pregnant or nursing a baby, seek the advice of a health professional before using this product.

EXP. 10/87

Usual Adult Dose: two tablets, four times daily. For children under twelve, consult a physician.

Each tablet contains: Aspirin (5 grains) 325 mg.

The Good Health Company
Main Town USA

Directions for safe use

Name and amount of all active ingredients

Name and address of manufacturer

Expiration date

Cautions or warnings

Exact measurement of the package content

Purpose

Name of medicine

Which OTC Drug to Buy?

Each drug has three names. This does not include any of the street names by which illegal drugs are called.

Drugs used in medicine have a **chemical** name and a *chemical formula*; a **generic**, or *universal*, name; and a **trade**, or *brand*, name.

- The *chemical name* for aspirin is acetylsalicylic acid (ah-**see**-tull-sal-ah-sigh-lick **ass**-id); the chemical formula is $C_9H_8O_4$.
- The *generic name* for acetylsalicylic acid is aspirin.
- The *trade name* for aspirin is different for each manufacturer.

The *chemical name* is of use only to a chemist, who sees the formula as a very precise description of the chemical composition of the drug. The *generic name* is simpler than the chemical name and is used internationally to identify the same drug. The *trade name* is the one that the manufacturer assigns to the drug.

All of this may seem confusing. What is *more* confusing is that the same aspirin may be sold under 10 to 20 different trade names. Of most importance to you are the generic name and the trade name for a drug.

When a drug is produced, it contains a basic chemical substance, such as penicillin or aspirin, which many drug manufacturers produce. These companies may then package the product as powder, liquid, tablets, or capsules under the generic name and sell it to pharmacies. They also may package the drug under a trade name to distinguish the drug from the same drug that other companies manufacture.

Some manufacturers sell only generic products both to pharmacies and to other manufacturers who, in turn, put their names on the product. A company usually spends money on advertising a trade name drug. This advertising cost is passed on to the consumer by increasing the basic price of the drug. This is not the case with a generic drug. Therefore, the cost of the trade name drug is often more expensive than the generic drug.

Pain Relievers—What You Need to Know

You can buy a number of products, without a prescription, for temporary relief of aches and pains. The most familiar and most widely used ones are aspirin and acetaminophen (aah-set-uh-**min**-uh-fen). They are analgesics, because they stop pain. There are two types of analgesics—nonnarcotic and narcotic.

Nonnarcotic Pain Relievers

Aspirin is by far the most widely used nonprescription drug in the United States with some 20 billion tablets sold annually. Aspirin contains a chemical—salicylic acid. Scientist still are not sure how aspirin makes pain go away. Aspirin also makes fever go down.

Because of aspirin's wide and common use, many people do not realize that aspirin can be dangerous. Even small amounts can irritate the stomach, especially an empty stomach. Aspirin can interfere with blood clotting, and large doses of it can cause dizziness and ringing in the ears.

Because of these problems, some who are sensitive to aspirin take a substitute—*acetaminophen*. It does not contain salicylic acid. While acetaminophen is free of most of the side effects of aspirin, an overdose can result in serious liver damage.

In some pain relievers, the aspirin is "buffered" with other ingredients that reduce, but do not eliminate, the side effects.

Cautions   Things to remember about *nonprescription* pain relievers:

■ *Keep these drugs out of the reach of children*. If anyone, particularly a child, takes a large dose, get medical help immediately.
■ *Don't use these drugs for extended periods of time without medical supervision*. If symptoms persist for more than 10 days (5 days in children under 12) or if new symptoms develop, see a physician.
■ *Read the label on the container carefully*. It will tell you how much of the drug to take, and when and how to take it.

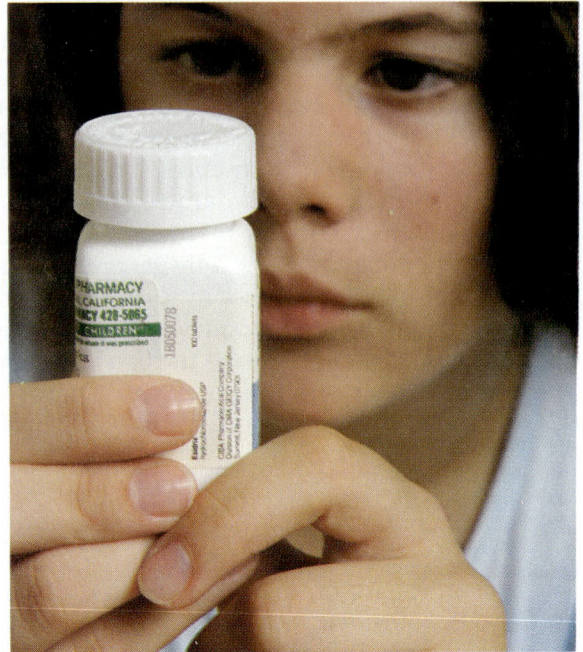

Keep drugs out of reach if there are children in the house. Read labels before using any medicine.

- *Do not take any medication that contains aspirin if you are allergic to aspirin or have ulcers or a bleeding problem.*
- *Seek medical help immediately if you experience any bleeding or vomiting of blood after taking aspirin.*

Narcotic Pain Relievers

Narcotics (nar-**kot**-ticks), analgesics such as *codeine* (**ko**-deen) and *morphine* (**moor**-feen), are much more powerful drugs than aspirin. By working on the brain and central nervous system, they stop very strong pain. Narcotics are used for some types of cancer, pain resulting from severe injury, or for postoperative care after surgery. Only a doctor can prescribe them because they are extremely addictive—causing both physical and psychological dependence. Narcotics are the one group of drugs that people widely abuse. We will discuss them further in this unit.

Antacids—Do We Need Them?

Americans spend over $100 million yearly on **antacids** (ant-**ass**-ids)—*medicines that reduce or alleviate stomach acidity.* Over 300 different brands of antacid tablets, pills, and gums are on the market. Under FDA guidelines, an antacid manufacturer can make only two therapeutic claims on its labels:

- that the product is safe;
- that it is effective for symptomatic relief of "heartburn, sour stomach, and acid indigestion."

The label is also to include warnings of possible side effects and a drug interaction precaution.

What Do Antacids Actually Do?

The stomach makes and secretes hydrochloric acid (HCl) for the purpose of digesting food, especially protein. The ingestion of food is a stimulus for the secretion of HCl. Certain foods especially stimulate the secretion of the acid in some people. By being aware of and avoiding foods that seem to cause this reaction in your stomach, you can avoid problems of acid indigestion.

Nervousness can also cause extra secretions of HCl. The extra acid in the stomach is responsible for the acid indigestion. In addition, gulping air while eating can also cause heartburn.

Antacids are nonabsorbable and contain ingredients that neutralize the acid in the stomach. However, some antacids contain aspirin, which can further irritate the stomach. Prevention is the best course of action and is relatively easy. Eat slowly, chew your food well, do not overeat, and avoid foods that seem to cause your stomach to react.

Antihistamines—Cold Remedies?

Your nose is dripping, your eyes are watering, your head aches—you have a cold and want relief. You *can* find shelves of nonprescription cold remedies. There are hundreds of them, and people spend millions of dollars a year trying to cure their colds. The fact is only *time* will cure a cold. Cold remedies may or may not relieve your symptoms.

A virus in the respiratory system causes colds. When the virus germs invade your body, special cells release a chemical called *histamine* (**hiss**-tah-men). This natural body substance causes the blood vessels in the respiratory tract to *dilate* (open wider). It also causes tissues to swell, which accounts for a stuffed-up nose and a seepage of fluid into surrounding spaces—thus, a runny nose and watery eyes.

When taken orally, *cold remedies* called **antihistamines**, block the effects of the histamine. They can reduce a swelling and runny nose for up to twelve hours. They can also reduce sneezing and watery eyes.

One of the side effects, however, is that these OTC drugs can cause drowsiness. You might also check the label closely, for common cold remedies often contain a variety of chemicals, some of which are not antihistamines at all.

Other Chemicals in Cold Remedies

Caffeine (caf-**feen**), a stimulant, is often an ingredient in cold remedies. It is used to counteract the drowsiness effect of antihistamines.

Aspirin or *acetaminophen*, according to the Consumer's Union, may be the only really valuable ingredients added to cold remedies, because each

Cold Prevention

Prevention of a cold is the best treatment you can give yourself. You can do that by keeping your body strong and healthy.

Manage stress in your life, eat well, and get adequate exercise and rest. If you do feel the symptoms of a cold developing, act immediately to counteract them, particularly with rest and good nutrition. You are not practicing wellness by taking a cold remedy and then going to school or work and spreading your germs to those around you.

If you take a cold remedy, be alert to the following side effects and stop taking the drug if these symptoms develop: upset stomach or vomiting, diarrhea, difficulty urinating, dizziness, ringing in the ears, loss of appetite, weakness, headache, blurred vision, nervousness, change in blood pressure, or insomnia.

When you are sick, getting rest is sometimes as important as taking a medicine.

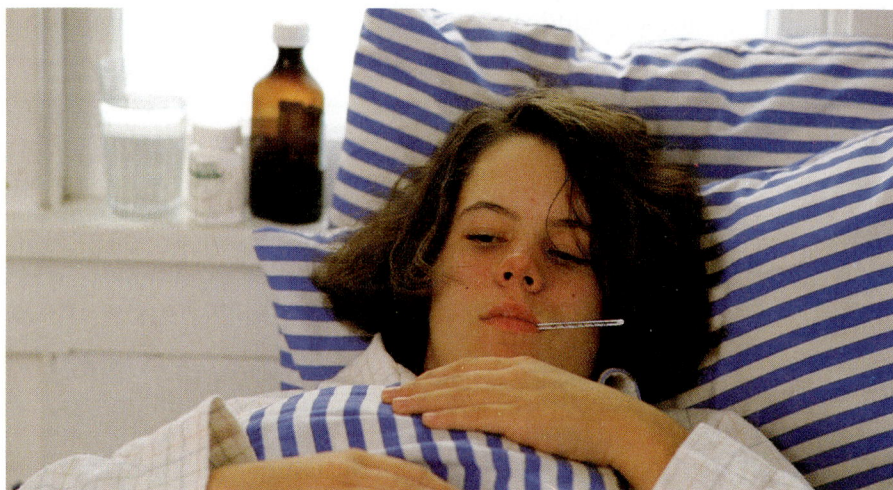

can lower a fever and relieve aching and inflammation. However, if a consumer takes cold pills that contain aspirin or acetaminophen, he or she may pay 20 times the cost for aspirin alone.

Antacids are sometimes added to cold remedies to try to counteract the burning quality of the aspirin and the nauseating effect of the antihistamine. However, the amount of antacid included is seldom enough to relieve either side effect.

All of this information points up to the fact that just because a product is sold over the counter, it does not mean that the consumer should not take precautions or should not consider side effects or dangers. If a person chooses to take a cold remedy, he or she must read the label and follow the directions.

CHECK YOURSELF

1. What are the three names given to each drug? To what do they refer?
2. What are analgesics?
3. How does aspirin differ from acetaminophen?
4. What do antacids do?
5. How does the common cold react to histamine and antihistamine?

3. Prescription Drugs

Certain drugs require more controls because of their potential harm and strength. Prescription drugs require a doctor's order. Only a licensed pharmacist can sell them.

The Pharmacist

A **pharmacist** (**far**-ma-sist) is *a person concerned with the preparation, distribution, and sale of legal drugs.* Both physicians and pharmacists are trained in drug therapy. They know what a drug is supposed to do and what adverse effects can occur. The biggest difference between the two is that a physician is trained to diagnose your illness, and a pharmacist is not. A pharmacist, however, may fill your prescription, inform you of any side effects or precautions to take when using the medication, and indicate the directions for taking the medication. A **prescription** (pre-**scrip**-shun) is *a physician's written order to a pharmacist to give a certain medicine to a patient.*

Your pharmacist can answer these questions about prescriptions:

- the name and dosage of the drug,
- how and when it is to be taken,
- the possible side effects,
- whether a prescription can be refilled,
- whether there is a cheaper generic drug that can be substituted,
- what the *shelf life* of a drug is—how long you can keep it before it becomes ineffective or dangerous,
- how to store the medication,
- whether to take two or more medicines together safely.

The Doctor's Prescription

The prescription from the doctor has the doctor's name and address on it, as well as the patient's name. It identifies the drug being prescribed, the dosage, the amount to be dispensed, and the directions for use.

In the lower left-hand corner of the prescription is a place for the doctor to circle the number of refills the patient may have before needing another prescription. The law requires that this information appear on the medicine's label when the consumer receives it.

J. D. Smith, M.D. —————————————— Doctor
1022 Pine Avenue
Main Town, Wisconsin

——————————————————— Patient

Name: Pam Finn ———————————— Patient's Address

Address: 232 Sunny Dr. ———————— Medicine and Quantity

Main Town, WI ————————————— Number of Capsules

RX ——————————————————————— Directions

tetracycline 100 mg

21 ——————————————————————— Refill

Sig: 1 tid

Refill 0 Time(s) J. D. Smith ———————— Doctor's Signature

Date 5/6/86 ———————————————— Date of Prescription

The doctor's prescription is in a type of shorthand. Some of the abbreviations used are on page 192.

Reading a Prescription

Have you ever tried to read a prescription? It may be difficult since some of the information is written in Latin. Here are a few abbreviations that will help you understand prescriptions.

Latin	Abbreviation	Meaning
recipe	℞	take
ad libitum	ad lib.	use freely as needed
ante cibum	a.c.	before meals
bis in die	b. i. d.	twice a day
quater in die	q. i. d.	four times a day
ter in die	t. i. d.	three times a day
capsula	caps.	capsule
guttae	gtt.	drops
per os	p. o.	orally
quaque quarta hora	q. 4 h.	every fourth hour
ut dictum	ut dict.	as directed
signa	Sig.	write on label
hora somni	h. s.	at bedtime

The Prescription Label

The prescription labels prepared in the pharmacy are as precise as the OTC medicine labels.

Prescription labels from the pharmacy contain the following information:

- Pharmacy name
- Identification number
- Patient's name
- Doctor's name
- Date prescription is filled
- Name of drug
- Instructions for use
- Special warnings or directions, for example:
  - Take with food or milk.
  - Refrigerate.
  - Do not take with milk.
  - Shake well.
  - Finish all of this medication.
  - May cause drowsiness. Alcohol may intensify drowsiness. Use care when operating car or dangerous machinery.
  - **Caution**: Federal law prohibits the transfer of this drug to any person other than the patient for whom it was prescribed.
  - For external use only.
  - Effectiveness expires (*month, year*).

Good Neighbor Pharmacy

500 Burnett Road
Main Town, WI
Phone 998-602-3478

5/6/86

Pam Green

Tetracycline   100mg

Take one capsule three times a day for infection.

No. 39610

Dr. Smith   TRN/0

Cautions to Remember

Some of the most commonly abused drugs, those that affect the nervous system, are prescribed by doctors. Narcotics, stimulants, and depressants have medical uses, some of which are very important. When the consumer uses them as directed for the purpose for which they are intended, these drugs can be beneficial.

When a consumer uses such drugs for nonmedical reasons, for reasons other than prescribed, or when not taken as directed, they are very dangerous. Use of these drugs must be closely supervised because they are highly addictive and they can cause death. More information about these drugs will appear in this unit.

It is important to always remember that drugs—even prescribed ones—bear close supervision because they can affect the body's chemical balance.

CHECK YOURSELF

1. What are the differences in information between the prescription drug label and the OTC drug label?
2. Why are the warnings on the prescription label very important to the consumer?

CHAPTER 10   Review

CHAPTER SUMMARY

■ Drugs, as medicine, are responsible for altering the structure and function of the body. They also can prevent or cure a disease or disabling condition.
■ One main way of grouping drugs is according to their primary effect on the body. This includes four basic groups: drugs that fight disease-producing organisms, drugs that prevent disease, drugs that affect the heart and blood vessels, and drugs that affect the nervous system.
■ The consumer is protected by drug regulations that the Food and Drug Administration enforces.
■ The FDA decides which drugs require a doctor's prescription and which drugs can be sold over the counter.
■ Information and directions on the drug label provide further assistance and protection for the consumer.
■ All drugs are potentially dangerous. To be healthful, a consumer must use drugs only as needed and exactly as directed.

REVIEWING WHAT YOU LEARNED

1. When is a drug a medicine? Why aren't all drugs considered medicines?
2. What are the major classifications of drugs outlined in this chapter?
3. What factors make each drug-taking experience a unique one?
4. Identify the similarities and differences between over-the-counter (OTC) drugs and prescription drugs, both of which are sold for health reasons.
5. How do the following OTC drugs work to restore health?
   a. aspirin
   b. antacid
   c. antihistamine
6. How do drugs that fight infection differ from those that prevent infection?
7. What is the role of the Food and Drug Administration in monitoring medicines and drugs used in medicines?

CHAPTER VOCABULARY

drug	diuretics	hallucinogens	withdrawal
medicine	vasodilators	toxic	over-the-counter (OTC) drugs
antibiotic	antiarrhythmics	intravenously	prescription drugs
tetracyclines	preventive agents	intramuscularly	chemical name
topical antibiotics	analgesics	pharmacist	generic name
sulfa drugs	antidepressants	prescription	trade name
vaccines	stimulants	drug interaction	narcotics
antibody	hypnotics	tolerance	antacids
antisera	barbiturates	dependence	antihistamines
digitalis	tranquilizers	addiction	

PUTTING VOCABULARY TO USE

On a separate piece of paper, write the following statements. Then supply the missing word or phrase from the chapter vocabulary list.

1. _____. A family of powerful pain relievers.
2. _____ _____. Cheaper than its trade or brand name equivalent.
3. _____. Physical or psychological need for a drug.
4. _____. Aspirin is the most popular of these.
5. _____. A substance that alters the structure or function of the body.
6. _____. Any unpleasantness when a drug is taken away.
7. _____. The need for a larger dose to produce the original effect.
8. _____ _____ _____ _____. Can be bought without doctor's supervision.
9. _____. Any type of drug that prevents or cures disease or disabling condition.
10. _____. Drugs that fight disease-producing organisms.
11. _____. Drugs used to prevent disease.
12. _____ _____. Only a pharmacist can sell these drugs.

APPLYING WHAT YOU LEARNED

1. Select an advertisement of a drug that a person uses to alleviate specific symptoms. Analyze the claims and benefits of the medication and determine the accuracy of the ad. Review how the ad influences the person's decision to buy the drug.
2. Identify three common physical complaints. Find the appropriate medicines to treat the symptoms. Then describe some alternatives to treating the symptoms besides drugs.
3. What are some appropriate questions to ask the doctor before he or she writes a prescription?
4. Select one of the following topics and write a one-page position paper on it. Include some facts to support your position.
   a. Is physical addiction more dangerous than psychological dependence?
   b. Are generic drugs really safe?
   c. Should aspirin be a prescription drug?
   d. Are the FDA's guidelines for approving drugs too rigid?
5. Look through a popular magazine and count the number of advertisements for over-the-counter drugs. What conclusions can you draw about the general public's attitude toward drugs? Pick one ad and rewrite it, giving suggestions for relieving a health problem without the use of a drug.
6. Select one of the following and write a one-page narrative paper on the person's contribution to a drug discovery: John J. Abel, Sir Frederick Banting, Sir Alexander Fleming, Edward Jenner.
7. Some medicines come from plants, especially flowering plants. Research the discovery of a drug made from a plant. How was it discovered? What is it used for?

FOCUS ON WELLNESS

Some drugs are taken to prevent disease, but most drugs are taken because there is something wrong in the body. *I can restrict my taking of drugs by . . .*

Tobacco—Pick Your Poison

"Smoking-related diseases are such important causes of disability and premature death in developed countries that the control of cigarette smoking could do more to improve health and prolong life in these countries than any single action in the whole field of preventive medicine." (*The World Health Organization*)

After studying this chapter, you will be able to:
- identify the health risks related to smoking,
- describe the effects of smoking on the body,
- assess your own attitudes toward smoking,
- describe the effects of cigarette smoke on a nonsmoker,
- explain the health problems associated with pipes, cigars, and smokeless tobacco,
- identify ways to successfully quit smoking or to help someone else in the effort to quit,
- point out the obstacles one faces in trying to change a habitual smoking habit.

Thirty million Americans have quit smoking and health professionals are leading the way—65% of the doctors, 61% of the dentists, and 55% of the pharmacists who once smoked have quit.

And, yet, one group of people have shown an increase in smoking. The number of teenage female smokers has more than doubled over the last 20 years. The number of teenage male smokers also has increased after a number of years of remaining constant.

Of the 50 million Americans who do smoke, almost all of them are well aware of the dangers—cancer, heart and lung disease, even death. One recent survey revealed that most of them—71%—would like to quit.

LIFE MANAGEMENT SKILL

Smoking vs. Not Smoking

Compile two lists—one on the reasons given for *not smoking* and the other on the reasons given *for smoking*. After you finish studying this chapter, look at your lists again. What adjustments would you make on them? Why? Why not?

Why Young People Smoke

Peer pressure, help in attaining self-confidence, an addiction (dependence) to tobacco, the desire to be an adult all contribute to teenage smoking.

Perhaps the greatest reason why young people continue to smoke is that they feel they can drop the habit at any time. Being young, they can stop before harmful effects begin. But statistics have shown that 80% of the adults now smoking started in their youth.

The surgeon general of the United States, in his "Report on Health Promotion and Disease Prevention," has said, "Cigarette smoking is the single most preventable cause of death." If you smoke, stop while you are young.

If you smoke, stop while you're young. You'll find good reasons to do so in this chapter.

Cigarettes and Health

Mouth. Just one cigarette causes "cigarette breath" and dulls the taste buds. The hot smoke is harmful to the mouth and throat tissues. Cigarette smoking plays a major role in causing cancer of the oral cavity and larynx.

Teeth. Tar stains the teeth, causing brown spots.

Bronchioles (**bron**-kee-ohls). As smoke is drawn into the breathing passages, harmful gases and particles settle into the surrounding membranes (bronchioles). One point of great concentration is where the bronchus divides into left and right bronchi. This is also where most lung cancer begins.

Fingers. Cigarettes cause yellow stains on fingers.

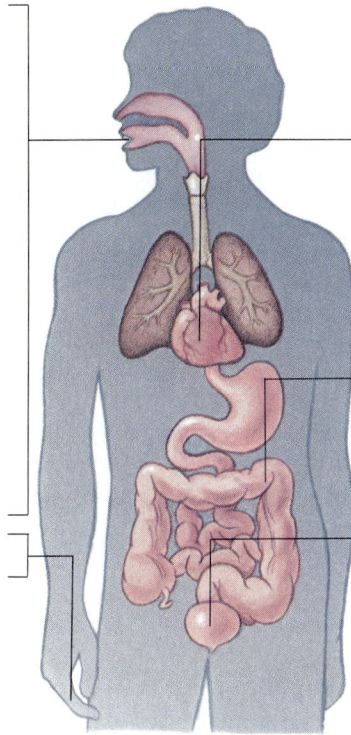

Heart and circulatory system. Nicotine causes blood vessels to constrict (to narrow), forcing the heart to pump faster and increase blood pressure. Smokers have a higher death rate from strokes. Smoking is also a risk factor in the development of vascular disease, affecting the circulation in the arms, hands, feet, and legs.

Gastrointestinal tract. Cigarette smoking appears to be connected to increased illness and a higher death rate from peptic ulcers. Cigarette smoking reduces the effectiveness of standard ulcer treatment and slows the rate of ulcer healing.

Bladder. Smokers have 7 to 10 times greater risk of bladder cancer than nonsmokers.

What Is in a Cigarette?

With each puff of a cigarette, a smoker comes in contact with more than 3,000 chemicals. Tobacco contains **nicotine**, (**nick**-ah-teen), *a poisonous drug stimulant that acts on the adrenal glands and heart tissue.* It is responsible for the rise in blood pressure and the increase in heartbeat that results from smoking a cigarette. Nicotine is also the addictive substance in cigarettes.

The "flavor" of a cigarette is due mostly to the tar in tobacco. **Tar** is *a thick, dark liquid obtained from burning the tobacco.* This tar consists of hundreds of known **carcinogens** (kar-**sin**-ah-jins), *cancer-causing agents.* The tar penetrates the smoker's airways and lungs. The tar forms a brown, sticky substance in the lining of the air sacs of the lungs, destroying some and damaging others.

Carbon monoxide (mah-**nock**-side) is a *colorless, odorless poisonous gas* in cigarette smoke that passes through the lungs and into the blood. This is the same gas that makes automobile fumes dangerous. It unites with the

See the Health Handbook, *page HB19, for tobacco smoke dangers to smokers and nonsmokers.*

body's hemoglobins, preventing them from carrying the oxygen needed for energy to the body's cells.

When tobacco smoke is inhaled, it causes the **cilia** (**sih**-lee-ah), *the hairlike projections along the respiratory tract that act as filters for air particles*, to slow down. Eventually, the cilia stop functioning, thus allowing foreign particles into the respiratory tract.

Dangers of Smoking

Cigarette smoking is responsible for approximately 320,000 deaths in the United States each year. Lung cancer, directly linked to cigarette smoking, is the leading cause of cancer death among men. With the increase in female smokers, lung cancer is becoming a more significant cause of cancer death among women.

Cigarette smoking during pregnancy is associated with small fetal growth, an increased chance of spontaneous abortion and prenatal death, increased stillbirths, and a low birth weight, as well as growth and developmental problems during early childhood.

Nicotine constricts the blood vessels of the fetus in the mother's uterus, as carbon monoxide reduces the oxygen level in the mother's and baby's blood. Smoking is especially harmful during the second half of pregnancy.

Smoking and the Respiratory System

Cigarette smoking is a major factor associated with the two principal diseases that constitute **chronic obstructive pulmonary diseases** (*COPD*). They are *chronic bronchitis* and *pulmonary emphysema.*

Chronic bronchitis (**kran**-ick bron-**kite**-iz) is a condition characterized by *persistent, recurring, excessive mucous secretion of the bronchial tree.* Its primary symptom is a chronic cough. (See also Chapter 18 on the respiratory system.)

Pulmonary emphysema (**pull**-mah-ner-ee em-fah-**zee**-mah) involves *the destruction of the tiny air sacs in the lungs through which oxygen is absorbed into the body.* As the walls between the sacs are destroyed, they lose their elasticity, becoming larger and thus providing less total surface from which oxygen can be absorbed. More breaths are required and, instead of using 5% of one's energy in breathing, a person with advanced emphysema uses up to 80% of personal energy strength just to breathe. (See also Chapter 18 on the respiratory system.)

Smoking and the Circulatory System

You already know that nicotine makes the heart work harder. Cigarette smoking also tends to increase the formation of fatty deposits in the arteries, increasing the chance of arteriosclerosis (hardening of the arteries) and gradually clogging the blood vessels to the heart.

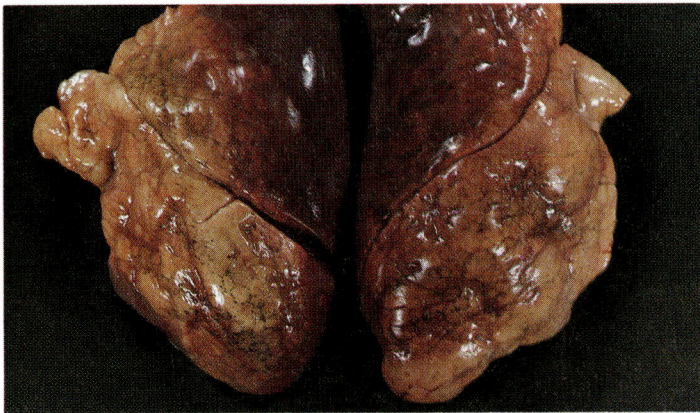
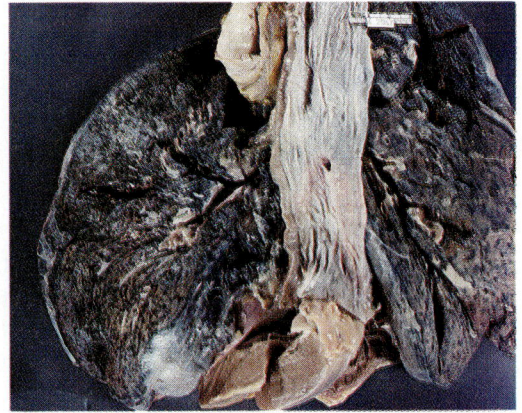

Left. *Normal lungs.* Right. *Smoker's lungs which are cancerous.*

Cigarette smoking also damages the heart. The risk of sudden death from heart disease is three times greater for smokers than nonsmokers. This risk increases to as much as five times greater for those who smoke more than a pack a day.

If a smoker has high blood pressure and/or high cholesterol, the risks of coronary heart disease are even greater. Experts estimate that if all Americans stopped smoking, deaths from heart disease could be cut by almost a third, saving more than 200,000 lives in a year.

Smoking Pipes and Cigars

While we have been mainly discussing cigarette smoking, the smoking of pipes and cigars cannot be excluded. Pipe and cigar smokers inhale less smoke, but they are more liable to contract cancer of the lip, mouth, and throat, since more tar and other chemicals are generated by pipes and cigars. If the pipe or cigar smoker makes it a habit to inhale the smoke, the chances of lung cancer increase.

Smokeless Tobacco

Many people believe that chewing tobacco is safer than smoking tobacco. These users claim they are not taking in smoke or putting smoke into the air. Advertisements using famous people to promote smokeless tobacco have contributed to an increase in its use, especially among teenagers. The picture of the cowboy or macho-type athlete using smokeless tobacco gives the impression that chewing and dipping contribute to one's masculinity.

Chewing tobacco is the process of *chewing on tobacco leaf*, usually storing it between the inner cheek and the gum. **Dipping** is the *use of small packets of pulverized* tobacco (also called *snuff*) placed between the inner cheek and gum. The pouch becomes wet with saliva and the tobacco taste fills the mouth. People are not supposed to chew these pouches, but some do.

Dangers of Smokeless Tobacco

Although smoke does not get into the lungs, smokeless tobacco presents some other health problems.

1. The nicotine in the tobacco is habit forming, or addictive.
2. Persons who chew or dip have an increased amount of saliva. Although the chewers usually spit out the saliva, they do swallow some without realizing it. This introduces tar and other chemicals into the digestive and urinary systems. Tobacco juices also contain chemicals that may delay wound healing.
3. Users of smokeless tobacco also develop bad breath and discolored teeth. Tobacco products decrease the user's ability to taste and smell, especially salty and sweet foods.
4. Tobacco and its by-products are extremely irritating to the sensitive tissues in the mouth. Irritation from direct contact with tobacco juices is responsible for **leukoplakia** (lou-kou-**plah**-key-uh), *thickened, white leathery-appearing spots on the inside of a smokeless tobacco user's mouth.* These areas can develop oral cancer. Cancer of the mouth and throat is four times more common among snuff dippers. Cancer of the gums and of the lining of the mouth is 50 times more common among dippers.
5. Smokeless tobacco users also tend to show greater tooth wear than nonusers. In the area where the tobacco is held, the gums tend to be pushed away from the teeth. The roots of the teeth become exposed and more susceptible to decay.

Specialty Cigarettes

Specialty cigarettes are *those prepared with tobacco and other ingredients.* The most common specialty cigarette is the clove cigarette, which contains about 60% tobacco and 40% cloves. Most of these cigarettes are imported from Indonesia and have been used in this country since the 1970s.

At one point in the early 1980s, young people started smoking them and sales increased from 15 million in 1980 to over 165 million in 1984. Because there have been complaints of lung problems and possible deaths as a result of smoking clove cigarettes, sales have dropped sharply in recent years. State boards are now investigating the possible harmful effects of the cigarettes.

CHECK YOURSELF

1. What do you think is the significance of the World Health Organization's statement in relation to wellness?
2. What are the main substances in cigarettes that affect our health?
3. What are the two major chronic obstructive pulmonary diseases?
4. What is the relationship between cigarette smoking and colds?
5. Compare the health hazards of smoking with chewing or dipping.

2. Consideration of the Nonsmoker

There is increasing concern and interest in this country and around the world that the nonsmoker is being affected by the smoke of those using cigarettes, pipes, and cigars.

Sidestream smoke—*smoke inhaled by nonsmokers*—contains the same harmful ingredients as the smoke inhaled by the smoker. However, smoke from a burning cigarette, which has not been filtered by the tobacco during inhaling, contains twice as much nicotine and tar and five times as much carbon monoxide as exists in inhaled smoke.

A smoke-filled room may have levels of carbon monoxide and other pollutants as high as those which occur during an air-pollution emergency. A nonsmoker could inhale enough nicotine and carbon monoxide in an hour to have the same effect as having smoked a whole cigarette.

Sidestream smoke causes eye irritation, headaches, and coughing. Lengthy exposure to these conditions can result in the same kinds of health problems that the smoker may experience.

If you smoke, it is considerate to ask others in an enclosed area if they mind your smoking. It is also appropriate to avoid smoking in very small, poorly ventilated areas, or in the presence of small children or people who have lung or heart problems.

Rights of a Nonsmoker

As a nonsmoker, you have a right to express that you prefer people not smoke around you. You are only protecting the air that you breathe. You will also find that your clothes and hair will smell of smoke if you are near smokers for any length of time.

If you are allergic to smoke, speak up and let people know. If you are out in a restaurant, ask for the nonsmoking section or at least to be seated

---

HEALTH UPDATE   HEALTH UPDATE   HEALTH UPDATE

Smoking Hazards

- Children of smoking parents have poorer lung function and a higher incidence of wheezing and respiratory infections.
- Annually, at least 25,000 people are injured and $313 million in propery is lost as a result of fires caused by smoking, especially in bed.
- Smokers who smoke a pack a day double their risk of heart attack and are ten times as likely to get lung cancer during their lifetime.

Supporting a New Nonsmoker

As a nonsmoker, you can be the support a person needs to be successful in kicking the habit. Encourage the person who is trying to quit.

Leave the person little treats —a candy cane, a nonsmoker's pin, an apple—with positive messages for keeping up the effort. Invite your friend to join you in activities where he or she will not be around smokers.

Exercise with your friend. Call the person at different times just to see how he or she is doing. Your supportive efforts could be what makes the difference.

away from the smokers. If you are a member of some group or club, ask that no smoking be allowed during meetings, or at least that the smokers are near ventilated areas or windows. Many cities have laws which restrict smoking in public places, such as restaurants, civic buildings, and business offices.

The Nonsmokers' Bill of Rights

In January 1974, the National Interagency Council on Smoking and Health adopted the **Nonsmokers' Bill of Rights**. The bill declared three basic rights of the nonsmoker:

- **The Right to Breathe Clean Air**. Nonsmokers have the right to breathe air that is free from harmful tobacco smoke.
- **The Right to Speak Out**. Nonsmokers have the right to express their discomfort when they are around tobacco smoke.
- **The Right to Act**. Nonsmokers have the right to work toward passing laws to prevent or restrict smoking, especially in public places.

CHECK YOURSELF

1. What is sidestream smoke?
2. How does sidestream smoke affect the nonsmoker?
3. What are your rights as a nonsmoker?

3. Kicking the Habit

Many programs are available for people who want to quit smoking. Some people use a series of filters over a period of weeks. Each filter reduces the tar and nicotine levels. Other people have used hypnosis and **aversion** (aah-**ver**-shun) **therapy**—*a technique in which the smokers experience unpleasant feelings each time they smoke, so that they make a negative association.*

Whatever technique a person uses, the critical key to being successful is that the smoker fully recognizes that the power for changing any habit or behavior lies within the individual. In the case of cigarette smoking, a person must feel in control over the habit, not the reverse. With this recognition, a person has a better chance of changing a behavior.

Tips for Quitting

Here are some positive steps that smokers can take to quit smoking:

- Identify the times when they reach for a cigarette out of habit.
- Change their daily routine so they do not think about smoking.

- Make a list of the reasons they want to quit smoking, and read it when they feel they want a cigarette.
- Chew gum, suck on a small piece of candy, or munch on a carrot stick when they feel a desire for a cigarette.
- Drink plenty of water.
- Avoid alcohol, coffee, and tea for the first week. These substances often stimulate a craving for tobacco.
- Exercise.
- Think in terms of quitting for a few minutes, then one hour, and then one day. Each hour, each day, a person can say, "I choose not to smoke today."
- Take deep breaths to aid relaxation when the craving to smoke gets strong.
- Brush their teeth often to remove the tobacco residue.
- Make an appointment to get their teeth cleaned so that tobacco stains are removed.
- If they are cutting down, they should set a goal for their zero-cigarette date.
- Get rid of smoking reminders—ashtrays, matches, lighters, etc.
- During the first few weeks, avoid people who smoke and situations that are conducive to smoking.
- When they get the urge to smoke, delay it for two to three minutes. During those few minutes, they should think of something else and change what they are doing.
- Plan a reward for themselves each time they resist lighting up.
- Become aware of improvements in how they feel, smell, and taste. They can use these as reinforcers for continuing.
- Get positive reinforcement and support from other nonsmoking friends.

Jogging and snacking on healthy foods are two ways to overcome the urge to smoke.

But Might I Gain Weight?

A common concern of smokers is the risk of weight gain if they try to quit. The U.S. Department of Health and Human Services reports the following information about people who have faced up to the habit and quit smoking:

- One-third gain weight because they substitute eating for smoking.
- One-third lose weight because they start a fitness program at the same time they stop smoking. They fill their need for smoking by eating carrot sticks or some other low-calorie snack.
- One-third of those who quit find their weight remains the same, neither more nor less.

CHECK YOURSELF

1. What is aversion therapy?
2. What is the most critical factor in successfully kicking the habit?
3. How can a support system help the smoker quit?
4. What points would you stress in helping someone set up a program to quit?

CHAPTER 11   Review

CHAPTER SUMMARY

- Some of the most conclusive research in the area of health behavior and wellness deals with the impact of smoking on one's health. Smoking is directly linked to respiratory and circulatory diseases, as well as a variety of other health-related problems.
- Smokeless tobacco contains the same chemicals as cigarette tobacco, but without the smoke. The chewer and dipper are both more susceptible to bad breath, stained teeth, and oral cancer than is the nonuser.
- Nonsmokers are also faced with health hazards when in the company of smokers. Sidestream smoke causes eye, head, and respiratory irritations. The nonsmoker inhales the same chemicals as the smoker.
- Many programs can help a person kick the habit. Motivation for quitting, however, must come from within. Smokers must recognize their personal desire to quit and believe they are in control.

REVIEWING WHAT YOU LEARNED

1. What are some of the benefits of being a nonsmoker?
2. What evidence could you cite that would support the idea that "cigarette smoking and tobacco use in general are hazardous to your health"? Give at least two examples.
3. Why should such attention be given to the rights of the nonsmoker?
4. Is smokeless tobacco a good choice as an alternative to smoking cigarettes? Explain your answer and present it to the class.
5. Why are pipe smoking and cigar smoking dangerous to your health?
6. What are specialty cigarettes?
7. What are three ways to quit smoking?
8. Name two obstacles one faces in trying to give up smoking.
9. Take the words *chronic, obstructive,* and *pulmonary* apart and explain what they mean. You can use a dictionary.

nicotine
tar
carcinogens
carbon monoxide
cilia

chronic obstructive pulmonary
   diseases
chronic bronchitis
pulmonary emphysema

chewing tobacco
dipping
leukoplakia
specialty cigarettes

sidestream smoke
Nonsmokers' Bill
   of Rights
adversion therapy

PUTTING VOCABULARY TO USE

Note the underlined words below. If the statement is false, substitute the correct word(s) from the chapter vocabulary. Do this on a separate piece of paper.

1. The flavor of the cigarette comes from the <u>nicotine</u>.
2. The <u>tar</u> consists of several cancer-producing agents.
3. Anything that causes cancer is known as a <u>pathogen</u>.

4. The two most common chronic, obstructive, pulmonary diseases are <u>lung cancer</u> and <u>pulmonary emphysema</u>.
5. The Nonsmokers' <u>Charter of Liberty</u> is primarily aimed at protecting nonsmokers.
6. Sidestream smoke is the <u>smoke of the smoker that the nonsmoker takes in</u>.
7. Leukoplakia is a condition associated with <u>cigarette smoking</u>.

APPLYING WHAT YOU LEARNED

1. Discuss the question of whether a physician has the right to refuse to treat a person for a disease related to smoking if the individual refuses to quit smoking.
2. Since cigarette smoking is clearly a hazard to health, what keeps it from being banned completely? (It kills thousands more people than illegal drugs.)
3. Do you know that over 95% of all people who quit smoking do so on their own, without the need for some organized program? What conclusions would you draw from this fact?
4. Even if you accept the tobacco industry's contention that there is no evidence that cigarette smoking causes cancer, what other arguments could you present against smoking?
5. You get home early one day and find your younger sister smoking a cigarette. What would you do?
6. Research shows that children whose parents smoke are more likely to smoke themselves. Why do you think this is true?

7. Your community is having a vote on whether or not to ban smoking in all public places—parks, grocery stores, etc. Write a one-page editorial expressing your views on this vote. Present it to the class.
8. Interview five ex-smokers to determine how they quit and how successful they have been. Draw some conclusions about their similarities in successfully kicking the habit.
9. Find out what current legislation is being considered relating to tobacco. How would the legislation affect the tobacco industry? How would it affect the health of the consumer?
10. Some individuals have filed lawsuits against the tobacco industry because family members died of lung cancer due to smoking. Find out what the arguments on each side were. Which side would you support? Defend your answer.

FOCUS ON WELLNESS

Cigarette smoking is the "number one" health risk in this country. *I will do my part to reduce this senseless risk and cause of illness and death by . . .*

Alcohol–A Risk to Your Well-Being

Perhaps the most misused drug in our society is alcohol. As a matter of fact, many people do not even consider alcohol to be a drug. A great deal of misinformation and misunderstanding about alcohol exists. Getting the correct facts will help you to know the dangers when someone asks you to take a drink.

After studying this chapter, you will be able to:
- explain the effects of alcohol on the body,
- describe what happens to alcohol when one takes a drink,
- explain what is meant by fetal alcohol syndrome,
- identify the factors that influence one's response to alcohol,
- list the reasons why young people drink and do not drink,
- list the indicators of a drinking problem,
- describe the stages of alcoholism,
- explain what kind of help is available to the alcoholic,
- describe the effects of drinking and driving.

Ethyl alcohol (**eth**-ull **al**-kuh-hall) is the active substance in distilled spirits, such as beer, wine, and liquor. *It is a natural substance formed by the chemical reaction of fermenting sugar and yeast.* **Fermentation** (fur-men-**tay**-shun) is *the process that produces alcohol by the action of yeast on sugar and starches.*

The source of the sugar varies with the type of alcoholic drink. The sugar source for beer is malted barley; for wine, it is berries or grapes; for whiskey, it is malted grains. Potatoes are the source of sugar for vodka, and molasses for rum.

Alcohol provides little of the taste, but all of the effect in intoxicating beverages. Because alcohol contains calories, it is a food substance. However, it has little or no nutritive value.

How Does Alcohol Work in the Body?

When someone has a drink, the alcohol follows the same path that food does in the digestive system. About 20% of the alcohol is absorbed directly into the bloodstream from the stomach. So within minutes after taking a drink, the alcohol is traveling through the body. The rest of the alcohol passes into the small intestine, where it is absorbed into the bloodstream.

12 oz. (340 g) of beer is equal to 5 oz. (142 g) of wine or 1½ oz. (42.5 g) of 80 proof liquor. "Proof" is an indicator of the concentration of alcohol in a beverage. Alcohol content is determined by dividing the proof number in half. (80 proof liquor has a 40% alcohol content.) The higher the proof, the greater the intoxicating powers of the liquor.

Alcohol in the Body

Brain. Alcohol reaches the brain almost as soon as it is drunk. It depresses the brain, slowing down the work of the nervous system. The brain loses its ability to control the mind and body.

Liver. The *liver changes the alcohol to water, carbon dioxide, and energy,* a process called **oxidation** (ox-suh-**day**-shun). The liver can oxidize only about ½ oz (14.2 g) of alcohol an hour. There is no way to speed up this process. Until the liver has time to oxidize all the alcohol, the alcohol keeps circulating through all body parts.

Bloodstream. The blood carries the alcohol to all parts of the body, including the heart, liver, and brain. As alcohol enters the circulatory system, it widens the blood vessels. This makes the skin feel flush and warm. Don't be fooled, however, for it is an artificial warmth. The rise of blood flow through the skin really causes the body to lose heat—body temperature actually decreases.

Kidneys. Alcohol affects the kidneys by causing them to produce more urine. (This is done indirectly. Alcohol affects the pituitary gland, which, in turn, acts on the kidneys.) This is one reason why a person feels dehydrated the day after heavy drinking.

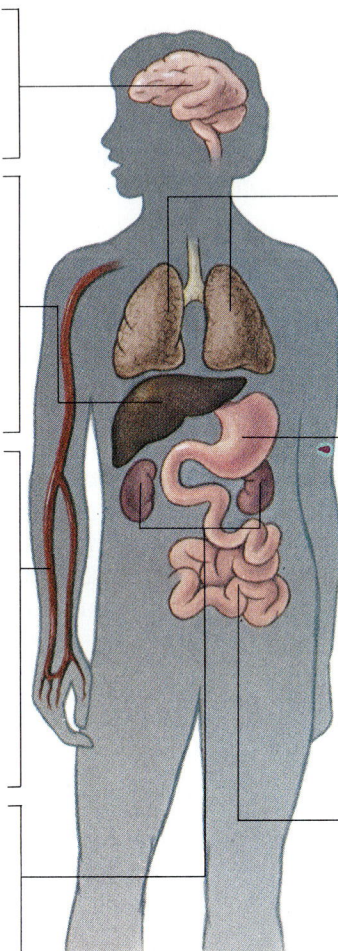

Lungs. When you inhale alcohol fumes, the alcohol is absorbed through the lungs, going quickly to the brain. Have you ever smelled someone's breath after a drink? Alcohol is eliminated in small amounts through the lungs as a person exhales.

Stomach. The alcohol molecule is very small and water soluble. It does not have to be digested. It can be immediately absorbed into the blood vessels in the stomach. By having food in the stomach, the absorption process is slowed. In small amounts, alcohol increases the flow of gastric juices from the stomach lining. Larger amounts of alcohol cause a larger flow of this high-acidity juice, irritating the stomach lining. Repeated irritation can cause an open sore called an *ulcer.*

Small intestine. Although some absorption of alcohol takes place in the stomach, most occurs in the first section of the small intestine. In contrast, food has to pass far into the latter two-thirds of the small intestine before absorption can take place.

Alcohol acts like a **sedative** (**sed**-uh-tive), *a substance that depresses or quiets the central nervous system.* Why then do people become talkative or more outgoing when they drink? As the inhibition center of the brain is slowed, the person relaxes. Drinkers may say and do things they normally would not say and do. Muscle coordination is impaired, a drinker becomes clumsy, and speech is slurred.

About 5% of the alcohol taken into the body is eliminated through the kidneys, lungs, and body perspiration. The remaining 95% is eliminated through the liver.

Special Consideration for the Liver

The liver is the largest gland in the body. It is also one that researchers are still studying. Scientists have identified over 500 functions of the liver, some of which include:

- a storage place for digested food,
- a regulator of the level of blood sugar,
- a chemical factory in which fats are changed,
- a filtering system for the blood,
- a digestive organ and an organ of excretion.

Alcohol interferes with the liver's ability to break down fats. As fats accumulate in the liver, a condition known as *fatty liver* develops. Excess fat interferes with normal metabolism in liver cells. It also causes a slowing of the reproductive activity of the liver cells.

As a result, worn-out cells are not replaced as quickly as they normally would be. Fat obstructs the normal blood flow in the liver cells, resulting in oxygen deficiency and cell death. This condition has been found in both heavy and moderate drinkers. It can be reversed when drinking stops.

Heavy alcohol use destroys tissues in the liver, and they are replaced with useless scar tissue. This condition is called **cirrhosis** (suh-**row**-sis), which means *scarring*. Blood flow through the liver is decreased and the functioning of the liver is impaired. The symptoms of cirrhosis are jaundice, a tendency toward infection, high blood pressure, hemorrhages, and abdominal swelling.

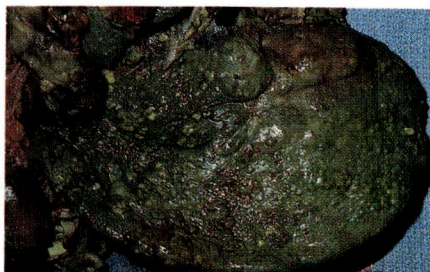

The left photo shows a normal liver. The right photo shows a liver scarred by heavy alcohol use. This condition is called cirrhosis of the liver.

Fetal Alcohol Syndrome

In recent years, researchers have found that women who drink heavily during pregnancy run a high risk of *giving birth to children who show physical, mental, and behavioral abnormalities and birth defects*. This condition is called the **fetal alcohol syndrome** (**feet**-ull **al**-kuh-hall **sin**-drum). The babies who had this syndrome were shorter and lighter in weight than normal, had impaired speech, cleft palate, general weakness, slow body growth, facial abnormalities, poor coordination, and heart defects.

Behaviorally, mental retardation, poor attention spans, nervousness, and hyperactivity are common. Some infants are born with all of these characteristics, and some are born with only a few.

The alcohol that the mother takes in is passed into her bloodstream, then across the placenta into the bloodstream of the unborn infant. So if the mother drinks enough to become drunk, the infant becomes drunk as well.

Unfortunately, the underdeveloped infant cannot rid the body of alcohol as an adult can, and so the alcohol remains in the body much longer. If this heavy drinking is done on a three-to-four-day-a-week basis, chances are that the unborn infant never fully rids its body of alcohol. And the unborn infant cannot say "No" when it has had enough.

What is important is that fetal alcohol syndrome is completely preventable. It does not occur in nondrinking pregnant women. Each woman has the choice. If one must drink, it is recommended that the person take no more than one drink a day. However, it is wise to remember that research has not yet found out precisely what is safe, and when the most critical period is in the pregnancy for consuming alcohol.

CHECK YOURSELF

1. How does alcohol absorption compare with the absorption of food?
2. What is the liver's role in processing alcohol in the body?
3. How is alcohol eliminated from the body?
4. What is fetal alcohol syndrome?

2. Factors Affecting Alcohol in the Body

Alcohol's effect on the body is measured by *the proportional weight of alcohol per 100 units of blood, expressed as a percentage*. This is called the **blood alcohol level**, or **BAL**.

The Blood Alcohol Level

The chart on page 211 describes the effects of alcohol on the body at various BALs. This is based on a 100-pound (45 kg) person and the amount of alcohol consumed over a two-hour period. Four factors affect the amount of alcohol in a person's blood:

1. the amount of alcohol a person drinks, not the number of drinks;
2. whether or not the person eats before or while drinking;
3. how much the person weighs;
4. how much time elapses after drinking stops or between drinks.

Individual Alcohol Intake

BAL	Approximate Alcohol Consumed in a Two-Hour Period	Effect on a 100-Pound Body
0.05%	1 to 2 oz (28.3 to 57 g) liquor 1 to 2 12-oz (340 g each) bottles of beer	Mild impairment in reaction time and judgment, careless behavior, some loss of coordination and self-control.
0.1%	3 to 4 oz (85 to 113 g) liquor 3 to 4 12-oz (340 g each) bottles of beer	Substantial impairment in muscle coordination, perception, and judgment. Emotions and inhibitions are relaxed.
0.2%	5 to 6 oz (142 to 170 g) liquor 5 to 6 12-oz (340 g each) bottles of beer	Increased loss of self-control, difficulty in thinking clearly, impaired memory. Unpredictable emotional behavior. Entire motor area of brain is depressed. Slurred speech, staggered walk. Simple tasks, like buttoning a coat, become difficult to impossible.
0.3%	7 to 8 oz (198 to 226 g) liquor 7 to 8 12-oz (340 g each) bottles of beer	Body thrown into state of confusion, sense organs seriously affected— double vision, hearing impaired, distances difficult or impossible to judge—may be in a stupor, walking is difficult and dangerous to person.
0.4%	9 to 10 oz (255 to 283 g) liquor 9 to 10 12-oz (340 g each) bottles of beer	Brain can barely function, nervous system shuts down, may experience vomiting or uncontrolled urination, unable to move, may slip into unconscious state.
0.5%	More than 10 oz (283 g) liquor More than 10 12-oz (340 g each) bottles of beer	Coma, brain unable to control body temperature—respiratory failure due to paralysis of breathing centers of brain. When this occurs, death will soon occur.

In almost all states, driving while intoxicated is defined as reaching the 0.1% BAL.

Factors Influencing the Effects of Alcohol

Some people get loud and silly when they have an alcoholic drink. Others get sleepy. Some get happy, others get sad. What factors determine how alcohol affects the drinker?

- *How much a person drinks.* The amount of alcohol taken into the body will affect the body's reactions.
- *How fast a person drinks.* The faster a person consumes alcohol or the more that a person drinks in a short period of time, the greater the effect.
- *How much a person weighs.* A heavy person has more blood and water in the body, thus diluting the alcohol. A light or smaller person is likely to feel the effects of alcohol sooner than a heavier person.
- *How much drinking a person has done in the past.* The body builds up a tolerance to alcohol. More alcohol is needed to feel its effects.
- *How much food a person has eaten.* Food in the stomach slows the effect of alcohol on the body.
- *What a person expects and may want drinking to do.* If a person believes that drinking will depress him or her, it probably will.
- *How a person feels when drinking.* The drinker's mood makes a difference.
- *Where a person drinks.* The situation and environment in which the person drinks can make a difference in the effect.

Alcohol's Effects on the Brain

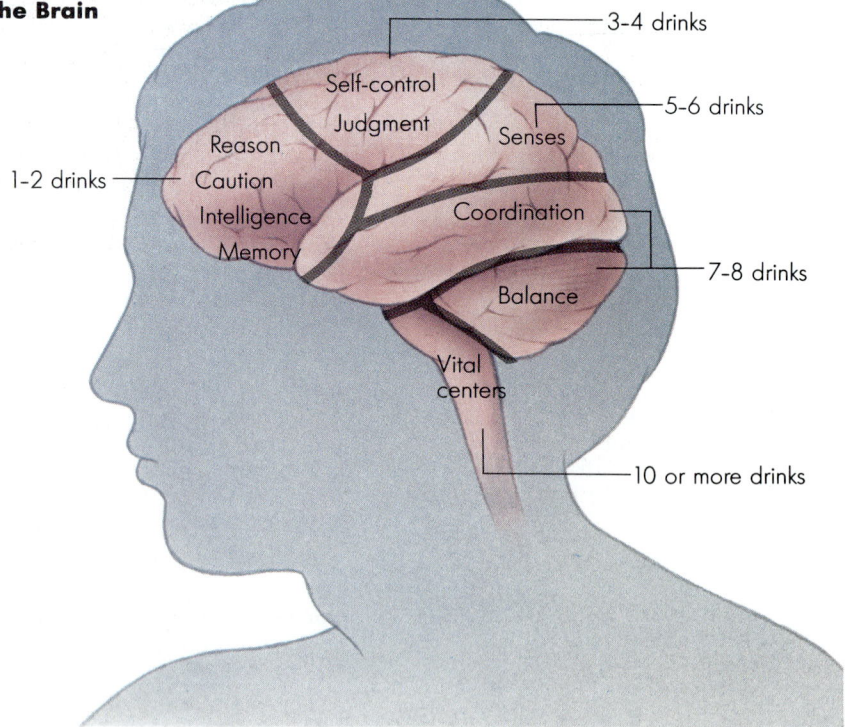

Brain diagram labels: 3-4 drinks, 5-6 drinks, 7-8 drinks, 10 or more drinks, 1-2 drinks. Self-control, Judgment, Senses, Reason, Caution, Intelligence, Memory, Coordination, Balance, Vital centers.

Alcohol not only affects the control centers of the brain, it can also kill brain cells.

Mixing Alcohol and Other Drugs— A Deadly Combination

When *a person takes alcohol with other drugs*, this is called the **multiplier effect**. When the person takes other sedatives, like tranquilizers, with alcohol, their effects are drastically increased. Almost all such accidental deaths result from combining alcohol with other drugs. Even over-the-counter drugs like aspirin alter the way that alcohol affects the body. Some of the reactions become unpredictable.

CHECK YOURSELF

1. What factors are considered in measuring a person's BAL?
2. List the effects of alcohol on the brain.
3. What reasons can you give for the various reactions people have to alcohol?
4. Why is the multiplier effect so dangerous?

3. Alcohol—A Social Problem

As we have already stated, many people do not even consider alcohol to be a drug. As the consumption of alcohol increases, evidence shows that people's attitude toward alcohol also may be getting more lax. The legal drinking age was reduced in many states. Now many states are reconsidering that decision in light of the great number of traffic fatalities that have been associated with drinking while driving, especially among young people.

Attitudes Toward Alcohol

In a survey of adults to determine how they perceived alcohol as a health threat, alcohol was ranked eleventh. The following list, compiled in the late 1970s and still valid, shows how the adults surveyed ranked the health risks.

Health Threat	% of Group		Health Threat	% of Group
1. Industrial waste	59%		7. Overweight	52%
2. Pollution	58%		8. Pesticides	47%
3. Marijuana	58%		9. Tranquilizers	43%
4. Crash diets	55%		10. Cholesterol	42%
5. Cigarettes	55%		11. Alcohol	41%
6. Diet pills	52%			

The survey results also show that only 19% of these adults considered alcoholism to be a health problem—a disease. Almost all saw it as a personal emotional weakness.

In our culture, which has 10 million alcoholics or problem drinkers, moderation in drinking is held as the acceptable standard. Drunkenness is not accepted, and chronic drunkenness leads to being a social outcast.

What does all of this have to do with you? Many factors influence decisions about drinking, one of which is society's general attitude toward alcohol. You can learn about all the problems associated with drinking and the effect of alcohol on the body. But what do you consider when you are making your decisions about alcohol?

Why Young People Drink

The reasons that teenagers give for drinking often are not very different from the reasons that adults give:

- to escape pressures or problems,
- to feel better, to get over being sad or lonely,
- to relax,
- to gain more self-confidence, to feel better about oneself.

Another important influence on teenagers' choice to drink is friends. There is pressure to drink, and it can be difficult to say no, especially when

Avoiding Drinking

Look at each of the reasons for drinking as they relate to emotional needs. Drinking to meet these needs is not a very healthy choice. Why? What other reasons do students give for drinking?

HEALTH UPDATE   HEALTH UPDATE   HEALTH UPDATE

Drinking Statistics

According to the Alcohol, Drug Abuse, and Mental Health Administration, alcoholism and problem drinking cost the economy over $71 million a day—$27 million in lost work, $23 million in health and medical costs, $18 million in motor accidents, $2 million in research and prevention programs, and $1.4 million in criminal justice costs.

According to the U.S. Department of Health and Human Services, alcohol plays a role in:

- 37 out of every 100 suicides,
- 70 out of every 100 murders,
- 50 out of every 100 arrests,
- 20,500 deaths a year and more mental hospital admissions than any other cause.

Other facts about drinking are these:

- Between 45 and 60% of all fatal crashes involving a young person are alcohol-related.
- Approximately one-half of all fire deaths involve drinking.
- Over 50% of drowning victims had been drinking.
- About 50% of those who died in falling accidents had been drinking.

you want to be accepted as a part of the group. When many social gatherings center around alcohol, it may be hard to feel a part of what is going on if you are not drinking.

Another factor that influences teenagers' drinking behavior is the family. The example the family sets regarding drinking influences the young person's attitudes and behavior. If the drinking behavior the young person sees is problematic, chances are greater that the young person will turn to alcohol when he or she has problems.

In Chapter 5, you read about emotional needs. Everyone has the need to belong, to feel loved, and to be important. We can go about meeting these needs in many ways. Does drinking to be part of a group meet an emotional need? For how long? Are you meeting the need if you are being accepted because of *what you are doing* rather than *who you are*?

Why Young People Choose Not to Drink

So much attention is focused on the reasons for teenage drinking that the nondrinking teenage group is often slighted. Why do 20 to 30 million young Americans choose not to drink?

The most common reason given for not drinking is, "I don't need it." This is a rather simple statement, but a very deep one. Perhaps the person is really saying, "I don't have to drink to be popular" or "I don't need to

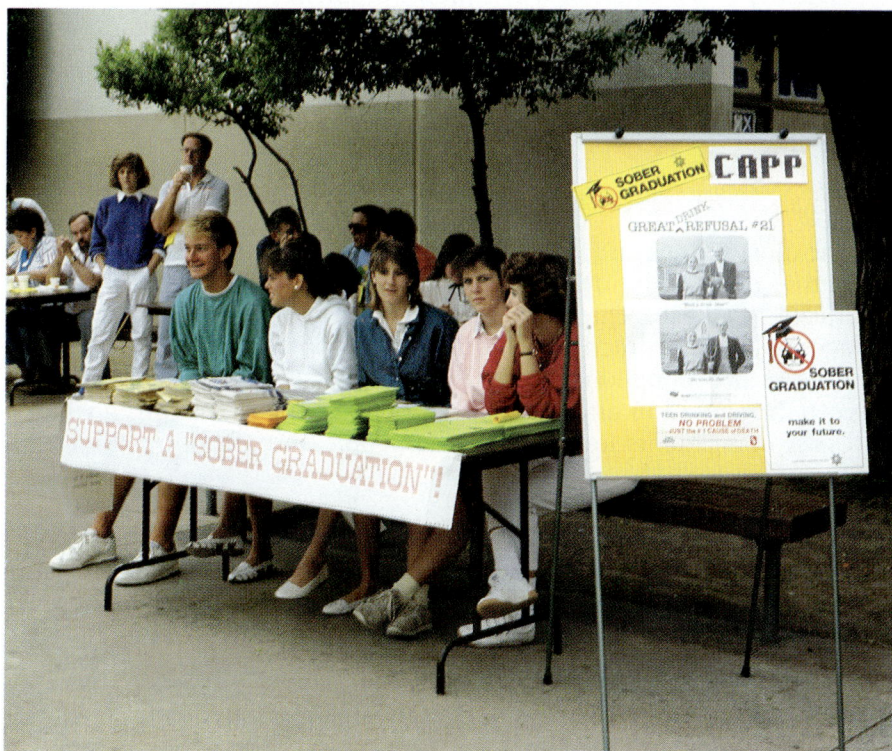

Drinking can harm the drinker, as well as friends and family. There are many school programs that encourage young people not to drink.

The Designated Driver

People going to a party now identify a "designated driver" when they leave for an evening. That person does not drink and is the one who drives the others home.

drink to be accepted, to have fun, or to relieve inhibitions." Can you say "I don't need it"? Other reasons given for not drinking include:

- It makes me sick.
- I hate the taste.
- It costs too much.
- It leads to other problems.
- I don't want to lose control of what is going on.
- I want to enjoy what is going on around me.
- It's harmful to my health.
- My parents are opposed to it.
- I would be breaking training rules.
- And last (but not least), it is against the law to buy or possess alcohol.

When Drinking Becomes a Problem

Problem drinkers are those who drink and lose control of themselves. Many are not yet alcoholics—people who are addicted to alcohol—but they may become so if they keep up their drinking habits.

It is estimated that 1.3 million teenagers are problem drinkers. Of this group, 750,000 are alcoholics. Usually the physical problems that develop with older alcoholics are not present in young alcoholics. This is due primarily to the fact that many of the problems that older people have are a result of many years of drinking.

Whether it is a cause or a symptom, problem drinkers have difficulties with family, school, and police. This becomes *circular*, meaning that if you had some problems at home in the first place, and then started drinking, the drinking would probably lead to more family problems. This points up the futility of drinking as a solution to one's problems.

Drinking and Driving

The most serious and widespread problem involving drinking and the law is that of drunken driving. This has become a serious problem for Americans of all ages. One reason why it is particularly a problem for the teenager is because much of the drinking is done in and around cars.

In 1983, over 6 million reported traffic accidents were caused by drivers between the ages of 15 and 20. Nearly 12,000 young Americans are killed each year in accidents involving young people and alcohol.

What Effect Can Alcohol Have on Driving?

Automobile driving experts have scientifically tested the driving ability of skilled racing drivers before and after giving them alcohol. These are the effects on one's driving after three or four average drinks:

- reduced ability to judge distances, speeds, turns,
- reduced ability to accurately judge one's own ability,
- greater tendency to take risks,

One-half of all auto accidents are caused by drivers who have been drinking.

- impaired reflexes,
- forgetfulness, such as failing to signal,
- sleepiness, and inability to concentrate.

Why is drinking and driving such a serious problem? Because people are killed and many of the victims are innocent people. A person crossing a street, a youngster riding a bicycle, a group waiting at a bus stop could all fall victim to someone who has chosen to drive and drink.

CHECK YOURSELF

1. Write a summary statement describing people's general attitude toward alcohol.
2. Compare reasons teens give for drinking with reasons teens give for not drinking.
3. Why is drinking and driving such a dangerous combination?

4. Alcoholism

Alcoholism is *the physical and psychological addiction (dependence) to alcohol.* It develops in stages, and it can be difficult to distinguish between a problem drinker and an alcoholic. **Alcoholics** are people who may have one or a combination of these behaviors:

- *They cannot keep from drinking.*
- *They cannot manage tension without drinking.*
- *They cannot stop drinking once they have started.*

Alcoholics usually cannot drink in social situations. One drink leads to continued drinking until they are drunk. Alcohol is a disease that can strike anyone, and in some people it may have a hereditary link.

Stages of Alcoholism

There are three clearly defined stages of alcoholism. They happen over a period of time. The time span can be long or short, depending on the individual.

Stage One of Alcoholism

Alcoholism typically begins with social drinking, often to relax or to relieve stress. Gradually, this kind of drinking becomes necessary to manage stress. A physical and psychological dependency on alcohol develops. The person begins to drink and becomes intoxicated regularly. The drinker cannot remember with whom he or she was or what was said or done after each drinking episode. Often at this stage, the drinker makes excuses and tries to rationalize his or her drinking behavior.

Stage Two of Alcoholism

Gradually, the person reaches a point where he or she cannot stop drinking. Physical and mental problems become evident. At this stage of the disease, defensive behavior is evident. The drinker denies or tries to hide the problem. The body has developed a tolerance and more alcohol is necessary. Drinking becomes the central event in the person's life. Performance on the job, at school, or at home decreases. Frequent absences from school, work, or other commitments occur.

Stage Three of Alcoholism

In the final stage of the disease, the drinking is visible. It can no longer be denied, and it is also uncontrolled. Alcohol becomes a constant companion. The alcoholic is isolated from friends and family. Malnutrition becomes a problem because the drinker has lived on an alcohol diet.

The body is physically addicted to the drug. If the alcoholic stopped drinking, he or she would experience the *withdrawal symptoms* associated with alcoholism, called **delirium tremens** (de-**leer**-ee-um **trem**-enz) (DTs). They consist of hot and cold flashes, tremors, nightmares, hallucinations, and fear of people and animals.

The alcoholic may require hospitalization in order to be medically supervised while the body goes through **detoxification** (de-tox-suh-fah-**kay**-shun), *the process by which the poisonous effects of alcohol are lessened in the body.*

Help for Problem Drinking and Alcoholism

Although alcoholism cannot be cured, it definitely can be treated and arrested. As many as two-thirds of all alcoholics recover with proper treatment. Several sources are available to help people with a drinking problem.

The National Council on Alcoholism

The *National Council on Alcoholism* is the only national health agency founded to combat alcoholism. The council offers a list of organizations in more than 100 cities that offer assistance for the problem drinker and treatment to the alcoholic and his or her family. The Council's headquarters are at 2 Park Avenue, New York, NY 10017.

Alcoholics Anonymous

Perhaps the best known source for help is **Alcoholics Anonymous** (AA). In groups all over the world, every member of AA is a "recovered" or "recovering" alcoholic. The members provide support and help to others who are trying to achieve sobriety. There are no membership dues or requirements. All one needs to do is attend a meeting and have the desire to quit drinking. The AA locations are listed in the telephone book.

HEALTH UPDATE   HEALTH UPDATE   HEALTH UPDATE

When Does a Person Have a Drinking Problem?

This questionnaire is intended to show a person who drinks if his or her drinking is on the way to becoming a problem. You may wish to take it, too. On a separate sheet of paper, answer *yes* or *no* to each question.

1. Do you lose time from school because of drinking?
2. Do you drink to lose shyness and build self-confidence?
3. Is drinking affecting your reputation?
4. Do you drink to escape from study or home worries?
5. Does it bother you if somebody says that maybe you drink too much?
6. Do you have to take a drink to go out on a date?
7. Do you ever get into money troubles over buying alcoholic beverages?
8. Have you lost friends since you started drinking?
9. Do you hang out with a crowd that can get liquor easily?
10. Do your friends drink less than you do?
11. Do you drink until the bottle is empty?
12. Have you ever had a loss of memory from drinking?
13. Has drunk driving ever put you into the hospital or jail?
14. Do you get annoyed with classes on drinking?
15. Do *you* think you have a problem with alcohol?

Scoring: If you answered *yes* to one or two questions, consider it to be a warning. If you answered *yes* to three or four questions, alcohol has become a serious problem.

LIFE MANAGEMENT SKILL

Problem Drinking

Mentally answer this questionnaire and check your results. If it looks like you might have a drinking problem, talk to your counselor or contact one of the groups discussed on pages 219–220.

Alateen and Al-Anon

Two other groups have used the AA model for helping relatives of alcoholics. This is important since one in every four Americans is closely affected by an alcoholic's behavior.

Alateen is *a group that helps children and teenagers whose parent(s) are alcoholics.* **Al-Anon** is *a group that helps the husbands and wives and other friends and relatives of alcoholics.*

In these groups, people learn what they can do to help the alcoholic. They also learn how to help themselves live with an alcoholic. In meetings, people learn facts about the disease and receive support and encouragement from other members. The phone numbers for these helping groups are in the telephone book.

What You Can Do

If you have a friend or relative who has a problem with drinking, there are organizations that can help you. Here are suggestions for some ways in which you can best help the problem drinker.

- Do let the problem drinker know you are concerned and willing to help.
- Do try to remain calm when discussing the problem with the drinker.
- Do refuse to ride with the person if he or she has been drinking and is driving.
- Do not preach, nag, or make emotional pleas to the drinker.
- Do not make excuses or cover up for the drinker.
- Do not take over the problem drinker's responsibilities.
- Do not argue with the person when he or she is drunk.
- Do not turn your back on the problem.

Some last points to remember about alcoholism:

- It is a public health problem because it affects many more people than the alcoholic.
- It is a treatable illness.
- If untreated, it gets progressively worse, leading to deterioration of personal health and the ability to function effectively in school, work, social, and family life.

Alternatives to the Use of Alcohol

People who use alcohol must know when they have had enough—so that they do not harm themselves or other people. Such a person must have effective judgment and self-evaluative skills, and the willpower to withstand pressures to continue to drink when the personal limit is reached.

ANTABUSE

"What is Antabuse? How does it help with a drinking problem?"

Antabuse is a commercial name for a drug known as *disulfiram* (dis-**sul**-fear-am). It was discovered by two Danish physicians in 1948. They found the drug to be useful in combating alcoholism. Disulfiram can only be used with a doctor's prescription. It is not a cure for alcoholism. When a person who drinks alcohol takes the drug, he or she becomes very sick. Dizziness and vomiting result when alcohol mixes with the drug, which discourages a person.

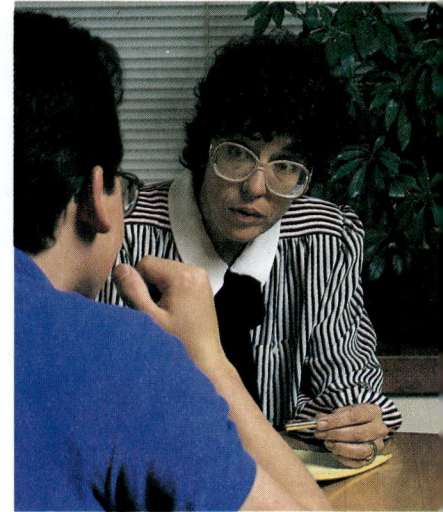

There are many alternatives to the use of alcohol—from asserting yourself to counseling.

Because a young person is still searching for the identity that usually comes with adulthood, these same decisions about *when* is enough, *when* to say "No," *when* not to drive, and *when* to get help are not so easy. In fact, they are very difficult, especially in the presence of the peer group.

If you are tempted to drink, try some of these suggestions:

- Find activities that do not center around alcohol.
- Challenge yourself to try new things or to find other ways to feel good about yourself and be accepted.
- Seek assistance for decision-making, problem-solving, and communication skills that will help to build your self-concept.
- Volunteer for programs to help others—Special Olympics, the elderly, Big Brothers and/or Big Sisters.
- Become a part of some group that supports your decision about alcohol and other values.
- Put yourself in positions that require some independent thinking, action, and responsibility, so that you can prove to yourself that you are capable and can make a contribution.
- Engage in regular physical activity as a way of telling yourself that you care about your body and your health enough to work at it on a regular basis.
- Practice asserting yourself. Say no to things you do not care to do. You will find it becomes easier with practice. You have a right to say no and a responsibility to care for yourself.

CHECK YOURSELF

1. Define alcoholism.
2. Describe the stages of alcoholism.
3. How would you describe problem drinking?
4. What help is available to problem drinkers?

ALCOHOL COUNSELOR

Alcoholism is a disease and reflects our problems with the most abused drug in our country. A large number of problem drinkers and alcoholics have not admitted that they have a problem with alcohol. For those who have decided to face their problem and to do something about it, many groups and organizations stand ready to help them. One of the vital components of any alcohol treatment program is the role of the **alcohol counselor.**

Alcohol counseling is a specialization in the general field of counseling. Degrees in psychology, social work, and counseling are good backgrounds for entering this field. Some colleges and universities offer specific training programs in alcohol and drug counseling. The laws and regulations that govern the licenses and credentials for these professionals vary from state to state.

Counseling of any kind requires individuals who relate well with many types of people and who have the ability to put their clients at ease. A counselor can gain great satisfaction from helping clients to deal with their personal problems and helping them to change and improve their personal lives.

The treatment of alcoholism takes many forms. There are volunteer agencies and groups designed to help the alcoholic. Special hospitals have been opened to deal specifically with the alcoholic. The alcohol counselor may work with alcoholics and with the families of alcoholics. The counselors also may engage in group counseling.

For more information about a career in this area, contact any college or university department of psychology, counseling, or social work.

CHAPTER 12   Review

CHAPTER SUMMARY

- Alcohol is absorbed directly into the bloodstream, and its effects can be felt almost immediately.
- Alcohol is a depressant drug. It reduces inhibitions, slows down the central nervous system, and affects all other systems.
- The primary task of ridding the body of alcohol rests with the liver. The rate at which the liver does this job, about one-half ounce of alcohol per hour, cannot be sped up.
- Several factors influence the effects of alcohol on the body, including body size, food in the stomach, the amount of alcohol consumed, and the span of time that elapses while drinking.
- Alcohol is both physically and psychologically addictive, and the body builds a tolerance to the drug—more is needed to feel its effects.
- Alcoholism is an addiction to alcohol that progresses in stages and in some way touches the lives of one in every four Americans.
- Groups and programs can help the alcoholic, as well as the alcoholic's family and friends. They include such organizations as Alcoholics Anonymous, Alateen, and Al-Anon.

CHAPTER VOCABULARY

ethyl alcohol	cirrhosis	alcoholism	Alcoholics Anonymous
fermentation	fetal alcohol syndrome	alcoholics	Alateen
sedative	blood alcohol level (BAL)	delirium tremens	Al-Anon
oxidation	multiplier effect	detoxification	alcohol counselor

PUTTING VOCABULARY TO USE

On a separate sheet of paper, answer the following questions about the vocabulary terms.

1. What is *ethyl alcohol* and how is it used in making beer, wine, or liquor?
2. Define *fermentation*.
3. Name two symptoms of *cirrhosis of the liver*.
4. Is *fetal alcohol syndrome* preventable? If so, how?
5. How is *blood alcohol level* (BAL) determined?
6. What is *Alateen*? How does it differ from Alcoholics Anonymous?
7. What makes the *multiplier effect* especially dangerous where alcohol in the body is concerned?
8. What are the *stages of alcoholism*? Describe each.

REVIEWING WHAT YOU LEARNED

1. Identify the reasons why two people can drink the same amount of alcohol and have very different effects from it.
2. Explain how blood alcohol level (BAL) is used to determine the amount of alcohol in a person's body.
3. Describe what happens to the brain with 2, 4, 6, and 8 alcoholic drinks.
4. What is fetal alcohol syndrome?
5. List three reasons why people drink.
6. List three reasons why people do not drink alcohol.
7. Describe the three stages of alcoholism which a person may go through.
8. Explain how alcohol affects the liver.
9. What effect does alcohol have on one's driving?
10. What help is available for the problem drinker?

APPLYING WHAT YOU LEARNED

1. You have been invited into a seventh grade health class to teach about alcohol as a health problem. Outline the major points you would cover. How would you present the concept of wellness in relation to alcohol?
2. An organization called Mothers Against Drunk Drivers (MADD) has become very active in promoting stricter legislation on handling drunk drivers. Find out how MADD got started and what impact it has had. Find out what the penalties are in your community and in your state for drunk driving. Write a report on your findings.
3. Why do you think people who drink at parties try to get everyone else to drink also? What would you do in a situation in which your friends would not take no for an answer from you?
4. In some communities, third parties are held liable for accidents involving drunk drivers. This means the people having the party where alcohol is consumed are responsible for a person's drinking too much at the party, especially if the person insists on driving home. Or a bartender might be held legally responsible for continuing to serve someone who has had too much to drink and then not keeping the person from driving. Do you think the third party should be held responsible? Why? Why not?
5. You are getting ready to leave a party with your friend who has had too much to drink. Your friend insists on driving and is your only means of transportation home. What would you do?

FOCUS ON WELLNESS

Drinking while driving has become a national health and social problem. Thousands of innocent people die or are injured each year because of such irresponsible behavior. *Even though I might not be a driver, I can work to reduce this tragic waste of lives by . . .*

Drug Abuse and Illegal Drugs

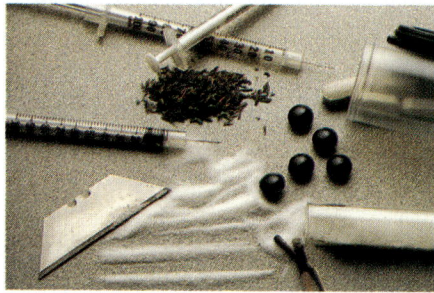

You have read elsewhere about alcohol abuse—perhaps the most prevalent drug abuse problem among young people. This chapter is primarily concerned with abuse of **illegal drugs,** or street drugs, *those that are unlawful to buy.*

After studying this chapter, you will be able to:
- differentiate between drug use, misuse, and abuse,
- explain the effects of stimulants and depressants, and the risks of misuse or abuse of each,
- describe the effects of narcotics and hallucinogens on the body,
- identify the health risks of marijuana,
- explain the problem of inhalants, as well as look-alike and designer drugs,
- list alternatives to drug abuse.

"I couldn't get to sleep, so I took a couple of extra pills."

"I was tired and had to stay up late studying."

"Everyone else was and I didn't want to be different."

"I was bored."

"Everything seemed to be going wrong—I was tired of the hassles and just wanted to relax."

Each of these statements is an excuse for misusing or abusing drugs. What do all of the reasons have in common? They each reflect an unhealthy way to meet personal needs. Using drugs may cover up problems, but it does not address or solve them. As a matter of fact, turning to drugs only makes the problems worse.

Abuse of these drugs presents an additional serious health hazard. Unlike other drugs, the illegal drugs are not controlled by any governing agency. This means a person never knows for sure what is being purchased, what strength it is, or what else has been mixed with it.

Drug Use, Misuse, and Abuse

Drug use occurs when *a drug is taken when needed, as directed, and only for the purpose that it is intended.*

Drug misuse occurs when *a drug is used in a way that it is not intended.* Taking someone else's medicine and increasing the directed dosage are examples of misuse of drugs.

Drug abuse is *taking drugs in ways for which they are not medically intended, or using substances that are illegal or not intended to be taken into the body.* Drug abuse is a major physical, mental, and social health problem.

The most commonly abused drugs are the **psychoactive drugs**—*those that affect the nervous system.* Psychoactive drugs include *stimulants, depressants, narcotics,* and *hallucinogens.* People looking for something to alter their feelings or their moods use these drugs. The first three of these drug types have some medicinal value, but when a person abuses them, serious health problems can occur. Hallucinogens have no proven medical use.

If you look closely at a drug habit, it will likely have these characteristics. Anyone having one or more of these characteristics may have a drug habit.

- Tolerance   The body becomes used to the drug's effect but starts needing more to obtain the same effect.
- Physical Dependence   The body develops a need for the drug, and if the drug is not taken the person becomes physically ill.

- Psychological Dependence   The person feels a strong emotional need to continue using the drug in order to feel better.
- Habituation   Taking the drug becomes a habit—a compulsion.

   See the caption on page 230 for more information on the drug habit, or compulsion.

CHECK YOURSELF

1. What is the difference between drug *use, misuse,* and *abuse*?
2. Why are psychoactive drugs the most commonly abused drugs?

2.   Stimulant Drugs

   The first major group of psychoactive drugs is the stimulants. **Stimulants** are *drugs that speed up the nervous system, making the person feel more alert and active*. A stimulant increases heart rate, blood pressure, and rate of breathing. Some foods, such as coffee, tea, and cola, have a stimulant called *caffeine* in them. However, the stimulants that cause the most concern when studying drug abuse are *amphetamines* and *cocaine*.

Amphetamines

   Amphetamines (am-**fet**-uh-means) are *stimulants used in medicine to reduce fatigue and drowsiness or to suppress the appetite*. A doctor prescribes them under close supervision since the body develops a tolerance toward them. Stronger dosages of such a drug are needed to feel the effect, and a person becomes dependent on them.

   People who use amphetamines to get a lift or stay awake for an extended period of time abuse amphetamines. Amphetamines interfere with muscle control and body movement. As the effect of the drug wears off, the user experiences a letdown and may become depressed. Sometimes the user needs a tranquilizer to calm down. This up-and-down cycle can become habit forming.

   Use of amphetamine suppressants in an effort to lose weight usually is not successful. As soon as the stimulant is discontinued, the person's appetite returns. If eating behaviors have not changed, the person will regain the weight in a very short period of time.

Cocaine—An Illegal Stimulant

   Cocaine (**koh**-kane) is a white powder made from the coca bush, which grows mainly in South America. **Cocaine** is *a stimulant, causing an increased heartbeat and a rise in blood pressure and body temperature. It produces a feeling of euphoria and high energy*. Cocaine is an illegal drug.

   The *euphoric lift*—the feeling of being confident—that comes from cocaine, is often followed by a letdown. Regular use can lead to depression, edginess, and weight loss. Usage tends to increase because the user wants

Because it is a white powder, cocaine is sometimes diluted with chalk dust, flour, baking soda, or poisonous substances. Buyers are never sure of what they are getting.

to avoid the letdown feeling. As usage increases, so does the danger of paranoia, hallucinations, and psychological dependence.

Also, growing clinical evidence shows that when cocaine is taken in the most potent, dangerous forms—injected in solution, or chemically converted and smoked in a process called *freebasing* — it is physically addictive. (See also *Crack* below.)

Effects of Cocaine

Cocaine affects the body in a way similar to that of the natural body stimulant—adrenaline. It puts the body in an emergency state. How cocaine works is still somewhat of a medical puzzle. It seems to intensify the action of body chemicals called *neurotransmitters* (new-row-trans-**mitt**-ers).

Firing off one nerve cell after another, much like a string of firecrackers, these chemicals send tiny electrical impulses throughout the nervous system. As these impulses multiply, they flood the peripheral nervous system, which controls involuntary functions like pulse and perspiration.

The impulses also flood three critical parts of the brain: the *cerebral cortex*, which governs higher mental activities like memory and reasoning; the *hypothalamus*, which governs appetite, sleep, and emotions; and the *cerebellum*, which controls motor activities such as walking and balance.

The brain cannot handle all of the messages at once. Like an overloaded telephone switchboard, too much information is coming in, so the user becomes *hyperaroused*, or overaroused. With regular use and higher doses, the alertness and exhilaration can quickly lead to insomnia and to "cocaine psychosis." A single dose can cause severe headaches and nausea. Each person's body is different, so response to chemicals is very individual. But total respiratory and cardiovascular collapse *can* result.

When cocaine is *snorted*, or sniffed up the nostrils, the drug is absorbed into the bloodstream through the mucous membranes of the nasal cavity. But it also *constricts*, or contracts, the many little blood vessels in these membranes, reducing the blood supply to the nose and causing it to become dry.

Repeated cocaine use can cause tissue damage in the nose and even *perforations*, or holes, in the nasal septum, the wall dividing the two halves of the nose. Cocaine can cause liver damage, malnutrition, and, especially, among those with cardiac problems, it can increase the risk of heart attack. Even in healthy individuals who are not heavy users of cocaine, the drug may disturb the electrical impulses of the heart and cause death.

Crack

Crack is *a very strong, pure form of cocaine.* It is possibly the most dangerous drug existing today in this country. What makes crack so dangerous?

Crack is usually purer than cocaine because crack is made through a process of heating cocaine and filtering out much of the impurities. This potent form of cocaine reaches the brain within seconds after being smoked or injected.

The result is a 10 to 15 minute intense "high," followed by an equally intense low. First, crack speeds up the body systems. The heart rate, blood pressure, and body temperature increase. The "low" then produces depression, anxiety, and difficulty concentrating.

Crack presents an increased risk of overdose since it is stronger than regular cocaine. Associated with this risk is the increased risk of heart failure.

Perhaps one of the most serious risks of crack is that it is considered to be one of the most addictive of drugs. Some experts believe that using crack *once* can cause a person to become an addict.

CHECK YOURSELF

1. What are amphetamines?
2. What are the medical uses of amphetamines?
3. What is cocaine?
4. What is crack?
5. How does cocaine alter the work of the brain?
6. What are the health problems associated with cocaine?

3. Depressant and Narcotic Drugs

The second and third major groups of psychoactive drugs are the *depressants* and *narcotics,* respectively.

Depressant Drugs

Depressants (dee-**press**-ents), or *sedatives,* are drugs that *tend to slow down certain body functions and reactions.*

Depressant drugs relax muscles, relieve feelings of tension and worry, and bring on sleep. They slow down the heart rate, blood pressure, and rate of breathing. The three main groups of sedative medications are *tranquilizers, barbiturates,* and *hypnotics.*

1. **Tranquilizers** are *sedatives that doctors use to calm a person's emotions without changing the patient's ability to stay alert or think clearly.* They also can lead to physical and psychological dependence.

2. **Barbiturates** are *sedatives usually prescribed for patients who suffer from insomnia*. Because barbiturates produce a relaxed feeling, they are often abused—used by people who do not need them as medicine. Abuse of barbiturates can lead to both psychological and physical dependence. Withdrawal from the drugs can be serious and requires medical supervision.

3. **Hypnotics** are *very strong sedatives that produce sleep*. Quaalude and Valium are the best-known drugs in this group. Hypnotic drugs cause physical and psychological dependence.

One of the deadliest combinations of drugs is the mixture of alcohol, which is a drug, with any sedative. (See Chapter 12.) Each drug multiplies the effect of the other. These effects can be stronger than the body can handle. Breathing can be slowed down to such a point that the brain becomes oxygen-starved. Coma, permanent brain damage, or death may result.

Ludes, Quads, Sopors

What are they? Here are some of their trade names—Quaalude (**kwah**-lude), Parest, and Sopor. Even though they have different names, they are basically all the same substance—*methaqualone* (meh-**thuh**-kwah-lone). Once thought to be safe and nonaddicting as a suitable sleep-producing substitute for the more addictive barbiturates, this hypnotic drug has become a popular one for abuse.

Methaqualone produces a relaxed feeling of well-being, accompanied by pleasurable euphoric sensations. This partially explains its popularity as a drug of abuse. Side effects of this drug include dizziness, nosebleeds, headaches, and diarrhea. Besides building a tolerance, the body becomes physically and psychologically dependent on this drug.

Narcotic Drugs

Narcotics are *drugs taken to bring on sleep or loss of feeling*. The narcotics are used to relieve pain in the body **(morphine)** (**mor**-feen), to stop severe coughing **(codeine)** (**ko**-deen), and to treat teething or stop diarrhea **(paregoric)** (par-uh-**gore**-ick). These types of narcotics are valuable drugs in medicine and relieve many people from pain and suffering. However, as much as they are used, narcotics are still very dangerous drugs.

The term *narcotic* comes from the Greek word meaning *"to numb."* Originally, the term narcotic referred to opium and pain-relieving drugs related to opium. Almost all narcotics are made from the opium poppy flower, grown in many parts of the world. Narcotics are also called hypnotic drugs because when they are taken in large dosages, the drugs will result in a coma.

Narcotics are *addictive* (dependent-forming). The United States carefully regulates the manufacture and import of narcotics. Physicians must state certain information on narcotic prescriptions, and pharmacists must keep records on their sales.

Drug Abuse and the Risk of AIDS

Since AIDS was first discovered in this country, intravenous (IV) drug users were second only to homosexual males for greatest risk of being infected with the AIDS virus. However, educators no longer refer to *high-risk groups*. Instead they talk about *high-risk behaviors*. Sharing needles is one of the surest ways of being exposed to the AIDS virus. Sharing IV drug needles allows for the exchange of blood from one person to another. The message is clear—DON'T.

Heroin

One opium-derived drug that was widely used in the nineteenth century was morphine. It was employed to relieve pain, but the drug was found to be highly addictive.

In 1874, the discovery of a substance derived from morphine, called **heroin** (**herr**-oh-win), was thought to be a major medical advance. Heroin was looked on as a cure for morphine addiction. But doctors soon discovered that heroin itself was the most dangerous addictive narcotic known. It is not used in medical work and is illegal in most countries, including the United States.

Heroin is sold illegally in the form of a white or brown powder that is usually sniffed or injected. Heroin is often mixed with other substances that look like it—starch, powdered milk, even strychnine, a deadly poison. The buyers never can be sure of what they are buying.

Heroin affects both the central nervous system and the bowels. It diminishes one's awareness of pain and depresses the respiratory center of the brain, causing breathing to become slower and shallow. This effect is very dangerous and can cause death if the user takes too much heroin.

Heroin can also cause nausea and vomiting. Regular abuse of heroin,

Drug addiction begins out of curiosity to experiment. *It leads to taking drugs in a* social group *which supports their use. The drug then becomes a source of escape from all the* problem-related situations *that it causes (for example, poor school work, trouble concentrating, loss of friends). The frequency of taking the drug then increases and its use becomes* habit-forming. *Finally, the person cannot live without the drug. He is a* compulsive user, *one who cannot break away from its use.*

as in the case of other narcotics, can stop proper functioning in the large intestine, causing painful constipation.

Besides being highly addictive, the body quickly develops a tolerance to heroin. When the body does not get heroin, or strong enough doses of it, severe withdrawal symptoms occur.

Treatment for heroin abuse often involves *methadone* (**meth**-uh-don)—a manufactured narcotic. It blocks the craving for the heroin, but it also is addictive. Heroin is an illegal drug.

CHECK YOURSELF

1. What are the three groups of sedatives, and what are their differences?
2. Why is the combination of a sedative and alcohol so lethal?
3. What are narcotics? Name four of them.
4. What makes heroin such a dangerous illegal drug?

4. Hallucinogens—Time Bombs in the Brain

The fourth major group of psychoactive drugs is the hallucinogens. For centuries, the natives of Mexico and South America have used **hallucinogens** (hal-**loos**-en-oh-jenz), *drugs that produce imaginary visions and objects in the brain*. Many tribes have used a certain type of mushroom in their tribal ceremonies. *Psilocybin* (sigh-luh-**sigh**-bin) is the principal hallucinogenic drug found in these mushrooms. *Peyote* (pay-**oat**-ee), a cactus, provides another hallucinogen. *Mescaline* (**mess**-kah-lean) is the hallucinogenic chemical found in peyote.

Today, mescaline most often is made illegally from laboratory chemicals. The effects of mescaline can be severe, including nausea, cramps, sweating, and vomiting. The abuse of mescaline may intensify existing psychological problems.

Hallucinogenic comes from a Latin word meaning "to dream." All hallucinogenic drugs are dangerous and illegal.

Angel Dust

Phencyclidine (feen-**sik**-luh-dine) **(PCP)**, or *angel dust*, is *a powerful and dangerous hallucinogen*. It is prepared **synthetically** (sin-**thet**-ick-uh-lee); that is, it is *composed from laboratory chemicals*. PCP, considered to be one of the most dangerous drugs, has acquired the nickname "bad drug."

Users report that PCP makes them feel distant and detached from their surroundings. Time seems to pass slowly, body movements slow down. Muscle coordination is impaired and the sensations of touch and pain are dulled. PCP can make the user feel strong and powerful. This feeling has

resulted in tragic deaths, serious accidents, and acts of violence. While under the influence of PCP, individuals have exhibited bizarre, destructive behaviors.

While overdoses of PCP can cause death, almost all PCP-related deaths are caused by the strange behavior the drug produces in the user. PCP users have drowned in shallow water because they were so disoriented they could not tell which way was up. Others have died in fires because of being disoriented and insensitive to the pain of the burning.

Abuse of PCP repeatedly makes it difficult to remember things and impairs speech, sometimes causing the abuser to stutter. Judgment and concentration are also impaired long after the abuser has stopped taking the drug. Serious mental problems have also resulted from PCP, causing users to need psychiatric care and, sometimes, institutional care.

The effects of PCP are widely unpredictable. Once taken, PCP remains in the body long after the effect has worn off. Flashbacks, even the bizarre behavior, may recur at later times from this illegal, dangerous drug.

Lysergic Acid Diethylamide (LSD)

LSD is probably the drug responsible for initiating the great awareness of hallucinogens in our society. **LSD** means "lysergic acid diethylamide" (lah-sir-**jik ass**-id die-eth-ul-**lam**-ide). The abuse of LSD during the 1960s and the resulting tragedies—deaths from a false sense of security or imaginings produced by hallucinations—received much publicity. Deaths resulting from people thinking they could fly, or standing on train tracks with the illusion that they could stop a train, made news across the country.

LSD causes an increase in the heart rate and a rise in blood pressure. The user may experience chills, fever, loss of appetite, or nausea. Fortunately, young people have gotten wise to LSD. Because of the unpredictable and extreme reactions to this illegal drug, people do not use it as much anymore.

Marijuana—A Dangerous Health Risk

The scientific name for **marijuana** (mar-uh-**wan**-uh), also *a hallucinogenic drug*, is *Cannabis sativa*. It comes from the hemp plant. Scientists have identified over 400 chemicals in marijuana. The chemical that produces the psychoactive effect is *tetrahydrocannabinol* (te-tra-hi-dro-ka-**na**-be-nul) (*THC*). The most chemical research has been done on THC because of its effects on important body organs. Scientists measure the strength of marijuana by testing how much THC it contains. The strength of the marijuana marketed today has increased almost four times over the past 10 years.

Hashish ("hash") is *the dark brown resin collected from the tops of the cannabis plant*. It is stronger than crude marijuana because it contains more THC. Dose for dose, it affects the user more strongly than the marijuana. Both marijuana and hashish are illegal drugs.

Recent research has shown that marijuana is a dangerous drug that has long-term negative effects on many of the body systems.

Immediate Effects of Marijuana

Marijuana has the effects of both a depressant and a stimulant. It lowers body temperature, but increases the heart rate and blood pressure. It stimulates the appetite, but reduces coordination and reaction time. It reduces a person's control over behavior. Some people may become talkative and giddy, others quiet and withdrawn. The effects vary from person to person and can be influenced by a person's mood and surroundings.

Long-Term Effects of Marijuana

It may take many more years before we fully understand the extent to which marijuana affects health. It took over 50 years to positively confirm the relationship between cigarettes and lung cancer. However, as the results of studies that are reported each year show, some of the findings about marijuana are becoming quite conclusive. That is, there is much less room for debate over whether marijuana is a serious health risk.

Physical Reactions   Unlike other chemicals, THC does not dissolve in water. This means that it is not as easily flushed out of the body. It may take as long as three weeks for the body to rid itself of the THC.

The highest concentration of fat cells in the body is in the brain cells, liver, lungs, kidneys, and gonads. In these cells, marijuana acts as a poison. It prevents the proper formation of DNA, proteins, and other essential building blocks for cell growth and cell division. (See Chapter 21.)

Latest research shows that marijuana smokers may be more susceptible than nonsmokers to infection by viruses, bacteria, and other disease-causing organisms. Although more studies are being conducted, initial evidence indicates that THC—the psychoactive chemical in marijuana—disrupts the body's closely interwoven network of immune cells.

Psychological Reactions   Young people who use marijuana tend to lose interest in other activities that are important for emotional and social development. This effect of marijuana has been termed the **amotivational syndrome** because *repeated users may become apathetic and lethargic, withdrawing*

Drugs and Athletes

In 1986, the National Collegiate Athletic Association adopted a plan to test college athletes at championship events and football games for the use of drugs.

The drugs include most of the *stimulant drugs*, which would increase energy and staying power, and the *narcotic drugs*, which would help to reduce pain. Also, the *hallucinogenic drug*, marijuana, was banned because of its initial stimulant properties.

Also banned were *diuretics* (**die**-your-eth-tics), which rid the body of sodium and water, *anabolic steroids* (**steer**-oids), which temporarily increase muscle size, and *sympathomimetic amines* (sim-**patho**-mim-eth-ic **am**-ines), which act as stimulants.

Here is a complete list:

- *Psychoactive stimulants*, such as amphetamines, cocaine, ethyl-amphetamine, norpseudo-ephedrine and related compounds.
- *Sympathomimetic amines*, such as chlorprenaline, ephedrine, methoxyphenamine, methyl-ephedrine and related compounds.
- *Miscellaneous central nervous system stimulants*, such as caffeine (if the concentration exceeds 15 micrograms per milliliter), strychnine and related compounds.
- *Anabolic steroids*, such as dehydrochlormethyl-testosterone, methenolone, testosterone (if the ratio of testosterone to epitestosterone exceeds 6) and related compounds.
- *Substances banned for specific sports*, such as alcohol, pindolol, atenolol, metroprolol, nadolol, propranolol, timolol and related compounds.
- *Diuretics*, such as bendroflumethiazide, benzthiazide, triameterne, trichlormethlazide and related compounds.
- *Street drugs*, such as amphetamines, cocaine, heroin, marijuana (based on a repeat testing), methamphetamine, and THC (tetrahydrocannabinol).

from involvement in academic and social activities. A report from the National Centers for Disease Control stated that recent national surveys report that 40% of heavy users experience some or all of the amotivational syndrome symptoms.

Regular marijuana users tend to have something in common: personality problems that include loss of willpower and motivation, lack of energy, and paranoia. These problems, if not present before the beginning of regular marijuana use, develop and intensify as a result of the marijuana.

Studies have shown that marijuana affects memory, making it more difficult to recall things and to pay attention. Concentration is impaired. Research is still going on to determine if marijuana causes permanent changes in the brain. There is general concern that over a period of time marijuana may destroy certain cells in the brain.

Body and Mind Dependence   The body builds a tolerance to marijuana. It needs more of the drug and stronger doses to feel marijuana's effects. A person can develop a psychological dependence on marijuana. Researchers are conducting studies to determine if the body also develops a physical dependence.

Driving and Marijuana

In 1976, the Department of Health, Education, and Welfare (HEW), now the Department of Health and Human Services, reported to Congress that marijuana use "definitely impairs driving ability." Drivers under the influence of marijuana react slower and make more accident-causing mistakes than drivers who are not under the influence. Since some of the effects of marijuana—delayed reaction time and poor concentration—seem to last longer than the actual high, a person may not think he or she is driving under marijuana's influence.

These conclusions drawn by HEW resulted from the extensive study of ". . . driving-related skills, driver-simulated studies, test course performance, actual street performance, and a study of drivers involved in fatal accidents."

Marijuana and the Respiratory System

Using much of the information collected from studying cigarettes, scientists have been able to draw some important conclusions about marijuana smoke. The smoke contains over 1500 chemicals and many more hydrocarbons—proven cancer-causing chemicals—than cigarette smoke. Deep, long breaths associated with smoking marijuana allow more time for harmful particles and gases to act on the lung cells. Smoking marijuana causes a narrowing of the breathing passages, making breathing more difficult.

The lungs have special cells that destroy disease-producing bacteria. Studies have shown that marijuana interferes with the work of these cells, making the user more susceptible to infections from the bacteria inhaled.

Federal and local governments are taking steps to destroy marijuana crops wherever they are found.

Taking Risks

To take a *risk* is to expose yourself to danger, or failure, or rejection.

A *reasonable risk* is putting yourself in a situation where you stand to gain something positive.

An *unreasonable risk* is putting yourself in a situation where you stand to gain nothing positive, lose something of value, cause physical or mental harm to yourself or another person.

Experimenting with drugs is an unreasonable risk. There is no growth—mental or social—involved. You have little or nothing to gain. Think of some reasonable risks that present a challenge to you, yet offer some positive outcomes.

Marijuana and Hormones

Marijuana affects the body's hormonal glands—most specifically, the pituitary and adrenal glands and the gonads (ovaries and testes). Presently, its effect on the adrenal glands is understood the least. However, its effect on testosterone—the male hormone responsible for the development of sex characteristics—is best understood.

Regular use of marijuana lowers the level of testosterone in the blood. Testosterone is responsible for the development of the male through puberty—voice change, growth of body hair, broadened shoulders, and the production of sperm—the male sex cell. Regular use of marijuana before and/or during the years of puberty can slow this developmental process.

Studies currently are being conducted to determine the effect of marijuana on the female reproductive system. Because the female has a more delicate balance of hormone levels than the male, there is cause for additional concern for long-term marijuana use among females. Marijuana smoking also may affect the menstrual cycle, as well as the developing egg cells.

Debates About Marijuana

With all of this evidence, why do people still support the use of marijuana? Some research is being done on the medical use of marijuana. This research is carried out under very close medical supervision and is still in the experimental stages. However, this has led some people to reason that if marijuana is used in medicine, it cannot be too harmful.

What these people do not realize is that, as a part of cancer research, marijuana is being given to sick people to relieve the side effects of cancer therapy. THC weakens the brain's usual message to the autonomic nervous system to vomit when a person is poisoned. For this reason, THC may help to reduce the nausea that cancer patients experience as a result of the chemical therapy they must take.

However, paralyzing the brain's vomiting center in a healthy person has some serious complications. Vomiting is a reflex action. THC weakens the natural defenses against accidental poisoning or drug overdose.

When all the current evidence has been collected, one conclusion about marijuana emerges. It is a dangerous drug.

Why Take It?

Here is a final thought on using marijuana to feel good, to get away from it all, or just to have a good time. We learn a variety of ways to face the ups and downs of daily life. We also develop patterns of behavior about feeling good, enjoying life, and, in general, liking ourselves. If young people depend upon a substance to feel good, they gradually develop a habit of looking outside of themselves for being happy and enjoying life.

It is easy to become dependent on other things or people. On the other hand, people who look for healthier ways to feel good—who look within themselves for answers—learn to gain strength from within. More likely, they are able to face life successfully and realistically because they have learned that they do not need an artificial means of escape.

CHECK YOURSELF

1. What is a hallucinogen?
2. Why are hallucinogens such as PCP and LSD very dangerous?
3. How is marijuana both a stimulant and a depressant?
4. What is the amotivational syndrome?
5. Explain why marijuana is a more serious health risk because the THC in it does not dissolve in water.
6. What is the effect of marijuana on the respiratory system?

5. Chemical Abuse—Problems You Can Do Without

Just as LSD was one of the most talked about drugs of the 1960s and PCP of the 1970s, the various *chemical-based inhalants, look-alike drugs,* and *designer drugs* are emerging as the danger drugs of the 1980s and 1990s, particularly among young people.

Inhalants—Not Meant for Human Consumption

Inhalants (in-**hay**-lants) are *substances whose fumes are sniffed and inhaled to give a hallucinogenic high.* Included among the inhalants are glue, spray paints, aerosols, and gasoline. A person who is sniffing an inhalant has trouble keeping his or her balance, has a glassy stare, and finds it hard to talk. Judgment is impaired, and the behavior of the user may resemble the behavior of someone who is drunk.

Effects of Inhalants

Since inhalants were never meant to be taken into the body, any use of them is considered drug abuse. It is a more common problem with pre-teens for several reasons, one of which is that inhalants are inexpensive. Other people, such as teenagers, recognize the extreme dangers of inhaling such substances and are wise enough not to take the risk.

Heavy use of inhalants can result in liver and kidney damage, changes in bone marrow, and even permanent brain damage. "Clowning around" under the influence of an inhalant has been the cause of many accidental deaths.

Inhalants are commonly found in most shopping outlets. Many states have passed laws prohibiting their sale to minors.

Lethal Look-Alikes

What are **look-alike drugs**? They are *drugs made from other drugs and deliberately designed to look like street drugs.* People may think they are buying the real drug, in most cases "speed," or amphetamines, when they are really buying large doses of caffeine mixed with decongestants. Such a combination can be just as lethal as amphetamines.

Law-enforcement authorities report that the sale of look-alike drugs has become a $500 million-a-year business in the United States. What is the problem that these drugs have?

In look-alikes, caffeine usually ranges from 0.0016 to 0.0064 ounces (50 to 200 mg). In addition to caffeine, many of these drugs contain phenylpropanolamine (feen-ul-pro-pah-**no**-lam-een) and ephedrine (ee-**fed**-rin). *Phenylpropanolamine* is used in cough and cold remedies and is found in some decongestant products. *Ephedrine* is used in cold and asthma products and as an appetite suppressant.

LIFE MANAGEMENT SKILL

Turning Down Drugs

There are many methods of staying away from, or turning down, drugs and other harmful substances. Review the discussions on self-concept (page 81), talking things over (page 91), decision-making (page 93), and goal-setting (page 94), and read about saying "yes" or "no" (page 397). All of these topics or processes will help you to turn down drugs.

HEALTH UPDATE   HEALTH UPDATE   HEALTH UPDATE

Drug Therapy

Drugs have been used to treat physical and emotional problems for centuries. But drug therapy has never been an exact science, one reason being the problem of dosage. The physician has had to depend on clinical judgment or trial and error to find the appropriate dose of a particular drug for a particular patient.

A physician has some guidelines to work from—the patient's past history, the body weight, and the manufacturer's recommendations. But individual differences are so great that it has been almost impossible to predict the effects of a dosage. Every body absorbs, breaks down, and excretes each particular drug at a different rate.

Laboratory techniques now have been developed to monitor drug therapy. The monitoring system is capable of analyzing extremely small quantities of substances—often one to two parts per million. With these methods scientists can determine the exact amount of a drug in body fluids and can understand more thoroughly the patient's response to a drug.

In the case of epilepsy, for example, medications to control seizure activity depend on a specific blood level for their effect. If the level of antiseizure medication is below the therapeutic range, seizures occur. If too much medication is given, the drug quickly becomes toxic, or poisonous, to the patient.

Drug therapy monitoring got its start in **toxicology** (tahk-suh-**koh**-lah-gee)—*the science dealing with the effects and detection of poisons,* or *the study of overdoses of medications and drugs*—but its usefulness is now expanding across all of medicine and is a growing field of study.

Effects of Look-Alike Drugs

Moderate doses of any one of these substances can produce nervousness, restlessness, insomnia, increased blood pressure and heart rate. Regular use of these look-alikes, and their use in combination with other drugs, can lead to the same psychotic behavior found to occur from the frequent use of amphetamines.

Look-alikes are hard to diagnose. Neither the user nor the medical profession, specifically the emergency room staff, knows for sure what the drugs really are. This makes treatment very difficult, since the procedure for an amphetamine overdose differs greatly from that of a caffeine overdose. Furthermore, the many interactions of caffeine with other drugs are not fully known. If the look-alikes are taken with other drugs, like alcohol, serious reactions can occur. If the abuser reaches the emergency room alive, the medical staff may not be able to treat the victim successfully as a result of all of the drug combinations.

Designer Drugs

Designer drugs are *drugs made with synthetic substances in such combinations as to produce products that are similar to the illegal drugs.* Until 1985, these drugs were not illegal, but because of the dramatic increase in one of these drugs, the Federal Drug Enforcement Agency took measures to make its selling illegal.

Sale of this drug, called *Ecstasy*, is punishable by 15 years in prison and a $150,000 fine. Ecstasy's chemical composition is related to that of amphetamines and mescaline. It is a combination of a stimulant and a hallucinogen. The National Institute on Drug Abuse reports evidence that shows Ecstasy is psychologically addictive and that it can cause brain damage.

Designer drugs continue to appear under many different brand names, and these brands are now under continual investigation by the Federal Drug Enforcement Agency. As these drugs are produced, many states are declaring them illegal.

Everyone's Chemical Makeup Is Different

The human body is made up of water, protein, fats, acids, chemicals, and minerals. Everything you put into your system mixes with or in some way reacts to your personal chemistry. In general, the chemistry of a human body might be thought of as containing the same amounts as follows:

- enough chlorine to sanitize 5 swimming pools,
- enough oxygen to fill a large closet,
- enough salt to season 25 chickens,
- 10 gallons of water,
- 5 pounds of lime,

- 31 pounds of carbon glycerin,
- enough magnesium for 10 flash pictures,
- enough iron to make one nail 3 inches long,
- enough gluten to make 5 pounds of glue,
- enough sulfur to rid a dog of fleas,
- enough sugar to make half a batch of cookies,
- enough fat to make 10 bars of soap,
- enough phosphorous to make 2,000 match heads,
- as much carbon as there is in the lead of 900 pencils.

See the Health Handbook, *pages HB20–21, for an alternative to taking drugs.*

Since each person's body chemistry is different, we each react differently to chemicals. Some people are fatally allergic to bee stings, others to penicillin. Certain creams or lotions make some people's skin break out—their chemistry reacts adversely to the chemicals in the lotion. When you put a chemical substance into your body, you have no way of knowing for sure how your body will react.

Doctors take this into consideration when prescribing drugs. They probably know their patients' health histories and can determine what will be reasonably safe for them.

However, when you abuse drugs, use illegal drugs, or—even riskier—mix drugs, your body may show no reaction one time and react violently the next. Is it worth the risk?

An Alternative to Drugs

People give many reasons for taking drugs. And the people who abuse drugs, along with the problems associated with drug abuse, tend to get a

COMMUNITY HEALTH EDUCATOR

Because of the increasing interest in fitness and healthy living and the discoveries about the risk factors of chronic diseases, the need for community health education is on the rise. People are assuming a greater responsibility for their own health, and they need the most current information available, given in terms they can understand. The primary goal of a **community health educator** is to bridge the gap between the latest advances in science and the information and practices of society.

Building this bridge requires a variety of skills. The ability to communicate through writing and speaking is very important. A community health educator must be aware of the background, cultural and religious beliefs, and the needs of the community. An educational background in both the biological and social sciences is necessary. A community health educator must keep abreast of new developments in science and education and continually update information.

Several points of access to the community are available for the community health educator. These include health-care institutions (e.g.,

hospitals, nursing homes, doctors' offices, and health-maintenance organizations) and volunteer or official health agencies (e.g., local health departments, the Red Cross, the American Cancer Society). Many businesses and private institutions also hire community health educators. Corporate health is one of the fastest growing areas in community health education.

The educational backgrounds of community health educators can vary widely. Although many universities have a health education department, not all of them offer a degree in community health. Community health education training is comprised of a wide variety of subjects to give students a broad base of experience. Some practical experience usually is included as well. Several postgraduate degrees are available to health educators seeking advancement in this field. For more information, write the American Public Health Association.

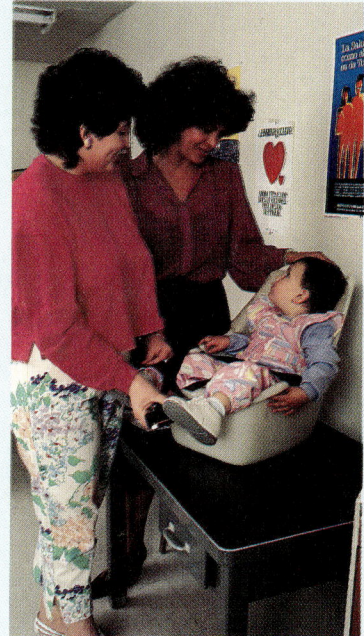

**American Public Health Association
1015 Fifteenth Street N.W.
Washington, DC 20005**

great deal of attention. But what about those who have said no to drugs:

- those who have found healthier ways to cope with day-to-day problems?
- those who have found ways to feel good about themselves without using drugs?

Turning to drugs is the easy way out. But many young people have decided it is worth the effort *not* to get involved with drugs.

Remember, turning down the offer to take a drug is your *right*. Any friend who leans on you about your decision is trying to chip away at your rights as a free individual. Furthermore, anyone who pushes you to do something you do not want to do is not a friend.

CHECK YOURSELF

1. What are the symptoms of inhalant abuse?
2. Why are inhalants such a dangerous risk?
3. What are lethal look-alike drugs?
4. What are designer drugs?
5. What are some healthy alternatives to drugs?

CHAPTER 13 Review

CHAPTER SUMMARY

- Drug abuse presents a major physical, mental, and social health problem.
- The most commonly abused drugs are the psychoactive drugs, those that affect the nervous system. These drugs fall into the stimulant, depressant, narcotic, and hallucinogenic categories.
- These drugs, because of their mind-altering characteristics, lead to addiction, or dependency—both physical and psychological.
- Recent chemical-based drugs have been inhalants, look-alike drugs, and designer drugs.
- The body also builds a tolerance for most drugs, meaning more of a drug is needed for the user to feel its effects.
- Illegal drugs present an additional problem because there are no controls over their production or sale. You have no way of knowing the strength or the purity of such drugs.
- Using drugs to feel good, escape problems, or be part of the group is not healthy and tends only to make problems worse. The responsible young person can find healthier ways to cope with day-to-day life.

REVIEWING WHAT YOU LEARNED

1. Give an example of drug use, misuse, and abuse.
2. What are the risks of abusing stimulants and depressants?
3. Why is cocaine a dangerous drug?
4. What is the amotivational syndrome? What medical problem does it cause for young people?
5. Why is PCP called the "bad drug"?
6. What health problems do look-alike drugs present?
7. Why are designer drugs dangerous?
8. Describe two effects of (a) narcotics and (b) hallucinogens on the body.
9. List three alternatives to drug use.

illegal drugs	hyperactive	codeine	hashish
drug use	depressants	paregoric	amotivational syndrome
drug misuse	*sedatives*	heroin	toxicology
drug abuse	*tranquilizers*	*hallucinogens*	*inhalants*
psychoactive drugs	*barbiturates*	phencyclidine (PCP)	*look-alike drugs*
stimulants	*hypnotics*	synthetically	*designer drugs*
amphetamines	*narcotics*	lysergic acid diethylamide (LSD)	community health educator
cocaine	morphine	marijuana	

PUTTING VOCABULARY TO USE

On a separate piece of paper, identify the characteristics below with the most appropriate drug group. Use the chapter vocabulary list above to find the correct drug groups. They are italicized.

1. _____. Glues, spray paints, aerosols, gasoline.
2. _____. Basic property is to distort reality.
3. _____. Some of this group are legal and some are illegal, but all relieve pain.
4. _____. A member of the stimulant group.
5. _____. Methaqualone belongs to this group.
6. _____. Heroin is a member of this group.
7. _____. Developed primarily to relieve anxiety and tension.
8. _____. Sleep-producing drugs.
9. _____. Drugs not used in medicine because of their highly unpredictable effects.
10. _____. LSD and PCP belong to this group.
11. _____. Given for weight control and hyperactive children.
12. _____-_____ _____. Designed to look like street drugs.
13. _____ _____. Made with synthetic substances to be similar to illegal drugs.
14. _____. Speeds up the nervous system.
15. _____. All natural forms are made from opium.
16. _____. Sleep producers that can lead to physical and psychological dependence.
17. _____. Cocaine fits under this drug group.
18. _____. Slow down heart rate, blood pressure, and rate of breathing.

APPLYING WHAT YOU LEARNED

1. Young drug abusers often started experimenting occasionally with drugs and then became dependent on them. Explain how such a change from experimentation to dependency can happen.
2. Drug abuse takes an enormous toll on society, as well as on the individual. Explain this statement and provide several illustrations of the costs to both the individual and society.
3. What arguments could you develop against the legalization of marijuana to be presented to a group of upper elementary students?
4. Collect current statistics on the use of illegal drugs in your city or town. Also find out what the statistics were five years ago. Make a bar graph to show the increase or decrease in use.
5. Write down three of your personal goals. Next to each goal write a statement about how involvement in drugs would interfere with your ability to reach your goal.
6. Review the problem-solving process presented in Chapter 5. A friend of yours is being pressured to go to a party where people will be smoking marijuana. She cannot decide what to do. Use the steps in the problem-solving process to help her reach a healthy decision.

FOCUS ON WELLNESS

Drug abuse is a widespread problem among young people. You may be aware of friends or other peers who are involved in some way with drug abuse. *To decrease this negative personal and social problem among young people, I, as an individual, can . . .*

U N I T

5

MAINTAINING A HEALTHY BODY SYSTEM

The Nervous System

Do you know that you have 12 billion nerve cells, and that a nerve impulse can travel well over 240 miles per hour? The nervous system is one of the most complex systems known to us, and through it we communicate with all the things around us.

After studying this chapter, you will be able to:
- describe the functions and characteristics of neurons,
- distinguish between the central and peripheral nervous systems,
- describe the functions of the parts of the brain,
- explain the action of a reflex,
- identify symptoms, causes, treatment, and prevention of various diseases and disorders of the nervous system.

1. Our Nervous System

Think of the series of events that take place when you eat a meal. Your eyes register that food is on your plate. Your hands move to a position to pick up the food. You then raise the food to your mouth, which opens at just the right time. You put the food in your mouth and start chewing. Your mouth has already begun secreting saliva to begin the digestive process.

You perform this act so regularly that it may seem to be automatic, but it is not. It is just one of the many processes the body goes through that requires coordinated movement. The nervous system controls the coordination of the process of eating and all other bodily processes.

The nervous system is the body's communication network and control center. There are nearly 45 miles of nerves running throughout your body. The two main divisions of this nervous system are the *central nervous system* (CNS) and the *peripheral nervous system* (PNS).

Basic Structure of the Nervous System

One of the most important parts of the nervous system is the *nerve cell* called the **neuron** (**new**-ron). Neurons form the basic structure of nerve tissue.

Parts of a Neuron

Every neuron is surrounded by a thin nerve membrane that has three basic parts: the *cell body,* the *axons,* and the *dendrites.*

Cell Body   The **cell body** is the *center for receiving and sending nerve impulses.* It is also responsible for manufacturing proteins and using energy for the maintenance and growth of the neuron. The shape of the cell body varies according to the type of neuron. Some sensory neurons are round, those on the surface of the brain are diamond-shaped, and motor neurons are star-shaped.

Axons   An axon (**aks**-on) is a threadlike extension of the cell body. **Axons** are *tubelike fibers that carry impulses away from the cell body.* An axon of one neuron may have enough branches to make contact with as many as 1,000 other neurons. Most of the axons in the CNS are very short—less than one twenty-fifth of an inch. In the PNS, however, axons are longer. Some axons extend from the spinal cord to muscles in the fingers and are as long as 40 inches (100 cm).

Many of the *axons in the PNS have a whitish coating of fatty material,* called **myelin** (**my**-uh-len), around them. This myelin sheath insulates the nerve fiber and speeds the transmission of impulses. Myelin also causes the distinction in gray matter and white matter in the nervous system. You will read more about gray and white matter on page 252.

The central nervous system is made up of the spinal cord and the brain.

The Nervous System

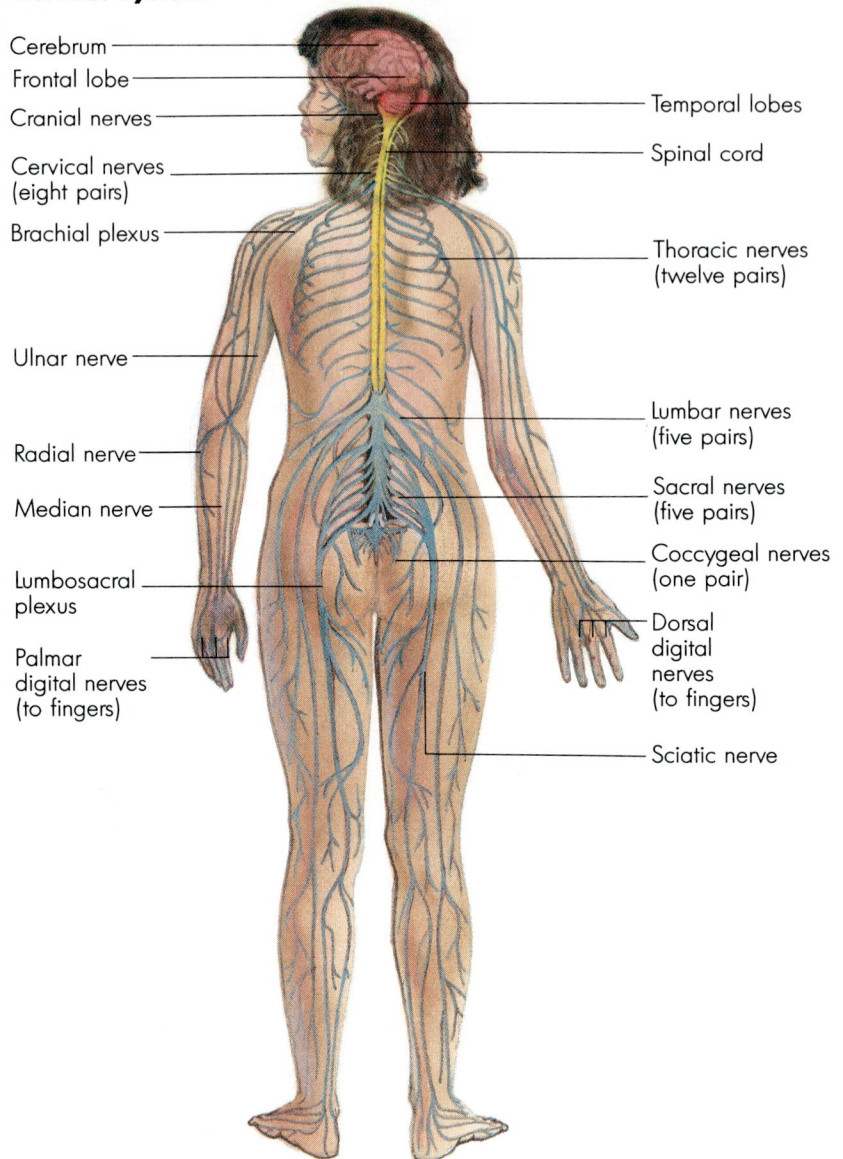

Cerebrum

Frontal lobe

Cranial nerves

Cervical nerves (eight pairs)

Brachial plexus

Ulnar nerve

Radial nerve

Median nerve

Lumbosacral plexus

Palmar digital nerves (to fingers)

Temporal lobes

Spinal cord

Thoracic nerves (twelve pairs)

Lumbar nerves (five pairs)

Sacral nerves (five pairs)

Coccygeal nerves (one pair)

Dorsal digital nerves (to fingers)

Sciatic nerve

Dendrites Dendrites (**den**-drites) also are threadlike extensions of the cell body. They are usually short and have many branches. They *receive and conduct impulses toward the cell center.*

Neuron Characteristics

Neurons are unique body cells in several respects. Unlike other cells, neurons cannot replace themselves. Damage to nerve cells is permanent. As you read in Unit 4, this is an especially important characteristic when we consider the effect of drugs on the nervous system.

Neurons are also unique in that they have an unusually high degree of *excitability* and *conductivity*. This means that they are very sensitive and can react to even the slightest stimulus. Once excited, a neuron can rapidly conduct an electrical charge from the point of stimulation to the brain or spinal cord. This charge can travel as fast as 248 miles per hour!

Types of Neurons

Neurons are classified according to their individual functions. The three main classes are *sensory neurons*, *connecting neurons*, and *motor neurons*.

Sensory Neurons

Sensory neurons *send impulses from special sensory neurons, called* **receptors,** *toward the central nervous system.* Receptors are located in different numbers throughout the body and are very specialized.

Receptor neurons located in the sense organs, for example, receive stimuli from the outside environment. There are sensory receptors for heat, cold, pain, hearing, taste, sight, smell, touch, and balance. Pain receptors are distributed unevenly in different parts of the body. Does it hurt more to be pinched on the skin below your eyes than on your back?

Another type of sensory receptor is located in the muscles, tendons, and joints. These receptors send messages to the brain to tell it when muscles are contracting and how much tension they are producing.

Still another type of sensory receptor receives messages about the digestion, circulation, hunger, thirst, and feelings of sickness. All of these receptors send impulses toward the brain or spinal cord.

Skin receptors are only one type of specialized sensory neuron in the body.

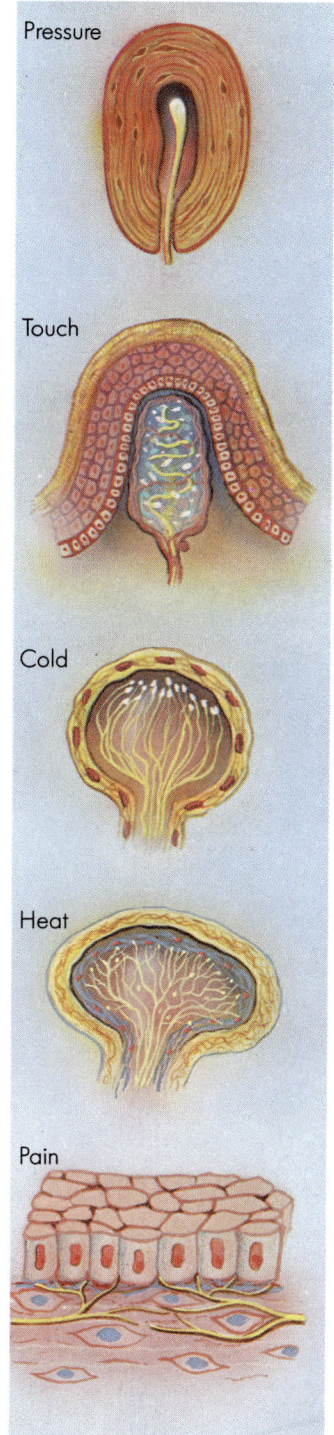

Pressure

Touch

Cold

Heat

Pain

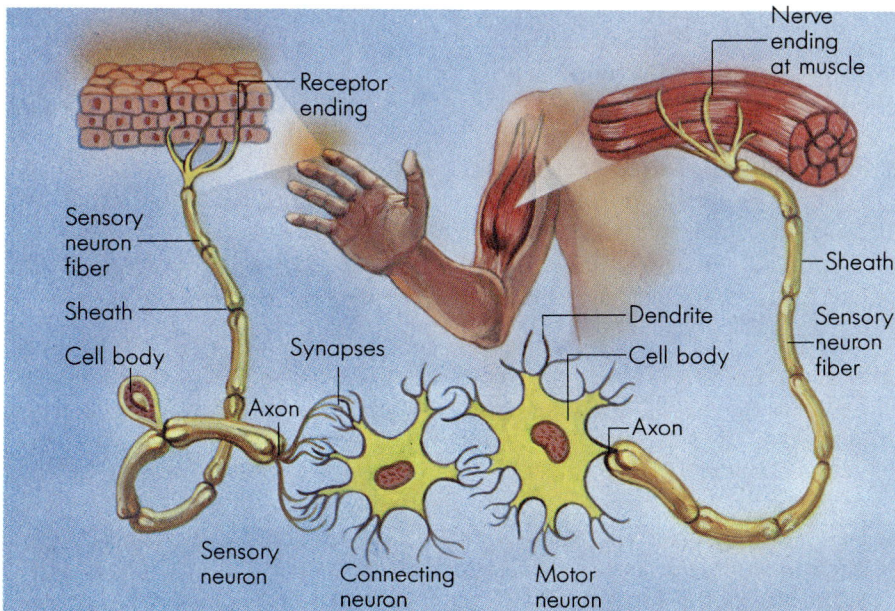

Nerve ending at muscle

Receptor ending

Sensory neuron fiber

Sheath

Cell body

Axon

Synapses

Dendrite

Cell body

Sheath

Sensory neuron fiber

Axon

Sensory neuron

Connecting neuron

Motor neuron

Connecting Neurons

The second classification of neurons is the connecting neurons, which are found only within the CNS. They are activated by impulses from the sensory neurons. **Connecting neurons** *provide the link between sensory input and muscle activity.* They relay impulses from sensory neurons to motor neurons.

Motor Neurons

Motor neurons, the third type of neurons, *carry impulses from connecting neurons within the brain or spinal cord to the muscles and glands.* These impulses bring about a coordinated response.

The Nerve Impulse

The **nerve impulse**—*an electrical charge that races from the point of stimulation to the brain or spinal cord*—is not completely understood, but some information is known. You are walking home with a friend. At an intersection the Don't Walk sign lights up in red. You stop, wait for the green Walk sign, and proceed. But during this time, you never stop talking with your friend. It sounds simple enough, but the event of stopping and waiting involves millions of nerve cells.

Sensory receptors in the eyes are stimulated by the signal light and translate the stimulation into a nerve impulse. Now each sensory neuron begins a series of electrical and chemical changes to transmit the impulse.

The impulse travels along the dendrites to the cell body. From the cell body, the impulse travels along the axon to the dendrites of the next sensory neuron. Before the impulse can be picked up by the dendrite, it has to cross an extremely narrow gap called a **synapse** (**sin**-aps), *the junction between the axon end of one neuron and the dendrite of another neuron.*

The nerve impulse is then picked up by neurons in the spinal cord, where connecting neurons carry the impulse to the brain. The brain translates the message and sends a message back through the motor neurons, telling the muscles to stop walking.

The axons of the motor neurons receive this message and instruct certain muscles to contract and others to relax. You stop at the corner. The same process repeats itself when the sensory receptors in your eyes receive the stimulus of the green Walk light.

CHECK YOURSELF

1. What are the two main divisions of the nervous system?
2. What characteristics make the neuron unique in comparison to other body cells?
3. Describe the basic parts of a neuron. Tell the function of each.
4. How are neurons classified? Describe what each classification does.
5. What are nerve impulses? Why are they important?

In one way or another, every bodily function involves the **central nervous system (CNS).** The *spinal cord* and *brain* make up this control center.

The Spinal Cord

The bones of the spinal column serve as protection for the spinal cord. *Three membranes,* called the **spinal meninges** (spy-nul men-**in**-jez), also *cover and protect the spinal cord.* The meninges are located between the bone and the soft tissues of the nervous system.

Spinal Cord

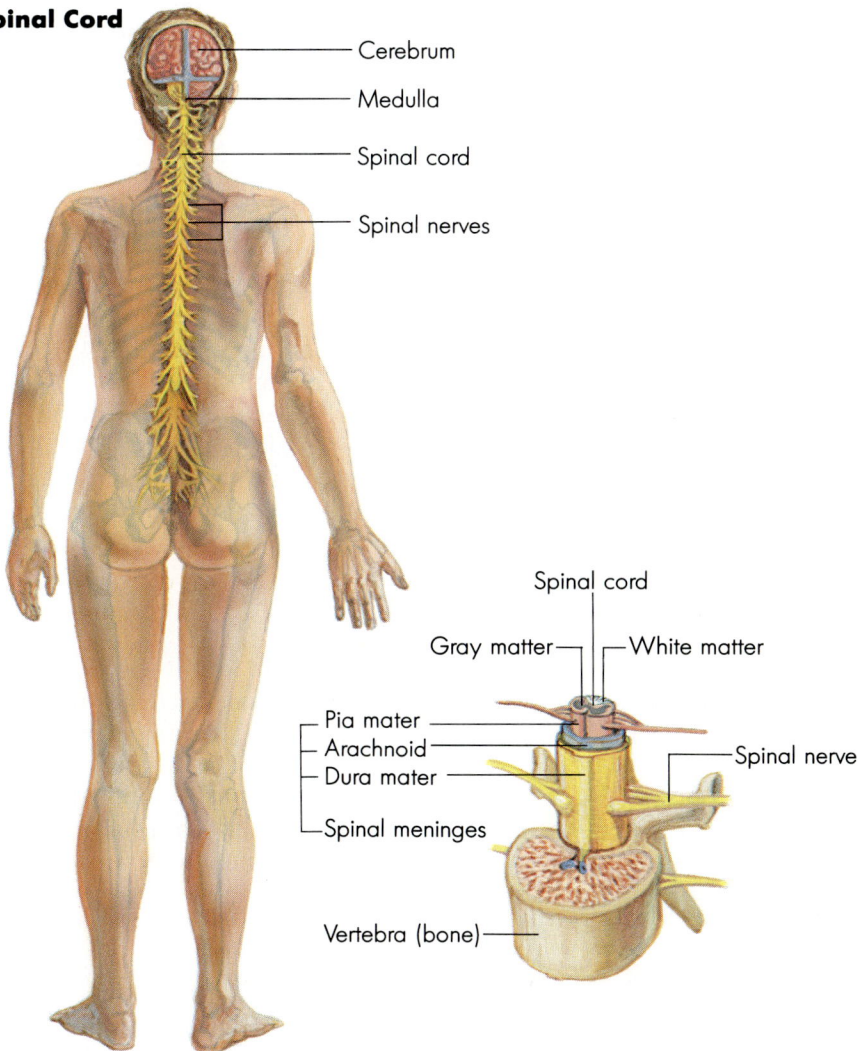

- Cerebrum
- Medulla
- Spinal cord
- Spinal nerves

Spinal cord

Gray matter — — White matter

- Pia mater
- Arachnoid
- Dura mater
- Spinal meninges

Spinal nerve

Vertebra (bone)

The spinal column and spinal meninges protect the spinal cord.

The outermost membrane, called the **dura mater** (**do**-rah **may**-ter), is *a tough protective covering.*

The middle membrane, called the **arachnoid** (uh-**rack**-noid), is *a thin, transparent sheath that lies directly under the dura mater.* It is like a spiderweb in appearance under a microscope.

The inner membrane, called the **pia** (**pea**-ah) **mater,** is *a delicate tissue that contains many blood vessels and provides nourishment to the cells of the brain and the spinal cord.*

Between the middle and inner membranes is a space filled with a special fluid, called *cerebrospinal* (ser-ree-bro-**spy**-nul) *fluid.* **Cerebrospinal fluid** *acts as a shock absorber and helps to protect the spinal cord from injury.*

Look at the cross section of the spinal cord on page 251. You can see that it consists of two different types of tissue. The central area resembles the letter H and is darker. This is gray matter and consists of nerve-cell bodies and dendrites and axons of connective and motor neurons.

You read on page 247 that certain axons have a myelin sheath. Myelin is white, composed of tightly packed myelinated axons, so the outer area looks white. The neuron-cell bodies and axons without myelin make up the gray matter.

The Brain

The human brain is a grayish-pink ball with many ridges on its surface. Weighing around three pounds (1.35 kg), the brain contains nearly 100 billion cells. At birth, the brain weighs about one pound (0.45 kg). In human beings, it reaches its full-grown size by age six.

The brain is supplied with the food and oxygen it needs from a vast network of blood vessels. Although the brain makes up only about 2% of the total body weight, it uses 20% of the oxygen that a person breathes in. The brain can go without oxygen for only four to five minutes before suffering serious damage.

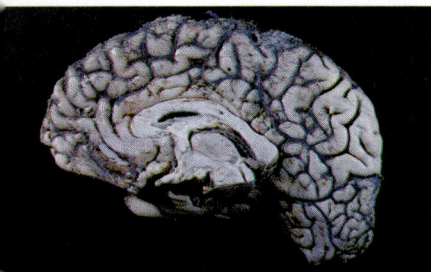

Cross-section of the brain, right side.

The Cranial Cavity

The brain lies in the *cranial cavity* (**kray**-nee-uhl **kav**-it-tee) and is protected by the eight cranial bones of the *skull. Additional protection is provided by the* **cranial meninges,** *membranes that are continuous with the meninges of the spinal cord.*

As in the case of the spinal cord, the cerebrospinal fluid fills the space between the pia mater—the meninges attached to the brain surface— and the arachnoid. This fluid plays a very important role in the nutrition and protection of the brain.

The Functioning of the Brain

The work of the brain is similar to a combination of a computer and a chemical factory. Brain cells produce electrical signals and send them from cell to cell along pathways called circuits. These **circuits** *receive, process, store, and retrieve information much like a computer.* Unlike a computer, however, the brain creates its electrical signals by chemical means. The proper functioning of the brain depends on the many complicated chemical substances that the brain cells produce.

The Brain's Divisions

The brain has three main divisions: the *cerebrum*, the *cerebellum*, and the *brain stem*.

The Cerebrum

The largest and most complex part of the brain is the **cerebrum** (ser-**ree**-brum). The cerebrum has two distinctively different types of brain tissue:

1. the irregularly shaped white matter, which is composed mainly of axons or fibers;
2. the *white matter* called the **cerebral cortex,** which is covered by a thin layer of gray matter and consists mainly of neuron-cell bodies.

Besides initiating every thought and voluntary action, this gray matter has great influence over all reflexes. Reasoning, memory, emotion, foresight, intelligence, and other mental activities all begin in and are stored in the cerebral cortex.

The Cerebral Hemispheres   *The cerebrum is divided into two identical halves,* called the **cerebral hemispheres** (ser-**ree**-bral **hem**-ess-fears). Each half has four lobes. Each lobe is named after the bone of the skull which is situated above it.

- The *frontal lobe* controls voluntary movements, personality, and at least some of the neurons involved with speech and memory.
- The *parietal lobe* (pah-**rye**-eh-tull **lobe**) is involved with a wide variety of sensory information—heat, cold, pain, touch, and body position in space.
- The *occipital lobe* (ach-**sip**-uh-tull **lobe**) contains our sense of vision. The impulse that results from stimulation of cells in the retina travels over the optic nerve to the occipital lobe.
- The *temporal lobe* contains our sense of hearing. The senses of taste and smell are also thought to be interpreted in the temporal lobe.

The Cerebellum

The cerebellum (ser-uh-**bell**-um) is the second largest portion of the brain. It is a mass situated beneath the occipital lobes of the cerebrum.

Midbrain

Parietal lobe

Occipital lobe

Meninges

Cerebrum

Frontal lobe

Thalamus

Interbrain
Pineal gland

Hypothalamus

Pituitary gland

Brain Stem

Temporal lobe

Pons

Medulla

Cerebellum

Spinal cord

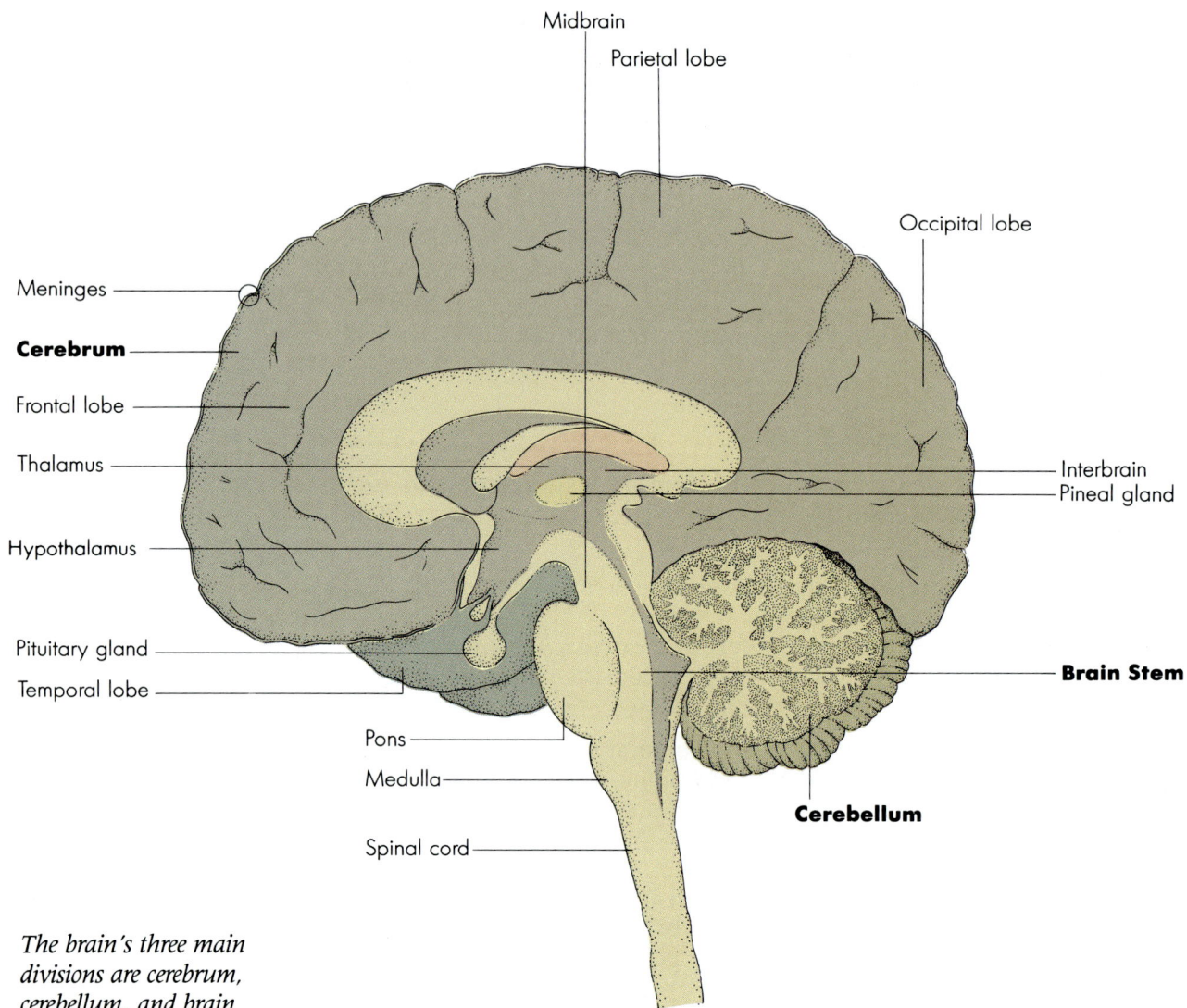

The brain's three main divisions are cerebrum, cerebellum, and brain stem.

The **cerebellum** *is responsible for smooth, coordinated muscle movements.* It receives impulses from the balancing centers of the inner ear, from muscles and joints, and from the motor areas of the brain.

The cerebrum determines the movements the body is to make, initiating the nerve impulses that activate appropriate muscles. The cerebellum coordinates these nerve impulses to ensure accurate and controlled movements. The cerebellum also maintains equilibrium during movement.

The Brain Stem

The **brain stem** is larger and more complex than the spinal cord. It *contains the important organs of the cranial nerves and the mechanisms for coordinating and integrating all incoming information.* The brain stem includes the *medulla, pons,* and *midbrain* with the *interbrain.*

The Medulla   The lowest part of the brain stem, called the medulla (meh-**dull**-ah) is an enlarged continuation of the spinal cord. The **medulla** *contains control centers that regulate heartbeat, breathing, and the diameter of the blood vessels.* Also situated in the medulla are the centers that control vomiting, sneezing, swallowing, hiccuping, and coughing.

The major sensory and motor pathways between the body and the cerebrum cross over as they pass through the medulla. Thus, each cerebral hemisphere controls the opposite side of the body.

The Pons   Just above the medulla, the brain stem enlarges to form the pons (**pahnz**). The pons connects the hemispheres of the cerebellum. The **pons** *serves primarily as a pathway for nerve traits passing to and from the cerebrum.* It contains nerve fibers that link the cerebellum and the cerebrum. The pons also controls respiration.

The Midbrain and the Interbrain   The shortest part of the brain stem is the midbrain, which lies just above the pons. The **midbrain** connects the brain stem with the cerebrum and the fibers from the cerebellum. *Its nerve centers help control movements of the eyes and the size of the pupils.*

Located above the midbrain is the **interbrain,** or *diencephalon* (die-en-**sef**-uh-lun). It is almost completely *covered by the hemispheres of the cerebrum.* The interbrain consists of two parts—the *thalamus* and the *hypothalamus:*

- The **thalamus** (**thal**-uh-mus) is a large mass of gray matter containing many nuclei. These nuclei *function as the relay stations for incoming sensory impulses.*
- The **hypothalamus** (hy-poe-**thal**-uh-mus) forms the lower part of the interbrain. It is situated just above the pituitary gland. Neurons from the hypothalamus *stimulate the pituitary gland* to release hormones that control many body functions. We will discuss the pituitary gland in Chapter 16.

  The hypothalamus also has nerve centers that control different body processes, keeping the conditions within the body balanced. For example, nerve centers in the hypothalamus regulate the amount of water in the body and the body temperature.

  Parts of the hypothalamus and the thalamus, along with parts of the temporal lobe, also play an important role in emotional responses.

CHECK YOURSELF

1. What makes up the central nervous system?
2. In what ways are the spinal cord and brain protected?
3. What are the main parts of the brain?
4. What are the four lobes of the cerebral hemispheres? Name a function of each.
5. What are the parts of the brain stem? Name a function of each.

Peripheral (pur-**rif**-er-rull) means "located away from the center." The **peripheral nervous system (PNS)**—the other main division of the nervous system—*carries all of the messages sent between the CNS and the rest of the body.* The PNS consists of 12 pairs of cranial nerves, 31 pairs of spinal nerves, and autonomic nerves. Within the PNS is a *somatic division* and an *autonomic division*.

- The **somatic** (soh-**mat**-ick) **division** includes *sensory neurons,* which send impulses to the CNS to be interpreted, and *motor neurons,* which carry impulses from the CNS to activate a response.
- The **autonomic** (ot-uh-**nom**-ick) **division** *maintains the equilibrium of the body's constant temperature, controls smooth muscles, and regulates the heartbeat.*

The Autonomic Nervous System (ANS)

You have read that the medulla controls basic body functions. Working with the medulla and midbrain to carry out these body functions is the autonomic nervous system. The **autonomic nervous system**'s constant regulation of the body processes enables the body to maintain a stable internal environment. The ANS consists of **ganglia** (**gang**-lee-uh) (singular form: *ganglion*)—*masses of nerve tissue*—and fibers connecting the brain stem and spinal cord with smooth muscle, heart (cardiac) muscle, and glands.

There are two parts of the ANS—the *sympathetic system* and the *parasympathetic system.*

The Sympathetic System

The **sympathetic** (sym-pah-**thet**-ick) **system** *responds to the body's needs during increased activities and in emergencies.* Sympathetic nerves lead to all of the vital organs and glands, including the liver, heart, kidneys, pancreas, stomach, salivary glands, and sweat and adrenal glands.

The Parasympathetic System

The **parasympathetic** (pear-uh-sym-pah-**thet**-ick) **system** *generally opposes the actions of the sympathetic system.* It slows down the heartbeat, opens blood vessels, and lowers blood pressure. If you have ever watched someone's eyes, you probably noticed changes in the size of the pupils. You can trace the nerve control of this reaction to the ANS.

The parasympathetic system is responsible for the *contraction,* or shrinking, of the pupil. The sympathetic system is responsible for the *dilation,* or

Unicycling and skateboarding call for the use of millions of nerve cells.

expansion, of the pupil. Similarly, the parasympathetic system increases digestive activities while the sympathetic impulses inhibit them. The balance of activity between the sympathetic and parasympathetic systems is controlled by the CNS.

Action of the Autonomic Nervous System

Organ	Action of Sympathetic System	Action of Parasympathetic System
Heart	Increases heartbeat	Slows heartbeat
Arteries	Raises blood pressure by constricting arteries	Lowers blood pressure by dilating arteries
Digestive tract	Slows movement Decreases activity	Speeds up movement Increases activity
Sweat glands	Increases secretion of sweat	Decreases secretion of sweat
Muscles of iris	Dilates pupil	Constricts pupil

Reflex Action

A **reflex** (**ree**-fleks) is *a spontaneous response of the body to a stimulus.* It occurs automatically, without conscious thought or effort. You cannot stop or keep some reflex actions from happening. In what ways do these reflex actions serve as protection?

The simplest type of reflex, such as occurs when the doctor taps the tendon below your knee, involves the interaction of only two neurons—a sensory neuron and a motor neuron. The impulse travels along sensory neurons to the spinal cord. Here the impulse moves across the synapse to the ending of a motor neuron. The impulse travels back to the leg muscle, causing it to contract and the knee to jerk.

In other reflexes, when a receptor is stimulated (for example, when your hand touches a hot stove), the axon of the sensory neuron makes contact with a connecting neuron in the spinal cord. This neuron, in turn, contacts a motor neuron that sends an impulse down its axon to the muscles. The muscles respond by pulling the hand away from the stove. All of this happens in a split second, even before pain is perceived by the brain.

The nerve chain of sensory and motor neurons involved in the reflex action is called a **reflex arc.**

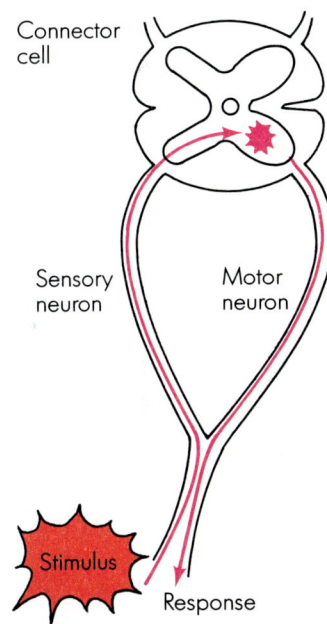

Connector cell

Sensory neuron

Motor neuron

Stimulus

Response

A reflex action can happen in a fraction of a second.

Sleep and the Nervous System

For reasons that are still unknown, human beings require a period of sleep on a regular basis. Deprived of sleep, humans become less efficient, lose their ability to concentrate, and become very irritable. Following a period of sleep, these symptoms disappear.

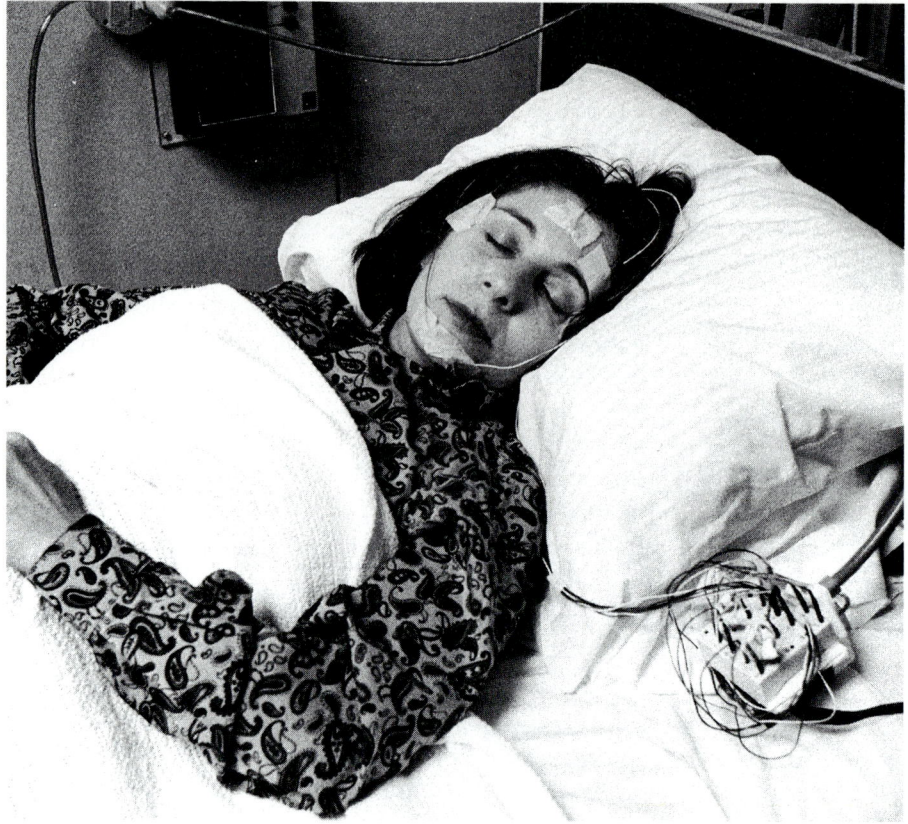

Brain waves are being recorded to chart this sleeping patient's unconscious activity.

By observing the brain waves of a person during sleep, scientists have been able to learn more about what happens to the nervous system during this time. Experiments show that there are periods of heightened activity in the brain during sleep. These periods are characterized by a period of **rapid eye movement** (REM).

This REM coincides with rapid, irregular low-voltage brain waves. Researchers have found that even though there is heightened brain activity that brings on dreaming, REM is a period when sleep is most relaxing.

During non-REM sleep, the metabolic rate and breathing rate slow down. Blood pressure is lowered, and nervous activity in the brain and spinal cord diminishes.

CHECK YOURSELF

1. The PNS consists of what nerves?
2. What is the basic function of the ANS?
3. Compare the work of the sympathetic and parasympathetic nervous systems.
4. What is a reflex arc?
5. Why do we need sleep?

4. Problems with the Nervous System

The normal functioning of the nervous system can be disturbed by any one of many diseases or disorders. An infectious disease, such as syphilis, can attack and destroy nervous tissue in the brain or spinal column. Accidents can physically damage or destroy nerve tissue. In addition, improper diet can lead to diseases that impair the functioning of the nervous system. Drug abuse, particularly alcohol abuse, destroys brain cells and can lead to a variety of serious nervous system disorders.

In general, disorders of the nervous system can be divided into four categories: *injuries, degenerative diseases, infectious diseases,* and *genetic disorders.*

Injuries

Injuries to the nervous system are common and painful. The major ones are injuries to the head, neck, and back.

Head, Neck, and Back

While participating in sports, riding in a car, lifting a weight, or using heavy tools, you can pull muscles and stretch, pinch, or crush a nerve.

It is best to use a safety belt in a car, dress correctly for motorcycling (see Chapter 26), and be careful when participating in sports. Warm up and cool down, wear the proper equipment, and be careful about taking undue risks.

One of the most common injuries is a **pinched nerve,** where *one of the spinal disks moves slightly as a result of a sudden jerking of the body, a blow, a fall, or a jolt due to a car accident.* The disk can press on or pinch a nerve, causing great pain and discomfort. Only a doctor can treat this condition.

Because of injury to the spine, some people must wear a neck collar or a special corset for the back. Others must go through *traction,* in which weights are used to balance out parts of the spinal cord and give relief from the pain. The last resort in spinal injuries is surgery.

Degenerative Diseases

In relation to the nervous system, **degeneration** refers to a *breakdown or deterioration of the structures of nervous tissue.* Three of the more common degenerative diseases of the nervous system are *Parkinson disease, multiple sclerosis,* and *Alzheimer disease.*

Parkinson Disease

The exact cause of Parkinson disease is not known. **Parkinson disease** *interferes with the transmission of nerve impulses from the motor areas of*

KEEPING FIT

The Nervous System and Drugs

Drugs that affect the nervous system are those that are most commonly abused. Some drugs, *stimulants,* cause the system to speed up. Other drugs, *depressants,* slow the system down.

What happens when the nervous system is depressed? The circulatory system and the respiratory system also slow down, and sometimes even stop. The leading cause of death by poisoning is *barbiturates*—drugs that slow down the nervous system. A certain group of drugs, *hallucinogens,* have a combined effect on the nervous system. That is, they speed it up and depress it.

Perhaps the greatest risk one takes with the misuse or abuse of any drug is the risk of damaging or destroying brain cells. Damage to brain cells is permanent since they are the only cells in the body that do not repair themselves. Say "Yes" to wellness and "No" to drugs.

Jonas Salk and Polio

Had you been a student in 1954, you might have been one of the million and a half American school children who took part in a major scientific experiment. You would have been living at a time when children were in fear of catching a crippling disease—polio. 35,000 to 50,000 people were infected by polio each year.

Intensive research against polio began in the late 1930s. In 1938, an organization was formed for the treatment of polio and for research. It was established by a famous polio victim, President Franklin D. Roosevelt.

Doctor Jonas Salk (1914–   ) joined the foundation a year after it opened. His first achievement was to determine that the 100 different virus strains that caused polio fell into three broad categories—Types I, II, III. This meant that all varieties of polio could be fought with a vaccine containing only the three virus types. It took Salk about 18 months to develop the anti-polio vaccine. But he only proved its effectiveness on monkeys.

Salk then began experimenting with children who already had had polio. They would have *antibodies*—proteins that were released into their blood to fight the polio virus. He found that the vaccine produced by the children's antibodies produced even more antibodies and was very powerful. He was ready to test his vaccine on children who had never had polio. He innoculated his own sons first.

Although Dr. Salk continued to accumulate evidence that his vaccine increased antibodies, he did not know if a child attacked by the polio virus would be fully protected by his vaccine. The only way to find out was to deliberately infect a child with polio. Because of the potential risk of death, this could not be done. So Dr. Salk helped organize a mass human experiment in schools.

Half of the students involved in the experiment received the vaccine, the other half did not. Both groups were watched closely during the epidemic season. The results caused great excitement in the medical community. Against Types II and III polio, the Salk vaccine was 90–100% effective. It was 65% effective against the more dangerous Type I. The vaccine was licensed for public use.

However, within two weeks, about 200 cases of polio were reported. With this alarming news, a hold was put on all vaccine production. It was discovered that each of the 200 victims had been given a vaccine made by the same drug company. The company did not know how to make a uniformly safe vaccine.

Dr. Salk, along with other polio experts, developed a detailed list of rules for making the vaccine. Since then, the Salk vaccine has been safe. Polio is no longer a threat to our health.

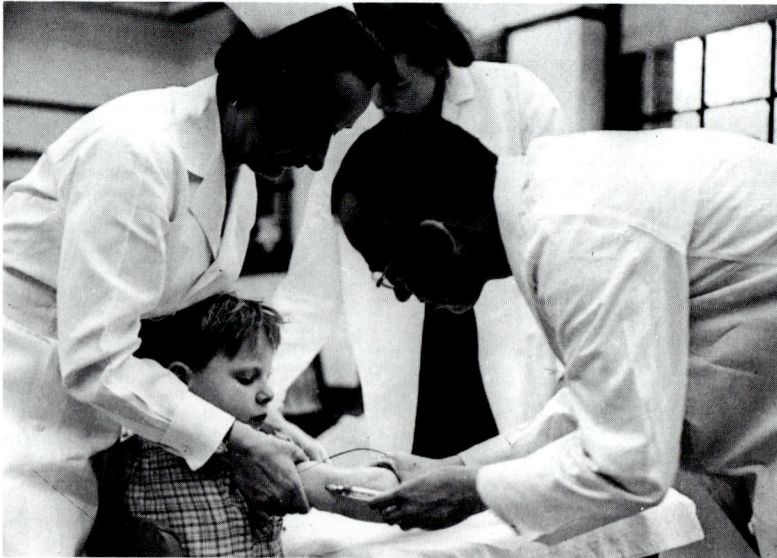

the brain. It is a progressive disorder, meaning that it gradually progresses to more nerves. The result is uncoordinated muscle movement. This disease is more common in men and usually occurs in people over 40 years of age.

In Parkinson disease, some muscles, especially those of the hands and feet, tremble. Other muscles, particularly those of the face, become rigid. With the discovery of a drug called L-dopa, the effects of this disease have been dramatically controlled in many patients.

Multiple Sclerosis (MS)

Multiple sclerosis (mul-tah-puhl skler-**roh**-sis) *destroys the myelin sheath that surrounds many nerve fibers.* For some unknown reason, this outer coating is gradually destroyed and scar tissue forms in its place. The scar tissue interferes with the ability of the nerve fibers to send impulses. The impulses may even be blocked completely. The brain's ability to control the muscles gradually decreases.

The effects of MS depend upon which nerves are involved. One person may have balance and coordination problems while another may have speech and hearing difficulties. MS may recede and not reappear for years. It is quite unpredictable. There is no known cure for MS, but by undergoing therapy, many patients are able to lead productive lives.

Alzheimer Disease

Alzheimer (**als**-high-mer) **disease** *attacks the brain, destroying brain cells.* At present, science does not know the cause of the disease or how it operates. Its origin may be a virus or a hereditary factor.

Alzheimer disease causes people to gradually lose their memory and powers of judgment. Speech and body coordination may also be affected. The disease seems to affect people who are over 40 years old. It increases in seriousness as people get older.

If the disease is detected in its early stages, it can be closely watched and the patient can be carefully treated for those everyday ills and infections that seem to help in the disease's spreading. Alzheimer disease is now recognized as one of the most serious causes of death among adults in their middle and later years. It ranks as the fourth largest noncommunicable disease that affects adults. This ranks it only after heart disease, cancer and diabetes.

Infectious Diseases

Infectious diseases of the nervous system are caused by pathogens, or disease-causing germs. These microorganisms live within tissue in the body, robbing it of nutrients and in some cases producing poisons. *Encephalitis, meningitis, poliomyelitis,* and *rabies* are infectious diseases that may result in damage to the nervous system.

Encephalitis

Encephalitis (en-sef-uh-**lite**-us) is *an inflammation of the cells of the brain.* It may occur as a complication of a virus, such as measles or mumps, although in many cases the cause is unknown. Symptoms can include headaches, fever, and sometimes convulsions. Almost all patients recover from encephalitis, although some have permanent brain damage.

Meningitis

What word does *meningitis* (men-in-**jite**-us) resemble? Does that give you a clue as to what part of the nervous system this disease affects? **Meningitis** is *an inflammation of the meninges.* It can be caused by certain types of bacteria, viruses, and poisons. Symptoms can include severe headaches, high temperature, vomiting, and sore or tight neck muscles. Antibiotic drugs are now used to fight this disease when bacteria cause it, making the chances for recovery excellent. Antibiotic drugs are not used when it is known that the source of the infection is viral.

Poliomyelitis

Poliomyelitis (poe-lee-oh-my-uh-**lite**-us), or polio, is caused by any one of three types of polio *viruses that enter the body through the mouth, reach the bloodstream through the stomach or lungs, and then attack the central nervous system.*

Children and young adults are especially susceptible to polio. Polio can result in paralysis of one or more of the limbs, usually the legs. If the brain

---

HEALTH UPDATE   HEALTH UPDATE   HEALTH UPDATE

Facts About the Nervous System

- Every night the average person has three to four dreams, each lasting 10 minutes or more.
- The longest recorded dream, timed by observing rapid eye movement (REM), is 143 minutes.
- There are more than four times as many cells making up your brain as there are people in the world today.
- The human skull is made up of 29 different sections.
- When you sit in some positions for too long, the main nerve in your leg gets squeezed and stops sending information to your brain. When this happens, you no longer feel your foot, and it seems like it is asleep. Moving around takes the pressure off the nerve and "wakes up" your foot.
- While you sleep, your fingers grow colder, your toes grow warmer, and you change position 30 to 40 times a night to let your muscles rest evenly to allow your blood to circulate freely.

---

or nerves controlling the diaphragm become infected, the respiratory system may become paralyzed. The development of the Salk and Sabin vaccines in the 1950s has brought this once life-threatening disease under control.

Rabies

Rabies (ray-bees) is *a viral infection of the brain and spinal cord.* The virus is found in the saliva of an infected animal. Humans become infected by being bitten by such an animal. Symptoms of rabies include restlessness, mental depression, and painful throat spasms. Rabies is a life-threatening disease. Death is rapid because of choking or paralysis. There is a vaccination for rabies that consists of a series of injections after a person has been bitten.

Genetic Disorders

Some diseases of the nervous system are hereditary; that is, they are passed from parent to child through inherited genes. These disorders include *phenylketonuria* and *Down syndrome.*

Phenylketonuria (PKU)

Phenylketonuria (feen-ul-ket-un-**nure**-ree-ah) is rare, occurring in about one out of every 25,000 babies in the United States, and is transmitted by a recessive gene (see Chapter 21). The presence of this gene results in *an inability of the body to break down a substance called phenylalanine* (feen-ul-**al**-uh-neen). The resulting buildup of this substance in the body interferes with the normal development of the brain. Symptoms of PKU appear in the first few weeks of life and may include vomiting, seizures, and dry skin. PKU can be detected by a blood test even before the symptoms appear. With early treatment, mental retardation can be prevented. Treatment consists of a special diet that ensures normal development of a growing brain.

Down syndrome is little understood at the present time.

Down Syndrome

Down syndrome is characterized by *mild to serious physical and mental retardation, a result of a chromosome abnormality in which an infant has inherited an extra chromosome.* Normal humans have 46 chromosomes, 23 pairs in each cell. In Down syndrome, a person has 47 chromosomes, with the extra chromosome being in the twenty-first pair. Although the reason for Down syndrome in a child is not completely understood, the incidence is greater when a woman becomes pregnant in her late 30s or 40s. There is no present cure for Down syndrome.

Other Disorders of the Nervous System

Two other important disorders of the nervous system are *epilepsy* and *cerebral palsy*.

Epilepsy

The term *epilepsy* comes from a Greek word meaning "seizure." **Epilepsy** (**ep**-uh-lep-see) is *a disorder of the nervous system caused by a sudden burst of nerve impulses in the brain*. This sudden burst of impulses is transmitted to the muscles and results in a *seizure*, a physical reaction that may be slight or intense.

The reason for this sudden discharge of nerve impulses is not completely understood. It may be the result of a chemical imbalance in the brain, a tumor, or an injury to the brain before or during birth. There may be other causes, such as a high fever in childhood, an infection, or an intake of poisons. Sometimes children who have epilepsy simply outgrow it as they reach their teenage years.

There are two kinds of seizures—*grand mal* and *petit mal*.

- **Grand mal** seizures usually last two to five minutes, and the person may fall to the floor, losing consciousness. During the seizure, the muscles become tense. They expand and contract, causing the body to shake. The person may be sleepy after the seizure, but usually has no memory of it.
- **Petit mal** seizures are so slight that they often go completely unnoticed. The person may go into a daze or have a blank stare for about 30 seconds. He or she may experience slight dizziness or faintness.

A person with epilepsy may lose control of his coordination and harm himself. Quick assistance is necessary during a grand mal seizure.

Cerebral palsy may result in poor coordination and balance; muscle spasms; or hearing, sight, and speech problems.

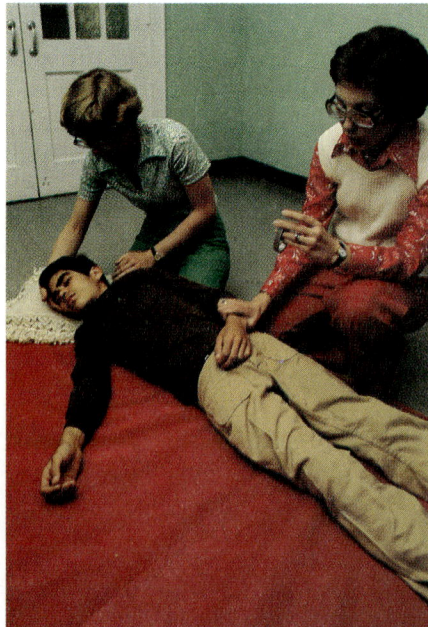

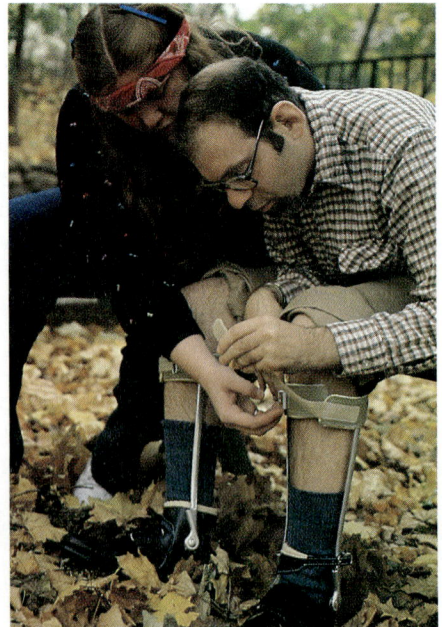

CERTIFIED SURGICAL TECHNOLOGIST (CST)

A **certified surgical technologist** is a member of the surgical team in the operating room who works with the surgeon, anesthesiologist, certified registered nurse, anesthetist, registered nurse, and licensed practical nurse, delivering direct patient care before, during, and after surgery.

The CST is a vital member of the health-care team who prepares supplies and equipment for use in surgery. Such a technologist usually scrubs the patients but may also assist the surgeon, work in delivery rooms or emergency rooms, or work as a private-duty scrub practitioner.

Like many other students in the health-care field, the potential CST has the opportunity to select from many

accredited schools. Certification means that the technologist has successfully completed a program of preparation and has passed a required examination.

Upon completion of an approved program, the CST will demonstrate the following:

1. knowledge of surgical aseptic (cleansing) techniques;
2. familiarity with basic surgical procedures, with anatomy, physiology, and microbiology, and with pathological processes;
3. the ability to meet patients' needs for comfort, safety, and reassurance;
4. the ability to anticipate and meet the needs of the surgical team and function in areas where qualified.

For more information on this career opportunity, contact the American Medical Association's Committee on Allied Health Education and Accreditation, or the Association of Surgical Technologists.

Committee on Allied Health Education and Accreditation
American Medical Association
535 North Dearborn Street
Chicago, IL 60610

Association of Surgical Technologists
8307 Shaffer Parkway
Littleton, CO 80127

There is no present cure for epilepsy, even though there are drugs that control most seizures. People with epilepsy generally live a normal, healthy life. The disorder does not affect their intelligence or ability to function.

Cerebral Palsy

Cerebral palsy (ser-**ree**-bral **pall**-zee) refers to *a group of nonprogressive* (that is, the illness does not worsen) *neurological disorders that are the result of damage to the cerebrum*. If oxygen to the brain is decreased or cut off, damage may occur before or during birth. Also during birth, pressure to a baby's head can cause damage to the cerebrum. Accidental injury, lead poisoning, and certain illnesses can also cause cerebral palsy.

The effects of cerebral palsy vary, depending on which part of the cerebrum is damaged and the extent of the damage. The effects are mainly physical and include muscle spasms; poor coordination and balance; or hearing, sight, and speech problems. People who have cerebral palsy can have normal or above normal intelligence. Physical therapy programs, braces, and walking aids all help people who have cerebral palsy lead full, active lives.

CHECK YOURSELF

1. What is the difference between the degenerative diseases of the nervous system and the infectious diseases of the nervous system? Name two of each type of these diseases and describe some of their symptoms.
2. What are two genetic disorders that affect the nervous system? Name some of their symptoms.
3. What is Down's syndrome?
4. Explain what happens when a person who has epilepsy has a seizure.

CHAPTER 14   Review

CHAPTER SUMMARY

- The basic structure of all nervous tissue is the neuron. Neurons are classified according to their functions—sensory, connecting, and motor.
- The most complicated body system is the nervous system. Made up of the brain, spinal cord, and a vast, complex network of nerves, the nervous system is the control center of the body.
- There are two basic divisions of the nervous system—the central nervous system (CNS) and the peripheral nervous system (PNS). The peripheral nervous system is further subdivided into the somatic and autonomic systems.
- The normal functioning of the nervous system can be disturbed by any one of many diseases or disorders. Accidents can physically damage or destroy nerve tissue. Alcohol and drug abuse can destroy brain cells.
- General disorders of the nervous system can be divided into three categories: degenerative diseases, infectious diseases, and genetic disorders.

REVIEWING WHAT YOU LEARNED

1. Compare the central nervous system (CNS) and the peripheral nervous system (PNS).
2. Describe the parts of a neuron and how each part functions.
3. Make a chart showing the lobes of the brain and what each lobe is responsible for.
4. What is the relationship between multiple sclerosis and the myelin sheath?
5. Explain the action of a reflex.
6. Name two degenerative diseases of the nervous system. Describe each of them.
7. Name two infectious diseases of the nervous system. Describe them.
8. Name two genetic disorders of the nervous system. Describe them.
9. What are (a) epilepsy and (b) cerebral palsy?

neurons
cell body
axon
myelin
dendrites
sensory neurons
receptors
connecting neurons
motor neurons
nerve impulse
synapse
central nervous system
   (CNS)
spinal cord
spinal meninges

dura mater
arachnoid
pia mater
cerebrospinal fluid
brain
cranial meninges
circuits
cerebrum
cerebral cortex
cerebral hemispheres
cerebellum
medulla
pons
midbrain
interbrain

thalamus
hypothalamus
peripheral nervous system
somatic division
autonomic division
autonomic nervous
   system (ANS)
ganglia
sympathetic system
parasympathetic system
reflex
reflex arc
rapid eye movement (REM)
pinched nerve
degeneration

Parkinson disease
multiple sclerosis
   (MS)
Alzheimer disease
encephalitis
meningitis
phenylketonuria
Down syndrome
epilepsy
grand mal
petit mal
cerebral palsy
certified surgical
   technologist

PUTTING VOCABULARY TO USE

On a separate piece of paper, write the following statements. Then supply the missing word or phrase from the chapter vocabulary list.

1. _____. Spontaneous response of the body to a stimulus.
2. _____. The basic structure of nervous tissue.
3. _____. Part of the brain stem that regulates heartbeat and breathing.
4. _____. Extensions that carry impulses away from the cell body.
5. _____. Extensions that receive and conduct impulses toward the cell body.
6. _____ _____. Neurons that send impulses from receptors toward the central nervous system.

7. _____ _____. Neurons found only in the CNS that provide the link between sensory input and muscle activity.
8. _____ _____. Neurons that carry impulses from the brain or spinal cord back to the muscles and glands.
9. _____ _____. Membranes that cover and protect the spinal cord.
10. _____. The largest part of the brain.
11. _____. The part of the brain responsible for smooth, coordinated muscle movements.
12. _____. Seizures that are intense and which last two to five minutes.
13. _____. The junction between the axon end of one neuron and the dendrite of another neuron.

APPLYING WHAT YOU LEARNED

1. Research the brain. How were various parts of the brain discovered? What are the most recent developments in brain surgery? Write a report on your findings.
2. Why do you think young people continue to use or experiment with drugs, knowing the risk to their nervous system?
3. Make a diagram illustrating the relationship of the nervous system to the other body systems.
4. Select one of the disorders of the nervous system to research. Find out how it was discovered and the latest information available on it. Include in your report how information is made available to the public.
5. Head injuries can be very dangerous. Find out the major causes of head injuries for people in your age group. Next to each cause, write a way that injury could be avoided.

FOCUS ON WELLNESS

The most complex, intricate system of the body is the nervous system. *I promote the health and full functioning of my nervous system by . . .*

The Skeletal and Muscular Systems

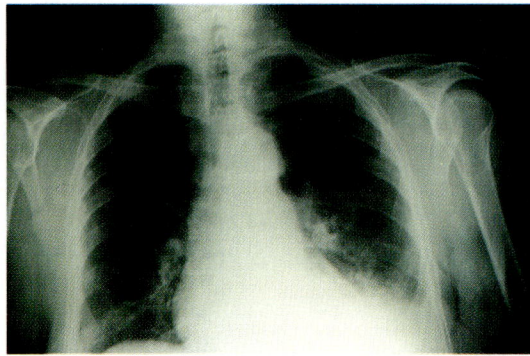

The skeletal and muscular systems are the body's means of locomotion. They are composed of bone and muscle, attached in such a way that we can perform amazing feats of mobility and power.

After studying this chapter, you will be able to:

- identify the functions of the skeletal system,
- describe the structure and function of bones,
- compare the various types of joints,
- describe illnesses of the joints and bones,
- describe the structure and function of muscles,
- explain the process involved in the muscles' obtaining necessary energy for work,
- define muscle tone,
- describe the work of the heart muscle,
- identify two diseases of the muscles.

Two of the body's major systems work together so closely that they are inseparable. They are the skeletal and muscular systems.

You might think of the skeletal system as the girders and crossbeams that make up the framework of a building. You also might think of your muscular system as the bricks and mortar that cover the framework.

But, unlike a building, which cannot move, your skeletal and muscular systems together allow you to run fast and to walk slowly, to jump high and to crouch low, to lift heavy weights, and to pick up small, comparatively weightless objects.

The Functions of the Bones

The structure of the skeletal system makes it possible for you to move. Bones serve as places where muscles attach to *joints,* the points of contact at which bones come together, making it possible for you to move in a variety of ways.

But this system serves many other purposes. Bones not only provide a supporting framework for your body, but they also protect internal organs. Bones are also the principal storage place for essential body minerals, such as calcium. *Calcium* is one of the minerals that promotes strong bones. Another important function of your bones is to serve as centers for the production of red blood cells and most white blood cells.

Bones Are Living Tissue

Just like other parts of the body, bones get the nutrients they need from the blood, and they grow and repair themselves. Just like other parts of the body, bones respond to the care that people provide them. Bones can be strong and healthy if people take care of them.

The body framework is made up of both bone and **cartilage** (**kart**-uh-ledge), a *strong, elastic material that gives form rather than rigidity.* A baby's skeleton is mostly cartilage. As the body grows, cartilage cells are replaced by bone cells and minerals through a process called **ossification** (os-seh-fuh-**kay**-shun), in which *calcium deposits form between the bone cells.* Ossification continues into early adulthood. Bones become harder and stronger, but they also become more brittle. This is why bones break more easily in adults than in young children.

At birth, 350 bones are in the human body. During early growth, many of the smaller bones fuse together. Adults have about 206 separate bones in their skeletal system.

Bones range in size from the smallest bone, the *stapes* in the middle ear, which is about 0.1 inch (0.25 cm) long, to the longest bone in the body, the *femur,* or *thighbone,* which is usually about 27% of a person's total height.

The Skeletal System

Parietal bone

Frontal bone

Temporal bone

Nasal bone

Cheek bones

Occipital bone

Atlas
(1st vertebra)

Axis
(2nd vertebra)

Cervical vertebrae
(neck)

Mandible
(jaw)

**Appendicular Skeleton
Shoulders, arms,
hips, legs**

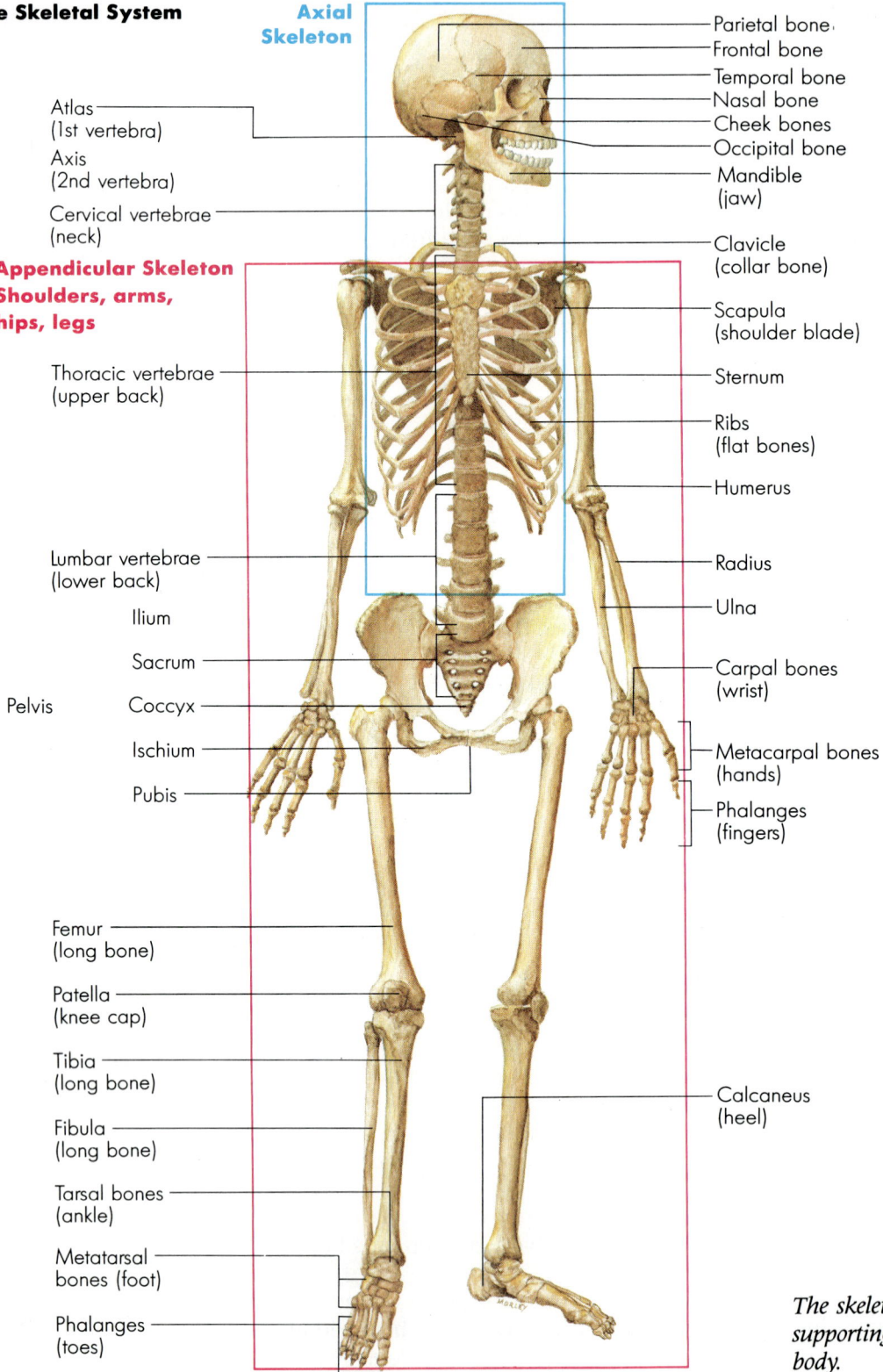

Clavicle
(collar bone)

Scapula
(shoulder blade)

Thoracic vertebrae
(upper back)

Sternum

Ribs
(flat bones)

Humerus

Lumbar vertebrae
(lower back)

Radius

Ulna

Ilium

Sacrum

Coccyx

Carpal bones
(wrist)

Pelvis

Ischium

Pubis

Metacarpal bones
(hands)

Phalanges
(fingers)

Femur
(long bone)

Patella
(knee cap)

Tibia
(long bone)

Fibula
(long bone)

Calcaneus
(heel)

Tarsal bones
(ankle)

Metatarsal
bones (foot)

Phalanges
(toes)

*The skeletal system is the
supporting framework of the
body.*

Types of Bones

Three basic kinds of bones are in the human body:

1. **Long bones,** like the femur, serve as levers. Long bones usually have a long, cylindrical shaft that has thicker ends shaped to fit the bones to which they are connected.
2. **Short bones,** like those in the wrists and ankles, are made of soft material covered with a thin layer of harder bone. Over one-half of all the bones in the body are in the hands and feet.
3. **Flat bones,** like the ribs, consist of two plates of hard bone with a softer material between them. These bones generally serve to protect vital body organs.

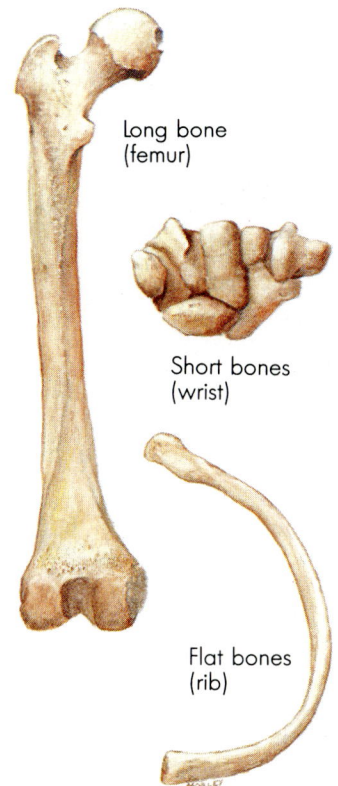

The Structure of the Bones

Different types of bones have different features and functions. Long bones have many of the features of other bones, which we will describe in more detail.

The Epiphysis

Long bones have enlarged ends called **epiphyses** (eh-**pif**-uh-sees) (singlar form: *epiphysis*). These *form a joint with another bone.*

Epiphyses are composed mainly of spongy bone tissue. The enlarged ends give stability to the joints at their points of entry. Muscles attach to the epiphyses, and the outer part of the epiphyses is covered with cartilage.

The cartilage serves as a buffer between bones. This spongy tissue is loose and acts as a shock absorber. In addition, cartilage supports the nose and ears, connects the ribs to the breastbone, or sternum, and acts as a cushion between joining vertebrae.

The inner part of the epiphysis contains red bone marrow. **Red bone marrow** *produces red corpuscles and most of the white corpuscles of the blood.* The

Long bone (femur)

Short bones (wrist)

Flat bones (rib)

The skeletal system contains long bones, short bones, and flat bones.

Cross-section of a long bone.

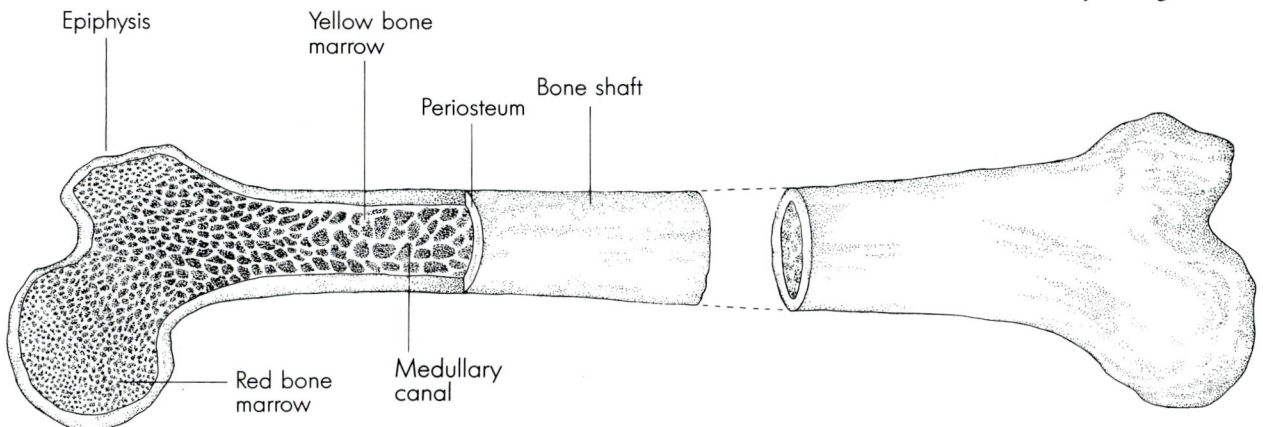

Epiphysis

Yellow bone marrow

Periosteum

Bone shaft

Red bone marrow

Medullary canal

corpuscles are also called *cells.* The red bone marrow's name is derived from the red color of the blood cells it produces.

The Periosteum

The **periosteum** (per-ee-**ahs**-tee-um) is a tough membrane that adheres tightly to the outer surface of the bone. This living membrane is richly supplied with blood vessels that branch into the bone at various points. The periosteum is vital in nourishing the bones and in producing bone cells. It contains *bone-forming cells* called **osteoblasts** (**os**-tee-oh-blasts) which are important in bone growth and repair.

The Shaft

Bones narrow into a thinner area, called a **shaft,** between the joint ends. Throughout the length of the shaft is a narrow space called the **medullary** (meh-**dull**-ah-ree) **canal.** This is linked with a tough connective tissue and filled with yellow bone marrow. Yellow bone marrow contains many blood vessels and a few cells that form white corpuscles. The main function of yellow bone marrow is to store fat. Yellow bone marrow gets its yellow color from the fat cells it stores.

Essential Minerals for Bones

In order to grow, harden, and repair, bones must have an adequate supply of minerals, especially calcium and phosphorus. Bones store the body's supply of these two minerals. If you have enough calcium and phosphorus in your daily diet, your body does not use the deposits in the bones.

However, if you have a mineral deficiency in your diet, your body takes away some of the mineral supply in the bones to provide minerals to the blood, muscles, and nerves. This creates a weakening of your skeleton and increases your chances of bone fractures.

The Joints

The point at which two bones meet is called a **joint.** Joints allow for movement of the body framework. Imagine that you did not have a joint at the point where your arm bones meet at your elbow. What activities would be impaired?

We can classify joints according to the movement they allow: *freely movable, partially movable,* or *immovable.* The illustrations on page 272 show the different types of joints.

Joints that allow for wide ranges of movement are often bound together by ligaments and muscles. **Ligaments** (**lig**-uh-ments) are *strong bands or cords of tissue that join bones or keep organs in place.*

The cavities of joint capsules are lined with a special membrane, the **synovial** (**cy**-no-vee-al) **membrane.** It secretes and fills the joint cavity

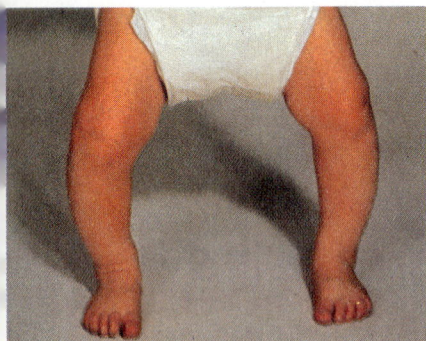

Bowed legs can be the result of lack of enough calcium and phosphorous in the diet.

Skull
(immovable joint)

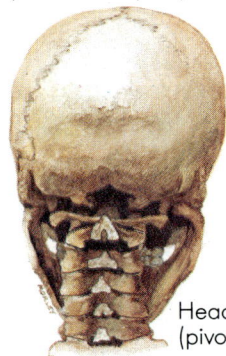

Head and neck
(pivot joint)

Shoulder
(ball-and-socket joint)

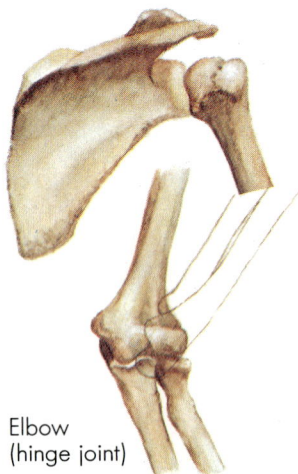

Elbow
(hinge joint)

There are three types of joints–immovable, partially movable, and freely movable.

with **synovial fluid,** which *lubricates the ends of the bones within the joint.* Many joints contain small sacs of fluid called **bursas** (**burr**-suhs) (singular form: *bursa*), which aid in the movement of muscles over bone. The synovial membrane lines all bursas.

You may have heard of **bursitis** (burr-**site**-us)—a painful condition occurring when a bursa becomes inflamed. It is common in the knee and shoulder joints.

Another joint illness is **gout**, *an inflammation of tissue around the joints by uric-acid crystals which form in the joint spaces.* The joints of the hands, elbows, feet, and knees are usually affected. In the feet, the big toe is the most common center for the illness.

It was once believed that people who ate rich food and drank heavy, sweet wines, like port, were thought to be the most likely victims of gout. But, the disorder may also be hereditary. Gout is now cured by medicines.

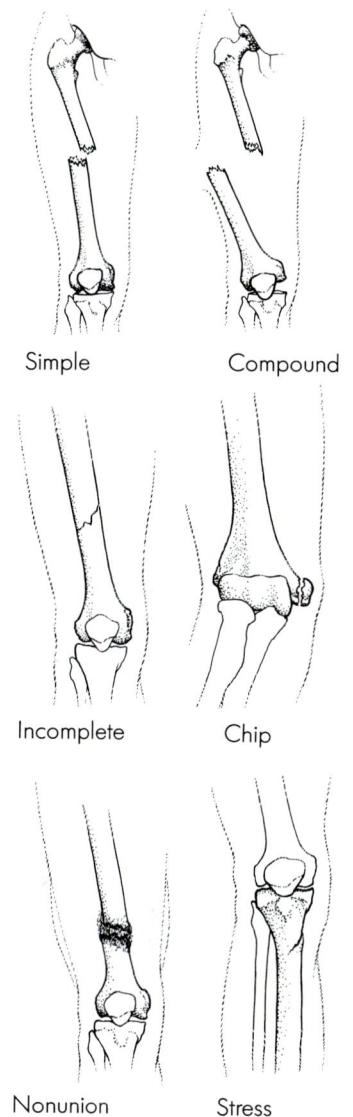

Simple   Compound

Incomplete   Chip

Nonunion   Stress

Bone Fractures

Fractures are *any type of break in a bone.* These types may be classified as *simple, compound, incomplete, chip, nonunion,* and *stress.* All of these fractures can be treated successfully.

- **Simple fractures.** The broken bone does not protrude (stick out) through the skin.
- **Compound fractures.** The broken bone protrudes through the skin and much blood can be lost.
- **Incomplete fractures.** The bone is cracked but not broken.
- **Chip fractures.** A piece of bone is broken off, or chipped.
- **Nonunion fractures.** The fractured bone does not heal properly. Sometimes this happens if the bone parts are not well fitted together, or if they shift.
- **Stress fractures.** A bone is strained in some way, so as to cause a weakness in it. Stress fractures happen through the repeated use of some part of the body. Sports figures and dancers are frequently victims of stress fractures in the legs and feet.

Bone Disorders and Diseases

Bone disorders and injuries to the bones are the result of many factors, including sports and recreational mishaps, viral infections, and poor posture. Chapters 2 and 3 will give you more information on injuries caused by participation in sports, and disorders as a result of poor posture.

Osteomyelitis

Osteomyelitis (os-tee-oh-my-uh-**lite**-us) is *a term given to many kinds of inflammation of the soft inner surface of the bones.* Many times, this inflammation is caused by a virus. In the past, osteomyelitis was a serious condition that required surgery to correct. Today, antibiotics, such as penicillin, are able to cure the infected bones.

Osteoporosis

Osteoporosis (os-tee-oh-**pore**-oh-sus) results from a low calorie diet, including a lack of calcium. The person *does not have enough nourishment to sustain the proper growth of the bones.* Elderly people, especially women, are prone to the disorder. Drinking milk and eating a balanced diet are important in containing the illness. (See page 151 for more information on calcium.)

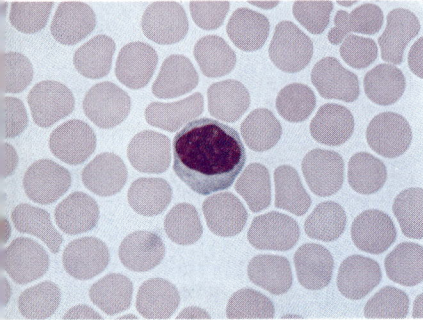

Leukemia

Leukemia (lew-**kee**-me-uh) is *caused by cancer cells that attack the marrow of the bone.* **Marrow** is the blood-forming matter inside the bones. The cancer keeps the marrow cells in an immature state, so that red and white blood cells and platelets are not produced in the quantities needed.

Leukemia can result in:

- anemia and a general tired feeling resulting from lack of red blood cells;
- abnormal bleeding from cuts or bruises, resulting from insufficient platelets to help clot the blood in a cut;
- general openness to infection, since the white blood cells that act as antibodies are underproduced.

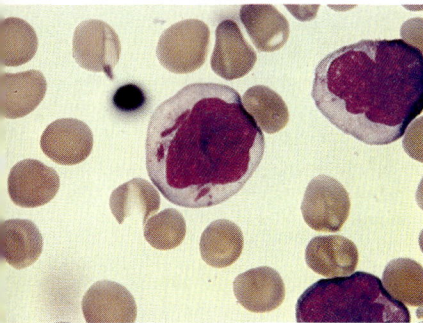

There are a number of types of leukemia, but all center around the marrow and the way the cancer affects it.

The causes of the disease are largely unknown. Some subtypes of the disease seem to be *genetic*, that is, passed on to offspring. Others may be traced to a virus. The disease and its type are determined by examining the bone marrow itself.

Leukemia sufferers are mostly children, and while there is treatment through certain drugs and radiation which may slow down the growth, the death rate is still high. More research is going on in the search for cures to leukemia and its subtypes. Marrow transplants have been very successful for some types of leukemia.

The top photo shows normal blood cells. The bottom one shows cells with leukemia.

CHECK YOURSELF

1. What are four functions of the skeletal system?
2. What is cartilage? What function does it serve?
3. Describe the three basic kinds of bones.
4. What is the difference between red bone marrow and yellow bone marrow?
5. What minerals are essential for healthy bones?
6. Name the three types of joints.
7. What is leukemia?
8. What is osteomyelitis?

Bones form the body's framework. Joints allow for the bones to move. But all body movements depend upon the most outstanding characteristic of muscles—the ability to *contract*, or shorten. Muscle tissue can shorten in length to a greater degree than any other type of tissue. The 600 muscles in your body are responsible for the movement of bones, pumping blood and carrying nutrients to all parts of the body, and controlling air movement in and out of the lungs. The muscle action in the esophagus, stomach, and intestine helps to break down food and to eliminate waste.

Almost all of the individual muscle fibers a person will ever have are present at birth. General muscle growth is an increase in the size of the muscles rather than an increase in the number of them.

Smooth Muscle Cells

Striated Muscle Cells

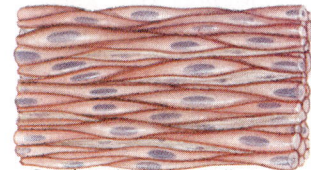

Cardiac Muscle Cells

Muscle tissue is composed of three types–smooth, striated (grooved), and heart.

Types of Muscles

The body has three basic types of muscle tissue—*smooth muscle, striated muscle,* and *heart muscle.*

1. **Smooth muscle,** sometimes called *unstriated* (un-**strye**-ated) *muscle,* is located in the gastrointestinal tract and blood vessels. Smooth muscles are involuntary because they work without a person's conscious control. Smooth muscle fibers are less than one-thousandth of an inch long.
2. **Striated muscle** is skeletal muscle. Skeletal muscles account for about 40% of the body weight.
3. **Heart muscle,** or *cardiac* (**kar**-dee-ac) *muscle,* is a special type of striated cell forming the fibers for the walls of the heart.

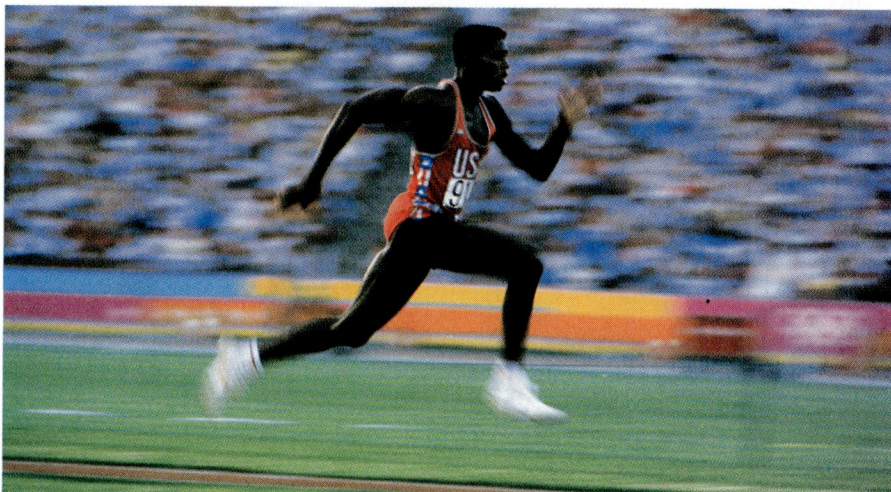

Runner Carl Lewis shows the importance of good muscular coordination in a race.

The Muscular System

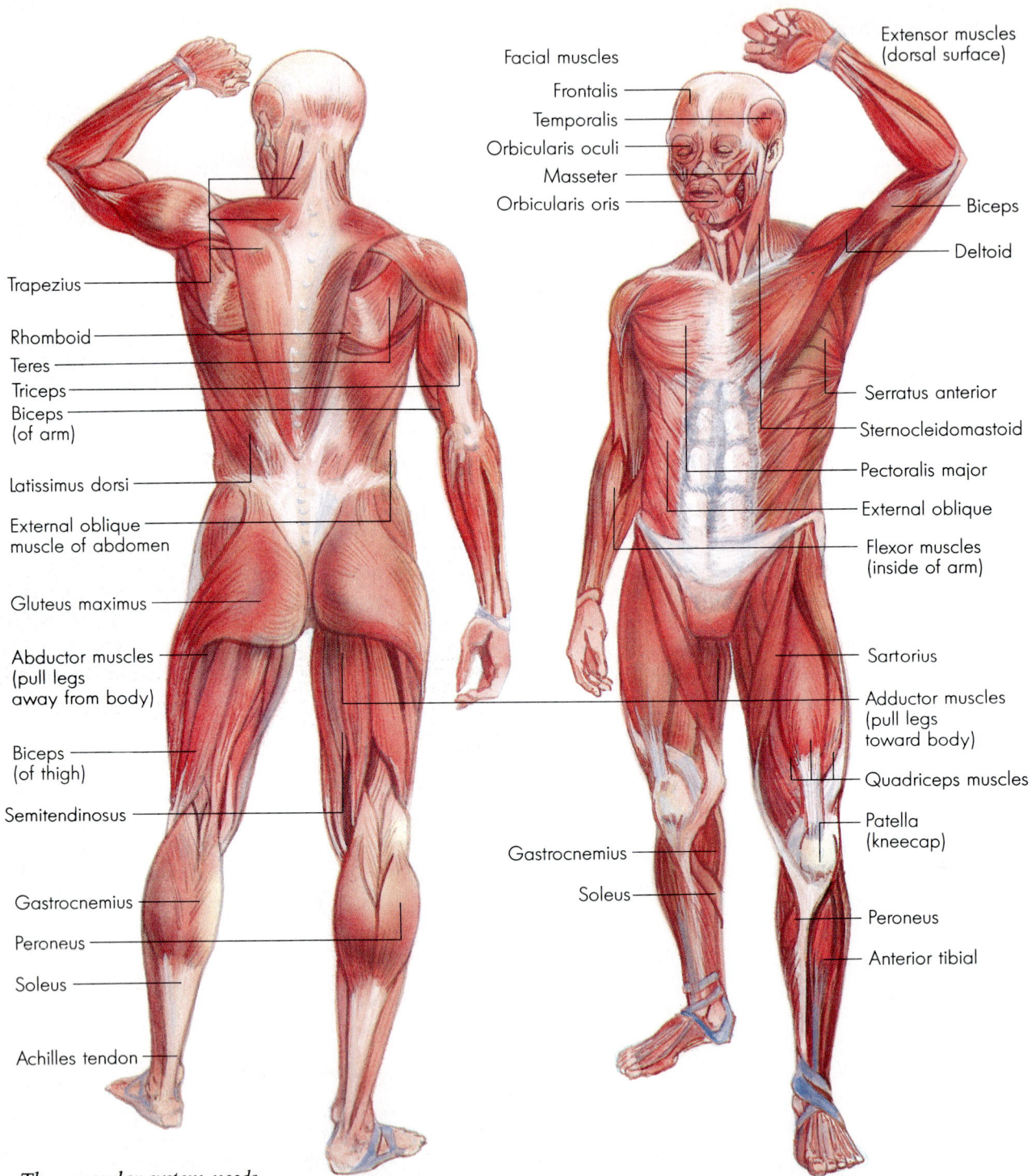

Facial muscles
Frontalis
Temporalis
Orbicularis oculi
Masseter
Orbicularis oris

Extensor muscles
(dorsal surface)

Biceps

Deltoid

Trapezius

Rhomboid
Teres
Triceps
Biceps
(of arm)

Latissimus dorsi

External oblique
muscle of abdomen

Gluteus maximus

Abductor muscles
(pull legs
away from body)

Biceps
(of thigh)

Semitendinosus

Gastrocnemius

Peroneus

Soleus

Achilles tendon

Serratus anterior

Sternocleidomastoid

Pectoralis major

External oblique

Flexor muscles
(inside of arm)

Sartorius

Adductor muscles
(pull legs
toward body)

Quadriceps muscles

Patella
(kneecap)

Peroneus

Anterior tibial

Gastrocnemius

Soleus

*The muscular system needs
exercise in order to keep it
functioning well.*

The Structure of Muscles

A muscle consists of a mass of fibers grouped together. Most skeletal muscles are attached to the periosteum by **tendons** (**ten**-dons), *strong parallel fibers massed tightly together that join muscle to bone, or muscle to muscle.*

Some muscles are attached directly to the periosteum. Small muscles in the face are attached directly to the inner lining of the skin. When you smile, these muscles contract, pulling the skin in and causing indentations in the cheeks called *dimples.*

Flexing and Extending

Many muscles work in pairs. While one *flexes,* its counterpart *extends.* Muscle contraction is started by the triggering action of nerve impulses. Nerves supplying most of the skeletal muscles originate at the spinal cord.

At the point where the nerve enters a muscle, it breaks up into numerous branch neurons, which in turn contact muscle fibers by means of tiny buttonlike endings called *motor end plates.* A neuron may branch to supply as many as 100 muscle fibers.

Muscles that bend a limb at the joint are called **flexors** (**flek**-sores), while *those that straighten a limb* are called **extensors** (ik-**sten**-sores). The tendons that connect muscle to bone must be connected to different bones, so that there is something to pull against when there is a contraction. If the flexors and extensors both contracted at the same time, they would work against each other, and there would be no movement.

Muscles are required to do a tremendous amount of work and, therefore, need large quantities of energy, supplied by oxygen. Muscles have a rich stock of arteries that supply them with food and oxygen via the blood.

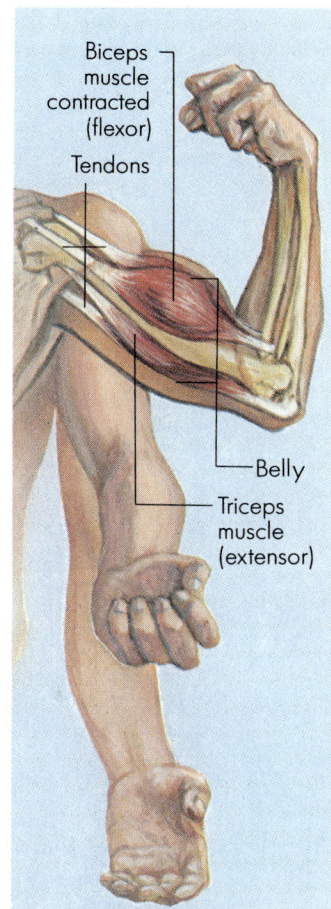

Extending and flexing involve different muscles.

What Makes Muscles Work?

Muscle tissue is actually about three-fourths water. The remaining one-fourth is made up of 20% protein substances and 5% nonprotein and mineral substances. One important nonprotein, chemical substance in muscle tissue is **adenosine triphosphate** (ah-**dean**-uh-sin try-**fahs**-fate) **(ATP).** An extremely important organic compound in muscles is *glycogen* (see Chapter 8).

Oxidation

Scientists still do not know exactly how the chemical energy stored in muscle cells is converted to the mechanical energy of muscle contraction. However, scientists do know something of the process.

The source of energy for muscle contraction is the same as that required for any cell: the oxidation of a carbohydrate, such as glycogen, to carbon dioxide and water. **Oxidation** is *the chemical breakdown of sugar in tissues to produce energy.* Food substances are broken down in the presence of oxy-

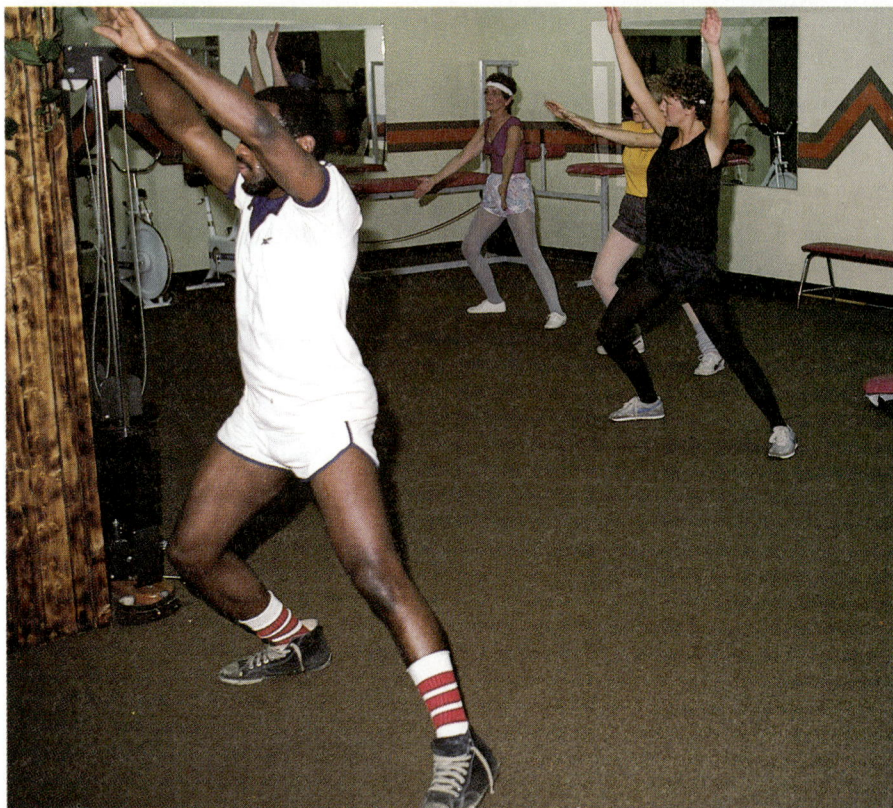

Aerobics exercises use body fat as the major fuel for the energy they need.

gen, and chemical energy is produced along with carbon dioxide and water, which are waste products. This energy allows us to move about and to live from day to day.

Adenosine Triphosphate (ATP)

This process of oxidation is too slow to be used as a source of immediate energy for the rapid contractions of which muscles are capable. The source of immediate energy for muscle contraction is the ATP found in muscle tissue. When ATP is broken down through chemical reactions, energy is released.

The Anaerobic and Aerobic Processes

The ATP is not stored in large quantities in muscle cells. Since it is constantly being used, it must be replaced. One of the ways that ATP is replaced is by means of the breakdown of *a sugar* called **glucose.**

When glucose is broken down, it is stored as glycogen in the liver and in the muscles, and it provides some ATP molecules. This process does not require the presence of oxygen and, therefore, is called *anaerobic* (an-uh-**row**-bick).

One of the waste products of this process is **lactic** (**lak**-tick) **acid.** The buildup of lactic acid *causes muscle pain and fatigue and interferes with the ability of muscle cells to contract.*

In the presence of oxygen, however, a glucose molecule is completely broken down, producing 18 to 20 times more ATP than does the anaerobic process. In the presence of oxygen, lactic acid does not accumulate. This aerobic (uh-**row**-bick) process is much more efficient than the anaerobic process, because it results in a higher yield of energy.

During exercise, both the anaerobic and aerobic systems are operating. When engaging in exercise that can be done for only short periods of time, like sprints, the body's main food fuel is glucose. Energy production comes mainly through the anaerobic process. The aerobic system does not have enough time to build up energy. Too much oxygen is needed in a short period of time, and the oxygen consumption cannot equal the demand.

In prolonged activity (15 minutes or longer), oxygen consumption has time to reach a new, higher level. Energy production is now at the aerobic level, which has fat as the major food fuel for the energy. This means that with prolonged activity the body begins to use stored fat for energy. It also helps to explain why aerobic exercises can be painful during the early phase, when there is a buildup of lactic acid. As the workout reaches the aerobic level, lactic acid is no longer building up in the muscle tissue. (See Chapter 2 and the *Health Handbook,* pages HB2–HB6, for more information on aerobic exercise.)

Muscle Tone

All muscle fibers do not contract at the same time. While some are contracting, others are relaxing. Even when you are sleeping, some cells are in a state of contraction, bringing about a certain degree of *firmness,* or **tone,** *to the muscles.* In the case of aging or poor health, muscles lose some or all of their tone. When you are in good health, a constant flow of impulses that the nerves send to the muscles maintains the muscle tone. Exercise and good nutrition improve muscle tone.

LIFE MANAGEMENT SKILL

Results of Exercise

Evaluate the amount of exercise that you get. How would you describe your overall muscle tone? List activities you could do to improve muscle tone and to increase aerobic workout.

Your Heart Is a Muscle

The most important muscle in your body is your heart. It works continuously, day and night. Just like other muscles, the more exercise the heart gets, the stronger it becomes. A strong heart works more efficiently; that is, it does the same amount of work with less effort.

The heart's job is to pump blood. Each time the heart beats, it is pumping blood through the rest of the circulatory system. A stronger, more efficient heart can pump the blood with fewer beats. It also has an increased **stroke volume;** that is, *it pumps out more blood with each beat.*

Exercise and the Heart

How does regular vigorous exercise help the heart and circulatory system? Regular exercise causes an increase in the number of capillaries, and this aids endurance. It also causes a decrease in the resting heart rate and an increase in the amount of the stroke volume.

This allows more chances for the heart to rest while pumping the required amount of blood throughout the body. As the heart becomes stronger, more oxygen reaches the body, meaning greater work performance.

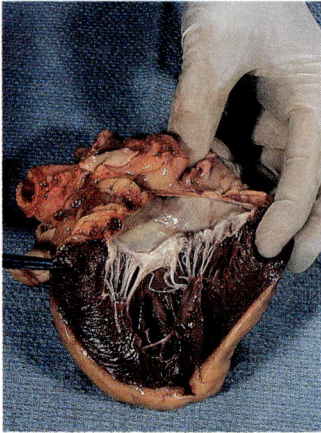

The heart is a natural pumping mechanism that never stops.

Regular vigorous exercise will help the heart and circulatory system.

Comparison of Average Heart Rate with Athletic Heart Rate

	Average Heart	Athletic Heart	Difference
1 minute	75	30	45
1 hour	4,500	3,000	1,500
1 day	108,000	72,000	36,000
1 month	3,240,000	2,160,000	1,080,000
1 year	38,880,000	25,920,000	12,960,000
Lifetime	2,799,360,000	1,866,240,000	933,120,000

Finally, exercise contributes to a lowering of blood pressure and a reduction in blood cholesterol and fatty substances in the blood. This reduces the risk of arteriosclerosis, or hardening of the arteries. (See Chapters 18 and 31 for more information on exercise and the heart and heart disease.)

Diseases of the Muscular System

Two common muscular diseases are also widespread. They are *myasthenia gravis* and *muscular dystrophy*.

Myasthenia Gravis

Myasthenia gravis (my-as-**thee**-nee-uh **grav**-is) is *a disease that is characterized by weakness and quick fatigue of the voluntary muscles.* The most commonly affected muscles are the eye muscles, which may result in drooping eyelids and double vision.

This disease can affect anyone, but for reasons unknown, it is most common in women of childbearing age. How does the disease develop? For some reason, victims develop an abnormal type of immunity in the blood. This immunity causes a muscle receptor to be nonresponsive to the chemical transmitter of nerve impulses.

Certain drugs are now used to increase the level of the chemical transmitter in the body, thus producing a temporary but dramatic recovery of muscle strength.

Muscular Dystrophy

Muscular dystrophy (**dis**-tro-fee), a crippling disease found most frequently in males, is characterized by *a progressive wasting away of skeletal muscles.* Muscular dystrophy, which is usually inherited, is caused by a defect

DOCTOR OF OSTEOPATHY

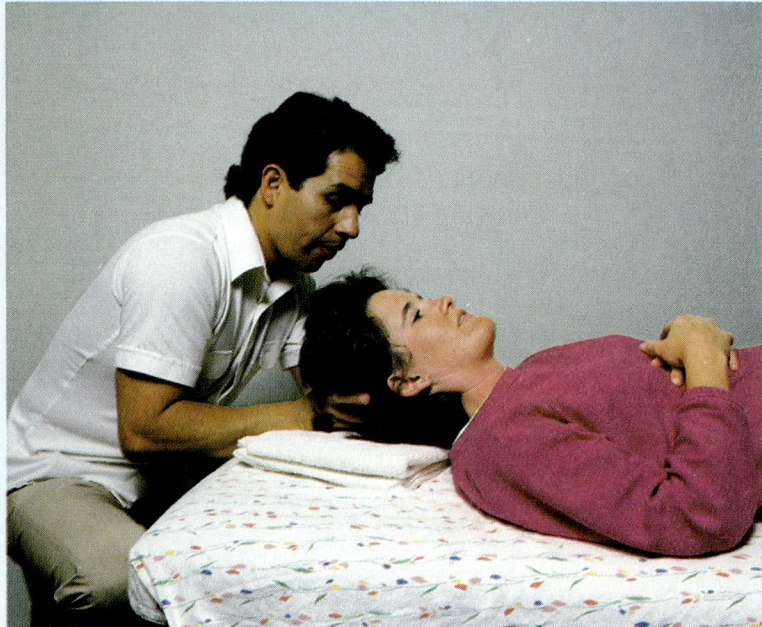

A career in medicine is one of the most challenging and rewarding professions you can choose. Most students are familiar with this field through their family physician. However, there is another alternative to the MD, doctors of osteopathy.

A **doctor of osteopathy** (os-tee-**op**-uh-thee) (DO) performs many of the same functions as a medical doctor and the training is very similar. Diagnosis, drug and therapy prescription, surgery and patient education are all part of the job. However, the DO adds something more in the approach to health care.

Osteopathy means *treatment of the musculoskeletal system*. The various organ systems of the body are all related by way of the circulatory and nervous systems. In osteopathy, manipulative therapy for the bones and muscles is a means of affecting the circulatory and nervous systems and, thus, the health of the entire body.

Doctors of osteopathy share the same work experiences as other doctors. They may work in a clinic or hospital, or set up a private practice. Teaching in a college of osteopathy or a hospital and doing medical research in various laboratory settings offer many possibilities for a DO.

To become a doctor of osteopathy requires completing the course of study at a college of osteopathic medicine and a year or more in residence at a hospital. A graduate will often continue this residency to pursue a specialty.

Success as a DO requires discipline, diligence, and common sense. The person must continue to study throughout his or her career.

Dealing with patients involves sensitivity and compassion. A DO must be able to work well with other health-care professionals and must be able to perform under extreme stress. Good health and a sense of humor are helpful assets in this challenging career.

For further information, contact:

American Osteopathic Association
142 East Ontario
Chicago, IL 60611

in the bones that control muscular function. When the muscle cells are unable to function properly, they die and are replaced by fatty tissue.

The symptoms of muscular dystrophy vary, depending on the part of the body that is affected. A person may experience muscle weakness, difficulty standing or walking, or frequent falls. Early detection of muscular dystrophy is crucial because muscle weakening can be delayed, even if the disease cannot be cured.

CHECK YOURSELF

1. What functions do muscles serve?
2. How are muscle contractions triggered?
3. What is the role of ATP in producing energy for muscles?
4. What is the role of glucose in energy production?
5. What is the difference between the anaerobic and aerobic production of energy?
6. Describe the effects of exercise on the heart.
7. Define myasthenia gravis.
8. Define muscular dystrophy.

CHAPTER 15   Review

CHAPTER SUMMARY

- The muscular and skeletal systems are closely related and make movement possible. The skeletal system is made up of about 206 bones, which have a variety of functions.
- Joints, the points where two bones meet, make it possible for bones to move. There are three types: freely movable, partially movable, and immovable.
- Bone disorders result from many factors, ranging from viral infections to poor posture. Two bone diseases are osteomyelitis and leukemia.
- The body has three basic types of muscle tissue: smooth, striated, and heart muscle.
- Muscles work in pairs. While one flexes, its counterpart extends.
- Nerve impulses and a complex process of chemical reactions control muscle activity.
- The most important muscle in your body is your heart, which exercise helps to keep healthy.
- Common muscular diseases are myasthenia gravis and muscular dystrophy.

REVIEWING WHAT YOU LEARNED

1. Why are the first few minutes of exercise usually the most difficult?
2. Describe the benefits of exercise on the skeletal and muscular systems.
3. What are the functions of the skeletal system?
4. What are the basic types of bones and where are they located?
5. Describe the features of a long bone.
6. How does the construction of joints allow for ease of movement?
7. Name six types of bone fractures and describe each one.
8. What are the functions of the muscular system?
9. What makes the muscles work? Describe this process.
10. What is muscle tone?
11. Describe the function of the heart muscle.
12. Describe two bone illnesses.
13. What is myasthenia gravis?
14. What causes muscular dystrophy?
15. What is the difference between a ligament and a tendon?

Skeletal System	shaft	*Muscular System*	muscle tone
cartilage	medullary canal	smooth muscle	myasthenia gravis
ossification	ligaments	unstriated muscle	muscular dystrophy
long bones	synovial membrane	heart muscle	osteopathy
short bones	synovial fluid	cardiac muscle	
flat bones	bursas	tendons	*Fractures*
epiphyses	bursitis	flexors	simple fracture
axial skeleton	gout	extensors	compound fracture
appendicular skeleton	osteomyelitis	adenosine triphosphate	incomplete fracture
red bone marrow	osteoporosis	oxidation	chip fracture
periosteum	leukemia	glucose	nonunion fracture
osteoblasts		lactic acid	stress fracture

PUTTING VOCABULARY TO USE

On a separate piece of paper, write the following statements. Then supply the missing word from the chapter vocabulary list.

1. _____. Chemical breakdown of sugar to produce energy.
2. _____. Spongy bone tissue that serves as a buffer between bones.
3. _____. Enlarged ends of long bones that form a joint with another bone.
4. _____. Tough membrane that adheres tightly to the outer surface of the bone.
5. _____. Strong fibers that join muscles to bone, or muscles to muscles.
6. _____. Muscles that bend a limb at the joint.
7. _____. Muscles that straighten the limb.
8. _____ _____. The amount of blood pumped out of the heart with each beat.
9. _____ _____. Crippling disease found most frequently in males.
10. _____. Small sacs in joints aiding in the movement of muscles over bone.
11. _____ _____. Nonprotein chemical substance in muscle tissue.
12. _____ _____. By-product of anaerobic conversion of sugar into energy.
13. _____ _____. Special membrane that lines the cavity of joints.
14. _____. Disease brought on by cancer cells attacking bone marrow.
15. _____ _____. Also called cardiac muscle.

APPLYING WHAT YOU LEARNED

1. Obtain a turkey or a chicken carcass. Mount the various bones and label them as bones, joints, breastbone, frame, etc.
2. Research the types of reconstructive surgery that are being done on bones and joints. If you know someone who has had such surgery, interview the person. How was the person rehabilitated? Write a one-page descriptive paper on your findings.
3. Imagine that for one day you had no joints in your body. Write a creative paragraph describing how your life would be different.
4. If you had to wear a full cast from your upper thigh to your ankle for several months, what would you expect to happen to your leg muscles? Why?
5. Find out how the Achilles tendon got its name. Report your findings to the class.

FOCUS ON WELLNESS

The ability to move about freely, exercise, and play is dependent upon the muscular and skeletal systems. *I can promote the health of these two systems by . . .*

The Endocrine System

There are eight key glands in the endocrine system.

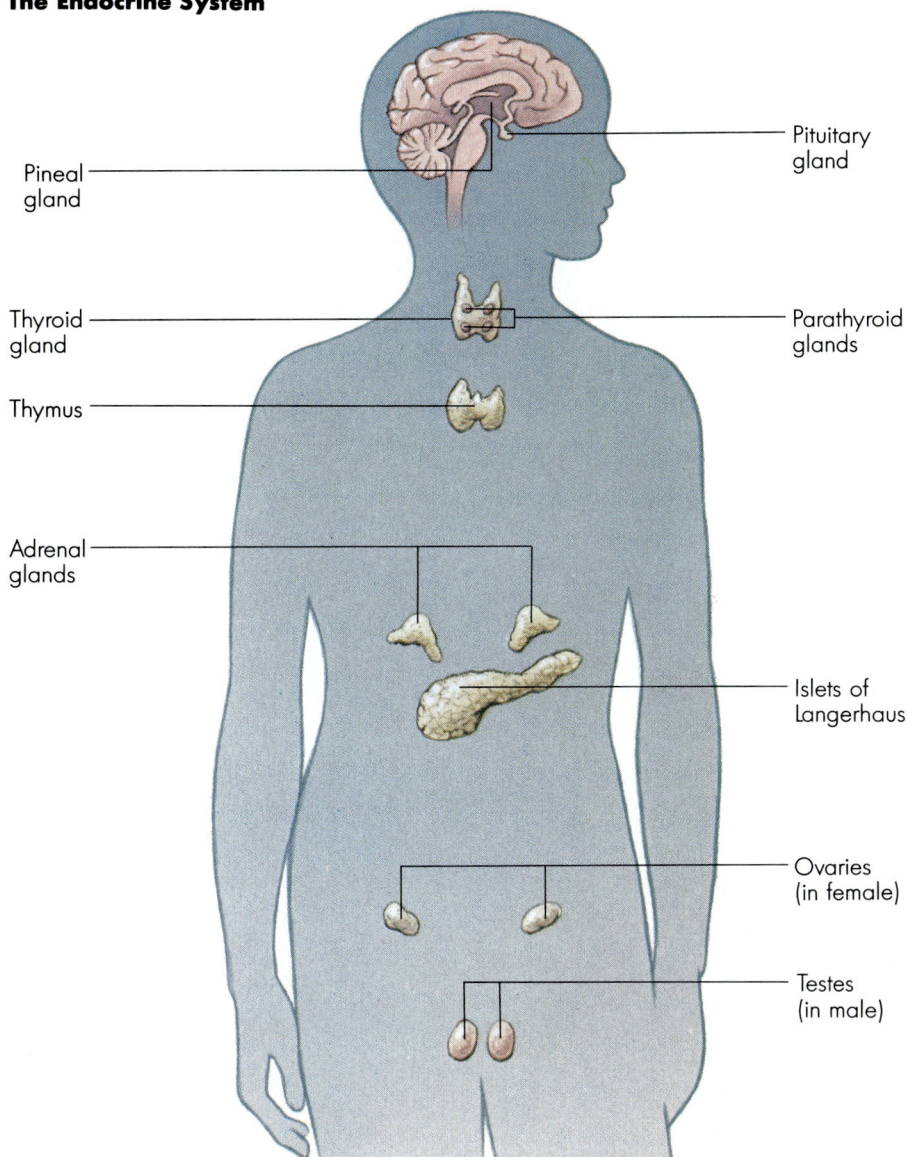

Pineal gland

Pituitary gland

Thyroid gland

Parathyroid glands

Thymus

Adrenal glands

Islets of Langerhaus

Ovaries (in female)

Testes (in male)

development, maturation of reproductive organs, and development of secondary sex characteristics.

3. *Hormones regulate the rate of* **body metabolism,** *the rate at which body cells produce energy.*

The Glands of the Endocrine System

Look at the illustration above. Eight glands make up the endocrine system: the *pineal, pituitary, thyroid, parathyroid, thymus, adrenals, islets of Langerhans,* and *ovaries* or *testes.*

The Pineal Gland

The **pineal** (pin-e-el) **gland** is around the size of a pea and is located within the brain. The functions of this gland are not fully known, but it seems to have a part in a person's sexual development.

The Pituitary Gland

The pituitary (pit-**tu**-uh-terry) gland is about the size of an acorn. It weighs about 0.021 ounces (0.6 g) and is situated at the base of the brain. Because of the **pituitary gland's** *many regulatory functions,* it is often referred to as the "master gland."

The pituitary gland has three lobes. The *anterior lobe* and the *posterior lobe* secrete different hormones and have a great effect on the other glands. The *intermediate lobe* is still not completely understood.

The Anterior Lobe of the Pituitary   The hormones that the anterior lobe releases control a range of bodily functions by regulating the metabolic activities of cells and by stimulating other endocrine glands. The anterior lobe produces at least five different hormones.

One of these, the **somatotropic** (soh-mat-toe-**tro**-pik) **hormone**, also known as the *growth hormone*, has a marked influence on muscles, kidneys, fat tissue, and the liver. It especially influences skeletal growth and height:

■ If the anterior lobe does not produce a sufficient amount of this growth hormone during the growth years, the person grows as a

The hormonal imbalance that produces a very small person or a very tall one is a rare condition.

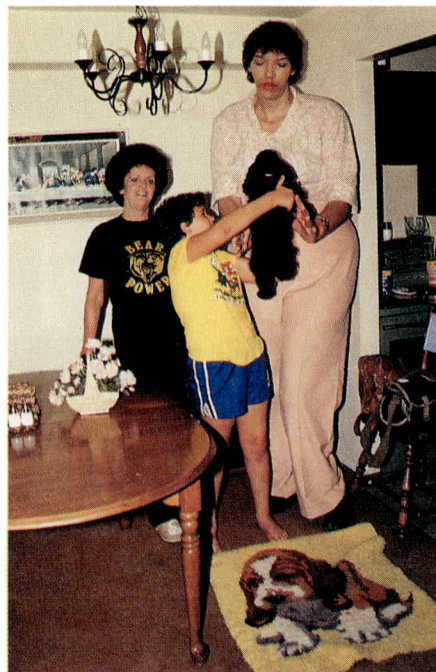

midget *(a very small person)* or as a **dwarf** *(a very small person whose arms and legs are quite short).*

- If too much of the somatotrophic hormone is produced during the growth years, the bones lengthen abnormally, resulting in a condition called **gigantism** (jie-**gant**-ism). The person becomes *abnormally tall.*

- If too much of this hormone is produced after the growing years, the bones thicken instead of lengthen. In this condition, called **acromegaly** (ak-row-**meg**-ah-lee), *the soft tissue over the bones enlarges, making the face look massive and the hands and feet large and awkward.*

- If the anterior lobe does not produce enough growth hormone after the growing years, a rare disease called **Simmond's disease** results. A person who has this disease suffers *premature aging, muscle weakness, and a wasting away of the body.* It is caused by the destruction of the pituitary gland.

Other Pituitary Gland Hormones of the Anterior Lobe   Other hormones that the anterior lobe of the pituitary gland produces are:

- The **thyroid** (**thy**-roid)-**stimulating hormone (TSH),** which regulates both the size and activity of the thyroid gland.
- The **adrenocorticotropic** (ah-dree-no-**kort**-eh-ko-tro-pik) **hormone (ACTH),** which triggers the manufacture and secretions of the outer layer of the adrenal glands.
- Two **gonadotropic** (go-nad-uh-**trop**-ick) **hormones,** which the pituitary gland secretes, control the growth, development, and functions of the *gonads,* the organs of reproduction. One of these hormones is called the **follicle** (**foll**-uh-kle)-**stimulating hormone (FSH);** the other is called the **luteinizing** (loot-in-eyes-**ing**) **hormone (LH).**

    In the female, FSH triggers the development of the cells that surround each egg in the ovary. In the male, FSH stimulates the testes to produce sperm cells.

    LH is responsible for ovulation, or the release of a mature egg from the ovary in the female. LH stimulates cells in the ovaries to produce *estrogen* (**es**-tro-jin) and *progesterone* (pro-**jes**-ter-rone), the female sex hormones. In the male, LH stimulates cells in the testes to produce *testosterone* (tes-**tos**-ter-rone), the male sex hormone.

The Posterior Lobe of the Pituitary   The posterior lobe of the pituitary gland secretes two hormones that are actually produced in the hypothalamus. One of the hormones is the **antidiuretic** (ant-ee-die-yur-**ret**-ick) **hormone (ADH)** and the other is known as **oxytocin** (ach-suh-**tow**-sin).

    ADH's principal effect on the body is to regulate the balance of water in the body. It stimulates the kidneys to retain water by returning it to the blood. If the kidneys did not return the water to the blood, a person would experience a serious internal water shortage. Oxytocin stimulates the smooth muscle found in the walls of the internal organs.

The Thyroid Gland

The **thyroid gland** is *the largest gland of the endocrine system*. It is a twin mass, consisting of a left and right lobe, located in the neck at the junction of the trachea and larynx. It produces a hormone called *thyroxine* (thy-**rok**-sin). Thyroxine contains iodine, which is necessary for normal thyroid activity. **Thyroxine** *affects all tissues by causing certain chemical reactions.*

Each cell in the body turns food into energy. The term **metabolism** (meh-**tab**-oh-liz-um) refers to *the rate at which cells in the body produce energy.* The cells depend upon the thyroid gland in order to change food into energy. If too much thyroxine is secreted in the body, a person experiences an increase in energy, making him or her overactive. If not enough thyroxine is secreted in the body, a person experiences a decrease of energy and becomes sluggish and tired.

As you have already read, the pituitary gland secretes a thyroid-stimulating hormone (TSH). This hormone is necessary to make the thyroid gland produce and secrete thyroxine.

Disorders of the Thyroid Gland   The metabolic action of thyroid hormones is very important during the growth years. A lack of thyroid hormones during the early growing years results in **cretinism (kree**-tin-iz-um). This condition *results in arrested growth, mental retardation, slow heart rate, and dry, yellowish skin.*

Myxedema (mix-eh-**dee**-mah) is a condition that results in *lack of growth in adulthood.* The metabolic rate drops, and mental and physical activity becomes sluggish. By administering thyroid hormones, all symptoms of myxedema usually disappear within a few weeks.

Goiter (**goit**-er) is another type of disorder of the thyroid gland. It is caused by a dietary deficiency of iodine. *The thyroid gland enlarges in an attempt to make up for the lack of iodine that is necessary for the production of its hormones.* Goiters are not a very common problem in the United States since most foods have iodine-fortified salt in them.

Goiters are common in countries whose food and water lack sufficient iodine.

The Parathyroids

The four brownish-yellow **parathyroid** (par-uh-**thy**-roid) **glands** are the smallest glands of the endocrine system. Two of them are located on the back side of each lobe of the thyroid. The hormone from these glands *regulates the body's calcium and phosphorus balance.* These minerals are necessary for growth as well as proper muscle contraction. They are essential to life, since their secretion helps to maintain normal functioning of muscle and nerve tissue.

The pituitary gland does not influence the secretion of the parathyroids, as it does the thyroid gland. The parathyroid secretions depend on the blood level of calcium. If the parathyroids are underproductive, producing low levels of hormones, the level of calcium in the blood drops. This results in an increased excitability in neurons, causing them to discharge spontaneously. This, in turn, causes *muscle spasms,* called **tetany** (**tet**-un-nee) that can be quite painful. If parathyroids are overproductive, greater than normal amounts of calcium are withdrawn from the skeleton, leaving bones weak and susceptible to fracture.

The Thymus Gland

The **thymus** (**tie**-mus) **gland** is located behind the breastbone, near the heart. The gland grows during childhood, but by adolescence it starts to shrink. It is very small in adults.

Like the pineal gland, the functions of the thymus gland are not fully known. The gland seems to have an important part to play in the body's immune system—possibly "setting up" part of the system during infancy and childhood.

The Adrenal Glands

The two adrenal glands are located at the top of each kidney. The **adrenal glands** consist of two parts—the outer portion, called *the adrenal cortex,* and the inner portion, called *the adrenal medulla.*

The Adrenal Cortex   The **adrenal cortex** (uh-**dree**-nul **kor**-teks), which is absolutely essential for life, *secretes a mixture of hormones that affect numerous bodily functions.* These secretions make up *a group of chemical compounds* known as **steroids** (**stir**-oids). Hormones from the pituitary gland stimulate the adrenal cortex to secrete its steroid hormones.

Aldosterone (**al**-doh-ster-rone) is the principal, most potent hormone that the adrenal cortex produces. Its function is *to maintain the body's water balance.* Aldosterone also regulates the kidneys' reabsorption of sodium and elimination of potassium. The production of aldosterone is regulated by the amount of sodium in the blood plasma. If the body lacks sodium or has an increase in potassium, the cortex increases its secretion of aldosterone.

The inner layer of the cortex produces a hormone called cortisone (**kort**-uh-zone). **Cortisone** *works to control the metabolism of carbohydrates, fats, and proteins.* Along with other hormones that the inner layer of the cortex secretes, cortisone also works to help a person cope with stress.

The Adrenal Medulla   The **adrenal medulla** is highly dependent upon the hypothalamus and the autonomic nervous system for regulation. It secretes the hormone **epinephrine** (ep-uh-**nef**-rin), more commonly called **adrenaline** (uh-**dren**-uhl-en), which *increases heart action, raises blood pressure, increases respiration, and suppresses the digestive process.*

This hormone is also known as the "emergency hormone" because it is released into the blood in greater amounts during highly emotional states, such as when a person experiences fear or anger.

If you look back at the effects of the sympathetic nervous system on the body, you will see that they are similar to the effects of epinephrine. The sympathetic nervous system stimulates the adrenal medulla to secrete its hormones. Unlike the adrenal cortex, however, the adrenal medulla and its secretion are not essential for life.

The Islets of Langerhans

The **pancreas** (**pan**-kree-us) is a gland that serves two systems: the digestive and the endocrine. The major portion of the gland secretes a digestive juice that breaks down nutrients. This elongated, flattened organ lies behind the stomach, attached to the first section of the small intestine by a duct that transports its digestive juice to the intestine.

Scattered throughout the pancreas are many small clusters of cells that are separated from those of the digestive pancreas by special fibers. These clusters of cells make up the endocrine part of the pancreas. They are called the **islets of Langerhans** for Paul Langerhans, a German scientist who first noticed them in 1869. There may be as many as a million of these tiny clusters that produce two secretions affecting the metabolism of glucose (blood sugar).

One hormone secretion, **insulin** (**in**-suh-lin), acts on the liver to *stimulate the formation of glycogen from glucose and causes the blood sugar to be transported across cell membranes.* The second hormone, **glucagon** (**glu**-kuh-gon), *stimulates the liver to convert glycogen to glucose.*

HEALTH UPDATE   HEALTH UPDATE   HEALTH UPDATE

Artificial Pancreas

Pumps are now being inserted successfully in diabetic patients to assist them in increasing their naturally low level of insulin. Researchers at the University of Minnesota inserted a pumping device, which is about the size of a hockey puck, in the upper chest. Every two weeks, the pump is refilled with insulin from a syringe in a simple outpatient procedure.

Insulin is necessary in helping the body to use sugar and other carbohydrates. Of the 12 million diabetics in this country, well over 1 million must take insulin daily to stay alive. This invention could mean a great deal to many of these people.

Insulin is a complex protein substance and is essential to life. Insulin must be present in the blood in order for the tissue to use carbohydrates. If it is not, the blood sugar level rises, and sugar accumulates in the kidneys instead of being metabolized. This condition is known as *diabetes mellitus* (die-uh-**bee**-tees **mel**-lite-us), which is discussed in more detail in Chapter 31.

The effect of glucagon is directly opposite to that of insulin. As the blood sugar level falls below a certain point between meals, glucagon is secreted. When glucagon stimulates the conversion of glycogen to glucose in the liver, the blood sugar level rises.

The Ovaries and the Testes

The **ovaries** (**oh**-var-rees) in the female and the **testes** (**tes**-tees) in the male are part of the *reproductive system,* and are both exocrine and endocrine glands. As exocrine glands, the ovaries produce and release the egg cell. The testes produce and release the sperm cell.

As endocrine glands, the ovaries and the testes produce hormones that are responsible for the development and maintenance of secondary sex characteristics (e.g, hair, breasts) during adolescence. The secretion of progesterone and estrogen by the ovaries is stimulated by hormones from the pituitary gland. Hormones from the pituitary gland stimulate the testes of the male to produce and secrete testosterone.

The endocrine system has its own built-in, highly complicated check-and-balance system. For example, a hormone that the pituitary gland secretes will cause another gland to secrete a hormone. As the level of the second hormone increases, this hormone acts upon the pituitary to lessen the release of any more of its own hormone. By means of this action, over-production of the hormone is prevented.

CHECK YOURSELF

1. What is the difference between an endocrine gland and an exocrine gland?
2. How do hormones act as chemical regulators?
3. In what ways does the pituitary gland influence other endocrine glands?
4. What are estrogen and progesterone in the female body?
5. What is testosterone in the male body?
6. Why is epinephrine, or adrenaline, called the "emergency hormone"?
7. What does insulin do for the body?

CHAPTER 16   Review

CHAPTER SUMMARY

- The nervous system regulates the endocrine system.
- Endocrine glands secrete hormones directly into the bloodstream, where they are carried to and influence changes in other parts of the body.
- Exocrine glands have ducts that carry their secretions to specific places in the body.
- The eight glands that make up the endocrine system are the pineal, pituitary, thyroid, parathyroid, thymus, adrenals, islets of Langerhans, and ovaries or testes.
- The pituitary gland is considered to be the "master" gland because many of its hormones control the functioning of other glands.
- The secretions from the endocrine glands influence body growth, metabolism, the body's reaction to emergencies, sex characteristics, reproductive abilities, and the maturation process.
- Overproduction or underproduction of certain of these hormones can cause serious illness.

endocrine system
endocrine hormones
gland
endocrine glands
exocrine glands
pineal gland
pituitary gland
anterior pituitary lobe
posterior pituitary lobe
somatotropic hormone
midget
dwarf

gigantism
acromegaly
Simmond's disease
thyroid-stimulating
    hormone (TSH)
adrenocorticotropic
    hormone (ACTH)
follicle-stimulating
    hormone (FSH)
gonadotropic hormones
luteinizing hormone (LH)
antidiuretic hormone (ADH)

oxytocin
thyroid gland
thyroxine
metabolism
cretinism
myxedema
goiter
parathyroid glands
tetany
thymus gland
adrenal glands
adrenal cortex

steroids
aldosterone
cortisone
adrenal medulla
epinephrine
adrenaline
pancreas
islets of Langerhans
insulin
glucagon
ovaries
testes

PUTTING VOCABULARY TO USE

Column A contains a list of endocrine glands. Column B contains a list of hormones and conditions resulting from hormonal imbalances. On a separate piece of paper, match the glands with their hormones and/or conditions. Several hormones and conditions may be appropriate for a particular gland.

Column A

1. anterior lobe of pituitary
2. posterior lobe of pituitary
3. thyroid
4. parathyroids
5. adrenal cortex
6. adrenal medulla
7. islets of Langerhans

Column B

a. thyroxine
b. tetany
c. TSH
d. gonadotropic hormone
e. goiter
f. aldosterone
g. myxedema
h. oxytocin
i. somatotropic hormone
j. cretinism
k. ACTH
l. ADH
m. cortisone
n. glucagon
o. insulin
p. epinephrine

REVIEWING WHAT YOU LEARNED

1. What is the function of hormones?
2. What is an endocrine and an exocrine gland?
3. Why is the pituitary called the master gland?
4. Diagram the relationship of the several endocrine glands on one another.
5. What is meant by the built-in check-and-balance system of the endocrine glands?
6. Which endocrine gland affects the body's response to stress? How?
7. Explain conditions resulting from improper functioning of two glands.

APPLYING WHAT YOU LEARNED

1. Interview a pharmacist or physician to determine which hormones are now synthetically produced. How are these hormones being used?
2. Research what an endocrinologist does. Write a narrative report describing this person's work.
3. Find out how a doctor determines whether or not the endocrine glands are working. What types of tests does the doctor perform?

FOCUS ON WELLNESS

All of the physical and many of the emotional changes experienced during adolescence are a result of hormones from the endocrine system. *By understanding the work of the endocrine system, I . . .*

The Reproductive System

The human reproductive systems in the male and female are designed to produce new life. Through this system, the human race produces offspring, thereby ensuring future posterity.

After studying this chapter, you will be able to:
- identify the structure and the function of the male reproductive system,
- identify some disorders of the male reproductive system,
- identify the structure and the function of the female reproductive system,
- identify some disorders of the female reproductive system.

The male **reproductive system** functions to produce the **sperm cell,** *the male cell that unites with a female egg cell to form a fertilized egg cell.* Males do not begin producing sperm until puberty—between the ages of 12 and 15. In Chapter 16 on the endocrine system, you learned that the pituitary gland secretes a hormone that causes the testes to begin producing testosterone. Testosterone causes the testes to begin producing sperm. Once a male reaches puberty, he is capable of producing sperm for the rest of his life.

The Testes

Sperm are produced in two small glands called **testicles (tes**-th-kills), or **testes (tes**-teez) (singular form: *testis*), a major part of the male reproductive system. These glands hang outside of the male's body in a sac called the scrotum. The **scrotum (skro**-tum) has the important function of protecting the sperm by keeping the testes at a temperature of 98.2°F (36.8°C), slightly below the normal body temperature of 98.6°F (37°C).

If the body temperature rises, the muscles of the scrotum relax, lower-

The male reproductive system consists of the testes, scrotum, epididymis, vas deferens, urethra, and penis.

The Male Reproductive System

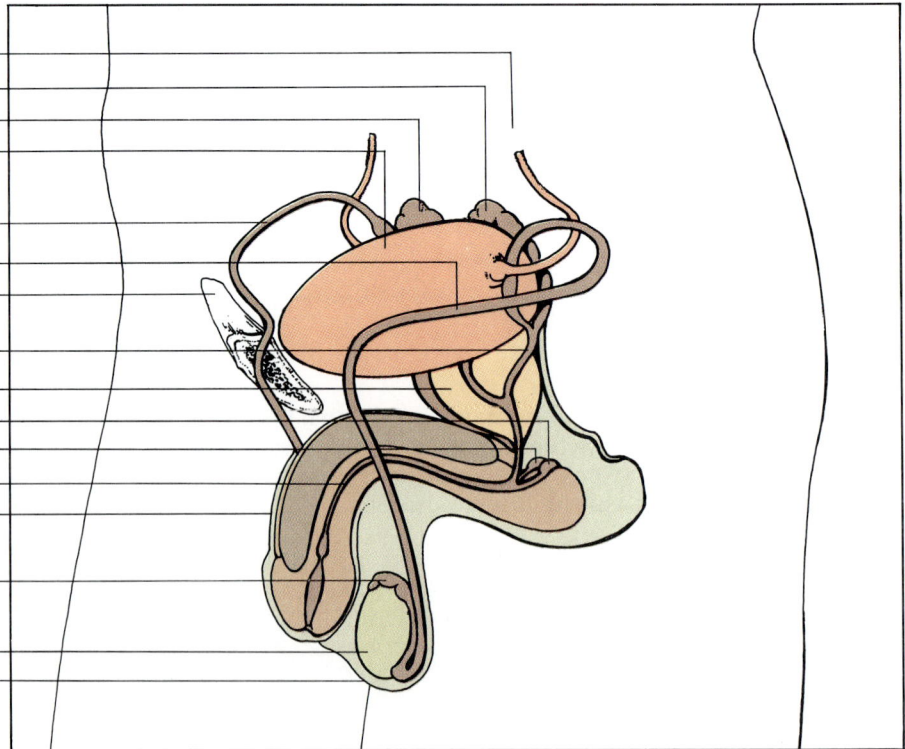

Ureter (from kidney)
Seminal vesicle
Seminal vesicle
Bladder

Vas deferens
Vas deferens
Pubic bone

Ejaculatory duct
Prostate gland
Cowper's gland
Cowper's gland
Urethra
Penis

Epididymis

Testes, (Testis, *sing.*)
Scrotal sac

ing the testes away from the body. If the body temperature is cold, the muscles contract, pulling the testes into the body. This is important because the sperm must be kept at just the right temperature to live.

Each testicle contains several hundred yards of coiled tubes. These tubes produce the sperm and provide a passageway in which the sperm can travel. A normal adult male produces about 200 million sperm a day. Each sperm is shaped somewhat like a tadpole, the head having the actual cell and the tail being the sperm's means of movement. Sperm cells are so tiny that 500 of them lined up end-to-end would only measure 1 inch (2.5 cm).

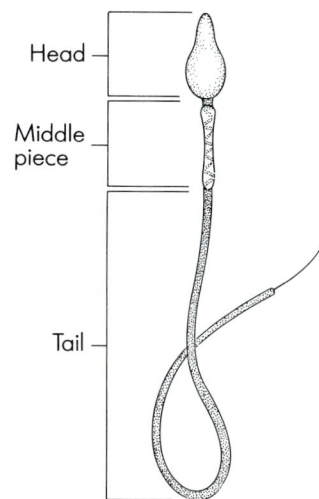

The sperm cell.

Other Major Parts of the Male Reproductive System

There are four other major male organs necessary for the production of life: the *epididymis,* the *vas deferens,* the *urethra,* and the *penis.*

The Epididymis

The tubes in each testicle join a larger coiled tube, called the epididymis (plural form: *epididymides*). The **epididymis** (ep-uh-**did**-uh-miss), located at the outersurface of each testicle, *stores the sperm after they are produced.* Sperm mature in the epididymis until they are ready to be released.

The Vas Deferens and Urethra

The **vas deferens**—a tube about 18 inches (45 cm) long—*connects with the epididymis at one end and the urethra* (you-**ree**-thruh) *at the other.* Sperm travel from the epididymis to the seminal vesicles through the vas deferens.

The **seminal vesicles** (**sem**-uh-nul **ves**-uh-kuls), two pouches that are each about 2 inches (5 cm) long, are attached to the vas deferens near the base of the bladder. They *secrete a fluid that mixes with the sperm to make them mobile and to provide nourishment.*

As sperm are ready to leave the body, they travel out of the seminal vesicles through the **ejaculatory ducts** (ee-**jak**-yuh-lah-tor-ee **ducts**). Fluids secreted from the **prostate gland** (**pros**-tate **gland**), located at the beginning of the urethra, and from the **Cowper's glands** (**Cow**-purr's **glands**), located below the prostate gland, mix with the sperm to form **semen** (**see**-mun) or *seminal fluid.*

A secretion from the Cowper's glands cleanses the urethra of any acidity to provide the safe passage of the sperm. A secretion from the prostate gland aids in the movement of the sperm.

The **urethra,** a tubelike organ, *connects with the bladder, as well as with the vas deferens.* The bladder stores urine, which leaves the body through the urethra. However, it is not possible for semen and urine to pass through the urethra at the same time. A muscle near the bladder contracts, preventing urine from entering the urethra when semen is passing out of the body.

Urine is highly acidic, which is why the urethra-coating secretion from

KEEPING FIT

Care of the Male Reproductive System

The male reproductive system consists of internal and external organs. It is important for males to keep the external organs—the scrotum and penis—clean. A daily shower will be a great help.

In athletic games, the use of a protector or supporter in the groin area will minimize injury. Very tight clothing may cause pain in the groin area. It is best to wear loose or fitted—but not overly tight—underwear and pants.

the Cowper's glands is important to ensure the sperm's safe passage. The substances from the Cowper's glands neutralize the acidity in the urethra before sperm pass through it.

The Penis

The urethra passes through the **penis,** *a tubelike organ, which is normally soft and hangs downward from the front of the body at the groin area.* The penis is made up of spongy tissue that, when filled with blood, causes it to become enlarged and erect. When the penis is in its erect state, semen is able to leave the body.

The lower trunk muscles provide the force that ejects the semen from the body. When these muscles contract, they cause an **ejaculation** (ee-**jak**-yuh-lay-shun). In the small amount of semen that leaves the body, there are about 300 to 400 million sperm.

When a boy reaches puberty, he begins to produce sperm cells, causing pressure to build in the reproductive system. The boy may experience a *nocturnal emission* (nock-**turn**-uhl ee-**mish**-shun) or a "wet dream." During sleep, the boy will have an erection and an ejaculation because the mind and body are in a more relaxed state. This is a normal process through which the body adjusts to the many changes taking place.

Males of every age experience erections. When a boy enters **puberty—** *the beginning of adolescence—*he may experience an erection during the day. The erection may occur for what seems like no reason at all. Sometimes an erection results from the friction of clothing. An erection does not need to be, and at almost all times is not, followed by an ejaculation.

Disorders and Diseases of the Male Reproductive System

Some disorders of the male reproductive system are *inguinal hernia* and *sterility.* Some diseases are *cancer of the prostate gland* and *testicular cancer.*

In any close contact sport, the groin area must be protected.

Hernia

A **hernia** (**her**-nee-uh) is *the pushing of a part of the body through the wall normally keeping it in*. Hernias, therefore, may occur in various parts of the body. A common hernia of the male reproductive system is called an **inguinal** (**in**-gwan-ul) **hernia**. This is *a weak spot in the abdominal wall near the top of the scrotum*. Sometimes, straining the abdominal muscles can cause a tear in this spot. A part of the intestine can then push through into the scrotum. Sometimes surgery is necessary to correct such a hernia.

Sterility

Sterility (stuh-**rill**-uh-tee) is *a condition wherein the sperm of the male is weak, malformed, or is unable to join an egg cell*. Therefore, fertilization does not take place. Temperature changes; exposure to certain chemicals; smoking; contracting mumps as an adult; syphilis or gonorrhea; and faulty operation of the epididymis, vas deferens, or the urethra can all result in a sterile condition.

Cancer of the Prostate Gland

Cancer is *any abnormal growth of the cells in the body*. The prostate gland has the second highest incidence of cancer in men, next to lung cancer. The risk of **prostate cancer** increases with age. Only a doctor can diagnose prostate cancer. Cancer specialists are working to improve methods for early detection since prostate cancer can be treated much more easily in the early, localized stage.

While few men die of cancer of the prostate, the cancer cells can spread through the bloodstream to other parts of the body. If the cancer spreads beyond the prostate gland, some 80% of patients will die within 10 years. Surgical removal of the prostate gland is the main remedy at the present time. (For more information on cancer, see Chapter 31.)

Testicular Cancer

Testicular (tes-**tic**-u-lar) **cancer** is a common cancer in males between the ages of 15 and 34. Hard lumps, or nodules, on the testes may be a sign of this cancer. If discovered early, it can be treated promptly and effectively.

Other diseases of the reproductive system are discussed in Chapter 30.

CHECK YOURSELF

1. What is the function of the scrotum?
2. What purpose do the secretions from the various glands serve in the reproductive process?
3. What are the major parts of the male reproductive system? What is the function of each?
4. What is a nocturnal emission?
5. Name two disorders or two diseases of the male reproductive system and describe them.

KEEPING FIT

Examination for Testicular Cancer

Males between the ages of 15 and 34 should do regular self-testicular exams for possible cancer. While showering, feel each testicle to see if there are hard lumps or a noticeable swelling. A person may also feel an ache in the groin area. See your doctor if any of these signs occur. Self-examination for testicular cancer should be carried out at least two times a month.

2. The Female Reproductive System

Unlike the male reproductive organs, most of the female reproductive organs are internal. The female reproductive system serves two important functions:

1. It provides the egg that will develop into a new human life.
2. It provides the nourishment and protection necessary for the fertilized egg cell to develop into a fully formed baby.

Major Parts of the Female Reproductive System

The major parts of the female reproductive system are the *ovaries,* the *Fallopian tubes,* the *uterus,* and the *vagina.*

The Female Reproductive System

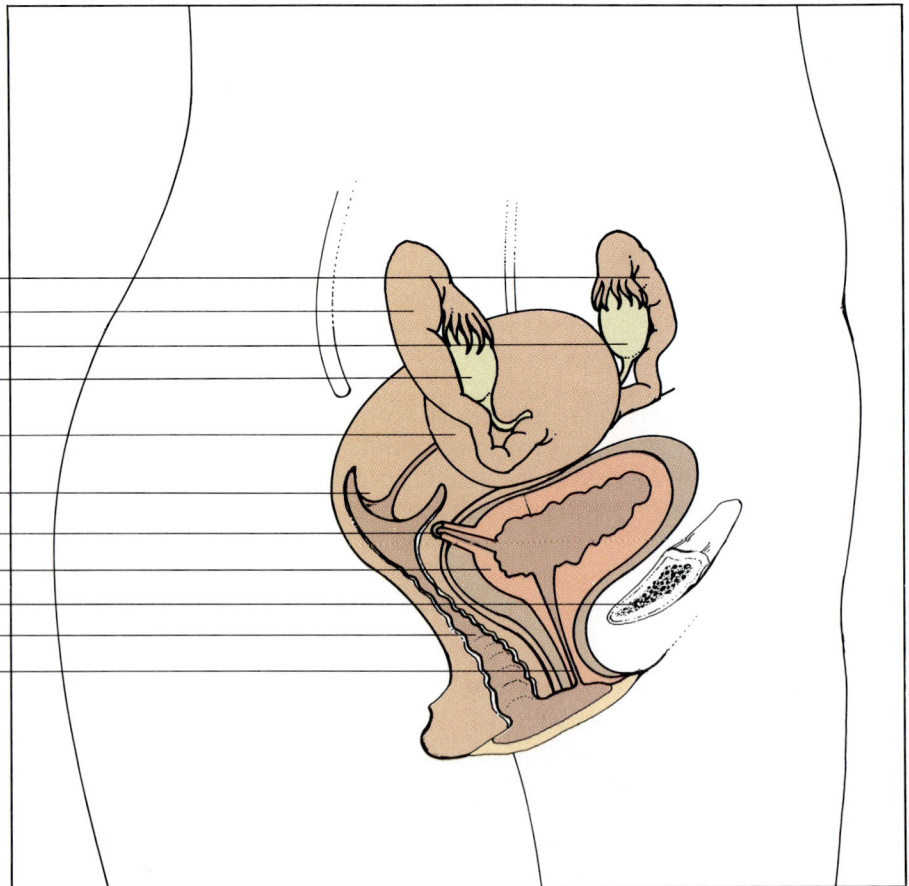

Fallopian tube
Fallopian tube
Ovary
Ovary
Uterus
Cervix
Ureter (from kidney)
Bladder
Pubic bone
Vagina
Urethra

The female reproductive system consists of the ovaries, Fallopian tubes, uterus, and vagina.

The Ovaries

Every female is born with over a million immature egg cells already present in her body. These *eggs are contained in two organs* called the **ovaries** (**oh**-var-eez) (singular form: *ovary*). The two ovaries, one located on each side of the body in the lower abdominal area, are small, almond-shaped bodies, about 1.4 inches (3.5 cm) in length, 0.8 inches (2 cm) in width, and 0.4 inches (1 cm) in thickness.

As a girl reaches puberty, hormones cause the egg cells to mature. As they mature, *the ovaries begin to release one egg cell each month*. This process is called **ovulation** (ahv-you-**lay**-shun). Usually the ovaries alternate, with one ovary releasing a mature egg one month and the other ovary releasing a mature egg the next month. As endocrine glands, ovaries also produce hormones that regulate the entire reproductive cycle in the female.

The Fallopian Tubes

When the ovary releases a mature egg, it travels into one of a pair of **Fallopian** (fa-**low**-pea-an) **tubes,** which *take the egg cell to the uterus, or womb*. These tiny, muscular tubes lie close to each ovary and have fingerlike projections that, with a waving motion, draw the egg into the tube. Each tube is about 4 inches (10 cm) long and 0.3 inches (0.8 cm) in diameter. Tiny hairlike structures and muscular contractions move the egg cell along the tube on its journey to the uterus.

If sperm cells are present while the egg is in the Fallopian tube, **fertilization** (fur-tuh-lie-**zay**-shun) can occur. *One sperm cell unites with the egg cell* in the upper one-third of the Fallopian tube, and cell division begins. At the instant of fertilization, a membrane forms around the egg cell to prevent any other sperm from penetrating it. The fertilized egg continues down the Fallopian tube to the uterus, where it attaches to the uterine wall to grow and develop.

The Uterus

The **uterus** (**you**-tur-us) is *a small, muscular pear-shaped organ, about the size of a fist, where the fertilized egg will grow.* The lining of the uterus has several layers and a rich supply of capillaries.

When the ovary releases its egg cell, the lining of the uterus begins to thicken with blood tissue. This is in preparation for the egg cell, if it has been fertilized. If fertilization has taken place, the egg cell attaches to the wall of the uterus, where it is nourished for the next nine months of growth.

The Vagina

If the egg cell is not fertilized, the rich lining of blood in the uterus is not needed. The uterus muscle contracts and gradually breaks down the lining. The lining of blood passes through the **cervix** (**sir**-viks), or *neck of the uterus,* and the vagina (vuh-**jine**-uh) to the outside of the body. The **vagina**, also called the birth canal, is *a muscular, very elastic tube that serves as a passageway to the uterus.* It is about 3.6 inches (9 cm) long.

Menstruation

The process of passing off the lining of the uterus is called **menstruation** (men-stru-**way**-shun). The name comes from the Latin word *mensis,* meaning "month."

During menstruation, about two to three tablespoons of blood and other tissue leave the body. This is blood and tissue that the body does not need. The menstrual flow usually lasts about three to five days. After the menstrual period ends, the entire cycle begins again. Soon the blood will be replaced as the lining of the uterus thickens again.

Although there can be great variations, the **menstrual (men**-stru-uhl) **cycle**—*the time from the beginning of one menstrual period to the onset of the next*—is usually 28 days.

The typical menstrual cycle lasts 28 days. Days 1–5: Menstruation occurs, while various hormones activate the formation of an egg in the ovary. Days 6–13: The egg continues to be formed while the lining of the uterus is being prepared to receive it. Around day 14: The egg is released from the ovary. Days 15–28: If the egg is fertilized, it implants itself in the wall of the uterus. If the egg is not fertilized, blood vessels in the wall of the uterus shrink, become oxygen-deprived, and break down. Then menstruation begins again, and the cycle repeats.

The Menstrual Cycle

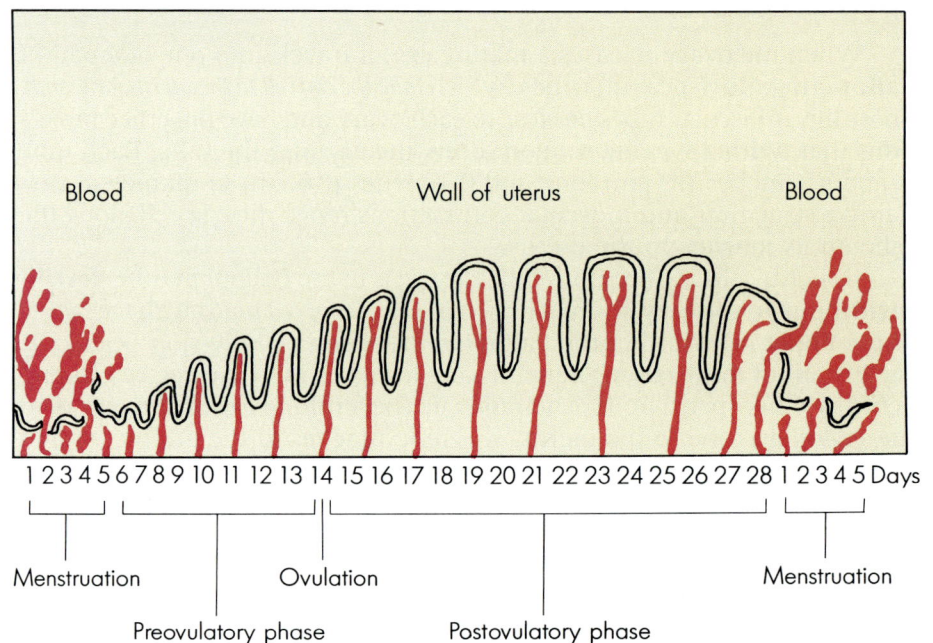

As a result of the uterus muscle's contracting to break down the lining, the female may experience abdominal cramps at the beginning of the menstrual period. Menstrual cramps are usually mild, lasting several hours. Light exercise can help to relieve cramps. A warm bath or a heating pad might also help to relax the muscles. However, severe or persistent cramping may be an indication that medical attention is necessary.

Almost all girls begin menstruating between the ages of 10 and 15. It takes the body a couple of years to adjust to all of the changes it is experiencing at this time. For this reason, the menstrual cycle is likely to be quite irregular.

Hormones control the menstrual cycle. However, nutrition, stress, and illness can also influence the cycle.

Disorders and Diseases of the Female Reproductive System

Some disorders of the female reproductive system are *sterility* and *premenstrual syndrome (PMS)*. Some diseases are *vaginitis, breast cancer,* and *cervical cancer.*

Sterility

One cause of sterility is an untreated sexually transmitted disease. Scar tissue develops in the Fallopian tube preventing fertilization. This is a serious consideration for females since they could have an STD and not know it.

Still another cause of female sterility is **endometriosis** (en-doe-**mee**-tree-oh-suhs), a condition in which the inner lining of the uterus—the *endometrium* (en-doe-**mee**-tree-um)—is present abnormally in the abdominal cavity. Surgery can usually correct this condition.

Premenstrual Syndrome (PMS)

Premenstrual syndrome (pre-**men**-stru-uhl **sin**-drum) **(PMS)** refers to a variety of symptoms that some females experience before their menstrual periods. Symptoms vary and may be experienced two weeks before the menstrual period or several days before it. Many females never experience PMS.

The symptoms of PMS include nervous tension, anxiety, irritability, bloating, weight gain, depression, mood swings, and fatigue. The causes of PMS are not completely understood, but it seems to be more common in women in their 30s. Some doctors believe that PMS is related to a hormonal imbalance. Others attribute the cause to a nutritional deficiency.

Most doctors recommend a diet and life-style changes as the first treatment of PMS. They also encourage women to find ways to reduce stress.

PMS sufferers need to evaluate their diet, reducing the intake of sugar, salt, caffeine, nicotine, and alcoholic beverages. They should also increase their intake of B vitamins, magnesium, leafy green vegetables, whole grains, and fruit. Finally, a regular exercise program should be developed.

Vaginitis

Vaginitis (vaj-uh-**nite**-us) is a very common condition in females. It will affect most females at some point during their lives. There are several types of vaginal infections. The three most common are *yeast infection, nonspecific vaginitis,* and *trichomoniasis.*

■ **Yeast Infection.** The signs of a yeast infection, which is caused by a fungus, are a thick, white discharge and *genital* (**jen**-uh-tul), or external reproductive area, *itching.*

■ **Nonspecific Vaginitis.** This infection is caused by bacteria. Symptoms include itching, an odorless discharge, and a burning sensation during urination.

LIFE MANAGEMENT SKILL

Menstrual Hygiene

Cleanliness during the menstrual period is very important. During this time, the body may perspire more, and the menstrual flow has an odor when it mixes with the air outside the body. For these reasons, daily showers or baths are important.

A female can use a sanitary pad to absorb menstrual flow. She may change pads frequently during the day. This, of course, will vary depending on how heavy the flow is. The *tampon* is sanitary protection worn inside the vagina. Tampons should also be changed regularly.

Because of the link between tampon use and Toxic Shock Syndrome, many doctors recommend that females not use super-absorbent tampons. They suggest alternating tampons with sanitary pads. If a female uses tampons, she should change them often and not use them at night.

It should not be necessary and may be unhealthy to use female hygiene sprays and deodorants. Odor can be a sign of a problem, possibly an infection. It is important that the problem be identified and treated rather than covered up with a perfumed product.

OBSTETRICIAN AND GYNECOLOGIST

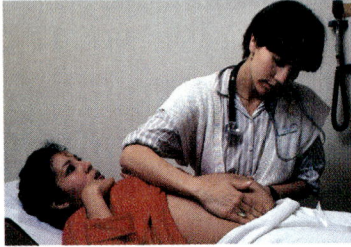

Obstetrics (ob-**stet**-ricks) (OB) and **gynecology** (guy-nuh-**kol**-o-g) (GYN) are commonly regarded as two separate fields of specialty. OB/GYN, however, have common reference points—female reproduction and health disorders and diseases of the female reproductive system.

The **obstetrician** (ob-**stet**-tre-shun) usually *assumes responsibility for care before, during, at, and after pregnancy.* The **gynecologist** (guy-nuh-**koh**-o-gist) *works with the female at all other times,* providing physical exams, and diagnosing and treating disorders or diseases of the reproductive system.

The OB/GYN tend to spend more hours in direct patient care per week than any other specialist. Almost 75% of OB/GYN patients are seen in follow-up visits.

After four years of post-doctoral training, the OB/GYN specialists are required to spend one year in clinical

practice, teaching, or in research in order to become a certified specialist. For more information, contact:

American Board of Obstetricians 100 Meadow Road Buffalo, NY 14216

■ **Trichomoniasis** (trik-uh-mah-**nigh**-uh-sus). This infection often occurs at the end of the menstrual period and is caused by a *protozoan* (pro-toe-**zoh**-un), a small living organism. The symptoms include an odorous discharge, genital itching, and occasionally a burning sensation during urination.

Breast Cancer

About 1 out of 11 women develop **breast cancer** at some time in their lives. About 90% of all breast lumps are found by the women themselves and about 80% of these lumps are **benign** (bee-**nine**) (harmless). That means the majority of breast lumps are noncancerous.

Early detection is still the best preventive health practice. The American Cancer Society recommends the monthly practice of breast self-examination. The best time to perform it is about one week after the menstrual period—the breasts are then least likely to be tender or swollen.

With one hand raised over the head and the fingers of the other hand flat, move your hand over every part of each breast. Use the left hand to inspect the right breast and the right hand to inspect the left breast. Pay special attention to the area between the armpit and the breast, checking for any lump, hard knot, or tissue thickening. If you find anything unusual, contact your doctor at once. Only a doctor can make a diagnosis.

For more information or to obtain a pamphlet on breast self-examination, contact your local American Cancer Society.

Cervical and Uterine Cancers

The cervix and the uterus are common sites of cancer in females. **Cervical** and **uterine cancers** are diagnosed by means of a *Pap smear*. The Pap test is highly effective in detecting early cancer of the cervix and uterus.

When early cancer is diagnosed, it can be treated effectively. A doctor should administer the Pap test. The American Cancer Society recommends that all women over 20 years of age have a Pap test at regular intervals.

Other diseases of the reproductive system are discussed in Chapter 30.

CHECK YOURSELF

1. What is meant by ovulation?
2. What is the function of the Fallopian tubes?
3. What is the function of the uterus?
4. Explain the process of menstruation.
5. When should a breast self-examination be performed?
6. Name two disorders or diseases of the female reproductive system and describe them.
7. What is the purpose of a Pap test?

KEEPING FIT

Breast Self-Examination (BSE)

Look in the mirror to see anything unusual—breast change in size or shape; discharge from the nipples; puckering, dimpling, or scaling of the skin.

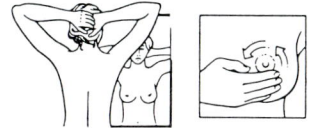

Explore the breasts by beginning at the outer edge. Press the flat part of the fingers in small circles, moving the circles slowly around each breast. Gradually work toward the nipple. Also examine the area between breast and armpit, including the armpit. Look for any unusual lumps or masses under the skin.

The same technique can be performed as you lie on your back. With your left hand behind your head, examine your left breast with your right hand. Repeat the same process for the right breast.

CHAPTER 17   Review

CHAPTER SUMMARY

- The reproductive systems of the male and female differ greatly in both structure and function. They serve the very important function of providing humans with a means of handing on life.
- The reproductive systems begin to mature at the onset of puberty. The male system begins to produce sperm cells, while the female system begins to produce egg cells.
- Major parts of the male reproductive system are the testes, epididymis, vas deferens, urethra, and penis.
- Some disorders of the male reproductive system are inguinal hernia and sterility. Some diseases are cancer of the prostate gland and testicular cancer.
- Major parts of the female reproductive system are the ovaries, the Fallopian tubes, the uterus, and the vagina.
- Some disorders of the female reproductive system are sterility and premenstrual syndrome. Some diseases are vaginitis, breast cancer, and cervical cancer.

reproductive system	urethra	Fallopian tubes	trichomoniasis
sperm cell	penis	fertilization	breast cancer
testicles	ejaculation	uterus	benign
testes	puberty	cervix	cervical cancer
scrotum	hernia	vagina	uterine cancer
epididymis	inguinal hernia	menstruation	obstetrics
vas deferens	sterility	menstrual cycle	gynecology
seminal vesicles	cancer	endometriosis	obstetrician
ejaculatory ducts	prostate cancer	premenstrual syndrome (PMS)	gynecologist
prostate gland	testicular cancer	vaginitis	
Cowper's glands	ovaries	yeast infection	
semen	ovulation	nonspecific vaginitis	

PUTTING VOCABULARY TO USE

On a separate piece of paper, write the following statements. Then supply the missing word for each from the chapter vocabulary list.

1. _____. Maintains constant temperature for sperm cells.
2. _____ _____. Secretes a substance that cleanses the urethra of any acidity.
3. _____. Site of the development of the egg cell if it is fertilized.
4. _____ _____. Their secretion provides nourishment for sperm.
5. _____. Contain all the egg cells.
6. _____. Combination of sperm secretions from glands.
7. _____. Storage place for sperm.
8. _____. The birth canal.
9. _____. The process by which the uterus sheds its lining.
10. _____ _____. The tube that connects the epididymis and urethra.
11. _____. A doctor specializing in the female reproductive system.
12. _____. The male cell.
13. _____ _____. Tubes through which a mature egg travels from the ovary to the uterus.
14. _____. Site of sperm production.
15. _____ _____. Secretes fluid that aids in the movement of the sperm.

REVIEWING WHAT YOU LEARNED

1. Describe the main parts of the male reproductive system.
2. Describe the process that takes place from the time that sperm are produced until semen is formed.
3. Why is it impossible for semen and urine to leave the body at the same time?
4. Why is the secretion from the Cowper's glands in the male especially important?
5. What are the functions of the female reproductive system?
6. Describe the main parts of the female reproductive system.
7. What causes menstrual cramps in the female? What can be done to relieve them?

APPLYING WHAT YOU LEARNED

1. Contact your local American Cancer Society for pamphlets describing self-examination for testicular cancer and breast cancer.
2. Explain why reproductive health is an important part of total health and wellness.

FOCUS ON WELLNESS

An understanding of and care for the reproductive system is an important part of total wellness. *I promote a high level of personal health by . . .*

The Circulatory and Respiratory Systems

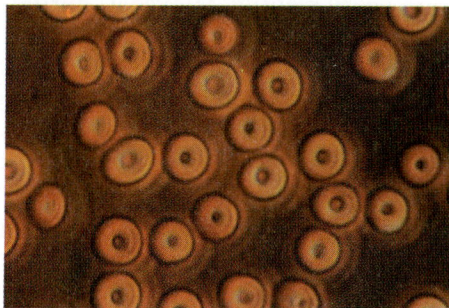

No body system works in isolation. Body systems are dependent upon one another. Just as all of the systems depend on the nervous system, they also depend on the circulatory and respiratory systems. The respiratory system processes the oxygen that the circulatory system carries to all of the parts of the body.

After studying this chapter, you will be able to:
- describe the anatomy and the function of the heart,
- identify the components of blood and what each component does,
- explain what blood pressure is and how it is measured,
- explain how blood is classified and what is meant by the Rh factor,
- name some illnesses of the circulatory system,
- explain the process of respiration,
- explain the anatomy and the functions of the respiratory system,
- name some illnesses of the respiratory system.

The blood is the body's transportation system, carrying oxygen and food to all of the cells of the body. Without a healthy circulatory system, the body could not function. The term, **cardiovascular** (kard-ee-oh-**vas**-kue-lur) **system,** refers to *the entire circulatory system.* This includes the heart, the blood vessels, and the blood.

Your Heart

Your **heart,** *the body's pump,* perhaps the most important organ in your body, started beating before you were born. It has been beating every minute of your life. The heart beats between 60 and 80 times a minute. In an average lifetime of 70 years, the heart beats 2.5 billion times. In the course of a day, the heart beats about 100,000 times, pumping more than 2,500 gallons of blood. During normal activity, the heart pumps about 5 quarts of blood every minute. However, during exercise, it can pump more than 21 quarts a minute!

The heart is a pear-shaped muscular organ about the size of your fist, and weighs less than a pound. It lies near the center of the chest between the lungs and just behind the breastbone, or sternum.

The heart is enclosed in a loose-fitting sac called the **pericardium** (per-uh-**kard**-ee-um). The pericardium consists of two layers. One layer is a thin, watery membrane that closely covers the heart's surface. The other layer is fibrous and is attached to the diaphragm, the sternum, and the spinal column, and to the large blood vessels that enter and leave the heart.

The heart is enclosed in a sac called the pericardium.

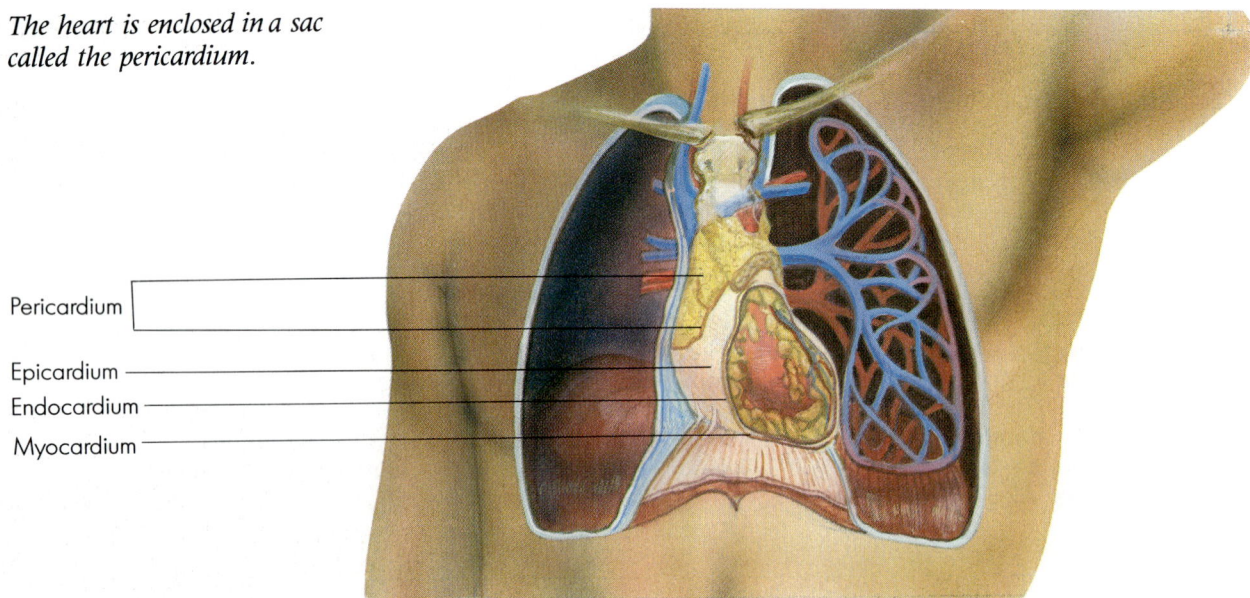

Pericardium

Epicardium

Endocardium

Myocardium

Layers of the Heart

A protective *outer layer of the heart*, called the **epicardium** (ep-uh-**kard**-ee-um), adheres to the heart wall. This epicardium makes up one of the three layers of the heart.

The *middle layer* of the heart, the **myocardium** (my-oh-**kard**-ee-um), *consists of cardiac muscle tissue* and is responsible for the contracting action of the heart.

The *inner layer,* or **endocardium** (en-doe-**kard**-ee-um), is *a thin membrane that lines all of the heart and chambers and covers structures, such as the heart valves, that project into them.*

Heart Chambers

The heart is divided into four hollow chambers, two on the left side of the heart and two on the right side. It consists of two pumps, separated by a wall of muscle. Each pump has an *upper chamber* called the **atrium** (**ay**-tree-um) (plural form: *atria*) and a *lower chamber* called the **ventricle** (**ven**-truh-kul). A set of valves lies between the atrium and ventricle on each side of the heart. The **valves** are *designed to keep the blood flowing in the proper direction.*

The pump on the right side of the heart receives blood from the veins, carrying waste from the body's cells. Blood enters the right atrium, flows to the right ventricle, and is then pumped to the lungs.

In the lungs, the blood leaves the carbon dioxide and other waste materials that it has picked up from the body's cells. The blood then picks up fresh oxygen from the lungs and returns to the heart, entering the left atrium. The oxygenated blood flows to the left ventricle and then is pumped through the arteries to all of the parts of the body.

The heart is divided into four chambers.

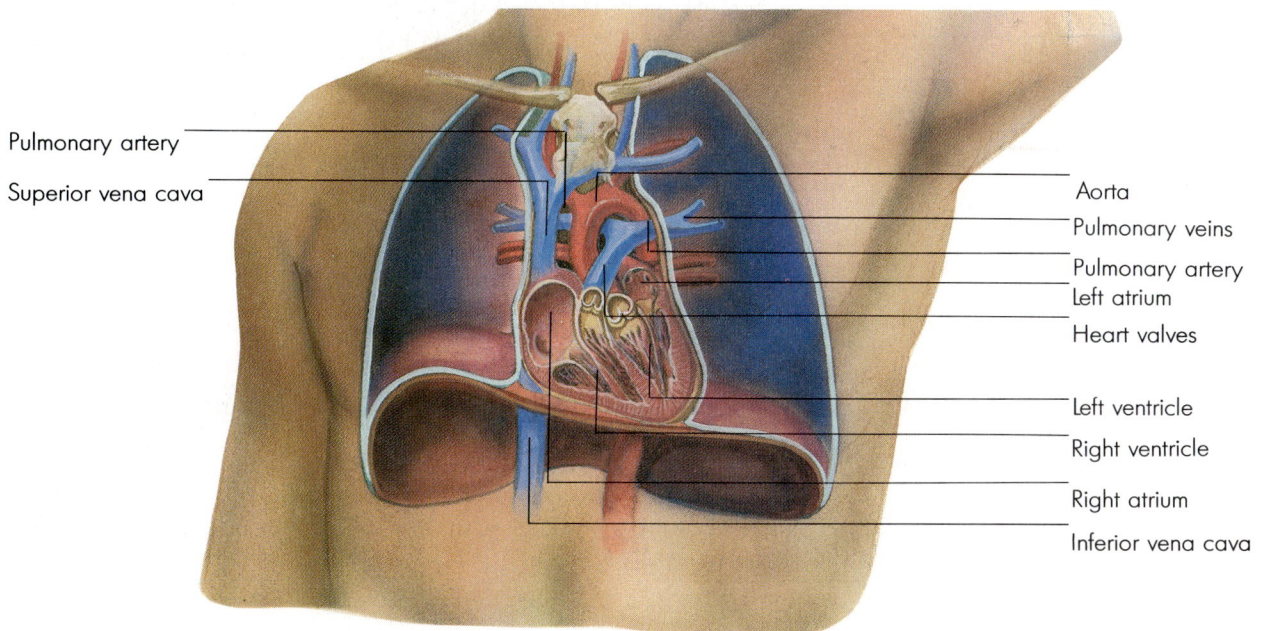

Pulmonary artery

Superior vena cava

Aorta

Pulmonary veins

Pulmonary artery

Left atrium

Heart valves

Left ventricle

Right ventricle

Right atrium

Inferior vena cava

What Makes the Heart Work?

The heart has a specialized conduction system consisting of three structures: the S-A node, the A-V node, and the A-V bundle.

1. The **sinoatrial node** (sigh-no-**ay**-tree-uhl **nohd**) **(S-A node)** is *a mass of specialized heart muscle tissue in the right atrium,* just beneath the epicardium. The S-A node *initiates each heartbeat, setting the pace for the heart.* The S-A node is often called the *pacemaker.*

2. The second structure, the **atrioventricular** (ay-tree-oh-ven-**trik**-you-lar) **node (A-V node),** is *located at the base of the right atrium.* The A-V node receives an electrical impulse from the S-A node, which *allows the atria to contract, thereby emptying the blood into the ventricles.*

3. Finally, the impulse travels to the **atrioventricular bundle (A-V bundle),** a cluster of special cardiac muscle fibers, which results in *the contraction of the ventricles, forcing the blood into the arteries.*

Influences Affecting the Heart Action

Several different influences can affect the action of the heart. As you already know, secretions from the thyroid and adrenal glands increase the heart rate. The heart is also under the control of the nervous system. Parasympathetic nerves slow down the heart rate, while nerves from the sympathetic nervous system speed up the heart rate.

In addition to the neural and hormonal control of the heart rate, many chemicals affect the heart. Nicotine is an example of a chemical that has an unusual effect on the heart. It initially stimulates certain receptors in the heart and then paralyzes them. Nicotine raises blood pressure and causes the coronary arteries to constrict, or to close.

CHECK YOURSELF

1. Describe the three layers of the heart.
2. Trace the path that blood follows through the heart.
3. Why is the S-A node called the pacemaker?
4. What factors affect the action of the heart?

2. The Blood Vessels

The **blood vessels** *distribute the blood throughout the body.* There are over 100,000 miles of blood vessels in your body. They are mainly divided into *arteries, capillaries,* and *veins.*

Arteries

Arteries (**art**-uh-reez), the largest blood vessels, *carry blood away from the heart*. Arteries have thick, three-layered walls.

- **The inner layer** of an artery is lined with a slick-surfaced membrane, which reduces friction as blood flows through it.
- **The middle layer** of an artery includes smooth muscle fibers and a thick layer of connective tissue.
- **The outer layer** of an artery is composed of elastic and fibrous tissues that strengthen the arterial wall. This elasticity also helps to maintain blood pressure. The artery walls are stretched as blood is pumped through them, and then they spring back between heartbeats.

Arteries branch into smaller vessels called **arterioles** (are-**tier**-ee-olls). These microscopic branches *regulate the flow of blood into the capillaries.*

Capillaries

Capillaries (**kap**-uh-lehr-eez) are the smallest blood vessels. Some capillaries are 50 times thinner than a single strand of hair. These thin vessels *allow for the passage of food and oxygen from the blood to the body cells.* Capillaries also *pick up the cells' waste products.*

Veins

The system of capillaries leads into tiny branches of veins called **venules** (**ven**-yules). These venules lead to **veins,** *the vessels which carry the blood back to the heart.*

Veins become larger in diameter as they get closer to the heart. The walls of the veins are thinner than those of the arteries. Just like the arteries, veins have a three-layered wall, but fewer elastic fibers.

The veins do not have to withstand the great pressure that the arteries do. Another difference between veins and arteries is that the inner lining of the veins forms valves that help to direct the flow of blood. These valves prevent the blood's flowing back into the capillaries. This is especially important in the lower extremities, where the blood must flow against the force of gravity.

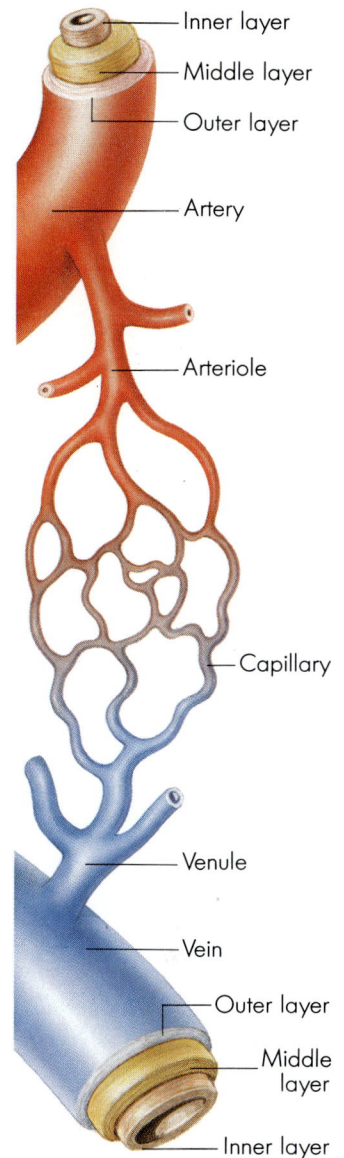

Inner layer
Middle layer
Outer layer

Artery

Arteriole

Capillary

Venule

Vein

Outer layer
Middle layer
Inner layer

Arteries, arterioles, capillaries, venules, and veins form the blood vessels of the circulatory system.

Blood Pressure

As blood flows from the arteries into the capillaries, the blood pressure lowers. **Blood pressure** is *the force of the blood on the walls of the blood vessels.* By the time blood reaches the venules, it has lost all but one-twentieth of its pressure. This is necessary, since the thin, tiny capillaries could not

The Circulatory System

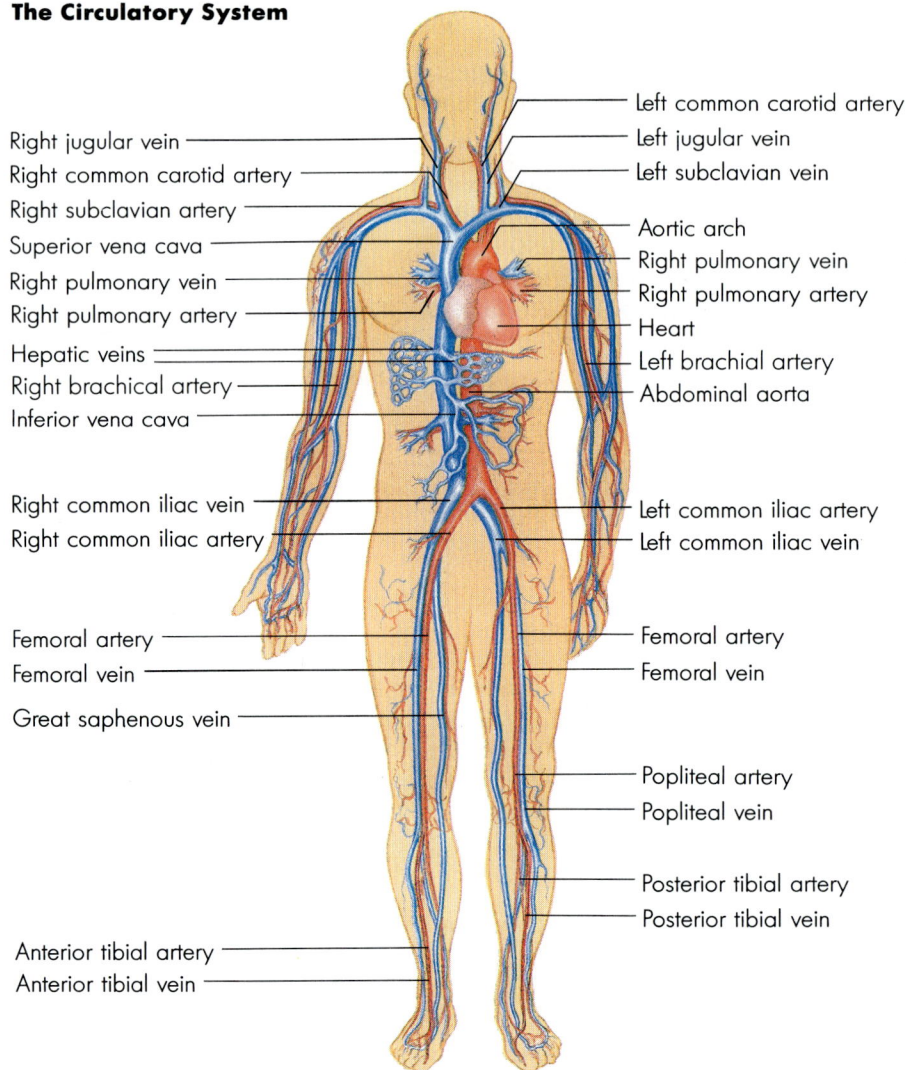

Right jugular vein

Right common carotid artery

Right subclavian artery

Superior vena cava

Right pulmonary vein

Right pulmonary artery

Hepatic veins

Right brachical artery

Inferior vena cava

Right common iliac vein

Right common iliac artery

Femoral artery

Femoral vein

Great saphenous vein

Anterior tibial artery

Anterior tibial vein

Left common carotid artery

Left jugular vein

Left subclavian vein

Aortic arch

Right pulmonary vein

Right pulmonary artery

Heart

Left brachial artery

Abdominal aorta

Left common iliac artery

Left common iliac vein

Femoral artery

Femoral vein

Popliteal artery

Popliteal vein

Posterior tibial artery

Posterior tibial vein

Why does our level of wellness depend so much on a healthy circulatory system?

withstand the force at which blood is pumped through the arteries. Blood pressure is reduced even more as the veins get larger. Muscular activity is necessary to maintain the blood flow through the veins.

Blood leaves the ventricles under a large amount of pressure. This pressure is necessary to pump the blood throughout the body. As you might expect, pressure is greater in the left ventricle and aorta than in the right ventricle and pulmonary artery. This is because the left ventricle must pump with a great enough force to send the blood throughout the body. The right ventricle is sending the blood a shorter distance—to the lungs.

Each time the ventricles contract, blood surges through the arteries with such a force that the walls of the arteries bulge. When *arterial pressure is greatest,* at this point in the cycle of heart action, the pressure is called **systolic (sis**-tahl-ick) **pressure.** As *the ventricles relax to refill with blood,* arterial pressure is at its lowest and is called **diastolic** (die-uh-**stahl**-ick) **pressure.**

Measuring Blood Pressure

A **sphygmomanometer** (sfig-moh-mah-**nom**-uh-ter) is an *instrument used to measure blood pressure.* You have probably had this done during a checkup.

A health professional wraps an air bag around your arm just above the elbow, then fills it with air until the artery in your arm collapses. As air is released from the bag, the professional uses a **stethoscope** (**steth**-uh-skope), an *instrument designed for hearing sounds produced by the body.* In this case, the professional listens for the return of a pulse in the artery.

The number on the sphygmomanometer gauge at this point represents your systolic blood pressure. It is the upper number of the fraction representing your blood pressure and is usually between 110 and 140.

As air continues to be released, the person taking the reading listens for a change in the tone of your pulse or for the sound of the pulse to disappear completely. The number on the gauge at this point represents your diastolic blood pressure. It is the lower number of the fraction and is usually between 70 and 90.

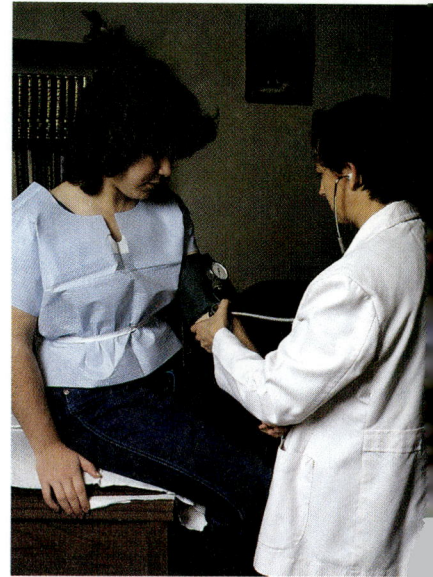

The doctor is using a sphygmomanometer on a patient.

CHECK YOURSELF

1. Why is the pressure in the veins so much less than in the arteries?
2. Compare the structure and function of the arteries and the veins.
3. What is the difference between systolic pressure and diastolic pressure?
4. How is blood pressure measured?

3. The Blood

The cells in your body are dependent upon the blood. Blood is the fluid that transports all of the substances that the body needs to sustain life. Blood delivers oxygen, hormones, and nutrients to the cells and carries away wastes that the cells give off. The blood also contains certain types of cells that help to fight infection.

The Composition of the Blood

Blood is *made up of a liquid component* called *plasma* and *other components* called *red blood cells, white blood cells,* and *platelets.*

Plasma

Plasma (**plaz**-mah) is a yellow fluid that makes up about 55% of the total volume of your blood. Plasma is about 92% water. The remaining

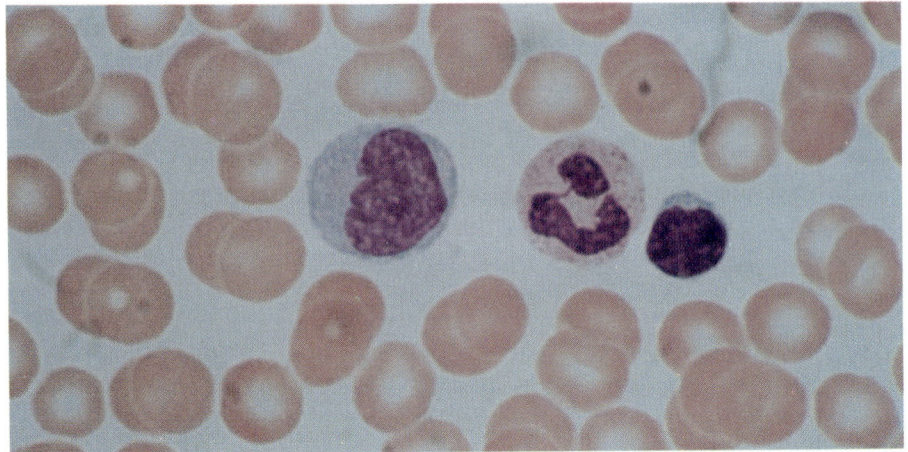

Blood is made up of plasma, red and white blood cells, and platelets.

fluid is about 8% protein. The water carries dissolved nutrients, waste products, and mineral salts. In addition, plasma contains varying amounts of hormones, enzymes, and vitamins. Plasma performs many of the functions of the circulatory system, including transporting food to the cells and carrying away the wastes.

The Red Blood Cells

Red blood cells, also known as **red corpuscles (kore**-pus-uls), have a life span of about 120 days. *They carry hemoglobin throughout the body.* Every second of every day millions of red corpuscles wear out or are destroyed or replaced. The body contains between 20 and 30 trillion red blood cells. Red bone marrow manufactures red corpuscles.

Red blood cells are doughnut-shaped, being thicker around the sides than in the center. Both sides of the red blood cells are curved inward.

The red, oxygen-carrying pigment in red blood cells is called **hemoglobin** (**hee**-muh-glo-bin). It is made up of a protein combined with iron. The iron makes hemoglobin capable of combining with oxygen. When carrying the oxygen, hemoglobin is a bright scarlet color. As oxygen is delivered to the cells, the hemoglobin becomes a very dark red.

Red Blood Cell Deficiency   A *person who has a deficiency in the number of red blood cells or a reduced hemoglobin level* has a condition called **anemia** (uh-**nee**-mee-uh). The body does not receive a sufficient amount of oxygen. Anemia has three main causes:

1. a serious loss of blood;
2. an excessive destruction of red blood cells or, as in the case of sickle-cell anemia, a defect in the hemoglobin;
3. a decrease in the production of red blood cells due to malfunctioning red bone marrow, or a nutritional deficiency, namely, the lack of a source of iron in the diet.

The treatment of anemia depends on the specific cause of it.

The White Blood Cells

The main purpose of **white blood cells,** or **leukocytes (lou**-kuh-sites), is to *destroy invading disease bacteria.* Some white blood cells secrete a poisonous substance that kills the bacteria. Other white blood cells surround the germs and literally *ingest,* or eat, them. These cells are produced in the lymph nodes and in the red bone marrow, and their production increases when there is an infection in the body. The shape of white blood cells varies. Their shape changes, allowing the cells to move through the tiny walls of blood vessels. There are far fewer white blood cells than red blood cells. The ratio of white to red blood cells is about 1 to 600.

The Blood Platelets

Blood **platelets (plate**-lits) are the smallest solid elements in the blood. There are about 15 trillion platelets in the blood. They are *crucial in preventing the body's loss of blood by initiating a chain of reactions that result in the clotting of blood.* Small fibers that the platelets produce trap red blood cells at the site of a cut, or a broken surface, forming a clot.

Blood Types

Do you know what your blood type is? This information could be very important to you if you needed a blood transfusion in an emergency. Tests for human *blood types* classify red blood cells as type A, type B, type AB, or type O, and as Rh-positive blood or Rh-negative blood. The blood types vary in their frequency among Americans:

- 33% are type O positive,
- 33% are type A positive,
- 15% are type A negative,
- 8% are type B positive,
- 6% are type O negative,
- 3.5% are type AB positive,
- 1% are type B negative,
- 0.5% are type AB negative.

A person who has type O blood is referred to as a **universal donor** because that person *can give blood to any other person with any type of blood.* On the other hand, a person who has type AB-positive blood is referred to as the **universal recipient** because *he or she can receive any type of blood.*

For transfusions to work, the blood types must match. Receiving the wrong type of blood can cause very serious consequences for the body. For instance, mixing certain blood types can *cause blood cells to mass together.* This process is called **agglutination** (uh-**glute**-en-ay-shun). Hospitals and blood banks take extreme care in checking blood types before giving transfusions.

The Rh Factor

About 85% of the population has *certain proteins in the blood,* called **Rh factors.** These people are said to be *Rh positive.* The remaining 15% are known as *Rh negative.* What significance does this have to your health?

A person with Rh-positive blood should not be given Rh-negative blood. Mixing the two factors causes antibodies to be produced. Rh-negative blood containing Rh antibodies has a violent effect on the red blood cells of Rh-positive blood. As in the case of mixing blood types, mixing Rh factors in blood also causes blood cells to mass together. This can cause serious complications and even result in death.

Blood Banks

Has your community ever had a blood drive? Most cities have blood banks; that is, they collect and store blood from healthy donors. At times when the blood supply is low, there may be a blood drive to encourage healthy people to donate a pint of blood.

Blood banks store *whole blood*, which is plasma and blood cells. It can be frozen and kept for long periods of time. When refrigerated, whole blood can be stored for several weeks. Whole blood transfusions are given most often when a patient has suffered a severe loss of blood.

In some cases, such as those involving burn victims, the need may be for blood volume rather than blood cells. Plasma transfusions are given in these situations. Plasma is separated from the whole blood by a **centrifuge (sen**-truh-fuge) **machine.** *This machine whirls the blood at a high speed, causing the blood cells to settle to the bottom, leaving a layer of plasma on the top.*

Blood banks always need blood. Find out when there is a blood bank call in your neighborhood and volunteer a pint of blood for the good of your community.

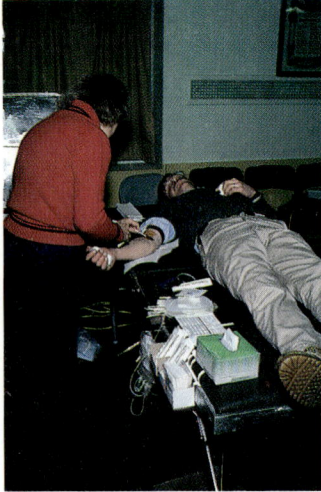

Blood donors are always needed. Donating blood is safe and easy and takes little time.

CHECK YOURSELF

1. Describe the makeup of plasma.
2. What is the function of the red blood cells?
3. What is hemoglobin?
4. What is the function of the white blood cells?
5. What are the different blood types?
6. Explain what is meant by the Rh factor.

4. Diseases and Disorders of the Circulatory System

Diseases and disorders in the circulatory system affect the heart and walls of the blood vessels, as well as the blood itself.

Diseases of the Blood

Among the diseases of the blood are *sickle-cell anemia, leukemia,* and *hemophilia.*

Sickle-Cell Anemia

Sickle-cell anemia is an *inherited condition, resulting from a defect in the hemoglobin within red blood cells.* The red blood cells develop a sickle shape and clump together, obstructing the blood and oxygen flow to the tissues. This leads to the death of tissues, since they are deprived of oxygen. The symptoms of sickle-cell anemia are severe joint and abdominal pain, skin ulcers, and chronic kidney disease.

There is no cure for sickle-cell anemia. However, it can be treated with blood transfusions.

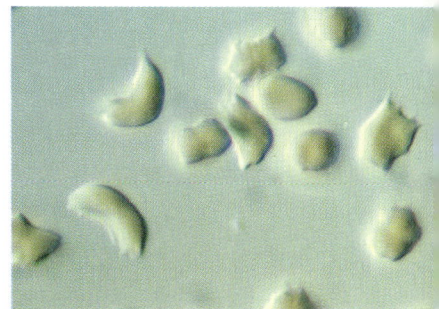

The sickle-shaped cells give sickle-cell anemia its name.

Leukemia

Leukemia (lou-**key**-mee-uh) can be regarded as both a bone and a blood disease. It has been covered in Chapter 15. As a blood disease, leukemia primarily attacks the white blood cells (leukocytes) which are produced in the lymph glands and the bone marrow. For reasons still not known, these structures sometimes begin to produce an abnormal amount of white blood cells. The *large numbers of white blood cells begin to crowd out the red blood cells.* The resulting disease is known as **leukemia,** which is a cancer of the bone or the blood that takes many forms. This disease is found mostly in young people. Certain drugs and radiation treatment can sometimes slow the growth of the disease, but there is no real cure yet.

Hemophilia

Hemophilia (he-muh-**fill**-ee-uh) is an inherited disease in which *the blood of males clots very slowly or not at all.* The hemophiliac, a person who has this disease, can, therefore, bleed to death very easily. The disease is not very common. A hemophiliac can take a medicine that causes the blood to clot.

Disorders of the Heart and the Blood Vessels

Three common disorders in this category are *heart murmur, varicose veins,* and *thrombosis.*

Heart Murmur

A **heart murmur** is an *abnormal sound in the heart.* The major cause of heart murmurs is a defective valve in the heart. A valve that is too narrow causes the blood to be pushed through the restricted opening with more force. A valve that does not close properly allows blood to leak back through it. Both situations cause the sound labeled a "murmur."

Most murmurs are slight and do not need correction. Others are more serious and may require treatment.

Varicose Veins

Varicose (var-uh-kose) **veins** are *swollen and enlarged veins,* especially in the legs, which affect both sexes and all ages. Some people inherit them, but other contributing factors include:

- standing for long hours, day after day,
- obesity,
- pregnancy,
- infection,
- injury,
- very tight clothes (this does not include support hose made especially for people with varicose veins),
- old age, which can cause the veins to lose their tone and elasticity.

HEALTH UPDATE   HEALTH UPDATE   HEALTH UPDATE

Balloons and Lasers to Unclog Arteries

Specially designed balloons are now being used in the treatment of heart disease, thanks to the development of a technique by a Swiss cardiologist. The technique, called PTCA for short, is a new development that opens blocked arteries without surgery.

A *catheter* (**kath**-uh-ter), a slender tube that has a tiny balloon at its tip, is inserted into the artery. When the tip has reached the narrowed area of the artery, the balloon is inflated. The expanded air opens up the narrow area so that the blood can flow normally again. Then the balloon is withdrawn.

Lasers. Experiments to unclog arteries are also being done with lasers. They have been used to successfully unclog leg arteries. In 1987 in Canada, lasers were first used to unclog a heart artery.

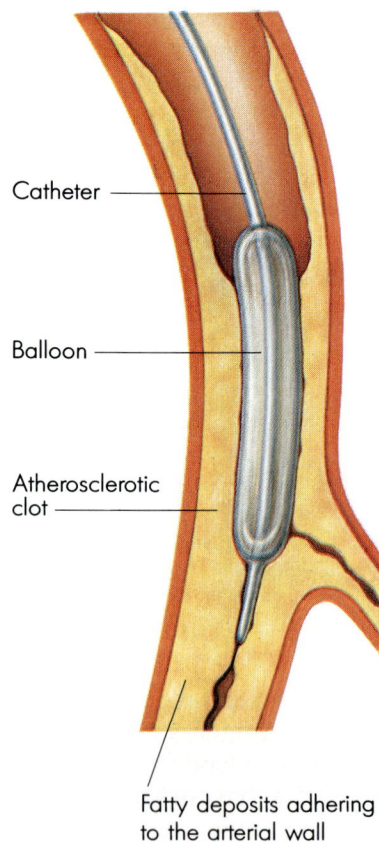

Catheter

Balloon

Atherosclerotic clot

Fatty deposits adhering to the arterial wall

Flow in the veins downward from the head and neck is easy with the assistance of gravity. But the flow from the legs to the heart is more difficult, since the upward route is in conflict with the gravitational pull.

Varicose veins are caused by the weakening of the **vascular system—** *the system of vessels that transports the blood.* Varicose veins develop when the valves in the veins are weakened.

When the valves become weak, they sag under pressure and stick out. The valves cannot close tightly to prevent the backflow of blood, so the blood collects and the veins are pushed to the skin. In advanced stages, the pressure resulting from this condition can cause pain.

The final treatment is surgical removal, or "stripping," of the veins. Exercise is not only a prevention but a recommended treatment. Through exercise, the circulation through the legs and back to the heart is improved. Exercise also massages the walls of the veins and helps them to regain their elasticity. If a person does become afflicted with the problem, strong healthy legs recover more quickly.

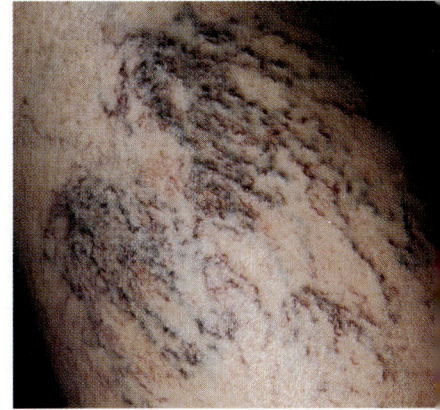

Varicose veins affect walking and they can be very painful.

Thrombosis

Thrombosis (throm-**boh**-sis), a blood vessel disorder, is *the presence or formation of a blood clot within a blood vessel.* A blood clot, called a **thrombus,** occasionally occurs in blood vessels. It remains attached to its place of origin. Clots that become too large interfere with the blood flow through the vessels.

A clot that becomes dislodged from its place of origin is called an **embolus** (**em**-buh-luhs). The danger of an embolus is that it can travel to other parts of the body, blocking important blood vessels. A **coronary embolism** (**kar**-uh-nare-ee **em**-buh-liz-um) is, therefore, *a traveling clot that blocks a coronary artery in the heart.* A **pulmonary embolism** is *one which blocks the pulmonary vein that carries blood from the lungs to the heart.*

Clots that move to the arteries carrying blood to the brain cause a *stroke.* The brain's supply of oxygen is blocked, resulting in damage to the brain cells. Strokes, along with other heart diseases, will be discussed in detail in Chapter 31.

Disorders of the Blood

You have already read about **anemia.** This is the most common blood-related problem. As a result of an insufficient number of red blood cells or lack of sufficient hemoglobin, the body tissues do not receive enough oxygen.

CHECK YOURSELF

1. Name three diseases of the blood and describe each of them.
2. Name a disorder of the heart and describe it.
3. Name a disorder of the blood vessels and describe it.

As you know, the body requires oxygen to convert food into energy. The body gets the oxygen it needs from the air you breathe in. You could live for days without water and weeks without food. But without air, you could live only a few minutes.

Breathing is *the means by which your body allows air to reach your lungs and to leave your lungs.* **Respiration** (**res**-pur-**ray**-shun) is *the process by which gases, oxygen, and carbon dioxide are exchanged in the lungs.* Cellular respiration takes place when these gases are exchanged between the cells of the body and the capillaries.

Breathing is a function of the autonomic nervous system. You breathe in about 16 to 24 times a minute every minute of the day without consciously thinking about it.

The main parts of the respiratory system are the *nasal cavity, pharynx, larynx, trachea, bronchi, alveoli,* and *lungs.*

One of the best ways to keep the respiratory system functioning well is to not smoke.

Posture and Breathing

When you stand erect, sit erect, or walk erect, you give the breathing mechanisms in your body the best opportunity to do their work. By slouching, you hinder efficient breathing. Practice sitting with your back straight in a chair that supports your head and back. Stand with your head up, neck straight, shoulders down and back, stomach and buttocks in, but hold yourself naturally, not stiffly. Also try standing with your arms down at your sides, then inhaling deeply as you raise your arms outstretched to shoulder level. Breathe out fully as you lower your arms.

The Respiratory System

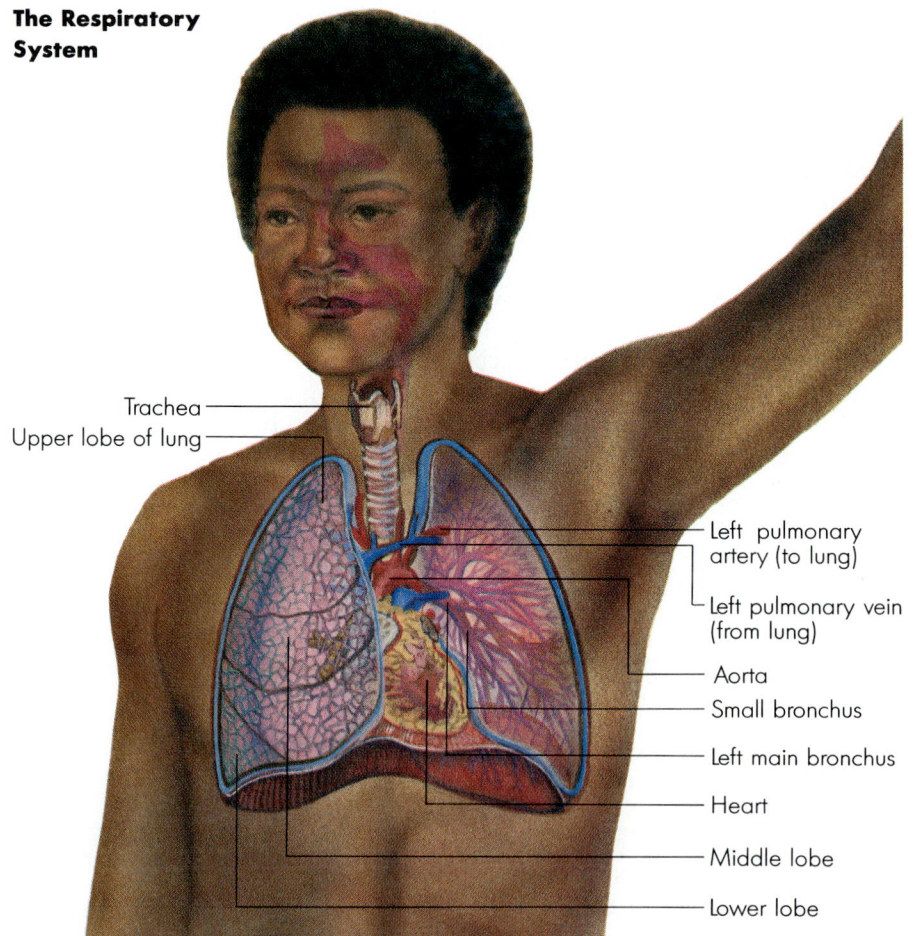

Trachea
Upper lobe of lung

Left pulmonary artery (to lung)
Left pulmonary vein (from lung)
Aorta
Small bronchus
Left main bronchus
Heart
Middle lobe
Lower lobe

The Parts of the Respiratory System

The Nasal Cavity

Air enters the body primarily through the **nasal cavity** in the *nose.* In the nose, the air is warmed. The nose is lined with mucous membranes and tiny hairs to clean the air. The mucous membranes secrete mucus to add moisture to the nose. All of the upper air passages are lined with mucous membranes.

The **sinuses** (**sigh**-nus-ez) are *air-filled spaces within the skull that open into the nasal cavity.* They, too, are lined with mucous membranes and normally aid in warming and moistening air. However, when mucous secretions from the sinuses drain into the nasal cavity and are blocked by swollen membranes in the cavity, sinuses can become painful.

The Pharynx and the Larnyx

From the nose, air moves into the **pharynx** (**fair**-inks), or *upper part of the throat,* down the **larynx** (**lair**-inks), or *throat,* and into the **trachea** (**tray**-key-uh), or *windpipe.*

The larynx is also known as the *voice box* because it is responsible for the production of sound. The larynx contains *folds of stretched tissue* called **vocal chords.** Air passes over this tissue, causing a vibration and producing sound. (The sinuses function here as a resonance chamber.)

A flap of tissue in the larynx is called the **epiglottis** (ep-uh-**glot**-us). When you swallow, the epiglottis closes, covering the opening to the larynx. This prevents solids and liquids from getting into your windpipe. The epiglottis opens to allow air to pass into the trachea.

The Trachea and Bronchi

The **trachea,** or *windpipe,* is about 1 inch (2.5 cm) in diameter and 5 inches (12.5 cm) in length. It is lined with a mucous membrane that is covered with *tiny hairs* called **cilia** (**sill**-ee-uh). Cilia are constantly making a fanning movement upward. To keep foreign particles out of the lungs, they move dust particles upward, or catch them on the mucous membrane.

The trachea extends into the chest, where it divides into two branches called **bronchi** (**bron**-khi) (singular form: *bronchus),* or **bronchial tubes.** The bronchi lead into the lungs. Within the lungs, each bronchus divides and then subdivides, forming a network of tubes that resemble tree branches. These *divisions of the bronchial tubes* are called **bronchioles** (**bron**-kee-ohls).

The Alveoli

At the end of each bronchiole is a cluster of thin-walled air sacs called **alveoli** (al-**vee**-ohl-lee). There are about 300 million alveoli in the lungs.

The alveoli are covered with a vast network of capillaries. The very thin capillary walls and equally thin alveoli walls allow for the exchange of gases that takes place here.

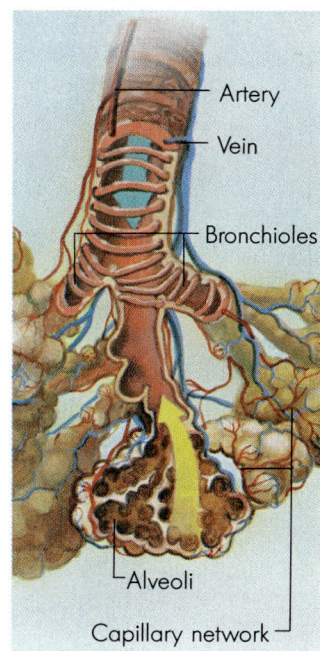

Oxygen passes into the bronchioles and the alveoli, and then into the blood. Carbon dioxide passes from the alveoli to the bronchioles and out of the body.

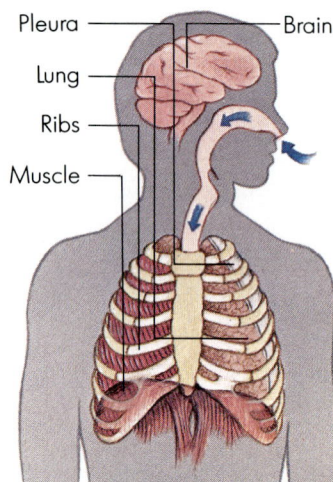

Inhale

Pleura — — Brain
Lung —
Ribs —
Muscle —

The Lungs

The **lungs** contain two *sections,* or **lobes.** Air is constantly being drawn into (inhaled) and expelled from (exhaled) the lungs by successive changes in pressure in the chest. However, the lungs do not actually use energy to do this work—the diaphragm and chest cavity do. The **diaphragm (die**-uh-fram) is *a muscle that separates the chest and abdominal cavities.* The chest cavity is made up of the ribs (which are attached at an angle to the spine), muscles, and skin.

When you inhale, your rib muscles and diaphragm contract. The diaphragm is lowered and the ribs are pulled upward and outward. This enlarges the chest cavity, creating a vacuum in the lungs. Air rushes into the lungs to equalize the pressure.

Just the reverse happens when you exhale. The diaphragm rises and the ribs move inward, increasing the pressure around the inflated lungs. As the lungs shrink, the air is forced out of the mouth and the nose.

Changes in Respiration

Two common changes in the normal pattern of respiration are *hyperventilation* and *hiccups.*

Hyperventilation

Hyperventilation (hi-per-vent-uh-**lay**-shun) means *overbreathing.* This occurs when a person takes too many breaths in rapid succession and loses too much carbon dioxide in the blood.

Hyperventilation can be caused by extreme fear or excitement. Dizziness, tingling in the skin, cramps in the hands, and a panicky feeling are all signs of hyperventilation.

An easy way to stop hyperventilation is to place a bag over the mouth. The person will then be breathing carbon dioxide, which will restore the balance between the oxygen level and the carbon dioxide level.

Hiccups

Hiccups (hick-ups) occur when *the diaphragm goes into spasms* (**spaz**-ums), *or contractions.* As the diaphragm contracts, air rushes into the lungs. To stop this rush, the epiglottis claps down over the windpipe. This stops the flow so quickly that the whole body suffers a jolt.

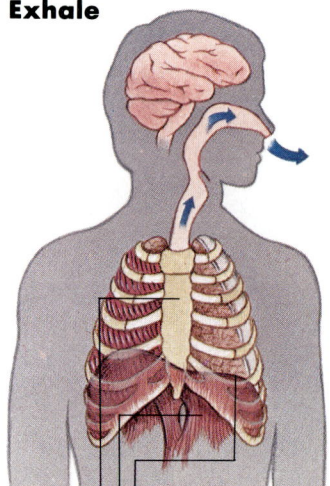

Exhale

— Top of diaphragm under the lungs
— Diaphragm
— Sternum (breast bone)

Caring for the Respiratory System

The respiratory system is highly susceptible to infections. Because of this, you should pay close attention to any nasal or sinus condition, and coughing or wheezing that lasts more than a few days. Hoarseness, or loss of voice, can also be a sign for concern.

Try to keep nasal passages open during cold or respiratory infection. The respiratory passages and organs are very delicate, so it is wise to avoid blowing your nose violently or to try holding back a cough or sneeze. A regular program of exercise helps to keep the lungs working efficiently. It also strengthens the lungs and aids in clearing out the other parts of the respiratory system.

CHECK YOURSELF

1. Name the main parts of the respiratory system.
2. What is the function of the larynx?
3. What are the bronchial tubes?
4. What do the alveoli do?
5. Name three ways to care for the respiratory system.
6. How does posture affect breathing?

6. Diseases and Disorders of the Respiratory System

Diseases and disorders of the respiratory system affect the throat and the bronchial tubes, as well as the lungs themselves.

Diseases of the Respiratory System

Bronchitis

Bronchitis (bron-**kite**-us) is *an inflammation of the lining of the bronchial tubes and the bronchi.* Acute bronchitis is usually caused by a virus or bacteria. A viral infection in the respiratory tract can lower the body's resistance to germs, thus allowing bacteria from the nose and mouth to infect the lower respiratory tract. A person with acute bronchitis usually has a fever and a cough. It can last several weeks.

Pneumonia

Pneumonia (new-**moan**-yuh) is *a lung infection.* The two main types are bronchial pneumonia and lobar pneumonia.

Bronchial pneumonia is *a bacterial infection of the bronchioles.* In the case of this disease, it is difficult to breathe, and pain results when the person takes deep breaths.

Lobar (**low**-bar) **pneumonia** is *a bacterial infection within the respiratory passages themselves,* affecting the entire lobes of the lungs, filling them with fluids and causing severe breathing problems.

Alexander Fleming and Penicillin

We see mold on bread and throw it away. In 1928 in England, when Doctor Alexander Fleming (1881–1955) entered his laboratory, he was annoyed to see mold growing on his bacteria cultures. He had been growing bacteria to study influenza. Now his cultures were spoiled. Being curious, however, he examined the cultures under a microscope. The mold formed a ring, leaving an area perfectly free of bacteria.

Much to his surprise, he had found a substance that killed bacteria. He had discovered *penicillin*—the miracle drug of the twentieth century.

Doctor Fleming had earlier discovered that certain antiseptics used to treat war wounds actually promoted infection. Instead of harming bacteria, they destroyed the body's chief defense against germs—the white blood cells. Fleming began his search for something to fight bacteria that would not harm other tissue.

After discovering the mold, Fleming began growing mold in test tubes. He found that the mold thrived best in cheese, bread, and meat broth. He proved his mold harmed bacteria but, in mice, it did not damage white blood cells. Despite his findings, he was unable to isolate the drug itself, so he published his work, hoping that someone might succeed where he failed.

However, most doctors did not accept the idea of using a mold to kill bacteria. Finally, at Oxford University, Doctor Howard Florey began experimenting with the mold samples he received from Fleming. He planted the mold in sugar solutions and soon discovered that shining gold droplets developed on the surface of the mold. When Florey dried the droplets they turned to a yellowish-brown powder —natural penicillin!

After experimenting with mice, Florey was ready to try his drug on humans. His first patient was a policeman who was dying with a blood infection. The policeman was much improved after five days on penicillin, but Florey's supply of the drug ran out and the policeman died. Though he lost a second patient, Dr. Florey then began to get positive results. Patients who otherwise had no hope began to recover with penicillin treatment. By 1945, penicillin was being mass-produced.

HEALTH UPDATE   HEALTH UPDATE   HEALTH UPDATE

Respiratory Facts

- The surface of your lungs is 1,000 square feet, 20 times greater than skin surface.
- Adult human beings breathe an average of 16,000 quarts of air each day.
- Although you can consciously control the rate of your breathing, you cannot stop breathing long enough to suffocate. As soon as carbon dioxide builds up in the body, a message is sent to the brain. The brain takes over and forces you to breathe. If you hold your breath too long, you simply pass out. Once unconscious, you automatically start breathing again.

Pleurisy

Pleurisy (plure-uh-see) is *a bacterial infection or an irritation of the pleural membrane, a double-wall lining covering the lungs.* The membrane becomes inflamed, and this causes a sharp pain in the chest and a shortness of breath.

Tuberculosis

Tuberculosis (too-ber-kue-**low**-sis) is *an infectious bacterial disease of the lungs characterized by the growth of tubercules, or sores, on the lungs.* Tuberculosis bacteria attack the alveoli and cause inflammation of tissues and organs. Symptoms include fever, weakness, loss of appetite, and severe coughing.

Tuberculosis is detected through a chest X ray. Although it used to be one of the great killers, it now can be treated quite successfully by means of antibiotics.

Disorders of the Respiratory System

Chronic Bronchitis

Chronic bronchitis (kron-ick bron-**kite**-us) is usually *caused by continual irritation, particularly by air pollution and cigarette smoke.* The cough associated with chronic bronchitis usually continues for an extended period of time. (See also Chapter 11 on smoking.)

Bronchial Asthma

Bronchial asthma (**bron**-kee-ohl **az**-muh) is a condition that can result from a sensitivity to pollen, dust, certain foods, or animal hair. Strong emotional responses also can bring on the attack of bronchial asthma. With

One of the main causes of bronchitis is industrial pollution.

BLOOD BANK TECHNOLOGIST

The **blood bank technologist (MTBB)** works for a blood bank. The person is a certified medical technologist (MT), who must first earn certification as an MT before becoming an MTBB.

Throughout this country, communities and organizations periodically conduct blood drives. The public's general response to these drives is usually very good because almost all people realize that they or someone in their family eventually will need a blood transfusion.

Sometimes the blood bank technologist travels to community centers, factories, business offices, schools, or any place where large groups of volunteers can be found.

The blood bank technologist takes a person's temperature, pulse, blood pressure, and a blood sample in order to protect both the donor and the eventual patient who will

receive the blood. It is also the blood bank technologist's responsibility to serve as the head of a department that takes, types, and stores blood.

If you are considering this profession, check your success in such high school courses as mathematics and chemistry. Doing well in those subjects will help you to be accepted into a program.

The blood bank technologist must deal directly with people. A kind, warm, understanding manner helps to calm anxious people who are donating blood for the first time or who might fear the sight of blood.

In preparation for a career as a medical technologist, you will need 3 years of college and 12 months of clinical training in an American Medical Association (AMA)-approved hospital laboratory school. After receiving your degree in medical technology,

you will also have to pass the examination that the Board of Registry of Medical Technologists gives to receive your MT certificate. To receive certification as a blood bank technologist, one additional year of study is required and includes some practical experience in an approved institution. A certification examination also follows this year of study.

There are over 800 approved hospital schools in which you can earn credits. Your guidance counselor can secure a list of them for you. For more information on this career, contact:

American Medical Technologists
710 Higgins Road
Park Ridge, IL 60068

---

bronchial asthma, these *reactions cause the bronchioles to become narrower, or to form a swelling of the bronchial linings, or to increase mucus in the bronchial tubes.* Bronchial asthma is characterized by difficult breathing and wheezing and coughing.

Pulmonary Emphysema

Pulmonary emphysema (**pull**-mah-ner-ee em-fah-**zee**-muh) is *a dis-*

order of the air sacs of the lungs. It is caused by breathing in foreign matter such as smoke and smog particles. Inhaled smoke is the primary cause of emphysema. The foreign substances breathed in cause the air sacs to lose their elasticity. Air, therefore, has a hard time passing into and out of the lungs. Symptoms include trouble with breathing and coughing.

Sometimes people who have emphysema lessen its harmful effects by taking breathing lessons in which they can force more air into and out of the lungs. (See also Chapter 11 on smoking.)

CHECK YOURSELF

1. Describe one disease of the respiratory system.
2. Describe one disorder of the respiratory system.
3. What relation does smoking have to some respiratory system disorders?

CHAPTER 18 Review

CHAPTER SUMMARY

- The circulatory system and the respiratory system are very closely related.
- The circulatory system transports life-giving oxygen and food to all the cells in the body.
- Consisting of the heart, the blood vessels, and the blood, the circulatory system provides a route for carrying food to the cells and picking up waste products from the cells.
- The heart is perhaps the most important muscle in the body. It serves as the pumping chamber to send blood throughout the body system.
- The respiratory system consists primarily of the nose, pharynx, larynx, trachea, bronchi, bronchial tubes, alveoli, and lungs.
- The lungs do not require energy to do their work. They are dependent on the diaphragm and chest cavity to expand and relax. This movement allows the lungs to take in air and to expel air.

REVIEWING WHAT YOU LEARNED

1. Describe the major parts of the heart and their functions.
2. What are the parts of the blood, and what does each part do?

3. Trace the path of a red blood cell through the body, beginning and ending with the lungs.
4. What is blood pressure and how is it measured?
5. How is blood classified and what is the Rh factor?
6. How are the circulatory and respiratory systems dependent on each other?
7. Describe the major parts of the circulatory system and their functions.
8. How does the body use oxygen?
9. What are the common causes of asthma?

APPLYING WHAT YOU LEARNED

1. What health behaviors affect the health of your circulatory and respiratory systems?
2. Why is it not possible to hold your breath until you suffocate?
3. What is the difference between respiration and breathing?

FOCUS ON WELLNESS

The body is dependent on the circulatory system and the respiratory system for life. Proper care of these two systems is necessary for them to work at an optimum level. *In relation to my circulatory and respiratory systems, I promote my own wellness by . . .*

Circulatory System

cardiovascular system	atrioventricular node	stethoscope	Rh factors
heart	(A-V node)	blood	centrifuge machine
pericardium	atrioventricular bundle	plasma	sickle-cell anemia
epicardium	(A-V bundle)	red blood cells	leukemia
myocardium	arteries	red corpuscles	hemophilia
endocardium	arterioles	hemoglobin	heart murmur
atrium	capillaries	anemia	varicose veins
ventricle	venules	white blood cells	vascular system
valves	veins	leukocytes	thrombosis
pulmonary artery	blood pressure	platelets	thrombus
pulmonary vein	systolic pressure	universal donor	embolus
aorta	diastolic pressure	universal recipient	coronary embolism
sinoatrial node (S-A node)	sphygmomanometer	agglutination	pulmonary embolism

Respiratory System

breathing	epiglottis	diaphragm	tuberculosis
respiration	cilia	hyperventilation	chronic bronchitis
nasal cavity	bronchi	hiccups	bronchial asthma
sinuses	bronchial tubes	bronchitis	pulmonary emphysema
pharynx	bronchioles	pneumonia	blood bank technologist
larynx	alveoli	bronchial pneumonia	
trachea	lungs	lobar pneumonia	
vocal chords	lobes	pleurisy	

PUTTING VOCABULARY TO USE

On a separate piece of paper, write the following statements and supply the missing words. Use the chapter vocabulary list for reference.

1. Blood is carried from the heart throughout the body by _____. It is returned to the heart by _____, and the exchange of food and oxygen for the body's cell wastes takes place in the _____.

2. The _____ _____ is in the right atrium and initiates each heartbeat. The _____ _____ is in the base of the right atrium and, stimulated by an electrical impulse, empties blood into the ventricles. The impulse then stimulates the _____ _____, forcing blood into the arteries.

3. _____ _____ is measured by an instrument called a _____. The point at which arterial pressure is greatest is known as _____ _____. The point at which arterial pressure is lowest is called _____ _____.

4. Blood is made up of a liquid called _____, oxygen-carrying red _____ _____, germ-fighting _____ _____ _____, and bloodclotting _____. The oxygen-carrying pigment in blood that gives it its red color is _____.

5. An insufficient number of red blood cells or lack of hemoglobin results in a condition called _____. _____-_____ _____ is a condition resulting from a defect in the hemoglobin in the red blood cells. Production of an abnormal amount of white blood cells causes a disease called _____. _____ results when the blood clots very slowly or not at all. A blood clot is called a _____. A dislodged clot that moves is an _____.

Write the following terms in the order that they receive air in the respiratory system. Next to each term, explain its specific function.

1. bronchial tubes	5. alveoli
2. lungs	6. pharynx
3. nasal cavity	7. trachea
4. bronchi	8. larynx

The Digestive System

The digestive tract is a complex collection of tubes that process the food we eat. It takes only nine hours for food to reach the large intestine, but it may take one to three days to pass through that organ. The stomach, the kidneys, and the small and large intestines all work together to provide nourishment for the body.

After studying this chapter, you will be able to:
- identify and explain the function of each organ of the digestive system,
- describe digestion and elimination,
- explain the cause of, and preventive measures for, digestive disorders,
- describe four kinds of food poisoning and how to prevent them,
- list the ways in which you can take care of your digestive system.

Digestion (die-**jest**-chun) is *the breaking down of food into microscopic molecules to be carried in the blood to the body's cells.* This process involves a muscular tube about 30 feet (9 meters) long, called the **gastrointestinal** (gas-tro-in-**tess**-tun-ul) **tract**, or **alimentary** (al-uh-**ment**-uh-ree) **canal.** During this one-to-two-day process of digestion, food is crushed, churned, mixed with powerful acids, and eventually turned into a form that your body can absorb and use or discard as waste.

Processes of Digestion

We actually are discussing three different processes when we talk about digestion:

- The first process is **digestion**—*the chemical and physical breakdown of foods* into simpler molecular units.
- The second process is **absorption** (ab-**sorp**-shun)—*the passage of digested food from the digestive tract into the circulatory system.*
- The third process is **elimination** (ee-lim-un-**nay**-shun)—*the expulsion of undigested food or body wastes.*

Digestion Begins in the Mouth

Food enters the gastrointestinal tract through the mouth, which is lined with nerve endings that respond to heat, cold, pain, and pressure. The mouth is the only part of the digestive system that has this sensitivity. When you take a bite of pizza or a hamburger, you probably do not think of everything that is happening in your body.

The Teeth and the Tongue

Your teeth and your tongue make the first contact with the food. The primary function of your teeth is to break the food into smaller bits. This *process of chewing,* called **mastication** (mas-tuh-**kay**-shun), prepares the food to be swallowed.

Your tongue is a muscular organ that plays a primary role in speech, but it is also needed for chewing and swallowing. The tongue contains nerve endings that detect cold, pain, and pressure, as well as the chemical substances that give flavor to food.

The *velvetlike look of the tongue is a result of small projections,* called **papillae** (pah-**pil**-lie) (singular form: *papilla), that cover the tongue's surface.* **Taste buds,** about 9,000 of them, cover the tongue but are most heavily concentrated around the papillae. To recognize the flavor of a food, it must be in a solution form. The salivary glands convert food into a solution.

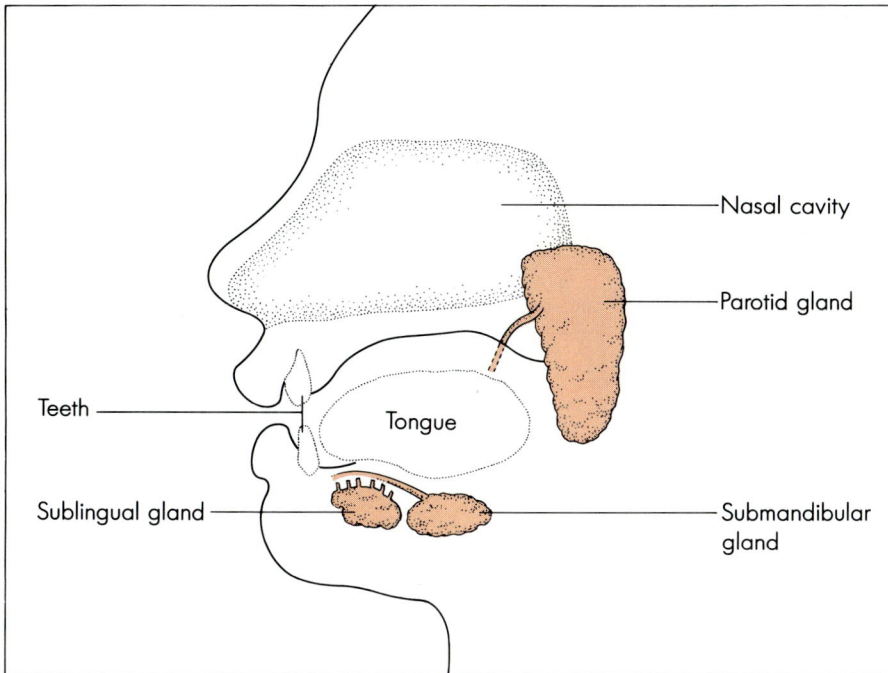

The Salivary Glands

Your mouth contains three pairs of salivary glands. **Salivary** (**sal**-uh-ver-ee) **glands** secrete **saliva** (suh-**lie**-vuh), *a mixture of water and various chemicals*. Saliva is 99% water. It also contains sodium, potassium, calcium, and protein.

Besides dissolving foods so they can be tasted, saliva softens and moistens the food, making it easier to chew and swallow. It also partly digests the starch in foods. Saliva cleanses the teeth and helps to neutralize acids in the mouth. Saliva also helps to keep the mouth moist and flexible, which is important for speech.

The autonomic nervous system controls the secretion of saliva. Have you ever found your mouth "watering" just as you were thinking about or smelling food? You secrete about a quart of saliva a day. Much of this saliva is secreted during times when there is no food in your mouth.

Swallowing—A Complex Process

Your tongue forms the food in your mouth into a ball to prepare for *swallowing*, which is also known as **deglutition** (dee-glue-**tish**-un). Swallowing involves numerous muscles in your mouth and pharynx. Although it begins as a voluntary process, swallowing quickly becomes involuntary. The smooth muscles of the esophagus take over.

As you begin to swallow, the tip of the tongue slightly arches, pushing the food to the back of your mouth. The back of your tongue elevates, and

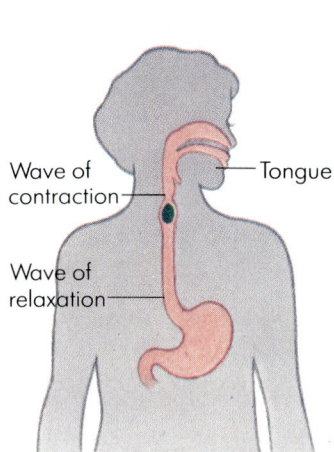

Wave of contraction — Tongue

Wave of relaxation

The process of swallowing is called deglutition.

Pharynx
Epiglottis
Esophagus
Food
Stomach

Before swallowing

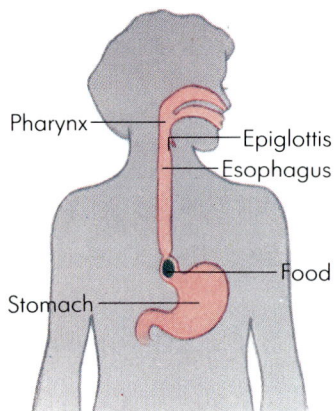

Food

During swallowing

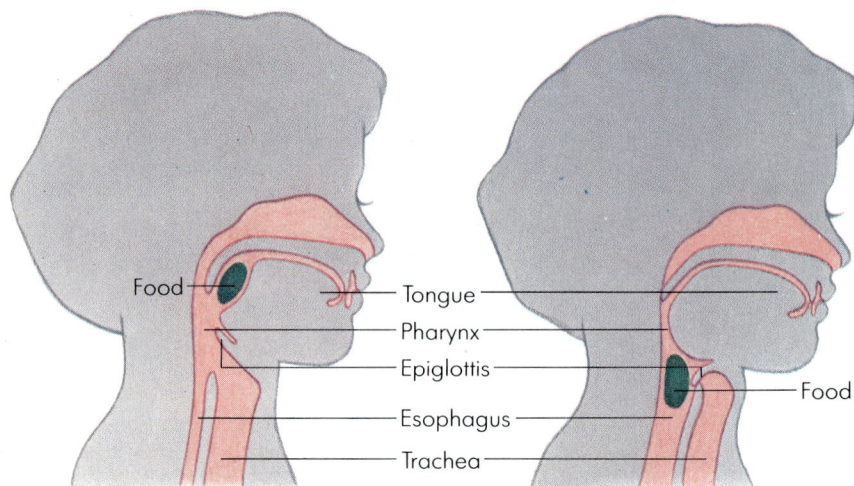

Tongue
Pharynx
Epiglottis
Food
Esophagus
Trachea

a wave of muscular contractions passes over your tongue, forcing food into your pharynx.

At the same time, the **uvula** (**you**-vuh-luh), *a small muscular flap of tissue suspended at the back of the mouth*, closes the opening to the nasal passages. The *epiglottis,* the flap of skin covering the trachea, or windpipe, closes to keep the food from entering the respiratory system.

Your body has another built-in protection against food's entering the respiratory system. When swallowing, the nervous impulses that are responsible for breathing stop, making it almost impossible to swallow and breathe at the same time.

When you swallow, food enters your **esophagus** (ee-**sahf**-ah-gus), which is *a tube that extends from the pharynx to the stomach* and is situated behind the trachea and heart. It is about 10 inches (25 cm) long.

The esophagus has two layers of muscle fibers. *A series of involuntary muscular contractions*—a process called **peristalsis** (per-uh-**stahl**-sis)—*moves food through the esophagus.* It takes solid food about 9 seconds to make this 10-inch trip.

A *sphincter* (**sfink**-ter) *muscle* at the entrance to the stomach allows food to move from the esophagus into the stomach. The sphincter muscle consists of rings of muscular fiber. When the fibers are relaxed, they form an opening. When the fibers contract, they close the opening. These muscles, located in several places along the digestive tract, prevent food from backing up as it moves through the digestive process.

CHECK YOURSELF

1. Both chemical and mechanical digestion takes place in your mouth. Explain what this statement means.
2. How do the teeth and the tongue aid in digestion?
3. List three functions of saliva.
4. What built-in protectors does the body have to prevent food from getting into the lungs?

2. Digestion in the Stomach and the Intestines

Digestion mainly takes place in the stomach and the small intestine.

The Stomach

The three main activities that take place in your stomach are:

- storage of the food until it is ready to enter the small intestine;
- *mixing of the food and gastric juices together to form* a substance called **chyme (kime)**;
- control of the rate at which food enters the small intestine.

Food is stored in your stomach for several hours. The stomach's capacity for food is thought to be about 1 liter (1.06 qt). When the stomach is filled, muscular contractions mix the food with gastric juices and move it toward the small intestine. This movement comes in waves, about every 20 seconds. Food moves into the small intestine through the process of peristalsis, as in the esophagus.

Gastric Juices

Your stomach is lined with mucous membranes that have a layer of cells which secrete gastric juices. **Gastric (gas-**trik) **juices** *contain hydrochloric acid, digestive enzymes, and mucus.* During the average meal, your stomach produces between 0.48 and 0.67 quarts (0.5 and 0.7 liters) of gastric juice. The autonomic nervous system and hormones both control the secretion of gastric juice.

Gastric juices digest proteins but not starches, sugars, or fats. The thick lining of the stomach prevents the stomach from digesting its own tissue. Very little absorption of food into the bloodstream takes place in the stomach because food has not broken down enough for absorption. However, some drugs (for example, aspirin and alcohol) are absorbed into the bloodstream from the stomach.

The Small Intestine

The major part of digestion and absorption occurs in the intestines, primarily the small intestine. The **small intestine** is about 20 feet (6 m) in length and 1 inch (2.5 cm) in diameter. Its three parts are the *duodenum* (due-uh-**dee**-num), the *jejunum* (jeh-**joo**-num), and the *ileum* (**ill**-ee-um):

1. The **duodenum** is *the first and widest division.*
2. The **jejunum** is *the middle division of the small intestine.*
3. The **ileum** is *the third and largest division of the small intestine.* It opens into the large intestine.

The small intestine is lined with millions of fingerlike projections called *villi* (**vil**-lie) (singular form: *villus*). These villi, especially those in the jejunum, increase the surface area of the small intestine about 600 times, making it an excellent site for the absorption of food.

Peristalsis moves food through the small intestine at a relatively slow rate, taking from 3 to 10 hours to complete its length. The motion of the villi, as well as other muscular contractions, breaks down food particles.

The Digestive System

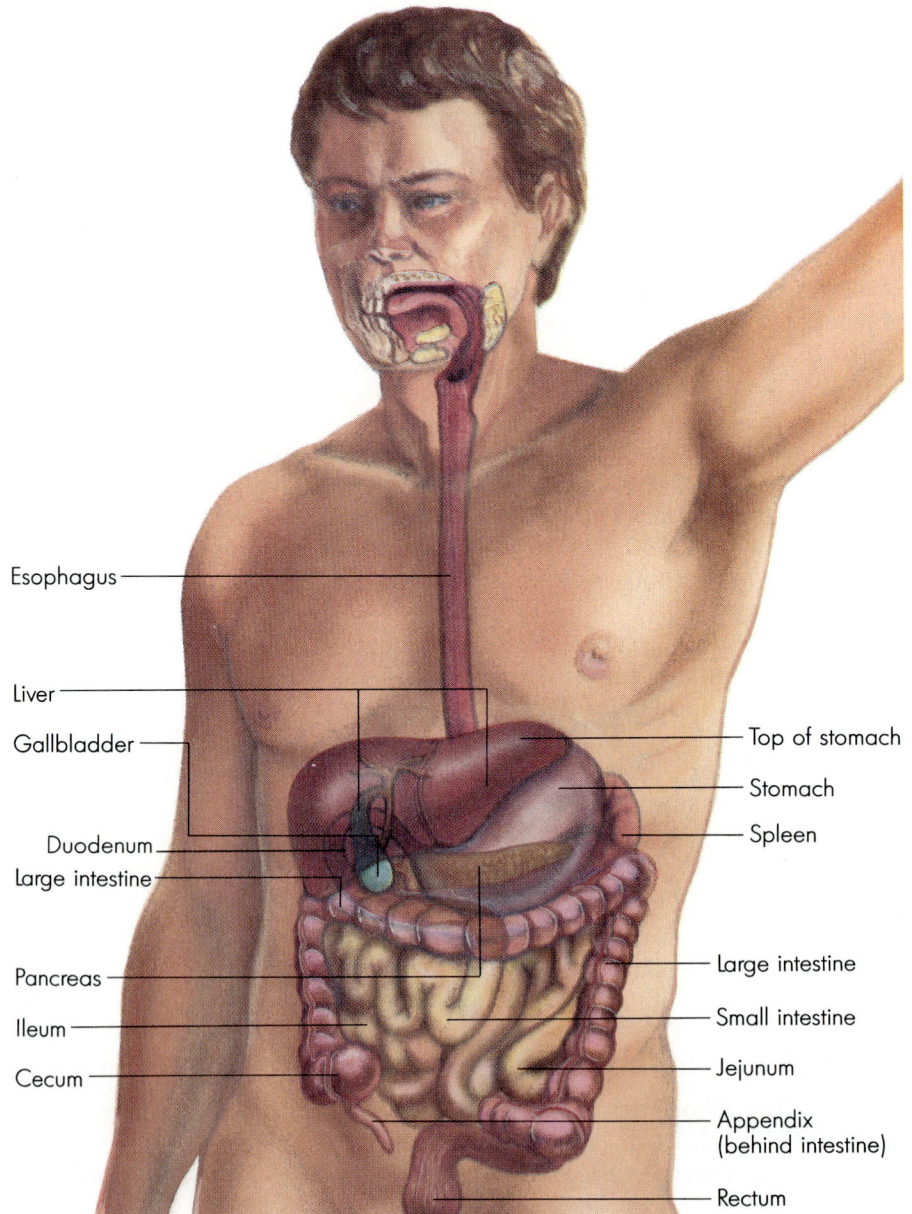

The major parts of the digestive system are the stomach, small intestine, and large intestine. The pancreas is behind the stomach while parts of the gallbladder and the duodenum are behind the liver.

Esophagus

Liver

Gallbladder

Duodenum

Large intestine

Pancreas

Ileum

Cecum

Top of stomach

Stomach

Spleen

Large intestine

Small intestine

Jejunum

Appendix (behind intestine)

Rectum

The majority of the chemical breakdown of food takes place in the small intestine. Intestinal juices, along with secretions from the liver and the pancreas, break down all of the food.

The *digestive juice*, **bile,** is produced in the liver, stored in the *gallbladder,* and secreted into the small intestine through the duodenum. Bile helps to break down fats and also promotes absorption.

The juices from the *pancreas* contain three main enzymes:

- **Trypsin (trip**-sin) breaks down partially digested proteins.
- **Amylase (am**-uh-laze) changes starches into simple sugars.
- **Lipase (lie**-paz) splits fats into fatty acids and *glycerol,* a sweet, syrupy substance.

The small intestine contains many blood and lymph vessels, making it especially adapted to the absorption process. Food molecules enter blood capillaries in the villi and are then carried throughout the body.

The Large Intestine

The lower part of the digestive tract is the **large intestine,** or the **colon (koh**-lun). It is about 2.5 inches (6 cm) in diameter and 5 to 6 feet (1.5 to 1.8 m) long. Unlike the small intestine, the lining of the large intestine contains no villi. The large intestine's main functions are the absorption of water and the elimination of the wastes of digestion.

Undigested food in the small intestine travels to the large intestine. The large intestine is filled with bacteria that act on undigested food. These intestinal bacteria also produce small amounts of vitamins K and B complex.

After water is absorbed from the contents of the large intestine, the action of the bacteria changes the consistency of its contents to a semisolid waste, called **feces (fee**-sees). As the lower portion of the large intestine fills up, the nervous stimuli begin to react on the abdominal muscles. This results in the passing of feces from the body through the **anus (ay**-nus), *the outlet of the digestive tract.*

Organs and Glands That Aid in the Digestive Process

The major aids in the digestive process are the *liver,* the *gallbladder,* and the *pancreas.*

The Liver

Besides being the largest gland in the body, the **liver** is perhaps the most versatile. The liver of an average adult weighs about 3.5 pounds (1.6 kg) and is dark reddish-brown. Scientists have identified over 500 functions of the liver, but it has six major functions:

1. The liver produces bile, a yellowish-green, bitter fluid important in the breakdown of fats. Your liver secretes up to 1.06 quarts (1 liter) of bile daily.
2. The liver converts glucose to glycogen. The liver can also form glucose from proteins and amino acids. Glucose and certain amino acids are absorbed in the small intestine and carried to the liver to be processed.
3. It maintains the body's balance of blood sugar.
4. It carries out the partial metabolism of carbohydrates, as well as fats and proteins.
5. It changes toxic wastes, such as ammonia, into a less toxic substance—**urea** (you-**ree**-uh), *the chief solid substance in urine.*
6. It stores fat-soluble vitamins A, D, E, and K and several water-soluble vitamins, such as B_{12}.

The Gallbladder

The **gallbladder** is *a small sac that stores bile.* It is located on the undersurface of the liver. The neck of the gallbladder forms a duct leading to the duodenum, the first division of the small intestine. This small pouch is only two-thirds of an inch in size. The gallbladder stores bile until the duodenum receives food from the stomach. It then releases a hormone into the bloodstream, which causes the release of bile into the small intestine.

The Pancreas

The **pancreas** is both an exocrine and endocrine gland. The exocrine function of this gland is involved in the digestive process.

Similar to the ducts of the gallbladder, the *pancreatic* (pan-**kree**-at-ick) *duct* enters the duodenum. The pancreas produces *alkaline enzymes* (**al**-kuh-line **en**-zimes) that are secreted into the pancreatic juice and flow into the small intestine. The alkaline enzymes, substances that are necessary to the digestive process, stop the activity of the acidic gastric juices, and then other chemical breakdown begins.

The production of *insulin* and *glucagon* in the pancreas is its endocrine function. Chapter 16 gives you information on these two hormones.

Elimination of the Body Wastes

Body wastes are eliminated through several body processes that make up the *excretory system.* The cells are continuously depositing their waste products in the blood. These wastes are delivered through the circulatory system to the various centers for elimination. Water and salts are excreted through the sweat glands of the skin. Carbon dioxide and some water are eliminated through the lungs when you exhale. As we have seen, the large intestine removes semisolid waste—feces. Urea and *Uric* (**you**-rik) *acid* are carried to the kidneys. The kidneys remove waste products that can be dissolved in water.

The Body Is Its Own Filter

All *filters,* no matter how large or small, have one basic function—to *remove impurities.* If a filter does not work, debris builds up, and soon the mechanism fails to work.

In the human body, the kidneys serve as filters for the wastes in blood and excess water. This valuable function keeps the body in a stable, working state. When kidneys do not work properly, an artificial blood-cleansing system called *dialysis* is used.

For years, dialysis equipment has been characterized by the use of a large machine. Now a new system for dialysis has been developed. It is called CAPD for short. This process costs about half that of the conventional dialysis, is less traumatic to the body, requires far less time, and can be done at home.

To use CAPD, a patient has a small, flexible catheter surgically implanted into the abdomen. A plastic bag, containing a sterile sugar and salt solution, is attached to the catheter and is held up, so that the fluid can drain, by gravity, into the bottom of the abdominal cavity. Then the catheter is clamped off, and the bag, which is still attached, is folded into a compact rectangle and stored in a pocket or inside the user's clothing.

Waste products normally drawn through the blood are drawn through the **peritoneum** (per-ut-un-**ee**-um), *the semipenetrable membrane that lines the abdominal cavity,* into the solution in the sterile fluid. Thus, the peritoneum does the work of the kidneys.

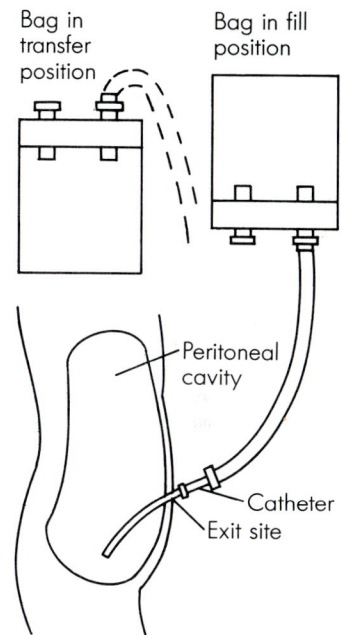

Bag in transfer position

Bag in fill position

Peritoneal cavity

Catheter Exit site

The Kidneys

There are two **kidneys,** the *organs that excrete the waste products of metabolism.* Both are bean-shaped and each is about the size of a fist. They lie on either side of the spine in the small of the back. The kidneys are embedded in a mass of fatty tissue that protects them. They also get support from the renal arteries and veins. (*Renal* (**ree**-nul) means "kidney.")

Each kidney is made up of three sections:

- the *outer layer,* or renal cortex,
- the *inner layer,* or renal medulla,
- the *renal pelvis,* which is a funnel-shaped sac that forms the upper end of the ureter.

The **ureter** (**you**-ree-tur) is *a tube that leads from each kidney to the bladder.* The **urethra** (**you**-ree-thra), in turn, is *a tube that leads from the bladder to the outside of the body.*

Renal cortex

Renal Medulla

Renal pyramids
(medulla)

Renal artery

Renal vein

Renal pelvis

Ureter

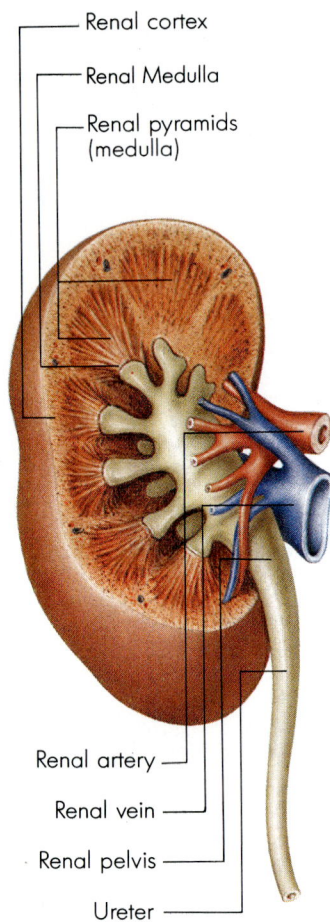

Cross-section of a kidney

The Function of the Kidneys

The kidneys act as a type of filter, removing waste products from the blood. They also maintain the correct proportion of water and other substances in the blood. Blood enters the kidneys through the *renal artery*. Inside each kidney, the renal artery splits into a network of over a million units called **nephrons**, which are the filters of the kidneys. Each of these forms *a twisted knot of small blood vessels,* called a *glomerulus* (glah-**mer**-uh-lus), which is surrounded by a special capsule of very thin, porous tissue, called the *Bowman's capsule.*

The section of blood vessel leading into each glomerulus is larger than the section leading away from it, so that pressure is built up as the blood flows through. Under this pressure, many substances in the blood pass in solution form through the tissue of the glomerulus and into the Bowman's capsule. From this capsule, the solution passes into a *tubule* (**too**-bule), or a small tube, which is intertwined with a network of blood vessels leading from the glomerulus.

The substances in the solution that the body needs are reabsorbed into the blood. The remainder of the solution becomes urine and continues along the tubule to the bladder. **Urine,** *the liquid waste material,* collects in the bladder until it is ready to be passed out of the body.

Kidney Problems

The kidney, because it is a complicated organ that is connected to other organs, may become infected or diseased. Common kidney problems are:

- **Cystitis (sis**-ti-tus). Bacteria may infect the kidneys. These bacteria usually come from the bladder, and the infection may cause a pain in the back or in the lower part of the abdomen.
- **Uremia** (you-**ree**-me-uh). The kidneys may become slowed down in their function of filtering wastes from the blood. Urea and other wastes then build up in the body and poison it.
- **Kidney stones**. Stonelike particles are sometimes formed from mineral salts and urea in a kidney. Some small stones may pass out of the body through the urine. Large stones can cause great pain as they try to pass out of the kidney through the ureter to the bladder. Sometimes a stone may get stuck in the ureter.

  In the past, an operation was necessary to remove the kidney stone. However, a new approach has recently been developed. High-frequency sound waves are focused in the area where the stones are. The sound waves literally crumble the stones. The technique is painless, and the resulting gravel is flushed out of the kidney in the normal way.
- **Nephritis (nef**-rite-us). The nephrons of the kidney become infected. The acute or chronic illness may take different forms, depending on the type of bacteria causing the infection.
- **Kidney failure**. When the kidneys fail, they stop working. Kidney failure may be caused by a blockage of urine, a very serious case of nephritis, or loss of blood.

Normally, a person can function on one kidney, but if both kidneys cease or have to be removed, the person will die. Two techniques are in use today for people without kidneys. One is **dialysis** (die-**al**-uh-sis), in which *a person is connected to a dialysis machine*. The machine filters wastes from the blood. The regular dialysis machine is the size of a washing machine, but today experts are working on a portable machine, which a person may use at home or while traveling.

The other technique in use today is that of a kidney transplant. A kidney donated to an organ bank is used to replace the nonfunctioning kidney.

CHECK YOURSELF

1. What are the main activities that occur in the stomach? in the small intestine?
2. How do chemicals affect digestion in the small intestine?
3. What is the role of the large intestine in digestion?
4. How does the large intestine differ from the small intestine?
5. How do the liver, the gallbladder, and the pancreas function as a part of the digestive process?
6. Explain the body's elimination process.

3. Digestive Disorders

The complex digestive system usually works as it should, digesting and absorbing the food you eat. However, as is the case of any system that is so complicated, a variety of things can go wrong. Some of the more common problems may be frequent, but they are also solvable.

Common Gastrointestinal Disorders

- **Halitosis** (hal-uhl-**toe**-sis), or *bad breath*, can result from disorders of the teeth or the gums, from eating certain foods, and from using tobacco. Contrary to advertisements, mints and mouthwashes do not prevent or cure halitosis, although they may cover up the odor.
- **Indigestion** occurs when *your body does not properly break down foods*. It can be caused by stomach disorders, by eating too fast or too much, by eating certain foods, or by indulging in an excess of alcohol.
- **Heartburn** is caused by *the stomach's acid content backing up into the esophagus*. This happens because the sphincter muscles do not close

LIFE MANAGEMENT SKILL

Good Eating Habits

Most of the disorders described on pages 339–340 are directly related to eating behaviors. What are ways to prevent each of these conditions with good eating habits?

tightly, or you may have an **abdominal hernia** (ab-**dahm**-uh-nul **her**-nee-uh), a condition in which the upper part of the stomach pushes through the diaphragm. If heartburn recurs or continues, a medical examination is necessary.

- **Flatulence** (**flach**-uh-lents), or *gas in the stomach or the small intestine,* can be caused by eating foods that have a lot of air in them, such as carbonated beverages, milk shakes, and certain vegetables. Some people's digestive system cannot break down lactose, or milk sugar; thus, consuming milk products might be a cause of gas. You may not realize how much air you swallow when you chew gum or drink soda pop, which often results in burping.

- **Nausea** (**nah**-see-uh), or *an ill feeling in the stomach,* and **vomiting,** *throwing up food through the mouth,* can be caused by motion (i.e., the rocking motion of a car, or a boat, or a plane), germs, drugs, or other substances in the stomach. Vomiting is a reflex response that can be a protection against the body's digesting a foreign substance. It occurs when the sphincter muscles at the base of the esophagus relax. The diaphragm then contracts and moves down over the stomach. Then the abdominal wall muscles contract so that the pressure inside the abdominal cavity is increased. As a result, the stomach is squeezed from all sides, and its contents are forced upward and out through the esophagus, pharynx, and mouth. The vomiting center of the brain is located in the medulla.

- **Diarrhea** (die-uh-**ree**-uh) is *a condition in which the feces become liquid and are expelled frequently.* It occurs when the digestive tract is irritated and food moves through it too rapidly. Numerous conditions can cause diarrhea, including a change in diet, food poisoning, overeating, emotional turmoil, nutritional deficiencies, or bacteria.

- **Dehydration** (de-high-**dray**-shun), or *excessive loss of body fluid,* is a problem caused by diarrhea, as well as vomiting. To prevent dehydration, a person should drink fluids often, especially water.

- **Constipation** (kahn-stuh-**pay**-shun) is *a condition in which the feces become massed or hard in the small intestine.* This makes expulsion infrequent. Constipation can be caused by a lack of fiber from fruits, vegetables, and whole grains; erratic eating habits; drinking too little water; or constant use of laxatives. Eating a well-balanced diet and exercising moderately are the best ways to avoid constipation.

More Complicated Digestive Disorders

Almost everyone has experienced at least some of the problems that you just read about. Most digestive problems are not serious and are only temporary. However, if any problem continues for a long period of time or is accompanied by fever or other symptoms of illness, a checkup may be necessary.

Doctors have a variety of instruments and tests that allow them to view the gastrointestinal tract. Problems can develop anywhere along the tract or in the glands that work as part of the digestive system.

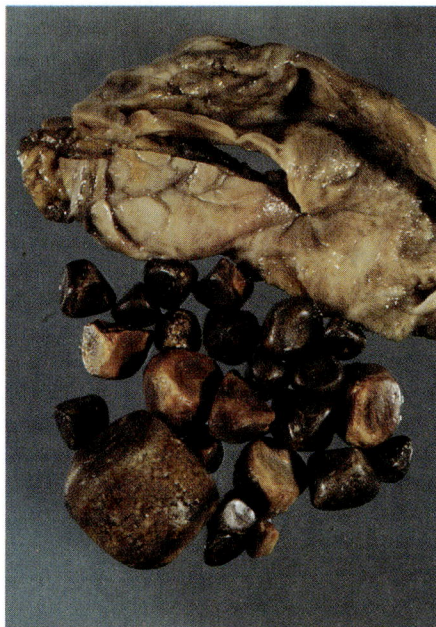

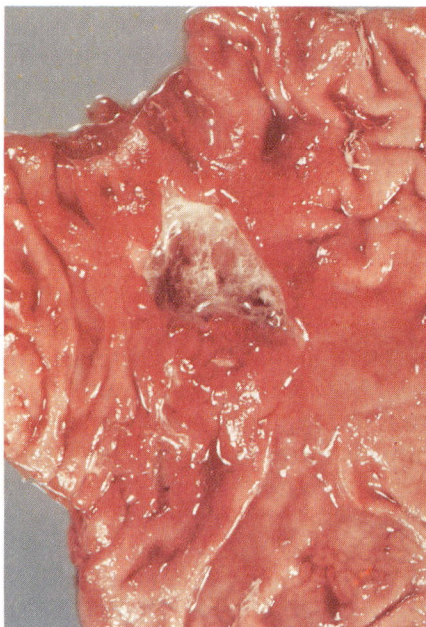

Gallstones

Gallstones are *small crystals formed from bile that can block the bile duct between the gallbladder and the duodenum.* Gallstones can be treated either with drugs to dissolve them or by surgical removal of the gallbladder. Experiments have also shown that some gallstones can be shattered by high frequency sound waves. (*See* also Kidney Stones on page 338.)

Ulcers

An **ulcer** (**ul**-sir) is *an open sore on the skin or in the mucous membrane.* As an ulcer develops, the surface tissue of the skin or mucous membrane breaks down and dies, leaving a raw, inflamed area.

Ulcers that develop in the digestive system are called **peptic** (**pep**-tik) **ulcers.** There are two main types of peptic ulcers:

- **Duodenal** (due-**odd**-un-ul) **ulcers,** *ones that develop in the duodenum,* resulting from an overproduction of hydrochloric acid and pepsin.
- **Gastric ulcers,** *ones that develop in the stomach* and that are also caused by the same two digestive juices.

Peptic ulcers are influenced by stress and the use of tobacco. Why do you think these two factors influence ulcers? Both of them stimulate acid production. Doctors think some people may have a hereditary tendency to develop ulcers. We also know that overuse of aspirin irritates the stomach lining and can promote the formation of ulcers.

A person who has a peptic ulcer will usually experience pain in the upper part of the stomach, usually when the stomach is empty. Peptic ulcers may be treated with drugs that neutralize stomach acid. In some cases, surgery may be necessary, but because of new drugs, it is becoming infrequent.

Gastritis

One of the most common disorders of the stomach is **gastritis** (geh-**strite**-us), which is an *inflammation of the gastric mucous membrane*. Gastritis can result from the presence of irritant foods—especially alcohol—or the presence of bacteria or viruses. In the case of gastritis, one usually experiences a painful burning sensation in the digestive tract.

Appendicitis

The appendix is a 3 to 4 inch (7.5 to 10 cm) long extension at one end of the large intestine. **Appendicitis** (uh-pen-duh-**site**-us) is the *inflammation of the appendix*. As a result of bacteria or foreign matter that gets lodged in it, the appendix becomes swollen and fills with pus. If it bursts, the pus spreads to other body organs, poisoning them.

The symptoms of appendicitis are usually pain and cramps in the lower-right portion of the abdomen. These symptoms may be accompanied by fever and vomiting. Under no condition should laxatives be given to a person with these symptoms. Such substances can cause the appendix to burst. A doctor's care is essential, for surgical removal of the appendix may be necessary.

Diseases of the Digestive System

Two diseases of the digestive system are *hepatitis* and *tooth decay*.

Hepatitis

Hepatitis (hep-uh-**tite**-us) is a *serious infection of the liver that is caused by a virus*. The virus germs destroy liver cells, allowing bile to enter the bloodstream. Bile in the bloodstream causes a yellowish coloring of the skin known as *jaundice* (**jaun**-dus).

Infectious hepatitis is transmitted through direct human contact or through contact with germ-laden food, water, or utensils. Recovery from infectious hepatitis is slow; the liver can remain enlarged and tender for weeks. Treatment involves bed rest and a diet low in fats and high in protein and carbohydrates.

Serum hepatitis is another form of liver infection. It results from a transfusion of contaminated human blood, from unclean needles used to administer drugs, from saliva, and from sexual activity.

Tooth Decay

Does it surprise you to see **tooth decay** listed as disease of the digestive tract? Tooth decay, in fact, is the most common noncommunicable (**nahn**-kah-mu-nee-kah-buhl) disease, that is, disease not capable of being transmitted. The first permanent molars of more than 95% of all American children begin to decay within a few years after they first show through

---

the gums. In the United States, tooth decay will cause over 20 million people to lose all of their teeth as they get older.

Tooth decay is also perhaps the most preventable disease of the digestive tract. A reduction in the amount of sugar that people consume and regular brushing and flossing do much to prevent this decay. (For more information about tooth decay, see Chapter 4.)

Food Poisoning

More than 44 million Americans are food poisoned annually. The cases range from people with a mild case of indigestion to people who have convulsions and die. Of the many sources of food poisoning, the three most common ones are *clostridium botulinum* (klah-**strid**-ee-um **botch**-uh-len-num), *clostridium perfringens* (klah-**strid**-ee-um **purr**-frin-gens), and *staphylococcus* (staf-uh-loh-**kahk**-us). There is also a common type of food infection known as *salmonella* (sal-mah-**nell**-uh).

These are all bacteria—one-celled organisms that multiply by dividing. To multiply, bacteria need food, warmth, and moisture. These bacteria may be found in all kinds of food. Because the organisms are so common, the chances of food contamination in the case of these bacteria are high.

Botulism

Botulism (**botch-uh**-liz-um) is the most serious kind of food poisoning. It is caused by *toxins, or poisons, formed by the growth of the botulism organisms common in soil.* These bacteria grow without air. That is why canned foods are a common place in which botulism develops. Botulism bacteria will not grow in acid, so nonacid foods are the major areas where botulism develops. These include such foods as beets, corn, and green beans.

You can recognize botulism by carefully examining food and watching for abnormal swelling in a can. Sometimes a bitter taste or an odor is an indication of botulism. Don't take any chances if the food looks or smells bad. Never use or eat a food product if the container is swollen or if the seal is broken.

The symptoms of botulism usually appear within 12 to 36 hours. Fatigue, double vision, headache, and dizziness are early symptoms. Seek medical assistance immediately. Botulism can be fatal.

A bulging can is a warning sign that the food may be spoiled. Discard the can.

Clostridium Perfringens

The **clostridium perfringens** are *bacteria found in soil, water, milk, dust, sewage, and the intestinal areas of humans and animals.* These bacteria are becoming the most common cause of food poisoning. They are heat resistant and therefore difficult to control. The poisoning occurs when food is stored at a warm temperature for several hours after it has been cooked. Meat, gravies, creamed chicken, and stew and soup are common sources.

Symptoms of diarrhea and cramps develop in 8 to 24 hours. Recovery is usually immediate without medical aid.

Left: *salmonella bacteria.*
Right: *clostridium botulinum bacteria.*

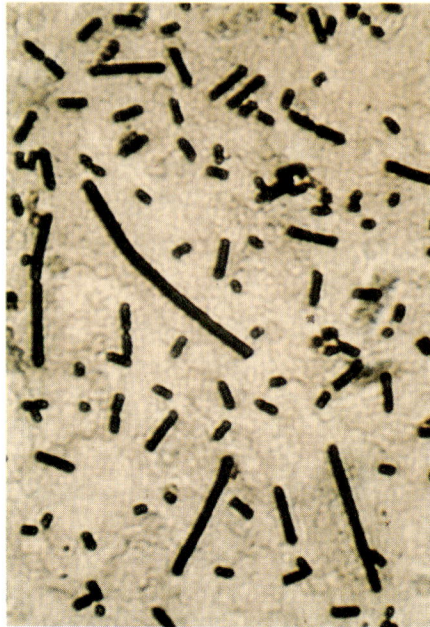

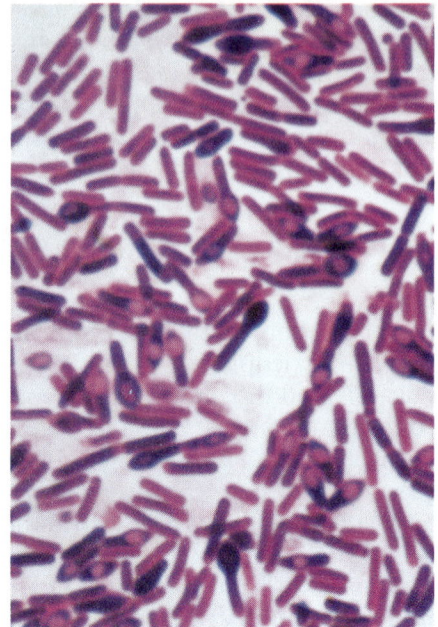

Staphylococcus

Staphylococcus is *a bacteria that is the number one food poisoner in this country.* Like most forms of food poisoning, staphylococcus needs a warm, moist place in which to grow and multiply. A wide variety of foods have been found to be good breeding areas for this disease-producing bacterium: milk, cheese, ice cream, cream-filled bakery goods, chicken or potato salad, dried beef, gravy, sausage, and ham. Usually, the situation occurs when food has been stored in a warm setting for several hours before being served.

The symptoms of staphylococcus occur very quickly, usually within three hours after a person consumes the **contaminated,** or *germ-laden* food. The person will suffer from vomiting, cramps, and diarrhea. The symptoms usually disappear in five to six hours. The only treatment is to replace the fluids lost during vomiting.

Staphylococcus contamination is best prevented by keeping foods that could spoil in a refrigerated area. The cold prevents the growth of the bacteria and the development of the poison.

Salmonella

Salmonella *are bacteria mainly present in the meat of sick animals, raw or improperly pasteurized milk, infected egg products, fertilizer, and foods contaminated by rats or flies.*

Salmonella is most serious when large amounts of food are prepared at one time, especially for outdoor activity, such as a picnic. This is because the bacteria spread so easily in exposed food. The danger is increased if the food is kept at a warm temperature instead of being stored in a refrigerator.

Stews, gravies, soups, milk and cream products, and custard are some of the more common sources of salmonella. Chicken and turkey dressing must also be watched because the poultry carcass serves as an insulator. Even canned foods may become infected if they are not eaten soon after being opened.

The symptoms of salmonella develop within 72 hours after eating contaminated food. Early signs of salmonella are headache, chills, cramps, and diarrhea. These are usually followed by nausea, vomiting, fever, muscle weakness, a bloated feeling, and thirst.

Treatment of salmonella includes a restrictive diet of liquids and soft, nonspicy foods. The symptoms should disappear within 72 hours.

Cleanliness is the best prevention against salmonella. Meat and eggs should be fully cooked, water and milk should be free from any bacteria, and fresh foods should be washed, covered, and kept away from flies, rodents, and other insects.

Helpful Hints on Preventing Food Poisoning

Here are five important categories that you should be aware of in preparing, serving, and eating food.

- **Sanitation.** In general, food poisoning is best prevented by proper sanitation. People who handle food should keep their hands and fingernails clean. When people mix food with their hands, they should keep their hands away from the mouth, nose, and hair.
- **Refrigeration.** Any food that could spoil should be refrigerated right after it is purchased. Leftovers should also be covered and refrigerated quickly. Temperature is a major factor in preventing food poisoning. Hot foods should be kept at 150° F (65° C) or higher, and cold foods should be kept at 40° to 45° F (4.4° to 7.2° C) or lower. Any temperature in between helps to breed bacteria. You can see that a normal room temperature of 65° to 75° F (21.7° to 24° C) is very conducive to food poisoning.

Proper refrigeration is one of the best ways to prevent food poisoning.

- **Refreezing.** Never refreeze thawed food. The frozen food becomes a perishable product once it has been thawed. Keep cold foods in the refrigerator until just before serving. Add dressings at the last minute so that they remain cold.
- **Appearance.** If there is any doubt about the color, texture, or odor of a food, throw it away. If it was spoiled when you bought it, take it back to the store and ask for a refund. If you exchange the product, make sure that the new product is satisfactory.
- **Buffets.** When eating out, be especially watchful of buffets where food is placed on a table for long periods of time without proper heat or refrigeration.

CHECK YOURSELF

1. How do your eating behaviors affect the more common digestive disorders?
2. What is hepatitis?
3. Why is tooth decay considered a disorder of the digestive tract?
4. List four ways in which you can prevent food poisoning.

CHAPTER 19   Review

CHAPTER SUMMARY

- The digestive system is an extremely complex system that involves both the chemical and physical breakdown of food.
- Beginning in the mouth, digestion prepares food to be in a form that all of the cells in the body can use.
- Secretions from glands and organs throughout the digestive tract work on foods to break them down chemically into usable form.
- The absorption of food molecules into the bloodstream takes place mainly in the small intestine.
- The waste products of digestion pass into the large intestine and eventually out of the body.
- A variety of disorders are associated with the digestive system, many of which are a result of personal eating behaviors and food selections.

REVIEWING WHAT YOU LEARNED

1. What are the major parts of the digestive system?
2. Match the major digestive disorders that were

discussed in this chapter with the location in the body where the condition is most likely to occur.
3. Make a list of the processes occurring in the digestive system that change food from the time you take it in until the time you release it as waste.
4. What are digestion, absorption, and elimination?
5. What are four major types of food poisoning? How can they be prevented?
6. Name three ways in which you can take care of your digestive system.

APPLYING WHAT YOU LEARNED

1. Visit a drugstore and find 10 items that are used to treat digestive disorders. Draw some conclusions after reading the directions and cautions on these products about their use. How could you avoid ever having to use them?
2. In magazines or newspapers, look for ads that describe various products for treating digestive disorders. In the same magazines or newspapers, look for any information that would encourage

digestion	*deglutition*	trypsin	dialysis	gastric ulcers
gastrointestinal tract	uvula	amylase	halitosis	gallstones
alimentary canal	*esophagus*	*large intestine*	indigestion	gastritis
absorption	*peristalsis*	feces	heartburn	appendicitis
elimination	*stomach*	anus	flatulence	hepatitis
mastication	*chyme*	*liver*	nausea	tooth decay
papillae	*gastric juices*	urea	vomiting	botulism
taste buds	*small intestine*	*gallbladder*	diarrhea	closteridium perfringens
salivary glands	duodenum	*pancreas*	dehydration	staphylococcus
saliva	jejunum	*kidneys*	constipation	contaminated
parotid glands	ileum	ureter	ulcer	salmonella
submandibular glands	villi	urethra	peptic ulcers	
sublingual glands	bile	nephrons	duodenal ulcers	

PUTTING VOCABULARY TO USE

Using the words italicized in the chapter vocabulary list, make a schematic outline of the digestive process. A schematic outline illustrates the relationship of the *processes* with their organs or glands, as well as the *order* in which they occur. Next to each vocabulary word on your outline, write a brief definition.

On a separate piece of paper, write the following statements. Then supply the missing word for each from the chapter vocabulary list.

1. _____. Bad breath.
2. _____. Result of the body's not properly breaking down food.
3. _____. Gas in the stomach or small intestine.
4. _____. Condition in which feces become liquid and are expelled frequently.
5. _____. The most serious kind of food poisoning caused by bacteria.
6. _____. The number one food poisoning source in the United States.
7. _____. A condition in which acid contents of the stomach back up into the esophagus.
8. _____. Condition in which the feces become massed or hard in the small intestine.
9. _____. Open sore in the skin or in the mucous membrane.
10. _____. Liver infection caused by a virus.
11. _____. Infection from eating meat of sick animals.
12. _____. Inflammation of the gastric mucous membrane.
13. _____. Small crystals formed from bile that block the bile duct.
14. _____. Excessive loss of body fluid.
15. _____. Ulcers that develop in the stomach.

proper nutrition and eating habits. Reach a conclusion about the discrepancies that you find.

3. As a specialist on the digestive system, you are asked to speak to a group of young adults who have poor eating habits, which could lead to any of the disorders that you have just studied. What key points would you tell them in order to prevent the occurrence of such problems?
4. Make a list of the digestive disorders that were discussed in the chapter. Next to each, identify the eating behaviors and/or the food choices that could lead to that condition.

FOCUS ON WELLNESS

The digestive system is a complex network of body parts and processes working together to keep a person alive and well. Numerous disorders can occur when the digestive system is not working properly. *I promote the health of my own digestive system by . . .*

U N I T

6

FAMILY AND SOCIAL HEALTH

A Healthy Family System

You have studied the various body systems. What things do all of the body systems have in common? The health and well-being of each part of a system affects the health of the entire system. Although the parts function separately, they are all interdependent and interrelated. We can say the same for the family.

After studying this chapter, you will be able to:
- describe the family in terms of a system,
- compare extended and nuclear families,
- summarize the changes in families over the past 50 years,
- describe the characteristics of a healthy family,
- explain how listening skills affect family health,
- explain the reasons for child abuse and how to treat it.

Many husbands and wives are learning to carry out all the household tasks, so that one spouse can substitute for the other.

One of the greatest concerns that arises from the mother's working outside of the home is that of quality day care. Over 28% of women who are working outside of the home have pre-school age children. Studies have shown, however, that when children receive quality care, the effects of day care are no different from care in the home.

Single-Parent Heads of Households

The number of households headed by women increased by more than a third in the 1970s and more than doubled in one generation. This change is largely the result of the increased divorce rate. One of the greatest changes in the American family has been the increase in single-parent homes. Over 11 million children—more than one out of every six under the age of 18—live in a single-parent home, either with a mother or a father.

This family structure can be, and many times is, a very healthy one. It does, however, put more stress on the family system, making it necessary for all of the family members to work together to cope with changes.

All of these transitions reflect the fast-paced, changing times in which we live. None are necessarily bad. As individuals, we have little control over some of them. The important point is that they all influence the health of a family system. The healthy family copes with the changes *while* maintaining the family structure.

CHECK YOURSELF

1. How has family interaction changed over the last 50 years?
2. What impact has television had on the family system?
3. What are the three most significant changes influencing families today?

3. Healthy Family Systems

What makes a family system work? Several factors are necessary, chief among them being *structure, flexibility, recognition of each family member's self-worth,* and *open communication* among the family members.

Structure and Flexibility

We all need **structure**—*a certain rhythm in our lives and the realization of where we fit into our society.* Going to school, eating at certain times, playing on a team all give structure to our daily lives. The family, too, needs structure. The members need to know their place in it and what their general functions are.

In families, one or more people must serve in a leadership role. The parent or parents can fill this role. The parents may delegate responsibilities to the children of the family, depending on their age level and capacities. A clear system of rules helps the family to function smoothly.

Such structure does not mean rigidity. The leaders of the family, as well as the other members, need to be flexible and open to change if it is best for the family. Such flexibility also lessens the stress factor. As you learned in Chapter 6, stress management is necessary for a high level of wellness.

We all need praise and encouragement to build up our self-worth.

Membership Self-Worth

In a healthy family, each member is recognized as a unique individual with his or her own self-worth. The family members express their thoughts and feelings, and they listen to the other members. As you read in Chapter 5, we all have basic emotional needs. We must meet these needs in order to feel good about ourselves. The family is the primary source of meeting these emotional needs.

Open Communication

Freedom of **communication,** or *openness among family members,* leads to another very important characteristic of healthy families. Family members express tenderness, warmth, and humor. They also express negative feelings. In general, family members interact with one another and approach life from a positive viewpoint.

One very important skill associated with this last point on communication is listening. Studies indicate that we spend 80% of our waking hours communicating, and at least 60% of that time is spent *listening.* Because listening takes up so much time, you would think that most people would be skilled at it—but the opposite is true.

Open communication helps everyone in the family contribute to its well-being.

According to studies that communication experts have done, immediately after listening to a 10-minute presentation, the average listener has heard, correctly understood, properly evaluated, and retained about 30% of what was said. With 48 hours, retention of the presentation will drop to about 20%.

What do you stand to gain from improving your listening? Better listening skills improve communication and job performance, increase self-confidence and motivation, and lead to increased concentration, which, in turn, results in better decision-making.

Good Listening Rules

Some of the rules of good listening are to:

- *Give your full attention to the person speaking.* Eliminate distractions. If a loud radio or television is distracting you from what someone is saying, turn it off.
- *Focus on the speaker's message by looking for the central concept.* Try to get the point of what someone is saying rather than trying to remember every fact the speaker mentions.

Listening Well

Take the inventory. Discuss how the various items contribute to being a good listener. Discuss the fact that good communication is a skill which we improve by repetition.

IMPROVING YOURSELF

Are You a Good Listener?

On a separate sheet of paper, indicate whether each statement describes you *most of the time, some of the time,* or *never.*

1. When listening, I assume I know what the other person is going to say. *ST*
2. I do not interrupt others when they are talking. *N*
3. I find myself thinking about what I am going to say while the other person is talking. *ST*
4. I make eye contact when listening to the other person. *MT*
5. I do several things while I listen. *ST*
6. I find my mind wandering while someone else is talking. *ST*
7. I make judgments on what is being said. *N*
8. I have to ask for things to be repeated. *ST*
9. I can carry on several conversations at one time. *ST*
10. I ask questions, without interrupting, if I am not sure I understand what was said. *MT*

Scoring. Give yourself 4 points for each *most of the time,* 2 points for each *some of the time,* and 0 points for each *never.*

0 to 10: You have very good listening skills.
11 to 20: You have some good listening skills, but could develop your skills more.
21 or more: Have you noticed people do not talk to you very much? It could be because of your listening skills, or lack of them.

- *Indicate your interest.* Lean toward the speaker; nod at or encourage the other person by saying "Uh-hh" or "I see," in a quiet voice.
- *Remember what the speaker has said and, to be sure you heard it correctly, repeat the point so the person can correct you, if necessary.* When it's your turn to speak, recap the highlights of what the other person has said, using a phrase like, "As I understood it, you were saying. . . ."

Have you ever noticed that good listeners are often well-liked people? Everyone wants to feel that he or she is being heard and is not going to be judged, corrected, or interrupted. People like a good listener.

CHECK YOURSELF

1. What are three characteristics of a healthy family?
2. How does involving the children in family decisions affect the health of the family?
3. What are three rules for being a good listener?

A family system can break down for numerous reasons. This breakdown may end in divorce, in which case the family system is restructured. In many cases, the family system, though troubled, remains intact. If family members do not seek help, depending on the problems, the health of individual members can be threatened.

Physical and Mental Abuse

The rising incidence of child abuse, battered spouses, and runaways is evidence of troubled family systems.

Spouse and Elder Abuse

People who have spouses that physically or mentally abuse them have recently been the subject of national attention. They are usually women who are married to men who are very authoritarian, who have a very low stress level, or who become violent when drinking alcohol.

In the past, many women felt trapped by their spouses, since they had no means of paid employment. Their friends and neighbors often ignored the problem.

Elderly family members may also be the object of violence. A family member may take out his or her frustrations on elderly grandparents or aunts or uncles, who cannot defend themselves.

The problem of battered spouses and elders cuts across all levels of society. However, helping agencies and outlets now exist in almost all communities to help provide support.

Child Abuse

No one knows for sure how many children are abused in families. The statistics are on reported cases, and it is likely that there are many more unreported than reported ones. **Child abuse** can be *physical, including sexual abuse and emotional abuse.* The emotionally abused child is perhaps the hardest to identify, since there may be no physical evidence of abuse.

Physical abuse of children can occur among any socioeconomic group, culture, or religious affiliation. Generally, the abusers are parents or close relatives, and the incidents *chronic*, meaning they happen repeatedly. In many cases, abusive parents were themselves abused children.

Abusive parents are generally isolated. They have no one to turn to for relief from everyday frustrations. In many cases, parents lack information about child development. They do not know what a child can reasonably be expected to do or how to act at certain ages. The tendency to abuse children is increased by such problems as unemployment, low self-esteem, poor stress management skills, marital conflicts, and drug and alcohol abuse.

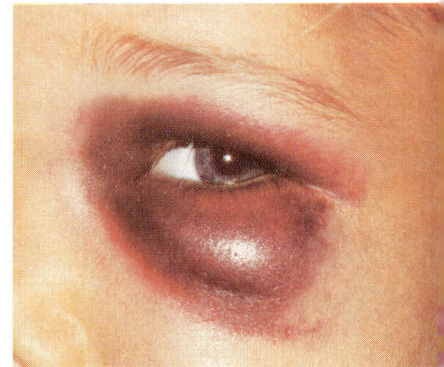

Child abuse is a serious social problem that must be corrected.

Over 2,000 children die each year from physical abuse. More than half of these deaths occur in children under the age of two years. One study found that if a child remains with the parents through two court hearings for abuse or neglect, the child is unlikely to survive to be the subject of a third hearing. Aside from the risk of death and physical injury, the abused child tends to be depressed, fearful, and withdrawn. The abused child may also exhibit destructive behaviors.

A large number of child-abuse cases involve sexual abuse. Typically, the sexually abused child is a junior high school girl victimized by someone in her own home—a father, stepfather, uncle, or some other trusted authority figure.

However, reports of sexually abused boys and young girls are becoming more and more common. This sexual abuse can last for years and never be reported. The child may be threatened with severe punishment, embarrassment, and even ridicule if he or she tells anyone.

It is most important that the victim in this situation know that he or she is not at fault. The child has done nothing wrong—it is the adult's behavior that is wrong. The victim should talk to some adult whom he or she trusts, so that the adult can get help for the victim.

Young Runaways

Some children try to get out of an abusive home by running away. However, the problem with this is that because of their need to survive, they often end up being exploited. Runaway children are prime targets for appearing in pornographic material and for prostitution.

Running away is not the answer, but help is available for the abused child. Before anyone can help an abused person, someone must report the abuse. All states now have laws requiring doctors and other health professionals to report suspected cases of child abuse. Anyone who suspects or knows of an abusive situation is urged to call the child welfare authorities.

Children can be removed from the abusive situation until it is corrected. But even more important, a needless tragedy may be prevented.

Family Counseling

Counseling help is available for both the child and the parents. Many communities now have crisis intervention hotlines. Parents who realize that they are losing control can get immediate help.

Parents Anonymous is a national organization that helps parents overcome their tendency toward violence. In meetings, parents make up a support system for one another. The organization functions much like *Alcoholics Anonymous*. Parents learn how to help themselves and one another as they talk about their feelings and problems.

Just as important as the rehabilitation of abusive parents is the long-range prevention of abuse in society as a whole. Parents and prospective parents need opportunities for learning about family life, child development, and parent-child relationships.

Rape

Sexual abuse is a term used to describe any sexual act brought on through force, threats, or domination. **Rape** is *sexual intercourse without a person's consent, brought on through threats, force, or sometimes, violence.*

Here are some facts to know about rape:

1. Any person of either sex and any age can become a victim.
2. Often the attacker is known to the person being attacked.
3. Heterosexual rape is by far the most common.
4. All rape is a type of violence committed by a person who wants to show hostility toward another person, particularly a female.

Acquaintance, or **date**, **rape** has become a serious social problem in recent years among young adults. *This action involves the rape of a woman, usually on a date with a particular man for the first or second time.*

A person who is raped should go immediately to the police and report the rape. Another choice is to call a rape crisis center, if there is one in the community. Both the police and this agency will help to get the facts and any physical evidence from the victim. The crisis center will also offer emotional and possibly legal support. See *Health Handbook,* page HB21, for information on rape prevention.

CHECK YOURSELF

1. What are battered spouses and relatives?
2. List three characteristics of abusive parents.
3. Why is running away not a solution to child abuse?
4. How does *Parents Anonymous* help abusive parents?
5. What is rape and what are at least two facts to know about it?

CHAPTER 20   Review

CHAPTER SUMMARY

- The family is a system and the basic unit of society. Like any system, the whole is only as healthy as its parts.
- Many factors influence the health of the family. Because the family is the basic unit of society, it is critical that we learn ways to improve and maintain the health of the family.
- The family has seen many changes over the past 50 years. Yet any family, regardless of its structure, has the potential to be healthy.

- Healthy families have some basic similarities. They are flexible, yet they have definite structure. The family members recognize one another's self-worth and communicate with one another.
- Battered spouses or relatives and abused children are the most frequent objects of the violence. However, there is help for the abused person through outside agencies.
- Rape is sexual intercourse without a person's consent, brought on through threats, force or, sometimes, violence.

| family | móbility | structure | child abuse | rape |
| nuclear family | extended family | single-parent families | communication | |

PUTTING VOCABULARY TO USE

Write the following paragraphs and supply the missing words for each from the chapter vocabulary list.

The _____ is the basic unit of society. Your immediate family—brothers, sisters, and parents—make up your _____ _____, while grandparents, aunts, uncles, and cousins are your _____ _____. One of the major changes in families over the past 50 years is a decrease in involvement with the _____ _____. This is primarily due to the increased _____ of families today.

In order to function, the healthy family must have a clearly identified _____. Although the leadership figure is important, there must be a freedom of _____ among family members. This _____ is enhanced as individual family members practice good _____ skills.

Two of the most significant changes in families are the _____-_____ _____ and the female head of the household.

Troubled family systems give rise to _____ _____, battered spouse and relative abuse, and runaways.

Age may not be a factor in _____.

REVIEWING WHAT YOU LEARNED

1. Compare the family system to the other systems you have studied. How does the concept of wellness apply to the family system?
2. Summarize the major changes in families over the past 50 years. How have these changes affected the health of the family?
3. Compare extended and nuclear families.
4. Describe the characteristics of a healthy family.
5. Explain the reasons for child abuse and how to treat it.
6. Summarize the benefits of being a good listener. How do listening skills affect family health?
7. Imagine you are a teenager in one of the 13 colonies in America just prior to the American Revolution. Pick your colony and your location. Then describe one day of your family life.

APPLYING WHAT YOU LEARNED

1. Find out what services are available in your community to assist families. Call one of them to find out what the most common family problems seem to be. Share your findings in class.
2. How can people use television to enhance the family system rather than to take away from it?

3. Evaluate a typical day in your life. How much time do you spend really listening to someone important to you? For a week, try to practice listening skills at least once a day with at least one person. At the end, evaluate your efforts.
4. For three days, keep a record of the types of interactions you have with people. Be aware of whether the other person listens, how well you listen, and whether your interactions are positive. At the end of three days, draw some conclusions about your personal interactions, especially with people to whom you are close.
5. In a one-page paper, describe a day in the life of a healthy family. Your description should reflect the characteristics of a healthy family.
6. The family has always been the basic unit of society. However, various eras and revolutions have had a significant impact on family life. Pick one of the following eras. Describe its influence on family health: Industrial Revolution, Agricultural Revolution, World War I, World War II.

FOCUS ON WELLNESS

A healthy society is dependent on healthy family systems. *I contribute to and promote my family's health by. . .*

Marriage and Parenthood

In the preceding chapter, we discussed family systems and the structure of healthy families. This chapter is concerned with the development of a family. Consider this development in relation to the cycle, much like the life cycle. Actually the family cycle is very much a part of the life cycle.

After studying this chapter, you will be able to:
- identify the major events of the family cycle,
- discuss the role of dating in the developmental process,
- identify reasons why teenage marriages have difficulty,
- summarize the factors that enhance successful marital adjustment,
- describe the significance of the parents' role in the healthy development of a child,
- describe the development of the fertilized egg through pregnancy,
- summarize the process of heredity.

The **family cycle** consists of *the majors events in the life of the family:*

- marriage,
- birth of the first child,
- birth of the last child,
- the last child's leaving home,
- death of a spouse.

Of course, the events that make up this family cycle reflect cultural factors and social change. For example, the average age for the family events from marriage to the last child's leaving home has decreased over the past 50 years. This is a result of earlier marriages and fewer children. The age of widowhood, on the other hand, has increased, since life expectancy is considerably longer than it was in the early 1900s.

What does this have to do with you and family health? These changes have a significant impact on family life. Middle-aged grandparents and four-generation families (great-grandparents)—two events that were almost unheard of in the late 1900s—are much more common today.

The phases of the family cycle suggest a progressive development of the family. Families may experience several phases at the same time, and this can be stressful. By understanding the family cycle, families are better able to adjust to the changes and thus to maintain family health. The two phases that we will discuss in this chapter are marriage and parenthood.

The first phase of the family cycle begins at marriage.

Marriage—The First Phase of the Family Cycle

The family cycle begins with the decision to marry. But before we study the important decision to marry, let us look at *why* people marry and some important considerations leading up to marriage.

In this country, there is great social pressure to marry. At least 90% of all Americans marry at some time in their lives. However, before people make such a major life decision, they must clearly identify their motives for marrying if they expect to be successful.

Reasons for Getting Married

If a person is getting married because of social pressure, it might be wise to reconsider. If a person is considering marriage to escape from problems at home or because a girl is pregnant or to prove a point, he or she is starting out on very shaky ground. With current statistics indicating that over one-half of all marriages end in divorce, such a start is potential for real concern.

Most people say they are marrying because they are "in love," and on

While the family cycle ends with the death of a spouse, the survivor can continue to live a rich and rewarding life.

the surface level that may be true. Often, however, these other motives, as mentioned above, may be hidden deep inside. Without close self-examination, a person may not even be aware of them. Other people may be aware of these motives, but may not be willing to admit them. If a person has any doubt or questions about the personal reasons for getting married or about the person that he or she is marrying, the best time to reconsider is before the marriage.

"But we are in love." The idea of romantic love is very glamorized in our society today. Countless movies and books portray the Romeo and Juliet type of romance. These stories are full of passion and excitement and usually end "happily ever after."

Unfortunately, they present an inaccurate picture of relationships. Almost all relationships do begin with romantic love, physical attraction, an aura of excitement and energy in the two individuals. Many couples are successful in maintaining this romantic side of their relationship.

However, all relationships go through various stages. When this first stage—the newness and excitement—settles, the couple must look closely to determine whether their oneness of mind extends to other aspects of their lives.

Marriage and Maturity   Unfortunately, many young couples make decisions about marriage based only on the romantic phase of their relationship. To be successful, marriage requires emotional and social maturity. Maturity can be difficult to define, yet it can be described:

- A mature person has the ability to establish and maintain relationships.
- A mature person has the ability to give as well as receive.
- A mature person can perceive others' feelings.

- A mature person is personally stable. Mature people have established values by which they live. They know their interests and, though open to new experiences, have goals and plans for achieving those goals.

The Most Important Factor   Perhaps the most important factor is that a mature person is aware of his or her emotional needs and how to meet them in healthy ways. How does this affect the success of a marriage? The marriage has a better chance of being successful if both individuals have found healthy ways to meet their emotional needs. They have friends, belong to a group, and are in some way making a contribution; that is, they feel worthwhile. Both individuals will not go into a marriage depending only on the marriage or the spouse to meet these needs.

As you can see, a person must consider many complex areas before getting married. Knowing your spouse is, of course, very important to the success of a marriage. However, knowing yourself—your innermost thoughts, feelings, fears, and dreams—is perhaps the most critical element for making a marriage work.

The Single Life

While the greater majority of people elect to marry, that still leaves many people who do not. These people remain single all of their lives or during some period in their lives. Some common reasons for living the single life are:

- the person prefers single independence, in which he or she is not responsible, directly or indirectly, for another person,
- the person has a type of job or responsibility that makes it difficult to marry or to help to rear children,
- the person has committed himself or herself to certain goals in life, and it would be hard to accomplish these goals if the person were married.

Whether a person marries or remains single, it is important to begin the socialization process. **Socialization** (sohsh-uh-luh-**zay**-shun) is participation in the processes particular to a cultural group. This process is important for people, whether they eventually decide to marry or to remain single. And it is usually explored through dating.

Dating as Part of Socialization

Dating provides an opportunity for you to get to know yourself better—to recognize your strengths and weaknesses. It also gives you the opportunity to interact with the opposite sex. By meeting and spending time with a variety of people, you learn what types of people you like and get along with best.

Getting to meet people in groups is a good way to learn how to interact with others.

The healthy young person uses dating as a testing ground. You can practice your decision-making skills and communication skills in your dating experiences. In doing so, you broaden your own development.

Going Steady

Dating often leads to going steady. There are some advantages to doing so. However, teenagers who go steady and who have dated very little may be closing themselves off from meeting other people too early in their social development. Going steady, even though it is convenient, saves money, and ensures you of having a date, may not be helpful in developing a healthy relationship.

Communication   Whatever the reason for going steady, if the relationship is to be healthy, you must identify and express your expectations— the rules or guidelines by which you are operating. By doing this, you open the doors to communication. Your steady can respond or react and also share his or her expectations. This open type of discussion is not easy. It takes practice, but it can be very helpful in preventing misunderstandings. When there is conflict in the relationship, you have already laid the groundwork for constructive communication.

The verbal or nonverbal expression of feelings, thoughts, and ideas is crucial to any relationship. How you communicate in dating relationships is a good indication of how you may communicate if you marry. The listening skills described in Chapter 20 are critical to successful communication.

Conflicts   Conflict is to be expected in any relationship. As you read in Chapter 7 on mental health, conflict can be constructive. However, communication must be open and good to resolve conflicts. Both people must

The teens are years of preparation for adulthood and for adult responsibilities. Young parents may never get the time to prepare adequately.

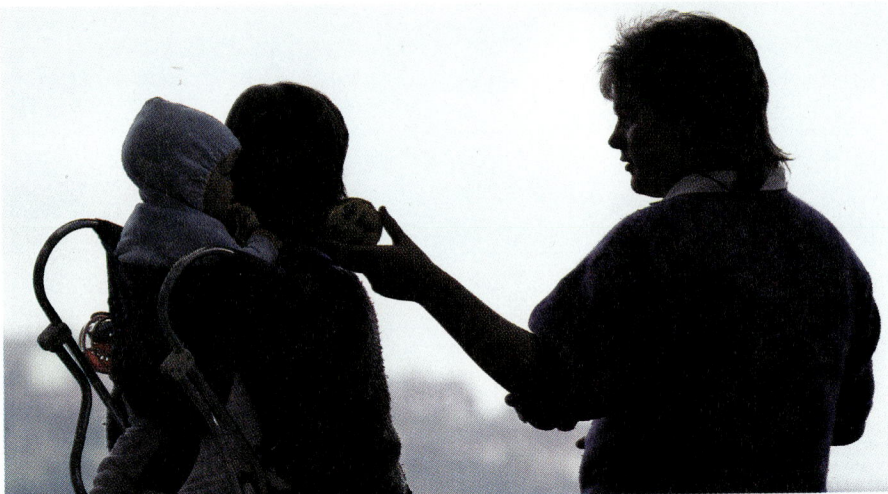

LIFE MANAGEMENT SKILL

Decisions and Consequences

Think of three goals that you have for the next three months. Next to each goal, describe how it would be affected by (1) marriage, and (2) pregnancy.

be willing to express themselves and to listen to what the other person is saying. Dating provides you an opportunity to work through conflicts and again practice your communication skills.

Teenage Marriage—A Risky Commitment

Although some teenage marriages do work, three out of four end in divorce. The teenage years are an important period of development. Since young people are just beginning to establish their own identities, it is unlikely that they are ready to make a choice of a marriage partner.

Reasons Against Teenage Marriage

In centuries past, young people 12 to 14 years married and quickly had children. This was encouraged in order to extend the family, provide workers, and start on the family cycle early. Since the average life expectancy of a person 300 years ago was between 35 and 40 years, the family cycle was short, indeed.

Today, because of modern medicine, people live longer. With the current need for a well-rounded education in order to get a job, people must spend more time training for a career. This training can go on into a person's 20s.

Marrying in the teens, therefore, has more negatives than positives going for it:

- *Marriage can interfere with the teenager's personal growth and development.* Many times, a young person gives up his or her personal interests and goals to direct attention to the marriage. This can result in unfulfilled, unhappy individuals. It may be difficult for the teenage couple to grow together and maintain a common bond.
- *Finances also present a problem for teenage marriage.* If the partners have

not finished high school, their earning power is severely limited. Trying to finish school and work at the same time puts great stress on the individuals. A young person may not yet have the skills to cope with such stress. As frustration builds, he or she may begin to take it out on the spouse.

■ *One of the main reasons for teenage marriage is an unexpected pregnancy.* Getting married under this condition puts an even greater stress—financially and emotionally—on the marriage.

It is possible for a teenage marriage to be successful. However, it is an exception rather than a norm.

Factors Affecting Marital Adjustment

Sociologists have conducted extensive research to develop measures of marital adjustment. In one study of over 7,000 couples, two researchers concluded that a well-adjusted marriage was one in which the husband and wife:

1. agreed on critical issues in their relationship,
2. shared common interests and activities,
3. demonstrated affection and shared confidences;
4. had few complaints about the marriage;
5. did not have feelings of loneliness or irritability.

The researchers went further to identify a number of social background factors associated with successful marital adjustment. Some of the more significant factors include:

■ similarity in family backgrounds,
■ domestic happiness of the parents,
■ lack of conflict with parents (in-laws),
■ increased educational achievement for both spouses,
■ having several friends of both sexes and belonging to organizations,
■ having a long period of close association prior to marriage,
■ having security and stability of occupation (this was more important than income),
■ agreement on having children.

These factors in isolation were not nearly as significant as they were when combined. That is, the more factors involved, the better the marital adjustment.

CHECK YOURSELF

1. What are the major events in the family cycle?
2. What are some reasons that people give for getting married?
3. How do emotional needs relate to a successful marriage?
4. Why do the majority of teen marriages fail?
5. Name five factors present in a well-adjusted marriage.

2. Parenthood

Without question, having a child requires a tremendous marital adjustment. Rearing a family is probably the most difficult job one can have. It is certainly one for which we are not usually prepared. A couple should give much consideration to this decision, since it has a significant impact on their health and thus the health of their relationship. All of the factors discussed in Chapter 20 that produce a healthy family are dependent upon a healthy parent or parents.

Why People Have Children

Couples give many reasons for having children. Some include:

- bringing stability to a shaky marriage,
- passing on the family name and heredity,
- giving one's parents a grandchild,
- having something to love,
- giving in to pressure from friends and parents,
- giving a child what a parent did not have.

The parent as teacher is important emotionally and socially for both parent and child.

Does it surprise you that one of the least mentioned reasons that parents give for having a child is a love for children?

The reasons for having a child may make the adjustment to parenthood a difficult one. A child is a full-time responsibility. If there were marital problems before the child, these problems are likely to increase with the birth of a baby.

Communicating becomes even more important when a child joins the family. The parents must make important decisions about the division of household tasks—especially if both parents work outside the home—and how the child will be reared.

The Parent as a Teacher

Parents are the most important teachers a child will ever have. They are responsible for the child's physical, emotional, social, and intellectual development and well-being—a task that requires much time and thought.

The child starts off totally dependent upon the parents. It is, or should be, the parents' goal to rear a responsible, healthy, independent person. What can parents do to successfully achieve this goal?

Maintaining One's Wellness

First, it is important that parents maintain their own wellness. A parent should not neglect his or her needs in the process of caring for the child.

A parent will not function well if he or she is tired, irritable, or pressed for time. Parents also need to get away by themselves for short periods of time to relax and enjoy a day or an evening out. The parent must keep his or her mental and physical stamina at a high level.

Maintaining Rules

Second, parents need to establish a clearly defined set of rules. The child learns not only the rules but the consequences for not following the rules. Parents must be consistent and carry through with discipline. That is, they discipline the child if he or she does not follow the rules.

Such an approach is different from random punishment. Discipline is structured. The child knows what the expectations are and knows what will happen if he or she disobeys.

Problems can arise when rules and consequences are not clearly defined. The parent may severely punish the child for disobeying on one occasion and not punish the child at all for the offense on another occasion. Such inconsistency is confusing to a child.

It can be helpful, especially as a child gets older, to *explain* reasons for limits or rules. This helps the child to begin to develop an understanding of cause and effect. For example, you cannot play in the street because you might get hit by a car.

Parents should try to make a distinction between *actions* (behavior) and the *person*. The parent disapproves of the behavior, but loves the child. This can be difficult for children to understand. But if the parents do not make the distinction, the child may develop low feelings of self-worth.

Children should be allowed to express their feelings, and parents can help children learn to express feelings in a healthy manner. Parents should also praise their children for their efforts. Children want to please. It is critical that parents should recognize and respond in a positive manner to their efforts.

Helping Children to Learn

What do we mean by the phrase "the person's potential to learn"? It is a person's ability to grasp new ideas, solve problems, and master new skills. It is a person's intelligence that is largely determined by his or her environment during the first five years of childhood.

Parents can help to develop this potential in a variety of ways. The child needs love and attention, a good example (a parent who enjoys learning), freedom to discover, and toys and games that make learning fun.

A parent can stimulate a child's senses at a very young age so that the child becomes sensitive to the environment. Bright colors stimulate eyes, soft music encourages talking and singing, and interesting noises stimulate hearing. Objects with a variety of textures develop a sense of touch, as does being held and cuddled.

Storytelling encourages imagination and creativity. Toys such as building blocks not only help the imagination grow but also further motor control and body coordination.

Children develop their comunication skills and master the language by talking with people. Parents can carry on conversations, point out interesting things to the child, and discuss various things that interest the child. Through all of the teaching, parents should find time every day to have fun with their child.

CHECK YOURSELF

1. What are four reasons why people have children?
2. What is the difference between discipline and punishment?
3. Name three things a child *needs* in order to learn.
4. Name three ways by which a young child might learn new things.

3. The First Nine Months

The **cell** is the *basic unit of structure of all living things.* Your body is made up of literally trillions of cells. Each has the ability to divide, reproduce, and repair itself, with the exception of the cells that make up the nervous system.

Cells that do similar work group together to form **tissues.** You have muscle tissue, nerve tissue, and blood tissue, to name a few. This tissue, in turn, forms **organs,** *certain body parts that have special structures and do special work.* The heart, brain, stomach, and lungs are organs.

As we have seen in Chapters 14 through 19, the organs then form **systems,** *collections of organs that work together to perform one overall function* (for example, the digestive system, the nervous system, or the circulatory system).

The **body system,** in turn, is made up of the *complex systems that work together and are dependent upon one another* for a totally functioning, healthy person.

The First Cell

The entire body system begins as one cell, so tiny that one can see it only with a high-powered microscope. This first cell is formed by *the union of an egg cell from the mother and a sperm cell from the father.* This process is called **fertilization**.

The union of an egg cell and a sperm cell forms a **fertilized** (**furt**-uhl-ized) **egg cell** that begins a complicated process of cell division. Over a nine-month period, this fertilized egg cell develops and grows into a complex, fully formed body system. This development is one of the most amazing feats of nature.

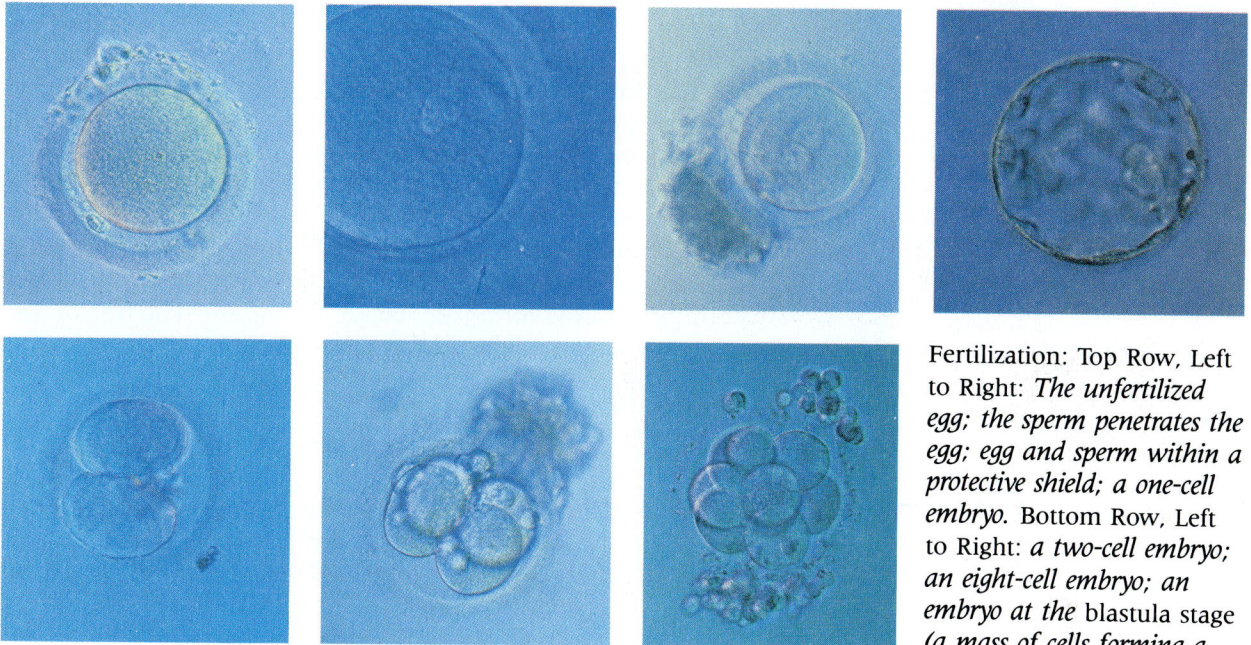

Fertilization: Top Row, Left to Right: *The unfertilized egg; the sperm penetrates the egg; egg and sperm within a protective shield; a one-cell embryo.* Bottom Row, Left to Right: *a two-cell embryo; an eight-cell embryo; an embryo at the* blastula stage *(a mass of cells forming a hollow ball).*

The Process of Fertilization and Implantation

In Chapter 17, you learned about the reproductive system. In order for fertilization to take place, sperm must be deposited in and travel up the female's vagina through the uterus and into the Fallopian tube. An egg cell must be present in the Fallopian tube, and the sperm cell must penetrate the outer lining of the egg cell.

When a sperm cell does unite with an egg cell, a protective covering instantaneously surrounds the egg cell. This prevents any other sperm cell from penetrating the egg cell.

Once fertilized, the egg takes about three days to reach the uterus. During this time, the egg cell has divided many times, forming clusters of cells. The cell is now called an **embryo** (**em**-bree-oh), *a cluster of constantly dividing cells in the first stages of development,* which begins to implant in the uterus. The implantation is complete about 10 days after fertilization. Then the embryo is about the size of the dot over an "i".

Prenatal Care

The sooner the mother confirms her pregnancy, the sooner she can begin prenatal care. This is important because the mother's health choices affect the developing baby's health. The pregnant woman should be having regular visits with an obstetrician, a doctor specializing in the care of a woman and her developing baby (see page 304).

The obstetrician gives the pregnant woman a complete physical examination, including blood tests and a pelvic examination. Possible complications may be identified and corrected early. The obstetrician monitors the developing baby. The doctor also helps to educate the mother in important health behaviors. Her eating behaviors are of special concern. She needs a well-balanced diet to ensure proper nourishment for her developing child.

The doctor may also discuss the importance of exercise during pregnancy. Depending on the mother's health and level of fitness, the doctor may have recommendations for a safe exercise program. The doctor will also monitor the woman's weight during pregnancy.

Development in the Womb

The cells that compose the inner layer of the embryo develop into the baby. The outer layer of cells develop into the **placenta** (pluh-**sent**-tuh), *a blood-rich tissue that transfers oxygen and nutrients from the mother's blood to the embryo.* It also transfers the embryo's wastes into the mother's circulatory system.

The placenta begins to form two to three days after implantation. The nourishment passes from the placenta through the umbilical (um-**bill**-uh-kuhl) cord to the embyro. The **umbilical cord** *connects the embryo to the placenta.*

The **amniotic sac** (am-nee-**ott**-ick **sack**) also forms at this time. *This sac is filled with transparent fluid that acts as a shock absorber for the embryo and insulates it against temperature change.* The developing baby floats in the fluid and is protected from jarring or bumps. The fluid in the sac changes about every hour. Thus, it is always fresh.

After two months, the developing individual is called a **fetus** (**feet**-us). At this time *all the vital organs have started to develop.*

The Three Stages of Birth

By the ninth month, the baby has turned to face head down in the uterus. The birth process begins with labor pains caused by contractions of the uterus. These contractions shorten the muscles of the uterus and begin to pull the **cervix,** *the neck of the uterus,* open.

For nine months, the cervix has held tightly shut, keeping the baby inside the uterus. Now it must open to a diameter of about 5 inches (13 cm) to allow the baby to pass through. The *dilation* (die-**lay**-shun), or opening, of the cervix is the *first* and, usually, the longest stage of the birth process.

During the *second* stage of birth, the baby passes through the vagina and out of the mother.

In the *third* and final stage, the uterus contracts to expel the placenta, now called the *afterbirth.*

Development in the Womb Before Birth

4 weeks

6 weeks

8 weeks

End of First Month
- One quarter inch (0.6 cm) long
- Heart, brain, lungs forming
- Heart starts beating on about twenty-fifth day

End of Second Month
- 1.5 inches (3.8 cm) long
- Muscles, skin developing
- Arms, hands, and fingers forming
- Legs beginning to form, along with knees, ankles, and toes
- Every vital organ starting to develop

End of Third Month
- 3 inches (7.5 cm) long
- Weighs 1 oz (28.3 g)
- Movement can be felt
- Can open and close mouth and swallow

End of Fourth Month
- 8 to 10 inches (20 to 25 cm) long
- Weighs 6 ounces (169.8 g)

End of Fifth Month
- About 12 inches (30 cm) long
- Weighs 1 pound (453.6 g)
- Eyelashes appear
- Nails begin to grow
- Heartbeat can be heard

End of Sixth Month
- Can kick and cry
- Can hear sounds
- Might even hiccup
- Has fingernails and footprints

End of Seventh Month
- Weighs 2 to 2.5 pounds (907.2 to 1,134 g)
- Can move arms and legs freely
- Eyes are now open

End of Eighth Month
- 16.5 inches (41.25 cm) long
- Weighs 4 pounds (1,814.4 g)
- Hair gets longer
- Skin gets smoother as a layer of fat develops under it

End of Ninth Month
- 18 to 20 inches (45 to 50 cm) long
- Weighs 7 to 9 pounds (3,175.2 to 4,082.4 g)
- Organs have developed enough to function on their own

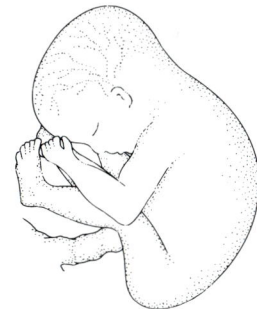

12 weeks

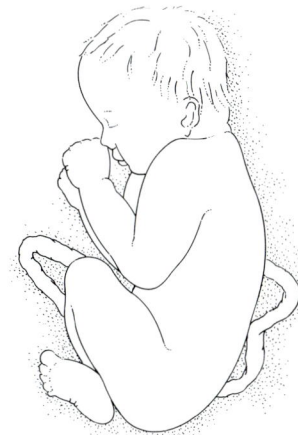

9 months

1. What is the difference between an embryo and a fetus?
2. Use one sentence to generally describe each of the nine months of development in the womb.
3. What are the three stages of birth?

4. From Generation to Generation

Perhaps no other area of health and the human body is as fascinating as the process of heredity. **Heredity** (huh-**red**-ut-tee) is *the passing on of the characteristics from the parents to the offspring.*

Chromosomes and Genes

The process of heredity is started in complex structures called chromosomes (**kro**-muh-zohmz). **Chromosomes** are *tiny structures within the nuclei (**new**-klee-eye) (singular form: nucleus) of cells that help to determine and continue the types of living things.* Through the chromosomes, humans give birth to humans, cats to cats, and horses to horses. Chromosomes are found in all body cells, except mature red blood cells, which have no nuclei.

Located within the chromosomes are the **genes (jeans)**, *tiny protein molecules that control hereditary characteristics.* Through the genes, special characteristics of the mother and father are given to the offspring. For instance, your genes determine your resemblance to your mother or father, the color of your hair, and the color of your eyes. This is because you receive some genes from your mother and some from your father.

Structure of the Chromosomes

Every living organism has a certain number of chromosomes. Human body cells, with the exception of the sperm and egg cell, contain 46 chromosomes. The egg and sperm cells have 23 chromosomes each. In fertilization, the union of a sperm and egg cell, the fertilized cell receives 46 chromosomes (23 from each parent), and the hereditary traits of the mother and the father have been passed on to another generation through the offspring.

As you know, the fertilized egg cell divides, eventually producing trillions of cells that make up the human body. In between each cell division, each chromosome in the cell nucleus duplicates itself. As the cell divides, the two sets of 46 chromosomes separate and each new cell contains 46 chromosomes, identical to those in the first cell. This process continues throughout life.

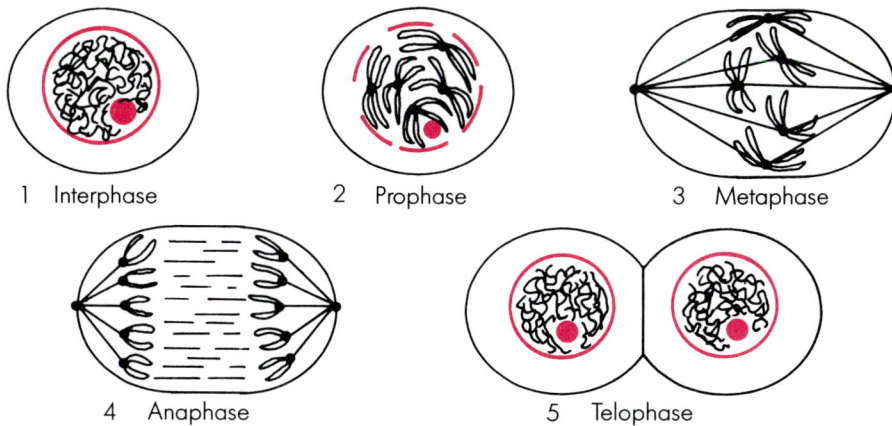

1 Interphase

2 Prophase

3 Metaphase

4 Anaphase

5 Telophase

Cell division is called **mitosis** *(my-**toe**-sis). It takes place in phases: (1) Interphase–the cell before mitosis; (2) Prophase– chromatin threads begin to appear as chromosomes; (3) Metaphase–separation of the chromosomes begins; (4) Anaphase–a complete set of chromosomes, equal in number, go to opposite ends of the cell; (5) Telophase– the cell separates to form two cells.*

A Girl or a Boy?   Will it be a girl or a boy? Of the 46 chromosomes in a fertilized egg cell, two are specialized sex chromosomes. In females, these two chromosomes look exactly alike and are called X chromosomes. In males, one chromosome is shorter and does not match the other. **Geneticists** (juh-**net**-uh-sists), *scientists who study* **genetics,** *the process of heredity,* call this smaller one the Y chromosome.

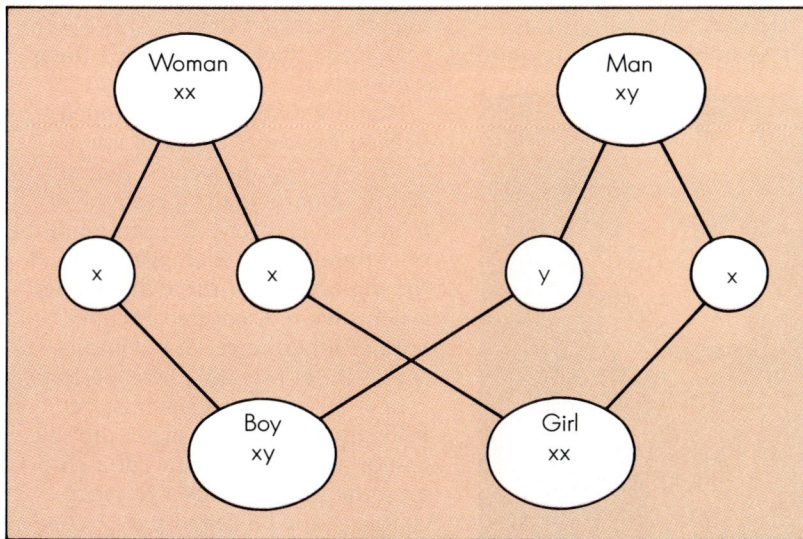

Gender is determined by specialized sex chromosomes, two of which are present in the female (xx) and two of which are present in the male (xy).

Remember that sperm and egg cells contain only half the number of chromosomes in other cells. This means that these cells contain only one sex chromosome, not two. Sperm cells may contain either an X or a Y chromosome. The egg cell only has X chromosomes. If an egg cell is fertilized by a sperm cell carrying an X chromosome, the baby is a girl because, as the chromosome pair, the combination is XX. If the sperm cell is carrying a Y chromosome, the pairing forms an XY combination, resulting in a boy. So the determination of the sex of a child is based on the father's sperm cell.

Gregor Mendel and Inherited Characteristics

Gregor Mendel (1822–1884) was an Austrian monk who wanted to be a high school teacher, but three times he failed the required examination for teaching. Discouraged, he turned his interest to his hobby—botany—the study of plants. In 1857, he began breeding plants to study the inheritance of physical characteristics.

Mendel was astonished when he began cross-pollinating tall and short pea plants. He discovered that every plant had two factors within it. These factors controlled the inheritance of each physical characteristic. Mendel had no idea what the factors were, but he knew that one was contributed by each parent. One factor was the dominant characteristic, the other the recessive one.

Mendel now faced the problem of sharing his discovery with other scientists. He was, after all, just a person whose hobby was botany and who had been unable to pass a teacher qualification test. In hopes of getting support, Mendel decided to send his work to Karl Wilhelm von Nageli, one of the most important botanists in Europe. Von Nageli returned Mendel's material to him.

Although Mendel later managed to get his research published in several scientific journals, no one paid much attention to it. He died in 1884, not knowing that he would someday be famous. Von Nageli died several years later, having no idea of the terrible mistake he made, or that he would be best remembered for *not* paying attention to Mendel's work.

During the 1870s, Walther Fleming, a German biologist, used dyes to study the nucleus of cells under a microscope. Fleming worked out the order of events in cell division. Fleming observed the tiny rods that form within the nucleus. He called them *chromosomes.*

Fleming's work was continued by a Belgian biologist, Edouard von Beneden, who discovered that all cells in a particular type plant or animal always have the same number of chromosomes. Biologists realized the importance of these discoveries when they rediscovered Mendel's laws of inheritance. The chromosomes fitted Mendel's laws perfectly.

In 1909, a Danish botanist, Wilhelm Johannsen, made the suggestion that each portion of a chromosome that controls a physical characteristic be called a *gene. Gene* was a Greek word meaning "to give birth to." From that point on, chromosomes were considered to be strings of genes.

Genes and the Genetic Code

As in the case of almost all other body-cell activity, the process of heredity involves complex chemical activity. The *special chemical compound necessary for the process of heredity* is **deoxyribonucleic acid** (dee-**och**-see-**rye**-bow-new-**clay**-ic **ass**-id) (**DNA**). The DNA molecule is about 1 ten-millionth of an inch in diameter (0.0000025 millimeter).

Each gene consists of a part of a DNA molecule. The DNA molecule resembles a twisted ladder, the rungs being made up of a chemical compound called *bases.* There are four kinds of bases that can be paired in only certain combinations according to their size, much like a jigsaw puzzle.

You have more than 10,000 genes in every cell, and they all contain the same four bases. The variation among genes is a result of the arrangement of these bases along the DNA molecule. Since several hundred pairs of bases are in each gene, a countless number of arrangements are possible.

DNA is responsible for the production of new cells and of protein. As you learned in Chapter 8, protein is made up of *amino acids.* There are 20 amino acids that may be joined in a variety of ways.

The order in which the amino acids join together is determined by the arrangement of the DNA bases. These 4 bases and the 20 amino acids that make up all proteins are the components of the **genetic** (juh-**net**-ick) **code,** *the code that regulates what the many body cells are supposed to do.* So in the sperm and egg cells, the genetic code regulates heredity.

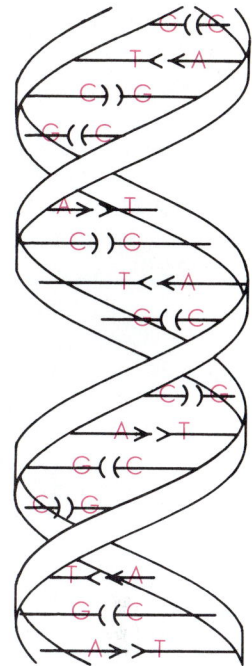

The four DNA bases and twenty amino acids are the components of the genetic code.

Dominant and Recessive Genes

As you can see, the process of heredity is extremely complicated. But what determines whether you have blue eyes or brown eyes, straight hair or curly? Every person inherits two genes for every trait—one from the mother, and one from the father. As the chromosomes divide and separate, the two genes for a particular trait line up next to each other.

HEALTH UPDATE   HEALTH UPDATE   HEALTH UPDATE

Dominant and Recessive Traits

Dominant	Recessive
curly hair	straight hair
black or brown hair	blonde or red hair
full lips	thin lips
dimples	smooth cheeks
straight nose	turned-up nose
brown eyes	blue eyes
long, full eyelashes	short, thin eyelashes
freckles	no freckles

Which are the fraternal and the identical twins?

In the case of many traits, one gene is **dominant** and the other **recessive.** This simply means that when the pair of genes lines up, the *dominant gene overpowers the recessive one and determines that particular trait.*

Let us take the trait of eye color as an example. Brown eyes (*BB*) are dominant; blue eyes (*bb*) are recessive. As you can see in the diagram, the child inherits the brown eyes.

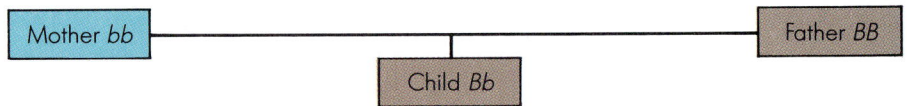

Mother *bb*		Father *BB*
	Child *Bb*	

However, consider the possible combinations if both parents have one dominant gene and one recessive gene for brown eyes. Since both parents have the dominant gene for brown eyes, their child will have brown eyes. There is one chance in four that their child will have blue eyes.

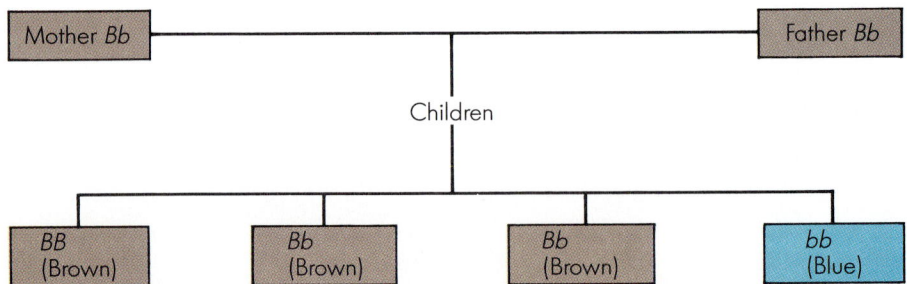

Mother *Bb*			Father *Bb*

Children

BB (Brown)	*Bb* (Brown)	*Bb* (Brown)	*bb* (Blue)

The Mystery of Twins

Twins, along with other multiple births, have been a puzzle to medical researchers for years. Identical twins are an accident of nature. Scientists do not agree on just how the accident happens.

In most cases, the woman's ovaries release two mature eggs instead of one. If a separate sperm cell fertilizes each egg cell, two embryos develop. The two embryos, called **fraternal twins,** *have different genetic makeup and therefore do not look any more alike than brothers and sisters normally do.*

In some cases, after one egg cell has been fertilized, it divides and two embryos develop. These embryos *have the same genetic information* and, therefore, are usually **identical twins.**

Research on twins has been expanding greatly. Researchers now use twins to study a variety of physical health problems, as well as questions about psychological development and adjustment.

Twins and Genetic Research

Researchers are currently using twins to study:

- genetic influence on temperament,
- genetic and environmental influence on fears and phobias, language development, and intelligence,
- genetic influences on antisocial behavior,
- the onset of alcoholism and affective emotional disorders,
- the causes of cancer and multiple sclerosis,
- the genetic components of coronary heart disease.

Researchers got an unexpected boost from the discovery of identical twins who had been separated from each other at birth. Neither twin nor his adoptive family knew about the other until the twins were reunited at age 39. The similarities in Jim Lewis and Jim Springer were startling. Researchers will try to determine how much was coincidental and how much was the result of being identical twins. What do you think?

- In school they both liked math and disliked spelling.
- Their first wives were both named Linda.
- They had both divorced and remarried, and their second wives were both named Betty.
- Both had a son named James Allen (one spelled Alan), and a dog named Tag.
- Both had gained weight at the same time, and had had the same kind of surgery.
- Both had a white seat around a tree in his yard.

CHECK YOURSELF

1. What is a chromosome?
2. What is a gene?
3. What is the relationship of the chromosomes to the genes?
4. What is the function of DNA?
5. What are dominant and recessive genes?

When you consider the countless number of divisions and processes that must take place to form a fully developed baby, it truly is amazing that almost all babies are born healthy and normal. However, it is estimated that as many as 250,000 children are born in the United States every year with major heredity conditions and disorders that will seriously impair their health.

According to the National Institute of Health, 15 million Americans have some kind of genetic condition or birth defect. At least 40% of all infant mortality is the result of genetic factors. Millions of Americans are healthy themselves, but are carriers of defective genetic information and do not know it until they have a child born with a birth defect.

It is estimated that everyone carries five to eight recessive genes for genetic disorders. Genetic diseases and disorders account for about one-fourth of hospital admissions and placements in institutions for the disabled.

Types of Genetic Disorders

A cleft palate and a clubfoot both have an incidence of 1 in 1,000 births.

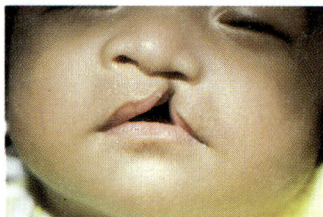

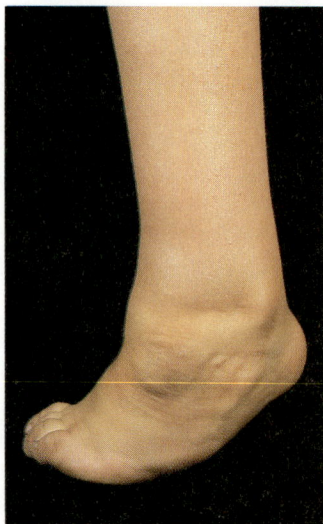

There are more than 2,000 known types of genetic conditions and birth defects. In the broadest definition, any quality an individual inherits is a **genetic condition.** However, as we use it here, genetic condition refers to *genetic diseases and disorders, illnesses, or other conditions of malfunction with which an individual is born.*

Any disease, disorder, or other condition present at birth can impair an individual's health. While a majority of birth defects are genetically related, some are the result of environmental factors—for example, handicaps that can occur when the mother has taken certain drugs or has become infected with *rubella* (rue-**bell**-uh) (German measles) during pregnancy. Thus, the term **birth defects** includes both *genetic conditions and many other types of diseases and disorders caused by a variety of factors.*

Some congenital defects are immediately observable at birth. These include physical malformations, such as **cleft** (**kleft**) **lip**, **cleft palate** (**pal**-ut), and **clubfoot**. While others may be present at birth, testing is required to confirm their presence.

Some conditions that may be present at birth do not generate observable symptoms until the infant is several months to a year or more old. Among these are **Tay-Sachs** (**tay-sacks**) disease (a disorder causing the destruction of the nervous system), **cystic fibrosis** (**sis**-tik fie-**bro**-sus) (a disorder that affects the mucous-secreting glands and the sweat glands), **sickle-cell** (**sick**-el-sell) **anemia** (an inherited blood disorder), **phenylketonuria** (feen-ul-ket-un-**nure**-ree-ah) (PKU) (an inherited enzyme deficiency), and hearing loss.

Various types of mental retardation, cerebral palsy, and minimal brain dysfunction cannot be observed, until the infant begins (or fails to begin) evolving through the normal stages of physical development.

Common Genetic Diseases and Disorders

Some genetic diseases and disorders show up at birth while others may not become apparent until later in life. Below is a list of the more common genetic diseases and disorders.

Condition	Incidence
Sickle-cell anemia	1 in 500
Cleft lip/cleft palate	1 in 1,000
Clubfoot	1 in 1,000
Down syndrome	1 in 1,000
Cystic fibrosis	1 in 2,000
Diabetes	1 in 2,000
Tay-Sachs disease	1 in 3,600
Hemophilia	1 in 10,000
Phenylketonuria (PKU)	1 in 10,000 to 20,000
Muscular dystrophy	1 in 20,000

Other **congenital** (kun-**jen**-uh-tul) **problems** (meaning, *existing at birth*) that may or may not be related genetically occur in even greater numbers. These include hearing and visual impairments, heart and circulatory defects, and prematurity. Nearly 250,000 babies are born with these problems every year.

The APGAR Test

Almost all American hospitals administer a routine test to determine an infant's physical condition at birth. It is named after the late Virginia Apgar, a noted **anesthesiologist** (an-ess-thee-**zee**-ahl-uh-jest)—*a doctor who administers anesthetics* (an-us-**thet**-iks). These are substances that cause loss of sensation, with or without loss of consciousness.

The APGAR test measures the baby's condition in five significant areas: appearance or coloring, pulse, grimace or reflex irritability, activity, and respiration. Any significant differences from the normal response in each of these areas may require further testing and observation.

Chromosome Abnormality

In spite of many years of advanced research, medical scientists still are uncertain about the exact causes of more than half of the congenital defects found in humans. While research continues, scientists do know that a principal cause of birth defects is chromosome abnormality.

Since the chromosomes contain genes responsible for inherited characteristics, even the slightest abnormality involves thousands of genes and can cause severe developmental problems in the fetus. Most miscarriages in early pregnancy are the result of chromosome abnormalities.

The most serious chromosome abnormalities are the result of the cells of the sperm, egg, or newly developed fetus containing more or less than the usual amount of chromosomal material. Down syndrome is the best-known result of such an error. It results in *abnormalities of the face and other parts of the body, and physical and mental retardation.* (See also Chapter 14 for more information on Down syndrome.)

Severe birth defects can also occur when parts of chromosomes break off and join onto other chromosomes, thus interfering with the normal transmission of genetic information.

Besides amniocentesis, which is discussed on page 386, there are other methods to investigate the health of the fetus. They are:

- **Ultrasonography** (ul-tra-**son**-og-raphy), in which sound waves are used to project light images on a screen.
- **Fetoscopy** (**feet**-oh-scopy), in which a tube containing a light is focused on parts of the fetus.
- **Chorionic villus biopsy** (**kor**-ee-on-ick **vil**-us bi-**op**-sy), in which a small piece of membrane is removed from the *chorion*, a covering for the fetus. This matter is examined for possible genetic defects. The procedure takes place around the ninth week of fetal development, so it is a procedure that can be performed earlier than amniocentesis.

Passing On Genetic Disorders

Genetic disorders are passed on much like other physical traits; that is, there are dominant and recessive traits.

Dominant Inheritance

One affected parent has a single faulty gene (D), which dominates its normal counterpart (n).

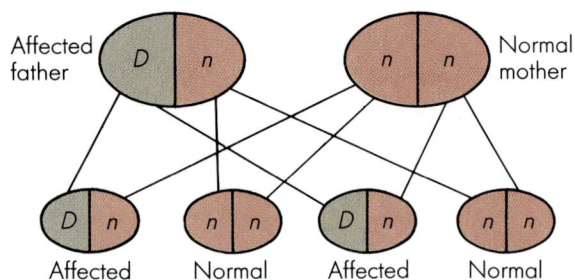

| Affected father | D | n |
| Normal mother | n | n |

D	n	Affected
n	n	Normal
D	n	Affected
n	n	Normal

Each child's chances of inheriting either the D or the n from the affected parent are 50%.

Recessive Inheritance

Both parents who are usually unaffected carry a normal gene (N), which takes precedence over its faulty recessive counterpart (r).

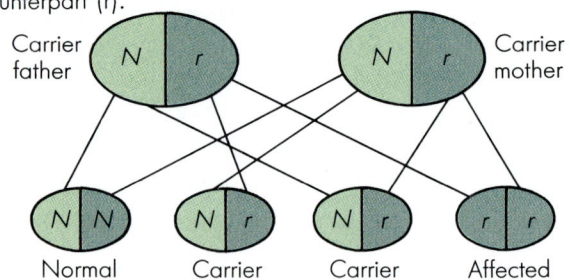

| Carrier father | N | r |
| Carrier mother | N | r |

N	N	Normal
N	r	Carrier
N	r	Carrier
r	r	Affected

The odds for each child are:

a 25% risk of inheriting a ''double dose'' of r genes, which may cause a serious birth defect.

a 25% chance of inheriting two Ns thus being unaffected.

a 50% chance of being a carrier as both parents are.

Wellness and Parenthood

Maintaining and promoting your own personal wellness is a great responsibility. This responsibility becomes magnified for the pregnant woman. She is responsible for the wellness of the developing fetus. This responsibility, however, also extends to the father. Certain drugs can damage chromosomes in the sperm cell.

Certain factors during pregnancy have been identified as the source of diseases, disorders, and malformations present at birth. Virtually any environmental factor known to have negative effects on a child or adult can have far more serious effects on the unborn. Some examples are:

Environmental Factor	Congenital Disorder
Rubella (German measles)	Cataracts, deafness, heart malformation, mental retardation
Radiation	Malformations, genetic defects in future generations
Certain drugs and medications	Prematurity, retarded physical and/or mental development
Poor diet	Prematurity, retarded physical and/or mental development

X-Linked Conditions

The mother is the carrier of *X*-linked conditions. While the mother is not affected, she carries one abnormal gene in her sex chromosomes and one normal gene. There is a 50% risk that each male child will be affected by a disease and a 50% risk that each female child will be a carrier. Among the more common *X*-linked conditions are certain forms of color blindness, hemophilia, and muscular dystrophy.

Advances in Genetics

Development of genetics as a science increased between 1900 and 1950. We gained much new knowledge about genetically related diseases and disorders, and new research techniques for diagnosing, preventing, and treating such conditions. This knowledge has produced a wide expansion of programs to deal with genetic conditions and birth defects.

More than a dozen states have implemented massive screening programs for such diseases as sickle-cell anemia. Forty-eight states screen all newborn infants for phenylketonuria (PKU). Both kinds of screening can be done with a simple blood test.

Amniocentesis

Amniocentesis (am-nee-oh-sen-**tee**-sus) is *a medical procedure that enables a physician to examine the chromosomes and to study the body chemistry of the unborn child.* The procedure is usually performed after the fourteenth week of pregnancy.

Amniocentesis involves inserting a syringe through the abdominal wall of the mother into the *amniotic* (am-nee-**ott**-ik) *fluid* surrounding the developing fetus. The physician removes an amount of fluid and then grows cells from the fluid in a culture.

It takes several weeks for all the chromosomal divisions in the cells to be complete. When they are completed, doctors can analyze the chromosomes for their content and number. Amniocentesis can detect Tay-Sachs disease and Down's syndrome. A side benefit is that the doctor can determine the sex of the fetus. This can be helpful to families who have sex-linked disorders.

CHECK YOURSELF

1. Name three genetic disorders and describe each.
2. Why are chromosome disorders so closely linked to birth defects?
3. What is meant by *X*-linked genetic conditions?
4. In a sketch, show how *X*-linked conditions can be passed on.

CHAPTER 21   Review

CHAPTER SUMMARY

- The family cycle is made up of a series of events over the years that have a direct impact on health.
- Considerations about marriage should involve much self-examination of needs, interests, and goals.
- Many factors affect the successful adjustment to marriage, including decisions regarding children.
- Communication is a critical element in the success of a relationship. It becomes even more important when a couple has a child.
- The parents are the most important teachers their child will ever have.
- Children's experiences in their first years lay the foundation for development throughout life.

- The process of fertilization is the beginning of the complex development that takes place during pregnancy.
- Through cell division, the fertilized egg, getting its nourishment and oxygen from the mother, develops into a complete human organism.
- Fertilization takes place when a sperm cell meets an egg cell.
- It is through this process that parents pass on their traits to their children. The tiny structures called chromosomes carry the genes that are responsible for heredity.
- This complex process of heredity is still being studied, especially from the standpoint of preventing birth defects.

CHAPTER VOCABULARY

family cycle	placenta	genetics	cleft palate
socialization	umbilical cord	fraternal twins	clubfoot
cell	amniotic sac	identical twins	Tay-Sachs disease
tissues	fetus	deoxyribonucleic acid (DNA)	cystic fibrosis
organs	cervix	genetic code	sickle-cell anemia
systems	heredity	dominant gene	phenylketonuria
body systems	chromosomes	recessive gene	congenital problems
fertilization	nuclei	genetic condition	anesthesiologist
fertilized egg cell	genes	birth defects	sidestream smoke
embryo	geneticists	cleft lip	amniocentesis

PUTTING VOCABULARY TO USE

On a separate piece of paper, write each sentence below. Supply the missing words for each from the vocabulary list.

1. The _____ is formed when a sperm cell unites with an egg cell. This process is called _____.

2. The developing baby is protected by fluid in the _____ _____, which acts like a shock absorber. The _____, as it is called after the second month of pregnancy, gets its nourishment though the _____.

3. Tiny structures within the nucleus of each cell are called _____. These structures carry the _____, which control heredity characteristics.

4. The study of the heredity process is called _____. One medical procedure, _____, gives doctors an opportunity to examine development while the fetus is still in the womb.

REVIEWING WHAT YOU LEARNED

1. What are the major events of the family cycle?
2. What might a person learn about himself or herself by going steady?
3. What is meant by using dating as a testing ground?
4. Why do so many teenage marriages have difficulties?
5. What are the three stages of birth?
6. What are the five factors researchers have identified as contributing to a well-adjusted marriage?
7. Describe what happens to an egg cell from fertilization through pregnancy.
8. Explain the relationship of chromosomes, genes, and DNA in the process of heredity.
9. Give two examples of how dominant and recessive traits are passed on to children.

APPLYING WHAT YOU LEARNED

1. Write a one-page descriptive paper on a noted genetic scientist.

2. Make a list of your 10 favorite activities. Next to each activity, write one sentence describing how your participation in that activity would change if you were married. Then write a statement on how it would change if you were a parent. Draw some conclusions about the impact of marriage and parenthood on one's life.
3. Contact the National Foundation of the March of Dimes to find out what types of activities it conducts to help fight birth defects.
4. Interview five people who have been married for at least 10 years to determine factors that they believe have contributed to the success of their marriage. Compare your answers with those that other class members found.

FOCUS ON WELLNESS

Marriage and parenthood are two of the most life-changing events that take place in a person's life. *I can better prepare myself for decisions regarding marriage and parenthood by . . .*

The Life Cycle

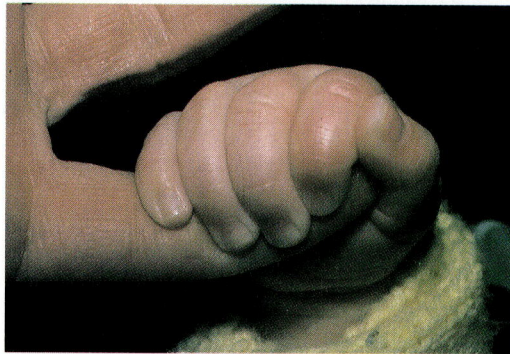

Growth and development are part of a continuous, life-long process. The process begins with conception and ends with death. Numerous scientists have studied this process and each of its stages. As a result, we can predict the type and rate of growth to be expected at each age level.

After studying this chapter, you will be able to:
- identify Erikson's eight stages of life development,
- describe the changes a person goes through during puberty,
- summarize the basic tasks of adolescence,
- explain the changes people experience as they age,
- explain the stages a person goes through in accepting death.

Although our growth and development are predictable, we each grow at a rate unique to our personal systems. As you will see, several factors influence this rate of growth.

Several noted scientists have presented theories, or models, of how we develop into who we are. Physical development is perhaps the best understood, while we are still learning about our emotional and social development.

Erikson's Stages of Development

Psychoanalyst Erik Erikson presents a theory that development progresses through stages and continues throughout life. In each stage, we must adapt to changes within ourselves and our environment. Our success in each stage has much to do with our experiences during that stage. However, Erikson believes that a failure at one stage can be overcome by successes at subsequent stages.

The following descriptions summarize Erikson's eight stages of development. They also provide the general characteristics of each age-group.

Stage 1: Infancy—Trust versus Mistrust

In the first year of life, one of the child's main tasks is that of developing trust. If the child's needs are met promptly and lovingly, he or she learns to regard the world as being a safe place and people as being dependable. If the child's needs are inadequately met or are rejected, he or she learns to be fearful of the world and people.

Stage 2: Early Childhood—Autonomy versus Shame and Doubt

During the second and third years of life, the child develops new physical and mental skills. He or she learns to walk, climb, push and pull, and talk. The child also begins to gain control over the elimination of body wastes. The child is proud of these accomplishments and personally tries to do as many things as possible. The crisis that now arises stems from the growing desire for independence.

If parents accept this need for the child's doing whatever he or she is capable of, then the child will develop a sense of **autonomy** (aw-**tahn**-uh-mee), *the confidence that one can control one's own body, impulses, and environment*. But if parents insist on doing everything for the child, or are critical when the child attempts things and fails, then the child will develop doubts about his or her abilities.

Stage 3: Childhood—Initiative versus Guilt

During the fourth and fifth years of life, physical capacities develop to the point where the child can initiate play activities rather than merely follow other children. Children often engage in playacting, imagining themselves in a variety of adult roles. They also begin to ask many questions, a sign of intellectual initiative.

If parents respect these efforts, the child's sense of initiative will be enhanced. If, however, the child is made to think that these activities are wrong or that the questions are a nuisance, he or she is likely to develop a sense of guilt about self-initiated activities.

Stage 4: Later Childhood—Industry versus Inferiority

Between the ages of 6 and 11, the child experiences a new socialization experience—school. As children at this age begin to acquire new skills, they are also developing a sense of industry. They begin to make things—mud pies, cookies, kites, etc. The child's sense of industry is reinforced if parents and teachers praise and reward these creative endeavors. But if the adults scold the child for making a mess or getting in the way, feelings of inferiority may develop.

Stage 5: Adolescence—Identity versus Role Confusion

People in the adolescent years, ages 12 to 18, are primarily concerned with the question of who they are. No longer young children, but not yet adults, adolescents are searching for a sense of identity, trying to find a continuity between what they have learned and experienced as children and what they are learning and experiencing as adolescents.

At this stage of their lives, they are much involved with peer groups. By assembling all of the images of themselves that they have acquired as a son or daughter, student, worker, and friend, adolescents arrive at a **role identity**—*a sense not only of who they are, but of where they are going as adults.*

However, if childhood produced feelings of mistrust, guilt, and inferiority, **role confusion** may result. *An adolescent will have difficulty in attaining a clear sense of identity.*

Stage 6: Young Adulthood—Intimacy versus Isolation

The crisis that confronts the young adult comes from efforts to share with, and care about, another person. If people are unsure of themselves, they will probably feel threatened by a close relationship. If fear of intimacy is greater than one's need for it, loneliness and isolation are likely to take over.

Stage 7: Middle Age – Generativity versus Self-Absorption

In middle age, a person's satisfaction is likely to come from helping young people. One doesn't have to be a parent to achieve this gratification.

Erikson's stages of human development are ones that we all go through. Pick the photo which represents your stage. What developmental characteristic must you work at within this stage?

A person who is concerned about the well-being of the young, and who works to improve the society in which the young will live and work as adults, is likely to achieve this gratification.

Erikson calls this *active concern for young people* **generativity** (**jen**-uh-rah-**tive**-uh-tee). By helping the young, a person strengthens his or her own feelings of self-worth. However, if, at this stage, one becomes completely absorbed in one's own personal needs and comforts, Erikson suggests that this person will probably find true satisfaction elusive.

Stage 8: Advanced Age—Integrity versus Despair

The last stage of life is one of reflection and evaluation. If a person reflects on the past and feels that he or she made a contribution, there is a feeling of self-acceptance and *integrity*, or completeness. But if one sees life as a series of missed opportunities, there is likely to be a feeling of despair.

Again, Erikson suggests that negative experiences at one stage can be overcome by positive experiences at another stage.

CHECK YOURSELF

1. What characteristics are common to two- and three-year-olds? six- and seven-year-olds?
2. What is meant by role identity and role confusion?
3. What growth and development do people experience in Erikson's seventh and eighth stages?

The first year of your life was the most rapid growth period. Your weight tripled and your height doubled! The second fastest growth period is adolescence. But there is one major difference—growth is rapid and uneven at this time. It is a result of a hormone secretion from the endocrine glands (the pituitary) and touches every aspect of your health and life. This growth period prepares you for adulthood.

As you already learned in Chapter 17, puberty is essentially the beginning of adolescence. Specifically, **puberty** is *the period of time when physical development, specifically the development of secondary sex characteristics, begins.* The **secondary sex characteristics** are *those dealing with such features as body hair, and the development of breasts in the female and muscles in the male.*

Puberty is a result of the release of hormones, primarily from the pituitary gland, that stimulate the testes in the male and the ovaries in the female to begin producing sex hormones. The *male hormone,* **testosterone,** and the *female hormones,* **estrogen** and **progesterone,** are responsible for the physical and emotional changes that take place during puberty. (See Chapter 16 for more information about the male and female hormones.)

HEALTH UPDATE   HEALTH UPDATE   HEALTH UPDATE   HEALTH UPDATE

Summary of the Physical Changes of Puberty

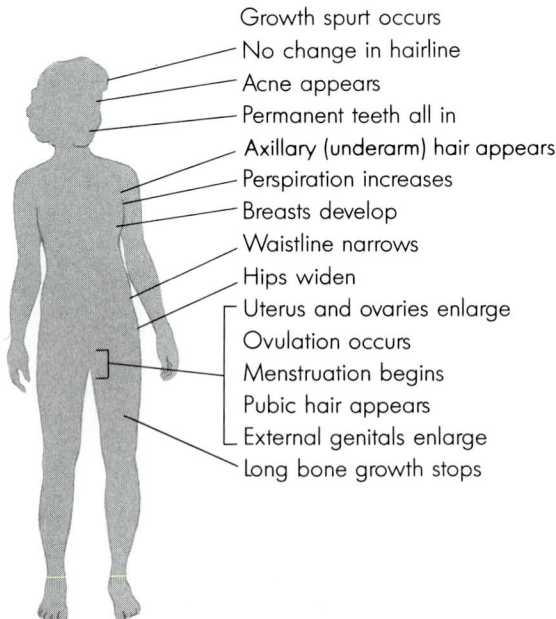

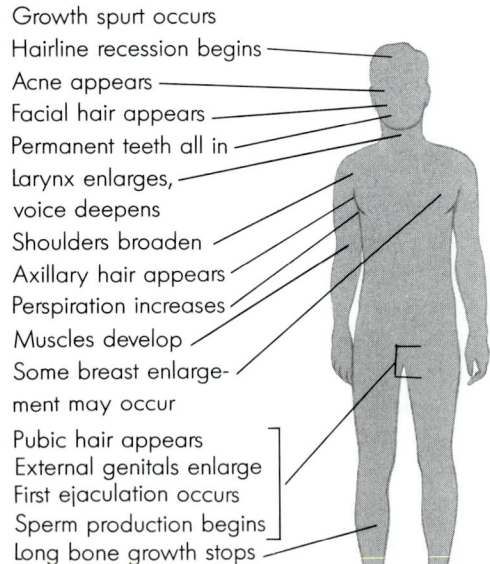

Growth spurt occurs
No change in hairline
Acne appears
Permanent teeth all in
Axillary (underarm) hair appears
Perspiration increases
Breasts develop
Waistline narrows
Hips widen
Uterus and ovaries enlarge
Ovulation occurs
Menstruation begins
Pubic hair appears
External genitals enlarge
Long bone growth stops

Growth spurt occurs
Hairline recession begins
Acne appears
Facial hair appears
Permanent teeth all in
Larynx enlarges, voice deepens
Shoulders broaden
Axillary hair appears
Perspiration increases
Muscles develop
Some breast enlargement may occur
Pubic hair appears
External genitals enlarge
First ejaculation occurs
Sperm production begins
Long bone growth stops

Physical Growth

Growth during puberty, unlike that during childhood, is rapid and uneven. The feet and hands grow first, and are often larger in proportion to the rest of the body. This causes awkwardness. Arms and legs must catch up. Then muscles grow to fill out the body's framework. Negative feelings about one's body may result, until a person becomes accustomed to some of the changes. All young people should know that this development is normal.

These boys are all the same age. They are developing physically according to their individual growth patterns.

Mental Growth

During adolescence, thinking skills also develop. By the time a person is between the ages of 13 and 15, mature capacities for thinking have emerged and are being refined. Adolescents are able to think in a more flexible, abstract, and logical way than they did as children.

Your Health Habits

Growth in adolescence is triggered by hormones, but your health habits, particularly diet and exercise, strongly influence your physical development. Your health habits affect your weight, posture, complexion, hair, and energy level. Are you promoting a high level of personal wellness by practicing good health habits?

In order to work through a problem or understand how something works, a child must have a very concrete example or explanation. Adolescents are capable of dealing with more complex problems in reasoning, without concrete terms.

In childhood, adults are mothers, fathers, and teachers. Young children accept the world as it is presented to them. The moon is about the size of a basketball. As they get older, children begin to realize that what they see or what is presented to them may not be the "whole." Now the moon just looks small because it is so far away. In adolescence, the ability to see parts of the whole develop more fully.

The ability to see other points of view also begins to develop. A person can explore ideas and develop concepts. Adolescents can begin to evaluate situations, think ahead about what might happen in a given situation, and recognize that they have choices in many situations. Perhaps the most important mental development is the ability to solve problems that require consideration of two or more variables at the same time.

During adolescence, memory skills improve, memory span increases, and a person can retain larger and lengthier bodies of information.

Schools help us to develop our mental skills and to apply them to many situations.

Emotional Growth

Emotional growth develops at a different rate among adolescents—perhaps more so than physical and mental development. Changes in the body may make young people very happy one minute and moody the next. These body changes may also arouse interest in the opposite sex and promote a desire for closeness.

Emotional changes cause the young person to begin looking at friends and family in new ways. As a child, a person is protected and is given what is needed for development. The child does not reflect on these things. With adolescence, there comes a feeling of giving, of helping people. The young person begins to see that he or she, too, can teach and share—to begin to enter a larger world of responsibilities.

Social Growth

Growth and development occur in adolescence in four ways. You have read about *physical*, *mental*, and *emotional* growth.

The fourth way, *social* growth, is also very important. In this area, some basic developmental tasks for adolescence have been identified. A **developmental** (de-vel-up-**ment**-tal) **task** is simply *something that needs to occur during a particular age period for a person to continue his or her growth toward becoming a healthy, mature adult.* Much of this development in adolescence centers around social growth. The major tasks include:

1. forming more mature relationships with peers of both sexes,
2. achieving a masculine or feminine social role,
3. accepting one's physique and using one's body effectively,
4. achieving emotional independence from parents and other adults,
5. preparing for marriage and family life,
6. preparing for a career,
7. acquiring a set of personal standards as a guide to behavior,
8. developing social intelligence,
9. developing conceptual and problem-solving skills.

To grow emotionally, we all need to be encouraged when we are unsure of ourselves and when we fail.

KEEPING FIT

Independence and Family Conflict

Developing independence is an important task of adolescence. It can also become a source of conflict between parent and teen. Can such conflict be resolved? Of course, but it takes work on both sides. Communication skills help.

Review the information on using ''I'' messages (page 91) and on resolving conflicts (page 120). Remember, communication is a skill that a person must practice repeatedly to effectively develop. If what you do doesn't work, evaluate what you might do differently and try again.

Major tasks of adolescence center around social growth.

Personal Identity

Perhaps one of the more critical undertakings that must be accomplished is achieving a **personal identity,** the *factors you believe make up the unique you.* This task has a great impact on all of the other factors and centers around one's self-concept. Questions like "Who am I?" "What do I want to be as a person?" are common in this search for identity. This is closely linked with one's emotional needs (see Chapter 5).

Here are some questions you can ask yourself as you form your personal identity, the unique you:

- Am I carrying out my responsibilities on my own, without needing someone to remind me of them?
- Do I get my schoolwork done as it is due?
- Can I make decisions on what to do, without my peers swaying me?
- Am I thinking of what type of work I am interested in doing after high school?
- Have I examined my beliefs on what types of behaviors are appropriate for males and females?
- Do I know the image I project as a male or a female?
- Does my behavior reflect a personal set of standards by which I live?
- Do I know what people like and do not like about me?
- Do I expect to work for what I get or want, rather than just "having things happen for me"?

HEALTH UPDATE   HEALTH UPDATE   HEALTH UPDATE

Sexuality and Adolescence

Young people are faced with pressures today about having sex. The decisions are difficult and can be confusing. The messages on television, radio, and in magazines and movies glamorize sex, promoting the idea that everybody is "doing it."

The fact is that everybody is *not* "doing it," and many young people have decided that it is best for them to wait. Nothing is wrong with a young person—or any person—who decides not to have sex. Making responsible decisions about sex is difficult. But it is important for young people to consider their personal values, feelings, and goals, and look at how those would be affected. Any time a person has sexual intercourse, a risk of pregnancy or sexually transmitted disease is present. True, protection is available, but it must be used properly, and no protection is 100% effective.

Consider that you have fifty or more years ahead of you as an adult—time to do and experience many different things. You only have a couple of years left to be a teenager. The activities of high school are once-in-a-lifetime experiences that are an important part of your development. The decisions you make now directly affect that development.

Saying "Yes" or "No"

- When to say "Yes" and when to say "No."
- When to move toward the peer group and when to back away.

These are all important decisions that you have probably been faced with and will continue to face. What do you do if your decision goes against what the group is doing? How do you follow your beliefs and not lose face with peers? You can learn to say "No" by following these simple steps:

- Use your decision-making skills, as outlined in Chapter 5.
- If your decision is "No," then say "No," without feeling you need to justify yourself.
- You will probably be asked to

justify why you have refused. This should alert you to the fact that the person asking you has not really accepted your decision, so any explanation will be challenged. Again, you can repeat "No."

Here you need to tell yourself that this is a good decision *for you*, that you will feel better when this pressure is over, and that you will not have to worry about selling yourself out because of others.

- Remember, you may need to repeat yourself several times.
- If the person persists, *leave.*
- Lastly, avoid compromise if you feel strongly about something. Compromise can be a slow way of saying "Yes."

Friends and Peers

Friendship and peer acceptance are very important during adolescence. However, in the process of developing into a healthy adult, it is important that you establish your own identity, separate from the group.

During adolescence, others occasionally will challenge what you stand for, what you believe, and what you think is right or wrong. Good friends will not challenge you to do something that goes against what you believe. They will not try to talk you into doing something that you do not want to do. This is one important guideline for evaluating friendships. See also page HB23 of the *Health Handbook* for advice on handling peer pressure.

CHECK YOURSELF

1. Define puberty.
2. What are the sex hormones?
3. How does the thinking process change as a person enters adolescence?
4. Name five questions that will help to form your personal identity.

Life expectancy has been greatly increased. In 1830, only 30% of the babies born could be expected to live to age 60. Today 83% of the babies born are expected to reach age 60. The actual average life span is 73 years, and it keeps lengthening.

Aging is a continuous process, beginning as soon as we reach maturity in our late 20s. Aging, like all phases of growth and development, is predictable but very individual.

Measures of Age

Gerontologists (jer-un-**tahl**-uh-jists), *people who study and work in the area of aging and often with the elderly,* cite three measures of age.

- The first is **chronological age.** It is simply *the number of birthdays one has had.*
- The second is **biological age,** that is, *how well different parts of the body are functioning.* Fitness standards for various chronological ages include how fast a person recovers from running up a flight of stairs or how fast blood clots. The rate of biological aging is influenced by heredity and life-style, including health habits, especially diet and exercise. Poisons taken in from the environment over a lifetime and illnesses a person has had also influence one's biological age.
- The third measure of age is **social age**, which is *the person's life-style.* At each phase of development, we have some general **age norms,** that is, *things a person is expected to be doing at a particular chronological age.* For example, our society expects a 16-year-old to be going to high school, meeting and socializing with a variety of people, possibly working part-time or preparing for a career after high school. Although these norms give people a timetable, the society in which we live imposes them. The norms do not always reflect what people want to do or can do.

The Physical Process of Aging

You have learned that body cells are being replaced continually. The life of a blood cell is about 120 days; that of an intestinal cell is about 3 days. As a person ages, this process of cell division slows. The cells that are capable of dividing and producing new cells gradually decrease.

As cells grow older, their nuclei change and age pigment accumulates in the cells. **Age pigment** is thought to be the result of *cells becoming less efficient in processing and ridding themselves of cell wastes.* With the gradual accumulation of age pigment, cell function slows and cells gradually deteriorate.

Aging is related to a person's own body processes as well as to overall life-style.

As a part of the aging process,

■ skin loses its elasticity and begins to wrinkle,
■ hair turns gray,
■ nails become brittle,
■ hearing and vision problems may develop,
■ bones gradually lose calcium, becoming more brittle,
■ basal metabolism slows,
■ kidney function slows,
■ the endocrine system decreases its secretion of hormones,
■ the body's immune system becomes less efficient,
■ a loss of lean body mass occurs, often accompanied by an increase of fat tissue,
■ joints become less mobile, muscle strength weakens,
■ vital capacity, the total amount of air that can be exhaled from the lungs after a deep breath, lessens,
■ the heart pumps blood less efficiently,
■ the body's ability to use glucose diminishes, lessening the body's available energy.

Although all of these physical characteristics of aging are inevitable, they are *very individual* and *directly related to a person's overall life-style.* If the person has been and continues to be active, eats well, and takes good mental and physical care of himself or herself, the function of these body parts remains more efficient.

Young and old can learn from each other. This is one of the greatest benefits of interacting with different age groups.

The Needs of the Elderly

Just like everyone else, the elderly have basic emotional needs. They need to love and to be loved, to feel they are making a contribution, and to feel they are worthwhile individuals.

A variety of factors affect a person's ability to adjust to growing old. People who have coped with changes all of their lives are better able to cope with the changes resulting from growing old. One's attitude toward aging and activity has a great influence on how a person adjusts to aging. People who remain active and involved tend to adjust better.

Family relationships are a very important factor in helping a person successfully adjust to aging. Older people who do not have relatives living with or near them face the greatest difficulty in adjusting to old age.

Elderly people who maintain friendships and contact with other people after retiring cope better with aging. Programs, such as Adopt a Grandparent, have been started in many communities to keep the elderly involved, especially with young people. The rewards for such involvement are two-sided. The elderly feel needed and useful. The young people get enjoyment from sharing and learning from the elderly.

In 1965, as a result of the Older American Act, the Administration on Aging (AOA) was started in the Office of Human Development Services. The AOA is responsible for serving the needs, addressing the concerns, and promoting the interests of older Americans. The greatest challenge of the future lies in reordering society to ensure older people broader outlets for their talents, skills, and energies.

CHECK YOURSELF

1. What are the three measures of age?
2. How does one's life-style affect each measure?
3. What does the Administration on Aging do?

4. Death—A Part of the Life Cycle

Although death is an inevitable part of the life cycle, it is a subject that is not often discussed. Yet, understanding and accepting one's feelings about death are an important part of mental health.

Clinical Death and Brain Death

Today there is not even a clear definition of death. **Clinical death** is when *a person's body systems stop working.* Sometimes, clinical death can be reversed, life can be restored, and the person can make a full recovery. For example, a person could be a victim of drowning and be revived through *cardiopulmonary resuscitation (***kard**-ee-oh-**pull**-mah-ner-ee ree-sus-uh-**tah**-shun) *(CPR),* a procedure to restore normal breathing after a cardiac arrest. You will learn more about it in Chapter 28.

If resuscitation (revival) is not successful, the brain cells do not receive the oxygen they need. **Brain death** happens when *oxygen is cut off from all of the brain cells.* When that happens, the person cannot be revived.

Stages in Brain Death

The first brain cells to die are those in the *cerebral cortex.* This area of the brain controls sensation and voluntary action, stores memories, and directs complex thought and the decision-making processes. The victim may continue to live, but without any of these functions.

If the brain continues to be cut off from oxygen, the *midbrain* dies. This area of the brain controls emotions, alertness, and consciousness. The victim lapses into a coma. However, heart function and breathing may continue.

If the lack of oxygen continues, the *brain stem* dies. It is this part of the lower brain that stimulates the action of the heart and lungs.

Understanding and Accepting Death

Several factors influence one's understanding of and attitude toward death, including personal experience, family attitudes and values, and one's age.

For instance, children's understanding of death increases in developmental stages. Infants up to two years have no real concept of death, other than the fact that things may be present at one moment and gone the next.

From ages two to five years, children recognize death but do not understand that it is permanent. Children at this age have considerable faith in their own ability to make things happen simply by wishing. Children may see death as being like sleep.

From ages five to about nine, children see death as a *personification*, that is, as an old man, a fairy princess, an angel, or a skeleton. They begin to see death as being permanent, but cannot relate it to something that could happen to them.

By age 10, children see death as final and inevitable. They are ready to deal with the reality of death but have difficulty accepting that it can happen anytime to anyone. Such an understanding develops as children enter adolescence.

Each of these stages and ages is general and will vary from person to person. They depend on what people have told the individuals about death and what experiences they have had with death.

Stages in Accepting Death

Elisabeth Kübler-Ross, a psychiatrist, has worked with hundreds of dying patients and their families. She has tried to better understand what a person goes through in coming to grips with his or her own death.

Kübler-Ross has identified stages in the acceptance of death that are similar to those we all experience when faced with any significant loss. Each person's reactions are individual and will vary in degree. These stages are simply a general guideline for understanding the dying process.

Stage 1: Denial and Isolation   *Denial* is a person's initial reaction to any loss. It may be a feeling of *isolation* or helplessness. It is an attempt to avoid reality: "It is all a bad dream and will go away."

Stage 2: Anger   A person moves from denial to the second stage—*anger*. Anger is a natural reaction, an outlet for resentment at being a victim. There is an envy of others who still have a life ahead of them. The person often takes out the anger on those close by—friends, family, and medical personnel.

Stage 3: Bargaining   Anger is often followed by a *bargaining* stage. The dying person attempts to postpone the end by praying, seeking better medical treatment, and promising to mend his or her ways—to be a better person.

Stage 4: Depression   The fourth stage, *depression*, follows feelings of isolation and loneliness. The dying person worries about family and money. The numbness, anger, and rage felt previously are now replaced with a sense of great loss.

Stage 5: Acceptance   The fifth stage of dying is that of *acceptance*. Depression involves facing reality, but it leaves a person feeling helpless. Acceptance involves facing reality in a constructive way. It allows for action.

Kübler-Ross identified another emotion that operates throughout all the stages just described. That emotion is *hope*. There usually is a hope that there will be a cure or a remission and that death will not come.

LIFE MANAGEMENT SKILL

The Grief Process

The grief process is usually associated with the effects of a death on a survivor. However, we experience this process with any loss. The loss of a job, the breakup of a relationship, or the loss of an important opportunity all prompt grief. We are likely to be able to cope better with such losses if we understand the grief stages we go through to reach acceptance.

Grief is a part of life that will pass as people come to accept the death of a loved one and realize that their own lives must go on.

Grief

The family and friends of the dying person also face coping with death. Grief and mourning develop through a series of stages much like Kübler-Ross's stages of dying.

Stages of Grieving   The survivors go through a stage of *denial* or disbelief, then a stage of *anger*. This anger may be directed toward the dying person. If there is forewarning of the death, the grieving person may *bargain* to prolong the dying person's life. As the grieving person realizes the futility of this, *depression* sets in. The survivors pass to a stage of *acceptance*, as they understand that the death of the person is a reality.

Coping With Grief   The death of someone you love is one of life's most shocking, and even shattering, experiences. Yet the grief that precedes and follows the death serves a very useful purpose for the survivors. It prepares them for the inevitable and helps them accept it when it comes.

Time and encouragement are needed to help survivors pass through their grief and mourning. The survivors need understanding and comfort. In the event of sudden death, there has been no time for preparation. Thus grief tends to last much longer. The real impact of death may not surface until months later.

In order to regain physical, mental, and emotional health, the survivors need to be able to talk about and express their feelings. Through such conversations, people can come to accept the death and continue to carry on their own lives.

CHECK YOURSELF

1. In what stages do children understand death? Describe the stages at various age levels.
2. Write a sentence summarizing each stage of dying.
3. How is the grief process of a survivor or other family member similar to that of a dying person?

MEDICAL RESEARCHER

The **medical researcher** is a scientifically oriented person who has an interest in finding answers to the unknown. This person uses proven facts and procedures to search further for new facts resulting in new medical cures and techniques.

You might think at first that a medical researcher is a medical doctor. Sometimes this is the case, since some doctors devote their time to research rather than to the practice of medicine with patients. However, there are others engaged in medical research who are not doctors.

In our country, medical researchers are employed by scientific organizations, medical foundations, hospitals, universities having research programs, pharmaceutical companies, companies manufacturing all types of compounds and drugs, governments—local, state, and federal—and other organizations engaged in medical research.

A medical researcher may be involved in the testing of products to see if they are effective or to see if a drug has any negative effects. A medical researcher may also be engaged in developing new medical equipment. Others in this field may be engaged in research to determine the cause of an outbreak of a rare disease or to analyze the experiments related to human "organ banks," including such organs as the heart, skin, bones, and liver.

The medical researcher works in a laboratory. This field provides the satisfaction of working to suit a person's skills. At the same time, the person has a hand in improving health care and the quality of life for many people. The scientist seeks answers to questions about the causes of disorders and diseases, and the ways in which ill people can be helped. Medical research can be very satisfying personally, as well as financially.

This career involves a long training period, including a demanding study of mathematics and science. Depending on the type of research, two to four years of training in specialist research work would be necessary.

For more information, contact the American Medical Association.

American Medical Association
535 North Dearborn Street
Chicago, IL 60610

CHAPTER 22   Review

CHAPTER SUMMARY

■ All people have various stages of growth and development which they grow through. One doctor, Erik Erikson, has outlined eight stages. They can serve as a useful model of human development.

■ Adolescence is a time of great physical, mental, emotional, and social growth.

autonomy
role identity
role confusion
generativity
puberty

secondary sex characteristics
testosterone
estrogen
progesterone
developmental task

personal identity
gerontologist
chronological age
biological age
social age

age norms
age pigment
clinical death
brain death
medical researcher

PUTTING VOCABULARY TO USE

On a separate piece of paper, indicate whether each statement below is *true* or *false.* Correct the *false* statements.

1. One of the basic tasks during adulthood is to develop a sense of *role identity.*
2. *Autonomy* develops as one gains confidence in one's ability to control the body, impulses, and environment.
3. A *developmental task* is something that rarely occurs during a particular age period.
4. *Puberty* is a period when you immediately develop into an adult.

5. *Gerontologists* study and work with terminally ill people.
6. One's *chronological age* is indicated by the number of birthdays.
7. *Biological age* is most influenced by *chronological age.*
8. *Social age* is basically standard and is easily measured.
9. *Clinical death* happens when the body systems stop working.
10. A person with *brain death* cannot be revived.

- There are clearly defined developmental tasks that adolescents carry out.
- Achieving a personal identity is one of the more critical tasks facing young people.
- There are three measures of aging: chronological, biological, and social.
- Aging is a continuous process, beginning as soon as we reach maturity in our late 20s.
- Death is a part of our lifecycle.
- There are five stages in accepting death, as outlined by Elisabeth Kübler-Ross.
- Stages of grief are also similar to the stages of accepting death.

REVIEWING WHAT YOU LEARNED

1. Summarize the changes that take place in young people during puberty.
2. What are Erikson's eight stages of life development?
3. How does a person's mental ability change as he or she enters adolescence?
4. What are the basic tasks of adolescence?
5. What happens to body cells as a person ages?
6. What factors influence a person's ability to accept or cope with death?

APPLYING WHAT YOU LEARNED

1. Find out what programs your community has for the elderly. As a health project, volunteer your time or put on a health-related program for a group of elderly people in your community.
2. Look up Jean Piaget's theory of intellectual development and compare it with Erikson's theory. Present your report to the class.
3. Give an example that compares the thinking ability of a 9-year-old and a 15-year-old. Explain the difference in the two thought processes.
4. What does the "generation gap" mean to you? What causes it? Suggest some ways to bridge the gap.
5. What are some of the advantages of being an adolescent? What are some of the difficulties?

FOCUS ON WELLNESS

The process of human development can be a rich and rewarding experience. *I can best participate in that experience at my present stage of development by. . .*

U N I T

7

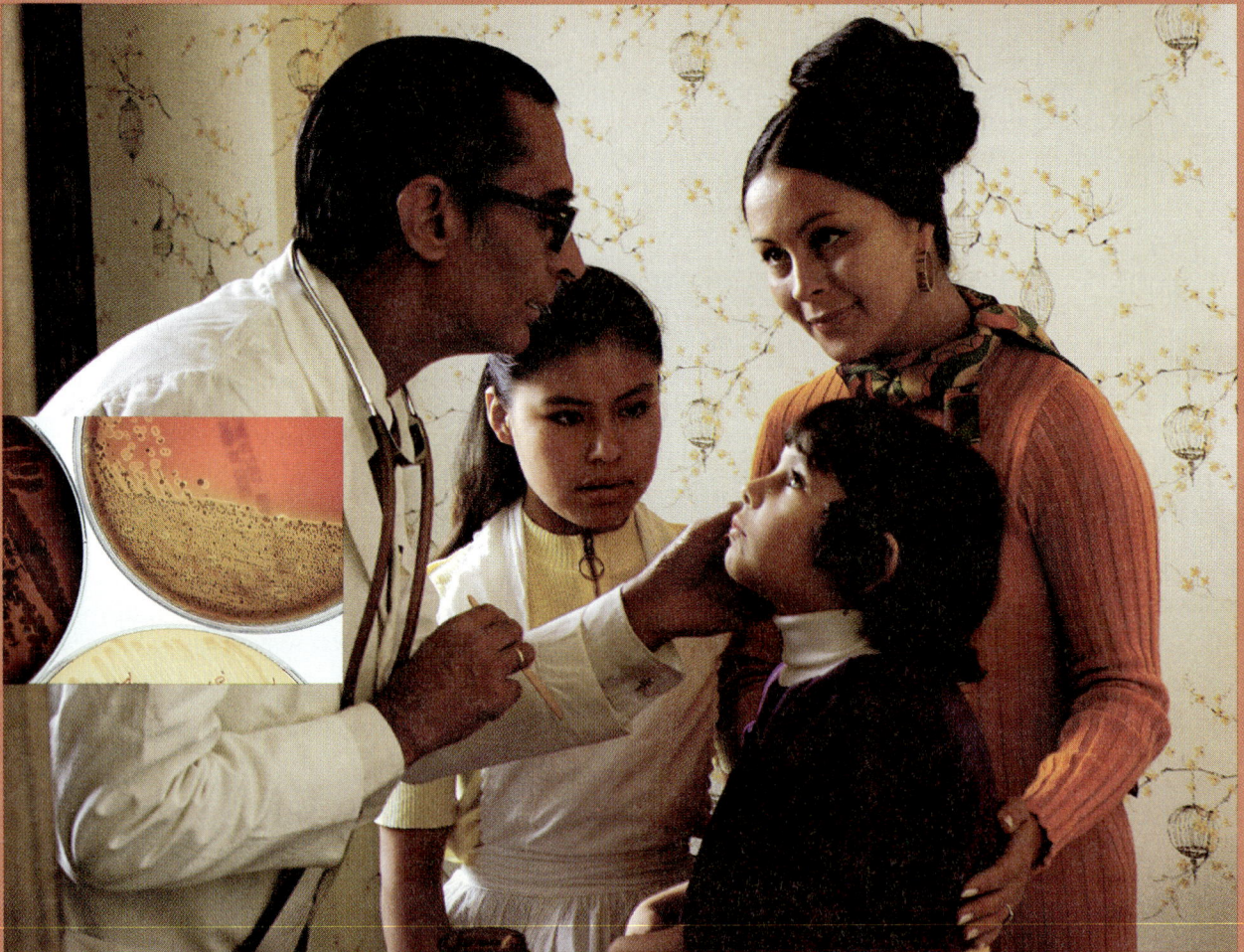

CONSUMER
HEALTH

You As a Health Consumer

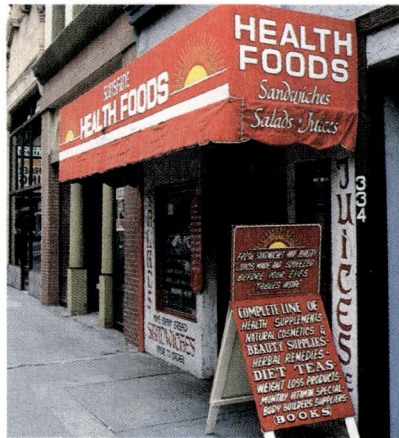

"Use the method doctors use to lose weight!"

"Buy one at the regular price and get one free!"

You are likely to see a number of such statements every day. Do such advertisements influence you? Do you know who or what influences you to purchase a particular health-related product? You will find the answers in this chapter.

After studying this chapter, you will be able to:
- identify the benefits of being a wise consumer,
- list your rights as a consumer,
- describe the five factors that influence your choices of products and services,
- define quackery,
- explain how to recognize quackery,
- describe the various agencies that help to protect the consumer,
- identify the appropriate person to contact for specific consumer complaints.

As you work to promote or take care of your health, you probably purchase many products and services. A **consumer** is *anyone who uses a product or a service.* Obviously, we have all been consumers for many years. When you consider the products that you buy that in some way affect your health, you also realize you are a health consumer.

Consumer health is concerned with helping you select products and services more wisely, and letting you know where to go or what to do if you have been cheated or need help.

Benefits of Being a Wise Health Consumer

There are three major benefits to being a wise health consumer:

1. *Being a wise health consumer saves money and time, and increases your satisfaction.* You are able to make the best purchases for the least amount of money and time. It may take preparation to collect information and compare products or services, but it usually pays off in the long run.
2. *Being a wise health consumer protects your health.* A wise consumer is not swayed into buying health products that are worthless and may be harmful. A wise consumer knows when to seek medical help and does so without delay. Recognition and treatment of early symptoms is an important consumer skill.
3. *Being a wise health consumer builds your self-confidence as you speak up for your rights.* If you have been sold a defective product or service, you protect yourself, as well as others, from future deception when you take action. Much of the progress that has been made in protecting consumers has resulted from people who were not afraid to speak up when they were cheated. Such basic assertiveness skills can be helpful to you in all facets of your daily life.

Your Rights As a Consumer

As a consumer you have several basic rights. In 1962, the late President John Kennedy introduced the "Consumer Bill of Rights." It includes:

- **The right to safety.** Consumers are protected from the selling of dangerous products.
- **The right to be informed.** Consumers are protected from misleading advertising. They can ask for all of the facts they need to make good choices.

- **The right to choose.** Consumers are given the right to make their own choices.
- **The right to be heard.** Consumers can speak out when they aren't satisfied. They have a voice in the making of consumer laws.

During the 1970s, former President Richard Nixon added another right: the **right to redress.** This means that consumers who have had a wrong done to them have the right to get that wrong corrected. There are many city, state, and federal agencies that help the consumer in these matters.

Former President Gerald Ford also added a right—**the right to consumer education.**

L I F E
M A N A G E M E N T
S K I L L

The Wise Consumer

Select one of the behaviors to which you answered "no." Write down three things you could do to improve in this area. List specific actions to help you become a healthier consumer.

How Wise a Consumer Are You?

On a separate sheet of paper, answer *yes* or *no* to each of the questions. The behaviors described give you a good idea of what is involved in being a wise consumer. These skills will be discussed in further detail in the chapter.

1. Are you aware of whether you are buying a product because you *need* it or *want* it? Yes
2. Before you buy, do you compare products for ingredients, price, packaging, warranties? Yes
3. Do you read the label before buying a product? Yes
4. Are you aware of factors such as advertising and peer pressure that might be influencing your purchase? Yes
5. Do you return products if you are not satisfied or if they are defective? Yes
6. Can you recognize gimmicks that sellers use to influence your purchase of often fraudulent products? Yes
7. Do you understand the purpose of advertising and how it is designed to make you Yes

want a product or feel that you need a product?

8. Do you check the material, product, or device before you buy it to be sure that the item is in good working order or is in its original packaging? Yes
9. Do you read advertisements closely so that you are clear about what they are saying and not saying? Yes
10. Do you avoid emotional or impulse buying? No
11. Do you feel intimidated by a high-powered, pushy salesperson? Yes
12. Do you let yourself be talked into things because they are on a special "just this one time" sale? Yes

Scoring: 9 to 12 Yes: *You are an alert consumer* and are probably getting the most for your money.

5 to 8 Yes: *Not bad,* you are on the right track.

Fewer than 5 Yes: *Buyer beware—* you may be just the customer the salesperson is looking for.

What Factors Influence Your Purchases?

Think of a health product you recently bought. What factors influenced your choice to buy that particular product? Did your friend have it? Maybe it was on sale, or you saw it advertised?

Five main factors influence your choices as a consumer: *price, convenience, tradition, quality,* and *advertising.* By being aware of these factors, you will be better able to make wise consumer health choices.

Price

Several factors influence price. Brand name products cost more. They are usually well advertised and the cost of advertising is passed on to the consumer. The size of the product also affects the price. You learned about *unit pricing* in Chapter 8. Unit pricing tells how much different sizes of the same product cost per unit. Many stores have unit price information on the shelves to help the consumer. The unit price is determined by dividing the price of the item by its weight, volume, or count—depending on how it is packaged.

Another factor that affects price is where the product is sold. Products in convenience stores and specialty shops usually cost more than those in grocery stores or general department stores.

Convenience foods can save time when you are in a hurry.

Convenience

Convenience—*the labor-saving feature of a product*—has a big impact on what we buy. In general, we pay more for convenience. Buying frozen macaroni and cheese may be much more convenient than buying the ingredients and making it. In this day and age when we are usually in a hurry or want to save time, convenience becomes a significant factor in our purchases. Sometimes it is worthwhile to pay more, but making a habit of buying convenience products becomes expensive and can put a sizable dent in your budget.

Every family has some favorite dishes that have been passed down to it.

Tradition

A **tradition** is a *custom, something that is passed down from generation to generation.* It may be a family, cultural, or religious custom. Perhaps your family has always used a certain brand or type of product. That will likely influence your choice of purchase.

Our friends also influence our purchases. Have you bought things just because everyone else had them? Did you use any other consumer skills in making your selection?

Quality

Have you ever bought a cheaper product only to have it not work or fall apart? Decisions about the quality of a product can be difficult. Just because something costs more does not mean it is of better quality. Examining the ingredients of a product and the guarantees that accompany the product will help you to assess its quality.

Advertising

Advertising is *all the ways used by which a manufacturer gains your attention for his product.* You may not be aware of how much advertising you are exposed to in a day. Think of the signs, the T-shirts, or the bumper stickers you have seen today that advertised something.

Advertising works in subtle ways, often on the subconscious level. It takes a very sharp consumer not to be influenced by advertising. Catchy jingles, tunes, and rhymes have a way of staying with us. That is just what the advertiser wants.

Manufacturers spend billions of dollars to advertise their products. They use many different techniques to sell health products. Advertisements play

Consumer Facts to Know

1. Frozen dinners cost 2.5 times what a home-cooked meal would cost.
2. Do you know what goes into fruit cocktail? Why are so few cherries in it? Because the government specifies how much and what goes into fruit cocktail:

- 30 to 50% diced peaches,
- 25 to 45% diced pears,
- 6 to 20% seedless grapes,
- 6 to 16% diced or sectioned pineapple,
- 2 to 6% halved cherries

Since there is a standard formula, all brands are virtually alike.

on our emotions and our needs. They promise popularity, sex appeal, or pain relief. Can you believe everything you read or hear in ads?

Let us look at some common techniques that are used in advertising.

Testimonials   Testimonials employ famous people to tell you how they use and like the product. A **testimonial** (tes-tuh-**mow**-nee-ul) is *another person's enthusiastic recommendation of a product*. Because you like that person, you may be influenced to buy the product. However, the law says that the person who gives the testimonial must have actually used the product. This does not mean that he or she really believes in the product. Companies pay famous people large sums of money for promoting their products.

Buy One, Get One Free   This is a common approach used in advertising. It makes consumers feel like they are getting something for nothing. Look closely at the advertisements. Often the price of one item has been raised so you pay more than you normally might. And remember, rarely, if ever, will you get something for nothing.

Emotional Pleas   Many ads play on people's emotional needs.

"Be the first on your block to have a . . ."
"Be happy, be smart, buy . . ."
"When you want only the best for you or your family . . ."

All of these ads encourage you to buy something for an emotional reason. Do not be tricked into spending more or buying something you normally would not buy.

CHECK YOURSELF

1. List two benefits of being a wise consumer.
2. What five factors influence one's choice of products or services?
3. What is a testimonial?

It is illegal to make false claims, promising that a drug or a food or a cosmetic will do something that it really cannot. You have probably heard of the terms **quack** and **quackery** to describe *a dishonest medicine promoter and his useless products or treatments.* Quackery plays on human emotions, weakness, and fear to get money from people who want fast cures or relief from pain. The most prevalent areas of quackery are those in which there is no cure or instant relief.

Be Alert to Health and Medical Frauds

Here are some ways that you can be alert to any signs of fraudulent practices or products. If you can answer yes to any of these questions, you should be wary. It is probably misinformation, and you are about to be the next victim of wasting your money.

- Is the product advertised as a "scientific breakthrough" without any particular reference to a medical school, study, or journal? If one is mentioned, have you never heard of it?
- Does the promoter claim that medical authorities and government agencies have ridiculed this product, asking you to be the champion of the underdog in the face of big medicine and government?
- Does the product claim to be effective for a variety of ailments?
- Do the promised benefits seem too good to be true?
- Does a "health consultant" sell the product door-to-door?

How Quackery Works

The promoter deals with magic, miracles, and fast, painless cures. Amazingly, otherwise very intelligent people become victims of these false claims. Many times it is because the people want to believe what they hear.

Take, for example, the person who is 20 pounds overweight and does not like to exercise. Exercise is hard work, especially for overweight people. Now "Slim-Ex," a new candy, enables this person to lose weight without exercise and while continuing to eat whatever he or she likes. An overweight person may purchase the product, wanting to believe that there is an easy way to lose weight.

Popular Types of Product Fraud

Here are types of products that are most susceptible to quackery:

1. **Beauty aids.** These play on people's fear of growing old or fat and promise youth, beauty, and sex appeal forever. Included are cures for baldness; quick, painless weight loss; prevention of wrinkles; bust developers; creams and lotions that promise youth and beauty.
2. **Diet aids.** Their appeal is to our need to be trim, vivacious, and energetic. They include energy restorers, body builders, pep pills, vitamin and diet supplements.
3. **Food.** Food fads represent one of the most lucrative areas of quackery. Relying on special foods, diets, or diet supplements is not only a waste of money—it is not healthy.
4. **Fraudulent devices.** This group of products includes devices that are promoted as being capable of curing ailments. By turning knobs and flashing lights, diseases are said to be cured or pain is relieved. Excess body weight is said to be "melted away" by wearing special clothing. Copper bracelets are promoted as being able to cure or prevent arthritis.

    Sometimes the devices are legitimate, but are promoted improperly, like getting eyeglasses, contacts, or dentures that are fitted for you, but ordered through the mail.

Medical Quackery

Quackery offers hope. Therefore, the most susceptible people are those ailing with diseases or conditions without known cures.

The problem with quack products is not so much the product's doing harm. Medical authorities point out that the danger is that quackery causes the patient to delay seeking sound medical advice and treatment until it may be too late.

Quack "cures" are offered most often for diseases or conditions for which treatment is apt to be lengthy and unpleasant, with uncertain results. The three areas most susceptible to quackery are *cancer, arthritis,* and *weight problems.*

Cancer

In contrast to the standard treatment for cancer—surgery, radiation, and chemotherapy—all of which may be painful and disfiguring—the quack remedy is usually simple and painless. It may be a pill, an injection, a trip to the mountains, or a nutritious diet. The quack remedy offers hope. And often, because hope is important, there may be apparent remission of the disease. This makes people more likely to believe in the product and continue to use it.

Have you ever heard of a **placebo** (plah-**chay**-bow)? It is *a substance that has no medical value, but which is given for its psychological effect.* The **placebo effect** comes about when *people think that they are taking medicine and the symptoms are relieved.* This illustrates the power of the mind over the body and the positive effect our beliefs can have on our wellness. But it also makes us quite susceptible to quackery.

The Placebo Effect

Placebo is a word that comes from the Latin, "to please." Placebos are made from harmless substances and are commonly called "sugar pills." Placebos can influence the mind. In one experiment, while 82 to 87% of chronic headache sufferers responded to real analgesics, 60% responded to placebos.

Placebos, however, can be harmful because they cannot relieve serious problems. Patients can acquire side effects and even become addicted to them. Doctors are very cautious about using them, since their effects are so unpredictable.

Some placebos seem to work better than others. One study has shown that placebo capsules are more effective than pills, while a placebo injection is the most effective. A bitter-tasting placebo works more "efficiently" than a sweet one. Blue is a good color for sedatives, while yellow works for anti-depressants.

Sometimes, even when a patient is told that he or she is getting a placebo, positive results happen. The power of the mind over the body, and the body's own power to heal itself, is one of the most important demonstrations of the placebo.

Why may wearing a copper bracelet be an example of the placebo effect?

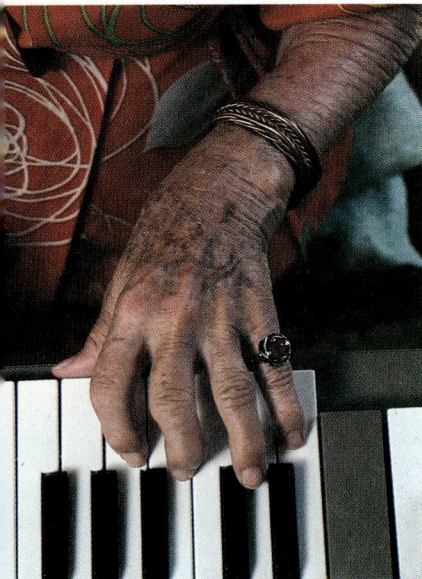

Arthritis

The pain and suffering of arthritis, a condition that afflicts more than 22 million Americans, is an open invitation to the quack's false promises. Medical science has no cure for arthritis, and even its control is complicated and not always effective. Some of the quack remedies are harmless enough, but they are still a waste of money. Wearing a copper bracelet, for example, is said to ease the discomfort of arthritis. It does no harm but cannot do what is claimed. However, other remedies that quacks offer are highly dangerous in themselves. The Arthritis Foundation estimates that arthritis victims spend $400 million a year on quack remedies.

Weight Problems

Unlike most quack remedies, many of the weight-loss plans that quacks offer may, if one faithfully follows them, actually work, resulting in a real loss of weight. The secret is not in the trick diet or the magic medicine the advertising features, but in the fact that most reduction plans involve a cutback in the amount of food consumed.

Weight control is perhaps the most lucrative area for unnecessary products and devices. As you learned in Chapter 9, there is only one way to lose weight—you must use up more calories than you consume. Buying products simply wastes your money. Yet people spend over $110 million annually on over-the-counter drugs that claim to aid in weight reduction.

1. Name three types of product fraud and describe what makes people susceptible to them.
2. What is the greatest problem with ill people who seek quack cures?
3. Why are cancer, arthritis, and weight loss the most susceptible areas of quackery?
4. What is the placebo effect? Give two examples of how it operates.
5. List three warnings that can tell you whether something may be a quack cure.

3. What to Do if You Get Cheated

Each of us is a consumer. We depend upon others to provide us with products and services to protect our health. Many fine companies and businesses do their jobs well in providing us with what we want and need. Most businesses depend on satisfied customers to stay in business. Reputable firms will make an honest effort to resolve problems, but you, as a consumer, must bring these problems to the attention of the company or store.

IMPROVING YOURSELF

Being an Assertive Consumer

Being a wise consumer not only can protect your health and save you money, but it can be fun and challenging. Think of a time when a salesperson was pushing or pressuring you. How did you feel—uncomfortable, nervous, imposed upon? Next time, assert yourself. Challenge the person with consumer-oriented questions. Or, if you are not interested or want to be left alone, simply state that. Compare what you stand to lose with your potential gains for being an assertive consumer.

Steps to Follow

Even the most careful shoppers find themselves buying products or securing services that do not work right or serve them well. Sometimes merchants and manufacturers are less than enthusiastic about resolving difficulties. This is why it is necessary for you, as a consumer, to know what to do and where to go for help. Here are some tips to follow:

1. Identify the problem and what you feel would be a fair way to solve it.
2. Have some documentation available to back up your complaint (for example, sales receipt, canceled check, warranty).
3. Go back to the person who sold you the item or performed the service. State the problem and what you would like to have happen to resolve the problem.
4. If this person is not helpful, then ask to see the store manager or supervisor. Repeat your story. Most problems are resolved at this level.
5. If you are not satisfied with the response at this level, do not give up. If the company operates nationally or the product is a national brand, write a letter to the president or the director of consumer affairs of the company. The points that your letter should include are:
   a. Your purchase,
   b. Name of product or serial number or model number or service,
   c. Date and location of purchase or service,
   d. Statement of the problem,
   e. History of the problem,
   f. Request for satisfaction,
   g. Copies of all documents,
   h. Request for action within a reasonable time,
   i. Your address and phone number.

Places to Get Help

If you are not satisfied with the company's response, even with your letter to the president, you may wish to contact one of several agencies outside the company for help. These sources vary greatly in services, approach,

Most large department stores have a customer complaint department.

and type of complaint. By becoming familiar with the existence and work of these agencies, you can improve your skill as a consumer.

The Better Business Bureau (BBB)

The Better Business Bureau (BBB) is a nonprofit organization sponsored by private business. It offers a variety of services. These services include general information on products and services, reliability reports, background information on local businesses and organizations, and records of companies' complaint-handling performances.

The BBB attempts to settle consumer complaints against local business firms. It accepts written complaints and will contact a local firm on your behalf. The BBB considers a complaint settled when one of these things has been done:

1. The customer receives satisfaction.
2. The customer receives a reasonable adjustment.
3. The company provides proof that the customer's complaint is unreasonable or unwarranted.

BBBs also handle false advertising cases. To find a BBB, check your local phone book, local consumer office, or local library. There are 147 BBBs, most of them located in the major cities of the United States.

Media Programs

If you live in or near a large city, you may be aware of one of the more than 100 newspapers and 50 radio–TV stations that offer "Action" or "Hot-Line" services for consumers who need help. These programs often get successful results because of the powerful influence of the press. Adverse publicity may be one of the best encouragers to get a merchant or business to take action to resolve a consumer complaint.

"Call for Action" is one of the larger media help lines. Staffed by 2,500 volunteers, it helps about 250,000 people each year. The volunteers relay complaints to the proper individuals, business people, or public agencies, and then check back with you—usually in about two weeks. If you have been satisfied, the incident is closed. If not, then "Call for Action" will intervene in your behalf. It generally turns public attention on a case to get results.

Small-Claims Court

You might imagine that seeking satisfaction in small-claims court is an expensive and long, drawn-out procedure. It is quite the contrary. If you have a complaint that you are not able to resolve, then consider going to the small-claims court. This is a very important alternative for consumers. Court procedures are simple, inexpensive, quick, and informal. There are court fees involved, but you often get most or all of them back if you win your case. Generally, you do not need a lawyer. In fact, in some states, lawyers are not permitted in small-claims court.

The small claims courts are a quick, effective means of settling minor claims problems.

Small-claims courts *deal with claims that range from $100 to $3,000,* with an average of around $500. To locate the small-claims court in your area, check your local phone book or state government headings for small-claims court listings. When you reach the court on the phone, ask the clerk how to use the court. Sit in on a court session before taking a case to small-claims court, so that you become familiar with the operation.

Occupational and Professional Licensing Boards

If you have a problem with professional or occupational services, such as in the case of a physician, a dentist, or a physical therapist, you may be able to get some help from a state licensing or regulatory board. There are an estimated 1,500 state boards that license or register more than 550 health-related occupations. The practice of licensing was first started to protect the public in matters of health and safety and to guard the public from incompetency and fraud.

To be licensed, a professional must have a certain amount of background and experience and must pass a qualifications test. State boards set licensing examinations; issue, deny, or revoke licenses; bring disciplinary actions; and handle consumer complaints.

If you contact a state board for help, it will usually bring your complaint to the attention of the person whom you filed against (known as the *licensee*). The board will seek a satisfactory solution to your problem. If necessary, the board can conduct an investigation. Some state boards even have consumer education materials to help you in selecting a health professional.

You can find out about a state licensing board by contacting your local consumer office. Check your phone book under state government offices or under professional listings. You can also ask professionals about the board that is responsible for their licensing. In fact, you should ask to see the person's license or registration before you use his or her services.

State, County, and City Consumer Affairs Offices

If you are not satisfied with a company's or person's response to your complaint about a product or service, a good place for an inquiry or a complaint is the local consumer affairs office. Local consumer offices can be particularly helpful since a person can contact them easily by phone or in person, and they are usually familiar with local businesses and regulations. Keep all receipts and other papers to show or to use when talking to the local agency.

If there is no consumer office where you live, contact a state consumer office. These consumer offices are set up differently from state to state. Many state and local consumer offices have a large selection of educational materials and information available. Your phone book should give you a listing under city, county, or state government.

Private Consumer Groups

In addition to the many governmental and business organizations that can be of assistance to the consumer, private consumer groups exist in all of the 50 states. In almost all cases, these are made up of *individual consumer members who join together to support consumer interests.* They are called **advocates** (**ad**-vuh-kates). An advocate is someone who speaks out for a position.

The private consumer groups are usually created and staffed by volunteers, although some have paid staff members. Some of the private con-

A Health Student Asks . . .

JUNK MAIL

"My family gets several pieces of 'junk mail' every day. Many times there are ads or offers for a variety of devices or 'free' gifts or prizes. Is there a way to stop companies from sending these? How are consumers protected from mail fraud?"

It is virtually impossible to keep from receiving such mail solicitation. However, you can protect yourself by not responding to offers, or, if you do respond, by doing so selectively. Be sure you know exactly what you are signing and what you are agreeing to purchase.

The U.S. Postal Service handles complaints of fraudulent or misleading promotions involving use of the mails in any way. You can contact your local postmaster, or write to the Inspector in Charge, Special Investigation Division, U.S. Postal Service, Washington, DC 20260.

sumer groups help individual consumers with complaints. Others are dedicated to serving the broad needs of special populations such as the elderly, women, minorities, and low-income people. They represent consumers by using their collective energy to focus on critical consumer issues in the marketplace.

For more information about consumer groups in your area, you can contact your local or state government consumer affairs office. If you fail to discover a group locally, you can try one of these organizations:

- The National Office of the Consumer Federation of America, 1012 14th Street, N.W., Washington, DC 20036
- National Consumers League, 1028 Connecticut Ave., N.W., Washington, DC 20036
- Ralph Nader's Public Citizen, PO Box 19404, Washington, DC 20036

Special Aids Through Government Services

The federal government has established a number of specialized agencies that deal with health-related products and services. Taxes support these agencies. You have a right as a citizen to make use of their services, and these agencies have a responsibility to help you.

The important skills of being an effective consumer are knowing where to get help and what services are provided. Such information will save you money, protect your safety and health, and often keep merchants honest in their dealings with consumers.

Product Safety   The Consumer Product Safety Commission (CPSC) protects consumers against the manufacture and sale of hazardous appliances, toys, games, and so forth. It has the power to ban hazardous products and also order a *recall* when a product is thought to be dangerous to the public. **Recall** means that *a product that is already on the market has been considered unsafe for use and that the CPSC has instructed the manufacturer to take the product off the shelves.*

Quality and safety labels are now found on toy packages (left). The U.S. Department of Agriculture regulates the quality of food products such as this side of beef (right).

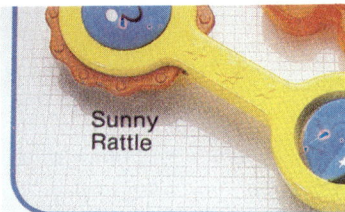

Sunny Rattle

©1985 Fisher-Price, East Aurora, NY 14052
Division of The Quaker Oats Company
Made in U.S.A.
Product specifications subject to change without notice.
Package printed in U.S.A.

Fisher-Price products are made to the company's traditionally high standards of quality, comply with all applicable government safety regulations and conform to the industry's Voluntary Product Standard for toy safety (PS 72-76).

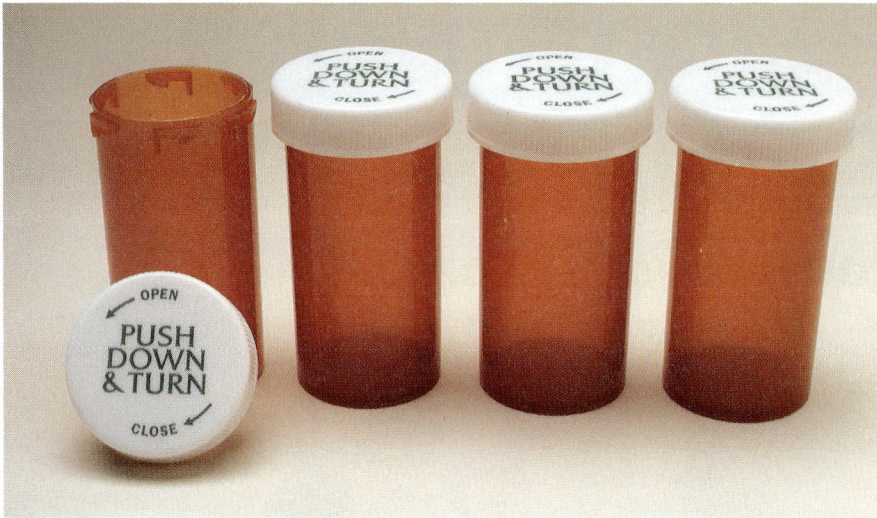

Child-resistant medicine containers have helped to decrease serious accidents among young children. Recently, tamper-proof seals on many food and drug containers have become widespread so that no one can add harmful matter to such products.

It is the CPSC that requires oral prescription drugs and aspirin to be packaged in child-resistant containers. These containers are designed so that children will have difficulty opening them, but adults can easily open them.

For more information about this agency, contact the Director, Office of Communications, Consumer Product Safety Commission, Washington, DC 20207.

Consumer Information   The Consumer Information Center (CIC) distributes consumer information that the federal government publishes. It also works with other related agencies to develop and distribute new consumer information materials. The CIC publishes a listing of over 200 federal consumer publications, many of which are directly related to health. For a free copy of the Catalog of Consumer Information, send a postcard to Consumer Information Center, Pueblo, CO 81009.

IMPROVING YOURSELF

Taped Information on Health Topics

In over 200 communities, a library of tape-recorded health information is as close as your telephone. The Tel-Med Tape Library includes more than 300 tape-recorded messages on various health topics. The service is free. You simply call the Tel-Med number, located in your telephone directory, and ask for the topic on which you want information.

For a list of topics and phone numbers, write to Tel-Med Corporation, PO Box 22700, Cooley Drive, Colton, CA 92324.

CONSUMER SAFETY OFFICER

Our federal government passes many laws and regulations and establishes numerous guidelines for our protection. The Food and Drug Administration (FDA) ensures the safety of foods, drugs, cosmetics, and medical devices. To see that its rules are followed, the FDA employs consumer safety officers.

The responsibilities of a **consumer safety officer** include the inspection of any facilities for the production, packaging, or storage of any item that the FDA regulates. The safety officers must document their findings carefully in case evidence is needed in a court case. They must advise plant officials of any deficiencies or violations and give recommendations for correction.

Consumer safety officers for the FDA inspect small manufacturing plants in rural areas as well as large corporations in cities. Extensive travel is part of the job. Some inspections take less than a day, while others require a week or more. In some cases, the consumer safety officer must make a follow-up inspection to ensure that the necessary corrections were made.

The consumer safety officer must be able to spot the problems and then determine the best course of action. Determination and diligence also contribute to the investigator's effectiveness. Inspections must be thorough, reports accurately detailed, and any follow-ups carried out effectively. Good communications skills are also important to a consumer safety officer.

To enter this field, you must pass the Professional and Administrative Career Examination and then be selected by the Office of Personnel Management. A bachelor's degree or three years of work experience are required before you may take the examination.

Training is offered through the FDA, as well as through college and university courses. The consumer safety officer may continue training at the agency's expense and advance through the U.S. Civil Service grades. Many other fringe benefits are available to government employees. For more information, contact:

**Food and Drug
  Administration**
200 C Street, S.W.
Washington, DC 20204

Food, Cosmetics, and Drugs   The Food and Drug Administration (FDA) ensures that all food and food additives, other than meat and poultry, or those containing meat and poultry, are safe, pure, and wholesome, and honestly and correctly labeled. If you find unsanitary, contaminated, or mislabeled foods, contact the FDA and it will review the complaint, which may lead to an investigation.

The FDA also ensures that cosmetics are safe and pure. The FDA requires that cosmetics be truthfully labeled and that the ingredients be listed on each package. If you have an unusual physical reaction to a cosmetic, report it to the FDA.

Last, the FDA ensures that drugs are properly labeled and safe and effective for their intended uses. The FDA determines if a drug should be a prescription drug, or obtainable only with a doctor's order, or a drug sold over-the-counter (OTC), which is available by individual choice. The FDA regulates the advertising of prescription drugs, while the Federal Trade Commission (FTC) regulates the advertising of over-the-counter drugs in all their forms.

For more information, contact the Director, Consumer Communications, HFJ-10, Food and Drug Administration, 5600 Fishers Lane, Rockville, MD 20857.

Meat and Poultry   The Food Safety and Quality Service (FSQS) of the Department of Agriculture ensures that meat and poultry and products made from them are safe, wholesome, and labeled properly. This branch ensures that meat-packing plants are clean and that any potential hazards are kept at safe levels. If you have suffered from suspected food poisoning from meat or poultry, contact a doctor of the local public health office who will contact the Meatborne Hazard Control Center, Agriculture Research Center, Beltsville, MD 20705.

This same agency also provides information on its activities and publishes a variety of educational materials on such subjects as food safety and purchasing.

For copies of any of these materials, contact the Information Division, Food Safety and Quality Service, Department of Agriculture, Washington, DC 20250.

Meat and poultry packing plants are constantly surveyed by the FSQS to see that the products are prepared, handled, and packed properly.

Advertising   As you have studied, advertising is designed to influence you and your decision about a product or service. Sometimes this advertising is honest, and sometimes it is not. The Federal Trade Commission (FTC) prevents the unfair, false, or deceptive advertising of consumer products and services. This includes television, radio, and printed ads.

For more information about false advertising of consumer products and services, contact the Office of the Secretary, Federal Trade Commission, Washington, DC 20580.

Transportation   The Bureau of Consumer Protection of the Civil Aeronautics Board (CAB) handles complaints against airlines. If you have been misled about discount fares or types of services, this is the agency with which to register a complaint. Usually you can get your problem taken care of by contacting the customer service representative of the airline. If this does no good, write to the airline's Consumer Affairs Department. If this fails, then the Bureau of Consumer Protection is a good choice. Its address is Bureau of Consumer Protection, Civil Aeronautics Board, Washington, DC 20428.

CHECK YOURSELF

1. What are the limits of a case that could be taken to small-claims court?
2. How might an advocate group help the consumer?
3. List five government agencies that protect consumers. Explain each agency's function.

CHAPTER 23 Review

CHAPTER SUMMARY

- Consumers are faced with thousands of products, high-powered advertising, and often inaccurate information, making their task of product selection a difficult one.
- Many factors influence one's purchases. Wise consumers are aware of how they are being influenced and choose their purchases accordingly.
- People who have incurable diseases or conditions spend billions of dollars on quackery. The quack offers hope along with quick, easy, painless cures.
- A wise consumer must be able to recognize fraudulent claims to protect his or her health and to save money.
- Many local, state, and federal agencies and organizations help to protect the consumer.

REVIEWING WHAT YOU LEARNED

1. Give two reasons why people turn to quack products.
2. Give five questions you should ask before buying a health product.
3. Why are cancer, arthritis, and weight control most susceptible to quackery?
4. Explain what is meant by the placebo effect. Give an example.
5. Give an example of each of the five factors that influence one's purchases.

6. Compare the benefits of being a wise consumer with the potential problems of not being a wise consumer.
7. Compare federal consumer-protection agencies with other such organizations.
8. Identify three organizations that would be helpful to you as a consumer if you bought a package of pills that guaranteed weight loss.
9. What are your rights as a consumer?

APPLYING WHAT YOU LEARNED

1. Make a list of five common advertising slogans or jingles. Next to each one, write a consumer-awareness warning. Your warning might point out something for the consumer to look for beyond what is being promoted in the ad.
2. Form a survey team to observe television commercials of different channels between 6:00 P.M. and 10:00 P.M. Answer the following questions and then report your findings:
   a. How many commercials were for health products?
   b. How many were beauty or beauty *and* health products?
   c. How many products used youth and beauty as part of the sales pitch?
3. Five classmates have been given $20 each to purchase health products. You are asked to give them

consumer	advertising	placebo effect	recall
convenience	quack	small-claims court	consumer safety officer
tradition	quackery	advocates	
testimonial	placebo		

PUTTING VOCABULARY TO USE

On a separate piece of paper, write the following paragraphs. Fill in each blank with the proper word. Use the chapter vocabulary list for reference. You may use some words more than once.

As a wise _____, I am aware of factors that influence my purchases. Family customs, or _____, may be a reason for buying a product, because I am familiar with it and my family has always used it.

_____ adds to the price of the product, but it is also a major factor influencing purchases.

Billions of dollars are spent every year in _____ to convince people that they need a certain product. One type of _____ is the _____, in which a famous person promotes a product.

One way I can save money as a _____ is to compare sizes, quantity, and prices.

Products and services that offer hope, but have no sound medical basis, are called _____. They cost the _____ money and often delay the person from seeking sound medical treatment.

People are often fooled because the quackery product has a _____ effect and the person may think he or she is cured.

A person who has been cheated may find assistance through an _____ group.

On a separate piece of paper, match the problem with the appropriate helping agency. You may use an agency more than once.

a. BBB
b. Small-claims court
c. Office of Consumer Affairs
d. CPSC
e. CIC
f. FDA

___ 1. The toy you bought for your little brother shattered, cutting him. You want to report it.
___ 2. You are tricked by what you think is false advertising.
___ 3. You want general information on a local business.
___ 4. You have a complaint about a local merchant.
___ 5. You want a catalog of consumer information.
___ 6. You break out in a rash after using a new skin lotion.
___ 7. You want to sue a company for a $500 loss; you feel it is responsible.

some suggestions about wise consumer practices in the use of their money. What major points would you share with them?
4. In a store, you observe two people shopping for shampoo. What are some ways that you can tell which one *is* and which one *is not* a wise consumer?
5. Make up a situation in which you, as the consumer, are cheated. Compose a letter of complaint to send to the president of the company.
6. In the Middle Ages, guild regulations were designed to protect consumers from spoiled foods.

Find out what some of these regulations were. Venice, for example, had regulations for the selling of fresh fish.
7. Research the use of herbal medicines to treat illnesses. Are they still being used today? How?

FOCUS ON WELLNESS

There are many benefits of being a wise consumer, including the positive feelings that come with asserting yourself in the marketplace. *I can improve my own consumer skills by . . .*

Health Services and Health Care

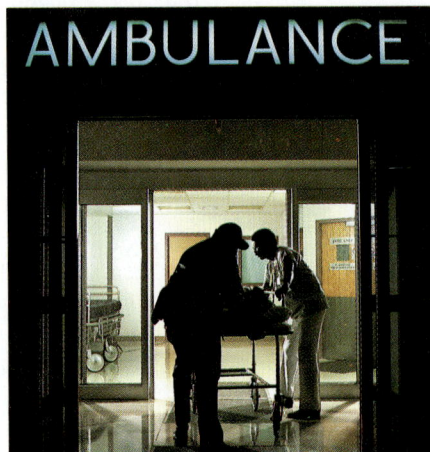

AMBULANCE

On your way to school, an ambulance speeds past you. It is one of the mobile intensive care units that services your neighborhood. Have you ever stopped to think about health-care services available in your community? Do you know where to seek help for various types of health problems?

After studying this chapter, you will be able to:
- recognize different health-care facilities and types of treatment,
- give examples of primary, secondary, and tertiary health care,
- list the variety of health resources available for inpatients and outpatients,
- describe new trends in the delivery of health care.

1. What Are Health Services?

In most of this book, the focus has been on *health education*, providing health information in such a way that it influences people to take positive action about their health. **Health services** is a different aspect of an overall health program. *It is concerned with the prevention of disease, the maintenance of and the promotion of health, and the treatment of and cure of disease.*

The Range of Health Care

The American public spends about $200 billion per year on health care. About $0.40 of every health-care dollar is spent for hospital services. Almost 5 million people are employed in some aspect of health-care delivery. The occupations and services range from very large hospitals to mobile vans, from air-pollution projects in large cities to tuberculosis checks in small towns.

When a person gets vaccinated against a disease that can spread, he or she is involved in preventive health services. People who are engaged in a fitness program are part of a health-promotion program, while people who are being treated for cancer or obesity are in a treatment or therapeutic type of program.

Health services can also be maintenance-oriented through the different types of assessments and examinations that are conducted periodically to make sure that individuals are free from disease.

Whatever the type of health service, it is a major part of the total health picture in the United States. *Health service* is more commonly referred to as **health-care delivery**.

Many different types of health resources exist in this country. Health resources are places that people can go to for various types of treatment. Think of some health resources in your community. Dentists' and physicians' offices, drugstores, nursing and retirement homes, hospitals, health-maintenance organizations, poison-control centers, psychiatric outpatient clinics, public health clinics, mental health centers, suicide-prevention centers, and neighborhood health centers are all examples of health resources.

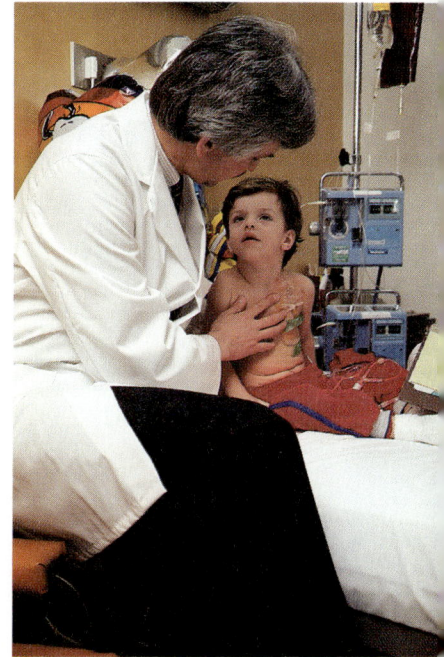

Health care delivery takes many forms and extends to all ages.

Types of Health Facilities

A **health facility** is a *place that a person goes to for health care.* There are basically two types: those facilities for *inpatient care* and those for *outpatient care.*

■ **Inpatients** are *people who require prolonged health care and who are admitted to and occupy a bed in a facility.* Such people may need nursing

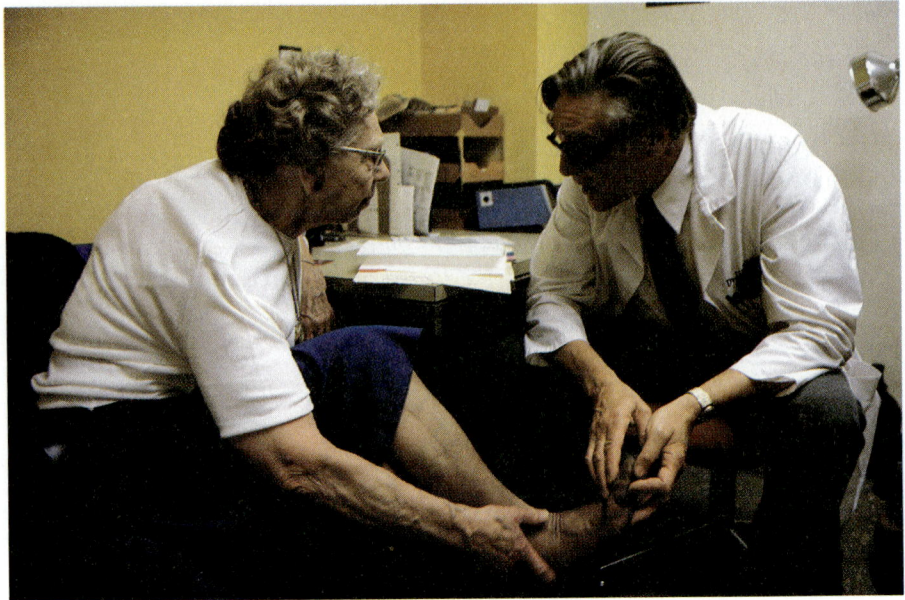

Geriatric care is that care given to older people.

service, extensive use of laboratory and X-ray services, or supervised rehabilitation.

■ **Outpatients** *receive various medical, dental, or other health services in the facility and then return home.*

Hospitals

The hospital is perhaps the most familiar type of facility. Hospitals are generally classified according to who runs them. In this country, three basic types of hospitals exist:

1. **Nonprofit, nongovernmental voluntary health facilities**. Most general hospitals in large communities are nonprofit. The community, a church group, or some other nonprofit group operates them.
2. **Governmental, tax-supported health facilities**. Federal, state, or county–city health agencies operate these institutions. Almost all of these hospitals are mental institutions, although the many Veterans Administration hospitals fall into this category.
3. **Proprietary, privately owned, independent facilities**. These hospitals are established as profit-making operations in the delivery of health care.

Two basic types of hospitals exist when we categorize them according to services:

■ **General hospitals**. These institutions provide for different types of personal health needs. The general hospital is often the core of the community health network.

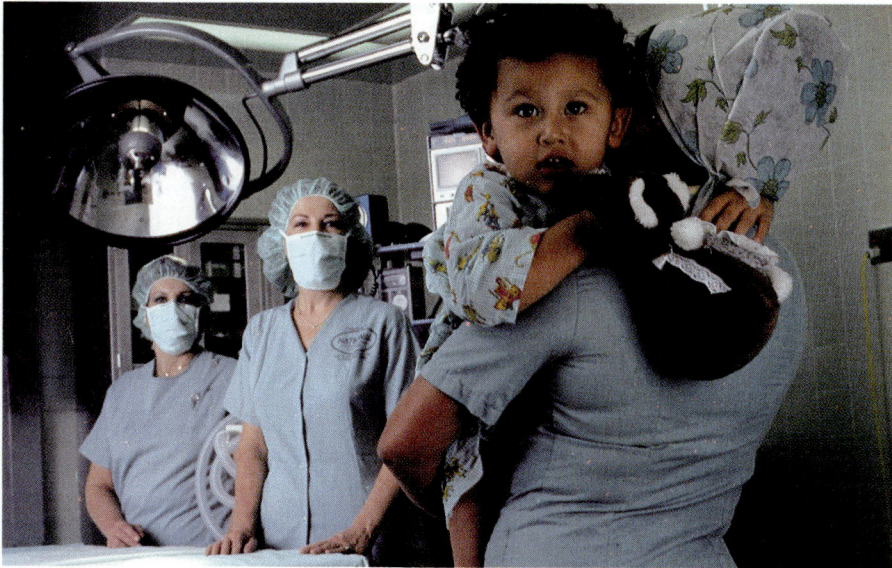

Pediatric care is care given to infants and children.

- **Specialty hospitals**. This type of facility tends to care either for certain kinds of patients (for example, children, Indians, veterans) or certain kinds of health needs (for example, mental health, tuberculosis).

Other Health-Care Facilities

Many other types of health-care arrangements exist, but the following ones are the most common:

- *Nursing care home*. A facility where a *registered nurse (RN)* or a *licensed practical nurse (LPN)* aids at least 50% of the people.
- *Personal care home with nursing*. A facility where an RN or an LPN aid less than 50% of the people.
- *Personal care home without nursing*. A facility where no full-time RN or LPN is employed, but the facility provides assistance in daily living activities and in the administration or supervision of medicine.
- *Domiciliary* (dom-uh-**sil**-uh-er-ee) *care home*. No nursing care is involved and no medicine is administered. It is more of a dormitory arrangement for people who can care for themselves.

The charts on pages 432 and 433 show a full range of health-services organizations.

CHECK YOURSELF

1. What is the primary concern of health services?
2. In your own words, define health-care delivery.
3. Give an example of inpatient and outpatient care.
4. Compare the three types of hospitals.

Health-Care Resources Available to Inpatients in the United States				
General Hospitals	**Specialty Hospitals**	**Nursing Homes**	**Mental Health Facilities Other Than Hospitals**	**Other Specialty Facilities**
Children's hospitals	Psychiatric	Nursing care	Alcoholism treatment	Dependent children and orphans
General public hospitals	Eye, ear, nose, throat	Personal care with nursing	Psychiatric halfway houses	Deaf
	Rehabilitation	Personal care	Alcoholism halfway houses	Blind
	Orthopedic	Home		Neurologically handicapped
	Tuberculosis	Domiciliary care	Residential treatment of emotionally disturbed, mentally retarded	Physically handicapped
	Chronic disease			Unwed mothers
	Maternity		Drug abuse treatment and rehabilitation units	
	Chemical dependency		Community mental health units	

2. Seeking Health Care

Today we have many facilities and medical specialists to care for our needs and to help us live longer lives. Presently, we have three major stages of health care and hundreds of different specialists in the health-care field.

Stages of Health Care

- **Primary care**. If you get sick and you call a doctor, most likely you call a general practitioner, a physician who is in family practice. This care, which *the patient seeks on his or her own*, is called primary care. It most often takes place in the doctor's office or a clinic.
- **Secondary care**. This care occurs when *the primary care physicians refer their patient to a specialist*. This care may involve a stay in a hospi-

Health-Care Resources Available to Outpatients in the United States			
Practitioners' Offices	**Hospital Outpatient Departments**	**Freestanding Clinics**	**Other Specialty Facilities**
Medical	Emergency	Health departments	Health-maintenance organizations
Dental	Organized outpatient	Industrial health units	
Chiropractic	Supportive services department	Family-planning clinics	Outpatient surgical areas
Podiatric		Psychiatric clinics	Pharmacies
Optometric		Community mental health centers	Poison-control centers
Psychologic			Kidney dialysis centers
		Residential treatment centers for emotionally disturbed	Blood banks
			Home health-care organizations
			Neighborhood health centers
			Rehabilitation centers

tal for more extensive testing than one could receive in a clinic or a doctor's office.

- **Tertiary care**. This care is needed when *the patient's condition requires advanced equipment or treatment*. This care takes place at hospitals equipped with special technology. Examples of tertiary care may include kidney dialysis treatment, or advanced heart or brain surgery, or cancer, or burn treatment.

Forms of Medical Practice

Traditionally, the physician has been the central figure in the delivery of health care in the United States. Physicians, for the most part, are in **private practice**; that is, *they are self-employed*, functioning in individual practices, operating out of their own offices, and not sharing personnel, facilities, or income with any other physicians.

An orthopedic surgeon is a specialist who performs surgery on bones and joints.

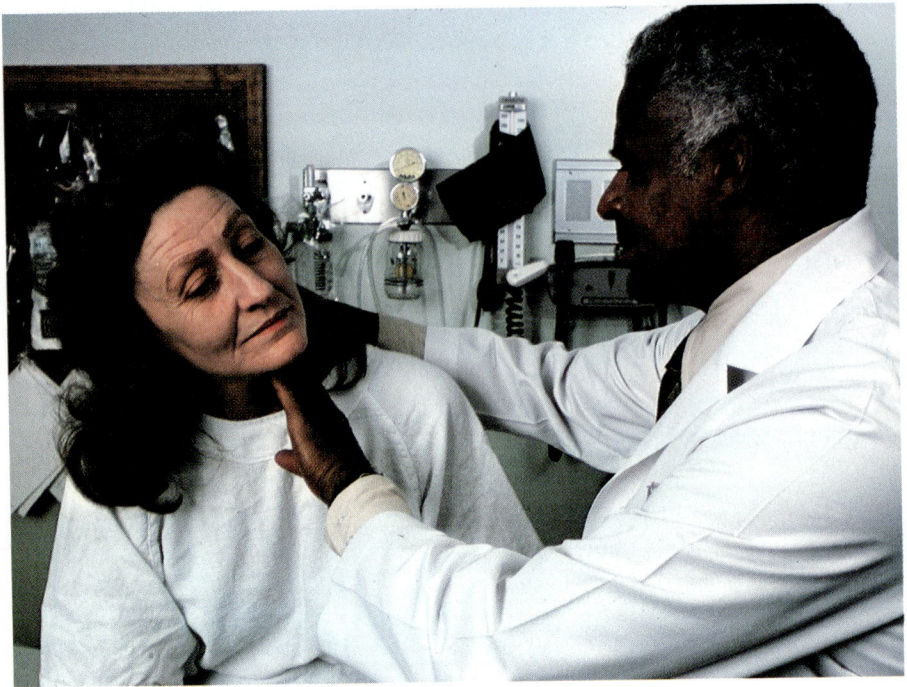

The Specialist

Physicians work as specialists in five major clinical areas: *internal medicine, obstetrics and gynecology, pediatrics, psychiatry,* and *surgery.* These primary care areas are broken down further into secondary care areas. For example, under internal medicine, there is a subspecialist who specializes in diagnosis and treatment for almost every organ and/or system of the body. Some of the common specialists are as follows:

- *Allergist* (**al**-er-jest). Diagnoses and treats patients for asthma, hay fever, hives, and other allergies.
- *Anesthesiologist* (an-es-**teez**-e-ol-o-gist). Administers anesthetics (drugs that cause insensitivity to pain) during surgery; checks the patient's condition before and after surgery.
- *Cardiologist* (**kard**-ee-aul-uh-jest). Diagnoses and treats heart diseases.
- *Dermatologist* (der-muh-**taul**-uh-jest). Diagnoses and treats all forms of skin diseases.
- *Endocrinologist* (en-doe-kri-**naul**-uh-jest). Diagnoses and treats problems related to the endocrine glands.
- *Gastroenterologist* (gas-tro-ent-uh-**raul**-uh-jest). Treats gastrointestinal (stomach and intestine) disorders.
- *Gynecologist*. Diagnoses and treats problems related to the female reproductive organs.
- *Neurologist*. Diagnoses and treats problems of the central and peripheral nervous systems.
- *Obstetrician* (ahb-stuh-**trish**-un). Specializes in all aspects of childbirth—care of the mother before, during, and after delivery.

- *Ophthalmologist* (op-thal-**mull**-uh-jest). Cares for and corrects eye problems.
- *Orthopedic* (or-tho-**pea**-dik) *surgeon*. Performs surgery on bones and joints.
- *Otolaryngologist* (**ot**-oh-lair-un-**gaul**-uh-jest). Treats ear, nose, and throat disorders.
- *Otologist* (**ot**-oh-uh-jest). Treats ear problems.
- *Pathologist* (puh-**thal**-uh-jest). Carries out laboratory tests of body tissues and fluids; studies the causes of death.
- *Pediatrician* (pead-ee-uh-**trish**-un). Specializes in the medical care of children.
- *Plastic surgeon*. Treats skin and soft-tissue deformities; performs surgery to improve external features.
- *Psychiatrist*. Specializes in mental and emotional disorders.
- *Radiologist* (raid-ee-**aul**-uh-jest). Examines and treats patients by using X rays and radium therapy.
- *Thoracic* (thu-**ras**-ik) *surgeon*. Performs surgery on the chest and the lungs.
- *Vascular* (**vas**-kue-lur) *surgeon*. Performs surgery on the heart and the blood vessels.
- *Urologist* (you-**raul**-uh-jest). Treats disorders of the urinary tract (kidneys, ureters, urethra); also specializes in the treatment of the male reproductive organs.

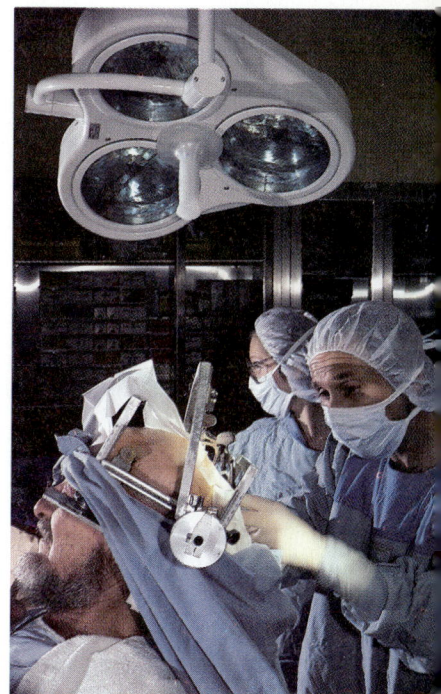

This doctor is a specialist who performs surgery on the brain and other parts of the nervous system.

HEALTH UPDATE   HEALTH UPDATE   HEALTH UPDATE

Choosing a Health-Care Professional

As you begin to take a more active, responsible role in promoting your personal health and wellness, it is important that you choose a health-care professional who will work with you in your efforts. The best time to select a health-care professional is before you need one.

- Ask a variety of people for recommendations.
- Use the yellow pages of the phone directory. They usually categorize doctors by their specialties.
- Call the local medical society. Their usual procedure is to provide three names, chosen in objective rotation from the society's membership roster.
- Ask your local librarian or consumer-protection agency whether a "doctor's directory" has been compiled for your community. It will provide detailed information about physicians.
- When you have compiled a list of several possible people, prepare a checklist, and call the office of each person to get the information you need to make your decision.
- Use the checklist in the *Health Handbook*, pages HB 24–25, to organize your information.

Group Practice

While group practice has existed for many years, it has become more popular in recent years because of the rising costs in setting up and maintaining a medical practice. The rapid advances in medicine and the demand for specialization also make this option more attractive today than in former years.

Group practice is a situation in which *three or more physicians unite to provide medical care*. They diagnose through consultation, and treat through the joint use of equipment, support staff, and funds for the maintenance and development of the practice.

Health-Maintenance Organizations (HMO)

When you go to physicians who are in private practice or in group practice, you pay for their services each time you use them. Another option is now available to the consumer—a **health-maintenance organization (HMO)**. The HMO physicians are paid by salary, not by a fee for each service. HMOs stress preventive medicine in an attempt to reduce the high cost of medical care.

The *consumer pays an initial membership fee and then is entitled to receive medical care for little or no additional charge*. The consumer uses the physicians that belong to the HMO. This may mean that you cannot choose your own physician. However, within the HMO, a wide range of physicians and specialists exists.

Members of HMOs are guaranteed treatment when they need it. HMOs save money by emphasizing preventive medicine and ambulatory care—treatment for patients who are not hospitalized—and by using expensive hospital care less often. Some HMOs pass the saving on to members in the form of reduced fees.

Health Insurance—Are You Covered?

One of the leading causes of bankruptcy in the United States is the cost of medical care. If you had to be hospitalized, could you and your family afford to pay from your savings each day that you would be in the hospital's care?

Many people protect themselves from incurring such debts by purchasing health insurance. Basically two types of health insurance exist—*government insurance programs* and *private insurance programs*.

Government Programs

Medicaid, insurance for low-income individuals and families, and *Medicare*, insurance for people 65 or older, are the two forms of government health insurance.

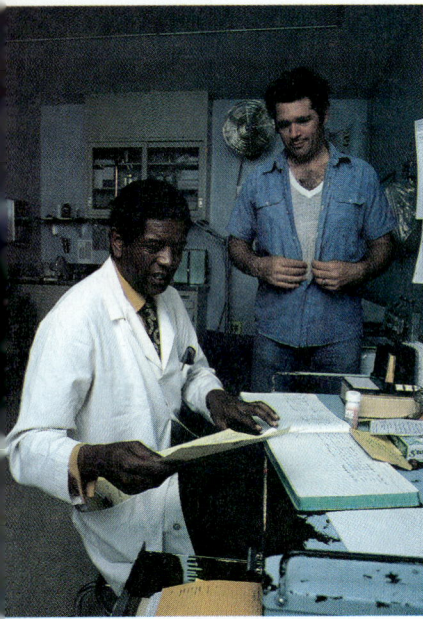

Regular medical examinations are an important part of any self-care health program.

Private Programs

The consumer can purchase private health insurance plans from insurance companies. Over 1,500 such companies offer a wide variety of insurance plans. Often a person's place of employment offers some kind of health insurance plan in which the employer pays a portion of the fee.

Elizabeth Blackwell and Women Doctors in America

America's first woman doctor was admitted into the medical department of Geneva College, New York, because the all-male student body at the college was in the mood for a practical joke.

No medical school wanted to consider admission to a woman. The Dean and the President of the college decided to handle the touchy situation by turning the decision over to the student body. They were sure that the student body would take a negative stand, and then they could politely decline Miss Blackwell.

However, the student body found this idea of voting entertaining and a nice diversion from their studies. There was even a rumor that the letter was a hoax planted by students at a rival college. They voted unanimously to admit Elizabeth Blackwell.

On November 7, 1847, Elizabeth enrolled in the medical department of Geneva College and had a transforming effect on the students. The usually rowdy medical students became orderly and gentlemanly. Later, Elizabeth graduated, but she knew the roughest road was still ahead. Because she was a woman, much more skill and knowledge would be demanded of her. After three years of work and study, Elizabeth began to practice medicine.

It was an uphill battle, but after years of struggle, Elizabeth opened her own hospital in a New York City slum and began training other women doctors. Although she had an all-female staff, Elizabeth had noted male physicians on her board, thus helping to ensure the success of her hospital, the New York Infirmary for Women and Children.

Elizabeth Blackwell retired from active participation in hospital work at the end of the Civil War. She went to England to study, write, and lecture. She knew that nothing could stop the program she had begun for women in the field of medicine.

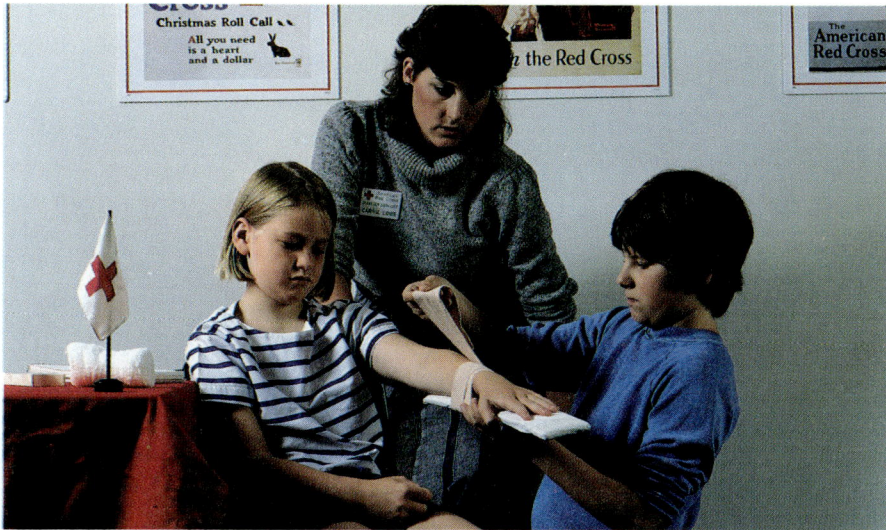

Insurance policies can be difficult to read and understand. Many consumers are not sure exactly what their insurance covers. It may come as a surprise to discover that one's insurance policy covers only a small portion of the medical bill. Some plans provide only minimal coverage. Hospital coverage is likely to be for a limited number of days. Other plans are quite comprehensive and may include dentist bills, drugs, and various psychiatric counseling.

As a consumer, the important point for you to remember is to treat health insurance just like any other purchase. Use your consumer skills. Read everything carefully before signing any agreement. Ask questions if you do not understand. Compare several different companies' prices and coverage.

New Trends in the Delivery of Health Care

In the last few years, other types of health-care outlets have developed. These outlets are designed to meet the needs of those people who are not covered by other health-care supports. The people who receive service in these centers often make too much money to qualify for government medical benefits, but they do not make enough to purchase their own private health insurance. Chief among these outlets are:

- **Adolescent health centers.** Most centers are located in large cities. They are designed specifically to deal with problems relating to adolescence. These clinics address adolescents' physical, mental, and social health. The practitioners, for the most part, specialize in adolescent medicine.
- **Holistic** (ho-**lis**-tik) **health centers**. These centers look at health in terms of the total person and put together a "wellness" plan for what the individual can do to improve personal health.

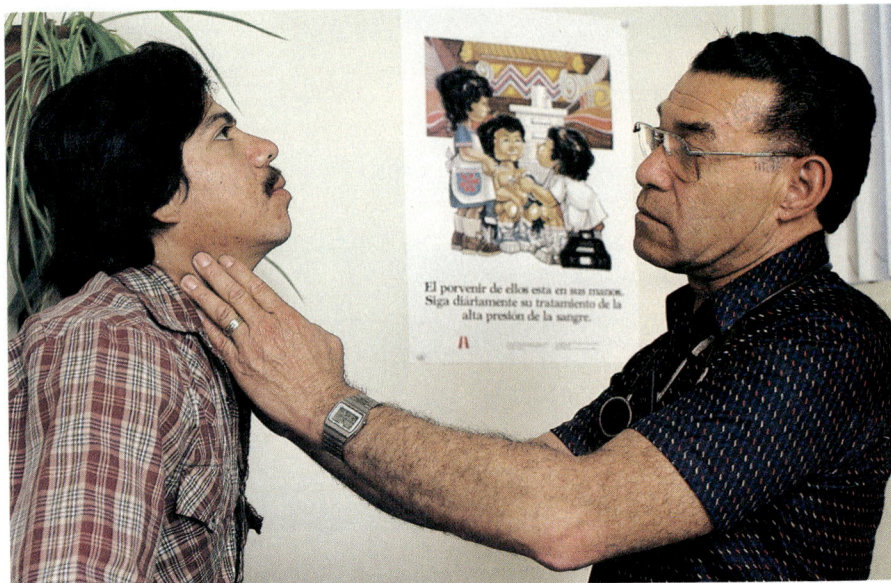

Neighborhood health centers are a new health care approach that meets local needs.

- **Neighborhood health centers**. These centers are designed to meet local needs, particularly those of ethnic and social groups who have difficulty gaining access to existing health-care programs.
- **Alternative maternal care birthing centers**. Over 60 of these facilities operate throughout the country. They are designed primarily to offer a homelike atmosphere, substantial savings on delivery costs, and opportunities to involve the entire family in the delivery of a baby.
- **Specialized cooperatives**. One example of a specialized cooperative is the Co-Op Optical Service of Detroit, where nonprofit groups offer consumers high-quality eye care for lower costs. The Co-Op is actually owned by the people it serves. Recently, estimates showed that 100,000 people in a year saved $10 each on glasses.
- **Hospice (haus-pus) care**. Care for the terminally ill is becoming part of the mainstream of the health-care delivery system. The **hospice** is *a way of caring for the dying, not just a place where the dying are cared for.* It unites the best techniques that have been devised for pain and symptom management with the provision of loving care.

The following list describes characteristics of almost all hospice care outlets:

- It is available 24 hours a day.
- It is provided with an interdisciplinary health-care team.
- Hospice patients and their families are a central part of the hospice care team.
- Volunteers are an integral part of the hospice program.
- Emphasis is on optimal control of pain and other symptoms.
- A qualified physician medically directs the programs.
- Programs provide inpatient and home care, as needed.

HEALTH

CAREER

LICENSED PRACTICAL NURSE OR LICENSED VOCATIONAL NURSE

The **licensed practical nurse (LPN)**, or the **licensed vocational nurse (LVN)**, as the person is known in some states, is a vital member of the health-care team. This branch of nursing is different from that of a registered nurse (RN). Administrators and supervisors are usually registered nurses. They may also be involved in the training of LPNs and LVNs.

LPNs and LVNs perform many of the patient-care duties, teaching them good health practices, assisting with rehabilitation, and offering comfort and emotional reassurance during times of suffering and crisis.

LPNs and LVNs are active in medical–surgical, geriatric, obstetric, and pediatric nursing. They work in operating rooms, intensive care units, and coronary-care units. In addition, these health-team members contribute to hospital staff meetings, including daily ward conferences and weekly staff consultations.

Among their most important responsibilities are interpreting and carrying out written orders. A doctor often visits a patient and leaves written orders for care for the next 24 hours. It takes a responsible person to follow the orders, and then to chart and write accurate reports to the physician so that the physician can make appropriate decisions about the patient. The patient's chart is a legal document, not just a means of communicating to the physician.

LPNs and LVNs work with all members of the health-care team, including physicians, surgeons, interns, residents, registered nurses, technicians, therapists, and other aides. Some work in hospitals, while others work in public-health agencies or in nursing homes. Some LPNs and LVNs even work in homes.

A career in practical nursing provides the opportunity to aid people who need help. It is a respected career that does not require the long, expensive education that is necessary for most other members of the health-care team.

The LPN or LVN is a person who enjoys responsibility, adapts to changing situations and conditions, understands and communicates with people, and treats all people with respect and dignity.

Generally, a high school diploma or equivalency is all that a person needs to enter into an LPN or LVN program. Over 1,000 programs for LPNs and LVNs exist in the United States. For more information about the location of an approved school, contact the National Association for Practical Nurse Education and Service.

Practical Nurse Education and Service
254 West 31st Street
New York, NY 10001

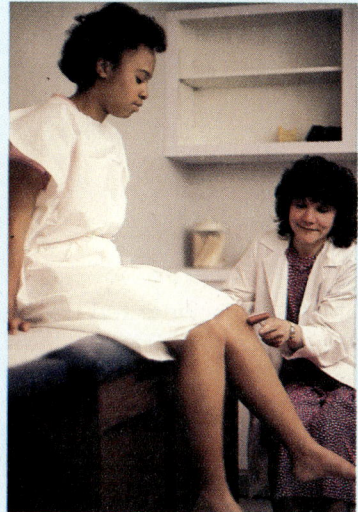

The Consumer and Health Care

The demand for health care by far exceeds the available services. As a consumer, what can you do to relieve some of this demand on the health-care system? The most important thing you can do is take greater responsibility in protecting and promoting your own health.

By supporting health-education programs in school and in the community, we provide people with the opportunity to learn about their bodies and health. This provides the basis for individual responsibility in the protection and promotion of one's health.

Knowing is not enough; people must act on the information that they have to reduce health risks.

- What good does it do to know that seat belts save lives if people sit on their belts?
- What good does it do to know that cervical cancer can be prevented through Pap smears if women do not take the time to have the test?
- What good does it do to smoke cigarettes in spite of the mounting evidence that smoking is a direct cause of cancer and heart disease?

The health-care delivery system cannot be expected to care for your health if you are not willing to invest yourself. You must see the relationship between yourself and the health-care system as a partnership, with both committed and motivated to care for and to be responsible for your health.

CHECK YOURSELF

1. Name the differences between primary, secondary, and tertiary care.
2. What are the major clinical specialties?
3. What is meant by HMO? Describe the service.

CHAPTER 24   Review

CHAPTER SUMMARY

- Many health facilities and resources are available to the consumer.
- Health-care delivery is a major part of the total health picture in the United States.
- As the cost of health services continues to increase, prevention becomes an even more critical part of the health-care delivery system.
- A variety of new trends are developing in our health-care delivery system.
- These trends generally involve the consumer in the more active role of participating in health services.
- This is in contrast to the traditionally passive role that consumers took in the past, for now consumers no longer totally depend on the doctor to get them well.

REVIEWING WHAT YOU LEARNED

1. How does health education differ from health services? Compare and contrast health services and health care.

health services
health-care delivery
health facility
inpatients

outpatients
general hospitals
specialty hospitals
primary care

secondary care
tertiary care
private practice
group practice

health-maintenance organization (HMO)
hospice
licensed practical nurse (LPN)
licensed vocational nurse (LVN)

PUTTING VOCABULARY TO USE

On a separate sheet of paper, write each statement and then mark it as *true* or *false*. If the statement is *false*, write a correct statement.

1. Neighborhood health clinics are an example of an *inpatient* health facility.
2. A domiciliary care home could be considered to be an *outpatient* health facility.
3. A visit to a psychologist's office would be considered to be *primary care*.

4. Belonging to a *health-maintenance organization (HMO)* can save the consumer money because the physician is not paid on a fee basis.
5. *Tertiary care* could take place in a holistic health center.
6. A *hospice* is an example of an outpatient facility.
7. If your physician sent you to a urologist, it is likely that you would be getting *secondary health care* from the specialist.

2. Give an example of primary, secondary, and tertiary health care.
3. Give three health resources available for (a) inpatients and (b) outpatients.
4. In the past, the hospital and the individual physician were the major, if not the only, providers of health care. Cite three examples to show that this traditional approach to health-care delivery is changing. Then cite three examples of traditional health care models that are still available.

APPLYING WHAT YOU LEARNED

1. Using the charts on pages 432 and 433, build up a directory of health-care resources in your neighborhood or town. You can compile one by using the local telephone directory as a resource.
2. Develop a set of criteria for selecting a physician or a dentist. Compare your list with your classmates' lists.
3. Interview several adults about their methods for selecting health services and find out what these services represent to them. Ask them the following questions:
   a. How do you go about selecting health services?
   b. What do you expect from health-care service people?
   c. How do you go about evaluating them?

   d. Do you give them any feedback about the care you receive?

   Draw some conclusions about health-care service utilization on the basis of your interviews.
4. Make a list of the health services and health facilities in your community. Using the public health department as a resource, try to determine whether the facilities are adequate. What are the most pressing health-care needs in your area?
5. During the 1800s, scientists made many important discoveries, especially in the field of medicine. Pick a scientific discovery from this time and discuss its impact on our health today.
6. Rebecca Lee was the first black woman to earn a degree in medicine. She accomplished this in 1864. In 1890, Ida Gray became the first black woman to earn a Doctor of Dental Surgery Degree. She was Chicago's first black female dentist. Research the contributions that other women have made to medicine.

FOCUS ON WELLNESS

Active participation in promoting health and wellness makes the consumer an important part of the health-care delivery system. *I do my part to contribute to health promotion by . . .*

Health Organizations

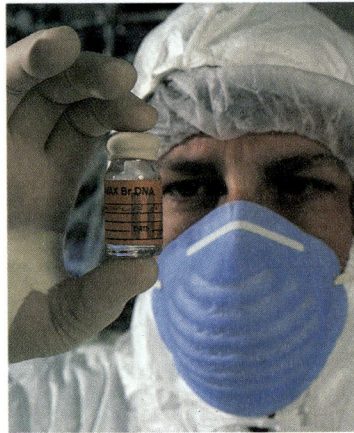

Joe's little brother had to have a polio shot before enrolling in elementary school. Sally's grandmother went to the city health department for a flu shot. Tina had to have a tuberculosis test before she could work as a cook in a local restaurant. Each of these people—whether voluntarily or by law—was taking advantage of local, state, and national health requirements to protect themselves and others.

After studying this chapter, you will be able to:
- describe the functions of voluntary health organizations,
- list the responsibilities of local and state health departments,
- outline the departments and divisions of the Department of Health and Human Services,
- explain the function of the World Health Organization.

Numerous organizations work at the local, state, and national levels to promote community and individual health. These organizations increase as the need exists. Presently, hundreds of these organizations are functioning across the country.

Professional and Voluntary Health Agencies

You are probably familiar with many of the voluntary health organizations. Most of them focus their efforts on a specific disease, disorder, or health problem.

Voluntary agencies receive almost all of their money from private donations and fund drives. Have you ever participated in a March of Dimes Walkathon or a Run for Cancer or a Dance-a-thon?

Voluntary agencies have three main functions:

- to educate the public about the disease or disorder they are fighting,
- to provide money for research on the disease they are fighting,
- to provide aid for people who have a disease or disorder, as well as education and support for the victim's family.

Many communities have fund-raising drives for different voluntary health agencies.

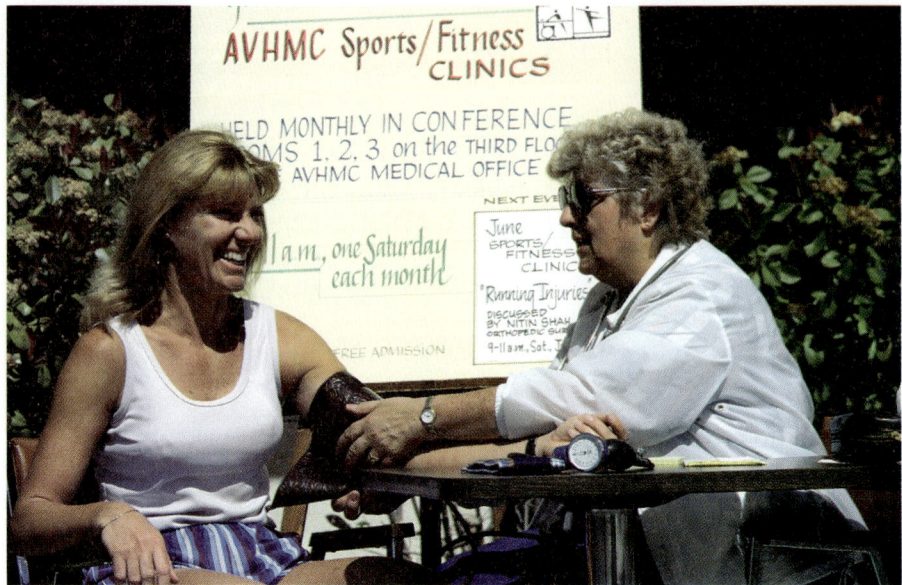

Many voluntary health agencies run community health fairs to check people's blood pressure.

Here are a number of the major voluntary agencies. Which of them have offices in your community?

- The American Heart Association
- The American Cancer Society
- The American Red Cross
- The National Foundation—March of Dimes
- The Multiple Sclerosis Foundation
- The Cystic Fibrosis Foundation
- The National Hemophilia Foundation
- The Kidney Foundation
- The American Diabetes Association
- The American Foundation for the Blind
- The National Council on Alcoholism
- The Arthritis Foundation
- The Leukemia Society of America
- Muscular Dystrophy Association
- The American Lung Association
- The Epilepsy Foundation of America
- The United Cerebral Palsy Association

The **National Health Council (NHC)** is *an organization of about 70 health agencies in the United States.* Many of the above health organizations belong to it. The main purposes of the NHC are:

- to help member agencies work together in an effective way,
- to assist in identifying and solving national health problems,
- to help in improving local and state health services.

The National Health Council also conducts health forums and health career and educational programs.

Local and State Health Departments

Almost all cities and counties have local health departments, concerned primarily with the prevention of disease and the health needs of the poor. Local health departments have the following responsibilities:

- inspecting restaurant and hotel kitchens,
- monitoring garbage pickup and disposal,
- enforcing minimum standards of water purity, as set by the federal government,
- picking up stray animals,
- ensuring that public buildings, hotels, and motels are sanitary,
- coordinating neighborhood health centers and clinics,
- tracking down epidemics and sources of diseases,
- administering vaccinations and immunizations,
- running clinics for treatment of sexually transmitted diseases,
- offering health-education fairs and awareness programs.

Every state has its own health department, which works in cooperation with federal and local agencies. Each state establishes its own disease-control laws and sanitary codes. State health departments may also inspect hospitals and nursing homes. They keep birth and death records, as well as records of diseases such as tuberculosis that must be reported to the federal government. State health departments may also offer a variety of educational programs.

HEALTH UPDATE   HEALTH UPDATE   HEALTH UPDATE

Water Filters and Cancer

You probably would be surprised to learn that the Environmental Protection Agency (EPA), water filters, and cancer all have something in common. Recently, tests that the EPA sponsored have shown that large, home-line water filters, the larger under-the-sink variety, can remove up to 99% of potentially **carcinogenic** (kar-sin-uh-**jen**-ik) or *cancer-producing*, substances called *trihalomethanes* (try-hal-uh-**meth**-anes) (THMS) that are widely found in drinking water.

Researchers have learned in recent years that the carbon in home filters absorbs foreign materials such as detergents, saturated oils, and pesticides from the drinking water. The longer the water is in contact with the carbon in the filter, the more effective the removal of the substance.

Some communities are taking the initiative to remove THMS from their drinking water supply. However, many communities either cannot afford it or have not yet chosen to do so. It is in these places that the individual consumer might well consider a home water-filtering system.

The primary concern of all of these organizations is the health of the individual. Just as in the case of all other systems, the health of a community will only be as good as the health of its members. Controlling disease, preventing disease, and regulating sanitation and waste disposal are all in some way an individual responsibility. Health departments can provide educational programs and health-screening fairs, but if the individual does not use what is learned, the programs will not be effective.

CHECK YOURSELF

1. What are the three main functions of the voluntary agencies?
2. Name three functions of the National Health Council.
3. Compare the work of a state health department with that of a local health department.

2. Health Promotion at the National Level

The protection and promotion of people's health and safety is a concern at all levels. Our world is relatively small and interdependent, so the level of wellness in one part of the world can have social and political ramifications in other parts. We are indeed living together on an island, and we are connected together by a mesh of health organizations.

The Department of Health and Human Services

At the national level, the federal government has a major involvement in health care. The national government first became involved in public health in 1798. At that time, Congress authorized a federally operated marine hospital to care for American merchant seamen. Today, the involvement has expanded considerably.

You have probably heard of the Department of Health, Education, and Welfare, better known as HEW. HEW began as the Department of Health, established in 1953. At that time, there was a division called the Public Health Service that was concerned with practically every phase of the health of Americans. In a reorganization in 1979, a separate department of education was established. The health department was renamed and became the **Department of Health and Human Services**.

The Department of Health and Human Services has four main divisions:

1. **Health-Care Financing Administration**. This division is concerned with the Medicare and Medicaid programs. **Medi-**

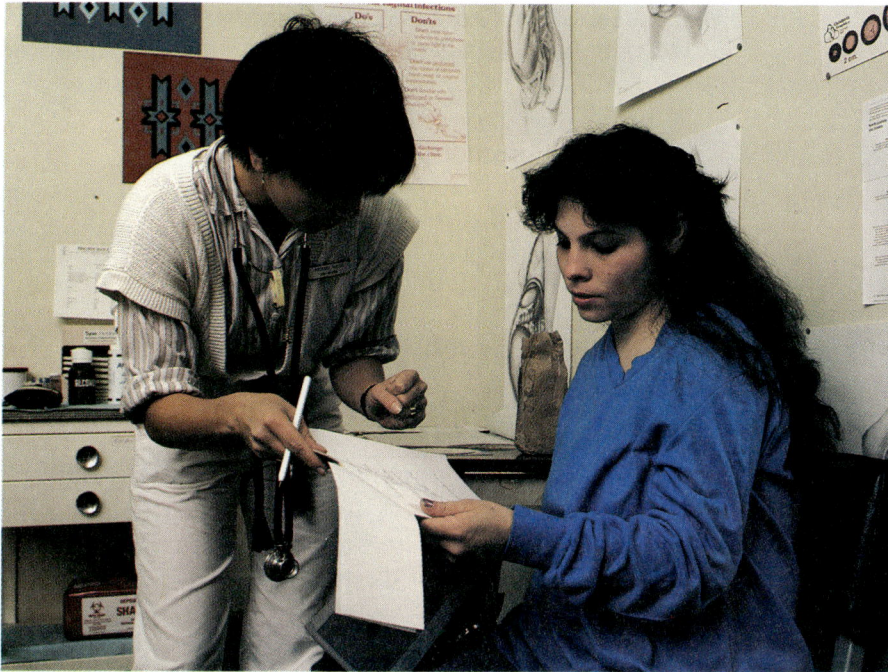

care *is the federal system of financing medical care for people 65 years of age and older.* **Medicaid** *provides health care for many people who could not otherwise afford it.*

2. **Office of Human Development Services**. This office is in charge of programs for groups with special needs, such as handicapped people, American Indians, and residents of rural areas.

3. **Social Security Administration**. This unit is responsible for federal social insurance programs.

4. The **Public Health Service** is the fourth division, and it consists of six agencies:

   ■ The **Health Services Administration** is responsible for community health and family-planning services. This includes maternal and child health programs.

   ■ The **Health Resources Administration (HRA)** supports education and training programs for health workers. It also conducts health services research and publishes health statistics.

   ■ The **Food and Drug Administration (FDA)** enforces laws that ensure the purity, effectiveness, and truthful labeling of food, drugs, and cosmetics.

   ■ The **Alcohol, Drug Abuse, and Mental Health Administration** is in charge of programs for the prevention of alcoholism, drug addiction, and mental illness. It is concerned with finding improved treatment and rehabilitation methods.

- The **National Institutes of Health (NHI)** supervise a broad range of biomedical research and provide funds for training research scientists. The NHI has 12 sections:
  - aging;
  - allergy and infectious diseases;
  - arthritis;
  - metabolism and digestive diseases;
  - cancer;
  - child health and human development;
  - dental research;
  - environmental health science;
  - eye;
  - general medical science;
  - heart, lung, and blood;
  - neurological and communicative disorders and stroke.
- The **Centers for Disease Control (CDC)**, based in Atlanta, Georgia, administers a national program for the prevention and control of disease. The CDC provides health information and conducts research to track down sources of epidemics. The CDC also helps to train doctors in **epidemiology** (ep-uh-dee-mee-**aul**-uh-jee), the *study of the causes, spread, and control of disease*. The CDC also works with local and state agencies to develop immunization services and programs.

CHECK YOURSELF

1. List the four divisions of the Department of Health and Human Services.
2. Name four areas of concern that the National Institutes of Health supervise.
3. What is the function of the Centers for Disease Control?

3. Health Promotion at the International Level

The best known international health promotion organization is the **World Health Organization (WHO)**, a United Nations' agency. The primary concerns of the WHO include providing health care and addressing the health problems of the poor and underdeveloped countries of Asia, Africa, and Latin America. The WHO provides communities with doctors and other health specialists, medicines, and supplies to combat the problems of disease and malnutrition. It is probably the most influential international organization, besides the International Red Cross, in the health field today.

WHO doctors are working in the jungles of the Amazon to eliminate disease.

Smallpox Elimination

This organization also tries to prevent the spread of disease. One of the WHO's greatest victories came in 1980 when the organization announced it had successfully eliminated smallpox. This came after the WHO started a worldwide vaccination campaign in 1960.

Smallpox had plagued countries for centuries and was the first disease in history to be completely conquered. But because it is no longer a threat, people have become lax. Some smallpox cases have been reported recently. These sprang up because the people had not been vaccinated.

Health for All

Presently, the WHO's theme and emphasis is "Health for All by the Year 2000." A major part of this worldwide effort centers on health education. But the WHO is continuing its fight against disease. It is now concentrating on six diseases—measles, tetanus (**tet**-un-us), whooping cough (pertussis) (purr-**tus**-us), polio, diphtheria (dif-**thir**-ee-uh), and tuberculosis—that presently kill 3.5 million children a year and cripple hundreds of thousands more throughout the world.

All of these diseases can be prevented by vaccination. In the developed countries, this largely has been done. The WHO is concentrating on children in Africa, Asia, and Latin America. Since it set its goal in 1974, the WHO has continued a steady vaccination program. Many officials think that by the end of the 1990s it will be successful—epidemics of the six diseases will be prevented.

Ethiopian children are being vaccinated by a doctor.

Many countries have joined in the crusade and have acted swiftly. In 1984, Columbia vaccinated 40% of its children, bringing the country's immunized child population to 80%. China vaccinated 85% of its children by 1988. India plans to immunize all of its children by the early 1990s. In 1985, Turkey vaccinated more than 80% of its children, following Columbia's example.

The WHO estimates that this program will cost $5 billion, but the vaccination program will not stop with the six diseases now being focused on. Research is being done on a vaccine for malaria, chronic diarrhea, and hepatitis B. Scientists are also experimenting on the development of a one-shot virus by planting many vaccines on a single virus.

CHECK YOURSELF

1. What is the WHO?
2. What are the six diseases that the WHO is presently trying to eliminate?
3. What other diseases or conditions is the WHO working to eliminate?

CHAPTER 25 Review

CHAPTER SUMMARY

- Organizations and agencies at the local, state, national, and international levels work to promote community health.
- Voluntary health agencies provide an invaluable service in a specific health area. They educate the public, fund research, and assist people who have health problems.
- Local and state health departments cooperate with federal agencies to promote the health of the people.
- At the national level, the Department of Health and Human Services is the umbrella organization for all of the federal health agencies.
- The best-known international health organization is the World Health Organization.

REVIEWING WHAT YOU LEARNED

1. Name four voluntary health agencies. What are two of the primary functions of such agencies?
2. What are three main concerns of a state health department?

3. What are five responsibilities of a local health department?
4. What are the four main divisions of the Department of Health and Human Services. What does each do?
5. Name three agencies of the Public Health Service. What does each one do?
6. What is the function of the World Health Organization?
7. Why would the United States not receive very much direct help from the WHO?
8. What are three national health-care agencies? What does each do?

APPLYING WHAT YOU LEARNED

1. Select a developed country other than the United States and find out how its health care compares with that of the United States.
2. Write or call a voluntary health agency. Find out how many people it services and what type of work its volunteers do.

National Health Council
carcinogenic
Department of Health and Human Services
Health-Care Financing Administration
Medicare
Medicaid
Office of Human Development Services
Social Security Administration
Public Health Service
Health Services Administration
Health Resources Administration (HRA)
Food and Drug Administration

Alcohol, Drug Abuse, and Mental Health
 Administration
National Institutes of Health
Centers for Disease Control (CDC)
epidemiology
World Health Organization (WHO)

PUTTING VOCABULARY TO USE

On a separate piece of paper, write the following statements. Then after each statement, put the name of the organization or term it describes. Refer to the chapter vocabulary list for help.

1. Assists in identifying and solving national health problems.
2. Study of the causes, spread, and control of disease.
3. Emphasizing "Health for All by the Year 2000."
4. Replaced what was formerly Health, Education, and Welfare?

5. Made up of 12 sections, conducting a broad range of research.
6. Concerned with Medicare and Medicaid programs.
7. Supervises medical research.
8. Offers programs for groups with special needs.
9. Administers national program for disease control.
10. Provides health care for the elderly.

3. Select one of the voluntary agencies listed on page 446 and research its origins: How and why did it develop? Write a one-page report on your findings.
4. Find out what disease at present is the primary concern of the CDC. What is the CDC doing to combat it?
5. Make a list of things you can do to contribute to community health. Compare your list with the lists of your classmates. Then develop a composite list. Write a statement summarizing the individual's responsibility in promoting community health.

6. Find out the immunization requirements for school children in your state.

FOCUS ON WELLNESS

The responsibility for the health of a community, though promoted by local, state, and national programs, ultimately rests with the individuals of the community. *I do my part to promote the health of my community by . . .*

U N I T

8

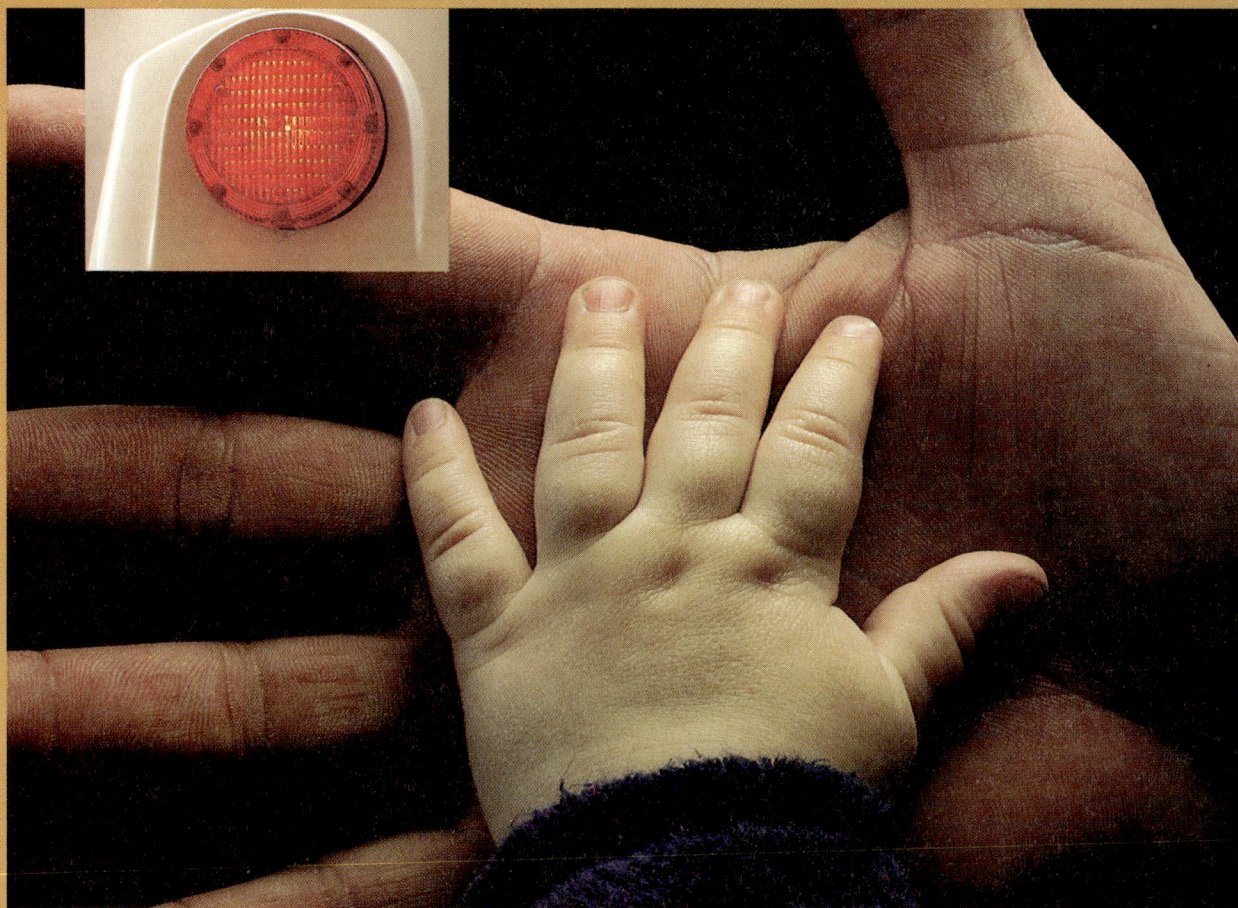

SAFETY
AND
EMERGENCY
CARE

Safety and Your Well-Being

"Over 80% of *all* accidents could be prevented."

If this statement is true, have you ever wondered why
we continue to have so many accidents? It is not because
we are lacking safety rules or knowledge of safety behavior.

After studying this chapter, you will be able to:
- explain how one's attitudes affect one's safety behavior,
- identify reasons why people take unnecessary risks,
- outline the costs of accidents,
- explain what is meant by the accident chain,
- describe appropriate safety behavior on the road, at home, and at recreation,
- list actions to take to prevent falls, poisoning, electrical shock, and fire,
- identify safety procedures for baby-sitting.

You have probably learned about safety ever since you began to crawl! Think about it. The commands probably took the form of "Don't touch that," or "Don't go out in the street," or "Don't put that in your mouth." The warnings were all to protect you from harm. Think of your present knowledge of safety rules. You have learned pedestrian safety, home and fire safety, and motor vehicle safety. Yet, with all of this knowledge, you are still overly prone toward accidents. Why?

Safety Attitudes and Behavior

Safety and accident prevention depends on each of us developing a safety-conscious attitude. The dictionary defines **attitude** as *a state of mind, behavior, or conduct regarding some matter shown to others through opinion or action*. **Safety consciousness** means *being aware of safety*.

So a **safety-conscious attitude** is one in which *you believe that you can prevent accidents by putting into action the rules you know*. Believing in prevention and acting according to this belief are the key.

Taking Risks

A **risk** is defined as a *chance of encountering danger or harm*. Of course, our environment is full of risks. However, much of our **behavior**, *our actions or reactions in relation to our environment*, can either reduce or increase our risk of accidents. Taking unnecessary risks not only threatens our personal safety but the safety of those around us. Have you ever been injured or involved in an accident because someone else acted in an unsafe manner?

How could the risks in this photo have been reduced by the parents?

Care must be taken during recreation. We are twice as likely to have an accident when we are enjoying ourselves.

Risks and Your Attitudes

Taking risks relates directly to our attitudes about safety. Some people take unnecessary risks to show off or to look important or to be like the crowd. Have you ever been in a situation in which someone coaxed you into doing something? Suppose a group of your friends decide to swim in a lake at night. They are good swimmers, and you are not. You stay on shore. They start to tease you, telling you the water is shallow, nothing will happen. What do you do? In situations like this, it takes strength to resist the taunts and to practice safe behavior.

People in dangerous work or sports do not take unnecessary risks. Skilled mountain climbers, balloonists, stunt flyers, sky divers, race car drivers, fire fighters, and police officers use all of the proper safety equipment and know their skill capabilities. They recognize the risks and respect the challenges involved in what they are doing. But they go to great effort not to *add* to the possibility of accident and injury.

Risks and How You Feel

How you feel also affects the risks you take. Have you ever been in a hurry to get somewhere? Did you practice safety on your way? When people are in a hurry or tired, they tend to get careless. Safety becomes less of a priority, and accidents are more likely to occur.

Did you know you are four times as likely to have an accident when you are depressed? You are twice as likely to have an accident when you are in an excited state. Anytime you are distracted or are not concentrating totally on what you are doing, you are adding to your chances of an accident.

The High Price of Accidents

Have you ever thought of the costs involved in accidents? If you have ever been involved in and injured in an accident, you are probably well aware of such costs. The loss of lives, pain, and disability from injuries are the most obvious and the highest costs. But let's look at other less apparent costs.

The Case of Jack and Jessica

Jack picked up Jessica after work, and they headed for the track. Both were on the high school track team, and Jessica had qualified for the state track meet. Today, however, they were late. Jack was upset because he had been delayed, and they were going to have to run extra laps if they missed the team meeting. Jack turned the corner too fast and never saw the truck that was stopped in the middle of the road. He put on the brakes, but could not avoid the collision.

Being in a hurry cost Jack and Jessica more than time. Although neither was seriously hurt, both were shaken up and sore. Jessica had to have several stitches in her head. Both had to miss one day of school, a week of work, and a week of practice. Their losses included earning power (money), physical fitness, and skill maintenance. In addition, Jack was responsible for damage to both vehicles and for towing expenses. He had insurance to cover the damage, but he will likely experience an increase in his insurance premiums to cover the damage because of his accident. His accident may even contribute to higher insurance rates for other people in the area in which he lives.

And what about the emotional costs that are not so easily measured? Jack and Jessica experienced a high level of stress as a result of the accident. They both now have additional stressors that they must handle. Both of their families were upset and inconvenienced. For a month, Jack lost his privilege to use the car. In addition, he has to attend Defensive Driving School, which means missing work on Saturday. Jessica will still compete in the state meet but will have to work harder to get prepared.

The experience of Jack and Jessica is not an uncommon one. Such events complicate not only their lives but the lives of others around them. If the accident is serious enough, these lives may be permanently changed. The waste from accidents like this one is needless because it could have been prevented.

CHECK YOURSELF

1. What does it mean to be safety conscious?
2. What is the relationship between safety attitudes and safety behaviors?
3. Why do people take unnecessary risks?
4. List the potential "costs" of an accident and the people who "pay" for accidents in some way.

2. Accidents Don't Just Happen

In studying accidents over the years, one important point has become clear—accidents don't just happen. In fact, most accidents follow a characteristic pattern. Let's look at an example and examine the characteristics of accidents.

Five Characteristics of Accidents

Five characteristics are present in almost all accidents. They are called the *situation,* the *unsafe habit,* the *unsafe act*, the *accident,* and the *injuries,* and make up an **accident chain**.

- **The situation**. You and a group of friends are driving to a concert. You are excited and anticipate having a good time. The road on which you are traveling is busy with others going to the same place. All of the people, in general, are rushing to get there.
- **The unsafe habit**. As a driver, you generally tailgate; that is, you follow too closely the car ahead of you.
- **The unsafe act**. This particular occasion is no different. While caught up in the excitement of getting to the concert, you again are driving too close to the car in front of you.
- **The accident**. You are on a main road and there are no lights, so the chances of the car in front of you having to slow down or stop are remote. But suddenly an animal darts out in front of the car

Auto accidents are the most frequent type of accident in the United States.

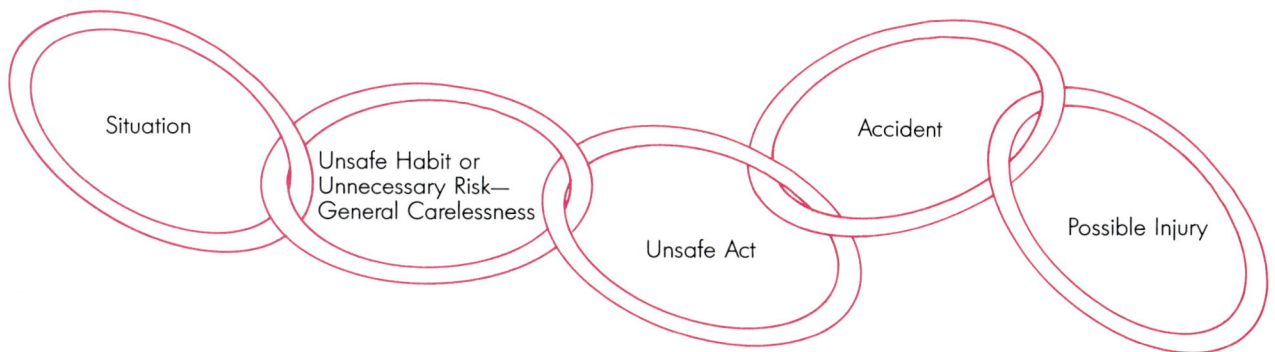

In the five characteristics of the accident chain, consider the first three as the links and the last two as the results.

ahead of you, and the driver slams on the brakes. You cannot react fast enough, and you slam into the car ahead of you.

- **The injuries**. Several people in both cars suffer minor cuts and whiplash from the jarring and sudden stop.

In the five characteristics of accidents, consider the first three as links in an accident chain and the last two as the result. If you break any one of the accident chain links, you prevent the accident.

You can see how you could have eliminated or controlled this accident. When you recall an accident, it seems so simple to see what you could have done to prevent it.

The safety-conscious person is alert to the risks of a given situation. The safety-conscious person breaks the accident chain by changing the situation, acting in a safe manner, or reducing or avoiding the risk.

Breaking the Auto Accident Chain

Over 80 million people—30% of our population—are injured as a result of accidents every year. Motor vehicles account for over half of these accidents. Over 55,000 people die each year in motor vehicle-related accidents. For people between the ages of 15 and 24, automobile accidents are the leading cause of death.

Eliminate Speeding

The majority of accidents and fatalities among young people do not involve a second vehicle. They involve overturned vehicles, a vehicle running off the road, or collisions with fixed objects, such as trees, light poles, and concrete restraining walls. They often involve high rates of speed.

Speed kills—this is another plain and simple message, yet one that people often ignore. By following posted speeds, you reduce your risk of accident and reduce your risk of injury if you are in an accident.

Driving the speed limit offers some other benefits. You do not have to worry about getting caught in a speed trap or getting a ticket. You can enjoy the ride more, thus reducing—even eliminating—a potential stressor. You save gasoline and wear on tires.

Use Seat Belts

How can we prevent motor vehicle accidents and fatalities? For every 100 young people killed in a motor vehicle accident last year, 80 would still be alive if they had been wearing a seat belt. Without question, seat belts save lives.

If you use your seat belt regularly, you are practicing prevention. If you do not, examine the reasons why you take such a risk. Seat belts are so important that states are now making it mandatory to use them.

Do Not Drink and Drive

One-half of all automobile fatalities involve drivers who are under the influence of alcohol. Drinking while driving is discussed in greater detail in Chapter 12. Yet it is such an important problem that it needs to be mentioned here because of its seriousness and direct relation to safety and health. If people observed the law and did not drink while driving, we could prevent millions of accidents.

You have a serious responsibility here since you not only risk your well-being but that of anyone else who may be on the road. The message is simple, but we cannot overemphasize it: If you drive, don't drink.

We can find numerous other ways to break the accident chain by using auto safety. Taking a driver's education or a defensive driving course can help you develop driving skills and learn to anticipate problems before they occur, but only if you apply what you have learned.

More and more people are becoming aware of the dangers of combining drinking and driving.

A Health Student Asks . . .

HEADPHONES WHILE DRIVING OR CYCLING

"I just got a set of radio headphones, but I have heard there might be some risks in wearing them. Is this true? If so, what are the risks?"

Health experts have expressed concern that radio headphones, if played too loudly and for long periods of time, could cause hearing damage. Follow these guidelines for safe listening:

- While wearing headphones, you should be able to carry on a conversation.
- Loud noises—car horns, shouts—should be audible.
- Never wear headphones while driving or riding a cycle.

Besides potential ear damage, headphones can be a distraction. Thus, you increase your risk of an accident. For this reason, some communities are passing restrictions that do not allow drivers, cyclists, or joggers to use them. The headphone users can turn them on when in parks and on sidewalks, but not when crossing intersections.

Headphones or not—don't forget your safety rules.

Safety Behavior Is Important

- Drunk drivers do about $18 million worth of damage every day in the United States.
- Hot weather kills an average of 450 Americans a year, snowstorms kill 97, and floods kill 83.
- According to the National Heart and Lung Institute, 350,000 people a year die from heart attacks before getting to the hospital. These victims wait, on an average, three hours before deciding to get help.
- One American dies in an accident every 5.5 minutes and one is injured every 20 seconds.
- Fire daily kills 32 people and damages 1,855 homes and 434 apartments.

Bicycle Safety

Bicycles are an excellent means of transportation. They use body power rather than mechanical power. They provide a good means of exercise, do not use gasoline, and do not pollute. However, bicycles are involved in more injury accidents that any other mobile product. About 80% of all bicycle accidents are related to either the cyclist or the environment.

Bicycle riders are very exposed to risks. What are some of them? What can be done to reduce these risks?

Main Causes of Bicycle Accidents

The main causes of bicycle accidents are:

- loss of control,
- entangled clothing in the bicycle,
- a foot slipping off the pedal,
- mechanical problems,
- collisions with another bicycle or a car.

Four out of every five collisions between bicycles and cars are caused by cyclists disregarding traffic rules. The most frequent error that the cyclist makes is riding on the wrong side of the road, against the flow of traffic.

Safe Cycling Guidelines

Here are National Safety Council guidelines for safe cycling:

- Always yield the right-of-way—you won't win a contest with a car.
- Keep to the right, close to the curb. Many streets have marked bicycle lanes. Ride in a straight, single-file line.
- Watch for parked cars pulling into traffic and for car doors that open suddenly.
- Except when signaling, hands should be on the handlebars at all times.

Motorcycle Safety

Motorcyclists are five times more likely to be killed in an accident than people traveling in a car. The reasons seem obvious. The motorcyclist is virtually unprotected. Regardless of whose fault the accident is, the cyclist loses.

Besides following safety rules on the road, cyclists increase their protection by wearing a safety helmet and proper clothing.

Safe motorcycle equipment includes a helmet with face shield, a jacket with sleeves, gloves, goggles, heavy pants, and boots.

1. What are the five characteristics of an accident?
2. What are three ways that people can prevent auto accidents and fatalities?
3. Why is there such emphasis on *not* drinking and driving?
4. Why is the motorcyclist's risk of injury so much greater than the car passenger's? What can be done to lower the risk?

3. Making the Home a Safe Living Area

Home should be the one place where we can go and feel safe and secure. Yet every year thousands of people are injured as a result of home accidents. Most are the result of **hazards**—*objects carelessly placed or in poor repair.*

Home accidents cause more disabling injuries than any other type of accident. One in every five accidental deaths occurs in the home, with the majority of victims dying from falls and fire. Others die from poisoning, drowning, suffocation, firearms, and electricity.

Electricity

Shocks from electrical appliances can kill. Every year electric shock kills more than 1,000 people and starts almost 150,000 fires.

If you become part of the circuit that an electric current travels, you will be shocked. You become part of the circuit when you touch an exposed wire while you are "grounded." The current can then pass through you to the ground.

Precautionary Measures

Here are some precautions you should take when using home electrical appliances and power tools. (See Chapter 27 for first-aid procedures in case of electric shock.)

1. Anytime anything seems to be wrong with an appliance or power tool, disconnect it immediately.
2. Never touch plumbing or metal and an electrical appliance or tool at the same time.
3. Inspect cords occasionally for signs of dried and/or cracked insulation. Replace frayed cords. Cords should not be placed under a carpet because they can be walked on and damaged.
4. Disconnect appliances by pulling on the plug, not on the cord.

Overloaded sockets are a prime cause of electrical fires in the home.

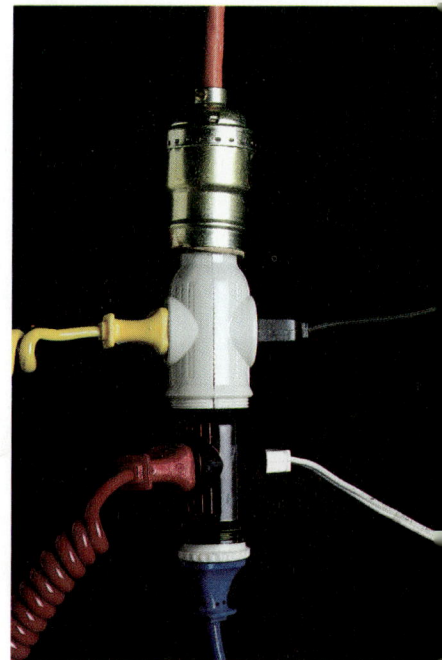

5. Never use an electrical appliance or power tool if your body, clothing, or the floor is wet. This includes hair dryers, radios, and electrical music equipment.
6. Call a trained electrician rather than try to make complicated repairs yourself.

First Aid for Electrical Shock

When electrical current passes through body tissue, heat is created and internal burns result. The current may paralyze the nerves and muscles that control respiration and circulation. Unconsciousness and death can result. On the next page are steps to take:

On the next page are steps to take:

LIFE MANAGEMENT SKILL

Correcting Dangerous Situations in Your Home

Review the *Danger Areas in the Home* given in the Health Update. What specific situations need to be corrected in your home? Make a list and give it to your parents for reference.

HEALTH UPDATE   HEALTH UPDATE   HEALTH UPDATE

Danger Areas in the Home

Hallway and Stairway
- Clear of objects
- Well-lit
- Railing on stairs
- Nonskid throw rugs
- No loose or turned carpet

Medicine Cabinet High on Wall
- All poisons and medicines out of reach of children
- All poisons and medicines well-marked
- Old medicines safely discarded

Bathroom
- No electric appliances near water
- Nonskid tape in bathtub
- Nonskid rug on floor
- No aerosols (hair spray, deodorants) near open fire
- Electrical cords in good condition

Kitchen
- Spills wiped up immediately
- Hands dried before operating electrical appliances according to manufacturer's directions

- Loose garments not worn near sources of flames
- Chemicals stored in a high place
- Fire extinguisher nearby
- Sharp and heavy utensils out of reach of children

Family Room
- Matches, lighters, cords out of children's reach
- Glass doors clearly marked
- Emergency numbers next to phone
- Nonskid rugs

Garage
- Tools kept in good condition and properly stored
- Spills or grease cleaned up
- All flammables properly stored
- Hoses and cords rolled up and stored out of the way

General
- Smoke detector on each floor
- Firearms unloaded and out of reach of children
- Fire-escape plan posted in a very visible place

1. You must break the chain of current. It is not safe to touch someone who is in contact with an electric current until you stop the current. If you do, you too will be shocked. Unplug the appliance or shut off the power at the switch box.
2. Your next most important consideration is to check for breathing. If the victim is not breathing, begin mouth-to-mouth respiration.
3. Next, check for a pulse; if there is none, begin to administer CPR. (See Chapter 28 for information.)
4. Once the breathing and pulse are stable, check for burns. You may also need to treat the victim for shock.

Fire Safety

Do you know what it takes to have a fire? That may seem like a very simple question. But think about it. What has to be present in order for a fire to take place? This is a very important set of principles, because unless these conditions are all present at the same time, there can be no fire. By understanding that *fuel*, *heat*, and *air* must be present to make a fire burn, you have the basis of fire prevention. If you take any one of the three away, you prevent a fire.

The *fuel* can be carelessly stored rags, wood, coal, oil, gas, or paper. There still won't be a fire unless there is some *heat* to make the fuel burn. This could be a match, an electrical wire, or a cigarette. Still, there will not be a fire unless there is *air*. The oxygen in the air feeds and fans the flames. Remove any one of these elements and there can be no fire.

The screen on this fireplace should be closed in order to keep sparks and cinders from flying into the room.

Fire-Safety Precautions in the Home

The majority of home fires could be prevented. Check the following fire-safety tips for the home.

Space Heaters

1. Every gas or fuel-burning space heater must be properly vented, unless the unit is specifically designed to be un-vented. In that case, make certain that a door or window is opened slightly in the room in which the unit is operating.
2. All space heaters should have tip-over shutoff switches and protective grilles around heating elements.
3. Use only extension cords that match the electrical require-ments of electric space heaters.
4. Never put a portable heater in a bathroom or near a sink.
5. To protect against carbon monoxide poisoning, use only space heaters with oxygen-depletion shutoff systems.

Matches and Lighters

1. Keep matches and lighters where children cannot get them.
2. Fill lighters in a well-ventilated area, away from flames. Avoid spills, or wipe them up immediately.

Improperly stored flammable liquids are a fire danger to all, as well as a health danger to young children.

Flammable Liquids

1. Store gasoline outside the house, and well away from ignition sources.
2. Store gasoline *only* in containers designed specifically for this purpose.
3. Never use gasoline for cleaning clothing, machine parts, or anything else.
4. Use only fluids labeled "Charcoal Starter" to light outdoor grills. Never throw *any* flammable liquid on a burning or smoldering fire.
5. Observe good safety rules with these flammable liquids:

Gasoline	Rubbing alcohol
Nail polish remover	Camp stove or lantern fuel
Kerosene	Paints and thinners
Furniture polish and wax	Paint strippers
Lighter fluid	Charcoal lighter fluid

Upholstered Furniture

1. Keep upholstered furniture away from stoves, ranges, space heaters, and fireplaces.
2. Caution smokers in the family against smoking when sitting on upholstered furniture, especially when they are drowsy. The smoking can be a double threat if the smoker is also tak-ing alcohol or medication.

Causes of Fire in the Home

Cause of fire	% of residential fires started
Cooking	18
Smoking	13
Heating	13
Incendiary/suspicious	11
Unknown cause	10
Electrical distribution	7
Appliances	7
Children playing	5
Open flame, spark	5
Other (i.e., fireworks, air-conditioning, flammable liquids, gas, etc.)	10

Clothing

1. Do not wear loose-fitting long sleeves or full skirts around flames or a stove.
2. Thin, lightweight fabrics ignite quicker than heavy, tightly woven fabric like denim.
3. By law, children's sleepwear (up to size 14) *must* be flame-resistant.

Smoke Detectors

The most valuable piece of home fire prevention equipment developed in the past 20 years is the **smoke detector**. It is *a device placed on a ceiling which sounds an alarm if smoke passes into it*. Smoke detectors are economical to buy, easy to install, and are now required by law to be installed in the important rooms of the home.

The smoke detector has saved thousands of lives since its use began in the 1960s.

In Case of Fire

If you are caught in a fire, acting quickly and remaining calm could save your life.

- If a fire starts in a frying pan, put a lid on the fire.
- If it starts in the oven, turn off the oven, and smother the fire with salt. *Never* put water on a grease fire, because it will make the grease spread.
- If your clothes catch on fire, roll on the ground or roll up in a rug or blanket. This smothers the flames. If you remain upright or run, the flames will spread.

Most fire deaths result from smoke inhalation rather than burns. Research indicates that it is not inhaling toxic fumes that kills, but rather not being able to get oxygen. The chemical by-products of combustion combine quickly with oxygen, preventing smoke-inhalation victims from extracting oxygen from the air.

The oxygen and toxic chemicals do not separate until the chemicals come into contact with another molecule with which they can combine. Once they combine, oxygen is released. That is why putting a wet towel over your face is a good idea. The toxic chemicals react with the water, giving you the freed oxygen.

Planning Your Escape

Most fatal home fires occur during the night. It is easy to become disoriented when you first detect smoke or fire. The best protection against injury or death from home fires, then, is to establish escape plans and periodically conduct practice drills.

The following steps are essential to all escape plans:

1. Turn on the bedroom lights.
2. Use a predetermined signal to alert everyone to fire. Smoke detectors, or fire alarms, which should be in every household, will do this job for you. Otherwise, you can use toy whistles, kept in all nightstands.
3. Before opening a closed door during a fire, test for warmth. If the door is warm, do not open it. Escape through a window.
4. Always stay close to the floor in a smoke-filled room. Smoke rises, so there is more oxygen near the floor. You can also see better.
5. Meet outside in a prearranged spot. *Do not* go back into the house.
6. Call the fire department from a neighbor's house. Rescue of a trapped person is safer and usually faster if left to the fire department.

Even these simple steps require advanced planning. You and your family should draw a floor plan. Use arrows to point to two escape exits

A lid is a very useful tool to use in putting out a pan fire.

KEEPING FIT

Safety on the Job

The one area in which there has been a steady decline in accidents and injuries is the workplace. This offers a good example of what awareness and prevention efforts can do. Many companies and businesses have safety programs for their employees. In many places, you will see posters indicating the number of workdays without an accident or injury.

All employees are required by law to meet minimum safety and health standards for their employees. The requirements are a result of the 1970 Occupational Safety and Health Act (OSHA). OSHA inspectors check factories, construction sites, and other work settings to ensure that employers are meeting the standards.

When You Are Left in Charge

Baby-sitting not only provides you with a way to make money but it helps you learn about the behavior of young children. Baby-sitting is a very responsible position. After all, parents are trusting you with one or more of the most important people in their lives. Knowing what to do and not to do can protect you and the children you are responsible for. Here are some hints:

1. Before the parents leave, get the names and phone numbers of the following:

    - where the parents will be,
    - nearby friend, relative, or neighbor,
    - child's doctor,
    - fire department,
    - police department,
    - poison-control center,
    - hospital.

2. Locate all exits.
3. Keep doors and windows locked for the safety of both yourself and the children.
4. Ask the parents what the children can and cannot do, and what time they go to bed.
5. Closely supervise the children. It only takes a couple of seconds for a curious young child to get into serious trouble.
6. Do not open the door for anyone.
7. Do not give any information to callers. Rather than telling a caller the parents are not at home, simply say they cannot come to the phone right now. Offer to take a message.
8. Do not hesitate to call for help or to report anything suspicious.

from each room. You need to plan alternate escape routes in case one is blocked. If an upstairs level is involved, a ladder or a readily available rope coil is essential so that the occupants can escape through windows.

Although the fire department cannot conduct routine inspections of individual homes, they may send you a variety of fire-safety information, upon request.

CHECK YOURSELF

1. What does being "grounded" mean in relation to an electric current?
2. What elements are necessary for a fire to start?
3. Why should a person wear a wet towel over the face when going through smoke?
4. Why should a person stay low to the floor when trying to escape from a fire?
5. List the steps for planning a safe escape from a home fire.

Sports and recreation can be fun. However, if people do not follow some basic safety behaviors, sports and recreation can end in accidents, injury, and even death. Prevention requires planning ahead and taking necessary precautions.

Here are three important points to remember:

1. Know your abilities and limits and stay within them. Many accidents happen when people get overconfident, try to show off, or get talked into trying something they are not able to do.
2. Take the time to properly warm up before and cool down after your activity.
3. Learn the safety rules specific to your activity *before* getting started.

Safety Precautions

Here are some guidelines to follow when you are enjoying yourself in recreational activities.

Pool Swimming

In the United States, it is estimated that 46 million people will take a swim in a pool on a hot summer day. One-half of all swimming pool drownings occur in home pools. Here are some precautions:

- Always swim with someone.
- Learn to swim well.
- Walk around the pool sides.
- If you get a muscle cramp, don't panic; relax and float, rubbing the muscle until it relaxes.
- Avoid running, pushing, and shoving.
- Follow the posted pool rules.

Ocean Swimming

Even in calm waters, think about safety precautions. Obey these rules:

- Swim only when the lifeguards are on duty. More than 80% of ocean drownings occur off unguarded beaches.
- Use the buddy system. Swim while someone watches you. Then watch that person while he or she swims.
- If you are pulled offshore by a high tide, swim on a 45° angle toward shore until you are freed by the current.
- Never dive into unfamiliar water or into shallow breaking waves.

Keep small children away from unattended pools.

Drownproofing

Drowning is a constant danger for all swimmers, no matter how well they swim. One of the most valuable *drowning prevention techniques* that you can know is **drownproofing**. For people who fall overboard or who are left in the water for some reason, this technique can save their lives. Both swimmers and nonswimmers could find drownproofing the difference between life and death.

Basically, the swimmer takes a deep breath, sinks into the water, and breaths the air out slowly. While below the water's surface, the swimmer moves hands up and down while kicking the feet back and forth. This action causes the swimmer to rise to the water's surface. When the swimmer arrives at the surface, he or she is to take another deep breath and repeat the process.

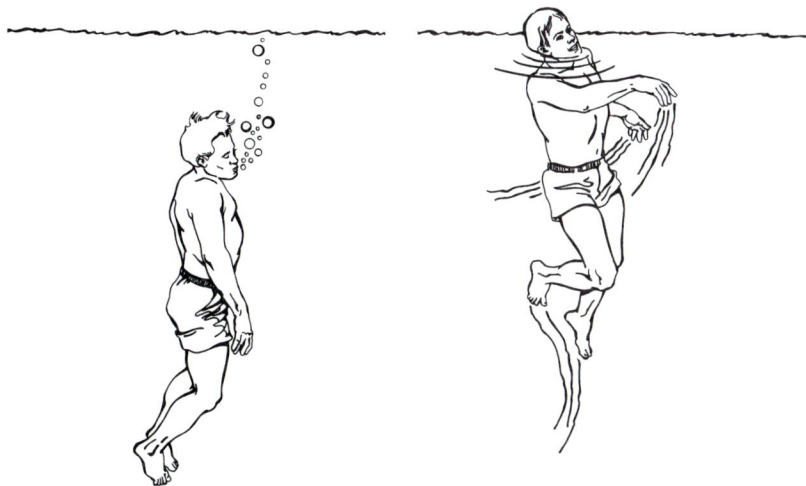

Diving

Sports are second to car accidents as the major cause of spinal injuries resulting in paralysis. Water sports—diving in particular—are major causes. Pay attention to these suggestions:

- *Always* check the water depth before diving.
- If you can't see the bottom through the water, it is safest not to dive.
- Be sure the area is clear of swimmers and floating objects before diving.
- Always dive straight ahead and not to the side of the board.
- Never go down a water slide headfirst.

Roller Skating

- Wear protective equipment—wrist guards, elbow and knee pads, and light gloves.
- As you fall, try to curl up into a ball and roll, staying loose. Tensing up increases your chances of injury.
- Watch for and slow down around pedestrians.
- Keep your speed under control.

Boating

- Learn how to handle a boat or a canoe correctly.
- Only use boats in good condition.
- Observe the load limit of the boat.
- Always wear a life jacket.

Camping

- Stay in specified campsites.
- Always let someone know where you are and when you will return.
- Be knowledgeable about the poisonous plants and insects.
- Have plenty of fresh water.
- Follow the campsite safety rules.

CHECK YOURSELF

1. With regard to sports and recreation, what are three important points to remember?
2. Name two important rules to remember while ocean swimming.
3. Name two important rules to remember while camping.

CHAPTER 26   Review

CHAPTER SUMMARY

- Accidents are almost always a result of human error, and the majority of accidents could be avoided.
- Prevention requires practicing safety rules, planning ahead, and anticipating problems before they arise.
- Our safety attitudes influence our safety behavior. We can be well aware of safety rules, but if our attitude is "It won't happen to me," or "I'll do it just this once," it is unlikely that we will practice the rules.
- Accidents are very costly.

- Besides the risk of loss of life and personal injury, accidents can have a high emotional price.
- Accident prevention is much less costly and can also be timesaving, since one of the large costs of accidents is loss of time.
- Safety and accidents touch every aspect of daily living: the home, the workplace, and recreation.
- Whether it is auto safety, fire safety, or water safety, or any other aspect of safe living, people should follow the basic rules of safety.
- Generally, it is within the control of the individuals involved to promote safe living and to prevent accidents from occurring.

attitude
safety consciousness
safety-conscious attitude
risk

behavior
accident chain
the situation
the unsafe habit

the unsafe act
the accident
the injuries
accident chain

hazards
smoke detector
drownproofing

PUTTING VOCABULARY TO USE

Give an example of each of the following terms that has some connection with safety:

1. attitude
2. behavior
3. unsafe habit
4. unsafe act
5. risk
6. prevention
7. accident chain
8. situation
9. accident
10. hazard

REVIEWING WHAT YOU LEARNED

1. Describe two examples of appropriate safety behavior while (a) driving, (b) working in the kitchen, (c) baby-sitting, (d) participating in your favorite sport.
2. List two actions that you can take to prevent (a) falls, (b) poisoning, (c) electrical shock, (d) fire in your home.
3. Discuss the accident problem in your community in relation to the following words:
   (a) cost
   (b) waste
   (c) innocent suffering
4. Explain the difference between safe and unsafe risk-taking behavior.
5. How would you describe the general daily behavior of a person who is safety conscious as compared to a person who is accident prone?
6. What are some common features that all accidents share?
7. Describe the links in an accident chain.

APPLYING WHAT YOU LEARNED

1. A congressman has proposed that all cars have a device added to the odometer so that no one can drive more than 55 mph. Write a one-page response to this proposed legislation, based on what you have learned about accident prevention and speed in this chapter.

2. Develop six original slogans for safety. They may be very general or very specific. Now choose your favorite three. If someone asked you to put one slogan on a billboard, which of the three would you choose? Be able to explain why you chose the one you did and why the people viewing it need to *see* it and *believe* it.
3. Using the checklist on home safety in this chapter, make a safety inspection of your own home. Evaluate specific areas and give a general evaluation of the entire home. Draw some conclusions about the safety of your home, based on what you have learned in this chapter.
4. You have been asked to speak to a group of eighth graders on some aspect of safety. Which one would you choose? Why? What three main points would you emphasize in your talk?
5. Certain house plants are poisonous. Find out which ones they are and check your house for those plants. Create a warning label to put on such plants.

FOCUS ON WELLNESS

The home is the place in which we spend most of our time, and yet it is a place in which many potential hazards exist. *I can reduce the hazards of potential accidents in my home by . . .*

Providing First Aid

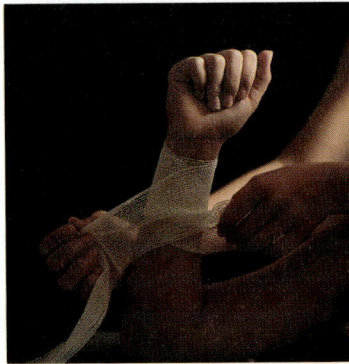

While the main purpose of safety education is to prevent accidents, first aid is concerned with reducing unnecessary suffering and preventing further damage to people involved in accidents. As you learn what to do in the event of an emergency, you can also examine the situation to determine how it could have been prevented.

After studying this chapter, you will be able to:
- define first aid,
- identify the priorities in responding to an emergency,
- differentiate between the types of wounds and know the first-aid treatment for each one,
- describe shock and its treatment,
- describe what to do in case of poisoning,
- tell the difference between poisonous and nonpoisonous snakes in the United States,
- explain procedures for treating snakebites,
- describe proper first-aid techniques for common emergencies,
- list various weather-related emergencies.

First aid, or *emergency care*, is *the immediate temporary care given to a person who has become sick or who has been injured.* First aid takes place until proper medical authority arrives. That could be a mobile emergency ambulance unit, a police officer, the highway patrol, a nurse, a physician, or the fire department.

Administering first aid is a responsible job. You must know what you are doing when you give it. If you do not, more harm can come to the victim. If you do, it can mean the difference between life and death, between temporary and permanent disability.

Knowing how to administer first aid is a valuable skill for anyone.

Priorities in an Emergency

What you do during the first five minutes in an emergency situation can mean the difference between life and death for the victim. Your task, when such a situation faces you, is to act calmly, quickly, and correctly. You have four important priorities to keep in mind. You may have to perform one or all of them:

1. **Rescue promptly**. Your first decision in an emergency situation is whether or not to move the victim. The rule to follow is to move a victim only when it is necessary to save life. For example, you would remove an accident victim from water; a room containing carbon monoxide, smoke, or toxic fumes; or a car that might explode or catch fire.

2. **Check breathing**. The second priority is to be sure the victim has an open airway. Clear the airway, by giving mouth-to-mouth artificial respiration, if necessary. Remember that a person can live only four to five minutes without oxygen. See a description of mouth-to-mouth resuscitation on pages 502–503.

3. **Control severe bleeding**. Your third priority is to control severe bleeding. Severe bleeding will likely be bright red and spurting. You can usually control it by applying direct pressure with the palm of your hand over the wound. If possible, elevate the body part so that it is above the level of the victim's heart. You will learn more about first aid for wounds and severe bleeding later in this chapter.

4. **Give first aid for poisoning**. The fourth emergency priority is to treat poisoning or infection from harmful chemicals. The American Red Cross defines a **poison** as *any substance—solid, liquid, or gas—that tends to impair health or cause death when introduced into the body or onto the skin surface*. We discuss poisons later in this chapter.

After Performing the Priorities

After you have carried out emergency procedures to ensure the victim's safety and life-support systems, you should follow some general procedures to further assist the victim:

- Send someone to summon medical help.
- Keep the victim still; do not let him or her get up or walk around.
- Keep the victim in the position most comfortable and suited to his or her injury or condition.
- Try to provide some privacy, protecting the victim from disturbance and unnecessary handling.
- Keep the victim from getting chilled; cover the victim with a coat or a blanket, if available.
- Loosen constricting clothing, being careful not to pull or jar the neck or spine.
- Look for emergency medical identification, such as a bracelet, pin, necklace, or card in a wallet or purse.
- As best as possible, find out exactly what happened.
- Plan what you are going to do and give the victim a reason for each thing you do. That will encourage the person.
- Reassure and encourage the victim. Part of your task is to keep him or her calm.
- Know and respect *your* own limits and abilities.
- Provide the best possible emergency first-aid care, but avoid further injury or complications.

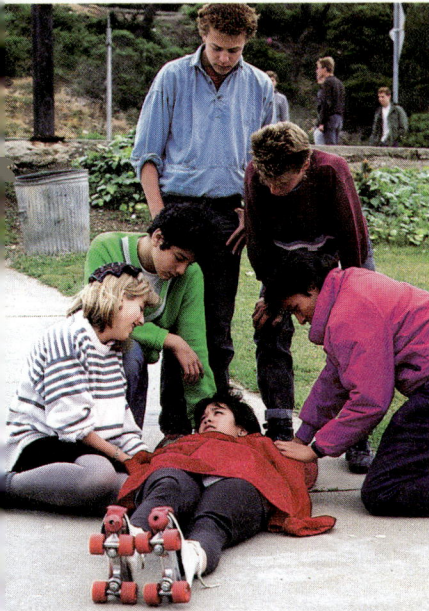

After carrying out any necessary emergency procedures, carry out the secondary procedures.

CHECK YOURSELF

1. What is the job of a first aider?
2. What are the four emergency priorities?
3. When should you move a victim?
4. Define poison.

2. Treating Wounds

Wounds are usually a result of external physical forces. Auto accidents, falls, and mishandling of sharp objects, tools, and weapons are the most common causes of wounds.

Types of Wounds

There are five types of wounds: *abrasions, incisions, lacerations, punctures,* and *avulsions.*

Abrasion (uh-**bray**-zhun)

- Damage to outer layers of skin
- Little or no bleeding
- Danger of infection

Incision (in-**sizh**-un)

- Usually a result of the body's being cut by a knife, glass, or sharp rock
- Bleeding may be heavy
- Deep cuts can damage muscles and nerve tissue

Laceration (las-uh-**ray**-shun)

- Jagged, irregular tearing of skin
- Bleeding may be heavy
- Chances of infection and damage to inner tissue is greater than in the case of an incision

Puncture (**punk**-sher)

- Wound produced by an object piercing the skin (e.g., bullets, pins, nails, splinters)
- Limited external bleeding
- Potential internal damage to organs, internal bleeding
- Possibility of infection increased (for example, **tetanus**—*a serious infection caused by organisms that live in the soil*—may develop)

Avulsion (aah-**vul**-shun)

- A wound that results when tissue is separated from the victim's body
- Occurs in auto accidents, animal bites
- A surgeon *may* successfully reattach the severed body part, so the body part should be sent with the victim to the hospital

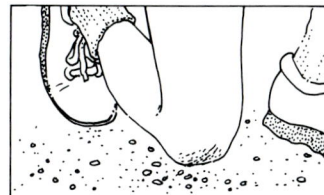

Abrasion

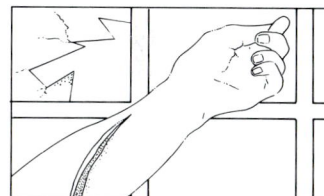

Incision

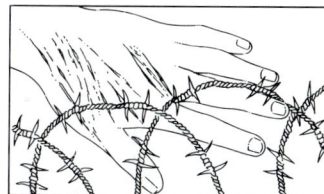

Laceration

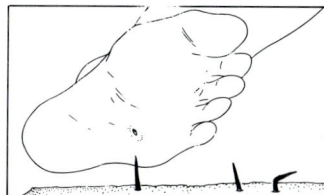

Puncture

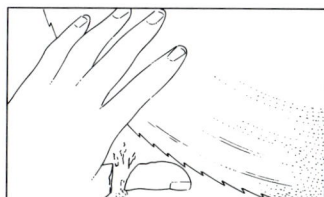

Avulsion

Joseph Lister and Antiseptics

It is 1850 in London. You are in an accident and have a compound fracture of your leg. You are taken to a nearby hospital for treatment. Your chances of surviving are very slim.

The smell of rotten human flesh is overwhelming. Diseases and infections from surgery are more life-threatening than most of the conditions requiring surgery.

One man was responsible for making dramatic changes in hospital care and treatment of surgical cases. Doctor Joseph Lister (1827–1912), though rejected by most doctors, worked for years to convince the medical profession that his theory on germs and disease was correct. He developed the first successful antiseptic to fight germs in wounds caused by accidents or surgery. He also developed internal sutures or "stitches" that were absorbed by the body.

Lister experimented with carbolic acid, applying it to wounds to prevent infection. His first experimental patient died because he remained at home without treatment for several days after his accident. Gangrene —the death of tissue—had already developed before Lister got to him.

However, his second patient—a young boy with a broken leg—received Lister's treatment, and to the amazement of the hospital staff, no infection developed.

Lister was met with hostility by the medical profession. It was not until the Franco-Prussian War in Europe (1870–1871) when, out of desperation, a surgeon tried Lister's methods and was successful, that Lister began receiving some acceptance. In the London hospital where he worked, his patients lived while other doctors' patients were dying. This made the other doctors begin to look more favorably on Lister's great discovery.

First Aid for Wounds

There are four steps in applying first aid to wounds:

1. Stop the bleeding immediately.
2. Protect the wound from contamination and infection.
3. Treat the victim for shock.
4. Seek medical care immediately.

Stop the Bleeding

Direct pressure to the wound is the best method for stopping the bleeding, because it prevents the loss of blood but does not interfere with circulation.

Applying Direct Pressure   Steps for applying direct pressure are:

■ Place a thick, clean cloth over the wound.
■ Place the palm of your hand over the cloth and press firmly.
■ Do not remove the cloth, for this might disturb blood clots that might have formed. If the blood soaks through the cloth, place additional layers of cloth over the first one.
■ Continue direct pressure until the bleeding stops.

Unless the bleeding involves a **fracture** (**frak**-chur)—*a broken bone*—the injured body part should be elevated above the level of the victim's heart. This uses the force of gravity to help slow the flow of blood.

Using the Pressure-Point Technique   If elevation and direct pressure do not stop the bleeding, you may need to use the **pressure-point technique**. This involves *applying pressure to the main artery supplying blood to the affected limb*. By compressing the artery against the body, circulation within the limb is stopped. You should use this technique *in addition* to direct pressure and elevation. In other words, do not stop applying direct pressure to administer the pressure-point technique. See *Health Update*, page 482, for the body's pressure points.

Protect the Wound

Normally, a clean cloth over a wound will help to protect it from **contamination** (kun-tam-uh-**nay**-shun), *the falling of substances into the wound*, and **infection**, *the introduction of harmful germs into the wound*. If a cloth is not available, a coat or any clean covering is better than nothing for the wound.

Treat for Shock

Shock is *a condition that results from a serious depression of the major vital functions*, such as breathing and circulation. Shock can result from injuries involving severe bleeding, heart attack, electrocution, poisoning, burns, or sudden changes of temperature.

You can recognize shock by these signs or symptoms: pale, moist, cold skin; weak or absent pulse; shallow, irregular breathing; and dilated pupils.

Procedures to Follow   The procedures for preventing and treating shock are as follows:

1. Keep the victim lying down.
2. Cover the victim *only* enough to conserve body heat.
3. Get medical help as soon as possible.

The Body's Pressure Points

As we have seen on page 481, the pressure point technique is the application of pressure to a main artery that supplies blood to the injured limb or the head. The main arteries that supply blood to the left and right limbs and the head are:

- the brachial artery, which brings blood to the arms,
- the femoral artery, which brings blood to the legs.
- the common carotid artery, which brings blood to the head.

Pressure points are used when the bleeding does not stop *after* applying direct pressure and elevation.

To place pressure at a pressure point, use your fingers or the heel of your hand. Press the artery toward the bone. This method should lessen the flow of blood. Keep applying direct pressure while you are using the pressure point technique. Slowly release the pressure on the pressure point, but keep applying direct pressure. Resume the technique if the bleeding continues.

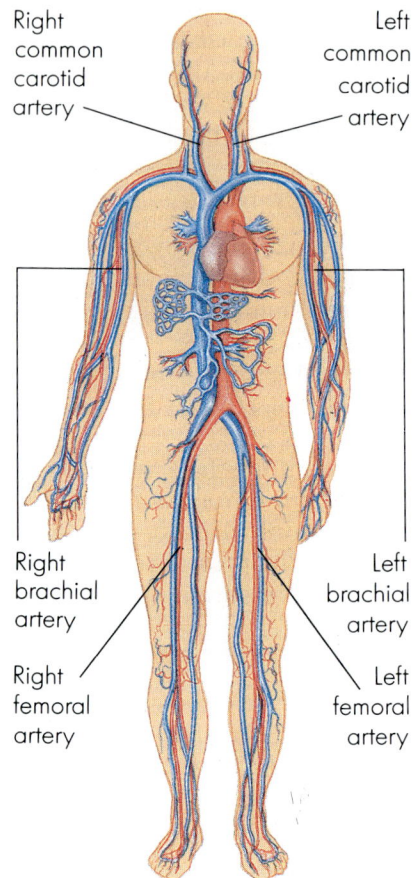

Right common carotid artery

Left common carotid artery

Right brachial artery

Left brachial artery

Right femoral artery

Left femoral artery

You should always place a shock victim on the back with the feet elevated higher than the head, usually about 8 to 12 inches. This position helps to return blood to the heart. If there is a chance of a head injury, do *not* elevate the feet.

Giving the victim fluids can help treat for shock, but you should give them *only* if medical help is delayed. Never give fluids to an unconscious victim or one who is vomiting or nauseated.

You should give the victim about half a glass of water, at room temperature, and preferably with a salt–soda solution. The salt–soda solution is made from 1 teaspoon (5 ml) of salt and one-half teaspoon (2.5 ml) of soda per quart (0.95 l) of water. You can give it to an adult every 15 minutes. Give about half the amount to a child.

Get Medical Help

Seek medical help immediately. Send someone or, if you are alone and near houses, shout for help. Leave the victim and go for help only after you have performed first aid and feel that you have lessened the margin of risk.

CHECK YOURSELF

1. Describe the five types of wounds.
2. What are the four steps in administering first aid for wounds?
3. What is the pressure-point technique?
4. What is shock? Describe its treatment.

3. Poisonings

Children have more frequent accidental poisonings than do adults. Today, most dangerous products come in containers with special tops that are difficult for children to unscrew. Snakebites are common to people of all ages, where certain snakes are found in rural areas. But suburban centers and even city parks are not free from some poisonous snakes.

Poisoning by Swallowing

What do drugs, snakebites, auto exhausts, insect sprays, house cleaners, and many plants all have in common? They are poisonous to the human body. **Poisonous** means that *a chemical substance can cause poor health, permanent injury, or death*. The emergency care that can be given in the first few minutes after poisoning can mean the difference between life and death.

About 3 million accidental poisonings take place each year. As you would imagine, most of those involve children under the age of six.

People can be poisoned by swallowing, inhaling, being bitten, and even by touching, as in the case of poison ivy. About four out of five poison cases are caused by swallowing. Mealtime is the most common time of day for poisonings, when small children get hungry and parents are involved in preparing meals. Swallowing medicines is the most common type of poisoning, but chewing leaves, asbestos, tar, and other materials by children is also common.

Poison-Proofing Your Home

To poison-proof your home:

- check to see that any chemicals, cleaners, or other poisons are clearly marked and completely out of a child's reach,
- properly dispose of any old, unused poisonous substances,
- use the phone book and write the phone number of the nearest poison-control center on a card. Place it next to the phone on the family's emergency number list.

Poison-control centers are found in most large cities and should be called even if you live far from one of them.

Procedures to Follow

Immediate procedures in treating for poisoning by mouth are to:

1. Dilute the poison as quickly as possible.
2. Seek medical advice from a physician or a poison-control center.
3. Maintain breathing and circulation.
4. Get the victim medical assistance without delay.

Dilute the Poison   If the victim is conscious, dilute the poison by giving him or her a glass of milk or water. Save the container of the suspected poison. Check the label for information on poisoning. You can obtain specified directions for what to do by calling a physician or a poison-control center.

Never induce vomiting unless a medical professional specifically advises you to do so. Some poisons, such as strong acids (bleach, toilet bowl cleaner) and a strong alkali (liquid drain cleaner), can do as much damage coming up as going down.

Seek Medical Advice   Call your physician and tell him or her what details you know. Follow the advice that the physician gives.

Since poisoning is such a major problem and the danger to life is great, especially in the first few minutes, a nationwide network of **poison-control centers** has been set up in and around large cities. People can contact these centers 24 hours a day.

When a person calls, the center will provide assistance on what to do

about the poison and where to go for help. Specific treatments for each type of poison are available. The staff person at the control center will look up the poison and tell the caller what to do.

About one out of five victims need hospitalization beyond the treatment. If this is needed, the staff person will tell the caller exactly where to get help and what to do in the meantime. To help the people at the poison-control center, a caller must be able to give the following information:

- the victim's age,
- the victim's weight,
- the name of the product or poison.

Maintain Breathing and Circulation You may have to perform some of the first-aid steps for keeping the victim's breathing and circulation going. You will find them on pages 502–503.

Get Medical Assistance You may not have time to seek medical advice. Dial the 911 phone number and tell the person the problem. Emergency service will then come and take over.

Animal Bites

Bites by any animal, especially if the skin is pierced by its teeth, should be washed with soap and warm water, and covered with a clean dressing or bandage.

Animals can transmit disease to humans, so it is important to observe the victim for unusual signs of illness. All animals should be watched for signs of **rabies—**_a virus disease of the nervous system that eventually causes madness and death._ Dogs, squirrels, and rats are the common carriers of this disease.

If at all possible, capture the animal and call the local health center to see where it is to be brought for examination. If the animal is a squirrel or rat, contact the health center for information on how to proceed. Rabies is treatable if it is caught in time in humans.

Poisoning by Snakebite

Of the hundreds of varieties of snakes, only four poisonous snakes are found in the United States. They are the _rattlesnake_, the _copperhead_, the _water moccasin_ (also called the _cottonmouth_), and the _coral snake_. Over half of the poisonous snakebites occur in Texas, North Carolina, Florida, Georgia, Louisiana, and Arkansas.

Only about 1% of the people bitten by poisonous snakes die. But a large number of deformities and amputations occur due to poisonous snakebites, so they should be considered serious. By knowing what poisonous snakes look like and by avoiding places where they often are located, you can protect yourself.

Poisonous Snakes of the United States

Notice the colored markings. Compare the shape of the head of a poisonous snake with that of a nonpoisonous snake. Notice the *arrowhead* form of the poisonous snake, while the nonpoisonous snake has a more *rounded* head. Rattlesnakes, water moccasins, and copperheads have the arrowhead characteristic.

The coral snake is more rounded, but it too can be distinguished from nonpoisonous lookalikes with this jingle: "Red and yellow—kill a fellow, red and black—poison lack." This simply means that if you spot a snake that has the red and yellow bands together, it is a coral snake and is poisonous. If the red and black bands are together, it is a nonpoisonous snake.

Another way to determine whether the snakebite is poisonous is by the *puncture wounds*. The poisonous bite will also be characterized by extreme pain and rapid swelling.

However, these signs are not present in the case of a coral snakebite. The coral snakebite is characterized by a chewed appearance on the skin. There might only be slight burning and mild swelling.

The venom of a rattlesnake, water moccasin, and copperhead affects the circulatory system, while the venom of the coral snake affects the nervous system.

Rattlesnake

Copperhead

Coral snake

Water Moccasin (Cottonmouth)

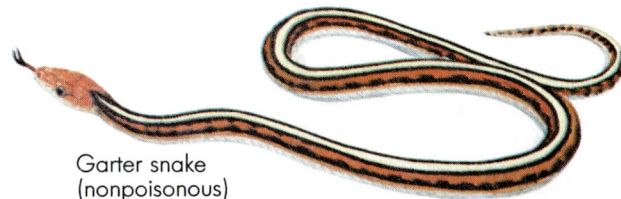

Garter snake (nonpoisonous)

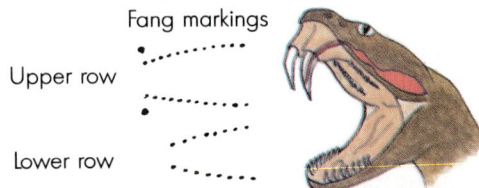

Fang markings

Upper row

Lower row

Poisonous snakebite

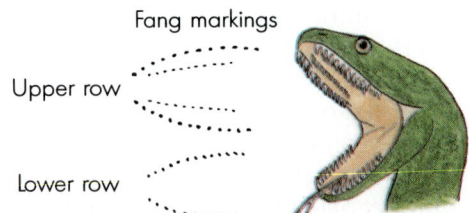

Fang markings

Upper row

Lower row

Nonpoisonous snakebite

Procedures to Follow

Immediate steps for treating poisonous snakebites are as follows:

1. Keep the victim calm.
2. Reduce circulation of the blood through the bite area.
3. Delay the absorption of venom.
4. Maintain respiration and prevent the aggravation of the wound.

Keep the Victim Calm   Your most important step is to get the victim to the hospital. In the meantime, keep the victim as quiet as possible, preferably lying down. The more the victim moves, the greater the possibility of the venom's being circulated. Keep the bitten area at or below the heart level.

Reduce the Circulation of Blood   If you know that you cannot get medical assistance within four hours, or if mild-to-moderate symptoms develop—rapid pulse, nausea and vomiting, shortness of breath, dimness of vision, a tingling sensation, weakness—apply a constricting band 2 to 4 inches (5 to 10 cm) above the bite. Slowing the circulation around the bite will help to localize the poison.

Do not apply a constricting band on a joint, around the head, neck, or trunk. The band should be 1 to 1.5 inches (2.5 to 3.8 cm) wide. It should fit snugly, but not tightly. You should be able to slip your finger underneath it.

If swelling develops, loosen the band. Be sure to check the pulse at the person's lower extremities to make sure the circulation is not cut off.

Delay the Absorption of Venom   Never put anything cold on a poisonous snakebite. Since snakes are coldblooded animals, their venom still works in a cold environment. You should also *not* give the victim alcohol, sedatives, or aspirin. Aspirin can adversely affect blood coagulation.

Maintain Respiration and Prevent Aggravation of the Wound   Make sure that the victim can breath comfortably. Get the victim to a physician as soon as possible, with the least amount of physical activity on his or her part. If the victim is alone, he or she should walk slowly and rest periodically, in order to keep blood circulation down to a minimum.

KEEPING FIT

Snakebite Prevention

Prevention is the best policy to follow with regard to snakes and snakebites. The following preventive measures will reduce your chances of being bitten:

- Do not keep poisonous snakes as pets.
- Do not disturb snakes.
- Avoid snake-infested areas or habitats where snakes are usually found.
- If it is necessary to enter snake-infested areas, wear protective clothing (mid-calf boots, long trousers of thick material, and mid-forearm gloves).
- Try to give advance warning of your presence by prodding the ground with a stick or by making noise.
- Never try to surprise or corner a snake.
- Do not reach blindly into holes, such as gopher holes, or onto rocky ledges.
- Do not disturb old wood or rock piles, and do not search around abandoned buildings.

CHECK YOURSELF

1. What are the primary procedures in treating poisoning by mouth?
2. What information do you need to give the poison-control center?
3. What are the characteristics for identifying the four poisonous snakes in the United States?
4. What are the first-aid procedures for treating poisonous snakebites?

4. More Common Emergencies

For each of the situations below, write down the steps you would take in administering first aid. Be specific in identifying what you would do:

1. You are baby-sitting; the little boy you are watching gets a nosebleed.
2. You are walking in a park and get stung by a bee. You can see the stinger in your arm.
3. Your friend slips going out the door and sprains his ankle. You are the only person around.
4. You are fixing breakfast and spill hot grease on your hand. Blisters begin to appear.
5. You and your friend are doing homework together when, for no apparent reason, he faints.
6. You are mowing the lawn and a piece of debris flies in your eye. Your eye begins to water, but the object does not come out.
7. Your little brother falls off a chair. As he hits the floor, landing on his arm, you hear a loud snap.
8. You have been exercising outside in the heat and begin to get painful heat cramps.

As you read this section, check your answers. Although these situations may not be life-threatening, proper first aid can avoid further injury or complications.

Apply a cold pack to a sprain.

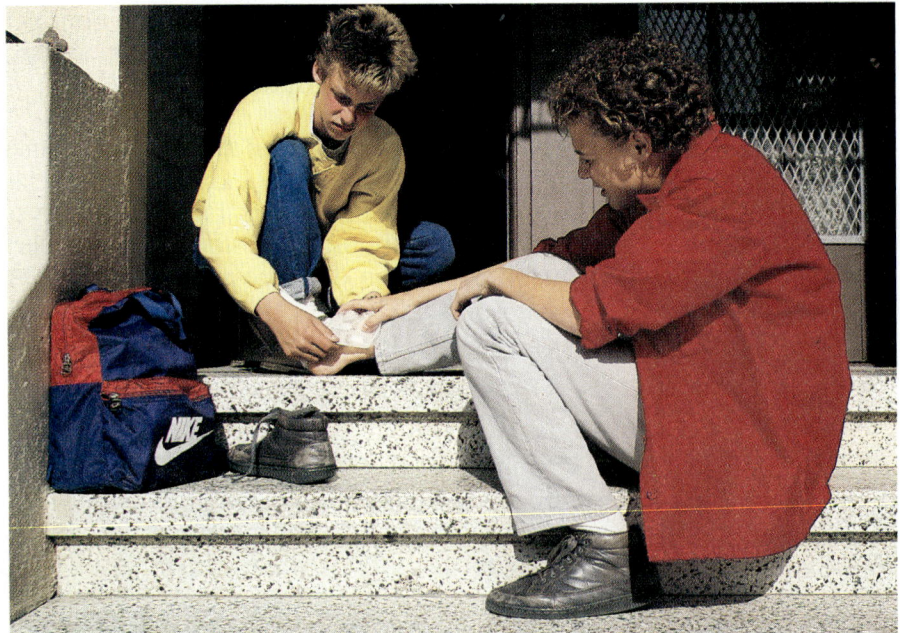

Nosebleeds

1. Keep the person quiet. Walking, talking, and blowing the nose may cause an increase in bleeding.
2. Place the person in a sitting position, leaning forward. You do not want to tilt the head back because the person may choke.
3. Apply direct pressure by pressing on the bleeding nostril.
4. Apply a cold towel to the person's nose and face.
5. If bleeding does not stop with these measures, insert a small, clean piece of gauze just inside one or both nostrils and apply pressure on the nose. Do not force anything up the nose.
6. If bleeding continues, seek medical help.

Bee Stings

1. Use a flat object, like a piece of cardboard, and scrape against the stinger until you pull out the venom sac. Do not try to pull out the stinger with tweezers. You will simply squeeze the venom into the skin, causing more pain.
2. Wash the area thoroughly with soap and water.

Sprains

1. Do not allow the victim to walk.
2. Elevate the foot to help reduce swelling. Swelling produces greater disability than does the actual injury.
3. Apply *cold* packs. Cold slows the swelling, while heat makes swelling worse.

Burns

Burns are classified according to the degree of skin damage involved:

- **First-degree burns** result from overexposure to sunlight, contact with hot objects, or scalding. Only the epidermis, the outer layer of the skin, is involved, and healing is usually rapid.
- **Second-degree burns** result from very deep sunburn and contact with hot liquids. They are more painful, and blisters form in the burn area. This type of burn destroys the epidermis and part of the dermis.
- **Third-degree burns** can be caused by flames, burning clothing, immersion in hot water, and electricity. Both the epidermis and dermis are destroyed. Initially little pain occurs since the nerve endings are damaged.

First Aid for First- and Second-Degree Burns First aid for first- and second-degree burns includes the following:

1. Submerge the burned area in cold water. Cold water helps to lower the skin temperature. *Never* put oil on a burn, because it holds the heat of the burn in the skin.

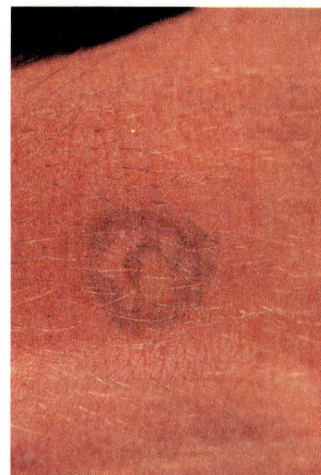

A bee sting on the wrist.

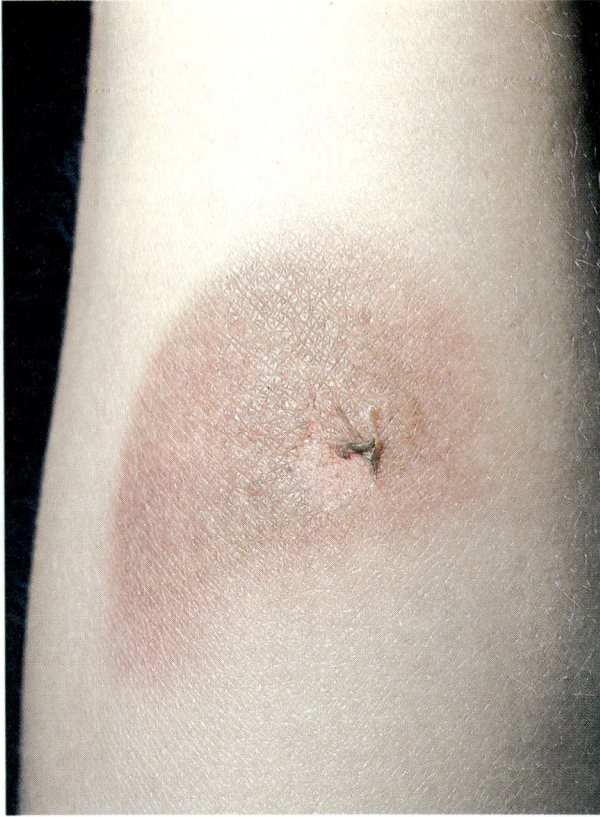
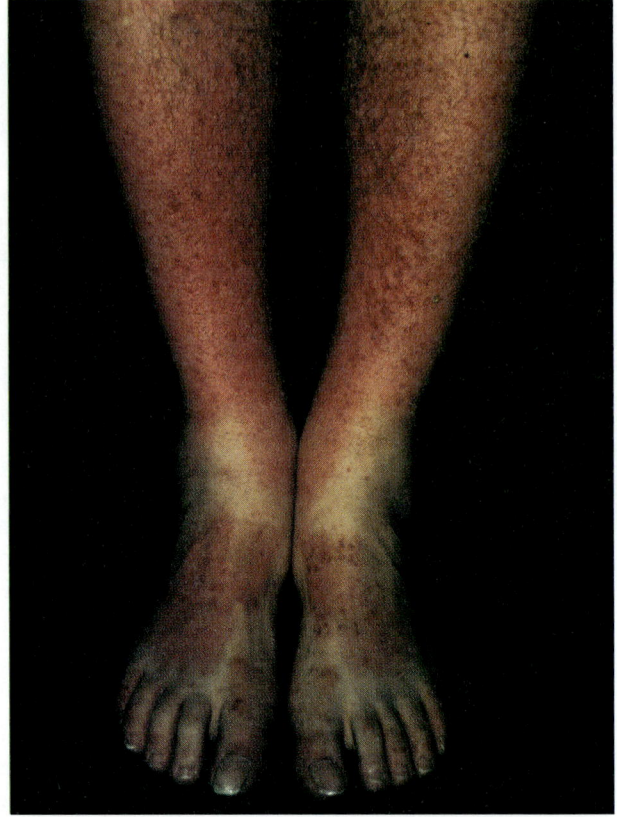

Left. *The photo shows a first-degree burn. The skin is blistered.* Right. *The photo shows a second-degree burn. The epidermis and part of the dermis have been destroyed in places on the skin.*

New Hope for Burn Patients

A method of treating patients who have suffered severe burns was developed at the Universtiy of Texas Medical School in Galveston. The technique is safer and less painful than the traditional method.

In this procedure, the entire burned area is surgically removed within a week of the accident and the area is temporarily covered with skin from a skin bank. Doctors then take the skin cells obtained from other parts of the patient's body and grow them in the laboratory to make a new sheet of skin to replace portions of the temporary foreign skin that was placed over the burn wounds.

By placing the temporary foreign skin over the wound, the risk of infection is greatly reduced. In the traditional method, the patient is given daily warm-water baths to loosen burned skin so that it can gradually be pulled or scraped off, bit by bit—a very painful procedure.

2. Apply a clean, dry dressing.
3. For second-degree burns, do not pop the blisters or remove any of the skin tissue.
4. If the burn is on an arm or a leg, keep the limb elevated.

First Aid for Third-Degree Burns   For third-degree burns, follow these directions:

1. Do not attempt to remove charred clothing. You may rip the skin.
2. If the burns are exposed, cover them with thick sterile dressings.
3. Elevate the hands and feet.
4. Do not treat the burns with cold water or ice because the cold may intensify the shock reaction.
5. Get the victim to a hospital immediately.
6. Watch for and treat possible shock.

Be very careful when removing a foreign body from the eye.

Fainting

Fainting is due to a reduced supply of blood to the brain for a short time. Follow these steps:

1. Leave the person lying down.
2. Loosen any tight clothing.
3. Maintain an open airway.
4. Sponge the face with water, but do *not* pour water over the face or the person may choke.
5. If the person does not revive, promptly seek medical help.

A Foreign Object in the Eye

1. Pull the eyelid down.
2. Try to lift out the object from the corner of the eye by using a clean cloth.
3. Do not rub the eye because the object could scratch it.

Fractures

A popping sound is a good indication that a bone has broken. (See Chapter 15 for information on fractures.) In any case, when you are not sure, always treat such an injury as if the bone were broken. Your objective is to keep the bone end from moving. *Never* attempt to set the bone. Instead:

1. Keep the body part in the position it is in.
2. Use a sling to hold the body part firmly in that position. Do not try to straighten it. Be sure the sling is not too tight, because you do not want to cut off circulation.
3. Seek medical care immediately.

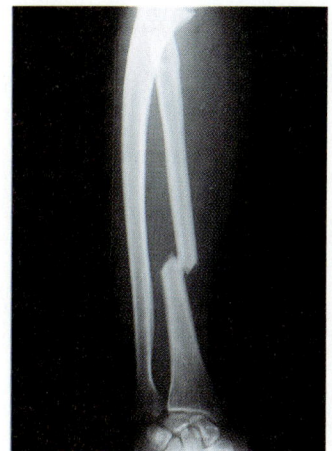

A simple fracture of a bone in the right forearm.

Heat Cramps

Heat cramps usually occur as a result of the body's loss of water and salt. Here are some procedures to follow:

1. If possible, the victim should go inside to get out of the heat.
2. The victim or another person should apply firm pressure with the hands on the cramped muscle. Gently massaging the muscle helps to relieve the spasm.
3. Give the person sips of salt water—1 teaspoon (5 ml) of salt per glass of water. The person should drink about one-half of the glass of water every 15 minutes. Be careful that the person does not take in too much salt at one time, for it may induce vomiting and nausea. Salt tablets are not recommended. You should not give salt to victims who have heart trouble or high blood pressure.

How Did You Score?

Now compare your answers to the eight situations on page 488 with the procedures listed above. Several steps were involved in each case. Check your responses to see how many of the steps you included. To be correct, they must be in the right order. Here is your score:

- **Excellent**: Listed all steps correctly for each of the eight situations.
- **Good**: Listed at least two correct steps for all situations. Your first aid would be helpful, but be careful and thorough in what you do.
- **Need to Improve**: Listed fewer than two correct steps in each situation. You may want to review what to do in everyday emergencies. You never know when you will be called on to help.

Many people wear the universal medical emergency identification symbol, usually as a bracelet.

Emergency Medical Identification

The American Medical Association has devised a *universal medical emergency identification symbol*. It is worn around the neck, wrist, or ankle, and indicates that the person wearing it has a medical condition that requires special attention. It also means that the person is carrying valuable information about what someone should do to help.

This information can be kept on a card in a wallet or purse. These cards are designed for the protection of a person in an emergency, when that person may be unconscious.

People who have diabetes and heart conditions, people who are allergic to penicillin or who have other common allergies, people who have seizures, and people who wear contact lenses commonly wear the emergency identification symbol. The back of the symbol gives vital information to those who might be called on to give the person first aid.

These devices are usually made of plastic or metal, and can be worn as bracelets or necklaces. They are available from many organizations. For more information, you may write to the American Medical Association, 535 North Dearborn Street, Chicago, IL 60610.

Weather-Related Emergencies

Most communities have emergency siren alerts to warn of potentially dangerous situations. However, some weather and environmental conditions occur without warning. Would you know what to do in such an emergency?

Hurricanes and Tornadoes

A **hurricane** is *a powerful rainstorm, characterized by driving winds*. It occurs around our coastal areas, mainly on the eastern and southern seaboards.

A **tornado** is *a powerful, twisting windstorm* that generally occurs in the central part of the United States. Tornadoes also occasionally occur in coastal areas and follow hurricanes. However, tornadoes have more recently struck sporadically in areas all over the country.

Knowing what to do in case of a hurricane or a tornado could save your life. The National Weather Service issues a **hurricane watch** and a **tornado watch** when *weather conditions are right for either of them to develop*.

It issues a **hurricane warning** to a locality when *the hurricane starts moving toward it*. The National Weather Service also issues a **tornado warning** when *it has spotted a tornado in an area and danger is imminent*.

To prepare for a hurricane, it is best to secure your property as fast as possible and leave it. The farther inland you go, the safer you will be from a hurricane.

A storm cellar or a basement is the safest place to go for protection from a tornado. If this is not available, stay in a hallway or a bathtub away from windows. If you are caught outside, get into a ditch and lie face down. Cover yourself, if possible, with a mattress, blanket, or clothing to protect yourself from flying objects.

Any weather storm can cause damage and take lives.

Most people are hurt or killed in an earthquake by falling objects and buildings that collapse.

Earthquakes

In some parts of the country, *heavy ground tremors* from **earthquakes** occur often. California averages almost 5,000 weak but noticeable quakes per year. Knowing what to do during and after an earthquake is important to your safety. Most casualties are not a direct result of the ground movement, but of falling objects or collapsing structures.

If you are at home during an earthquake, stay there. Stand in a strong doorway, get under a sturdy bed, or move into a hallway. Stay away from bookcases, tall shelves, sliding doors, and chimneys, because they may collapse. If you are outdoors, stay away from electrical wires, telephone poles, or other objects that might fall on you.

Snowstorms or Blizzards

A **blizzard** is a *snowstorm with winds of 35 miles per hour or more*. Visibility is less than 500 feet (150 m), so it is easy for a person to get lost. The safest place to be during a blizzard is indoors. If you are caught outside, keep your mouth and nose covered and keep moving so you do not freeze. Try to follow a road or a fence to the closest safe place.

If you must go outside in a blizzard, wear protective clothing. Thermal, woolen undergarments; outer garments that will repel wind and moisture; head, face, and ear coverings; extra socks, warm boots, and woolen-lined mittens will help to protect you from the freezing temperatures. (See Chapter 2 for more information on frostbite.)

SNOW SKIING

"My friend and I are snow skiers. We recently read of skiers suffering frostbite due to the windchill. We estimate that we move down a slope at about 10 to 15 miles per hour. When do we risk danger?"

Any windchill of −25°F (−33°C) or colder presents a danger, with −72°F (−58°C) presenting a critical danger. The following chart illustrates the windchill factor.

Wind speed (mph)	Temperature			Windchill		
	A	B	C	A	B	C
5	−10	−20	−30	−15	−26	−36
10	−10	−20	−30	−33	−46	−58
15	−10	−20	−30	−45	−58	−72
20	−10	−20	−30	−53	−67	−82
25	−10	−20	−30	−59	−74	−88
30	−10	−20	−30	−63	−79	−94

Example: With a 15-mph wind at −20°F under B, the windchill is −58°F, also under B.

You also protect yourself by wearing proper wool clothing, especially on your head, face, hands, and feet. Take regular breaks and remember that if any wind is on the slopes, you increase your risks. Always be aware of the windchill factor.

Frostbite

Frostbite is a common injury to those who spend time in the outdoors during cold weather. During extreme cold, the body tries to conserve heat for its more vital internal organs, so less and less blood is sent through the extremities, mainly the fingers and the toes.

If the temperature in the cells gets low enough, **frostbite** may occur. This happens when *ice crystals begin to form in the spaces between the cells. This ice expands and kills tissue, in the process causing the skin to become white and insensitive to any feeling.*

The loss of circulation in the area also increases the chance of **gangrene** (**gan**-green), which is *the actual death of tissue in a part of the body.* Gangrene often requires amputation of the dead part.

Several factors can increase the prospect of suffering from frostbite, some outside our control and others within it. The temperature, how long the person is exposed, wind velocity, humidity, the amount of protective clothing used, and how wet the clothing is must always be considered.

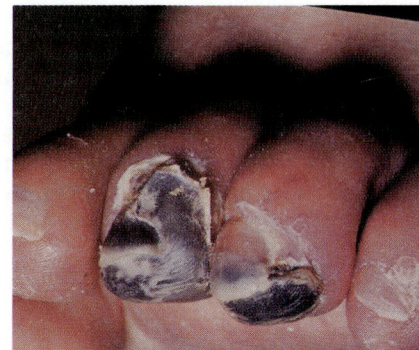

Gangrene of the toes has set in due to frostbite.

HEALTH

CAREER

HOME HEALTH AIDES

Many families and individuals face circumstances in which they need extra help. Someone must look after children if a parent is admitted to the hospital or is bedridden at home. Many people need household help and sometimes nursing care during recovery from an accident or an illness. Elderly people and invalids often require various degrees of care in their homes. **Home health aides** provide these services to individuals or their families.

The work of a home health aide depends on the needs of the client. **Child-care workers** often take full responsibility for the child or children during the day. This may include meal preparation, bathing and dressing, playtime and recreational activities, and in the case of older children, some tutoring.

Companions are workers who take care of the elderly or disabled. A companion usually prepares meals and spends the day with the client reading, playing cards or games, and doing other things to keep the client as active as possible. Light housework may be included, as well as some basic nursing care. A companion does not administer medication or therapy. However, a companion may take care of business matters for the client.

The positions filled by a home health aide may be temporary, lasting a few weeks, or relatively permanent, as in the case of a terminal patient who prefers to be at home and does not require hospitalization.

Becoming a home health aide requires relatively little formal education. Employers consider a high school diploma to be a sign that a person can complete necessary work. Helpful courses in high school or junior college would include home economics, English, health, mathematics, and psychology. A home health aide learns many of the needed skills through experience. Household chores and babysitting are good practical experiences for students while in high school.

Helpful personal traits for a home health aide are patience, a warm personality, and a willingness to work and follow directions. To do a good job, home health aides must *want* to help their clients. They must be able to get along with many different people under a variety of

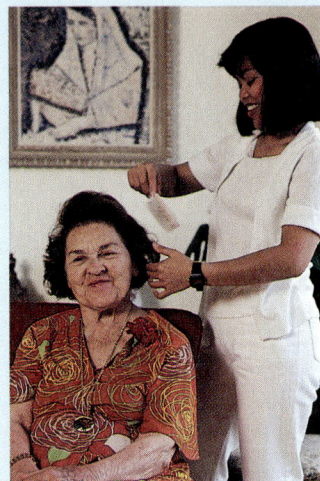

circumstances. For more information, contact Helping Hand Services, Inc.

**Helping Hand Services, Inc.
801 Princeton Avenue, S.W.
Birmingham, AL 35211**

First Aid for Frostbite   When you are giving first aid to someone who has frostbite, you have three priorities:

1. Protect the frozen area from further injury.
2. Warm the affected area rapidly.
3. Maintain respiration.

Take the victim indoors, cover the victim with blankets, and give him or her a warm *nonalcoholic* drink. (Alcohol would slow down the system further.) Warm the frozen body part quickly by immersing it in *warm, not hot*, water. Test the water by pouring it over the inner surface of your forearm. If water is not available, wrap the affected body part in sheets or blankets. *Do not rub* the body part, as this will further damage the tissue. Get the victim to a doctor as quickly as possible.

CHECK YOURSELF

1. How are burns classified? What is the appropriate first aid for each?
2. Why do you use cold instead of heat on sprains?
3. What is the difference between a *watch* and a *warning*?
4. What is the proper treatment of frostbite?

CHAPTER 27   Review

CHAPTER SUMMARY

- Your quick, calm, knowledgeable actions can mean the difference between life and death.
- The four priorities in administering first aid are:
  1. rescue the victim from the life-threatening environment, if necessary;
  2. check to ensure that the victim is breathing;
  3. control severe bleeding;
  4. treat for poisoning.
- In addition, you can help by providing reassurance and by keeping the victim calm.
- Remember that first aid is immediate, temporary care—seek medical attention immediately.
- You may never be faced with a life-threatening emergency, but you may need to administer first aid in an everyday situation. Knowing what to do and acting quickly can prevent further injury.

REVIEWING WHAT YOU LEARNED

1. What is first aid?
2. List priorities in responding to an emergency?
3. Name five kinds of wounds, define each, and describe each one's treatment.
4. Define shock and describe its treatment.
5. Describe three types of poisoning and what to do to treat each of them.
6. Name the poisonous snakes of the United States.
7. Explain the procedure for treating snakebite.
8. Describe first aid for three of the following:

   - nosebleed
   - sting
   - sprain
   - fainting
   - fracture
   - foreign object in the eye
   - heat cramps

9. Describe the three classifications of burns. What first-aid technique would you employ for each?
10. List the life-saving procedures to follow when you first approach an accident victim.
11. Explain the function of the emergency medical identification symbol.
12. What general suggestions can you make about protecting yourself in the event of a weather disaster, such as a tornado?
13. What information should you give when you call a poison-control center?

first aid	fracture	hurricane	blizzard
poison	pressure-point technique	tornado	frostbite
abrasion	contamination	hurricane watch	gangrene
incision	infection	tornado watch	home health aids
laceration	shock	hurricane warning	child-care workers
puncture	poisonous	tornado warning	companions
avulsion	poison-control centers	earthquakes	

PUTTING VOCABULARY TO USE

On a separate piece of paper, match the characteristic of the wound in column B with the type of wound in column A. Several characteristics may be appropriate for each wound.

Column A
1. _____Avulsion
2. _____Abrasion
3. _____Laceration
4. _____Puncture
5. _____Incision

Column B
a. Carries with it the danger of tetanus.
b. Limited external bleeding.
c. Hardly bleeds, adding to the danger of infection.
d. Bleeding may be heavy.
e. Skin is pierced.
f. Tissue is separated from body.
g. Usually caused by glass, a knife, or a sharp rock.
h. Jagged, irregular tear.
i. Potential internal damage to organs.

Select the symptoms that characterize (a) shock and (b) snake poisoning. Write them on a separate piece of paper.
■ rapid pulse ___
■ moist, pale skin ___
■ weak pulse ___
■ vomiting ___
■ shallow, irregular breathing ___
■ nausea ___

On a separate piece of paper, write the term that defines each description. Use the chapter vocabulary list for reference.

1. The basic procedures of providing assistance to the sick or injured until medical assistance arrives. _____
2. The introduction of foreign microorganisms into the body when a wound occurs. _____
3. A method of stopping bleeding if direct pressure fails. _____
4. A twisting windstorm _____
5. Especially dangerous to fingers and toes. _____
6. Death of tissue. _____

APPLYING WHAT YOU LEARNED

1. Now that you have studied about first aid, you have some impressions of what it takes to be a good first aider. Write down and discuss these characteristics.
2. How can the development of skill in first aid decrease the need for emergency health services in a hospital?
3. Make up an auto first-aid kit to help care for the kinds of injuries discussed in this chapter. List the items and be sure to identify for which injury the items would be used.

4. It has been said that we prevent shock by treating for shock. Is this true? What does it mean?
5. Check to see the extent of first-aid supplies and first-aid knowledge at home. Make suggestions to your parents or other adults on the items that are lacking, which need to be there just in case of an emergency.

FOCUS ON WELLNESS

A thorough knowledge of first aid increases a person's efforts at accident prevention. *I will improve my first-aid skills by . . .*

A Matter of Life and Death

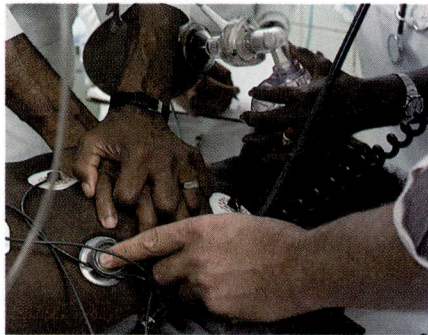

More than half of all emergency victims are dead before they reach the hospital. In many cases, these victims would have had a good chance of surviving if someone at the scene of the accident had known and had been able to practice a lifesaving technique.

After studying this chapter, you will be able to:

- demonstrate the universal distress signal for choking,
- list the steps for aiding a choking victim,
- know how to check for breathing and pulse,
- describe the process for giving mouth-to-mouth resuscitation,
- explain the steps involved in administering CPR,
- compare CPR for adults with CPR for small children.

The most common cause of sudden death is a heart attack. Drowning, electrical shock, drug overdose, stroke, smoke inhalation, and suffocation can also result in the stoppage of breathing and circulation and result in sudden death. A knowledge of first aid to use in these cases is, literally, a matter of life and death.

First Aid for the Choking Victim

Just as in the case of heart and lung failure, choking is responsible every year for many preventable deaths. More than 3,000 Americans choke to death annually. Two-thirds of the deaths reported apply to children under age four. Choking is the sixth leading cause of accidental death in the overall population. It is the leading cause of accidental death in the home for children under one year of age.

In order for a choking victim to survive, immediate recognition and treatment of choking are a must. Would you know what to do to help a choking victim? Would you know what distress signal to give if you were choking?

It may seem hard to believe, but oftentimes people do not respond to a choking victim because they mistake choking for a heart attack. This is why fatal *choking accidents in restaurants* have acquired the name **café coronaries.** The universal distress signal for choking is clutching the neck between the thumb and index finger. What is the proper response for immediate first aid?

Choking in Infants or Small Children

Families with young children should take a first aid course to learn to dislodge an object from a child's windpipe. The local EMS, American Health Association, or American Red Cross provides training in the use of effective techniques. See the illustration on page 501 for one technique.

Choking in Older Children and Adults

Ask, "Are you choking?" If the victim cannot respond, begin first aid immediately. Begin **abdominal thrusts,** also known as the *Heimlich Maneuver:*

1. Wrap your arms around the victim's waist, with the thumb side of your wrist against the victim's abdomen. Place your hand just above the navel.
2. Grasp your fist with your other hand and press it into the abdomen with quick, upward thrusts until successful. It may be necessary to repeat the thrust six to ten or more times until successful.

Clutch the neck between thumb and index finger to show the universal distress signal for choking.

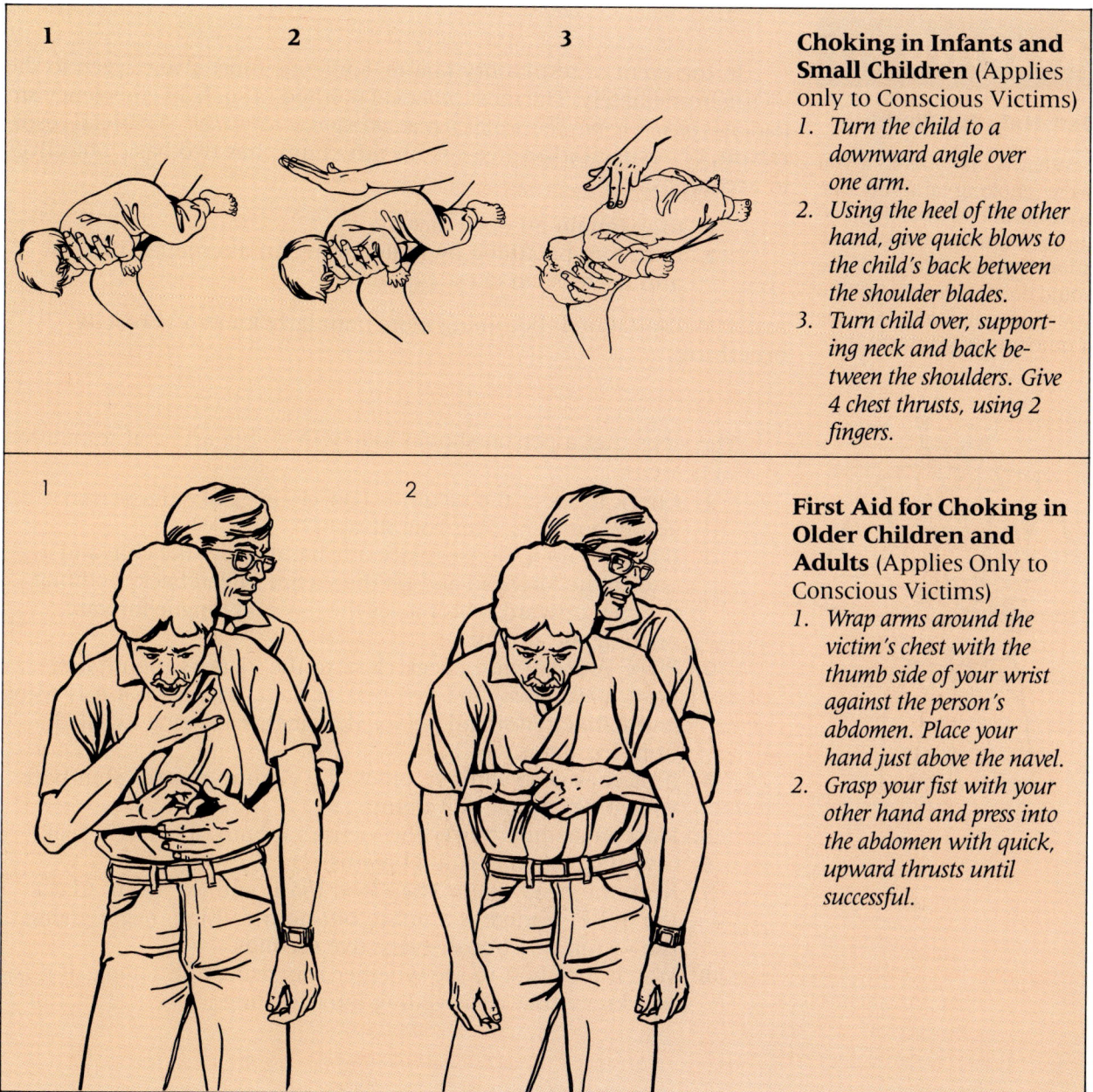

Choking in Infants and Small Children (Applies only to Conscious Victims)

1. Turn the child to a downward angle over one arm.
2. Using the heel of the other hand, give quick blows to the child's back between the shoulder blades.
3. Turn child over, supporting neck and back between the shoulders. Give 4 chest thrusts, using 2 fingers.

First Aid for Choking in Older Children and Adults (Applies Only to Conscious Victims)

1. Wrap arms around the victim's chest with the thumb side of your wrist against the person's abdomen. Place your hand just above the navel.
2. Grasp your fist with your other hand and press into the abdomen with quick, upward thrusts until successful.

You Can Prevent Choking

Some simple practices can help to prevent choking:

- Take small bites of food.
- Eat slowly, chewing food thoroughly.
- Do not talk or laugh with food in your mouth.
- Do not go to sleep at night with chewing gum or any other matter in your mouth.

When Breathing Has Stopped

KEEPING FIT

Self-Help for Choking

What would you do if you were choking and no one were around? The abdominal thrust maneuver can be self-administered. That is, you could press your own fist into your upper abdomen by using a quick, upward thrust.

In the event of respiratory failure, someone must give oxygen to the victim immediately. The most practical method in such an emergency situation is *mouth-to-mouth respiration or mouth-to-nose respiration*. **Artificial respiration,** or **resuscitation** (ree-sus-uh-**tah**-shun), has two basic objectives to accomplish:

1. to maintain an open airway,
2. to restore breathing by maintaining an alternating increase and decrease in chest expansion.

Artificial respiration is becoming more popularly known as **rescue breathing**.

Giving Artificial Respiration to Adults

The steps that a person should follow in giving artificial respiration to adults are:

1. Check to see if the victim is conscious. Shake the person gently and ask, "Are you all right?"
2. If there is no response, place one hand under the chin and one on the forehead and tilt the victim's head back, pointing the chin upward. This moves the jaw and tongue forward, opening the airway.
3. Place your ear and cheek close to the victim's mouth and nose. *Look, listen,* and *feel. Look* at the chest to see if it is rising and falling; *listen* and *feel* for the air that is being exhaled from the lungs.
4. If there is no breathing, pinch the victim's nostrils shut with your index finger and thumb.
5. Place your mouth over the victim's mouth, forming a seal.
6. Give the person two full breaths.
7. Keep the head tilted. Then *look, listen,* and *feel* again. Check the pulse. If there is a pulse, but no breathing, begin giving the victim one breath every five seconds.
8. Watch the chest to see whether it is rising and falling. If it is, you know that air is getting into the lungs.

Giving Artificial Respiration to Children

For children (ages one to eight) and infants (up to one year of age), do not tilt the head as far back. Your mouth will cover and form a seal around the infant's mouth and nose. Use full breaths for the infant, at the rate of one every three seconds. Give a child about one breath every four seconds.

If you check for a pulse, and the victim is not breathing and has no pulse, it means that the victim's heart has stopped. The air is not being pumped to the brain, and the brain can die after about five minutes without oxygen. You must begin *cardiopulmonary resuscitation* (**kard**-ee-oh-**pull**-mah-ner-ee ree-sus-uh-**tah**-shun) immediately, but only if you are trained to do so.

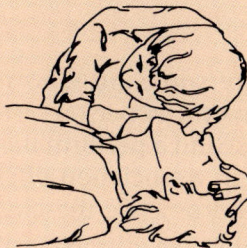

Artificial Respiration for Adults

1. *Position head to clear airway. Then pinch nostrils shut with index finger and thumb.*
2. *Keeping nostril pinched shut, place your mouth over the person's mouth, forming a seal.*
3. *Give the person two breaths (1–1.5 seconds each). Allow deflation between breaths.*
4. *Keep head tilted. Look, listen, and feel again.*
5. *Continue at the rate of 1 every 5 seconds.*

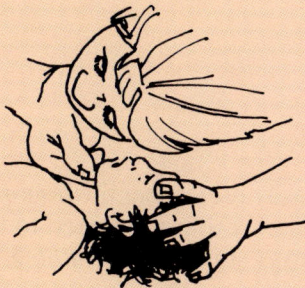

Artificial Respiration for Infants and Young Children

1. *Position head to clear airway, but do not tilt head far back.*
2. *Seal the child's mouth and nose with your mouth.*
3. *Give breaths for an infant, one every 3 seconds. Give one breath every four seconds for a child.*

CHECK YOURSELF

1. What is the universal distress signal for choking? Why would this signal be necessary?
2. Explain the steps in giving first aid to a choking victim.
3. What are the two major objectives of artificial respiration?
4. What are the steps in giving artificial respiration?

Cardiopulmonary resuscitation (CPR) is a lifesaving technique that requires no special tools, instruments, or equipment. CPR involves *breathing for the victim, while forcing the heart to pump blood by applying pressure to the victim's chest.*

Who Can Perform CPR?

Only someone who has successfully completed a CPR course can perform CPR. A person certified to administer CPR must pass both a knowledge test and a performance test. The American Red Cross and the American Heart Association offer courses throughout the country. Anyone can learn and practice the lifesaving skill through these courses.

If these health agencies are not located in your community, contact the local emergency medical service, police, or fire or health department for information about classes.

The Steps to Learning CPR

By learning the ABCs of CPR, you can easily remember the major *responsibilities* that the rescuer must perform in *the order* that they need to be performed. *A* always stands for *airway*; *B* always stands for *breathing*; and *C* always stands for *circulation*.

Remember that these steps are the same each time, and the order never changes: *airway–breathing–circulation*.

Airway

If you come across a person who has collapsed, your first task is to determine whether the victim is conscious. Gently shake the victim's shoulder and ask loudly, ''Are you all right?'' If the victim does not respond and other people are around, point directly to one person and direct that person to go call for help. Give the person the emergency phone number, which is 911 nationwide. You want the person to act quickly, so you should be brief and direct.

Now you are ready to open the victim's airway. If the victim is not lying flat on the back, you need to roll the victim to this position. Carefully roll the body as an entire unit. In other words, you do not want the upper body to turn, followed by the lower body. If there is any evidence of possible neck injury (for example, in the case of a driving accident), do not move the victim. You must open the airway without moving the victim's head.

Breathing

Only a matter of seconds should have passed since you first found the victim. If the victim shows no signs of breathing, the rescuer must begin artificial respiration.

To open the airway, follow the procedures just described on pages 502–503 for giving artificial respiration. Remember the three checks for breathing:

- *Look* for the rise and fall of the chest and/or abdomen, indicating breathing.
- *Listen* for the sound of air's being inhaled or exhaled.
- *Feel* for exhaled air on your cheek.

Circulation

The next step involved in CPR is to provide artificial circulation by applying external pressure on the victim's breastbone. Remember that you must be properly trained and certified to administer this procedure.

First, you must determine whether the victim's heart is beating. You do this by feeling the **carotid** (kuh-**rot**-id) **pulse**. It is *on each side of the neck, just below the ear*. Find your own carotid pulse.

With the index and middle fingers, feel for the pulse. If there is none, the victim is suffering from cardiac arrest, and you must start artificial circulation. You must carry out the following three basic steps:

1. With the middle and index fingers of the hand nearest the victim's legs, locate the lower margin of the victim's rib cage on the side next to the rescuer. The fingers are then moved up the rib cage to the point where the *ribs come together to meet the breastbone*. This bony structure is called the **xiphoid** (**zigh**-foid) **process**. You must be careful not to press the xiphoid process because of the risk of puncturing a lung. Place two fingers at the xiphoid process; then put the heel of the other hand just above the fingers. This gives you proper hand placement. Place the other hand on top of the first one, with the fingers interlocked and slightly raised. Only the heel of the hand touches the victim's chest.

2. Kneel so that your shoulders are directly over the victim's chest, and keep your arms straight. Elbows must remain in a locked position. Compress the breastbone 1.5 to 2 inches (3.8 to 5 cm) on an adult. Then completely relax the pressure, but never let your hands lose contact with the victim's chest.

3. You must also continue breathing for the victim. Give 15 chest compressions, then 2 full breaths, and 15 more compressions. The compressions should be at a rate of 80 to 100 per minute. Each time you return to do chest compressions, you must measure up from the xiphoid process to be sure of proper hand placement. Continue CPR until help arrives and takes over.

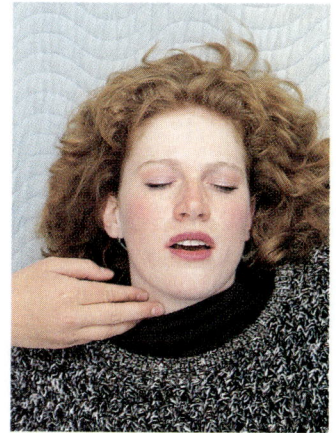

Feel for the carotid pulse with your index and middle fingers.

Finding the xiphoid process and proper hand placement in CPR.

Position for compression in CPR.

CPR for Adults

1. Position the person flat on his back. Roll him over as an entire unit.
2. Open the person's airway.
3. Provide artificial circulation by applying external pressure on the person's breastbone. See the description on page 505. Remember that you must be properly trained to administer this procedure.
4. Give 15 chest compressions, then 2 breaths, and 15 more compressions. The compressions should be at a rate of 80–100 per minute. Continue until help arrives.

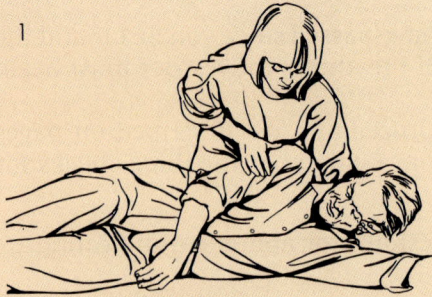

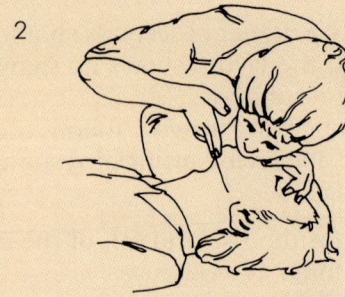

CPR for Infants and Small Children

1. Tip infant's head back a little in order to open airway.
2. Cover your mouth over baby's mouth and nose and give breaths of air.
3. Check for pulse by placing middle fingers over infant's brachial artery (artery at upper part of the arm).
4. Draw an imaginary line between infant's nipples. Place 2–3 fingers on sternum, one finger's width below the middle of the imaginary line. Compress

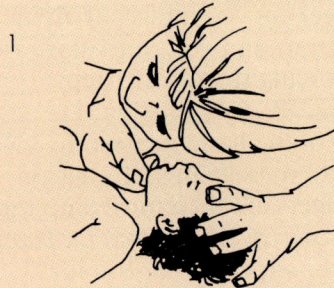

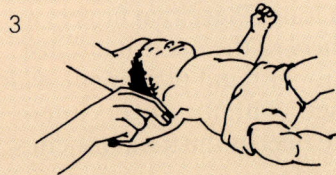

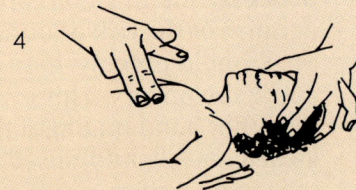

downward 0.5 to 1 inch at a rate of 100 per min-

ute for infant, 80–100 for a young child.

CPR for Infants and Small Children

Because of size, some adjustments are needed when using CPR for infants. For step A, *airway*, tip the infant's head back a little in order to open the airway. Tilting the head too far will close the airway.

Once you have cleared the airway, move on to step B, *breathing*. Check the breathing in the same way as for an adult—*look, listen,* and *feel*.

If there is no breathing, rather than pinching the nose, cover your mouth over the baby's mouth and nose, and give breaths of air. Give breaths at the rate of one every three seconds.

In step C, *circulation*, check for the pulse by placing your middle index finger over the infant's upper arm. If there is no pulse, then chest compressions are needed.

For infants and young children, draw an imaginary line between the nipples. Place 2–3 fingers on the sternum, one finger's width below the imaginary line. Compress 0.5 to 1 inch (1.3 to 2.5 cm).

For children, place the middle and index fingers on the notch where the ribs and breastbone meet. Place the heel of your hand next to your index finger. With one hand, compress the breastbone about 1 to 1.5 inches (2.5 to 3.8 cm).

For infants, do compressions at the rate of 100 per minute. For young children, do 80–100 per minute. You must also continue artificial breathing. After five chest compressions, give a breath.

CPR is a skill that a person must properly learn and practice before being ready to use it in an emergency situation. You may never need to use the skill, but by being prepared, you may save a life some day.

A Health Student Asks . . .

THE GOOD SAMARITAN LAW

"I have read of several cases where a person tried to help someone who was injured and the injured person later tried to sue the rescuer. Am I taking a risk of being sued if I try to help a victim of an accident or injury?"

According to the **Good Samaritan law,** *no person who administers emergency care in good faith is liable for civil damages unless such acts are "willfully or wantonly" negligent.*

This means that if you know first aid and are a layperson— that is, not a medical person who will receive pay for services ren- dered—and act in good faith, you cannot be sued.

Keep yourself familiarized with the various first-aid procedures. You never know when you may need to respond to an emergency, and your calmness, quick think- ing, and actions may make the difference.

CHECK YOURSELF

1. What are the ABCs of CPR?
2. Compare the CPR given to an adult with that given to an infant or a child.
3. What is the xiphoid process?

EMERGENCY MEDICAL TECHNICIAN (EMT)

The quality of first-aid care often makes the difference between life and death for many accident victims. This is the responsibility of an **emergency medical technician,** or EMT.

An EMT must respond to calls from the emergency medical dispatches to provide care for accident victims and other types of emergencies. Many EMTs drive ambulances, but others work in hospital emergency rooms, emergency clinics, intensive care units or coronary care units, or in the rescue squads of police and fire departments.

To become an EMT, you must complete high school and be at least 18 years old. The U.S. Department of Transportation has devised a formal training program. Other agencies, such as the American Heart Association, the American Red Cross, and the Civil Defense also offer emergency training courses.

Training for an EMT includes instruction and practice in managing severe bleeding, cardiac arrest, fractures, airway obstruction, emergency childbirth, and other first-aid techniques. An EMT can also learn rescue and extrication techniques. With advanced training and under a physican's radio supervision, an EMT may administer drugs.

Because of the life-threatening nature of emergency work, an EMT must be able to work quickly and effectively under extreme stress. The EMT must not only treat the victim but also deal with frightened family members and curious by-standers. Success as an EMT requires some physical strength, manual dexterity and coordination, and emotional maturity.

Emergency work can be frustrating, tiring, and very stressful. On the other hand, great satisfaction can come from doing the job well and saving lives. For further information, contact:

The National Registry of Emergency Medical Technicians
6610 Busch Boulevard
PO Box 29233
Columbus, OH 43229

CHAPTER 28   Review

CHAPTER SUMMARY

- You can be trained to administer basic life-support techniques. You may never need to use them, but in the event of an emergency, your skill could save a life.

- Choking claims thousands of lives every year, most of which could have been saved if someone had known how to administer first aid for choking.
- Artificial respiration is a process by which the rescuer breathes for the victim.

café coronaries   cardiopulmonary resuscitation (CPR)
abdominal thrusts   Good Samaritan law
Heimlich Maneuver   carotid pulse
artificial respiration   xiphoid process
artificial resuscitation   emergency medical technician (EMT)

PUTTING VOCABULARY TO USE

On a separate piece of paper, supply the following information.

1. Develop a short set of instructions that could be used in places where *café coronaries* take place.
2. Give another name for *artificial respiration*.
3. Locate the *xiphoid process* and explain what role it plays in CPR.
4. Draw a diagram that shows the steps in CPR.
5. List reasons why no one should give *CPR* without training.

- In CPR, the rescuer breathes for the victim and manually compresses the heart to pump blood through the body.
- In both instances, time is critical. If the heart is not beating, the brain cannot get the oxygen it needs. The brain dies after about five minutes without oxygen.

REVIEWING WHAT YOU LEARNED

1. If you are alone and are choking, what is the best thing to do?
2. What are the steps for aiding a choking victim?
3. Outline the steps to follow in giving artificial respiration to adults.
4. How can you determine the following:
   a. no breathing,
   b. no swallowing,
   c. no pulse?
5. Explain the steps in administering CPR.
6. How does the application of CPR differ for children and adults?

APPLYING WHAT YOU LEARNED

1. Now that you have studied about artificial respiration and cardiopulmonary resuscitation, identify three places where you think such occurrences might take place. Check to see whether the people at those locations are trained and certified to administer these procedures. If not, provide them with information about where they can obtain this certification and training at no cost.
2. What would be your response to an individual who made one of the following statements: "There is too much responsibility in administering any of these lifesaving techniques," "That just isn't for me," "I don't want to get involved in some hassle," "Let someone else do it."
3. Check to see who is the closest person to your home who knows how to apply artificial respiration and cardiopulmonary resuscitation. Ask the person if you could call on him or her for assistance if the need arose. Get the person's phone number and keep it in a safe place.
4. Research and write a report on the beginnings of the American Red Cross and its work today.
5. The American Red Cross is to provide free training for CPR in the evening at your school. In two minutes, present a sales pitch to your parents on why the three of you need to attend and be trained in this important lifesaving technique.

FOCUS ON WELLNESS

The prevention of choking and the administering of artificial respiration and CPR are all-important lifesaving skills. *I can contribute to the saving of lives in at least one of these areas by . . .*

U N I T

9

TREATING, CONTROLLING, AND PREVENTING DISEASES

Communicable Diseases

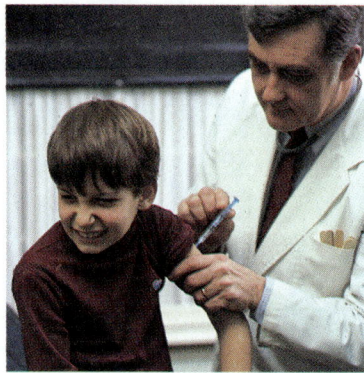

In the United States alone, diseases kill nearly 2 million people each year. Millions more people survive diseases, but are left handicapped in some way. Even millions more have mild diseases, such as colds and flu.

Regardless of the seriousness of the diseases, they are all costly. Americans spend more than $500 million a year on nonprescription drugs alone to treat colds. In a one-year period, colds alone were responsible for absences of 30 million days from school and 30 million days from work.

After studying this chapter, you will be able to:

■ differentiate among the disease-causing microorganisms,
■ describe the body's defense against disease,
■ explain the infectious disease process,
■ describe how the body's immune system works,

■ differentiate between natural and artificially acquired immunity,
■ identify symptoms and treatment of common infectious diseases,
■ describe preventive measures for infectious diseases.

You know that total health encompasses one's mental and physical well-being. It is understandable then that when we define diseases, we consider both the mind and the body. Disease can develop in almost any part of the body and can also affect one's mental and emotional well-being.

In Unit 2, you learned about mental health problems and mental illness. This unit is concerned with diseases of the body. How can a physical disease affect the level of one's mental health? Think of a time when you had a bad cold and missed a big event you had looked forward to. How did you feel?

Two Basic Groups of Diseases

Many of the most common diseases are caused by *tiny germs* called **microorganisms** (**my**-krow-**or**-guh-niz-ums) that invade the body. These diseases are known as **infectious** (in-**feck**-shus) **diseases,** that is, *diseases you can catch.* Some infectious diseases are also **communicable** (kuh-**mu**-nuh-kuh-bull), meaning that *you can pass on the germs to another person.*

All other diseases are called **noninfectious diseases.** These diseases *occur from sources within the body itself,* usually through some malfunction of a body system. They are also called **noncommunicable diseases,** in that *they are not passed on to others.* As you will see, noninfectious diseases have a variety of different causes, many of which are related to the way in which we live.

A damp, wet climate is a perfect breeding place for certain types of microorganisms that cause disease.

1. How might disease influence one's mental health?
2. What is an infectious disease?
3. What is the main difference between the communicable infectious diseases and the noncommunicable infectious diseases?

2.   Infectious Diseases

Infectious diseases, the most common type of disease, are caused by *microorganisms* called **pathogens** (**path**-uh-jens). Pathogens infect, or *invade,* the body and attack its cells and tissues. As the pathogens grow and reproduce, they damage or destroy the body cells and tissues. *Bacteria, viruses, rickettsias, fungi, protozoans,* and certain *worms* are all pathogens.

Bacteria

Bacteria are *one-celled microscopic organisms that rank among the most widespread of all living things.* Some bacteria are so small that a single grain of soil may contain over 100 million of them. Of course, most bacteria do not cause disease.

Resident Bacteria

The trichinella spiralis *is a parasitic worm that lodges itself in living animal muscle and feeds off it. (See p. 518 for more details.)*

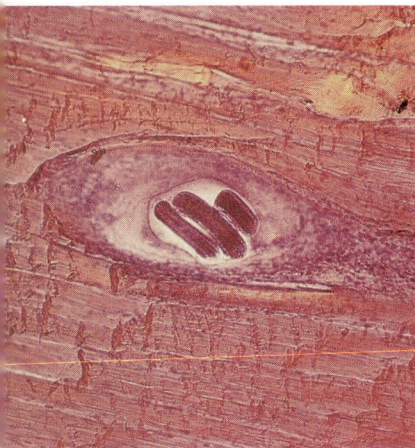

Many kinds of bacteria called **resident bacteria** *live in your mouth and intestines and on your skin, and help to protect you from the harmful bacteria.* *Lactobacilli* (lak-toe-buh-**sil**-eye) (singular form: *lactobacillus*), found in the gastrointestinal tract, produce lactic acid from simple carbohydrates. *Coliform* (**koh**-luh-form) *bacilli,* found in the intestines, help to break down carbohydrates and combat disease-carrying bacteria.

As you will read later in this chapter, the resident bacteria form one line of defense against disease. They only cause disease if they move to a place in the body where they do not belong. For example, if bacteria from your mouth moved into your middle ear, you could develop an ear infection.

Saprophytes and Parasites

In order to live, all bacteria must have a food supply, as well as suitable temperature, moisture, and darkness. Some *bacteria digest nonliving food materials, such as milk and meat.* These organisms are called **saprophytes** (**sap**-ruh-fites). *If the food supply is a living plant or animal,* the microorganism is called a **parasite** (**par**-uh-site). *The plant or animal that the parasite feeds upon* is called the **host.**

The Spread of Bacterial Infection

What happens when a bacteria germ infects the body? Most diseases caused by bacteria result from microorganisms that are not present in the body. These bacteria enter the body and multiply at a very rapid rate through cell division. A fully grown cell divides, forming two new cells. If conditions are good, this division can occur at intervals of 30 minutes. That may not sound like much, but calculate what this multiplication rate can mean.

If a single bacterial cell divides, 30 minutes later the two cells become four. Thirty minutes more (1 hour lapsed), the four cells become eight. In just fifteen and one-half hours, there would be 4.3 billion bacteria!

Obviously, this multiplication could not continue for long or the bacteria would soon completely take over. Because the bacteria must compete with one another for food, competition kills many of them, which helps to control their numbers.

Toxins

Other bacteria cause disease by producing certain *poisons* called **toxins** (**tahk**-suns). Food poisoning is a result of this type of bacteria.

Bacteria that normally live in the soil can enter the body through a wound and produce a poison that affects muscles and nerves in the body. *Tetanus,* or lockjaw, is an example of such bacteria.

Bacterial diseases include certain types of pneumonia and food poisoning, diphtheria, tetanus, tuberculosis, strep throat, syphilis, and gonorrhea. We will discuss some of these diseases in greater detail in this unit.

HEALTH UPDATE　　HEALTH UPDATE　　HEALTH UPDATE

Groups of Bacteria

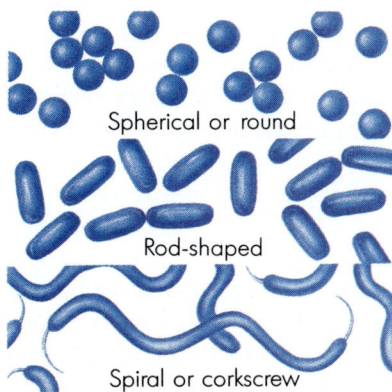

Spherical or round

Rod-shaped

Spiral or corkscrew

Picture 1 illustrates spherical, or round bacteria called **cocci** (**kock**-eye) (singular form: *coccus*). They may appear in long chains (*streptococcus*) (strep-tuh-**kock**-us). They may be clustered like grapes (*staphylococcus*) (staf-uh-low-**kock**-us). *Picture 2* illustrates rod-shaped bacteria called **bacilli**. In *picture 3*, the bacteria cells are spiral, or twisted. These are called **spirilla** (spy-**ril**- uh) (singular form: *spirillum*).

Types of Viruses

As in the case of bacteria, there are many types of viruses. Here are a few and the diseases they cause.

- **Rhinoviruses** (rye-no-**vie**-rus-ez) cause about 50% of all colds. They attack the cells in the nasal passages and tend to cause colds in the summer and fall.
- **Corona viruses** (kuh-**row**-nuh **vie**-rus-ez) cause about 15 to 20% of all colds, mostly in the winter.
- **Adenoviruses** (ad-ee-no-**vie**-rus-ez) cause cold symptoms in the early spring and summer. Since over 200 viruses cause the symptoms we call a cold, you can see why we do not have a vaccine against colds!

- **Coxsackie viruses** (**kock**-sak-ee **vie**-rus-ez) cause poliomyelitis, meningitis, fevers, and heart disease in infants.
- **Enteroviruses** tend to cause gastrointestinal disorders, sometimes misnamed stomach or intestinal flu. They are not types of influenza but diseases in their own right.
- **Echoviruses** can cause meningitis and diarrhea.
- **Epstein-Barr virus** has been implicated in infectious mononucleosis.
- **Herpesviruses** (hur-peas-**vie**-rus-ez), such as herpes simplex, type I, are responsible for cold sores, and herpes simplex, type II, causes sexually transmitted disease.

KEEPING FIT

The Retrovirus

Scientists are discovering new information about viruses with their study of the AIDS virus. The AIDS virus is known as a *retrovirus*. Retroviruses have a different chemical makeup than ordinary viruses. And it appears that the chemical makeup of the AIDS virus is even more complicated than other retroviruses. Most retroviruses have three types of genes. Genes control the reproduction of the virus. The AIDS virus has as many as eight. Some scientists believe that there are still more to be discovered.

Viral Diseases

The **virus** (**vie**-rus) germ is *the smallest known, simplest form of life—* between 10 and 100 times smaller than bacteria. It is also one of the human body's worst enemies. Scientists had not actually seen viruses until 1932, when the high-powered electron microscope was developed. Using an electron beam instead of light and a photographic plate instead of the human eye, the electron microscope made the study of viruses possible.

An examination of viruses reveals that they are not cells. They have no nucleus, no cytoplasm, and no cell membrane. The virus particle consists of *nucleic acid*, a complex chemical that is an acid present in the cells of all organisms.

Viruses at Work

All viruses are parasites, requiring living cells for survival and reproduction. Viruses are highly specific in the kind of cells they invade. Only certain viruses invade animal cells, and then these various viruses can only attack specific types of cells, not just any cells. For example, the rabies virus can only enter brain cells, polio viruses attack the nervous system, and cold viruses enter the cells lining the respiratory system.

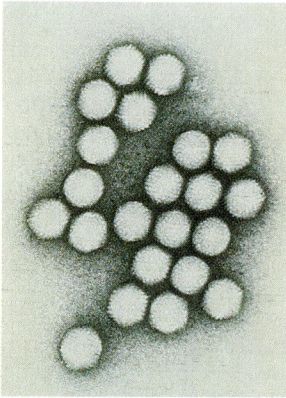

Adenoviruses cause the common cold in early spring and summer.

The lone-star tick is the carrier of Rocky Mountain spotted fever in the Southeast United States.

Viral hepatitis is caused by a virus that affects the abdominal organs. Mumps and mononucleosis (**mahn**-oh-new-klee-**oh**-sus) are caused by viruses that infect glandular tissues. Smallpox, chicken pox, shingles, and warts are infections caused by viruses that attack the skin tissues.

When a virus enters the human body, it attaches itself to a cell and releases its nucleic acid into the host cell. The substance disrupts the cell's activities and causes it to begin producing more of the viruses identical to the one that attached itself to the cell wall. These viruses then spread to other body cells, where the process is repeated.

Rickettsias

Rickettsias (rik-**et**-see-uhs) are *organisms that are considered intermediate, that is, somewhere between a virus and a bacterium.* They are smaller than bacteria. Most of them grow in the intestinal tracts of insects, which then carry them to their human hosts. A rickettsia requires a living cell in order to grow and multiply.

Blood-sucking insects such as lice, mites, and ticks carry the rickettsia germ to humans. *Typhus* (**tie**-fus) *fever* and *Rocky Mountain spotted fever* are diseases caused by these organisms.

Ringworm can spread quickly, especially among children. (See page 45 for more information.)

Fungi

Fungi (**fun**-guy) (singular form: *fungus*) are *simple plants that cannot make their own food.* Many feed off dead animals, insects, and leaves. Fungi are, therefore, saprophytes. They prefer dark, damp environments. Some of the best known fungi include yeast and mushrooms.

Disease-producing fungi mainly invade deep tissues of the hair, nails, and skin. Fungi cause infections of the scalp, such as *ringworm,* and of the feet, such as *athlete's foot.* Pathogenic fungi can also cause *brain inflammation* and serious lung infection.

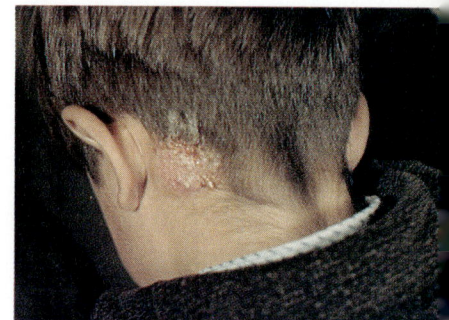

Protozoans

Protozoans (**prote**-uh-zoe-uns), or protozoas, are *single-celled organisms that are larger and have a more complex cellular structure than bacteria.* Most protozoans are harmless. The disease-producing protozoans are most common in tropical areas that have poor sanitation. Protozoans cause *malaria, African sleeping sickness,* and *amebic dysentery* (uh-**mee**-bic **dis**-in-terr-ee), a severe intestinal infection.

Other Pathogens That Can Cause Infections

Certain flatworms and roundworms, while not microorganisms, are regarded as pathogens and cause diseases in the human body. Disease-producing flatworms include *flukes,* which can invade the blood, intestines, liver, or lungs, and *tapeworms,* which live in the intestines. *Pathogenic roundworms* can infect the intestines, muscles, and fluids under the skin. You may have heard of **trichinosis** (**trik**-uh-no-sus), *a disease caused by an intestinal roundworm and transmitted primarily from eating improperly cooked meat—specifically, pork.*

CHECK YOURSELF

1. Name six types of pathogens that cause disease.
2. How do disease-causing bacteria work in the body?
3. How are viruses different from the other pathogens?
4. What is the difference between a parasite and a saprophyte? Give an example of each.

3. The Infectious Disease Process

What happens when a person becomes infected by a pathogen? Why do some people get sick and others do not? Every infectious disease develops and follows the same general pattern. As you begin to understand this process, you can better identify ways to prevent diseases.

Factors Necessary for an Infectious Disease

Certain factors must be present for a disease to develop. By removing or controlling only one of these factors, a disease can be stopped or prevented. The pathogen needs:

1. An **intermediary host.** The pathogen needs a place to live before it invades a noninfected organism. This could be a human, an animal, a plant, food, or soil.
2. A **means of transmission.** The pathogen has to leave its intermediary host and travel to the noninfected organism.
3. A **host.** The host must be a person, in this case, whose body has a lowered resistance to the pathogen, thus being susceptible to the infection.

The Spread of Pathogens

Pathogens are spread in basically four ways:

1. **Close contact with an infected person.** Many infectious diseases spread as a result of close contact with an infected person. Colds, flu, mumps, measles, and pneumonia are diseases spread through coughing and sneezing. The pathogens are in tiny droplets of moisture expelled when a person coughs or sneezes. They become airborne, and people near the contagious person breathe in the pathogens.
2. **Direct contact with the infection.** Other pathogens are spread when an uninfected person comes into direct contact with an infected area on another person's body. Some skin infections, as well as the sexually transmitted diseases, are spread in this way.
3. **Contact with animals.** Animals spread many serious diseases. When insects like fleas and mosquitoes feed on an infected person, they may take the disease-causing germs into their own body. The pathogens continue their development within the insect.

   When the insect bites an uninfected person, it injects some of the pathogens into the person's body, thus spreading the disease. Some infectious diseases, like rabies, are spread by direct contact with infected mammals and birds.

Cold germs are spread by sneezing and by adhering to surfaces. So not only cover your nose and mouth while sneezing, but wash your hands frequently, too!

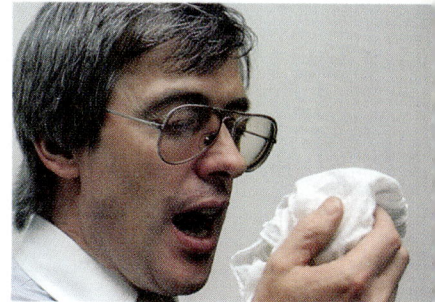

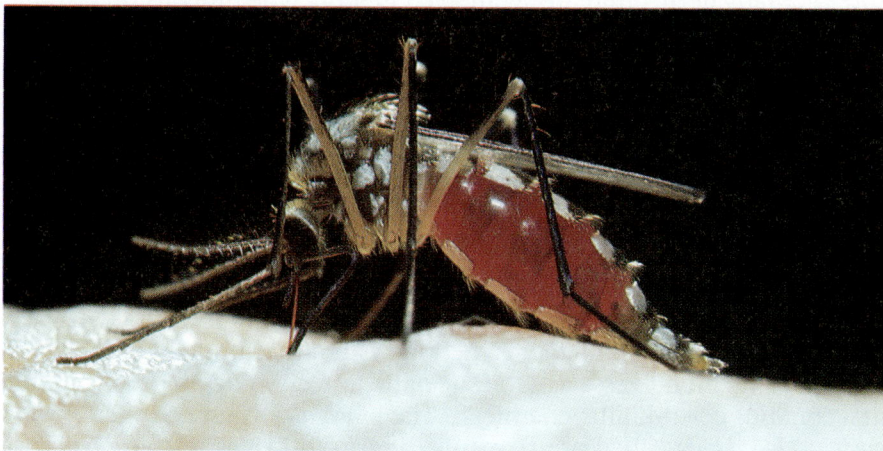

Mosquitoes are common carriers of infectious diseases.

4. **Contact with objects.** Certain pathogens can live for long periods of time on nonliving things. They are spread when an uninfected person comes into contact with objects that the contagious person has used. In certain diseases, like chicken pox, the disease-carrying germ enters the body and can spread to other people before the symptoms of the disease appear. This is known as the "contagious" period.

Other infectious diseases can be spread through contaminated drinking water. This is especially a problem in communities that have poor sanitation.

Have you ever had food poisoning? Contaminated foods or improperly cooked foods, like pork, also transmit infectious diseases.

Defense Against Infectious Diseases

In order for the infectious disease to spread, the pathogen must have a host. With all of the germs that are present in our environment and all of the available human hosts, why are there not more disease epidemics?

The body has three major defense systems to protect itself against infections. It has *mechanical, chemical,* and *biological barriers* that prevent the pathogens from entering the body.

Mechanical Defenses

First, the tough, dead cells that make up our outer layer of skin form a very effective barrier to germs. Membranes in the mouth, nose, and bronchial tubes are covered with mucus that traps many pathogens. They are then expelled when a person coughs or sneezes.

Chemical Defenses

The body has several chemical barriers, including tears, that fight many infectious pathogens. The digestive juices of the stomach are high in acid and kill many germs that are swallowed in food. The mucous membranes also release a protective chemical that fights disease-causing germs.

You read earlier that some bacteria, called *resident bacteria,* are helpful in fighting germs. They work in two ways to protect the body against infections. First, they produce substances that kill certain germs. Second, resident bacteria crowd out many of the pathogens that otherwise would grow and multiply in the body.

Biological Defenses

What happens when germs manage to penetrate these barriers? The body has an internal biological reaction system that protects it against infections. Tiny blood vessels at the site of the infection begin to release fluid that contains germ-killing chemicals. The *vessels also release cells, most of which are white blood cells,* called **neutrophils** (**new**-trah-fils). These *neutrophils sur-*

Immunology Terms

Immune response—the body's production of disease-fighting cells and antibodies.

Immunologists (im-yah-**nahl**-uh-jests)—scientists who study the process of immunity.

Immunization (im-yah-nigh-**zay**-shun)—any medical procedure that enables a person to develop immunity to specific disease-producing organisms which he or she might have caught.

round and literally eat up the invading bacteria germs. This process is known as **phagocytosis** (fag-uh-suh-**toe**-sus), the prefix *phago* meaning "eating." The cells surround the invading bacteria and digest them.

Monocytes (**mahn**-uh-sites) are *produced in the bone marrow and, like neutrophils, carry out phagocytosis.* They work with neutrophils to destroy bacteria and are especially important in killing bacteria that cause tuberculosis. Monocytes also work with *lymphocytes,* which you will read about in the next section.

In reacting to an invading virus germ, the body cells that have been infected release **interferon** (int-ur-**fear**-ahn), *a protective protein.* Researchers are still studying interferon. It does not protect the infected cell that produces it, but it protects the uninfected cells by signaling them to begin producing antiviral chemicals.

Not all cells or all viruses trigger the interferon. However, the body can use the interferon manufactured as a result of one virus to protect itself against other viruses.

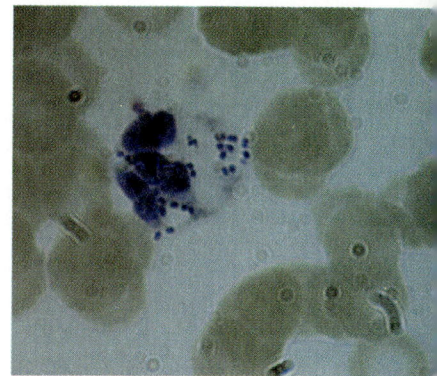

In phagocytosis, the neutrophils devour the invading germs.

Fever   Fever is another way that the body reacts to and fights infections. Many internal chemical reactions speed up when germs invade the body. **Fever** happens when *internal heat is formed faster than the body can get rid of it, thus raising body temperature.* In some cases, invading bacteria manufacture poisons called *pyrogens* (**pie**-ro-gens) (firemakers), which cause fever by affecting the body's temperature-control centers. Even though fever's function is not completely understood, doctors think that some pathogens cannot live or reproduce at temperatures higher than the normal body temperature. The fever weakens or kills these germs.

For information on reading a thermometer, see page HB27 of the *Health Handbook.*

CHECK YOURSELF

1. What factors must be present for an infectious disease to develop?
2. How are pathogens spread?
3. What defenses does your body have against pathogens?

Immunity (im-**you**-nuht-ee) is *the body's ability to resist harmful substances known as* **immunogens** (im-**mune**-nuh-jens). Immunogens include disease-producing germs as well as poisons from certain insects, spiders, and snakes.

The Body's Immune System

The body's immune system has two helps—*phagocytosis,* which has been described on page 521, and *antibodies* (**ant**-uh-bod-eez). When a pathogen enters the body, specialized cells react. Certain cells directly attack the germs, while others produce **antibodies,** which are *proteins released into the blood to neutralize or destroy the germs.*

Both of these responses depend on *a type of white blood cell,* the **lymphocyte** (**lim**-fuh-site). Lymphocytes are manufactured in the bone marrow and are transported through the lymph system.

The Lymphatic System

As you know, blood passes through the capillary walls into the body cells and is the body's primary means of transporting oxygen, nutrients, and cell wastes. The body has *a secondary circulatory network*—the **lymphatic system.** This system *provides a means of returning fluids from the body tissues to the heart.*

Such a system is necessary because fluid pressure in the body continuously causes water and other materials to seep out of the capillaries. This fluid, called **interstitial** (int-ur-**stish**-ul) **fluid,** *nourishes body tissues.* If there were no way for it to return to the blood, the tissues would become swollen. *This fluid returns by way of the lymphatic system* and is called **lymph.**

The lymphatic system also serves as one of the body's defenses against infection. The lymph flowing through this system can carry larger molecules and particles than the blood can. The lymph also carries a number of white blood cells, particularly granulocytes (**gran**-yuh-low-sites) and lymphocytes. Some of these white blood cells are returned to the larger veins, while others are stored in **lymph nodes,** *glandlike structures that serve as filters to screen out bacteria.*

Types of Lymphocytes

There are two main types of lymphocytes. One type, called **B cells,** is *responsible for producing antibodies that destroy or neutralize the invading germ.* Invading germs stimulate the B-type lymphocytes in the lymph nodes to divide and become plasma cells, which, in turn, produce antibodies. *The microbes or foreign bodies that stimulate the production of antibodies* are called **antigens** (**ant**-uh-jens).

The Lymphatic System

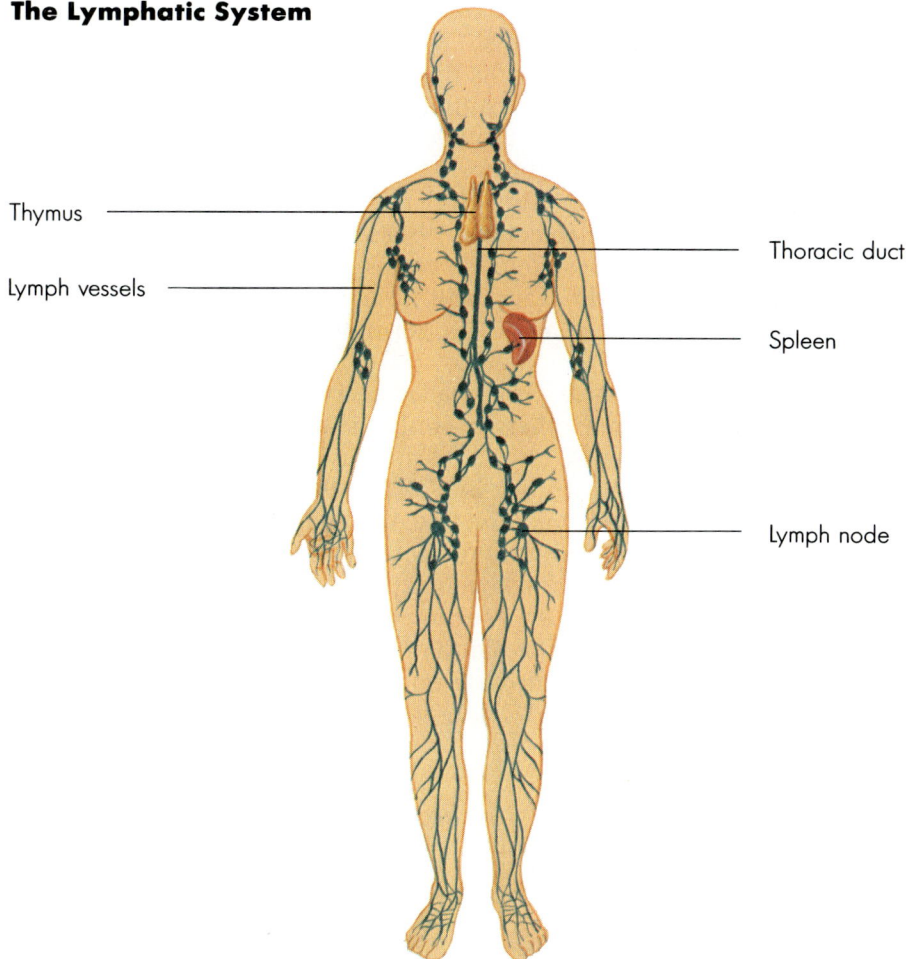

Thymus

Lymph vessels

Thoracic duct

Spleen

Lymph node

The lymphatic system is the body's secondary circulatory network.

The second type, called **T cells,** are produced in the bone marrow and then travel to the thymus gland. Here they undergo changes and then end up with the B cells in the bloodstream. *They attack the invading substance or organism directly.* They actually surround the invading germs and digest them.

Antibodies—A Complex Operation

As we have seen, antibodies are proteins that certain cells manufacture to defend the body against some disease-causing germs. Some antibodies cause chemical changes that dissolve the bacteria germs, while others alter the surface of the bacteria, causing the germs to clump together. The white blood cells then digest the clumps.

A third way that antibodies work is by attaching themselves to and then covering the virus or poisonous substance. This destroys the activity of the substance.

Antibodies are highly specialized. This means a specific antibody works on or against only one kind of germ. The body produces different antibodies for different disease-causing germs.

Immunity

As you have read, immunity is the human body's natural resistance to many diseases. Certain germs cannot live in the body, while others are quickly destroyed if they enter the body.

One important feature of the body's immune system is that it remembers the pathogens it meets. This gives the body long-term protection—immunity—against many infectious diseases. For example, if you had chicken pox, your immune system remembers the chicken-pox virus germ. If the germ enters the body again, cells designed specifically to combat it will attack the germ immediately. The germ doesn't get a chance to make you sick again.

This *immunity the body develops* is called **active immunity.** Some types of immunity last a lifetime; others last only a short period of time. A single virus causes chicken pox, so once a person has had the disease, the body is usually protected against it for life. However, many different kinds of viruses cause the common cold. Because the body is continually exposed to different cold germs, immunity to the cold lasts for only a short time.

In cases where a person has been exposed to disease-causing germs, a doctor can give the person an injection of serum containing antibodies. The serum is obtained from the blood of a person who developed an immunity. It gives a person immediate but temporary protection against a disease.

Vaccines Provide Active Immunity

Through the use of vaccines (vak-**seens**), the body can develop active immunity against a disease without actually having had the disease. **Vaccines** are usually *preparations that are composed of dead or weakened viruses.* Vaccines provide immunity by causing the body to produce antibodies. The vaccine contains substances that are strong enough to cause the production of antibodies, but not strong enough to actually cause a disease. Through the process of a **vaccination** (vak-suh-**nay**-shun), *vaccine is injected into the body.*

The first vaccine was developed by Dr. Edward Jenner in 1796. In an effort to control the deadly smallpox disease, he injected people with pus from the sores of cowpox. (The cowpox and smallpox viruses are closely related.) People developed a mild case of cowpox, but also developed an immunity to smallpox. Jenner's technique has been refined, and vaccinations are now used to protect people from a variety of crippling or fatal diseases.

At birth, babies carry in their blood small amounts of the antibodies that protected their mothers. They are thus protected from the same diseases as their mothers. This immunity lasts for a few months until the baby can produce antibodies of his or her own. This *temporary immunity that the infant acquires from the mother* is called **passive immunity.**

KEEPING FIT

Your Immunization Record

Find out if you have an up-to-date immunization record. When was the last time that you had a booster or a tetanus shot? You can begin keeping your own health records.

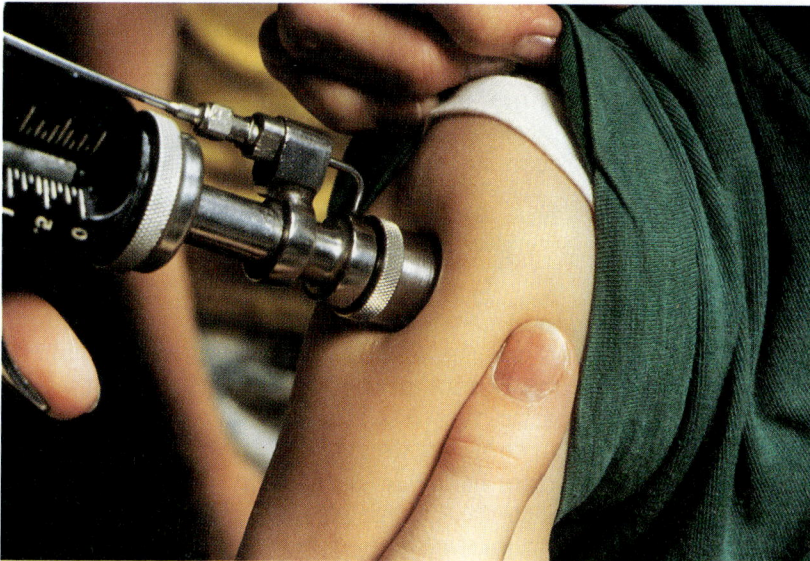

Most individual injections for illnesses are given with a conventional needle. Group vaccinations are given with a "gun" that is quick and painless.

Types of Vaccines

Some of the major types of vaccines include *live-virus vaccine, killed-virus vaccine,* and *toxoids.*

Live-Virus Vaccine

Some vaccines are made from weakened-virus germs. By using mechanical means or chemicals and *growing the virus over and over until it is a very weak germ,* scientists develop a **live-virus vaccine.** In this weakened state, the virus cannot cause a disease, but it does make the body form antibodies. Measles, rubella, and oral polio vaccines all contain live viruses.

Killed-Virus Vaccine

Another type of vaccine is the killed-virus vaccine. Scientists use mechanical means or chemicals to kill the viruses. The **killed-virus vaccine** *causes the body to produce antibodies, but it is not as powerful as the live-virus vaccine.* This is why people need booster shots of killed-virus vaccine. **Booster shots** are *injections given to add strength to the antibody in guarding against infection.*

Toxoids

Diphtheria and tetanus are diseases caused by bacteria that release a poisonous chemical called *toxin.* Scientists have discovered that by chemically treating bacteria toxins, they can make very effective vaccines. The treated toxins, called **toxoids** (**tahk**-soids), *stimulate the production of antibodies and establish active immunity against diphtheria and tetanus.*

Reactions to Vaccines

Vaccines are as safe as modern medicine can make them. However, vaccinations sometimes cause minor reactions, usually in the form of mild fever and skin rash. On rare occasions, more serious reactions may occur. Yet, the risks from vaccines are far less than the risks from the diseases themselves.

Immunization for All

Immunization is more than just a good idea—the law often requires it. Each state has its own laws governing immunizations and school attendance. In most states, students cannot enter kindergarten without up-to-date immunizations. Several states now enforce laws that prevent teenagers from attending school without complete immunization. Why do you think immunizations are so important in the school setting?

The chart in your *Health Handbook*, page HB32, shows you the recommended vaccines to take from infancy. Other vaccines are available and may be needed on different occasions. Influenza vaccines are often recommended during epidemics. For people traveling to other countries, vaccines against typhoid, yellow fever, cholera, and bubonic plague are available. They may be recommended if these diseases are a danger in the part of the world in which the person is traveling. In Chapter 25, we learned how the World Health Organization is using immunization to eradicate a number of world diseases.

CHECK YOURSELF

1. What relationship does the lymph system have to the body's immune system?
2. What is the difference between active and passive immunity?
3. How do vaccinations work to provide immunity?

5. Communicable Diseases—Symptoms, Treatment, and Prevention

Some communicable diseases are more common than others. Diseases that were once dreaded can now be controlled through immunizations. Some have even been completely eradicated. However, because some diseases are no longer the threat they used to be, people have gotten lax in their immunization programs, and isolated cases of some diseases, such as polio, are being reported. An immunization program is essential, just as is the practice of simple biofeedback.

Your Disease-Prevention Efforts

Disease Prevention and Wellness

Take the *Your Disease Prevention Inventory* and score yourself. Review the statements in relationship to your practice of wellness. Each statement relates to good health habits, preventive measures, or listening to one's body. Only a healthy body can fight disease. As the body's resistance is lowered by poor eating habits, stress, drugs, and lack of sleep and exercise, it becomes more susceptible to disease. There is no way to separate one's daily health behaviors and choices from one's level of wellness.

On a separate sheet of paper, answer *most of the time, some of the time,* or *never* to each statement as it relates to your behavior.

1. I keep my immunization records up to date. *MT*
2. I have periodic medical and dental checkups. *MT*
3. I eat a daily balanced diet. *ST*
4. I get at least eight hours of sleep a night. *N*
5. I exercise vigorously at least three times a week. *ST*
6. I do not smoke. *ST*
7. I avoid using towels that others have used. *MT*
8. I avoid using other people's combs and brushes. *MT*
9. I take a few minutes each day to relax. *ST*
10. I stay home at least the first day that symptoms of illness appear. *ST*
11. I listen and respond to my body's messages that it is tired or that something may be wrong. *ST*
12. I wash my hands before every meal. *ST*
13. I shower or bathe regularly. *MT*
14. I do not share eating utensils or glasses with other people. *MT*
15. I cover my mouth when I cough or sneeze. *MT*
16. I avoid walking barefooted in locker rooms and shower rooms. *MT*

You have read of most of these health behaviors before in other chapters. Some of them sound simple—even elementary—yet many people fail to practice them regularly. Are you being responsible for promoting your own wellness?

Scoring. Give yourself a 4 for each time you answered *most of the time,* a 2 for *some of the time,* and a 0 for *never.*

35 to 60: Your disease-prevention efforts are very good.

15 to 34: You practice some prevention but could do more.

14 or below: Watch out! You are allowing yourself to be more susceptible to infectious diseases than necessary. You need to practice more prevention.

Biofeedback

One way to keep checking on yourself is through **biofeedback—** *biological feedback about your body.* It is the process of becoming aware of physical events in your body that you normally are not aware of, with the intent of gaining voluntary control of such events.

Simple and basic examples of biofeedback include:

1. weighing yourself,
2. taking your pulse when exercising,
3. taking your temperature when you are sick.

Walter Reed and Yellow Fever

In the Spanish-American War (1898), Spanish guns killed few American soldiers, but disease wiped out entire battalions. Doctor Walter Reed (1851–1902), an army surgeon, was assigned the task of studying the cause and spread of typhoid fever.

Reed worked for over a year, discovering that flies were the carriers of typhoid. With this information, he was able to show the military how to prevent the spread of typhoid.

But conquering typhoid was just the beginning. Reed's most outstanding work was battling yellow fever. It is hard to imagine, but this dread disease killed 100,000 Americans in the late 1800s. Florida, Texas, and Louisiana were dangerous places to live during certain months, and at times the disease spread as far north as New York. In only 30 days, Philadelphia lost one-tenth of its entire population.

Doctor Reed dispelled the theory that yellow fever was spread by humans. He believed it was carried by mosquitoes. Since there was no way to test this theory on animals, doctors allowed themselves to be bitten by mosquitoes to see if they would get yellow fever. Doctor Jesse Lazear did get it and within one week was dead. Another doctor also died of the disease. Reed confirmed his theory.

Yellow fever became the first human disease discovered to be caused by a virus. Efforts began to control the mosquitoes. In 1905, the U.S. experienced its last epidemic of yellow fever—in New Orleans.

Walter Reed did not live to witness the eradication of yellow fever. He died in 1902, and in 1945 he was elected to the Hall of Fame for Great Americans.

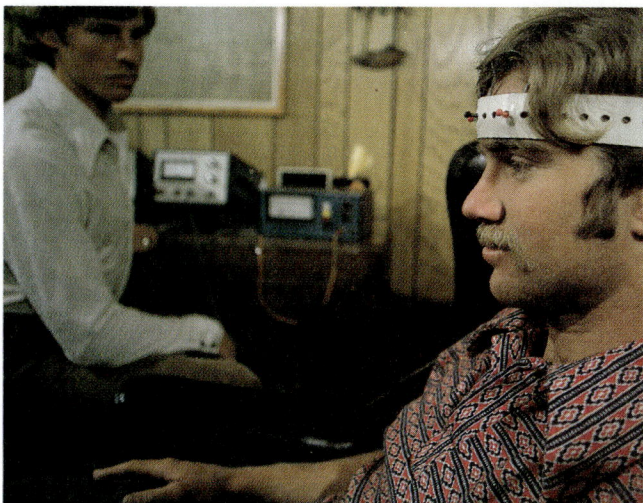
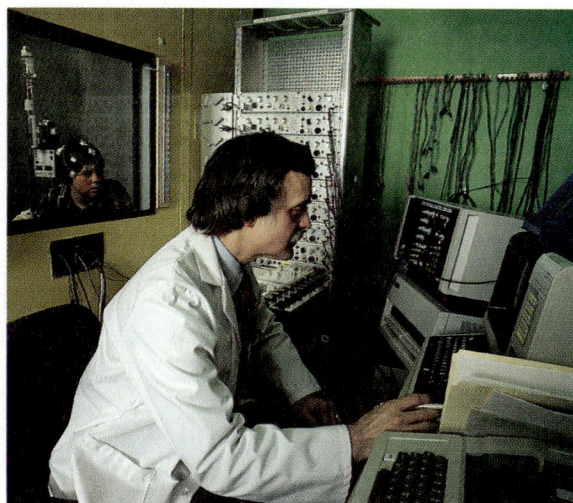

Biofeedback provides a means for receiving feedback on areas of the body that are *involuntary*—that is, areas that function under the control of the autonomic nervous system. These include the brain, the heart, and the circulatory system.

Biofeedback instruments, such as this electro-encephalogram (EEG), are one of the most important medical developments of the last 20 years.

Other Uses of Biofeedback

Besides using the personal methods of biofeedback, other methods can be used to help restructure many body malfunctions. Using sophisticated instrumentation, muscle tension, brain waves, skin temperature, skin resistance, and other physical processes can be regulated.

The implications of biofeedback in preventive medicine and health maintenance are tremendous. Changes in the body's balanced healthy state can be prevented or overcome by consciously reestablishing normal body conditions. Biofeedback is used clinically for stress management, migraine and tension headaches, anxiety neurosis, neuromuscular rehabilitation, and gastrointestinal disorders.

Biofeedback Instruments

The principal instruments used in biofeedback training are:

1. **Electromyogram** (ee-lek-troh-**my**-uh-gram) **(EMG).** The feedback of bioelectric information from the muscles regarding muscle tension.
2. **Electroencephalogram** (ee-lek-troh-en-**sef**-uh-luh-gram) **(EEG).** The feedback of bioelectric information from the brain regarding changes in the brain-wave status.
3. **Thermal trainer.** The feedback of changes in skin temperature, a result of blood flow.
4. **Electrodermal** (ee-lek-troh-**der**-mul) **response (EDR).** The feedback of changes in skin resistance, a result of perspiration.

Biofeedback will become increasingly popular in the future. But, the simple disease-prevention steps that we all take day after day are also invaluable. Consult your *Health Handbook*, page HB32, for a list of these steps.

The Common Cold

Colds are caused by viruses that are spread through the air, water, or by any direct or indirect contact with a contagious person. Once you have been exposed to a cold virus, it usually takes one to two days for the symptoms to appear.

The cold virus is most contagious during the first 24 hours after symptoms appear. Symptoms can include a mild fever, aching, sneezing, congestion, a runny nose, a cough, a mild sore throat, and a headache.

At present, there is no cure for the cold. Getting rest, drinking liquids, and maintaining good nutrition are the best methods of treating the cold virus. Americans spend about $500 million a year on over-the-counter cold remedies. Some of these may help to relieve the symptoms, but many are useless and some may even be harmful.

One problem with many cold remedies is that they cover up or temporarily relieve symptoms, so people go back to school or work rather than stay at home. This presents two problems:

1. the body does not get the rest it needs to recover energy to fight the germs,
2. the infected person spreads the disease germs to those he or she is around.

Although it may be difficult to completely prevent colds, you can keep your body healthy so it can better resist infection. Good nutrition, regular exercise, adequate sleep, and good hygiene all contribute to prevention. Controlling stress levels and relaxing also help to ward off infections.

Not smoking is another way you can directly work to prevent infections. People who smoke get more colds, and their colds tend to last longer.

Colds can be dangerous. Call a doctor if any of these symptoms lasts two or more days:

1. a fever of 101°F (0.38°C) or over,
2. sore throat with a 101°F (0.38°C) fever,
3. pains or shortness of breath in the chest,
4. continued coughing,
5. pains in the back of the throat or in the ears,
6. any of the above, even after taking over-the-counter medicines.

Mononucleosis

Mononucleosis is *an infectious disease, common among young people, that develops as a result of a large, abnormal increase in the number of lymphocytes in*

L I F E MANAGEMENT S K I L L

Infectious Germs and Your Well-Being

An infectious germ has less of a chance to survive in a healthy body. Persons who have been under a great deal of stress, are not maintaining a well-balanced diet, or are not getting adequate rest are not fully capable of resisting infection. Do you promote your own wellness and practice prevention? Review the list of seven basic health habits and the suggestions for reducing stress (both on page HB18).

HEPATITIS

"My brother recently contracted hepatitis, and we all had to get shots to protect us. What exactly is hepatitis? How is it contracted?"

Hepatitis is *a disease involving an inflammation of the liver.* There are two main types—*viral hepatitis* and *toxic hepatitis.* There are two forms of viral hepatitis—*infectious hepatitis,* type A, and *serum hepatitis,* type B.

Infectious hepatitis, type A, results from eating contaminated food or drinking contaminated water. Symptoms include weakness, loss of appetite, vomiting, and *jaundice*—a yellowing discoloration of the skin. Symptoms usually appear three to four weeks after being exposed to the virus germ and last from two to six weeks.

You probably received a shot of *gamma globulin* (**gam**-uh **glob**-yuh-lun), a protein fraction of blood rich in antibodies. If this vaccine is administered within a week of a person's being exposed to the hepatitis virus, the disease can be definitely prevented.

Serum hepatitis, type-B virus, used to be transmitted through blood transfusions from an infected donor. However, tests that detect the virus in the blood have helped to eliminate this means of transmission. Unsterile medical instruments, contact with an infected person, and hypodermic needles shared by drug abusers are the main ways the B virus is spread. Symptoms usually appear 6 to 12 weeks after the infection. The treatment is the same for types A and B, and bed rest is prescribed for both.

Toxic hepatitis results from exposure to certain chemicals. The chemicals can enter the body by being swallowed, inhaled, injected, or absorbed through the skin. Symptoms will depend on the particular chemicals causing the hepatitis.

the blood. It gets its name from these mononuclear (singular form: *nucleus*) cells. It is believed to be caused by a virus and is spread primarily through direct contact, such as kissing. Symptoms include chills, fever, sore throat, fatigue, and swelling of the lymph nodes. Complete bed rest is usually prescribed, since treatment and recovery can take as long as three to six weeks.

CHECK YOURSELF

1. How can biofeedback be used to benefit us?
2. What can be done to relieve the common cold?
3. What is mononucleosis, and what is the best treatment for it?

CHAPTER 29   Review

CHAPTER SUMMARY

- Infectious diseases are caused by microorganisms called pathogens.
- Pathogens that cause infectious diseases are bacteria, viruses, rickettsias, fungi, and protozoans.
- In order for a disease to be present, there must be an intermediary host, a means of transmission, and a host.
- By controlling any one of these three variables, disease can be prevented.
- Pathogens spread by close contact with an infected person, by direct contact with the infection, by contact with animals, and by contact with objects.
- The body has mechanical, chemical, and biological lines of defense that help it to fight the invasion of pathogens.
- The most complex of these defenses is the body's immune system. The body itself has naturally acquired immunity and, through vaccines, artificially acquired immunity.
- The body's immune system has two parts—phagocytosis and antibodies.
- The body's ability to fight infection depends on how the individual takes care of his or her own body and health.
- The body's resistance to diseases increases with the practice of good health habits.

REVIEWING WHAT YOU LEARNED

1. What makes viruses so much more difficult to deal with than the other pathogens?
2. Describe how the immune system works.
3. Describe three steps to take to prevent infectious diseases.
4. Distinguish between the various types of immunity.
5. What are some major factors that would cause one's immune system not to function at the level at which it is capable?
6. Identify symptoms of three common infectious diseases.
7. Explain the role of the antigen in the immunization process.
8. Outline the necessary steps for the development of communicable disease in a human being.
9. Why might it not be a good idea to attempt to reduce a slight fever during an illness?

APPLYING WHAT YOU LEARNED

1. In recent years, some groups have challenged the right of government to make laws requiring immunization of children before they enter school. If you were given the task of explaining the need for such laws, what would you say? Make your response within two paragraphs.
2. Interview four people who are in their late 30s or older about polio. What were some of the myths about the disease? What were some of the fears that people had? Compare what these people say with what is known or feared today about polio. Report your findings to the class, and compare all the findings.
3. Research Jonas Salk and A. B. Sabin. What was the difference in their discoveries? What impact did they have on the health of the public? Write a one-page information report on your findings and read it to the class.
4. On one side of a poster board, made a collage of ads for cold remedies. On the other side, create your own ad for preventing the cold and treating it with good health habits.
5. Find out what some of the myths were surrounding the great plague that broke out in Europe in the Middle Ages. It was called the Black Death. How did people's fear of the plague affect their way of dealing with it? When did the plague disappear, and why?
6. Research Rocky Mountain spotted fever. What is it? How did it get its name?
7. In the 19th and 20th centuries, Ellis Island in New York City harbor was a clearing house for millions of immigrants who came to this country. Find out about the disease-prevention efforts that were carried out with the immigrants. Draw some conclusions about their effectiveness.

FOCUS ON WELLNESS

Communicable disease requires a suitable environment in which to continue to spread and cause health problems. *As an individual, I can help to break the continuance of communicable disease and control the spread by . . .*

microorganisms
infectious diseases
communicable
noninfectious diseases
noncommunicable diseases
pathogens
bacteria
resident bacteria
saprophytes
parasite
host
toxins
cocci
bacilli
spirilla
virus
rhinoviruses
corona viruses
adenoviruses
coxsackie viruses
enteroviruses
echoviruses

Epstein-Barr virus
herpesviruses
rickettsias
fungi
protozoans
trichinosis
neutrophils
phagocytosis
monocytes
interferon
fever
immunity
immunogens
antibodies
lymphocyte
immune response
immunologists
immunization
lymphatic system
interstitial fluid
lymph
lymph nodes

B cells
antigens
T cells
active immunity
vaccines
vaccination
passive immunity
live-virus vaccine
killed-virus vaccine
booster shots
toxoids
biofeedback
electromyogram (EMG)
electroencephalogram (EEG)
thermal trainer
electrodermal response (EDR)
hepatitis
mononucleosis

PUTTING VOCABULARY TO USE

Use the clues below to find the correct term in the chapter vocabulary list. Write the answers on a separate piece of paper.

1. _____. A preparation injected into the body that is strong enough to cause immunity and yet not strong enough to cause disease.
2. _____. An injection given to add to the antibody strength in guarding against infection.
3. _____. An infectious disease common among young people that is caused by an abnormal increase in lymphocytes and that spreads through direct contact.
4. _____. Any disease-producing organism.
5. _____ _____. Organisms that are helpful to the body in that they protect us from harmful bacteria.
6. _____. An organism that actually lives off another living plant or animal.
7. _____. The place where a parasite feeds.
8. _____. The body's ability to resist disease-producing substances.

9. _____. A proteinlike substance that is produced in the body to fight infection.
10. _____. Agents that stimulate the production of antibodies; foreign substances in the body.
11. _____. A secondary circulatory system that helps fight infection.

Match the description with its pathogen. Write the answers on a separate piece of paper.

1. _____. Rocky Mountain spotted fever is an example of a disease caused by this type of pathogen.
2. _____. Some of these cause infections of of scalp and the feet.
3. _____. Most of these are harmless.
4. _____. Organisms that may be shaped like corkscrews, rods, or round clusters.
5. _____. A parasite that requires a dead cell in which to grow and multiply.
6. _____. Caused by intestinal roundworm.

Sexually Transmitted Diseases

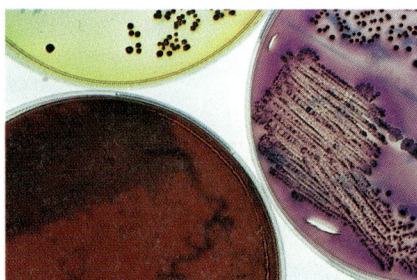

Sexually transmitted diseases (STDs) represent a serious threat to the health of all Americans, but particularly to young adults. About 85% of all cases of STDs involve people between the ages of 15 and 30. The highest rate of increase in the diseases is among the teenage population. About 2,000 teenagers become infected with an STD every day.

After studying this chapter, you will be able to:

- define the term sexually transmitted disease,
- identify and describe the symptoms and treatment for the most serious sexually transmitted diseases,
- identify the serious complications of each sexually transmitted disease, if not treated,
- discuss the importance of seeking medical attention for any sign of a sexually transmitted disease,
- identify how the spread of sexually transmitted diseases can be prevented or curtailed,
- view sexually transmitted diseases as a serious threat to one's *total* health.

A **sexually transmitted disease (STD)**, or a **venereal** (vuh-**neer**-ee-ul) **disease (VD)** as it is more commonly called, is a *communicable disease that is spread from person to person through sexual contact*. While many of the common communicable diseases are being controlled, rates of STDs are rising steadily.

Although epidemics of STDs are current in this country, there are ways to control and even prevent the diseases completely. The first step to do so is to obtain accurate information about the diseases and to recognize inaccurate information.

Gonorrhea (gahn-uh-**ree**-uh) is the third most common communicable disease, the common cold being the first and an STD called chlamydia (kluh-**mid**-ee-uh) (see page 541) being the second. Despite the fact that gonorrhea is a treatable disease and can be cured, about 2 million cases of it are reported in the United States each year. There is no way of knowing how many unreported cases there are.

Why do people fail to seek medical attention? A social stigma exists about STDs, and some people are embarrassed. Others are not willing to take responsibility for their actions. Still others just will not believe that "it *could* happen to them." Through denial and rationalization, they ignore the signs and symptoms. In many cases, no symptoms are obvious, and the person does not know that he or she has the disease.

Gonorrhea is *a disease caused by a bacteria germ that lives in warm, moist areas of the body*, primarily in the lining of the urethra of the male and in the cervix of the female. The bacteria are transmitted during sexual contact. A person cannot pick up the germ from towels or toilet seats, because the bacteria cannot live outside the body.

The gonorrhea bacteria germ lives in warm, moist areas of the body and is highly contagious.

Symptoms of Gonorrhea

In the case of gonorrhea, one problem is that symptoms are not always obvious. This is true particularly in the female, who may never know that she has gonorrhea. The symptoms may not be present or may be so slight that an infected person does not notice them.

In the female, symptoms may include a slight discharge from the vagina, a burning sensation during urination, abnormal menstruation, and abdominal pain or tenderness. In the male, symptoms may include a whitish discharge from the penis and a burning sensation during urination. The lymph glands in the groin may also become enlarged and tender.

These symptoms usually appear between three days and three weeks after sexual contact with an infected person. These symptoms may go away on their own, but the disease is still present in the body.

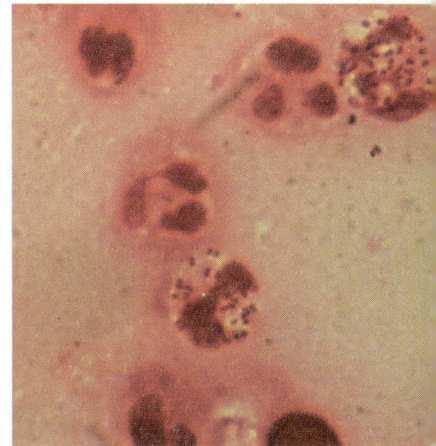

Diagnosis and Treatment

A physical examination, which includes a laboratory test of secretions from the male's penis or from the female's cervix, is necessary to diagnose gonorrhea. If gonorrhea is diagnosed early, it can be cured.

Most cases of gonorrhea can be safely and effectively cured by using antibiotics—either penicillin or tetracycline (tet-**rah**-syck-lean). But now there is a new, more serious strain of gonorrhea that resists penicillin. Patients must use strong antibiotics to treat it. It is also very wise to pay a follow-up visit to the health clinic or doctor's office to be sure the treatment was effective.

The body does not develop an immunity to gonorrhea or any other STD, so a person can contract the disease again. Furthermore, since a different germ causes each of the different STDs, a person can have more than one STD at a time.

There is only one sure means of preventing gonorrhea—no sexual contact.

Problems from Untreated Gonorrhea

In both males and females, untreated gonorrhea can lead to *sterility,* the inability to reproduce. In the male, this is a result of damage to the tubes through which the sperm travel. In the female, scar tissue forms in the Fallopian tubes, blocking the pathway of the egg cell. In the female, this complication can result even if the disease is treated.

Infections in both males and females can cause damage to joints, heart tissue, and other body organs. In the female, **pelvic inflammatory** (in-**flam**-uh-torr-ee) **disease** (**PID**) is another possible complication. This is a *painful infection of the Fallopian tubes, ovaries, and pelvic area.* Symptoms may include pelvic pain, chills and fever, irregular menstrual periods, and lower

---

HEALTH UPDATE   HEALTH UPDATE   HEALTH UPDATE

Battling Gonorrhea

Each year gonorrhea affects about 2 million people, more than half of whom are between the ages of 15 and 24. It is spread easily because the symptoms are hard to recognize. About 80% of the women and 15% of the men who contract gonorrhea do not know they have it.

A new test now makes detection faster and more accurate. This test might also help to limit the spread of the disease. It takes only about an hour to complete, compared to a 72-hour wait for the traditional test. The increased speed helps to get the patient into treatment much earlier.

---

back pain. Gonorrhea also increases the chance of premature labor and *stillbirth*—a full-term child born dead—in pregnant women.

If a female has gonorrhea when she gives birth, the baby can develop eye infections that may lead to permanent blindness. For this reason, most states have a law that requires all newborns to be treated with special eye drops.

CHECK YOURSELF

1. What are the symptoms of gonorrhea?
2. How is gonorrhea diagnosed and treated?
3. List one misconception about gonorrhea.
4. What is PID?

2. Syphilis

While syphilis (**sif**-uh-lus) is not as common as gonorrhea, it is one of the most dangerous of all the sexually transmitted diseases. Syphilis, too, is spread by sexual contact.

Historically, syphilis is supposed to have first been brought to the Old World 500 years ago by Christopher Columbus' crew. In 1494, syphilis appeared in Europe. It is likely that some of the crew or passengers on Columbus' ships had contracted the disease and brought it back to Spain on the return voyage after the discovery. It was present among the Indians in the New World, but in a mild way. In Europe, the disease took the most destructive form.

Syphilis *is a disease that attacks many parts of the body and is caused by a small bacterium called a spirochete* (**spy**-roh-keet). Syphilis is dangerous because, when left untreated, it can damage the vital organs, such as the heart, the liver, the kidneys, and the central nervous system, including the brain. It can cause heart disease, blindness, paralysis, and insanity.

Symptoms of Syphilis

Syphilis develops in stages. Symptoms appear and then go away on their own. However, the disease remains.

The First Stage

The first sign of syphilis is a **chancre (shang**-kur), *a reddish sore at the place where the germ enters the body, usually on the genitals.* It is a painless sore that appears within 10 to 90 days after contact with an infected person. The chancre lasts one to five weeks and will then go away, even if not treated. However, the disease continues to develop in the body.

The Second Stage

The germ, if not treated early, will travel into the bloodstream. Within one to six months after contact, the highly contagious second stage of syphilis appears. This is commonly characterized by a nonitching rash on the chest, back of the arms, and legs. In women, the rash is most often found on the outer edges of the vagina. Sores may develop from the rash. These sores will likely give off a clear liquid filled with the infectious spirochetes. Also, some swelling may occur in the lymph nodes under the arms and around the groin.

Fever, sore throat, and a generally sick feeling all over are also common symptoms. Without treatment, these symptoms will disappear.

The Third Stage

The third stage of syphilis, called *latent syphilis*, usually begins about two or more years after the initial infection. All signs have disappeared, leading the individual to think that he or she is cured, or never had the disease in the first place.

It is in this third stage that syphilis begins to attack the heart and blood vessels and the central nervous system. It actually destroys the tissue of these organs. The damage to these areas is slow and steady. This stage may appear 10 to 20 years after the latent stage. It may last a few months, or 20 years, or until death. Even though people have reached the third stage, they can relapse into the second stage.

Heart disease or nervous disorders may appear and no one will really know, without examination, that syphilis is responsible. A person may experience blindness or insanity. About 25% of all people who allow syphilis to progress to this late stage become *senile* (**seen**-ile), that is, exhibit a loss of mental abilities.

Treatment of Syphilis

While gonorrhea is detected by means of a microscopic slide exam, the test for syphilis, called the Venereal Disease Research Laboratory, or VDRL, is a blood test. The presence of the spirochete in the blood or from the sores indicates the presence of the disease. Some states demand that couples who plan to marry have a blood test for syphilis before doing so.

Penicillin is the main drug used in the treatment for syphilis. Doctors strongly recommend follow-up to be sure that the disease has been cured. No matter how effective the treatment can be, it can only stop the disease from progressing and not continuing. It cannot restore any harm that has already been done, so early treatment of syphilis is crucial.

Just like gonorrhea, syphilis has no immunity. A person may become reinfected at any time. If an individual goes through too many treatments, the body may become immune to penicillin as a means of treatment. As in the case of all STDs, the only sure means of prevention is no sexual contact.

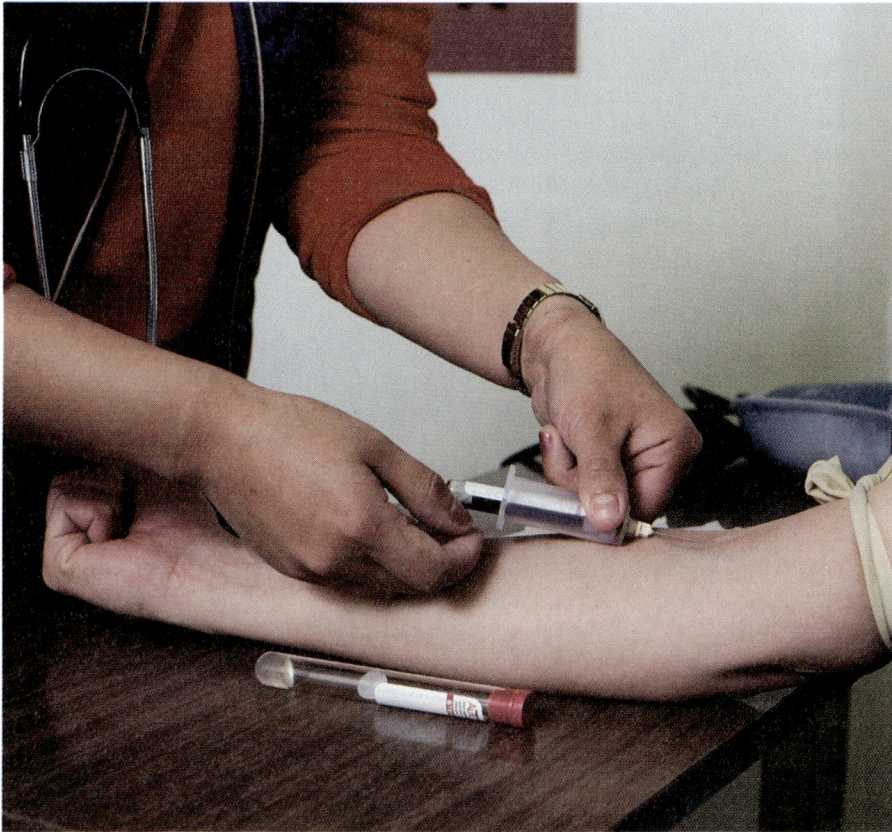

Many states require a blood test for syphilis before they will issue marriage licenses.

Congenital Syphilis

A pregnant woman who has syphilis is likely to transfer the infection to her unborn child. This condition is called **congenital** (kahn-**jen**-uh-tul) **syphilis**. *Congenital* means existing at or dating from birth. The unborn child can develop syphilis any time after the fifth month of pregnancy. The mother's chances of having a *miscarriage*—the expulsion of a human fetus that is not capable of living—are four times greater if she has syphilis, and her chances of having a stillborn baby are doubled.

If the baby is born, symptoms of congenital syphilis begin to appear within three to four weeks. If syphilis is diagnosed early enough in the mother, penicillin treatment will usually protect the unborn fetus.

CHECK YOURSELF

1. What is a chancre?
2. How are complications resulting from syphilis more serious than those resulting from gonorrhea?
3. How is syphilis diagnosed and treated?
4. What is congenital syphilis?

Four serious diseases transmitted through sexual contact are *herpes simplex II, NGU, chlamydia,* and *AIDS.* Cures are available for NGU and chlamydia, but at present, no cures for herpes II or AIDS exist.

Herpes Simplex II

Herpes (hur-peas) **simplex virus type I** is *a virus that causes cold sores on or around the mouth.* (See page 44.) This virus can be transmitted to other parts of the body through direct contact with mucous membranes. However, this viral infection is not a sexually transmitted disease.

Herpes simplex virus type II is *a virus that causes blisterlike sores in the genital area.* Herpes type II is sometimes called **genital herpes.** It is transmitted by sexual contact and is at present an incurable STD. The Centers for Disease Control has declared this STD to be an epidemic.

Recently, medical professionals have decided not to distinguish between Herpes I and II, because it is possible to find a Type II infection on the mouth and a Type I infection on the genitals. However, for the purposes of this text section, the virus, when transmitted through sexual contact, is described as Type II, and it does have certain characteristics.

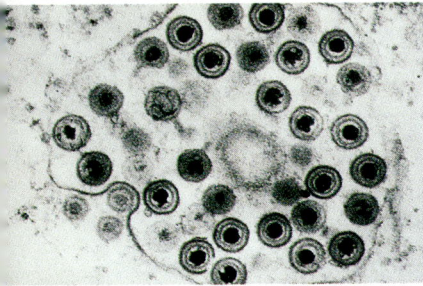

Symptoms

Symptoms of herpes II include painful, itching sores in or around the genitals. Sores usually appear 2 to 20 days after contact with an infected person. They may last as long as three weeks. Other symptoms include fever and a burning sensation during urination. With the help of moisture and friction, the herpes II virus can spread to other areas of the body. This is why a person who has herpes II is told not to rub the skin and to keep it dry.

Diagnosis and Treatment

A medical examination of genital sores is the usual means of diagnosis for herpes II. Currently, no cure exists for herpes II, but there is treatment that may arrest (stop) it in an individual.

The blisterlike sores of herpes II go away, but the virus germ remains in the body. Blisters may reappear at any time. Also, when the blisters are present, the disease can be transmitted to another person.

However, one of the problems with this virus is that the disease may be contagious for a period of time *before* the blisters appear and *after* they go away. There is no sure way of knowing when the disease is in its contagious state. This makes controlling its spread very difficult.

Although the symptoms of herpes II go away, the virus remains in the body in such a state that it may be reactivated to cause another rash. After the healing from the initial outbreak has taken place, the virus germ enters nerve endings near the initial rash. The virus moves away from the surface of the skin, thus escaping the body's defenses. It moves to nerve-cell bod-

Symptoms of the herpes simplex virus type II can come and go, but the virus remains in the body.

ies near the spinal cord, where it becomes *dormant* (inactive). Dormant herpes II virus can remain in this state indefinitely without causing damage.

Some people never have another outbreak of the virus, while others experience periodic outbreaks. Different factors, which are very individual, influence recurring outbreaks. Stress is one factor thought to bring on recurrences.

Infected women should have regular Pap smears, since herpes II infections have been linked to the development of cervical cancer cells. Pregnant women who have a herpes II infection run a higher risk of miscarriage or premature birth. There is also a high death rate among babies born to mothers who have the herpes II infection. Babies have a higher risk of brain damage if they pass through the birth canal at a time when the infection is active.

A pregnant woman should inform her doctor if she knows or suspects that she has herpes II. A doctor can perform *caesarean* (suh-**zar**-ee-un) *delivery*—birth by surgical means—to avoid any risk to the baby.

Nongonococcal Urethritis (NGU)

Nongonococcal urethritis (non-gon-uh-**kock**-ul yur-i-**thrite**-us) **(NGU)** is *a disease caused by several different kinds of bacterialike organisms that infect the urethra in men and the cervix in women*. This STD is called *nonspecific*, because the specific cause of it has not yet been discovered. Like all STDs, NGU is transmitted through sexual contact.

Symptoms and Treatment

Men notice symptoms of NGU more than women do. In men, there may be a discharge from the penis anywhere from one to three weeks after infection. Males may also experience a mild burning during urination. Women may have a vaginal discharge and pain in the lower abdomen.

NGU can be treated and cured. Treatment consists of an antibiotic, usually tetracycline.

Chlamydia

Chlamydia (kluh-**mid**-ee-uh) may not be a familiar STD, but it is probably the most prevalent one in the United States. It is *an infection that attacks the male and female reproductive organs and is caused by several different microorganisms that are similar to bacteria but are closer in size to viruses*. Annually, about 3 million cases are reported—1 million cases more than gonorrhea.

Symptoms

In men, the symptoms include pain and burning during urination and a discharge from the penis. These symptoms usually occur one to three

STDs—A Major Public Health Problem

Why do STDs continue to be a major public health problem? Many reasons exist, but they all add up to ignorance about the diseases, embarrassment about discussing them, fear of what others may think, and complacency regarding early treatment. The "social stigma" has also made it difficult to combat STDs.

Most STDs could be completely eradicated if people practiced responsible health behaviors. Ignoring signs of a disease is not being responsible. Responding to symptoms, seeking treatment, and following medical-care instructions will combat this serious epidemic.

But, the best way people can combat this serious health problem is by having no sexual contact. It is not only okay to say "No"—it is healthy.

weeks after exposure. If left untreated, chlamydia can result in a chronic (on-going) inflammation of the urethra. The disease is also linked to infertility in men.

In women, the symptoms are not obvious. If symptoms do occur, they may include an unusual discharge from the vagina, pain in the pelvic region, and painful urination. If left untreated, chlamydia can cause pelvic inflammatory disease (PID). (See page 536.)

A pregnant woman who has chlamydia can spread it to her baby during delivery. In infants, the disease can cause eye infection, blindness, and sometimes pneumonia.

Treatment

Chlamydia is diagnosed through a laboratory test. Certain antibiotics can cure chlamydia. However, if scar tissue has already formed, treatment cannot undo that damage. Chances of infertility in the male and sterility in the female will remain.

AIDS

Acquired immunodeficiency syndrome (uh-**kwired** im-you-no-duh-**fish**-un-see **sin**-drum) (**AIDS**) is *a virus that attacks one of the key lymphocytes in the body*—the T4 lymphocyte cell. This cell controls and regulates the immune system of the body. When the AIDS virus gains control of the T4 cell, the whole body is open to disease-causing germs, because the T4 cell then cannot activate the cells that make antibodies. As you know, antibodies are the agents that recognize and help to destroy disease-causing germs in the body. (For more information about the body's immune system, see Chapter 29.)

Human immunodeficiency virus (HIV) is *the name of the virus that causes AIDS*. HIV is a very fragile virus. It cannot live outside the body. HIV lives in certain body fluids. It is spread from person to person through *blood, semen,* and *secretions* from the vagina. In order to infect a person, the virus must gain entrance to the bloodstream. The AIDS virus is spread through

- sexual intercourse—oral, anal, or vaginal,
- sharing contaminated needles or syringes,
- transfusion of blood or blood products,
- pregnancy of a woman with the AIDS virus.

According to a final report from the Centers for Disease Control in 1988, the virus is not transmitted by saliva, tears, urine, vaccines, or insects, although the virus may be present in some quantity in these things. It is also not transmitted by eating utensils or casual contact. There is a possibility that the virus may be transmitted through breastfeeding, but the Centers for Disease Control is still evaluating this possible form of entry.

KEEPING FIT

Donating Blood and AIDS

A person cannot get the AIDS virus by donating blood, because only sterile needles are used and all blood is tested to make sure that the AIDS virus is not present.

Testing for AIDS

A blood test is done to test for the AIDS virus. If a person has been infected, AIDS antibodies will be present in the blood. These antibodies are produced by the immune system to fight the AIDS virus. However, the time between exposure to the AIDS virus and the presence of antibodies could be two weeks to three or four months—perhaps longer. This means a person could have a negative test *even though he or she is infected.* Being retested about six months later would be necessary to confirm a negative test.

The AIDS virus can affect people in three main ways.

Virus Carriers. A person could have the AIDS virus in his or her body, but have no signs or symptoms. In essence, these people are healthy. However, they are carriers of the virus and can spread it to others. Three, five, seven, ten, maybe twelve years later, such virus carriers could start having symptoms and actually develop the disease.

AIDS-Related Complex (ARC). People infected with the AIDS virus could develop AIDS-Related Complex (ARC). With ARC, a person has some of the early symptoms of AIDS, but does not have one of the diseases used to diagnose an official case of AIDS. ARC *symptoms may include persistent fatigue, diarrhea, fever, swollen lymph nodes, loss of appetite and/or weight, skin rashes, or night sweats.*

AIDS. Finally, a person infected with the AIDS virus can develop the disease, AIDS. The disease could appear six months after being infected or seven to ten or more years later. Once a person develops AIDS, he or she may live six months or as long as about three years. There have been people who have lived even longer. AIDS victims do not actually die of AIDS. They die from **opportunistic infections.** These are *infections that would not have had a chance to do damage in a body with a healthy immune system.*

Pneumocystis carinii (**new**-mo-sis-tis-kar-**in**-i), a form of pneumonia, is one of the most common such infections. Symptoms may include difficulty breathing, shortness of breath, fever, and persistent cough.

A form of cancer, *Kaposi's sarcoma* (**cap**-o-zees **sar**-co-ma) is another common infection in AIDS patients. Symptoms of the cancer include purple blotches and bumps on the skin.

Some AIDS patients will develop AIDS *dementia* (**dee**-ment-she-uh) *complex.* This progressive disorder destroys brain tissue. It is a result of the AIDS virus attacking the nervous system. The victim may have loss of memory, coordination, partial paralysis, and personality changes.

L I F E MANAGEMENT S K I L L

Treatment of AIDS

At present, there is no cure for AIDS. The treatment available can only help to relieve some of the symptoms and, in some cases, prolong the lives of the AIDS patients.

Scientists all over the world continue to work at developing a drug, a vaccine, or a genetic device that will prevent healthy people from getting the disease, and a cure to save the lives of those already infected.

CHECK YOURSELF

1. Compare herpes simplex virus type I with type II.
2. Why is NGU called nonspecific?
3. What are the symptoms of NGU?
4. What is chlamydia?
5. In women, to what disease can chlamydia lead?
6. How does AIDS attack the body?

4. Other STDs

Several other STDs exist. Some are more serious than others, but they all require medical attention. The chart on page 544 provides a description of the most common ones.

Treatment

Treatment for STDs is an important personal responsibility. Having an STD is not like having a cold. It will not simply go away if a person waits long enough. The *individual* must do something about it. No one else can do it for that person.

It is also not a time for embarrassment. A person who seeks treatment from a private doctor or a public health clinic is guaranteed by law that all information will remain confidential. But it is important that the infected person notify all people with whom he or she has had any sexual contact at all.

Sexually Transmittable Diseases

Disease	What it is	Cause	Symptoms	Treatment
Vaginitis (vaj-uh-**nite**-us)	A common inflammation of the female genitals. Many types exist. Can be carried by males.	Microscopic organisms	*Female*—severe itching, discharge *Male*—few or no symptoms	Antibiotics
Trichomoniasis (trik-uh-muh-**nigh**-uh-sus)	A vaginal infection that can lead to urethra and bladder infections. (This disease is a form of vaginitis that infects about 1 million people a year.)	A protozoan parasite	*Female*—yellowish discharge, strong odor, irritation, itching *Male*—slight or no symptoms (Men are rarely infected, but they can be carriers.)	Prescription drug
Genital warts	Pink or reddish warts that have cauliflower-like tops.	A virus	Warts appear on genitals 1 to 3 months after infection	Application of a prescription skin medication
Pubic lice	Parasites that feed on tiny, human blood vessels. They are usually in body hair. (When they infect the pubic hair, they are often called *crabs.*)	Parasite	Intense itching, small nits (eggs) on pubic hair, small spots of blood on underwear	A special medicated shampoo
Scabies (**skay**-bees)	Tiny parasitic mites that burrow under the skin— not always acquired through sexual contact.	Tiny mites	Itching in the genital area 4 to 6 weeks after infection. Mites can be spread to forearms or fingers	Hot baths and medicated creams

PUBLIC HEALTH NURSE

Surely you have heard of a nurse in a hospital setting or a doctor's office—but have you ever heard of a **public health nurse**? This interesting career choice is also referred to as **community health nursing.** In contrast to the hospital nurse or the patients in the doctor's office or clinic, the community as a whole is the public health nurse's patient.

As a community health nurse, one must tend to more than just a patient's physical needs. The nurse must consider a patient's stability, age, education, housing, and cultural attitudes. Public health nursing has changed in recent years. At one time, it was restricted to the enforcement of rules and regulations. Today it has taken on a more positive and challenging role—that of prevention and care, and the promotion of health.

A public health nurse may be involved in the diagnosis, planning, and treatment of patients that he or she may visit in their homes, at work, in schools, in clinics, and so on. It is truly a community-type job.

Who employs public health nurses? By far, local public health agencies hire the majority of public health nurses. These include city and county health departments and other official agencies and private agencies such as the Visiting Nurse Association, American Red Cross, and others.

The most attractive aspects of this type of career include being able to earn a good living while enjoying the satisfaction of caring for those in need. The job usually offers an opportunity to get to know the patients very well, because the public health nurse often works with people for a long period of time. Constant variety appears in the type of patient and the area in which the nurse gives treatment.

Public health nursing is a specialty within general nursing. A potential candidate for becoming a public health nurse can further his or her education in two ways: through an associate degree program offered in a hospital, or through a B.S. program that many colleges and universities offer. For more information, visit your school counselor for assistance in locating the approved schools in your area that offer such programs.

For information, contact the National League for Nursing.

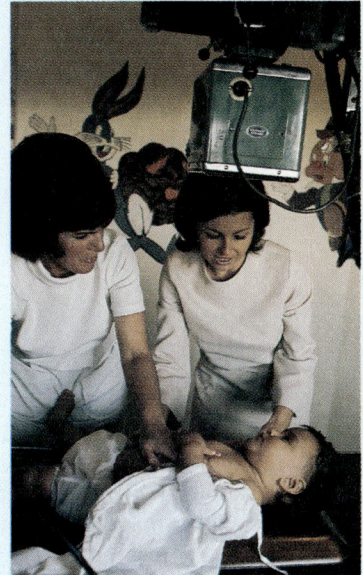

Committee on Careers
National League for Nursing
10 Columbus Circle
New York, NY 10019

Prevention of STDs

The body does not build up an immunity to any of the STDs. No vaccination is available to prevent the diseases. The only one sure way *not* to contract an STD is *not* to be sexually active. More and more young people are recognizing this as a much preferred alternative to contracting STDs and experiencing their crippling effects.

CHECK YOURSELF

1. What is vaginitis?
2. What is the difference between genital warts and lice?
3. What is the best way to prevent STDs?

CHAPTER 30   Review

CHAPTER SUMMARY

- A sexually transmitted disease, STD, is one that is spread from person to person through sexual contact.
- The most serious epidemics in our country today are the sexually transmitted diseases.
- One of the problems of this epidemic is the amount of misinformation surrounding these diseases.
- Gonorrhea, the third most common STD, is caused by a certain bacteria and can be treated and cured.
- Syphilis, one of the most serious STDs, is caused by a bacterium. It progresses in stages, and in its later stages causes serious, even fatal, damage to certain body organs. Syphilis can be treated and cured, if caught early.
- Herpes simplex type II is a virus infection that is a current epidemic, for which there is no cure.
- Nongonococcal urethritis is caused by bacterialike organisms and affects a female's cervix and a male's urethra. It can be treated and cured.
- Chlamydia is a microorganism infection that attacks the reproductive organs. It is the most widespread STD in the United States. It can be cured.
- AIDS is a virus that attacks a key part of the body's immune system. It leaves the body open to serious infection. There is, at present, no cure for AIDS.
- The other types of STDs, all different, can be treated and cured.

- The best prevention for STDs is to avoid sexual contact.

REVIEWING WHAT YOU LEARNED

1. Define sexually transmitted disease.
2. Compare and contrast the germs, symptoms, and treatment of gonorrhea and syphilis.
3. What makes sexually transmitted diseases different from other communicable diseases?
4. Identify three sexually transmitted diseases other than syphilis, gonorrhea, and herpes II. Describe their causes, symptoms, and treatments. Also describe what happens if each is not treated.
5. Why are AIDS and herpes II of special concern today?
6. How is it possible for a person to have more than one STD at the same time?
7. Why are sexually transmitted diseases a serious threat to one's total health?
8. Name three ways by which the spread of STDs can be prevented or curtailed.

APPLYING WHAT YOU LEARNED

1. What factors have led to the continuing spread of sexually transmitted diseases? How can these factors be reduced?
2. What steps could the public health agencies take to further control the spread of STDs?

sexually transmitted disease (STD)
gonorrhea
pelvic inflammatory disease (PID)
syphilis
chancre
congenital syphilis
herpes simplex virus type I

herpes simplex virus type II
genital herpes
nongonococcal urethritis (NGU)
chlamydia
acquired immunodeficiency
    syndrome (AIDS)

vaginitis
trichomoniasis
genital warts
pubic lice
scabies
public health nurse

PUTTING VOCABULARY TO USE

On a separate piece of paper, fill in the blanks
with the appropriate words or phrases.

Disease	Symptoms	Treatment
1. _____	genital warts	skin medication prescription
2. _____	chancre	_____
3. _____	painful urination in males	antibiotics
4. _____	pain in pelvic region and painful urination in females	_____
5. _____	yellowish discharge, strong odor in females	prescription drugs
6. _____	blisterlike sores in genital area	_____
7. _____	intense itching and small nits on pubic hair	special medicated shampoo
8. _____	female—severe itching; male—few or no symptoms	antibiotics
9. _____	itching in the genital area	_____
10. _____	males have a mild burning during urination	usually treated by antibiotics, such as tetracycline
11. _____	thymus gland swells, general tiredness	_____
12. _____	pelvic pain or chills and fever	antibiotics

3. Using reference material, write a report on what is being done to help people infected with herpes II or AIDS cope with the disease.

4. STDs are completely preventable and, with the exception of herpes II and AIDs, are curable. Yet, they continue to spread in epidemic proportions. What do you think people could do to help combat the spread of these diseases and gain control over them? Make a list of steps you would take and compare them with your classmates' lists.

5. Contact your local health department to find out what programs it has to educate people about the prevention of STDs.

FOCUS ON WELLNESS

There is no doubt that sexually transmitted diseases are at the epidemic stage, particularly among young people. *I can protect myself and help to control the spread of these diseases by . . .*

Noncommunicable Diseases and Disorders

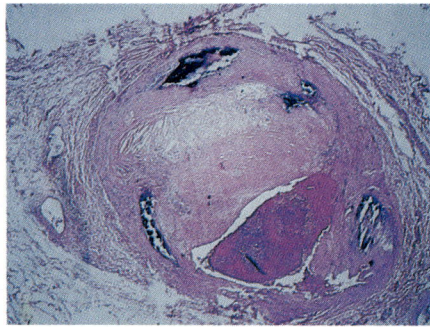

While some illnesses are new—having been caused by changes in life-styles and the environment—others have been with us for thousands of years. Some—like heart disease, cancer, diabetes, and arthritis—have been found in the bodies of ancient Egyptians. Yet many scientists feel that in the 21st century, these illnesses will be curable.

After studying this chapter, you will be able to:

- describe how one's life-style relates to chronic and degenerative diseases,
- describe hypertension as a silent, mysterious killer,
- identify the factors related to hypertension,
- define and describe atherosclerosis,
- explain what happens when a person has a heart attack,
- identify preventive measures for heart disease,
- explain how cancer develops,
- describe cancer symptoms and treatment,
- define the two main types of diabetes,
- describe the two most common types of arthritis.

1. Chronic and Degenerative Diseases and Disorders

There are many illnesses called diseases that pathogens do not cause. These are **noninfectious diseases**, *ones that are not contagious and that have a variety of causes*. Each noninfectious disease is grouped according to its general cause. Each disease is also a **noncommunicable disease**, meaning *not capable of being transmitted through contact with an infected or afflicted person*.

A variety of conditions cause these diseases, many of which relate to a person's life-style and health habits. You have studied many of the degenerative (deteriorating) and chronic (long-lasting) diseases and disorders in Chapters 14–19 on the body systems—among them, Parkinson's disease, multiple sclerosis, Alzheimer's disease, myasthenia gravis, and muscular dystrophy. In this chapter, we will concentrate mainly on heart disease, cancer, diabetes, and arthritis.

Cardiovascular Diseases

Perhaps the diseases most closely related to one's life-style are the **cardiovascular** (card-**eo**-vasq-u-ler) **diseases**—*those of the heart and blood vessels*. These diseases are a major killer in the United States.

Over half of all Americans die of some form of cardiovascular disease. While it is less common as a killer of the young, its importance to young people is great because many of the risks of cardiovascular disease are due to life-style choices and habits that people adopt early in life.

Exercising and eating low fat and low cholesterol foods will help all of us reduce the risk of heart disease. See your *Health Handbook*, pages HB14–HB18 for information on wise food selection.

Learning about cardiovascular diseases is also important because knowing how to recognize these diseases, what to do in an emergency, and where to get help may mean the difference between life and death.

Approximately 35 million people, or one in every six adults, have some elevation of the blood pressure, and one-half of them do not know it. Hypertension has been detected in children as young as six years old.

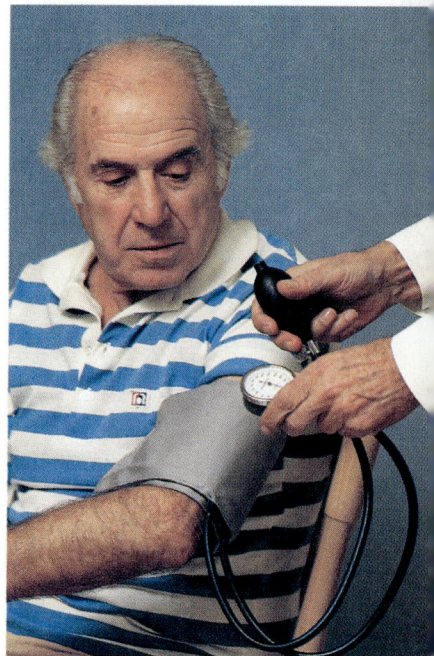

Young and old alike should have frequent readings for high blood pressure.

High Blood Pressure

Blood pressure *moves blood through the circulatory system*. Blood pressure is created by the contraction of the heart muscle, which pumps blood through the vessels, and by the resistance of the arterial walls. With each beat of the heart, blood pressure goes up and down within a limited range. *When blood pressure goes up and stays up*, a person has **high blood pressure**, or **hypertension** (**high**-purr-ten-chun).

High blood pressure is a silent, mysterious killer. It is mysterious because in more than 90% of all cases, the cause is unknown and no cure exists. It is silent because in its early stages, it produces no symptoms that require medical attention.

Damaging Effects of High Blood Pressure

High blood pressure is dangerous because it:

- excessively works the heart and left ventricle,
- causes excessive pressures, which may lead to damaged arteries,
- causes *sclerosis* (skler-**roh**-sis) (hardening) of blood vessels,
- weakens blood vessels,
- possibly leads to *hemorrhages* (**hem**-uh-ruh-jehs) (uncontrollable bleeding), especially in the brain and kidneys.

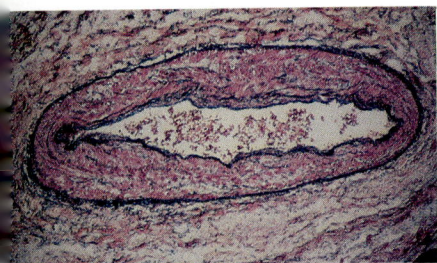

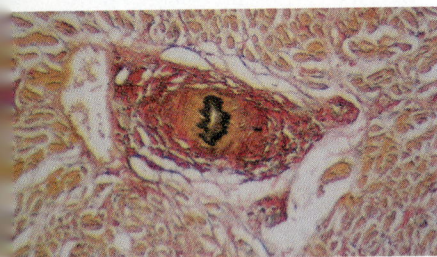

The normal coronary artery on the top is unblocked. The coronary artery on the bottom shows thickening fatty deposits along the wall—a sure sign of atherosclerosis.

Only after years of stress on the cardiovascular system does this disorder result in major complications, such as stroke, heart attack, heart failure, or kidney failure. As a result, high blood pressure leads to premature disability and death in hundreds of thousands of people each year.

Causes   Although the exact cause of high blood pressure is not known, many factors have been identified as being related to it. People in highly stressful environments seem to be more susceptible to high blood pressure. Emotional stress or tension causes the arterioles to constrict and thus causes blood pressure to rise.

A factor we must also consider is heredity. When parents have high blood pressure, the odds are greater that their children will have high blood pressure.

One factor that has definitely been identified as a contributor to high blood pressure is excessive salt intake. What is excessive? The recommended daily allowance is three to eight grams (.11 to .28 oz), five grams (.18 oz) being equivalent to a teaspoonful. The average American consumes two to three times this amount.

As you read in Chapter 8 on nutrition, sodium is essential for cellular function, but the body needs it only in small amounts. Table salt (sodium chloride) provides more than enough sodium for almost all people. You can reduce your salt intake by checking food labels and limiting foods high in salt. Taste your food before salting it, and try other seasonings.

Treatment   Hypertension cannot be cured, but 90% of the cases can be controlled with medicine and by diet. Diet controls, besides limiting salt intake, include maintaining ideal weight, reducing sugar consumption, and reducing intake of foods high in cholesterol and saturated fats. Regular exercise also helps to reduce blood pressure.

Arteriosclerosis

Arteriosclerosis (are-tier-ee-oh-skler-**roh**-sis) means *hardening of the arteries*. It is by far the most common cause of death in the United States. Arteriosclerosis refers to any disease in which the walls of the arteries thicken and lose their elastic quality.

Atherosclerosis   About 86% of all of the deaths from coronary heart disease, stroke, and the other diseases of the arteries occur because of a type of arteriosclerosis, called atherosclerosis. **Atherosclerosis** (ath-uh-roh-skler-**roh**-sis) is the *thickening of the arterial wall due to fatty deposits*. These deposits clog the artery so that blood cannot flow through the blood vessel.

At birth, the lining of the blood vessels is very smooth. Over the years, *fatty deposits*, called **plaque**, build up along the inner lining of the arteries. This buildup is due mainly to dietary choices.

When about two-thirds of the vessel is blocked, symptoms may develop that indicate signs of coronary heart problems. These fatty deposits slow the flow of blood in the arteries, so the heart does not get enough blood. Atherosclerosis also can result in a heart attack.

Angina Pectoris

Many people who have atherosclerosis experience a condition known as angina pectoris (an-**jigh**-nuh **peck**-tah-rus). In the case of **angina pectoris**, *pain and tightness or pressure in the chest occur as a result of the heart's not getting enough oxygen.* People who have never had a heart attack may experience angina pains (intense attacks of chest pain). Medication can relieve the pain. These people may have to limit their physical activity to avoid the pain.

Thrombus and Embolus

The rough surface of the artery walls, combined with the slower blood flow, may cause the formation of *a blood clot*, called a **thrombus** (**throm**-bus). If a thrombus breaks away from the artery wall and is carried in the blood flow, this *moving clot* is called an **embolus** (**em**-buh-luss).

Heart Attack

A thrombus or an embolus can block the artery completely. *If blockage occurs in an artery leading to the brain*, a **stroke** results, blocking the brain's

---

HEALTH UPDATE   HEALTH UPDATE   HEALTH UPDATE

New Breakthroughs in Heart Disease Research

Heart Attack Blood Test. A new and simple blood test is now being developed to gauge a person's susceptibility to heart attack. With this test, early treatment will mean fewer deaths and lower health costs.

Researchers have found that genetic factors play an important role in heart attack. The test involves examining certain characteristics found in genes that are linked to high blood pressure, arteriosclerosis, and the development of fatty deposits on the walls of arteries.

With the test, early preventive measures could begin for people whose genes indicate a high risk of heart disease. Diet, exercise, and drug treatment could be started before an attack.

Blood Vessel Replacements. Currently, Dacron® tubes are used to replace large blood vessels that have been damaged. But, the Dacron® tubes do not work as replacements for smaller vessels.

Now, two new techniques are being developed to replace weakened or damaged small blood vessels. They involve *growing blood vessels* and creating a new form of *pliable plastic* that has all the flexible qualities of a normal blood vessel.

Growing blood vessels deals with the use of certain skin cells that cause a growth of *collagen*—a fibrous tissue found in bone, cartilage, and connective tissue. Under certain conditions, this material can grow a type of skin useful in the treatment of burns and the forming of blood vessels.

---

supply of oxygen and thus damaging the brain cells. If *the blockage occurs in a coronary artery*, a **heart attack** results.

A heart attack occurs because the heart is not getting the oxygen and nutrients it needs. The part of the heart that does not get this nourishment dies. The severity of the heart attack is determined by how much heart tissue dies.

The heart can keep functioning if this area is not too great. Scar tissue will gradually form over the damaged area, and other arteries will assume the work of the blocked ones. However, since scar tissue is not elastic, it does not contract when the heart does, so the heart is never again able to function at its fullest capacity.

Signs of an Attack   A heart attack can occur at any time; it usually is sudden and happens without warning. However, immediate response to the early signs of such an attack can mean the difference between life and death. These early signs include discomfort in the center of the front of the chest. The sensation may be one of pressure, fullness, squeezing, or aching. The distress may extend into one or both arms, the neck, jaw, upper abdomen, and even the back. Nausea, vomiting, sweating, and shortness of breath may also accompany the attack.

A person can easily mistake some of these signs for other problems, such as heartburn or indigestion. He or she should seek medical attention immediately. Self-diagnosis in this case could be fatal.

Cardiac Arrest

Cardiac arrest occurs when *the heart stops completely*. In the case of cardiac arrest, circulation stops, and the brain can live for around five minutes.

Cardiac arrest can occur at any time, even in a normally healthy person.

If cardiac arrest occurs in the hospital, the doctors and hospital staff will attempt external heart massage first. If that does not revive the heart, they may administer electric shock.

If cardiac arrest occurs when medical assistance is not available, the victim's life may be saved if someone administers CPR (cardiopulmonary resuscitation). This lifesaving skill, explained in Chapter 28, forces the blood out of the heart and into the arteries. It includes mouth-to-mouth resuscitation, so the victim gets the oxygen needed. Only someone properly trained in the technique should administer CPR.

Fibrillation

Fibrillation (fib-ruh-**lay**-shun) is a *condition occurring when the muscle fibers of the heart work without coordination, having an irregular rhythm and contracting usually at a very fast rate.*

When this condition occurs in the ventricles, it is called *ventricular (ven-**trik**-cue-lur) fibrillation*. It is usually fatal because it prohibits the ventricles from pumping blood out of the heart. Doctors can sometimes correct ventricular fibrillation by giving the heart a powerful electric shock.

Stroke

As we have seen, a stroke occurs when the blood supply to a part of the brain tissue is cut off, and as a result, the nerve cells in that part of the brain cannot function. The nerve cells of the brain control the way we receive and interpret sensations and most of our bodily movements.

In order to function, the brain cells must have a continuous and ample supply of oxygen and nutrients carried in the blood. If the brain cells are deprived of blood for around five minutes, they will die.

Interference with the blood supply to the brain may be due to a number of causes. It is sometimes difficult to determine the cause or causes of a particular stroke, and a doctor may need time to make a definite diagnosis.

Cerebral Thrombosis

One of the most common causes of strokes is *the blocking of a cerebral artery by a clot* (called a thrombus) that forms inside the artery. This condition is known as **cerebral thrombosis** (throm-**boh**-sis). Sometimes the clot occurs in one of four neck arteries that supply the brain with blood.

A clot is not likely to occur in a healthy artery. But sometimes atherosclerosis damages arteries.

Cerebral Embolism

Sometimes a **cerebral embolism** occurs. *A wandering blood clot*, called an embolus, *is carried in the bloodstream, usually from a heart that is damaged by disease, and becomes wedged in one of the cerebral arteries.* This process also interferes with the flow of blood to the brain.

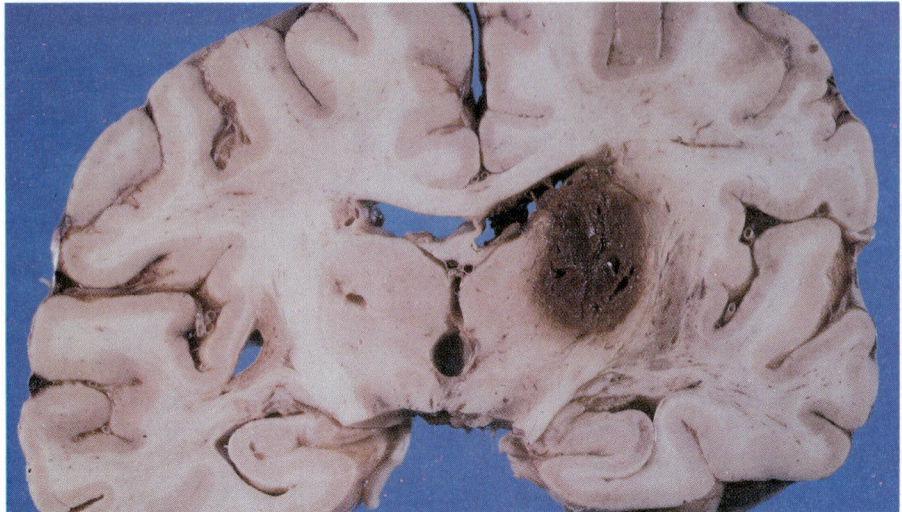

This cerebral hemorrhage was brought on by hypertension, or high blood pressure.

Cerebral Hemorrhage

A diseased artery in the brain can burst and flood the surrounding brain tissue with blood. This is called a **cerebral hemorrhage**. The brain cells that the artery nourished do not get the food and oxygen they need. A cerebral hemorrhage is more likely to occur when the person suffers from a combination of atherosclerosis and high blood pressure.

How Does a Stroke Affect a Person?

Any part of the body can be affected by a stroke—it all depends on where the stroke takes place. Because the brain controls the body's movement, a stroke may affect any part of the body. Suppose an artery is blocked in the area that controls speaking. Then speech will be affected. If the blocked area controls the leg muscles, then those muscles will be affected. Even memory can be affected.

Sometimes a stroke will have little effect on the person. At other times, the effect will be severe. Some people recover quickly, while others may not recover at all.

Warning Signals of a Stroke

These are the major signs of a stroke:

- Sudden, temporary weakness or numbness of the face, arm, and leg on one side of the body,
- Temporary loss of speech, or trouble in speaking or understanding people,
- Temporary dimness or loss of vision, particularly in one eye,
- Unexplained dizziness, unsteadiness, or sudden falls.

If you notice one or more of these signals, be sure to tell your doctor.

Implantable Defibrillator

About 300,000 Americans die each year from ventricular fibrillation because they do not get medical care in time. A team of Baltimore researchers has developed an electric device that can be permanently implanted in the body. It detects ventricular fibrillation and automatically brings it under control.

The implanted defibrillator works on the same principle as the electric defibrillator used in a coronary-care unit. (See page 556.) The device is implanted under the skin of the abdomen. It is connected to the heart by means of electrode wires passed under the skin. One electrode is placed in the vena cava just above the heart. (The vena cava is one of the large veins in which blood is returned to the right atrium of the heart.) The other electrode is stitched to the membrane covering the lower part of the heart.

Once in place, the battery-powered device monitors the heart's natural electrical discharges. As soon as it senses an abnormal pattern, it sends out a 700-volt shock that can be repeated three times. The artificial pacemaker delivers a much smaller amount of stimulation to correct a less lethal defect in heart rhythm. (See page 558.)

The Baltimore researchers suggest that the implantable defibrillator, along with drug treatment, may drastically reduce the number of sudden deaths from cardiac arrest.

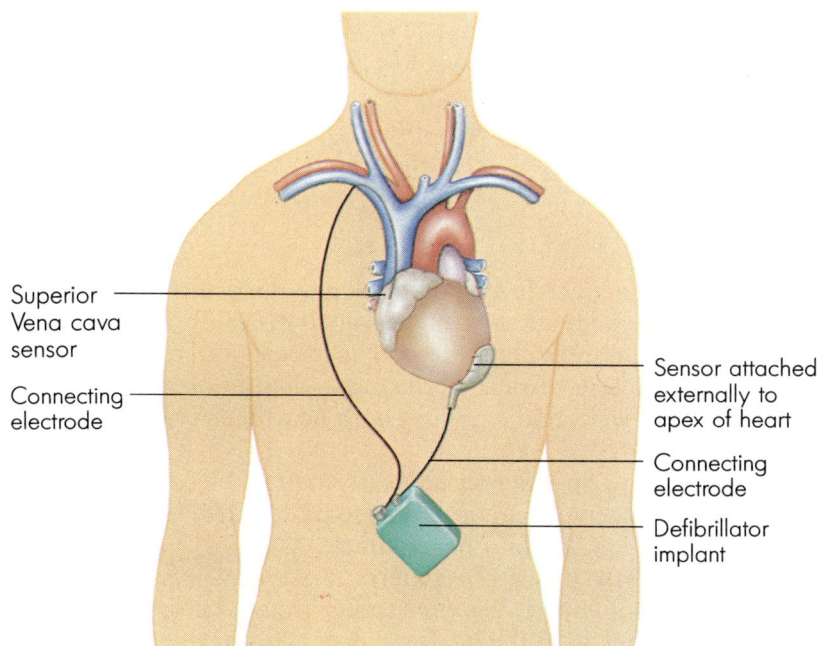

Superior Vena cava sensor

Connecting electrode

Sensor attached externally to apex of heart

Connecting electrode

Defibrillator implant

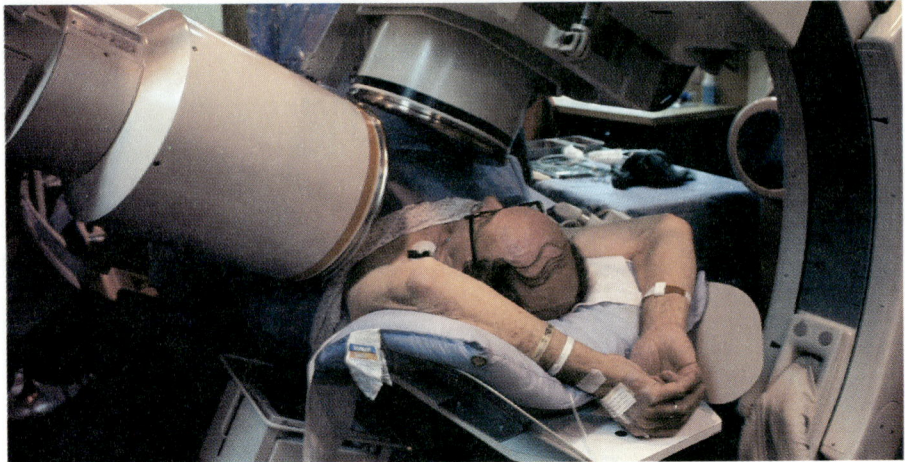

This patient is undergoing fluoroscopy.

Medical Care for the Heart Patient

The doctor usually gives an electrocardiogram test to the patient to detect the nature of the heart attack and how the heart is behaving. Is the heart beating regularly or irregularly? Is the heart beating fast or slow? Is the heartbeat weak or strong? The **electrocardiogram** (e-**leck**-tro-card-eo-gram) (**EKG** or **ECG**) *provides a graphic picture of the electric activity of the heart by tracing it on graph paper.* The type of marking can indicate the heart activity and rhythm.

Sometimes during a heart attack, after rapid and erratic beating, the heart will stop entirely. Ambulances now often carry defibrillators. The electric **defibrillator** is *an instrument that allows the medical professionals to shock the heart with an electric impulse that can correct the irregular beat or get the heart beating again.* This has been a valuable lifesaving technique that medical professionals use when other techniques to revive the person have failed.

Coronary-Care Units

Many hospitals have developed coronary-care units to treat heart attack victims. These areas are specially designed to rapidly and continuously check a person's vital signs (temperature, heartbeat, and respiration). Blood pressure and blood tests are also performed. In addition, the patient is put on a system that checks and regulates both heartbeat and blood pressure.

Instruments   Many special tests are performed in the coronary-care units, and in hospitals in general, in order to accurately detect the nature, location, degree, and damage of a heart attack.

The **fluoroscope** (**flure**-uh-scope) is *a machine similar to a chest X-ray machine, except that it gives a live picture* rather than a still photograph. The doctor can look directly at the heart shadow. This device is helpful in determining the irregular size or function of any of the heart chambers, in addition to the development of any hardening of the arteries.

Phonocardiography (**foe**-no-kard-ee-**og**-ruh-fee) is *the placing of a microphone on the chest* to record heart sound signals, transfer them through photography to graph paper, and trace them, so that a professional can examine the heartbeats for irregularities.

Perhaps the most valuable tool in a coronary-care unit is the **angio-cardiography** (**an**-jee-oh-kard-ee-**og**-ruh-fee), *a device that provides a picture of the heart, its vessels, and the chambers.*

A common way to get pictures of these organs and tissues is by **cardiac catheterization** (kath-at-ah-ruh-**zay**-shun). A **catheter** is *a thin, flexible tube that can be guided into the body organs.* It is made of plastic so that the blood will not cling to it. The catheter is inserted into an artery or vein in either an arm or leg. It is threaded to the heart, which a doctor observes by using a fluoroscope.

This device enables the doctor to measure blood pressure and oxygen content of the blood in the heart. In addition, special materials can be injected through the catheter, making the blood flowing through the heart and arteries visible in X rays. (For more information on catheters, see page 318.)

New Developments in Treating Heart Disease

Open-Heart Surgery

In 1952, the first successful **open-heart surgery** was performed by an American surgeon, Dr. F. John Lewis. He used ice to lower the body temperature and slow circulation so the heart could remain dry during sur-

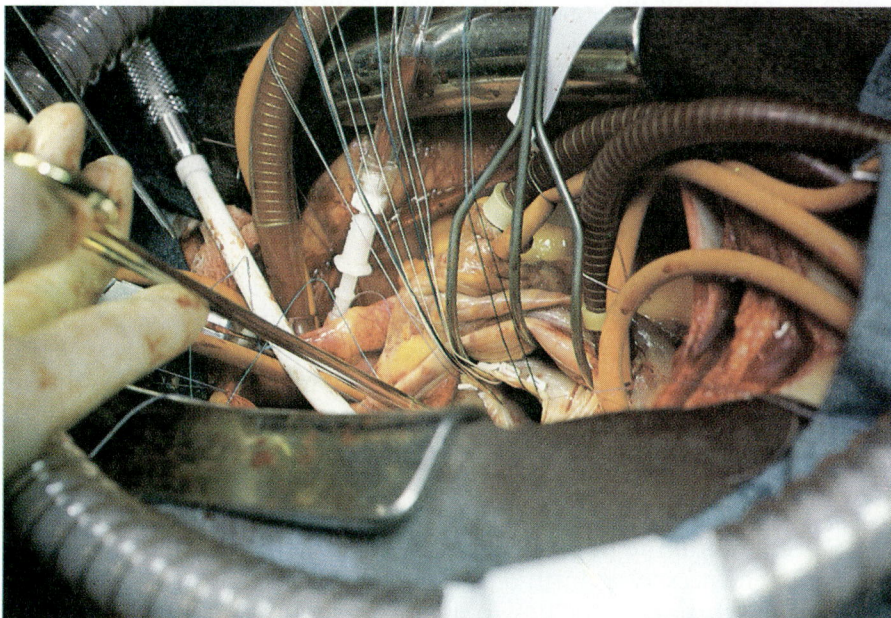

Open heart surgery has saved thousands of lives since 1952.

gery. Today, a heart–lung machine performs the job of the heart and lung for several hours during the operation. The development of this machine has resulted in many advances in open-heart surgery.

Coronary Bypass Surgery

In 1967, a surgical technique for coronary heart disease—**coronary bypass surgery**—was introduced to the medical profession. The purpose of this surgery is *to create detours around obstructed or narrowed coronary arteries* so that more blood can reach the heart. This, in turn, reduces *angina*—chest pain caused by an insufficient blood flow—and decreases the risk of total blockage.

In this operation, a portion of a vein is removed from the patient's leg. One end of the vein is connected to the coronary vessel below the blocked area. This allows blood to flow to the area that is not getting enough blood. Between 50,000 and 70,000 of these operations are performed each year. Whether the surgery adds to the length of life has not been determined, but it has been successful in reducing the physical pain of heart disease.

Heart Transplants

Imagine having *your heart completely removed and another one put in its place*. In South Africa in 1967, Dr. Christiaan Barnard first used this procedure, called a **heart transplant**. Most patients, however, died within the first year, mainly because their bodies rejected the organ. By the late 1970s, the Stanford University Medical Center had achieved a 70% survival rate after the first year.

In the United States in 1985, a man whose heart was expected to collapse within hours was given an artificial heart as a stopgap measure until a human transplant was arranged. Experiments involving the transplantation of an artificial heart are still going on.

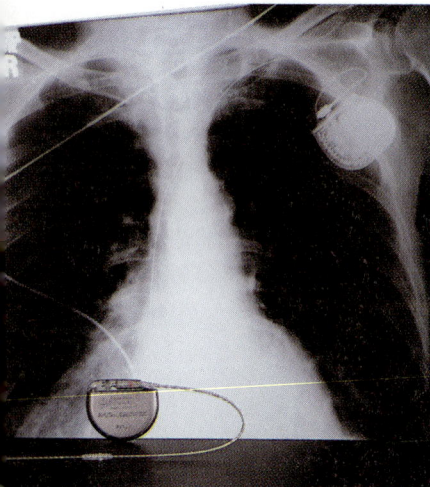

The artificial pacemaker is seen in the upper right hand corner of the X-ray.

The Artificial Pacemaker

Electrical impulses cause the heart to beat. Thus, the heart has a natural pacemaker that is responsible for initiating this electrical impulse. When something interferes with this pacemaker, it does not initiate regular strong heartbeats.

In the case of an **artificial pacemaker**, *a small unit is implanted in the chest muscle and is wired to the heart. It transmits an electrical impulse to the heart, causing the heart to beat*. Many pacemakers are battery-operated and the batteries must be replaced every four to five years. In the 1970s, surgeons began using nuclear-powered and rechargeable battery-powered pacemakers.

Heart Valve Surgery

Valves control the proper flow of blood through the heart. Defective valves may be present at birth or develop later in life. The valves may be too tight, in which case the flow of blood into the ventricles is restricted.

The other type of defect involves the valves being too loose, in which case blood leaks out of the ventricles.

To repair a tight valve, the surgeon may separate the flaps of the valve, preventing them from sticking together and making the opening too narrow. Another surgical procedure involves replacing the valve with an artificial one. A surgeon also uses this procedure to repair valves that are too loose.

Surgeons use two types of artificial valves. One is made from a valve of a pig's heart and functions much like a human valve. The other, called a cage-ball valve, consists of a tiny stainless steel cage. Enclosed in the cage

---

IMPROVING YOURSELF

Prevention of Heart Disease

Throughout this section, the focus has been on identifying heart disease, its causes and signs; what to do when it happens; its care, treatment, and rehabilitation. These are all important areas, and many lives have been saved through scientific and medical advances.

But prevention offers the *most* promise. To prevent heart disease and the other cardiovascular diseases, it is necessary to look at the risk factors associated with contracting these diseases. A **risk factor** is *a characteristic that has been shown to increase the chances of getting heart disease.*

Obviously you have no control over the factors of age, sex, race, and family medical history. However, you can significantly lower your risk by paying attention to the factors over which you do have control.

- People who smoke a pack of cigarettes a day are twice as likely to have heart attacks as nonsmokers. The risk increases with the amount smoked. Cigarette smoking also increases a person's risk of having a stroke.

- Within two years of non-smoking, the risk of heart attack drops significantly. Within 10 or 15 years, the ex-smoker's risk of heart attack is no greater than that of a nonsmoker.
- Diet is perhaps the single most important factor in atherosclerosis. Reduce your intake of cholesterol and fat simply by cutting down on butter, mayonnaise, beef, pork, and lamb.
- Obesity is a contributive factor to heart disease. A middle-aged overweight person is two to three times more likely to have heart disease than a similar person of normal weight.
- Salt intake is directly related to hypertension. You can control it by not adding salt to food and limiting your intake of salty, prepared foods.
- People who exercise regularly reduce their risk of heart disease.
- Managing stress in your daily life is an important factor in reducing your risk of heart disease.

---

is a heat-treated carbon ball. The valve is sewed into the heart and allows blood to pass only in one direction. It is able to do this because the pressure from the blood as it tries to flow backward forces the ball into the mouth of the cage, closing the valve.

Some scientists are now working on a device that would substitute for the work that the left ventricle does. This part of the heart often wears out before the other parts. The device would take blood leaving the left ventricle and pump it into the aorta for distribution throughout the body. (See diagram of the heart on page 309.)

Artificial Blood Vessels

Presently, experiments are being done on artificial blood vessels. Some as large as the diameter of a pencil and others smaller than a pencil lead are being worked on. If the research is successful, 300,000 to 500,000 people may benefit from them each year.

CHECK YOURSELF

1. What factors relate to the development of hypertension?
2. How does atherosclerosis develop?
3. What are the warning signs of a heart attack?
4. How does an artificial pacemaker work?
5. What causes a stroke?

2.   What Is Cancer?

Cancer is the second leading cause of death among adults in the United States. Cancer is not one disease, but many diseases, and it is difficult to define cancer by using only one definition. Generally, all **cancers** constitute *abnormal, uncontrolled cell growth*. Cancer cells are more powerful than normal cells because they can travel beyond their environment and invade other cells. In the process of growth, the cancer cells take over and destroy normal cells and tissues.

Abnormal Cell Growth

The growth of abnormal cells is not unusual in the body. The body replaces 500 billion cells each day. These numbers of cell divisions must be perfect in order for the body to exist as the complex, functioning organism that it is.

When cell divisions are not perfect, abnormal cells develop. The number of abnormal cells is estimated to be between 10,000 and 1 million per day. Many of these cells are so defective that they die, but scientists still do not know how some abnormal cells survive and grow as cancer cells. We do know that the body has some natural defenses that destroy abnormal cells. If these defenses were not present, many of us would suffer from cancer very early in life.

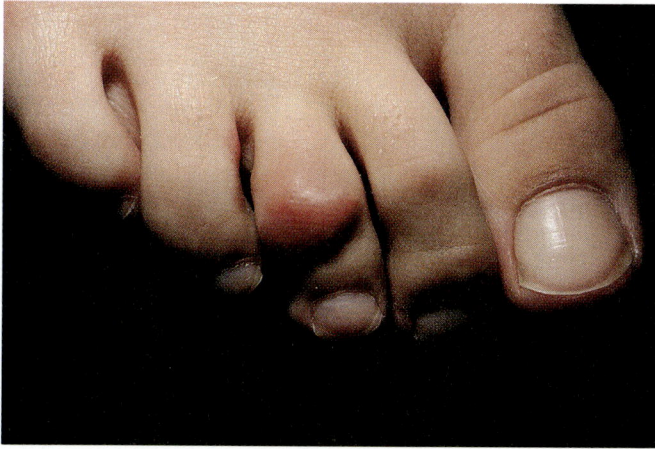
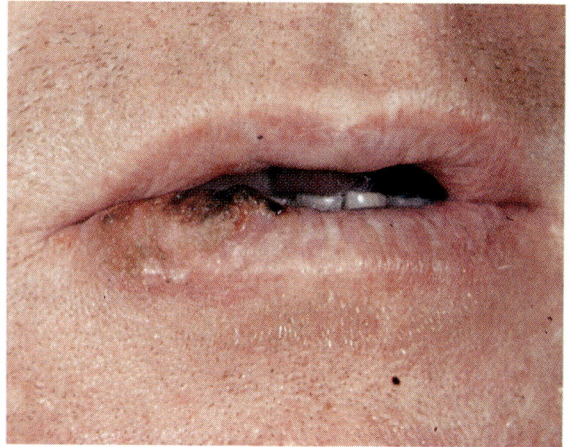

The sore on the mouth is an example of a malignant tumor. The growth on the toe is an example of a benign tumor.

As you know, cell division produces new cells. Normal cells reproduce at exactly the rate required to replace dying cells, never at a faster rate. Just like normal cells, cancer cells reproduce by dividing, but they do not reproduce at the controlled rate that a normal cell does.

As these cells reproduce and multiply, *a mass of tissue*, called a **tumor**, develops. Some of these tumors are **benign** (buh-**nine**), that is, *noncancerous*. They do not spread to healthy tissue or other parts of the body. **Malignant** (muh-**lig**-nunt), or *cancerous*, tumors invade and eventually destroy surrounding healthy tissue.

Cancer cells can break away from the malignant tumor and travel through the lymphatic system and the blood to other parts of the body. At these new locations, they set up new colonies and attack the healthy tissues. This process is called **metastasis** (meh-**tass**-tah-sis), *the further invading and destroying of the tissues and organs involved*. Although scientists do not know why, certain tumor cells spread to certain sites. This knowledge helps the doctor predict where to check for the spread of cancer. Once cancer has metastasized, it is very difficult to control. This is why early detection of cancer is so important.

Types of Cancer

About 250 different types of cancer exist. They are classified in two ways: the part of the body where the cancer cells first develop, and the type of body tissue where the cancer begins. The chart on page 563 shows some of the different types of cancer, as well as which types are the most common.

Cancers that start in the epithelial (ep-uh-**thee**-lee-ul) *tissue*, the tissue that forms the skin and linings of the body organs, are called **carcinoma** (kar-sin-**oh**-muh) **cancer**. Cancers of the skin, breast, and body systems are carcinomas and are the most common. **Sarcoma** (sar-**koh**-muh) **cancers** are those cancers which *begin in the tissue that forms the body's supporting structures*, such as bones, muscles, and cartilage. Leukemia, because it affects the blood, is classified as a sarcoma.

Diagnosing Cancer

During a physical examination, a doctor can detect many of the types of cancer. This is one reason why regular physical exams are important. Through a *Pap smear*, for example, the doctor can check for cervical and uterine cancer in women. The Pap smear detects unusual cells or potential cancerous tissue long before any outward physical signs of a problem appear. The doctor can also use X-ray technology to detect cancer.

If the doctor detects a tumor, final and sure diagnosis is made through a biopsy (by-**op**-see). The **biopsy** involves *removing a small piece of tissue from the tumor and examining it under a microscope to determine whether the tumor is malignant or benign*.

Cancer's Warning Signs

Early detection of cancer is the most critical factor in treating or curing the disease. The individual should be alert to the seven warning signals of cancer:

1. unusual bleeding or discharge,
2. a lump or thickening in the breast or elsewhere,
3. a sore that does not heal,
4. change in bowel or bladder habits,
5. hoarseness or a continuing cough,
6. indigestion or difficulty in swallowing,
7. change in a wart or mole.

Carcinogens

As we have seen in Chapter 11, certain *cancer-causing agents*, called **carcinogens** (kar-**sin**-ah-jins) exist. These include human-made and natural

We are becoming increasingly aware of the dangers of human-made carcinogens in the air.

Different Types of Cancer

Body-Site Type	Organ(s) Most Often Affected	Occurrence
Skin cancer	Skin	Most common type in United States
Digestive system	Colon (large intestine) and rectum (excreting tract)	Most common type in United States next to skin cancer
Respiratory system	Larynx and lungs	Mainly occurs in men; increase in incidence of lung cancer in women
Breast	Breast	Mostly women
Reproductive system	*Males*—prostate gland *Females*—cervix, ovaries, uterus	
Blood and lymph system	Bone marrow, lymph (cancer of the bone marrow is called *leukemia)*	Occurs in men and women

chemicals found in small quantities in air, water, food, and the workplace. Carcinogens are also found in X rays, sunlight, and certain viruses. Not everyone is equally susceptible to the same carcinogen. But you can control your exposure to, and ingestion of, many carcinogens.

The Sun

It is perhaps ironic and hard to believe that the most important source of energy for life itself, the sun, is also a cancer stimulus. The cancer-producing effects come from the ultraviolet radiation that only seems to affect the skin. Skin cancer is highest in those areas where it is warmer and where there is more opportunity for exposure to direct sunlight.

People who work out-of-doors and people who have fair skin are particularly susceptible to skin cancer. This is why those who spend work or recreation time out-of-doors need to use sunscreen lotions that protect the skin from the ultraviolet rays of the sun. See Chapter 3 for more information on sunburn and sunscreen lotions.

Although radiation is often used in the treatment of cancer, it is in itself a cancer-producing agent in humans. The overuse of X rays in past years exposed people unnecessarily to high risks and potential harm of radiation. Since we are constantly being exposed to the cosmic rays in the universe, it is unwise to add any unnecessary exposure through X rays. When it is absolutely necessary in medicine, X rays are used in diagnosis.

The Air

We inhale about 20 breaths per minute. Our quality of health is directly related to the air we breathe. Lung cancer has shown the greatest increase of any form of cancer in the past 35 years. This increase is essentially due to two main factors: cigarette smoking, and air pollution that is caused by industrial wastes, automobile exhausts, and household sources.

General air pollution or pollution from industrial sources is really a matter of community responsibility. The decision about cigarette smoking is largely an individual one.

Treatment of Cancer

In the last 50 years, cancer treatment has improved greatly. In the 1930s, the disease was *arrested*, that is, *stopped*, in only 20% of patients. Today that figure is near 41%.

From earlier study in this chapter, you know that cancer cells are different from normal cells. Cancer cells continue to grow at an uncontrolled rate until they reach a number that eventually kills the patient.

You should recall that cancerous tumors often shed cancerous cells into the blood and lymphatic system, which makes early control very important. Once the cancer cells are in the lymphatic system or bloodstream, they can spread anywhere.

Since over 250 forms of cancer exist, each cancer has a specialized treatment. But, in general, there are some basic approaches to treatment that involve three different strategies: surgery, radiation, and chemotherapy.

Surgery

Surgery has been the method that doctors use most often for treating cancer of the breast and intestines. Doctors have had some success by using surgery in these areas, but improved success will not come until researchers make some progress in capturing the shed cancer cells that are in the bloodstream.

Radiation

When *cobalt* (**koh**-balt) *units* are used in the treatment of **radiation**, the radiation energy penetrates a tumor without damaging the skin. The energy destroys the cells by disrupting chemical actions, especially in the nuclei. The radiation may affect cell enzymes or cause chromosome changes to limit a cell's ability to divide. Radiation affects cells that divide more rapidly than normal cells do.

There is always the risk of the radiation's causing damage to the normal cells near the cancerous area. This is a characteristic shared with surgery. Normal cells are often sacrificed in order to kill cancer cells. Another similarity between the treatments of surgery and radiation is that both surgery and radiation therapy are used when the cancer is located in

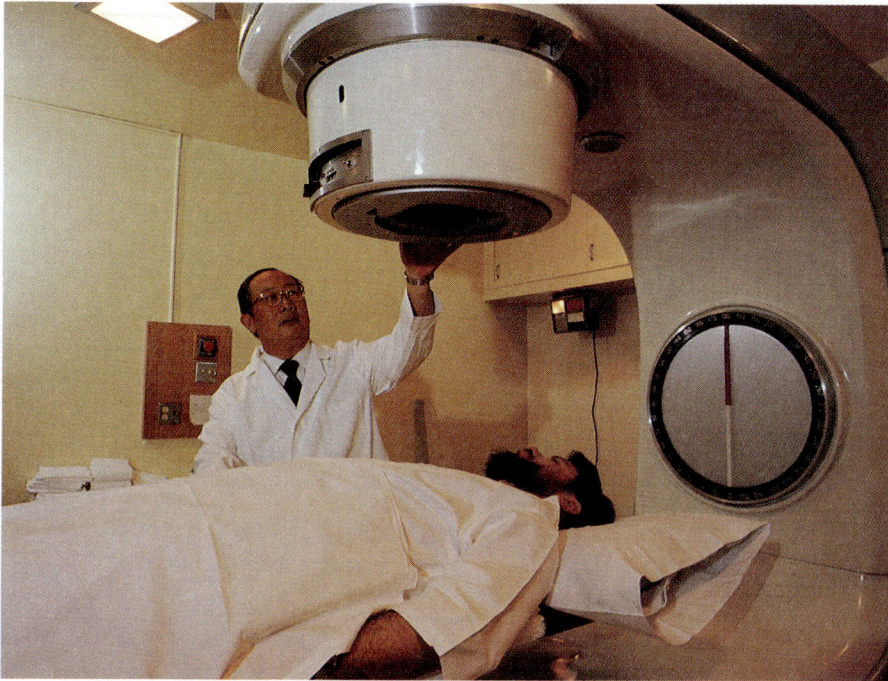

a local, well-defined area, and has not spread all around the body. The advantage of radiation therapy over surgery is that there is no external disfiguration, as there can be with surgery.

Unfortunately, as is the case in surgery, radiation treatment also does not affect the cancer cells that have been shed into the bloodstream. Its influence is only on those cancer cells that are in the direct path of the radiation beam.

Radiation therapy is very successful in arresting some forms of cancer, such as cervical cancer. It is also very helpful in areas of the body where cancerous tumors are difficult to operate on, such as in the head and neck.

Chemotherapy

Chemotherapy (key-moh-**ther**-uh-pea) is *the use of chemicals in the treatment of cancer.* The goal of chemotherapy is to destroy malignant cells without excessive destruction of normal cells. One advantage of drugs over surgery or X rays is that when a drug is administered, it will distribute all over the body, and its effect will be available wherever there is need to attack the cancer cells.

Unfortunately, some unpleasant side effects occur with the use of chemotherapy, since normal cells are also exposed to the drugs. Severe nausea and vomiting are common, as is loss of hair on top of the head.

The anticancer drugs work to interfere with the cell division that cancer cells undergo as they attempt to spread. The idea is that if the drug can break up the process of growth, then the cancer will cease from spreading and the cancerous area will remain localized, or limited.

Avoiding Unnecessary Cancer Risks

While conclusive results are not yet available, many cancer specialists recommend that people follow the dietary guidelines listed below to avoid unnecessary cancer risks:

- Limit your consumption of preserved foods,
- Limit your consumption of prepared meats,
- Avoid artificial sweeteners,
- Limit foods with artificial flavors and colors,
- Increase dietary fiber and bulk,
- Maintain an ideal weight.

What Is Being Done to Combat Cancer?

Cancer is being attacked on many fronts. The categories below show many important areas that can and do contribute to control of cancer.

Education

- Informing the medical profession of the latest findings
- Informing the public of ways to prevent and detect early cancer

Services

- Professional clinics, detection centers, nursing, rehabilitation
- Volunteers—helping cancer patients and their families

Research Programs

- Major study in hospitals, universities, and institutes
- Study by individual scientists

Cancer Organizations

- American Cancer Society
- National Cancer Institute
- Private cancer research

Public Support

- More careers in medicine and research
- Public education, interest, and support
- Voluntary activity
- Financial backing and support

HEALTH UPDATE   HEALTH UPDATE   HEALTH UPDATE

A New Breakthrough in Cancer Research

In the latter part of the 1980s, scientists at the National Cancer Institute found a way to transform white blood cells—lymphocytes—into killer cells that will attack and destroy cancer cells, but not normal ones. The scientists removed lymphocytes from the body and incubated (warmed) them with a large amount of body protein called *interleukin-2*. This protein is produced in very small quantities by our bodies.

In an experiment with 25 patients with cancers so serious that they no longer responded to radiation or chemotherapy, it was found that the killer lymphocytes reduced tumor size by 50% in 11 of the patients.

More experimentation needs to be done on the technique. It has been found to have negative side effects in many people. Not since the development of chemotherapy in the 1950s has there been a completely new treatment for cancer.

Marie Curie and Radium

The greatest single medical discovery ever made by a woman was made by a physicist, Marie Curie (1867–1934).

Born Manya Sklodowska, she registered herself at the Sorbonne, the great French University in Paris, as "Marie." Marie finished her master's degree in physics, graduating first in her class. Later, she married another scientist, Pierre Curie, in 1895, and they began working together.

After two years of marriage, Marie decided to complete her doctoral degree. She had only her doctoral research paper to do and began searching for a subject. She became interested in the discoveries of two other scientists—Wilhelm Röntgen, who had accidentally discovered X rays, and M. Henri Becquerel, who was studying certain substances that take in and give off electromagnetic waves.

Becquerel's work especially fascinated Marie. He discovered that uranium ore gave off invisible rays—though he did not know what the rays were. Uranium is an *element*, one of the 103 known basic materials from which all substances are made.

While studying the uranium rays and their strange behavior, Marie Curie would invent a new word—*radioactivity*—for the special energy that the uranium held. Her research expanded to the study of radioactive properties in the other known elements. In a short time, Marie eliminated all but two elements—uranium and thorium—as effective radioactive ones.

Marie began calculating the amounts of uranium and thorium in an ore called pitchblende when something went wrong. The pitchblende registered a greater degree of radioactivity than she had ever recorded. Marie had discovered two new elements. She named the first polonium and the second radium. It took Marie four years to force 3/10ths of an ounce of pure radium from a ton of pitchblende.

The Curies also discovered what Marie called the "temperamental" nature of radium. It burned the skin tissue painlessly. Pierre used himself as a human experiment, studying the powerful effects of radium on the skin. Along with two other colleagues, Pierre discovered that radium had a selective action against diseased cells. It destroyed the diseased cells, while healthy tissue would heal without permanent damage. The realization that radium was to become a powerful weapon against cancer made it the most sought-after substance in the world.

Marie's happy life came to an abrupt halt in 1906 when Pierre was killed in an accident. Marie went on to be awarded the Nobel Prize two times and to head the newly built Institute of Radium in France.

LAETRILE

"Why do people go to the expense and risk of obtaining drugs like Laetrile for treating cancer?"

In the United States, *Laetrile* (**lay**-uh-trill) is an illegal drug that cannot be used in the treatment of cancer. It is available in Mexico, and some people from the United States go there in the hope of finding a cure.

Laetrile contains cyanide, a potentially lethal poison, as well as many impurities. Drugs like Laetrile will always be available as long as cancer exists, because people want to be free of pain, either from the cancer itself or the effects of chemotherapy.

When a person reaches the "hopeless" stage, he or she is more likely to try anything. This is when people in the cancer quackery business can influence a desperate person and make money.

As long as we have no known cure for cancer, there will be the many drugs, treatments, and devices that people will sell to the uneducated and the desperate. Sometimes the cancer patients convince themselves that such unproven practices work, often because they want to believe it. Also cancer patients tend to have periods when they "seemingly" improve. The patient often interprets this as a sign that this unproven practice or drug is actually working. Sadly, these people invest money in worthless attempts to cure their cancer. They waste valuable time in getting medical assistance that can provide them with the only real chance they might have for cure and survival.

Prevention

Prevention is possible in the case of some cancers, but not all. By avoiding exposure to harmful chemicals and excessive radiation, the individual can greatly reduce the risk of some forms of cancer. Right now, early diagnosis and treatment remain the most effective ways of treating cancer.

In the United States, approximately 462,000 people die each year of cancer. Cancer kills more children between 3 and 14 years of age than any other disease. Today, three out of eight cancer patients will live at least five years after diagnosis and treatment. However, thousands who could have been saved by earlier diagnosis and treatment will die.

CHECK YOURSELF

1. What is the difference between normal cells and cancerous cells?
2. What are the warning signs of cancer?
3. Why are early diagnosis and treatment of this disease so critical?

Diabetes (die-uh-**bee**-tees) is one of the leading health problems in the United States, and it is the third leading killer of adults. It affects at least 12 million Americans, and the problem seems to be increasing. Almost half of this number do not know they have diabetes.

About 600,000 new cases of diabetes occur each year. Diabetics are twice as apt to suffer from heart disease and stroke. They are 25 times more prone to blindness and 17 times more prone to kidney disease than non-diabetics.

A diabetic female lessens the chance of carrying a pregnancy to term and increases the frequency of birth defe[...] nomic toll of diabetes in hours of work los[...] billion dollars annually.

How Diabetes Functions

Diabetes, *a chronic disease that can be con[...] affects the way the body uses food.* In the nor[...] starches, and other foods are changed to *a fo[...] bloodstream carries this glucose to the bod[...] of **insulin**—*a hormone produced in the pancreas[...]* use by the cells. In the case of diabetes, th[...]

Diabetes develops either because the b[...] insulin or because what the body produces[...] the body cells. When glucose is unable to [...]

Self-injection of insulin is the common way to administer the hormone.

in the blood until the kidneys eliminate some of the surplus and pass it off in the urine.

Too much sugar in the urine and in the blood is one of the surest signs of diabetes. The high levels of sugar in the blood are thought to cause the eye and kidney damage to which diabetics are prone.

Types of Diabetes

In 1979, the National Diabetes Data Group established two classifications of diabetes: *type I, insulin-dependent diabetes* and *type II, noninsulin-dependent diabetes.*

In Case of a Diabetic Emergency

Type I

Source

Low blood sugar
(insulin reaction/*hypoglycemia* (high-poh-gly-**see**-mee-uh), an abnormal decrease of sugar in the blood)

Time Span

Sudden onset (minutes to hours)

Signs

- Staggering, poor coordination
- Irritability, belligerence, hostility
- Pale color
- Sweating
- Eventual stupor or unconsciousness

Causes

- Delayed or missed meals
- Too much insulin, by overdose or error
- Extreme exercise

Treatment

- Provide sugar.
- If the person can swallow without choking, offer *any* food or drink containing sugar, such as soft drinks, fruit juice, candy.
- Do not use diet drinks!
- If the person does not respond in 10 to 15 minutes, take him or her to a hospital.
- Look for a diabetic identification bracelet or necklace.
- The diabetic may carry candy or special quick-sugar commercial preparations in plastic, soft-tipped containers. Squeeze the contents into the person's mouth.

Type II

Source

High blood sugar

Time Span

Gradual onset (hours to days)

Signs

- Thirst
- Very frequent urination
- Flushed skin
- Vomiting
- Fruity or winelike odor or breath
- Eventual stupor or unconsciousness

Causes

- Undiagnosed diabetes
- Insulin forgotten or omitted
- Stress, such as illness or injury
- Overindulgence in food or drink

Treatment

- Get the person to a hospital.
- If you are uncertain whether the person has high blood sugar or low blood sugar, give some sugar-containing food or drink. If the person does not respond in 10 to 15 minutes, he or she needs a physician's help.
- Do not give food or drink if the person is unable to swallow. Take the person to a hospital if he or she has no response to treatments.

Symptoms of Types I and II Diabetes

Type I	Type II
Frequent urination	Excess weight
Abnormal thirst	Drowsiness
Unusual hunger	Blurred vision
Weight loss	Tingling, numbness in hands and feet
Irritability	Skin infections
Weakness and fatigue	Slow healing of cuts (especially feet)
Nausea and vomiting	Itching

Type I, Insulin-Dependent Diabetes

This type of diabetes (formerly called juvenile) occurs most often in children and young adults and accounts for about 500,000 of all cases of diabetes. It usually appears abruptly in children and young adults and progresses rapidly.

Because the pancreas produces little or no insulin, these patients must take daily injections to stay alive. Before the discovery of insulin, type I diabetics usually lived no more than two years after diagnosis. Today, because of advanced methods of treatment, many diabetics live near-normal life spans.

Type II, Noninsulin-Dependent Diabetes

This type of diabetes (formerly called maturity-onset) usually occurs in adults over 40 years of age. This is the more common form of diabetes and accounts for over 95% of the total diabetic population. In this type of diabetes, the pancreas produces some insulin, but because of a cell receptor defect, the body cannot use the insulin effectively.

People can often control type II diabetes by diet and exercise and, in some cases, by use of oral medications. Problems related to the circulation and heart are common in this type of diabetes. Because the onset of type II diabetes is gradual, the disease often goes undetected for years.

Type II diabetes has been linked to heredity, obesity, and inactivity. About 80% of all patients are overweight at the time they are diagnosed. People can prevent many cases of type II diabetes if they maintain a desired weight and keep physically active.

CHECK YOURSELF

1. How do the two types of diabetes differ?
2. How can a person prevent type II diabetes?
3. What happens in a diabetic emergency?

4. Arthritis: America's Chief Crippling Disease

The term arthritis (are-**thrite**-us) literally means "inflammation of a joint." **Arthritis** covers at least 100 different *conditions that cause aching, pain, and swelling in joints and connective tissue throughout the body*. It can and does occur at all ages, from infancy on. The National Center for Health Statistics estimates that about 37 million people have arthritis severe enough to require medical care. Arthritis costs the national economy over $18 billion yearly in lost wages and medical bills. It is likely that you or someone you know has arthritis. It affects one in seven people and one in three families. The two most common kinds of arthritis are *rheumatoid arthritis* and *osteoarthritis*.

Rheumatoid Arthritis

Rheumatoid (**rue**-muh-toid) **arthritis** is the most serious type of arthritis and is mainly a *destructive and disabling inflammation of the joints*, especially the joints of the hands and arms, the hips, the legs, and the feet. But rheumatoid inflammation also attacks connective tissue throughout the body. This is what can cause symptoms such as fever, fatigue, and swollen lymph glands.

Rheumatoid arthritis causes joints to stiffen and swell.

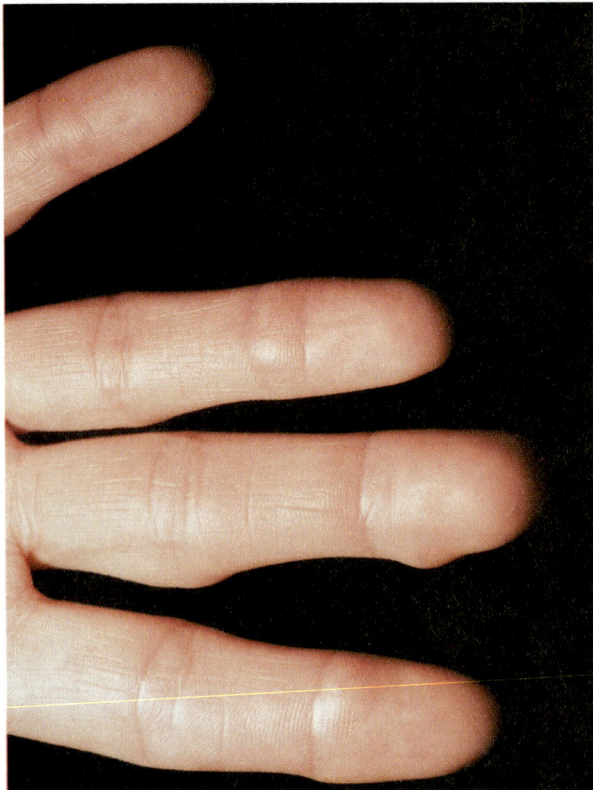

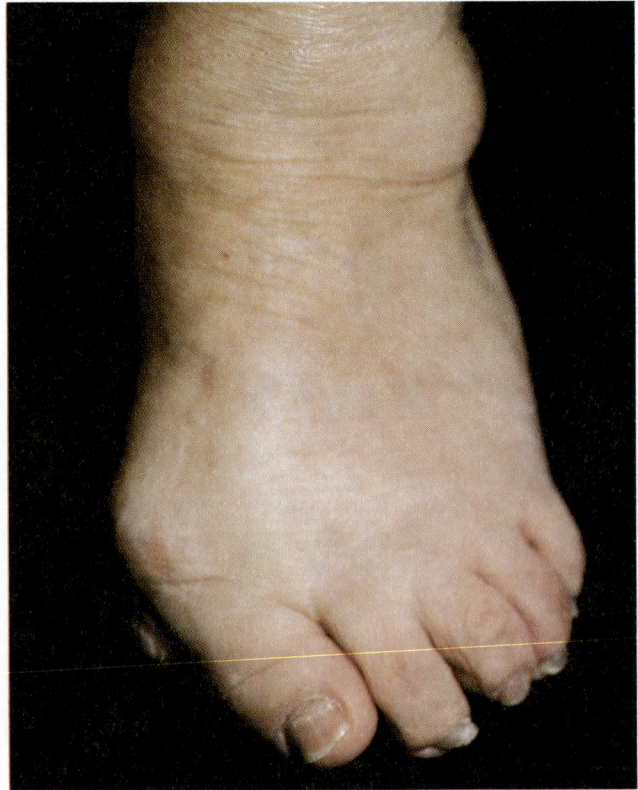

Rheumatoid arthritis causes the joints to stiffen, then swell, and become tender. The inflammation can do progressive damage inside the joint if it is not diagnosed and properly treated.

What Rheumatoid Arthritis Does

The area where two bones meet is enclosed in a capsule, containing fluid. The capsule has an inner lining called the *synovial membrane*. (See Chapter 15 on the skeletal and muscular system for more information.)

Inflammation starts here, swelling the membrane, and spreading to other parts of the joint. Outgrowths of inflamed tissue invade the cartilage surrounding the bone ends, eventually eating it away. Finally, scar tissue can form between the bone ends and sometimes change to bone, so that the joint becomes fused, permanently rigid, and immovable.

Inflammation can also lead to distortion of the joint. This is most apparent when the disease attacks the hands. The fingers become drawn back and angled sideways, so that the hands are deformed and difficult to use properly in performing common daily tasks.

These conditions can develop in anyone. But under proper treatment, started early, people can prevent them in almost all cases.

Treatment of Rheumatoid Arthritis

Scientists do not know the cause of rheumatoid arthritis, the most serious arthritic disease, and at the present time there is no cure for it. Treatment programs are designed to relieve pain, reduce inflammation, prevent damage to joints, prevent deformities, and keep joints movable and functioning properly.

All of the following may be involved in a full treatment program for rheumatoid arthritis: medication (aspirin is the most frequently used anti-inflammatory medicine), rest, exercise, posture rules, splints, walking aids, heat, surgery, and rehabilitation.

Osteoarthritis

Osteoarthritis (ahs-tee-oh-are-**thrite**-us) is the most common type of arthritis, affecting about 16 million people. *It results from wear-and-tear in the mechanical parts of a joint.* Unlike rheumatoid arthritis, inflammation is rarely a problem. Osteoarthritis primarily affects the weight-bearing joints of the knees and hips.

In the case of osteoarthritis, the cartilage becomes pitted and frayed and, in time, may wear away completely. Bone ends then become thicker and bony spurs may develop. As a result, surrounding ligament and membranes become thickened, changing the whole structure and shape of the joint.

Aching and soreness around the joints, especially when a person moves, is the major symptom of osteoarthritis. Although there is no cure for it, treatment can slow down and even control the disease process.

KEEPING FIT

The Warning Signs of Arthritis

- Persistent pain and stiffness on arising
- Pain, tenderness, or swelling in one or more joints
- Recurrence of these symptoms, especially when they involve more than one joint
- Recurrent or persistent pain and stiffness in the neck, lower back, knees, and other joints

Aches and pains in or around joints can mean different things. Early detection and diagnosis of arthritis is essential and can prevent unnecessary damage and pain. Yet, arthritis specialists report that people suffering from arthritis wait an average of four years after their first symptoms appear before seeking assistance.

CHECK YOURSELF

1. What are the early warning signs of arthritis?
2. How do rheumatoid arthritis and osteoarthritis differ?
3. How is arthritis treated?

CHAPTER 31   Review

CHAPTER SUMMARY

- Some diseases are not caused by pathogens and are not communicable. These diseases and disorders have a variety of causes.
- One of the most serious of these—the cardiovascular diseases—is often caused by one's life-style or personal health habits.
- Hypertension and atherosclerosis are two of the most serious heart diseases.
- Both can result in heart attacks. By controlling or avoiding certain risk factors, heart disease can be controlled, even prevented.
- Cancer is the second leading cause of death among adults in the United States.
- The exact cause for the development of cancerous cells is not known. However, certain health behaviors and exposure to certain carcinogens tend to increase one's risks of cancer.
- Cancer is treated through surgery, radiation, and chemotherapy.
- Diabetes is the third leading cause of death among adults in the United States. It results from the inability of the pancreas to produce enough insulin, and it can be controlled through medication.
- Finally, the major crippling disease, arthritis, is not completely understood and can strike anyone at any age. However, with prompt treatment, arthritis can be controlled.

REVIEWING WHAT YOU LEARNED

1. What life-style practices have led to the significant deaths due to cancer and heart disease?
2. Define and describe atherosclerosis.
3. What happens when a person has a heart attack? What brings on a heart attack?
4. What medical treatment might a victim of heart attack expect upon arriving at a hospital?
5. Explain the ways that cancer is treated.
6. Explain the importance of early detection and treatment of cancer.
7. How does arthritis develop? Identify the major symptoms and the current treatment for the condition.
8. Define and describe the two main types of diabetes.
9. What role does diet play in the following diseases?
   a. Hypertension
   b. Cancer
   c. Diabetes
10. Why do you think hypertension is called the "silent killer"?

APPLYING WHAT YOU LEARNED

1. Choose a noncommunicable chronic or degenerative disease. On a sheet of paper, explain how

noninfectious diseases
noncommunicable diseases
cardiovascular diseases
high blood pressure
hypertension
arteriosclerosis
atherosclerosis
plaque
angina pectoris
thrombus
embolus
stroke
heart attack
cardiac arrest
fibrillation
cerebral thrombosis

cerebral embolism
cerebral hemorrhage
electrocardiogram
defibrillator
fluoroscope
phonocardiography
angiocardiography
cardiac catheterization
open-heart surgery
catheter
coronary bypass surgery
heart transplant
artificial pacemaker
risk factor
cancer
tumor

benign
malignant
metastasis
carcinoma cancers
sarcoma cancers
biopsy
carcinogens
radiation
chemotherapy
diabetes
glucose
insulin
arthritis
rheumatoid arthritis
osteoarthritis

PUTTING VOCABULARY TO USE

On a separate piece of paper, write the answers to the following:

1. *Chronic.* Supply a phrase or word that is synonymous with chronic.
2. *Arteriosclerosis and atherosclerosis.* Explain the relationship between these two conditions.
3. *Rheumatoid arthritis and osteoarthritis.* Cite two ways that these diseases are both similar and different.
4. *Diabetes.* In one sentence, describe this disease.
5. *Hypertension.* Define "hyper" and "tension." Write your own definition for this term.

6. *Carcinogen.* Cite three examples of carcinogens.
7. *Malignant.* What is the opposite of this word?
8. *Sarcoma.* Identify the major areas of the body where this type of cancer is most prevalent.
9. *Chemotherapy.* Name two potential problems in using this treatment.
10. *Metastasis.* Give two words that mean the opposite of metastasis.
11. *Cardiac arrest.* Identify three warning signs of cardiac arrest.
12. *Carcinoma.* Compare cancerous tissue with normal tissue.

biological, psychological, sociological, and cultural factors can play a role in the development of the disease.
2. Why do you think that the noncommunicable diseases have replaced the infectious diseases as the leading causes of death?
3. Research the recent discoveries and developments in heart surgery. Write a one-page descriptive report on your findings.
4. Make a list of reasons why you think people delay going to a doctor when they have a warning sign of cancer. Develop a poster encouraging people to respond to cancer's warning signs. Display your poster.

5. Call or write to the American Cancer Society in your community and find out what current research is being done on cancer. Share your findings with the class.

FOCUS ON WELLNESS

Cardiovascular disease and cancer are the major killers of American adults. Even though these are usually diseases of mid-life and later life, early habits and attitudes play an important role in their prevention. *I can work to reduce my vulnerability to these diseases by . . .*

UNIT

10

THE HEALTH OF THE ENVIRONMENT AND THE COMMUNITY

CHAPTER 32
The Environment and Your Health

CHAPTER 33
Energy and Conservation

The Environment and Your Health

Look at the beautiful scene in the picture on this page. Do you realize that this area is in danger from any number of environmental problems? In this chapter, you will be reading about the most serious of them.

After studying this chapter, you will be able to:
- describe an ecosystem,
- explain the effects humans have had on ecosystems,
- identify the components and hazards of air pollution,
- describe the impact of air pollution on weather,
- list the health problems resulting from water pollution,
- describe the environmental problems associated with waste disposal,
- explain the health hazards of noise pollution.

1. The Environment and You

Ecology (ee-**kahl**-uh-jee) is *the branch of science that deals with the inter-relationships between living organisms and their environment.* Our actual environment consists of a *thin layer of soil, water, and air near the earth's surface* called the **biosphere** (**bye**-uh-sfear). This sphere of life is made up of **biotic** (bye-**ot**-ick) **communities** (i.e., *plants and animals providing one another with life-sustaining material*).

The *biotic communities are the living part of larger units* called **ecosystems** (**ee**-koh-sis-tums). Ecosystems also encompass the **abiotic** (ay-bye-**ot**-ick), or *nonliving* environment, which includes air, water, and soil. The parts of an ecosystem make up a working relationship that sustains life.

In an ecosystem, every element is an essential part of the whole. When ecosystems are left to function on their own, they maintain the delicate balance of nature necessary to sustain life. However, the delicate balance of these intricate systems has been and continues to be seriously threatened by pollution. Altering or eliminating even one component of the system threatens the entire system.

Our Environment Sustains Our Lives

Why study about the environment in a health class? What does this have to do with you? Literally, everything has some bearing on environmental health. We are dependent upon our environment for sustaining life. The health of the environment directly affects our personal level of health.

CHECK YOURSELF

1. What is ecology?
2. What is the biosphere?
3. What is a biotic community?
4. What is an ecosystem?
5. What is an abiotic community?

2. The Air We Breathe

The most vital resource that we, as humans, need to sustain life is air. We could not live more than a few minutes without air. The quality of the air we breathe has a great impact on our health. Yet, each year the living organisms that need air most—humans—release more than 200 million tons of pollutants into the air.

KEEPING FIT

Fluorocarbon Gases

Fluorocarbon (floor-oh-**kar**-bun) **gases** are *gases used in spray cans to force out their contents.* These fluorocarbons float up into the air when they are released from the aerosol can. In the atmosphere, the fluorocarbons release chlorine, which destroys ozone.

In 1974, scientists confirmed the dangers of this gas, and, within a year, sales of aerosol can products dropped 25%. In most states, the use of **aerosol**, *a suspension of fine liquid or solid particles in gas,* in such products is banned.

Check for any aerosol cans in your home. Is their use necessary? Could you use a nonaerosol alternative?

The Environmental Protection Agency monitors air pollution.

Protecting Your Environment

Do you do your part to protect your environment and prevent pollution? On a separate sheet of paper, indicate whether each statement describes you *most of the time* (M), *some of the time* (S), or *never* (N).

1. I use nondisposable plastic materials rather than paper napkins, cups, or plates.
2. I save glass and aluminum for recycling.
3. I buy returnable bottles or recyclable cans.
4. I keep my stereo, radio, and TV at a moderate volume.
5. I use non-aerosol sprays.
6. I limit my shower time or take baths to conserve water.
7. I do not let the water run in the sink unnecessarily.
8. I use a car pool or public transportation when possible.
9. I combine trips in the car and avoid unnecessary driving.
10. I keep the exhaust system in my car in good condition (for car owners only).
11. I do not waste paper.
12. I save all paper products for recycling.

Scoring. Give yourself 4 points for every *most of the time*, 2 points for every *some of the time*, and 0 for every *never*. Add up your totals.

48 to 34: *Excellent,* you are environmentally conscious and are doing your part.
33 to 15: *Good,* you are trying.
Below 15: *You are a hazard* to your environment.

To be more specific, our activities release yearly in the atmosphere 10 billion tons of carbon dioxide, 14 million tons of nitrogen oxides, 50 million tons of hydrocarbons, 1,500 tons of fluorocarbons, along with 3 million tons of toxic metals.

Air pollution is *the contamination of the atmosphere by waste products* at levels that are unhealthy for humans and for the environment. You have already studied about the respiratory diseases asthma, lung cancer, and emphysema. While air pollution alone does not cause these diseases, it is estimated that about 15,000 excess deaths occur because of air pollution.

In addition, about 7 million sick days and 15 million days of restricted activity per year are related to this problem. The total affected population of 40 million represents about one out of every six Americans.

The Environmental Protection Agency (EPA) developed the Pollutant Standards Index (PSI) to describe the quality of air throughout the United States. The chart on page 581 shows what the ratings mean.

The Ingredients of Air Pollution

The materials that pollute the air include *hydrocarbons, nitrogen dioxide, ozone, carbon monoxide, sulfur dioxide,* and *particulates.*

Hydrocarbons

Hydrocarbons are the *unburned chemicals in car exhausts.* Hydrocarbons react with sunlight to form **photochemical pollution**, that is, *pollution that restricts the food-processing capabilities of plants.*

Besides being harmful to plants, hydrocarbons can cause the nose and throat to become irritated and the eyes to water. Scientists are now studying the relationship between hydrocarbons and lung cancer.

Nitrogen Dioxide

Nitrogen dioxide (nigh-truh-jun di-**ach**-side) is *one of the ingredients that contributes to ozone* (**oh**-zone), *or photochemical, smog.* When you see **smog**, *a blend of smoke and fog,* on the horizon or over an area, the yellowish-brown color comes from nitrogen dioxide.

Ozone

Perhaps you have studied about the ozone layer of the atmosphere. In the atmosphere, ozone serves as a screen, protecting us from the sun's harmful ultraviolet rays. As chemicals enter the atmosphere and break down this ozone layer, we risk being exposed to more harmful sun rays, as well as a change in world climates.

Air Pollution Chart

Index Value	PSI Descriptor	General Health Effects	Cautionary Statements
400 300	hazardous	Premature death of ill and elderly. Healthy people will experience adverse symptoms that affect their normal activity.	All persons should remain indoors, keeping windows and doors closed. All persons should minimize physical exertion and avoid traffic.
200	very unhealthful	Premature onset of certain diseases in addition to significant aggravation of symptoms and decreased exercise tolerance in healthy persons.	Elderly and persons with existing diseases should stay indoors and avoid physical exertion. General population should avoid outdoor activity.
100	unhealthful	Significant aggravation of symptoms and decreased exercise tolerance in persons with heart or lung disease with widespread symptoms in the healthy population.	Elderly and persons with existing heart or lung disease should stay indoors and reduce physical activity.
50	moderate	Mild aggravation of symptoms in susceptible persons, with irritation symptoms in the healthy population.	Persons with existing heart or respiratory ailments should reduce physical exertion and outdoor activity.
0	good		

Older plants are being replaced by ones with more efficient pollution controls.

The automobile is a major source of air pollution. Every day, almost 60 million Americans rely on the automobile for transportation. Of these, 40 million drive alone, with their cars' consuming 290 million gallons of gasoline each week. One of the most effective ways to reduce the automobile pollution is by carpooling. Here are some of the advantages of carpooling:

- *It saves energy.* An increase in car occupancy from 1.6 to 2 people per car would result in an annual national fuel savings of almost 5 billion gallons of gasoline.
- *It would improve air quality.* High levels of pollution are especially present during morning and evening traffic periods. Fewer cars on the road would lead to lower pollution levels.
- *It would reduce congestion.* If the number of people could be increased to 2 per car, 20% of all cars would be taken off the road during rush hour.
- *It provides an alternative to driving in places where mass transit is unavailable.*
- *It saves money.* Estimates are that about $500 per year is saved on tire wear, gasoline, and parking costs.
- *It allows free time.* On those days when the rider is not driving, he or she can relax and engage in last-minute studying.
- *It saves time.* In some communities, there are incentives for carpooling. Special lanes are open so that the carpoolers can get a headstart on the traffic jams that otherwise would be present.

When nitrogen dioxides and hydrocarbons combine in the presence of sunlight, the ozone gas is formed. **Ozone** is *one component of photochemical smog.* When ozone is near the ground, it is a harmful pollutant. Ozone damages the tissues of plants. In humans, it damages the small airways in the lower respiratory tract, causing a resistance to airflow. This prevents the transfer of oxygen from the lungs to the bloodstream.

Ozone also damages the alveoli of the lungs, where the oxygen transfer occurs. This leads to *fluid's building up in the air sacs of the lungs,* a condition called **pulmonary edema** (**pull**-mah-ner-ee eh-**dee**-muh).

Carbon Monoxide

Carbon monoxide is a *poisonous gas, mainly released into the air by car exhausts.* When a person inhales carbon monoxide, it attaches to the hemoglobin (the red coloring matter in the blood) 245 times more easily than oxygen, thereby reducing the blood's oxygen-carrying capacity. Carbon monoxide can also lead to blood clotting and can prevent the oxygen being released from the blood to the cells.

A deficiency of oxygen can cause dizziness, blurred vision, headaches, and fatigue. Over a long period of time, this can lead to anemia and heart and lung disease.

Sulfur Dioxide

Sulfur dioxide is *a poisonous gas, a product of the burning of fossil fuels such as oil or coal*. Factories and power plants are major producers of this pollutant. Sulfur dioxide irritates the respiratory system and makes breathing more difficult. It is associated with the rapid increase in chronic bronchitis and emphysema in the United States. Sulfur dioxide also kills plants and rusts metals. Steel corrodes two to three times faster in air-polluted cities than in rural areas.

Particulates

Particulates (par-**tik**-you-luts) are *actual particles of soot, ash, and fall-out, solid and liquid matter suspended in the air*. Some particulates carry harmful gases and even pesticides into the breathing passages of the human body. Plant life helps to filter particulate matter, but as more and more trees and foliage are destroyed for building purposes, the problem gets worse. Particulates soil clothing, reduce visibility, and affect the climate.

A Word About Lead

Lead is a naturally occurring material in our environment. However, the content of lead in the air and our general exposure to lead has dramatically increased over the years. The greatest contributing factor is the automobile. Until laws were passed requiring automobiles to operate on

These photos show a clear day and a smoggy day in the San Fernando Valley of Los Angeles County.

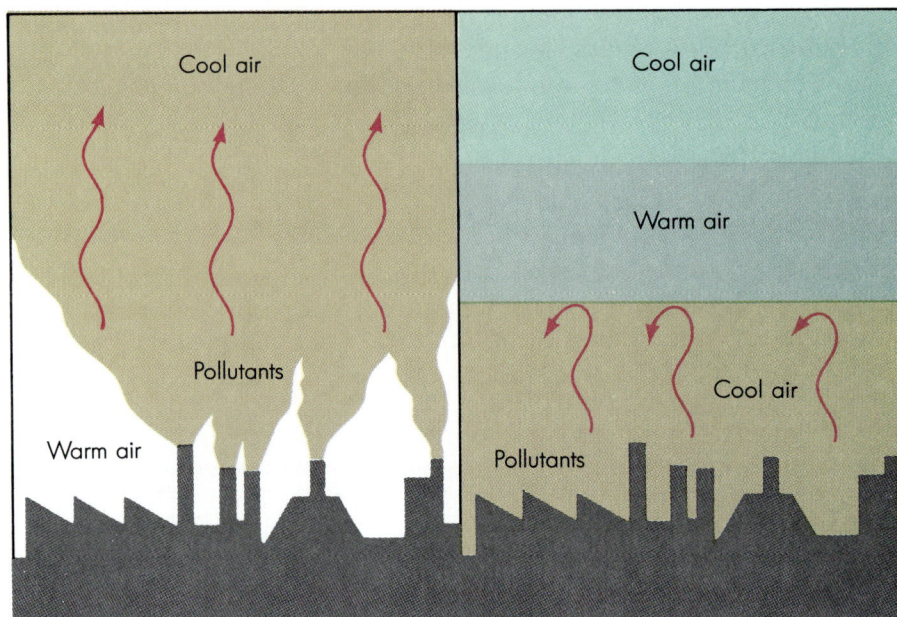

Left. *The picture shows warm air rising normally into the atmosphere.*
Right. *The picture shows temperature inversion. A warm air mass is trapped between two cool air masses, causing pollutants to remain near ground level.*

unleaded gasoline, lead was the most used additive in gasoline. Lead is also used in paints, ceramics, glassware, pipes, and many other products.

Lead is absorbed into the bloodstream through the lungs. *If too much lead enters the body,* **lead poisoning** results. The symptoms of lead poisoning include loss of appetite, anemia, and damage to the nervous system. Scientists are still studying the long-term effects of lead poisoning.

Protection Against Air Pollution

Protect yourself during pollution emergencies or when pollution levels are high:

- Avoid strenuous outdoor activities.
- Do not smoke.
- Do not drink alcoholic beverages. Alcohol, when combined with high levels of carbon monoxide caused by air pollution or smoking, will affect judgment more than usual.
- Eat well-balanced meals, for good nutrition helps your body to better handle toxic substances.

Air Pollution and Weather

How do weather conditions affect air pollution? When the wind blows, fresh air helps to carry away some of the smog and harmful gases—temporarily "clearing the air." Air pollutants rise and usually spread over a wide area.

However, under certain conditions, temperature inversions develop, trapping the pollutants in an area and increasing the seriousness of air pollution. A **temperature inversion** (in-**vur**-zhun) occurs when *a warm air mass moves over cooler air below, trapping the cooler air, at ground level, with whatever pollutants it contains.* Because cooler air is also above the warm layer of air, the warm air is also trapped.

Climate Change and Carbon Dioxide

Some of the air pollutants, such as sulfur, nitrogen, and the toxic metals, return to earth rapidly, while others, such as carbon dioxide, remain in the atmosphere for years.

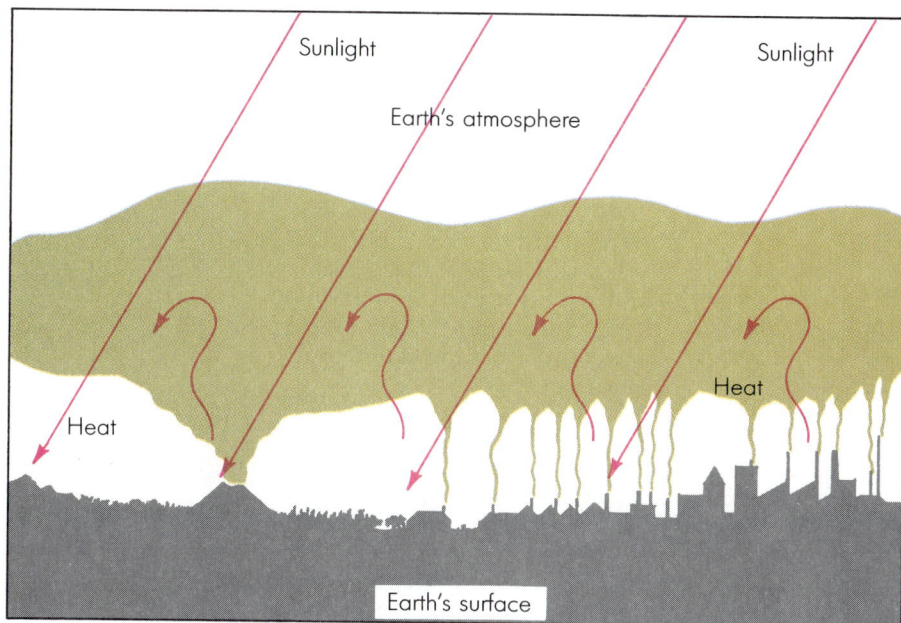

In the greenhouse effect, large quantities of carbon dioxide, caused by the burning of fossil fuels, form a cloud around the earth. Heat is kept near the surface, thus causing higher temperatures and humidity.

Carbon dioxide enters the atmosphere as a result of human and animal respiration and decay. The burning of fossil fuels, such as kerosene, gasoline, coal, and oil, adds more carbon dioxide.

Plants take some carbon dioxide from the air during **photosynthesis** (foe-toe-**sin**-thuh-sus), *the process by which plants make food*, while the world's oceans absorb some carbon dioxide. Thus, the chemical permeates our atmosphere.

The Greenhouse Effect   How can carbon dioxide change the world's climate? It creates a situation called the **greenhouse effect**, the *process by which the earth is gradually warmed*. If you have ever been in a greenhouse, you can understand why this effect using carbon dioxide is so named.

In a greenhouse, visible sunlight passes through to the plants and infrared radiation is absorbed, resulting in higher temperatures, an increased amount of water vapor, and a steaming effect. Go into a greenhouse and you will notice the immediate humid feeling. The humidity cannot escape because the glass of the greenhouse contains it. The situation is the same with the earth's surface.

Sunlight passes through the carbon dioxide cloud that encircles the earth. The heat that the earth gives off cannot escape because of the cloud. This cloud also causes more heat and moisture to be trapped in the earth's atmosphere, making temperatures much warmer.

A Warmer Environment   If the earth became warmer, the way of life for millions of people would be altered. For example, a 2-degree average increase in the world temperature would put New York City, and many other cities of the world, under water. It is estimated that a 2-foot (60-cm) rise in sea levels will occur in the next 100 years. Carbon dioxide probably has

A Health Student Asks . . .

ASBESTOS

"Our schools have been inspected for problems with asbestos. Several of the schools were found to have problems. What is wrong with asbestos and why is it used for building if it is dangerous? What is being done to correct the problem in schools?"

Asbestos is a naturally occurring mineral fiber. It is fireproof, and a good insulator of heat and electricity. Asbestos also is virtually indestructible. All of these characteristics have led to its having over 2,000 uses, including vinyl flooring, insulation, and fireproof clothing.

Asbestos is an example of a product that people used extensively before officials realized just how potentially dangerous it is. Officials knew that people who mined or manufactured asbestos products or who installed asbestos insulation were 10 times more likely to contract *asbestosis* (as-bes-**toe**-sus), or white lung disease. This is a potentially fatal disease that blocks the lungs with thick fibrous tissue. Asbestos has also been linked to certain cancers. Government regulations now require workers to wear protective clothing to limit the hazards of asbestos.

What officials did not know until more recently was that the small amounts of asbestos fibers in the products consumers use are also a health hazard. As a result, many public places have been inspected for hazardous levels of asbestos fibers. Some cities have banned the use of asbestos for fireproofing or insulation. Government regulations now protect consumers from certain types of asbestos products.

The Environmental Protection Agency (EPA) wants to phase out all asbestos products for safety's sake and is now working toward that goal.

You can obtain more information on asbestos by writing to **Asbestos, National Cancer Institute, Bethesda, MD 20205.**

helped to warm the temperature of the earth by about half a degree. Many believe that the greenhouse effect has caused this condition. Over the last 40 years, 20,000 cubic miles of ice have melted at both poles.

Although carbon dioxide makes up only 0.03% of the atmosphere, it plays a critical role in keeping the earth's surface warm enough to support life. Without the insulating layer of carbon dioxide, surface temperatures would be 60 degrees lower, which would be much too cold for life in most places. The activities of humans and the increasing population of the earth, however, threaten to tip the balance to a hotter earth.

Acid Rain

We have always needed rain for good crops and a sufficient water supply. Is acid rain the same as ordinary rain? No, acid rain is a rather new phenomenon, and is not helpful like ordinary rain. **Acid rain** occurs when *ordinary rain passes through atmosphere polluted with sulfur and nitrogen oxides, and picks up these chemicals.* In small amounts, these oxides are important in nature to nourish plant and aquatic life. However, industries, auto exhausts, and other outlets that burn fossil fuel have disrupted this delicate balance and created an overabundance of these two oxides.

The falling rain mixes with these pollutants to produce a form of precipitation that is a mixture of sulfuric (sul-**few**-rick) acid, nitric (**nigh**-trik) acid, and water. We call this precipitation acid rain, but in reality it includes all forms of precipitation, including acid snow, acid sleet, acid hail, and even acid fog.

Wells Cathedral in England was completed 700 years ago. Only recently have its statues been eroding from acid rain.

The Effects of Acid Rain The effects of acid rain are being felt in the Northeast, where many lakes no longer have fish. In some cities, statues that have been standing for decades are beginning to erode. Automobile finishes corrode more rapidly, and the paint on houses lasts only a few years.

The high acid content in a lake or stream destroys the eggs of aquatic life. This not only brings an end to the inhabitants of the water but also to the animals that feed on the fish.

An additional problem has developed in some lakes because of acid rain. When the acid precipitation mixes with certain types of soil, aluminum is released and seeps into nearby lakes. Aluminum is deadly to fish. Mercury, when combined with acid rain, mixes to form methylmercury (meth-ul-**mer**-kue-ree), which is also deadly to fish. You can see how these chemicals easily enter the human food chain, as humans eat fish that have consumed the deadly chemicals.

Acid rain causes open sores or wounds to develop on plant leaves, reducing plant growth. Litter in the form of bacteria accumulates on the plant leaves. The development of nitrogen, which is important in plant growth, is inhibited. Finally, calcium, potassium, and magnesium are taken from the leaves and the soil of the plants. Thus, acid rain threatens our crop production, our forests, and all of our wildlife.

The damage resulting from air pollution costs the American public an estimated $12 billion a year in cleanup and health-related expenses. Crop damage alone is estimated at $500 million yearly.

CHECK YOURSELF

1. What effect does air pollution have on one's health?
2. List and define four ingredients of air pollution.
3. How does the weather affect air pollution?
4. Explain what is meant by the greenhouse effect.
5. What is acid rain and what are three of its dangers?

3. Water—A Vital Resource

Like air, water is necessary for human existence. We could not survive more than about five days without water. Water makes up about 65% of the human body. The human brain is about 80% water.

Water is a vital part of the ecosystem. Countless one-celled plants and animals live in the oceans. All forms of animal life in these bodies of water depend on plants and small animals for food. In turn, millions of people depend on the ocean for their food. Again, you can see the cycle and the interdependence of all elements of the system.

Water is one of our limited resources. Although about 70% of the earth's surface is water, only 3% of the world's water supply is free of salt. Most of that 3% is solidified in polar ice. Our increasing use of water, combined with severe pollution of our waterways, has us headed for a serious fresh-water shortage problem.

Saving Water

Clean water is a precious resource, one that people often take for granted. The increasing amount of waste water throughout the country has caused communities to take a close look at ways to conserve clean water. One-third of all waste water comes from homes.

Even after treatment, waste water is usually dumped into rivers and streams. Eventually, its harmful substances find their way into drinking-water supply systems downstream.

Steps toward Conservation

People can conserve water in individual homes. With each family's doing its part, utility bills can be reduced and more fresh water can be conserved. Here are some practical suggestions:

- Each time the toilet is flushed, 5 to 8 gallons of water are used. About 40% of the municipal water supply is used to flush toilets. Avoid unnecessary flushing and carelessly using the toilet to dispose of nonwater-soluble items.
- A 5-minute shower uses over 50 gallons of water. Water could be saved by taking briefer showers, turning off the water while lathering, and using water-saving showerhead accessories.
- Repair leaking faucets. Even small leaks can lose up to 400 gallons of water per day.
- Turn off water when not in use, such as while shaving or brushing teeth.
- Let rain water the garden. Usually one soaking per week is enough. Capture rainwater for use in the house, especially to water plants.
- Avoid leaving any water (indoors or outdoors) on and unattended.

Water Pollution

Water pollution is *the condition in which wastes accumulate to a point that the water's natural purification processes are unable to break them down into harmless forms.* Daily, we send billions of gallons of dirty water down drains. *Food and human wastes, detergents, and other substances* form **sewage**, which must, in some way, be treated or disposed of. Most of the pollutants that humans put into the water come from sewage, agricultural drainage, and industrial wastes.

Industrial Water Pollution

Industrial plants and factories are the largest consumers of water. They use water for cooling, for power, and for transportation. In addition to consuming tremendous quantities of water, industries are also responsible for polluting the nation's water supply. It is estimated that American industries produce 770 billion pounds of waste each year.

Nearly 1,000 chemicals are developed each year in the United States, which means countless new pollutants. Chemicals and metals from industrial wastes, oil leaks, and accidental oil spills, along with mine drainage and wastes from mining operations, account for the millions of tons of toxic substances dumped into our waterways each year.

Chemical pollutants are dangerous to all living organisms.

Agricultural Water Pollution

Farmers use fertilizers to get a higher crop yield. Many of these **fertilizers** are made up of chemicals, pesticides, and herbicides, in addition to processed animal waste. When these fertilizers enter lakes and streams, they encourage growth of small plants called *algae* (**al**-jee). As algae multiply, die, and decay, the supply of oxygen in the water is reduced. Plant and animal life cannot survive. This process, called *eutrophication* (you-troh-fuh-**kay**-shun), eventually causes the body of water to dry up completely or turn into a slimy bed of algae.

This form of water pollution can eventually affect humans directly, especially in areas where people get their food from the water.

Water Pollution by People

Sewage disposal is an increasing problem that contributes to our water-pollution problem. Millions of people in this country do not have waste-treatment facilities. A number of communities still dump raw sewage into the freshwater supply. Sewage includes human wastes, garage and sink wastes, laundry water and bathwater. What happens to this sewage when it leaves the pipes in your home? Some communities have sewage-treatment plants. Others rely on septic-tank disposal. The end products of sewage treatment are mainly nitrates and phosphates, which add to the problem.

Other Forms of Water Pollution

Perhaps a less obvious source of water pollution in communities is the sediment, salt, and sand that build up in rivers and streams. This buildup is a result of erosion from highway construction and development sites. Urban construction increases normal erosion rates by about 100 times.

Finally, our use of waterways for navigation and recreation adds to the water-pollution problem. No doubt you have read about oil tankers colliding or leaking. You do not have control over preventing this type of pollution. But what about exhausts from motor boats, or the litter and waste dumped into recreational lakes?

Sewage treatment plants are helping reduce water pollution in many communities.

The Effects of Water Pollution

Water pollution has a devastating effect on the delicate balance of the ecosystem. It can destroy organisms that provide food for large animals while encouraging the growth of other plant life. Besides killing some fish, water pollution contaminates other fish.

Human industrial wastes, the largest water pollutants, contain many organisms that cause serious illness to humans. Industrial wastes—chemicals, oils, detergents—cause illness and poison wildlife.

The breakdown of sewage takes oxygen from the water, and so fish cannot get enough oxygen to survive. Chemicals—detergents, fertilizers, pesticides—have long-range ill effects on people who eat the fish or drink the water.

Checking Water's Purity

Under the standards of the Safe Drinking Water Act, you should check your water in the following ways:

Test	How often
1. **Bacteria.** This test indicates whether disease-causing bacteria may be present. It is a simple test, but requires a specially prepared sampling bottle, which a lab will give to you if you do the sampling yourself. This is often called the "coliform" test.	Once every three months
2. **Nitrate.** Nitrate in drinking water doesn't bother most adults, but it can be very bad—even deadly—for babies six months old or less. The test calls for a specially prepared sample bottle, available from a lab.	Just once
3. **Turbidity** (ter-**bid**-ut-ee). This word refers to *the tiny particles suspended in most water that comes from surface sources.* Really high turbidity means cloudy, silty water. It looks bad, but that isn't the danger. Those little particles hide bacteria and make proper disinfection nearly impossible.	Every day, but only for surface sources. If you use well water, you don't have to do this test at all.

Epidemics of hepatitis, typhoid fever, and different kinds of diarrhea have been traced to polluted water supplies. Finally, water shortages present a serious problem to communities and are a greater threat because of pollution.

What can individuals do to be sure that the water that they are drinking is safe? If you live in or near a town, check with the local water utility and ask how it handles the sampling and testing of drinking water. You can also find the answers to these questions from the local health department or the regional office of the Environmental Protection Agency (EPA).

CHECK YOURSELF

1. What role does water play in an ecosystem?
2. List three ways by which water becomes polluted, and explain the effect of each type of pollution.
3. Explain what is meant by turbidity.

4. Solid-Waste Disposal

Solid waste includes everything humans produce, use, and discard—paper, plastics, glass, cars, furniture, food scraps, etc. Yearly, Americans dispose of enough solid waste to fill 5 million large truck trailers. What happens to all this waste?

You have probably seen some of this solid waste scattered on the roadside, in parks, or floating in water. Litter is perhaps our most visible form of pollution. It is also a costly form of pollution. It costs the taxpayer about $0.50 per item to have city employees pick up litter.

Some waste is burned, which adds to the air-pollution problem. Some cities have large dumps for disposing of waste. Some communities have sanitary landfills. Solid wastes are collected, compacted by bulldozers, and buried under many layers of soil.

It is estimated that 80% of solid wastes produced yearly could be **recycled,** that is, *re-formed in some way and used again.* Yet only 6% of wastes actually are recycled. Recycling not only helps to reduce solid-waste problems but also helps to conserve resources.

About 50% of the nation's paper, 8% of the steel, 75% of the glass, 40% of the aluminum, and 30% of the total plastics output are used solely to wrap and decorate consumer products. One dollar out of every $11 spent on groceries goes to packaging. This amounts to $400 per year for a family of four—not to mention the contribution to the solid-waste problems.

This waste dump will eventually be bulldozed over with layers of soil.

Recycling stations for paper products and aluminum cans are found in any medium to large community today.

Hazardous Wastes—A Special Case

A **hazardous waste** is *a solid waste that may cause or significantly contribute to serious illness or death, or that may pose a threat to the environment if it is not handled properly.*

Hazardous wastes are the results of high technology in our society. Industry creates many products that result in hazardous wastes, such as automobiles, tires, plastics, fuels, clothing, paper, paint, pesticides, and medicine. Since almost all Americans need or want these products, it is unlikely that we will solve this problem by not making these products. The problem then becomes what to do with the wastes.

Why These Wastes Are Dangerous

Hazardous wastes possess four characteristics that make them dangerous. These include:

1. **Ignitability** (ig-**nite**-uh-bil-uh-tee). These *wastes pose a fire hazard.* The fire and smoke can often spread harmful particles over a large area.
2. **Corrosivity** (kuh-**roh**-siv-uh-tee). These *wastes require special containers because of their ability to corrode, or eat away, standard containers.*
3. **Reactivity** (ree-ack-**tiv**-uh-tee). These *wastes react when exposed to air or water, or when exposed to shock or heat.* They may also generate toxic gases or explode.
4. **Toxicity** (tahk-**sis**-ut-ee). These *wastes release poisonous substances* into the air if they are not properly managed.

The first three characteristics will cause acute effects, resulting in almost immediate damage to human health or the environment. The fourth characteristic, toxicity, creates chronic effects, which are most likely to appear over a longer time period.

Of all of the hazardous waste in the United States, only 10% is disposed of in a safe manner. Industry accounts for 60% of the hazardous waste developed in this country.

Environmentally safe and effective ways of disposing of or treating hazardous waste do exist. It becomes a matter of whether the producers are willing to invest the dollars and make the disposal of these materials their responsibility.

Toxic Substances and Health

In 1977, the Toxic Substances Control Act became effective. It was a move to protect the public health and environment from chemical harm. The law is designed to give the Environmental Protection Agency (EPA) authority to watch all aspects of development and use of chemical substances—including product development, testing, manufacture, processing, distribution, use, and disposal.

About 44,000 chemicals fall under the control of this act. The EPA must consider:

- the benefits the chemical substances contribute to the nation's economic and social well-being;
- the risks associated with the use of any alternatives;
- the possible health and environmental problems that can result from continued exposure or a catastrophe.

There used to be poor controls over dumping cans of dangerous chemical and radioactive waste. Now these cans must be gathered by communities and disposed of safely at great expense.

Rachel Carson and Environmental Protection

What comes to mind when you think of spring? Trees getting new buds, grass turning green, flowers blooming, and birds singing? It may seem hard to believe, but in some parts of our country, spring has become quiet—many of the birds are dead. They became victims of pesticides, chemicals used to kill insects. Thus, the title for Rachel Carson's book on protecting the environment—*Silent Spring*—was selected.

Rachel Carson (1907–1964) was the first woman scientist employed by the U.S. Bureau of Fisheries. She spent four and a half years gathering data from all over America and from other parts of the world on the effects of pesticides. She found that the lethal chemicals which had been produced were being made stronger. Rachel Carson also discovered that insects these chemicals were meant to kill were having the last laugh! Many of them were breeding stronger offspring —immune to the chemical attack.

Perhaps the most frightening finding was the possibility of these chemicals ending up in the food we eat and the water we drink. Rachel Carson also had a serious concern over the possible connection between the widespread use of certain chemicals and the incidence of cancer in humans.

Her book *Silent Spring* was finished in 1962 and it shocked the nation. For the first time, most people heard of the dangers of pesticides, especially DDT. Her book made the best-seller list. Chemical companies fought back, spending thousands of dollars to disprove Rachel Carson's findings. They were not successful. Rachel Carson set in motion concerns for environmental protection that have resulted in legislation, as well as a continued high level of consumer awareness.

As you know, **toxic substances** are *poisons*. These poisons may cause immediate death if an individual is exposed to them in sufficient amounts, such as in the case of a train derailment where chlorine gas leaks into the air.

Many of the dangers from exposure to toxic substances are slow to show their effects on humans. They may be *carcinogenic* (cancer-producing) over a long period of time. The toxic substance somehow breaks down the healthy process of cell development in the body and begins the growth of

Pollution Facts

1. Sitting quietly and breathing normally, the average person breathes about 16,000 quarts of air a day.
2. On the average, each person in the United States uses over 70 gallons (267 l) of water a day in the home.
3. Of the 18,500 known land-disposal sites, only 6,000 even meet minimal state standards for disposal of garbage on the land.
4. The average American family buys about 1 ton (0.8 metric tons) of food every year and throws away about 10% of it.
5. Recycling 2,000 tons (1,600 metric tons) of newsprint would save 34,000 pine trees per month. A middle-sized city uses about 2,000 tons of newsprint every month.
6. 2,000 tons (1,600 metric tons) of disposable plastics, dry-cleaning bags, Styrofoam cups, plates, and plastic eating utensils are thrown out daily in the United States.
7. If all the one-way beverage containers manufactured in 1978 were laid end to end, they would stretch over 500 million miles (800 million km) —200 times around the earth.

malignant cells. Toxins may also cause **mutagenic (mute**-ah-jen-ick) **changes,** which means that *the cells containing the inherited traits of the male and female are altered*, and that a person may pass on altered genetic material to his or her offspring, causing birth defects.

Sometimes these toxic substances will affect a pregnant woman in such a way that birth defects are present at the time of birth. The defect was not in the parents' genes, but was passed from the mother to the unborn child just before the time of birth.

The Occupational Safety and Health Administration (OSHA) regulates all potentially dangerous substances. It works to protect people's health and safety in their work environment. Many jobs include occupational hazards. This means the employee is being exposed to potentially dangerous substances.

CHECK YOURSELF

1. What are three ways to dispose of solid waste?
2. What are the characteristics of hazardous wastes that make them dangerous?
3. What are the health risks of toxic substances?

Noise pollution has not received the attention in the past that water and air pollution have. Perhaps this is because people cannot see noise pollution. However, we are becoming increasingly aware of the serious health problems that it causes.

The problem of noise pollution generally occurs more in urban areas, where there are more people, traffic, construction, structures being torn down, and aircraft noises from jets. Aircraft flying over residential areas is one reason why the topic of noise pollution began to receive increased publicity and attention.

The constant noise of overhead jets through neighborhoods is more of a disturbance than a health hazard. Yet noise, when it exceeds the disturbance level, can result in hearing loss, especially if the exposure to the noise is for an extended period of time. A study of Eskimos in their remote Arctic world showed that 85% of all adults suffered hearing loss after the introduction of snowmobiles and hunting rifles.

As technology increases, so does noise. Sixteen million people in the United States suffer some hearing loss because of exposure to noise. In a recent study, degrees of **sensory deafness,** *an incurable hearing loss caused by excessive noise over a long time,* were detected in 60% of college freshmen.

Sensory deafness is caused when the special sensory hair cells in the inner ear are damaged. These hair cells bend down when vibrations pass along them. The hairs spring back up if the sounds are not too loud. After years of exposure to damaging sound levels, the hair cells do not spring back anymore. They stay flattened out and eventually die.

For more information about the ear and sensory deafness, see Chapter 4.

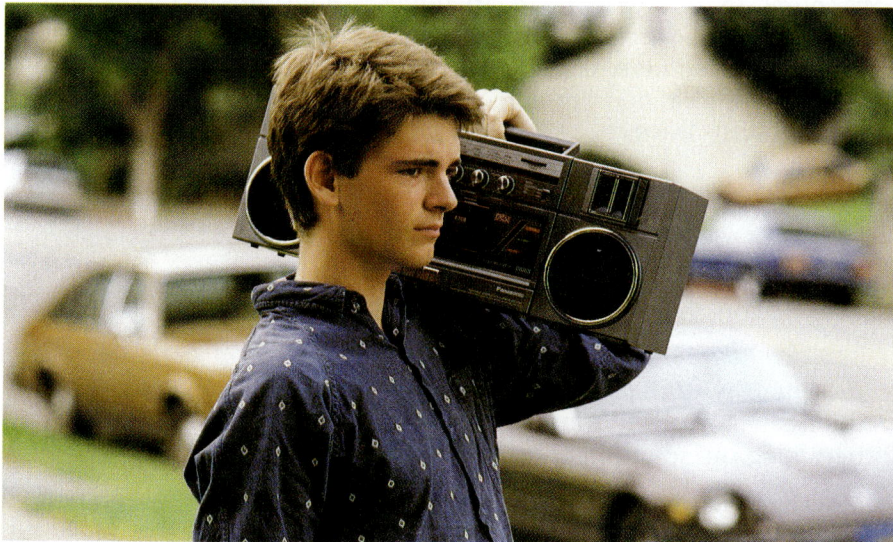

Excessive noise invades privacy and can cause sensory deafness.

HEALTH UPDATE   HEALTH UPDATE   HEALTH UPDATE

Table of Sound Levels, in Decibels (dB)

Source

Armored personnel carrier—123
Oxygen torch—121
Rock-n-roll band—108 to 114
Riveting machine—110
Jet flying at 1,000 ft —103
Newspaper press—97
Subway at 35 mph—95
Motorcycles at 25 ft (750 cm)—90
Food blender—88
Garbage disposal—80
Clothes washer—78
Dishwasher—75
TV audio—70
Vacuum—70
Near freeway and auto traffic—64
Conversation—60
Air conditioner at 20 ft
  (600 cm)—60
Leaves rustling—20

Code in Decibels (dB)

Uncomfortably loud	130
Very loud	100
Moderately loud	80
Quiet	50
Very quiet	30
Just audible	20

Effects of Noise Pollution

Noise pollution can come from the sound of stereos, washers, dryers, dishwashers, TVs, dogs barking, people yelling, workers hammering, or children playing. Studies have shown that excessive noise causes people to become distracted, tense, and even aggressive. The entire body reacts to noise. If the noise is sudden, a person's eyes blink, the muscles tense, and the person may perspire. Blood pressure and cholesterol levels rise.

Constant noise may cause blood vessels to constrict. Skin becomes paler, pupils in the eyes dilate, heart and breathing rates increase, muscles tighten, adrenaline is pumped into the bloodstream, and stomach acid increases. Prolonged noise causes stress that is linked to headaches, fatigue, nausea, and high blood pressure. Sound levels in schools can affect students' ability to learn.

Factors in Noise Pollution

The factors that make noise a polluter and a disturbance to the individual are:

- the intensity of the sound,
- the frequency of the sound,
- how long the sound lasts.

As we have seen in Chapter 4, the *intensity of sound is measured* in **decibels,** abbreviated dB. Pain is caused by noises measured over 140 dB.

MICROBIOLOGIST

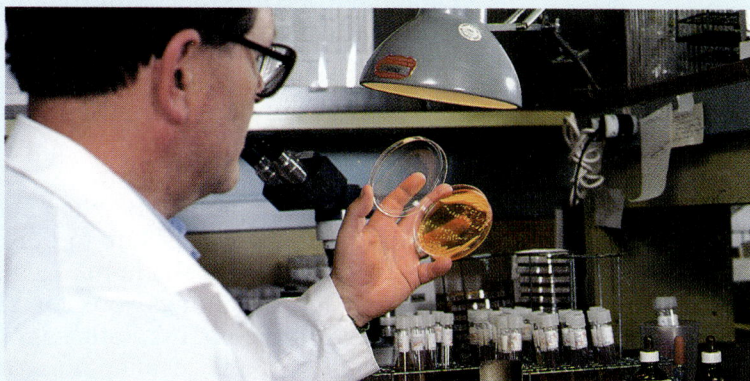

Microbiologists (my-kroh-by-**aul**-uh-jests) work in the health sciences field. They work together with scientists in the medical field to investigate different types of illness and to find ways to overcome them. They work in the public health field in keeping the public food and water supplies clean and pure, and they investigate the sources of epidemics when they occur.

An education in microbiology would help you answer such questions as:

1. Can life exist without oxygen?
2. How does fermentation take place and why is it important?
3. Can living organisms exist in sulfur?

Some microbiologists become university professors and researchers. Others work for the government at either the federal, state, or local level. Microbiologists also work for health facilities in all parts of the country. Their work may be in hospitals, clinics, or research laboratories. Industry also employs microbiologists to do research in production plants. In agriculture, microbiologists work in research laboratories and also do fieldwork, con-ducting experiments on crops that microorganisms may have infected.

Both space and marine explorations make use of microbiologists because of the need to consider possible contamination and disease in these relatively unexplored environments.

Microbiology is a field that demands much mental exertion and challenge. It is a field that offers excellent career opportunities. As a professional, the microbiologist enjoys high respect in the scientific community because of years of study and contribution to society.

On the personal side, microbiologists must have good eyesight, as well as color and depth perception. They should be able to work with their hands, and should have good health and enough stamina to stand for long periods of time.

Microbiologists must be able to work well alone. They must be self-starters who have plenty of initiative and the persistence to see a job through to the end. The demands of scientific investigation mean that the microbiologist cannot expect regular hours on the job.

If you are interested in such a career, contact your academic counselor at school now, and try to get as much scientific background as possible during the rest of your high school years. Virtually every college and university has a program in biology or microbiology. You can receive further information by contacting the registrar's office at the school of your choice.

Sound above 70 dB can eventually damage your hearing. A survey carried out in New York City found that the decibel level of headphone sets averaged 120 dB—well above that of a rock-n-roll band (108 to 114 dB).

Noise Reduction

Over 20 million Americans suffer from environmental noise. A serious problem with noise-induced hearing difficulties is that damage is permanent. Congress has passed laws to require manufacturers to label equipment and toys that harm your hearing. This helps, but it is not enough. Everyone can help. This can become a family project. Here are some tips for reducing noise in your home:

- Tell your family what noises bother you and ask them to tell you what noises bother them.
- Have your hearing tested.
- Wear hearing protectors when you cannot avoid loud noise.
- Limit periods of exposure to noise.
- Advocate quiet in the home.
- When you buy things, look for EPA noise-rating labels.
- Lower volume on TVs, radios, and other appliances.
- Carpet floors and insulate noisy areas.
- Become aware of community noise standards and of groups in your area that deal with noise.

CHECK YOURSELF

1. What is sensory deafness?
2. What are three effects of noise pollution on the body?
3. Name three things you can do in your home to reduce noise.

CHAPTER 32   Review

CHAPTER SUMMARY

- Our personal level of health and wellness is dependent on a healthy environment. It is virtually impossible to separate the two.
- An ecosystem is a balanced relationship between the living and nonliving environment and is necessary to sustain life.
- However, as this ecosystem becomes imbalanced, primarily because of pollution, all forms of life are threatened.

- Air, water, land, and noise pollution are now posing serious health threats to humans.
- All forms of pollution can be controlled and many prevented, if we will do our part to preserve and conserve our environment.

REVIEWING WHAT YOU LEARNED

1. What is an ecosystem?
2. Explain one effect that humans have had on an ecosystem.

ecology	ozone	greenhouse effect	reactivity
biosphere	pulmonary edema	acid rain	toxicity
biotic communities	fluorocarbon	water pollution	toxic substances
ecosystems	aerosol	fertilizer	mutagenic changes
abiotic	carbon monoxide	sewage	sensory deafness
air pollution	sulfur dioxide	turbidity	decibels
hydrocarbons	particulates	recycled	microbiologist
photochemical pollution	lead poisoning	hazardous waste	
nitrogen dioxide	temperature inversion	ignitability	
smog	photosynthesis	corrosivity	

PUTTING VOCABULARY TO USE

On a separate piece of paper, identify at least one other word that has the same prefix as each of the words listed below. You may use the glossary in this book or the dictionary. A suggested answer for the first word is provided.

Term   **New Word**
1. *eco*logy   *eco*system
2. *bio*tic
3. *hydro*carbons

Term   **New Word**
4. *nitro*gen dioxide
5. *car*bon monoxide
6. *sulf*ur dioxide
7. *parti*culate
8. *sew*age
9. *fert*ilizer
10. *tox*ic substances
11. *deci*bel
12. *micro*biologist

---

3. What are the major causes of air pollution? Identify the important health hazards of air pollution.
4. Explain what is happening in the case of the greenhouse effect. Describe its potential harm and the changes in weather that can result from it.
5. What are the effects of water pollution on humans?
6. What factors have led to an increase in all forms of pollution in the United States?
7. Explain the health hazards of noise pollution.
8. How is lead poisoning caused?
9. Give three examples of possible health-related expenses due to waste disposal.

APPLYING WHAT YOU LEARNED

1. Research the Clean Air Act of 1963 and its 1970 amendment. What does it require? How is it enforced? What additional amendments would you add for your community?
2. Research the Love Canal and find out what has happened to the residents. Report your findings to the class.
3. Find out how your community treats water before it is consumed. Report your findings to the class.
4. Mount St. Helens' eruption caused serious pollution problems in the northwestern part of the country. Write a one-page descriptive report on the health problems caused by this volcano.
5. Select one form of pollution or chemical pollutant and describe the cost of it to the consumer in terms of health, money, and any other factors. Include suggestions for eliminating the problem.
6. If you could pass one law to protect our environment and address the pollution problem, what would it be? How would you enforce it? Explain why you chose the law that you did.
7. Compare the geographic setting and environment of the Eastern Woodlands or the Southwest and its impact on the life-styles of native Americans.

FOCUS ON WELLNESS

People are dependent on a healthy environment to maintain a high level of wellness. *With this understanding, I will adapt my health behaviors to promote a healthy environment by . . .*

Energy and Conservation

In the past few decades, science has discovered a whole array of energy sources and conservation measures. One among them is the use of solar energy to heat the home. But scientists still need to invent other conservation methods in order to provide a safe environment for the twenty-first century.

After studying this chapter, you will be able to:
- Compare the various sources of energy on the basis of their effect on the environment,
- list a variety of energy-conservation measures,
- describe the government's role in environmental protection,
- explain how an individual can promote environmental conservation in the community,
- describe some successful efforts at cleaning up the environment.

1. Energy—The Ability to Do Work

Energy is *the ability to do work* and is an essential component of an ecosystem. All human life depends on energy. Most of the earth's energy has originally come from the sun.

Sources of Stored Energy

About 90% of the stored energy we use comes from **fossil fuels**—*coal, petroleum, and natural gas*. In the United States, half of the energy used is obtained from petroleum. Coal provides about 20%, and natural gas about 25%. Fossil fuels, however, are limited resources. The amount of fossil fuels that people have burned has doubled every 20 years since 1900. The continued increase of energy use threatens to exhaust the world supply.

Water power and nuclear energy are the two other main sources of energy in the world today. In the United States, about 4% of the energy we use comes from water and 4% from nuclear power. Although water power does not pollute, it requires the construction of a dam, which is a considerable expense and which seriously alters the ecosystem.

Nuclear Power

The use of nuclear power as a practical means of producing energy for an alternative to power steam turbines and large generator stations is now a reality. Since the early 1950s, when President Dwight D. Eisenhower first proclaimed "atoms for peace," the Atomic Energy Commission (AEC) has endeavored to make possible the use of nuclear power for peaceful uses.

Nuclear energy has received much attention over the past few years. The most powerful form of energy known, nuclear energy comes from the splitting of the atoms of certain elements, especially uranium. Atoms have nuclei (singular form: *nucleus*) that are held together by a strong force. **Nuclear fission** (**new**-klee-er **fish**-un) is a *process by which the nuclei of heavy atoms are split, releasing large amounts of energy*, primarily in the form of heat.

Nuclear reactors—*the containers in which the fission process takes place*— form the bases of nuclear power plants, in which the heat energy released by fission generates steam. The steam, in turn, runs electric generators. Although making this form of energy does not contribute to air pollution, nuclear energy has other problems.

Nuclear-Power Problems

Nuclear-power plants produce more waste heat than power plants that burn ordinary fuel. If nuclear-power plants return the water that they use to the rivers and streams before cooling it down, **thermal** (**thur**-mal) **pollution** results. This term refers to *heat pollution*. Certain fish and plant life cannot live in the warmer water. The warmer water also causes algae to grow at a faster rate, clogging the water and killing other forms of life.

In addition, the waste products produced in nuclear fission are **radioactive** (raid-ee-oh-**ak**-tiv), meaning that *changes in the nuclei of atoms occur, and they give off radiation, or heat.* Disposing of the radioactive nuclear wastes presents a serious health and environmental problem. The wastes must be stored until they "cool" down or lose their radioactivity. The problem is that radioactive wastes take hundreds of years to cool down.

Government Regulatory Bodies

The development of nuclear energy has become a very clouded issue. The government has spent a great deal of money on the development of nuclear reactors around the country. But after the Three-Mile Island incident in Pennsylvania in 1979, the public is not as confident about the safety of this energy source as it had been.

In 1974, Congress divided the functions of the Atomic Energy Commission between the Energy Research and Development Administration (ERDA) and the Nuclear Regulatory Commission (NRC). In 1977, Congress abolished the ERDA and transferred its functions to the newly created Department of Energy (DOE).

The NRC licenses and regulates the operation of civilian nuclear facilities, primarily nuclear plants. This agency must approve the design and operation of all commercial nuclear reactors. The NRC may fine or close down any operation that it believes is a potential danger to public health and safety.

The DOE investigates, develops, and promotes new sources of energy and new ways to save existing supplies. It also develops and coordinates national energy policies and programs—controls oil-import programs and regulates electric power, national gas, and oil-pipeline companies that conduct interstate operations.

Nuclear power plants have great energy potential, but they can be dangerous and must be regulated closely.

The Energy Problem

There is much talk about energy today. Politically, our country is attempting to reduce its dependence on foreign oil. This move would save large amounts of money, too. However, it would lead to further development of the Alaska-pipeline area, which might have some strong negative environmental impacts.

The DOE is hoping that the American public will reduce gasoline consumption by 10%. This will also amount to an improvement in air quality.

The development of two energy sources, coal and nuclear, will increase. Both will have some adverse effects on the environment. With almost all coal coming from strip mines, mines that are worked from the earth's surface, this could be a major problem.

The main pollutant in coal is sulfur. Unless the sulfur is removed when coal is burned, the amount of sulfur dioxide in the air could double.

CHECK YOURSELF

1. How is nuclear energy produced?
2. What are some of the problems of nuclear energy?
3. What three sources of energy provide a hope for the future? Why?

2. Environmental Conservation

Conservation is a familiar word to most of us. What are the main objectives of conservation? **Conservation** is concerned with *maintaining the environment while also maintaining a high standard of living.* Conservation is concerned with preventing the degradation of the earth through pollution in all of its forms. Is this possible? Yes, because people who pollute are also people who can conserve. That is our greatest hope for preserving the environment. What can you do to reduce the waste of our limited resources?

Saving Energy at Home

Conservation of energy not only helps to protect the environment but it avoids using up irreplaceable resources. Of the greatest significance to our health, conservation of energy reduces pollution of the environment.

About 70% of the energy we use at home is to heat or cool the environment. We use an additional 20% for heating water, and the remaining 10% goes for lighting, cooking, and running small appliances.

Following are some things that you can do in the home to conserve energy. Some may not be your decision, but you might discuss them with your family as ways to save money and conserve energy.

L I F E
M A N A G E M E N T
S K I L L

Conservation and Your Well-Being

Select four statements in the second column of *Saving Energy at Home* and describe how each directly affects your well-being.

Things to Do

1. Seal indoor leaks between living areas and the attic.

2. In hot weather, use exhaust fans when cooking, bathing, or doing laundry.

3. Close window drapes at night.

4. At least 6 inches (15 cm) of insulation should be over the top floor ceiling and 3 inches (7.5 cm) on an exterior wall.

5. Keep doors and windows shut during the air-conditioning season. Close fireplace vents.

6. Keep air conditioning at a constant temperature and on automatic control.

7. Put a flow controller in the shower or sink. It is inexpensive to buy.

8. Wash clothes with cold-water detergents, and wash in warm or cold water.

9. Fix leaky hot-water faucets.

10. Never leave hot water running unnecessarily.

11. At night, turn down the thermostat 5 or 10 degrees.

12. If you have a food disposal, use cold water rather than hot water.

13. If you have a gas stove at home, be sure that it has a blue flame in the pilot light.

14. When you have a choice, cook on top of the stove rather than in the oven.

15. Let the dishes air dry.

16. Be sure appliances have a full load when you use them.

17. Keep windows near the thermostat tightly closed.

18. Use only white bulbs, instead of colored bulbs.

19. Use low-wattage bulbs.

How It Helps

1. Prevents heat loss from the living areas.

2. Reduces heat gain that would increase the need for artificial cooling.

3. Reduces heat loss.

4. Helps to keep hot air in and cold air out during the cold season, and does the reverse during the hot months.

5. Reduces the strain on the air-conditioning unit.

6. Reduces the load on the system.

7. Reduces flow through shower or faucet, and saves $25 to $30 per year.

8. Reduces energy costs and saves $40 to $50 per year.

9. Saves electrical or gas energy.

10. Saves electrical or gas energy.

11. Savings of 9 to 15% of energy bills.

12. Using cold water saves energy costs.

13. A blue flame is a sign of a more complete burn and saves fuel.

14. This saves energy and uses less heat.

15. This saves heating costs.

16. You get the most for your money by getting maximum use.

17. Variations in temperature near the thermostat will cause the unit to run hotter or colder.

18. This saves energy; colored bulbs are about 60% less efficient than white bulbs.

19. This saves energy.

The Origins of Environmental Conservation

You might think that the concern of the environment is a recent event in American history. However, this is not so, for the roots of this interest began in the late nineteenth and early twentieth centuries. Concern at that time was limited to the destruction of the forests as a result of post-Civil War industrial expansion.

Such events sparked the founding of the two oldest environmental organizations, the Sierra Club and the Audubon Society. They both attempted to organize public opposition to exploitation of the environment.

Theodore Roosevelt, the president of the United States between 1901 and 1909, is the best known of all presidents who supported the cause of environmental conservation. He is known as the father of the National Park System, because of his great interest in, and love for nature. He is honored as one of the four presidents on the face of Mt. Rushmore for his contribution to the preservation of the natural environment.

President Theodore Roosevelt, along with Presidents Washington, Jefferson, and Lincoln, are represented on Mt. Rushmore, South Dakota.

Recent Developments

Mining, grazing, and lumbering were brought under government control by laws passed around the turn of the century. Compared to what has happened since 1962, when Rachel Carson's book *The Silent Spring* was published, these past efforts were rather small. Carson's book was an emotional warning about the dangers of the overuse of pesticides and their effect on people and wildlife.

In the 1960s, fear of radiation also became more widespread, and people in cities began to recognize the relationship between industrial- and traffic-pollution emissions and their health.

A comparison of the results of opinion polls between 1965 and 1970 show the public's increased interest in the environment. An increase from 17% to 53% of people rated "reducing air and water pollution" as two of the three major problems to which government should devote more attention.

Conservation Today

Perhaps our failure to recognize the potentially harmful effects of environmental pollution is related to the way we lead our lives. Civilization and industrial development have created life-styles that separate almost all people from direct contact with the precious resources that actually keep all of us alive. We buy food from stores and get water from faucets. We tend to take for granted our essentials for life.

However, all is not lost. A tremendous amount of power lies within each individual to turn some of the environmental problems around and to promote environmental quality. While we cannot control industry, each of us can do our part on a local or individual level. Much of this has to do with our attitudes toward the environment and our control over events that affect our environment.

The Government's Role

The environmental movement of the 1960s and 1970s helped produce some environmental quality legislation. The National Environmental Policy Act of 1969 recognized the need to give environmental consideration to any federal project. This act came to be known as the Environmental Impact Statement, which must accompany all of the federal government's activities. In addition, this act provided for the establishment of a Council on Environmental Quality, which was responsible to the president for making suggestions and preparing an annual Environmental Quality Report.

The federal antipollution efforts were increased through the establishment of the Environmental Protection Agency (EPA) in 1970. The federal government gave the EPA the responsibility to do research, propose new laws, and implement and enforce existing environmentally related laws.

In 1970, with the support of labor unions and independent occupational health organizations, the Occupational Safety and Health Administration (OSHA) was created. OSHA's focus is on special problems in the workplace.

Legislation concerning pollution was first passed in 1967 in the form of the Air Quality Act. It was designed to reduce automotive hydrocarbons, carbon monoxide, and nitrogen oxide emissions by 90% by 1975. This deadline has been extended several times and the standard has never been reached.

The standards for waste water were passed by the Water Pollution Control Act of 1970. The Safe Drinking Water Act of 1974 authorized the EPA to establish federal drinking-water standards. The Environmental Pesticide Control Act of 1972 gave the EPA authority to regulate pesticide use and sale. In 1976, the federal government gave the EPA the responsibility of enforcing standards for the disposal of hazardous industrial wastes under the Resource, Conservation, and Recovery Act, but it was not until 1980 that anything in this area began to happen.

Finally, in 1976, the Toxic Substances Control Act became law. As you have read, this provided for protection of the public against any toxic material not covered by any other legislation.

As you can see, legislation does promote environmental quality, and the government is making some strides in trying to control environmental destruction. The ultimate responsibility, however, rests with the individual and, as you will see, you can do a great deal.

Your Involvement in Legislation

Sometimes the public holds a negative view of those people who get involved in policy-making decisions on the political front. This is unfortunate, because the very basis of a democracy is the strength of the people. Governmental policies directly affect the quality of the environment. If the government adopts weak environmental policies, then we risk losing the beauty of our wilderness and national parks, recreational opportunities,

SOLAR ENERGY

"I have seen several solar energy homes in our community, and one of the neighborhood schools is heated by solar energy. How does it work?"

Solar energy is becoming increasingly popular as a source of safe energy.

Solar energy is *heat energy that sunlight produces as it strikes a surface.* Have you ever gotten into a car that has been closed up on a hot day? If so, you experienced solar energy! Because the heat gets trapped inside the car, it is hotter in the car than outside. Then as you open the windows, heat escapes (called *heat loss*), and the car cools. The same basic idea is used in solar-heated buildings.

The architect's main objective is to maximize the amount of the sun's heat trapped inside the house and to minimize the amount of heat loss. Solar-heating and cooling systems, in combination with energy-conserving architecture, could reduce the need for conventional oil, gas, and electricity by 70%. Solar-heating systems require a means to collect, store, and distribute heat throughout the building. Some solar-heating systems, called *active systems,* require fans or pumps to produce and move the heat. *Passive systems* trap the heat, using it without the means of mechanical power.

In a passive system, the building's design, position to the sun, wind direction, and the materials used in construction allow the sun's thermal energy to flow naturally. In a passive solar house, the heat-collecting windows face south to trap the rays of the sun. Heat losses are minimized by superinsulation and concrete-block construction. A wood stove may be used as a back-up heating system.

Solar supporters point out the following advantages of active or passive solar applications to homes, farms, and community buildings:

- the supply is inexhaustible and readily available;
- solar installations, though initially higher than conventional ones, offer long-term savings in money and energy;
- solar use does not damage the environment; it is safe and clean and conserves energy.

and even our health. As inhabitants of this environment, directly affected by these policies, we have a right to let our voices be heard.

You may not realize that you are already involved in the decision-making process which affects environmental decisions for today and tomorrow. How are you already involved in these decisions when, perhaps, you are doing nothing? The policymakers of environmental standards may consider you and others to be uninterested when you do not try to influence a policy decision about the environment. What kinds of decisions are these policymakers involved in? Here are some:

■ whether a dam will be built in the Grand Canyon;
■ whether offshore oil leases will be granted near some of our finest fishing and beach areas;
■ whether wilderness and national park areas are given to lumbering and mining companies for exploitation;
■ whether nuclear reactors are built and operated near large population areas and water supplies.

By deciding not to get involved, you still influence positions such as these.

As an individual, you can have considerable impact on environmental policy when you reach voting age. You can keep yourself informed on issues and let your political officials know how you feel about the issues.

LIFE MANAGEMENT SKILL

Becoming Involved

After you finish *Your Efforts to Change*, tally your score and see how you can improve it if you fall below 16. Take three areas that you need to work on and prepare a plan to improve them within the next month.

IMPROVING YOURSELF

Your Efforts to Effect Change

Are you someone who takes action, who believes an individual's efforts can make a difference? On a separate sheet of paper, indicate *yes* or *no* to each of the following statements, depending on whether or not they describe you.

1. I sometimes think about conserving energy, but then I think, "What's the use, I'm just one person."
2. I write to my legislature to support legislation on environmental quality.
3. I say something to people who are littering.
4. If I pass a piece of litter, I pick it up and put it in a garbage container.
5. I keep informed on environmental issues, especially those in my community.
6. I seldom concern myself with environmental issues because they are out of my control.

7. We will always have land and air, so I really don't worry too much about the environment.
8. If my community were trying to rezone a park area to make a parking lot, I would petition against it.
9. I know what the zoning laws are in my community.
10. I would participate in an Earth Day or Ride Your Bike to School Day.

Scoring. If you answered *yes* to numbers 2 to 5 and 8 to 10, give yourself 4 points each. If you answered *no* to numbers 1, 6, and 7, also give yourself 4 points for each. Add up your score.

40 to 28: *Excellent!* You think you can contribute and act accordingly.
27 to 16: *You are on the right track.* Every little bit helps.
15 or below: *Beware!* You might find you do not have much of an environment left to enjoy.

Working with Others

It is easier to work with others on such projects, because an individual's time, resources, and stamina are limited. By joining an organization that promotes what you support, you can work on problems that interest and concern you.

Knowing about the environmental problems you are dealing with is important. Scientists are still researching some environmental questions, but others are well covered, and much material is available on them.

Good sources of information are libraries and government agencies. Sometimes industry and trade associations and foundations provide information and assistance. Most environmental concerns are issues, with more than one side. Become aware of both sides of the issue.

CHECK YOURSELF

1. Define conservation.
2. List five things you personally can do to conserve energy.
3. What are four laws (acts) that have been enacted to promote environmental quality? Describe them.

3. The Bright Side—Turning the Tide

For years, the story of the environment was a story of pollution, of crisis, of problems. There were no bright spots because all that existed were the problems. Until the 1960s, people had little awareness of the environmental decision maker's commitment, and they also didn't seem to care.

Today, it is different. Politicians are keenly aware of the environmental issues in their districts. They are often reelected or defeated depending on their stand on certain issues. The public is more aware than ever before.

Some Successes

No longer are the messages of the environment all negative, full of problems. Some dramatic changes and some wonderful accomplishments have occurred, which demonstrate what can happen when individuals take an interest and become involved. If nothing else, through the last few decades we have learned that the power of the people and the business community can be directed to save the environment.

St. Paul Harbor

In St. Paul Harbor, Kodiak Island, Alaska, the water was polluted by 16 seafood-processing plants. Now all are screening the waste products that are put into the harbor. The solids that are collected are converted into pet food. The harbor is free of the masses of solid waste that once were common.

Escambia Bay

In the mid-1960s, Escambia Bay, near Pensacola, Florida, was the site of some of the biggest fish kills ever reported in the United States. Programs by major industries in the area to control the pollution have ended all of this. The State Fish and Game Commission reports fishing has dramatically improved.

Lake Erie

Lake Erie was dying a few years ago as sewage and other pollutants took away the oxygen that the fish needed. Now most biologists agree that the cycle has been reversed. The credit is due to an extensive program to control nutrients, sewage, pesticides, and other toxic materials, as well as to curb commercial overfishing. Sport fishing is now back to what it was over 20 years ago.

The Willamette River

Along the Willamette River, including the cities of Portland and Salem, Oregon, for 187 miles people can fish or swim anywhere. That was not always the case. The state of Oregon has worked for years to improve the quality of its most polluted river. It took nearly 20 years to get all of the municipalities along the Willamette to provide primary treatment of sewage.

So ambitious are the people in this area that the goal for 1983 was zero discharge of polluted wastes into the river—and it was a realistic goal! So alive is the river that a $3.7 million system of fish ladders to accommodate salmon moving upstream to spawn has been developed.

Private groups volunteer cleanup of very polluted waterways. These two people are cleaning up an oil spill. Hay is used to trap the oil; then it is shoveled away.

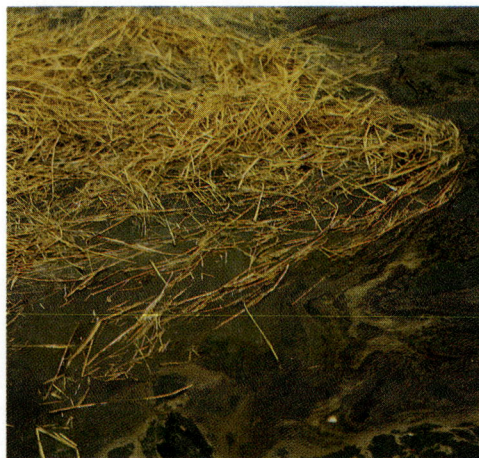

Houston Ship Channel

Between the city of Houston, Texas, and the Gulf of Mexico, 40 miles to the south, lies the Houston Ship Channel. This narrow bayou was once so polluted with oil that it actually caught fire in 1966. Cleaning up this waterway was one of the greatest environmental challenges people have faced.

The ship channel is located in the heart of one of the world's largest oil–chemical refining areas. The waterway not only received pollutants from these plants but also from the city and the port of Houston, which is the nation's third busiest port. The battle is far from over, but fish and plankton have now returned and the waters are clear—something that no one would have believed possible 25 years ago.

Corporate Cooperation

Twenty years ago, the automobile and steel industries were among the biggest polluters in the United States. But both industries now report great progress in promoting environmental quality. General Motors has designed cars that have emission standards 90% lower than they were in the 1960s. These have included reductions in hydrocarbons, carbon monoxide, and nitrogen dioxide. The catalytic converter, tough state laws, engine modifications, and stricter penalties for violation are all helping to combat the air-pollution problem.

The U.S. Steel Corporation, the nation's largest steel producer, has spent over $1 billion dollars to control pollution. U.S. Steel is now using processes, such as a water-recycling system, that prevent polluted water from entering nearby lakes.

State and City Involvement

After a heated battle with the canning industries, the environmentalists succeeded in getting the Oregon legislature to pass a bill requiring five-cent deposits on carbonated soft-drink and beer cans, and two-cent deposits on refillable bottles. The law also outlawed detachable tabs on cans.

The results of this action were dramatic. Cans were replaced with the new, button-down cans and bottles. Consumers were returning containers of all kinds so they could recover the deposits. Surveys have shown that Oregonians not only learned to live with the law, but learned to like it. The law and its effects have been enormously successful. Litter has decreased significantly. Citizens take an active part in preserving their beautiful environment.

The city of Anchorage, Alaska, has put into effect a vehicle-inspection and maintenance program in an attempt to improve air quality. The city has bad air pollution in the winter, when carbon monoxide in the air often exceeds acceptable levels. The city's immediate goal is to stop further deterioration of air quality.

Some states give a money refund if cans are collected and brought to a recycling center.

El Paso, Texas, celebrated its 100th anniversary by opening a new, 10-million-gallon-a-day water-recycling plant. It is believed to be the nation's first large community to stretch its dwindling water supply by pumping reprocessed sewage into the city's major underground aquifer.

In addition, El Paso has an effective program to reduce individual water consumption. The city encourages the use of vegetation that uses less water. These and other conservation actions have reduced daily water use from 216 gallons (821 l) per person in 1977 to 185 gallons (703 l) per person in 1984.

One Person's Fight to Protect the Environment

If you still question your ability as an individual to have an impact on improving the environment, perhaps you will be interested in Andy Lipkis' story. In 1970, as a high school student, Andy attended a summer camp in California's San Bernardino National Forest. It was there that he first learned that pollution was killing the trees. He decided to do something about it.

Over the next 11 years, with the help of many volunteers, he planted over 150,000 smog-tolerant trees in the Los Angeles area. His organization, Tree People, became well known and provided very effective conservation education programs.

Where to Get Help

Many agencies and groups have a direct connection and interest in environmental quality. These organizations and governmental bodies can be basically divided into private nonprofit groups and federal- and state-regulated agencies.

The private nonprofit organizations usually have stated goals and purposes, and may or may not be interested in the environment as a whole, but, at least, they will have some specific interest in or position on a particular environmental issue. You can contact these organizations for information, and to find out more specifically about them.

Private Nonprofit Agencies

Organization	Interest
Center for Auto Safety 2001 S Street, N.W. Washington, DC 20009	Concerned with auto pollution and safety.
Environmental Action Foundation 1525 New Hampshire Avenue, N.W. Washington, DC 20036	A lobbying group for lower-energy utility bills; conserving the utility dollar.

Organization	Interest
National Fire Protection Association Batterymarch Park Quincy, MA 02269	A nationwide group that promotes fire protection in all forms.
National Audubon Society 950 Third Avenue New York, NY 10022	All three groups are intimately concerned with all forms of pollution.
Sierra Club 703 Polk Street San Francisco, CA 94109	
Friends of the Earth 530 Seventh Street, S.E. Washington, DC 20003	
National Safety Council 444 North Michigan Avenue Chicago, IL 60611	A nationwide group that promotes personal and environmental safety in all aspects.
Environmental Defense Fund 257 Park Avenue South 16th Floor New York, NY 10010	Nationwide group of business people and scientists working toward the public interest in environmental quality.
Environmental Action, Inc. 1525 New Hampshire Avenue, N.W. Washington, DC 20036	A lobbying group for legislation and federal regulation on such environmental issues as water pollution, energy conservation, and utility-rate reform.

Nonprofit agencies call the public's attention to such problems as the effects of acid rain on the trees of Mt. Mitchell, North Carolina.

Federal Agencies

In this unit, we have discussed the work of several federal agencies that are involved in some aspect of environmental quality, health, and protection. Use these agencies to obtain up-to-date information on particular topics. Most of them provide free public information pamphlets. You can also write these agencies to make them aware of violations of laws concerning pollution of the environment.

- **The Environmental Protection Agency (EPA)**. This agency, which was created in 1970, is primarily concerned with air-pollution control, solid-waste management, radiation, quality drinking water, water pollution, the use of pesticides, and the dumping of toxic substances in the environment.
- **The Department of Energy (DOE)**. This department came into being in 1977. This branch of the government is designed to supervise all energy-related federal programs, from gasoline to the development of nuclear weapons. It is involved in such diverse

activities as ensuring adequate electricity in given areas and monitoring the effects of different chemicals used in synthetic fields on the environment.

- **The Department of the Interior**. This department administers over the National Park System. These parks are the designated areas of natural beauty and wonder that have been set aside for all people to enjoy.
- **The United States Forest Service (USFS)**. This agency is part of the Department of Agriculture. It maintains supervision of our forest lands and protects large wilderness areas. Permits for backpacking, camping, and the like for given areas can be secured from this government agency.

State Agencies

Each state usually has some level of state parks, wildlife, and recreation that concerns itself with hunting and fishing regulations, maintenance of state parks, protection of special natural attractions within the state, and outdoor recreational permits.

Many states have offices that parallel those of the federal government in the supervision of pollution laws and standards, the dumping of chemical toxic waste, solid-waste disposal, and safe drinking water.

A phone call to your local city government will put you in touch with the state office that can provide you with information about environmental problems in your particular area.

CHECK YOURSELF

1. What is one example of environmental action that made a difference?
2. Where would you write for information if you wanted to start a recycling program?
3. What is the function of the Department of the Interior?

CHAPTER 33   Review

CHAPTER SUMMARY

- Producing enough energy to meet the demands of the American people poses a serious threat to the environment. However, we can conserve energy in numerous ways. In addition, research continues to find alternate sources of energy.
- Active, well-informed, interested citizens can have

a significant impact on promoting environmental quality issues.
- Since the people of the land have become aware of some of the environmental problems, much progress has been made to clean up the environment. People still need to do more and to give more consideration to prevention.

energy	nuclear reactors	solar energy
fossil fuels	thermal pollution	conservation
nuclear fission	radioactive	Environmental Impact Statement

PUTTING VOCABULARY TO USE

On a separate piece of paper, match the terms in column A with the correct definition in column B.

Column A

1. nuclear fission
2. energy
3. Environmental Impact Statement
4. solar energy
5. conservation
6. nuclear reactors
7. nuclear energy
8. fossil fuels

Column B

a. source of 90% of the energy we use
b. the most powerful form of energy we know
c. process of splitting the nuclei of atoms
d. form the basis of nuclear power plants
e. the ability to do work
f. National Environmental Policy Act of 1969
g. heat energy produced by the sun
h. prevention of the degradation of the earth

REVIEWING WHAT YOU LEARNED

1. Name three governmental and three nongovernmental agencies that have the responsibilities of or an interest in the protection of the environment. Be specific in identifying their unique role or contribution.
2. Summarize the important points you should make if you were to write your elected official about an environmental problem.
3. What evidence can you point to that, as a people, we are making progress in our battle to overcome environmental problems?
4. What reasons can you give for the need for individual involvement in environmental issues?
5. Identify at least three available alternatives to fossil fuel energy. What are the major advantages and disadvantages of each?
6. Form at least three general principles from the "saving energy" list (page 606) to conserve energy in the home.

APPLYING WHAT YOU LEARNED

1. Research the nuclear power issue. Take a side and develop a two-minute presentation supporting the side you chose.
2. Read Rachel Carson's *The Silent Spring*. What are three major points that she makes in her book? Report back to the class.
3. Find out more about the pollution problems at the Great Lakes. Select one of the lakes and write a report describing cleanup efforts.
4. Show your awareness of environmental protection by writing an environmental impact statement for a new airport that is to be built near a large suburban community.
5. If you were to design a house or an apartment, what are some features you could include that would be helpful to foster environmental protection?
6. Pick one of the following people and research his involvement as an environmentalist. Prepare a one-page narrative paper written as the environmentalist might have to describe his own efforts and concerns: Jay Norwood Darling, Gifford Pinchot, John Muir, John J. Audubon, or Charles Richard Van Hise.

FOCUS ON WELLNESS

People can protect the environment just by personally being more careful of what they have and what they use. *I feel that I can make my most consistent and meaningful contribution to the improvement of environmental quality by . . .*

HANDBOOK

E. Communication and Relationships

F. Consumerism and Health

G. Safety and Emergency Care

H. Disease Prevention

I. Conservation and the Environment

A. Your Physical Health and Fitness

1. Basic Warm-Up Body Movements

For Use with Chapters 1 and 2

The first component of physical fitness is flexibility. As you improve your flexibility, you improve your efficiency of movement. This means you do not have as much wasted movement. More efficient movement means more efficient use of energy. Warm-up exercises are excellent for improving basic body movements because they involve stretching the muscles. Movements should be long and slow-stretching with very gentle bouncing. Avoid quick, hard bouncing because you risk injuring a muscle.

When warming up, begin slowly, repeating each of your exercises twice. Add to repetitions each week until you have built up to a maximum of 30. This is a critical part of any exercise program. Too many people start out overenthusiastically and attempt 30 repetitions the first day. The results are usually very sore muscles and a discouraged person. Begin slowly, giving your body time to adjust.

Warm-Ups for the Leg Muscles

1. **Sitting Toe Touches.** Sit with legs extended in front of you. Feet together and legs flat on the floor. Reach for toes with hands, bringing forehead as close to knees as possible.

2. **Calf Tendon Stretcher.** Stand two to three feet from a wall. Lean forward, body straight. Place palms against the wall at eye level. Step backward. Continue to support your weight with your hands. Remain flat-footed until you feel your calf muscles stretching.

3. **Calf Stretch.** Assume a stride position with right leg forward. Place hands on hips. Lean upper body forward. Simultaneously bend your right leg at the knee to a 130° angle. Extend your left leg so that it is in line with the upper body. Your left foot should be flat on the floor. Return to starting position. Repeat with left foot forward.

4. **Sprinter.** Assume a squatting position with hands on the floor. Extend right leg backward as far as possible. The left leg should be bent at your knee and kept under your chest. Hold. Then repeat with left leg back and right leg forward.

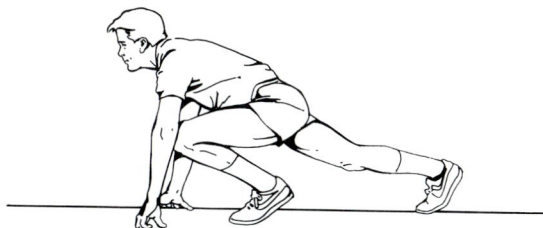

5. Standing Leg Stretcher. Find a chair or table 2½ to 3 feet in height. Place left foot on the chair or table. Keep this leg straight and parallel to the floor. Your right leg should be firmly planted on the floor. From this position, slowly extend fingertips toward your outstretched leg on the chair. Hold and return. Eventually you should get your forehead to your knee. Repeat with other leg.

6. Side Stretch. Stand erect with hands on hips, feet spread wider than shoulder width. Progress to the right, bending the right leg, keeping the left leg extended. Return to starting position and repeat on opposite side. This firms thighs, hips, and buttocks.

7. Leg Crossover. Lie on back, legs together, arms extended sideward for balance. Raise the left leg to a vertical position. Keeping the left leg straight, lower it to the floor on right side. Return to starting position. Repeat with right leg. Leg crossovers firm hip muscles and stretch muscles on the back of the leg.

Warm-Ups for the Abdominal Muscles

1. Bicycle Pumps. Sit with legs extended and hands resting on the floor on or beside the hips. Lift right leg slightly off the floor and bend it so that it almost touches the buttocks, then return it. As you return the right leg, start to bring the left leg forward. Repeat in a rapid manner. This exercise is good for both the abdominal muscles and the thighs.

2. Abdominal Curls. Lie flat on your back with the lower back touching the floor, knees bent. Curl the head and upper part of the body upward and forward to about a 45° angle. At the same time, contract your abdominal muscles. Return slowly to the starting position. Repeat. Abdominal curls tone the abdomen.

3. **Curl-Down—45° Angle.** Start from a sitting position with knees bent and hands placed behind head. Lower the upper body to a 45° angle. Hold that position and return. Repeat. This also tones the abdominal muscles.

Warm Ups for the Torso and Shoulders

1. **Side Stretch.** Stand with feet shoulder-width apart, legs straight. Place one hand on hip and extend the other hand up and over your head. Bend to the side on which the hand is placed. Move slowly. Hold. Repeat on the other side.

2. **Shoulder Stretch.** With arms over your head, hold the elbow of one arm with the hand of the other. Slowly pull the elbow behind your head. Do not force. Hold. Repeat on the other side.

2. Twelve Suggestions for a Safe Workout

For Use with Chapters 1 and 2

1. *Begin each workout with loosening-up exercises (warm-ups); do the same at the end of each workout.* Start out slowly at the beginning of the activity and cool down slowly.

2. *Set realistic goals.* Short-term goals are better because they give you positive reinforcement to keep going.

3. *Listen to your body for pain signals.* Stop if pain occurs. Continuing to exercise during pain may lead to long-term or permanent injury.

4. *If you are not used to the heat, exercise less than your normal amount, giving your body time to adjust.* On extremely hot and humid days, exercise during the cooler parts of the day, such as early morning or late evening.

5. *Wear light-colored, loose-fitting clothing.*

6. *Drink plenty of fluids, particularly water.*

7. *On cold days, wear one layer less of clothing than you would normally wear outdoors if you were not exercising.* Wear layers of clothing, rather than one very heavy layer in cold weather. Wear a hat while exercising in cold weather.

8. *Wait about two hours after eating a meal before exercising strenuously.*

9. *Exercise on soft surfaces, such as a track, grass, or dirt, which are easier on the body.* By avoiding uneven surfaces, you also reduce the risk of ankle, knee, hip, and back injuries.

10. *If you are moving about during exercise, try to land on your heels rather than the balls of your feet.* This reduces the chance of injury to the feet and lower legs.

11. *Don't shortcut in the equipment or footwear that you use.* Give particular attention to the care of your feet. If your feet get injured, activity stops. Be sure to get shoes that fit comfortably and have well-cushioned soles.

12. *If you walk, ride, or jog at night, wear light-colored clothing that headlights can easily pick up.* Put reflective tape on clothing and shoes. Walkers and joggers should face oncoming traffic. Bicycle riders should ride with the flow of traffic.

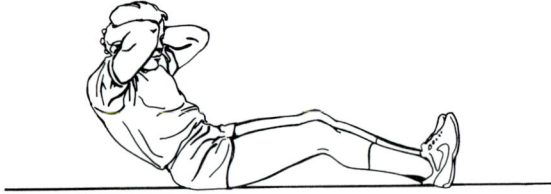

3. Walking/Jogging Program

For Use with Chapters 1 and 2

	Day	1	2	3	4	5	Totals
Week 1	Distance	W 2 mi	W 2 mi	W/J 2 mi J total ½ mi	W/J 2 mi J total ½ mi	W/J 2½ mi J total ¾ mi	12.25
	Time	36 min	36 min	34 min	34 min	32 min	172
	Calories burned	195	195	218	218	225	1051
Week 2	Distance	W/J 2½ mi J ¾ mi	W/J 3 mi J ¾ mi	W/J 3 mi J 1 mi	W/J 3 mi J 1 mi	W/J 3 mi J 1 mi	17
	Time	32 min	50 min	48 min	48 min	48 min	226
	Calories burned	225	274	290	290	290	1369
Week 3	Distance	W/J 3 mi J 1¼ mi	W/J 3 mi J 1¼ mi	W/J 3 mi J 1½ mi	W/J 3 mi J 1½ mi	W/J 3 mi J 1½ mi	22
	Time	45 min	45 min	42 min	42 min	42 min	216
	Calories burned	300	300	310	310	310	1530

Key:
W = Walk
J = Jog
mi = miles
min = minutes

Note: Continue adding about ¼ to ½ mile to the distance you jog, subtracting the distance you walk. Then, depending on your goal, you can add more total distance or increase your speed. Remember to monitor your pulse rate. Also begin each activity with a warm-up and end it with a cool down.

4. Bicycling Program

For Use with Chapters 1 and 2

	Day	1	2	3	4	5	Total
Week 1	Distance	5 mi	5 mi	5.5 mi	5.5 mi	6 mi	27
	Time	30 min	30 min	33 min	33 min	36 min	162
	Calories burned	185	185	195	195	205	965
Week 2	Distance	6 mi	6.5 mi	6.5 mi	7 mi	7 mi	33
	Time	36 min	39 min	39 min	42 min	42 min	198
	Calories burned	205	215	215	225	225	1085
Week 3	Distance	7.5 mi	7.5 mi	8 mi	8 mi	8.5 mi	39.5
	Time	45 min	45 min	48 min	48 min	51 min	237
	Calories burned	235	235	245	245	245	1205

5. Calories Burned Through Various Activities

For Use with Chapters 1, 2, 8, and 9

The following calories will be burned per hour by a 150-pound person in various activities.

Activity	Calories per hour
Archery	264
Badminton	396
Basketball	564
Billiards	174
Circuit-training	756
Climbing hills	
w/no load	492
w/5-kg load	528
w/10-kg load	570
Fishing	252
Football	540
Ax chopping, fast	1212
Ax chopping, slow	348
Digging	516
Hedging	312
Mowing	456
Raking	222
Golf	348
Gymnastics	270
Judo	798
Running	
11 min., 30 sec. per mile	552
9 min. per mile	786
8 min. per mile	852
7 min. per mile	936
6 min. per mile	1038
5 min., 30 sec. per mile	1182
Skiing, cross country hard snow	
Level, moderate speed	486
Level, walking	582
Uphill, maximum speed	1116
Skiing, downhill soft snow	
Leisure (F)	402
Leisure (M)	450
Snowshoeing, soft snow	678
Squash	864
Table tennis	276
Tennis	444
Volleyball	204

6. Avoiding Back Problems

For Use with Chapter 3

Sitting

- Sit in a firm chair with a supportive back. Do not sit in very deep or overstuffed chairs or sofas.
- When sitting, keep your knees about one-half to one inch higher than your hips.
- Avoid sitting in one position for long periods. At least every 20 minutes, get up and move around.
- When driving, make sure the front seat of your car is far enough forward so that your knees are higher than your hips. This will reduce the strain on your lower and upper back muscles.

Standing

- Do not stand in one position for longer than a few moments. Shift your weight from one foot to the other.
- Women should change from high to low heels if they have to stand for a long period of time.

Sleeping

- When sleeping, lie on either side and draw one or both knees up toward your chin.
- Sleep on a flat, firm mattress or use a bed board one-half to three-quarters of an inch thick, placed between the mattress and box springs.

Lifting

- Bend at the knees, not at the waist. Let your legs, not your back, do the work, even if you are only picking up a pen.
- When carrying packages, keep them as close to your body as possible to relieve back strain.
- If you must carry a heavy load, divide it into two parts.
- Don't bend over furniture to open or close windows.

Pushing and Reaching

- When moving a large object, *push* it, don't *pull* it.
- Use a step stool for reaching high objects.

B. Your Mental Health

You probably will not use such a detailed process for every problem with which you are faced. However, you might find it easier to practice your skills on easier problems. Then, when faced with more difficult decisions, you will be better prepared.

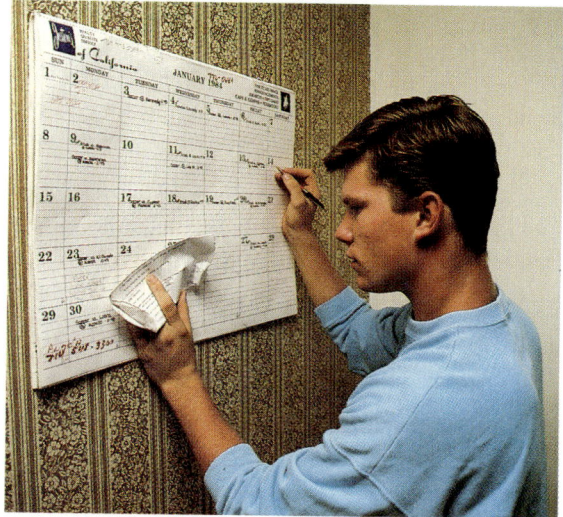

1. Problem Solving

For Use with Chapter 5

Problem-solving Steps

Problem solving is a skill that you can learn. Problem solving involves making a decision, so let us look at the process involved in solving a problem. Note the word *process*. Process implies that some *procedures or steps are involved in developing a skill*.

1. *Clearly identify the problem.* This sounds easy, however, it is not only the most important step, but it can also be a difficult one. Be sure that you have a grasp on the real problem and that it is well defined.

2. *Identify all of your possible choices.* Picture what the situation would look like if the problem were solved. What choices do you have? Try to think of as many as possible. Ask for input from your parents, other adults you can talk to, or others that the problem may involve.

3. *Consider and evaluate the consequences of each choice.* One way to identify the consequences is to ask yourself, "What will happen if I . . .?" Again, you may want to seek input from others. The objective is to examine all parts of the problem and the possible solutions. Will the alternative you are considering solve your problem or just temporarily ease it? How will other people important to you be affected?

4. *Select the best choice and act.* This means that you know and accept the consequences of your actions.

5. *Evaluate the results of your choice.* Did your actions solve the problem or create a new problem? What did you learn?

2. Goal Setting

For Use with Chapter 5

Much like problem solving, goal setting is a skill. It involves a process that gives you some direction within which to work.

1. *Decide on one thing on which you want to work.* It involves a process that gives you some direction within which to work.

2. *List what you will do to reach your goal.* Identify others who can help you and support your efforts.

3. *Give yourself an identified period of time to reach your goal.* Build in several checkpoints to evaluate how you are doing.

4. *State a reward for yourself for achieving your goal.* Relax and enjoy your reward. The recreation will help you to look back, evaluate how you did, and prepare some mental notes on handling the task (the same or differently) in the future.

3. Steps to Managing Time

For Use with Chapter 6

1. *Start by keeping a log of all your activities for one day.* Identify the amount of time spent on each activity. Analyze your log to determine how much of your time is productive and how much is wasted.

2. *The next step is to set goals for yourself.* One way to do this is to think of yourself at the end of a day or week. Imagine what you would like to have accomplished at the end of that period of time to feel good about yourself. This will help you identify what you want to do.

3. *Next, make a list of all your tasks.* What are the things you are responsible for getting done.?

4. *Combine your two lists and set yourself some priorities.* Rank the items on your list in order of importance.

5. *Now plan your day to include getting your priority items accomplished.*

Reinforce yourself by checking off your list as you go. Some people need more structure than others. If you find yourself floundering, make yourself a timetable.

After-School Tasks to Accomplish	
4:30–6:00	Get home, relax, exercise, do something that is fun.
6:00–6:45	Help with dinner, eat.
7:00–7:30	Do math project.
7:30–8:00	Finish health project.
8:00–8:30	Review science for test.
9:00–9:30	Call Janie.
9:30–10:00	Read library book
10:00–10:15	Get ready for bed

Be sure to provide a reward for yourself for accomplishing your table. Remember to be realistic about your time planning. Schedule only half of your day to allow for interruptions.

4. Reducing Stress

For Use with Chapter 6

One technique that has been developed for reducing stress is called **progressive relaxation.** This is simply a method of *consciously relaxing each body part.*

Preparation

- Sit in a comfortable position, close your eyes, take slow, deep breaths.
- Tune out the noises around you.
- As you exhale, consciously relax your muscles, releasing tension. (Be especially aware of your forehead, jaw, and shoulders.)
- Let your mind wander, picture yourself in a serene environment.

Relaxing the Muscles

Muscles cannot be tensed and relaxed at the same time.

- Sitting comfortably, take several slow, deep breaths.
- Beginning with your forehead muscles, tighten the muscles and hold for 5 seconds.
- Slowly release, letting the muscles relax.
- Continue with the face and jaw muscles, neck and shoulder, arms and hands, stomach, legs and feet.

Relaxation techniques are designed to help people lower stress by *first,* becoming aware of tension in the body and, *second,* by relaxing the mind, taking thoughts off other situations momentarily.

5. Preparing for Test-Taking

For Use with Chapter 6

One stressor that all students have in common is tests. However, some students are able to use this stress to help them do well on tests. Others can know the material well, yet fall apart at the time of the test by letting the stress destroy them. Prepare yourself by following these directions.

1. *First of all, you must be prepared for the test.* Use your time-management skills to build in study and preparation time.

2. *Listen to yourself.* Become aware of the message you give yourself about your ability and about the test. "I'll never finish," "I have to make a B or I'll fail the class," "This is my worst subject" are all negative messages. All of these messages have a strong, subtle effect on how you perform on the test, as well as increasing your test anxiety. Go into the test saying, "I'm prepared. I'll do the best I can." This sounds simple, yet it has a significant impact on managing your test anxiety.

3. *Before beginning the test, take a little time to physically and mentally relax.* Close your eyes; take several long, slow, deep breaths. Clear all other thoughts and distractions from your mind. Develop a mental picture of yourself successfully completing the task at hand. This takes only a few minutes, and no one else will even be aware of what you are doing. But it prepares you to do your best.

4. *Go through the test.* First, answer all the questions you know or are relatively sure of. Then go back and answer those you are less sure of. Pace yourself. If essay questions are involved, make a brief outline of your thoughts before writing. This will help you organize your answer. Remember, you can take control of your life and your stress and make it work for you.

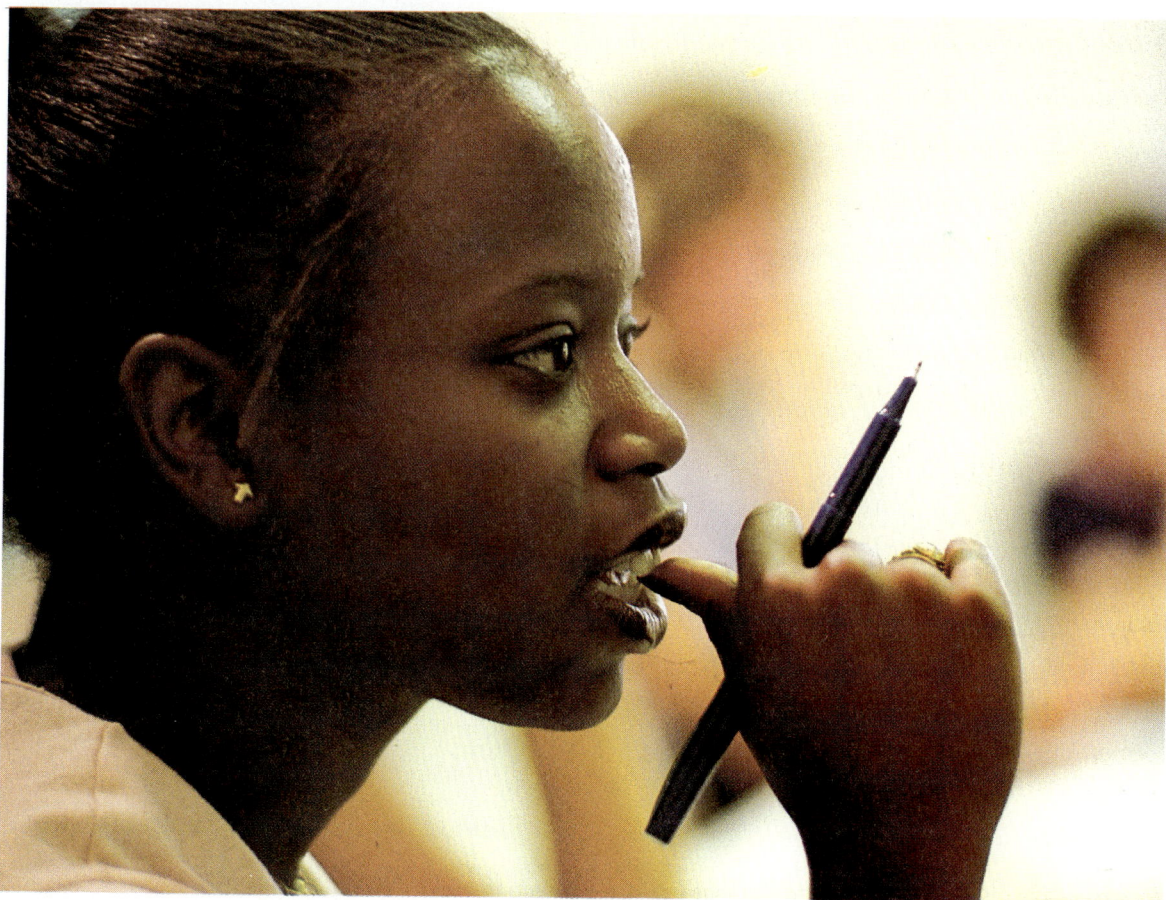

C. Nutrition and Your Health

crackers, and nondairy creamers. Coconut and palm oils are almost always listed in the ingredients. Without being aware of it, you may be consuming a greater amount of saturated fat than is healthy.

1. Types of Fats and Their Contents

For Use with Chapter 8

Notice that coconut oil and palm oil have a considerably higher percentage of saturated fats than the other oils. Check the labels on cookies,

Type of Fat (1 tbsp)	Calories	Cholesterol (mg)	Fatty Acids (as percentage of calories)		
			Saturated	Monounsaturated	Polyunsaturated
Butter	100	31	64	30	4
Lard	115	13	40	41	10
Liquid safflower oil	101	0	14	23	60
Liquid corn oil	102	0	18	41	40
Imitation diet margarine	49	0	20	40	37
Mayonnaise	100	0	18	22	50
Vegetable shortening (hydrogenated)*	110	0	26	47	24
Sesame oil	120	0	16	41	43
Soybean oil	120	0	16	24	60
Olive oil	120	0	14	73	8
Coconut oil	120	0	91	6	2
Palm oil	120	0	54	37	10
Sunflower oil	120	0	11	22	67

* Hydrogenation is a process of adding hydrogen to vegetable oils to make them more solid.

2. Water Soluble Vitamins

For Use with Chapter 8

Vitamin	Role in Body	Food Source	Recommended Daily Allowance*	Vitamin Disease	Deficiency Symptom
C (ascorbic acid)	Protects against infection, formation of connective tissue; helps wounds heal; maintains elasticity and strength of blood vessels.	Citrus fruits, tomatoes, cabbage, broccoli, potatoes, peppers	Men: 60 Women: 60	Scurvy	Rough, scaly skin; anemia; gum eruptions; pain in extremities; retarded healing
B₁ (thiamine)	Changes glucose into energy or fat; helps prevent nervous irritability; necessary for good appetite.	Whole-grain or enriched cereals, liver, yeast, nuts, legumes, wheat germ	Men: 1.4 Women: 1.1	Beriberi	Numbness in toes and feet, tingling of legs; muscular weakness; cardiac abnormalities
B₂ (riboflavin)	Transports hydrogen; is essential in the metabolism of carbohydrates, fats, and proteins; helps keep skin in healthy condition.	Liver, green leafy vegetables, milk, cheese, eggs, fish, whole-grain or enriched cereals	Men: 1.7 Women: 1.3	Ariboflavinosis	Cracking of the mouth corners; sore skin; bloodshot eyes; sensitivity to light.
Niacin	Hydrogen transport; important to maintenance of all body tissues; energy production; needed by body to utilize carbohydrates, to synthesize human fat, and for tissue respiration.	Yeast, liver, wheat germ, kidneys, eggs, fish	Men: 18 Women: 14	Pellagra	Diarrhea; skin rash; mental disorders
B₆	Essential to amino-acid and carbohydrate metabolism.	Yeast, wheat bran and germ, liver, kidneys, meat, whole grains, fish, vegetables	Men: 20 Women: 20	—	Greasy scaliness around eyes, nose, and mouth; mental depression
Pantothenic acid	Functions in the breakdown and synthesis of carbohydrates, fats, and proteins; necessary for synthesis of some of the adrenal hormones.	Liver, kidney, milk, yeast, wheat germ, whole-grain cereals and breads, green vegetables	Not known	—	Enlargement of adrenal glands; personality changes; low blood sugar; nausea; headaches; muscle cramps
Folacin (folic acid)	Necessary for the production of RNA and DNA and normal red blood cells.	Liver, nuts, green vegetables, orange juice	Men: 400 Women: 400	—	Anemia yielding immature red blood cells: smooth, red tongue; diarrhea
B₁₂ (cyanocobalamin)	Necessary for production of red blood cells and normal growth.	Meat, liver, eggs, milk	Men: 3.0 micrograms Women: 3.0 micrograms	Pernicious anemia	Drop in number of red blood cells; irritability; drowsiness and depression

*Based on men and women ages 15–18; expressed in milligrams unless stated otherwise.

3. Fat Soluble Vitamins

For Use with Chapter 8

Vitamin	Role in Body	Food Source	Recommended Daily Allowance*	Vitamin Disease	Deficiency Symptom
A	Maintenance of epithelial tissue; strengthens tooth enamel and favors utilization of calcium and phosphorus in bone formation; growth of body cells; keeps eyes moist.	Milk and other dairy products, green vegetables, carrots, animal liver	Men: 1000 Women: 800	Night blindness; growth decrease; eye secretions cease	Swelling of feet and ankles; weight loss; lassitude; eye hemorrhages
D	Promotes absorption and utilization of calcium and phosphorus; essential for normal bone and tooth development.	Fish oils, beef, butter, eggs, milk; produced in the skin upon exposure to ultraviolet rays in sunlight	Men: 10 micrograms Women: 10 micrograms	Rickets: a softening of the bones causing bow legs or other bone deformities	Thirst, nausea, vomiting; loss of weight; calcium deposits in kidney or heart
E	May relate to oxidation and longevity; may be a protection against red blood cell destruction.	Widely distributed in foods: yellow vegetable oils, and wheat germ	Men: 10 Women: 8	Increased red cell destruction	—
K	Shortens blood-clotting time.	Spinach, eggs, liver, cabbage, tomatoes; produced by intestinal bacteria	Not known	Poor blood clotting (hemorrhage)	Jaundice in infants

*Based on men and women ages 15–18; expressed in milligrams unless stated otherwise.

4. Minerals for the Body

For Use with Chapter 8

Mineral	Primary Function	Food Source	Daily Requirement (millograms)	
Calcium (Ca)	Building material of bones and teeth; about 99% of the calcium in your body is in your skeleton; regulation of body functions: heart muscle contraction, blood clotting.	Dairy products, leafy vegetables, apricots	Men: 1200 Women: 1200	
Phosphorus (P)	Combines with calcium to give rigidity to bones and teeth; essential in cell metabolism; helps to maintain proper acid-base balance of blood (calcium and phosphorus are the 2 most abundant minerals in the body).	Peas, beans, milk, liver, meat, cottage cheese, broccoli, whole grains	Men: 1200 Women: 1200	
Iron (Fe)	Part of the red blood cell's oxygen and carbon dioxide transport system; necessary for cellular respiration; important for use of energy in cells and for resistance to infection.	Liver, meat, shellfish, peanuts, dried fruits, eggs	Men: 18 Women: 18	
Iodine (I)	Essential component of the thyroid hormone, thyroxine, which controls the rate of cell oxidation; helps maintain proper water balance.	Iodized salt, seafood	Men: 150 micrograms Women: 150 micrograms	
Chromium		Meat, cheese, whole grains	*	
Manganese (Mn)	Enzyme activator for carbohydrate, protein, and fat metabolism; also important in growth of cartilage and bone tissue.	Wheat germ, nuts, bran, green leafy vegetables, cereal grains, meat	*	
Copper (Cu)	An essential ingredient in several respiratory enzymes; needed for development of young red blood cells.	Kidney, liver, beans, Brazil nuts, wholemeal flour, lentils, parsley	*	
Zinc (Zn)	The function is unknown, although it is a component of many enzyme systems and is an essential component of the pancreatic hormone insulin.	Shellfish, meat, milk, eggs	*	
Cobalt (Co)	An essential part of Vitamin B[12].	Vitamin B[12]	*	
Fluorine (F)	Essential to normal tooth and bone development and maintenance; excesses are undesirable.	Drinking water in some areas	*	

*These minerals are called trace minerals. Some have only recently been included on the RDA charts. Although the body needs only about 100 milligrams of each of these daily, they are still vital to a healthy body.

(continued on page HB 14)

(continued from page HB 13)

Mineral	Primary Function	Food Source	Daily Requirement (milligrams)
Molybdenum (Mo)	Essential for enzymes that make uric acid.	Legumes, meat products, some cereal grains	*
Sodium (Na)	Regulates the fluid and acid-base balance in the body.	Table salt, dried apricots, beans, beets, brown sugar, raisins, spinach, yeast	*
Chloride (Cl)	Associated with sodium and its functions; a part of the gastric juice, hydrochloric acid; the chloride ion also functions in the starch-splitting system of saliva.	Same as sodium	*
Potassium (K)	Part of the system that controls the acid-base and liquid balances; thought to be an important enzyme activator in the use of amino acids.	Readily available in most foods	*
Magnesium (Mg)	Enzyme activator related to carbohydrate metabolism.	Readily available in most foods	*
Sulfur (S)	Component of the hormone insulin and the sulfur amino acids; builds hair, nails, skin.	Nuts, dried fruits, barley and oatmeal, beans, cheese, eggs, brown sugar	*

*These minerals are called trace minerals. Some have only recently been included on the RDA charts. Although the body needs only about 100 milligrams of each of these daily, they are still vital to a healthy body.

5. Low Cholesterol/Fat Snacks
For Use with Chapters 8 and 9

Snack foods often are high in cholesterol or fat or both. Here are some suggested snacks from the American Heart Association that will not contribute to cholesterol problems. An added bonus is that they are also low in calories.

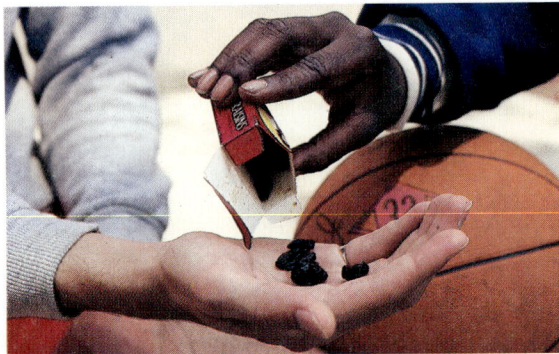

- 10 roasted almonds mixed with ⅓ cup raisins,
- 2 celery ribs filled with peanut butter,
- 1 fresh apple, either plain or cut into wedges and spread with a little peanut butter,
- 2 cups dry popcorn (season with onion, garlic, or chili powder),
- 3 or 4 dried figs and herbal or spiced tea,
- 4 whole-grain crackers with 2 tablespoons peanut butter,
- 1 medium-size banana,
- 4 graham crackers and 1 cup skim milk,
- 1 hard-boiled egg, the yolk removed, and the hollow center stuffed with seasoned, finely chopped fresh vegetables moistened with a small amount of mayonnaise.

6. Fast Food and the Basic Food Groups
For Use with Chapters 8 and 9

Fast Food Item	Estimated Number of Calories	Milk Group	Meat Group	Fruit Vegetable Group	Grain Group	Other
A. Main Dishes						
Hamburger	560–675		Hamburger	Onions, lettuce, tomato	Roll	Ketchup, pickles, mayonnaise
Beef taco	190	Cheese	Beef	Lettuce	Taco shell	
Bean burrito	345	Cheese	Refried beans	Onions	Flour tortilla	Sauce
Fish dinner	840–900		Fish	French fries, coleslaw	Muffins	
Chicken dinner	650		Chicken	Mashed potatoes, coleslaw	Roll	Gravy
Meat and mushroom pizza	380–450	Cheese	Beef	Mushrooms, tomato sauce	Crust	
B. Desserts						
Banana split	540–630	Ice cream	Nuts	Banana		Whipped cream, strawberry topping, pineapple topping, chocolate syrup
Ice cream cone	150					Cone
Other desserts	240–250					Pies, cookies, turnovers, Danish pastry
C. Other Dishes (calories)						
				French fries (220), coleslaw (121), corn on the cob (169), mashed potatoes (64)	Roll (61), hush puppies (153)	Onion rings (270), gravy (23)
D. Beverages (calories)						
		Whole milk (150), 2% milk (120), chocolate shake (390)		Orange juice (80)		Soft drinks, coffee (2)

7. Recommended Daily Dietary Allowances Revised 1980

For Use with Chapters 8 and 9
Food and Nutrition Board, National Academy of Sciences—National Research Council
Designed for the maintenance of good nutrition of practically all healthy people in the U.S.A.

	Age (years)	Weight (kg)	Weight (lb)	Height (cm)	Height (in)	Protein (g)	Water-Soluble Vitamins C (mg)	Thiamin (mg)	Riboflavin (mg)	Niacin (mg NE)[e]	B-6 (mg)
Infants	0.0–0.5	6	13	60	24	kg × 2.2	35	0.3	0.4	6	0.3
	0.5–1.0	9	20	71	28	kg × 2.0	35	0.5	0.6	8	0.6
Children	1–3	13	29	90	35	23	45	0.7	0.8	9	0.9
	4–6	20	44	112	44	30	45	0.9	1.0	11	1.3
	7–10	28	62	132	52	34	45	1.2	1.4	16	1.6
Males	11–14	45	99	157	62	45	50	1.4	1.6	18	1.8
	15–18	66	145	176	69	56	60	1.4	1.7	18	2.0
	19–22	70	154	177	70	56	60	1.5	1.7	19	2.2
	23–50	70	154	178	70	56	60	1.4	1.6	18	2.2
	51+	70	154	178	70	56	60	1.2	1.4	16	2.2
Females	11–14	46	101	157	62	46	50	1.1	1.3	15	1.8
	15–18	55	120	163	64	46	60	1.1	1.3	14	2.0
	19–22	55	120	163	64	44	60	1.1	1.3	14	2.0
	23–50	55	120	163	64	44	60	1.0	1.2	13	2.0
	51+	55	120	163	64	44	60	1.0	1.2	13	2.0
Pregnant						+30	+20	+0.4	+0.3	+2	+0.6
Lactating						+20	+40	+0.5	+0.5	+5	+0.5

Note: The Recommended Daily Dietary Allowances are revised every 5 years. The 1985 revision has been postponed pending further research into the advisability of certain changes.

[a] The allowances are intended to provide for individual variations among most normal persons as they live in the United States under usual environmental stresses. Diets should be based on a variety of common foods in order to provide other nutrients for which human requirements have been less well defined. See text for detailed discussion of allowance and of nutrients not tabulated.

[b] Retinol equivalents. 1 retinol equivalent = 1 μg retinol or 6 μg β carotene.

[c] As cholecalciferol. 10 μg cholecalciferol = 400 IU of vitamin D.

[d] α-tocopherol equivalents. 1 mg d-α tocopherol = 1 μ-TE.

[e] 1 NE (niacin equivalent) is equal to 1 mg of niacin or 60 mg of dietary tryptophan.

Fat-Soluble Vitamins					Minerals					
Folacin[f] (μg)	B-12 (μg)	A (μg RE)[b]	D (μg)[c]	E (mg α-TE)[d]	Calcium (mg)	Phosphorus (mg)	Magnesium (mg)	Iron (mg)	Zinc (mg)	Iodine (μg)
30	0.5[g]	420	10	3	360	240	50	10	3	40
45	1.5	400	10	4	540	360	70	15	5	50
100	2.0	400	10	5	800	800	150	15	10	70
200	2.5	500	10	6	800	800	200	10	10	90
300	3.0	700	10	7	800	800	250	10	10	120
400	3.0	1000	10	8	1200	1200	350	18	15	150
400	3.0	1000	10	10	1200	1200	400	18	15	150
400	3.0	1000	7.5	10	800	800	350	10	15	150
400	3.0	1000	5	10	800	800	350	10	15	150
400	3.0	1000	5	10	800	800	350	10	15	150
400	3.0	800	10	8	1200	1200	300	18	15	150
400	3.0	800	10	8	1200	1200	300	18	15	150
400	3.0	800	7.5	8	800	800	300	18	15	150
400	3.0	800	5	8	800	800	300	18	15	150
400	3.0	800	5	8	800	800	300	10	15	150
+400	+1.0	+200	+5	+2	+400	+400	+150	h	+5	+25
+100	+1.0	+400	+5	+3	+400	+400	+150	h	+10	+50

f The folacin allowances refer to dietary sources as determined by *Lactobacillus casei* assay after treatment with enzymes (conjugases) to make polyglutamyl forms of the vitamin available to the test organism.

g The recommended dietary allowance for vitamin B-12 in infants is based on average concentration of the vitamin in human milk. The allowances after weaning are based on energy intake (as recommended by the American Academy of Pediatrics) and consideration of other factors, such as intestinal absorption.

h The increased requirement during pregnancy cannot be met by the iron content of habitual American diets nor by the existing iron stores of many women; therefore the use of 30–60 mg of supplemental iron is recommended. Iron needs during lactation are not substantially different from those of nonpregnant women, but continued supplementation of the mother for 2–3 months after parturition is advisable in order to replenish stores depleted by pregnancy.

8. Assessing Your Eating Behaviors

For Use with Chapters 8 and 9

Read each statement below. Decide how it describes your eating behavior. On a separate sheet of paper, mark *sometimes, always,* or *never* for each statement.

1. I eat "on the run" or standing up. *sometimes*
2. I eat when I am emotionally upset. *sometimes*
3. I eat just to be social.
4. I eat when I am bored and can think of nothing else to do. *sometimes*
5. I eat when commercials I see tell me I'm hungry.
6. I eat when the clock says I should eat.
7. I feel I need to clean my plate.
8. I eat my meals in less than 15 minutes.
9. I eat even when I am not hungry.
10. I continue eating even after I am full.
11. I eat within an hour of bedtime.
12. I find myself eating, and my mind is a million miles away.
13. I chew my food thoroughly before swallowing.
14. I put my fork down between bites.
15. I eat breakfast daily.

Scoring. For statements 1 to 12, give yourself a score of 3 points for each *never,* a score of 1 point for each *sometimes,* and a score of 0 for each *always.* For statements 13, 14, and 15, give yourself a score of 3 for *always,* 1 for *sometimes,* and 0 for *never.* Now you can assess yourself:

30 to 36: *Very good*—you practice some healthy eating behaviors.

24 to 29: *Good*—be aware of eating behaviors that might be habits.

15 to 23: *Room for improvement.*

14 or below: *Poor*—take a close look at your eating patterns to see what changes you can make.

9. Seven Rules for a Healthful Diet

For Use with Chapters 8 and 9

Dieting, maintaining weight control, and staying healthy can sometimes become very confusing. The National Dietary Guidelines of the U.S. Department of Agriculture provide seven guidelines that underpin the principles of a sound diet for a healthy person.

1. Eat a variety of foods.
2. Maintain a desirable weight.
3. Avoid too much fat, saturated fat, and cholesterol.
4. Eat foods adequate in starch and fiber.
5. Avoid too much sugar.
6. Avoid too much sodium.
7. If a person drinks alcoholic beverages, he or she should do so in moderation.

D. Tobacco, Alcohol, and Drugs

1. Tobacco Dangers for Nonsmokers

For Use with Chapter 11

The following 16 compounds, found in tobacco smoke and thought to be the most dangerous to nonsmokers, are listed in the order of "risk priority."

1. **Acrolein.** A toxic, colorless liquid with irritating vapors.
2. **Carbon Monoxide.** A highly toxic, flammable gas used in the manufacture of numerous chemical products. Inhalation of carbon monoxide interferes with the transportation of oxygen from the lungs to the tissues in which it is required.
3. **Nicotine.** A poisonous alkaloid; also used as an insecticide, and to kill parasitic worms in animals.
4. **Ammonia.** A gaseous alkaline compound of nitrogen and hydrogen used as a coolant in refrigeration and air-conditioning equipment, and in explosives, artificial fertilizers, and disinfectants.
5. **Formic Acid.** A liquid acid used in processing textiles and leather. Exposure to the acid irritates the mucous membranes and causes blistering.
6. **Hydrogen Cyanide.** An extremely poisonous liquid used in many chemical processes, including fumigation.
7. **Nitrous Oxides.** A group of irritating and sometimes poisonous gases which combine with hydrocarbons to produce smog. Nitrogen dioxide can weaken bodily tissues and increase susceptibility to respiratory ailments.
8. **Formaldehyde.** A pungent gas used primarily as a disinfectant and preservative. It is extremely irritating to the mucous membranes.
9. **Phenol.** A caustic, poisonous acidic compound present in coal and wood tar, which is used as a disinfectant.
10. **Acetaldehyde.** A highly toxic, flammable liquid, which irritates the eyes and mucous membranes and accelerates the action of the heart. Prolonged exposure causes blood pressure to rise and decreases the number of blood cells.
11. **Hydrogen Sulfide.** A poisonous gas that is produced naturally from decomposing matter and which is used extensively in chemical laboratories.
12. **Pyridine.** A flammable liquid used in pharmaceuticals, water repellents, bactericides, and herbicides.
13. **Methyl Chloride.** A toxic gas used in the production of rubber, in paint remover, and as an antiknock agent in gasoline.
14. **Acetonitrile.** A toxic compound found in coal tar and molasses residue and used in the production of plastics, rubber, acrylic fiber, insecticide, and perfumery.
15. **Propionaldehyde.** A colorless liquid with a suffocating odor used as a chemical disinfectant and preservative, as well as in plastic and rubber production.
16. **Methanol.** A poisonous liquid alcohol used in automotive antifreezes, rocket fuels, synthetic dyestuffs, resins, drugs, and perfumes.

2. Blood Alcohol Levels and Drunkenness

For Use with Chapter 12

Body Weights	Number of Drinks*											
	1	2	3	4	5	6	7	8	9	10	11	12
100 lbs.	.038	.075	.113	.150	.188	.225	.263	.300	.338	.375	.413	.450
120 lbs.	.031	.063	.094	.125	.156	.188	.219	.250	.281	.313	.344	.375
140 lbs.	.027	.054	.080	.107	.134	.161	.188	.214	.241	.268	.295	.321
160 lbs.	.023	.047	.070	.094	.117	.141	.164	.188	.211	.234	.258	.281
180 lbs.	.021	.042	.063	.083	.104	.125	.146	.167	.188	.208	.229	.250
200 lbs.	.019	.038	.056	.075	.094	.113	.131	.150	.169	.188	.206	.225
220 lbs.	.017	.034	.051	.068	.085	.102	.119	.136	.153	.170	.188	.205
240 lbs.	.016	.031	.047	.063	.078	.094	.109	.125	.141	.156	.172	.188

Under .05	.05 to 0.10	.10 to .15	Over .15
Driving is not seriously impaired (although some research indicates fine motor skills may be impaired at .02 or .03 level).	Driving becomes increasingly dangerous. .08 is legally drunk in Utah.	Driving is dangerous. Legally drunk in most states.	Driving is very dangerous. Legally drunk in any state.

*One drink equals 1 ounce of 80–100 proof liquor, or 12 ounces of beer, or 5 ounces of wine.

3. Breaking Records— An Alternative to Drugs

For Use with Chapter 13

You have probably heard of many world records, but do you know that many teenagers hold world records? How do you break a world record? Here is what to do:

- First, get a copy of the *Guinness Book of World Records*.
- Look through it, decide what you want to do, plan carefully, and practice.
- Let the media—your local newspaper or radio or television station—know what you are attempting.
- You must have one or two adult observers to witness your actions all the time. (The observer cannot be a parent, relative, or friend.)
- The adult observer must write and sign statements about your feat.

- Send the signed statements from the observer, the write-ups or pictures, or any formal public announcement of your feat to:

  Guinness Superlatives Ltd.
  2 Cecil Court
  London Road, Enfield
  Middlesex, England

- The Guinness editors will respond to your letter if they think your claim is valid.

Are you up to the challenge? Here are some records that the *Guinness Book of Records* recorded:

- A teenager from California swung 58 hula hoops around her body from a dead start.
- A 13-year-old boy tied six Boy Scout Handbook knots—the square knot, sheet bend, sheepshank, clove hitch, round turn and two half hitches, and the bowline—on individual ropes in 10.9 seconds!
- The previous musical chairs' record that a California high school held was broken in 1982 when 4,514 participants played the longest musical chairs' game and ended up with one winner—an 18-year-old.
- Two high-school students in Missouri threw a fresh hen's egg 316 feet plus 5¾ inches on their eleventh try—without breaking it!
- The greatest distance walked by a person continuously balancing a full one-pint milk bottle on his head is 18 miles plus 880 yards.
- In 1976, a 17-year-old girl in New York recorded the longest single unbroken apple peel—172 feet, plus 4 inches. It took her 11 hours and 30 minutes. The apple weighed 20 ounces.
- How many high-school students does it take to leapfrog 100 miles? It took 14 from a high school in Texas. They averaged 42 leaps for each of 400 laps, and it took them 23 hours and 11 minutes.

Some records may seem of little importance, but that is not the point. The people who made them poured their energies into the project. They used their creativity and talents to complete a task well. It was not so much the outcome that was important, but how they increased their skills while working.

People who participate in a task and who do it well come away with a sense of accomplishment and self-worth. They are, consequently, ready to move on to other tasks. Little or nothing of such outcomes can be said for the person locked into drugs.

E. Communication and Relationships

1. Listening Skills

For Use with Chapter 20

Listening is a skill that helps the person talking to deliver the message and the listener to receive it accurately. Here are some guidelines for becoming a good listener.

1. When listening, I never assume that I know what the other person is going to say.
2. I do not interrupt others when they are talking.
3. I do not concentrate on what I am going to say while the other person is talking.
4. I make eye contact when listening to the other person.
5. I cease activities while I listen to the other person.
6. I concentrate on what the person is saying while he or she is talking.
7. I do not make judgments on what is being said.
8. I listen carefully so the other person does not have to repeat the message.
9. I carry on one conversation at a time.
10. I ask questions, without interrupting, if I am not sure I understand what was said.

2. Rape Prevention

For Use with Chapter 20

Here are some steps to follow that will help you to prevent rape:

1. Do not hitchhike.
2. Do not accept rides from strangers.
3. Do not park your car—day or night—in remote spots away from people.
4. If you are attacked, try to run away and get help.
5. If you cannot run away, decide what is best

to do: scream, fight, disable in some way, bluff your way out through verbal abuse or convincing talk.

6. Act carefully if the attacker has a weapon. Look carefully for a moment of escape when the attacker may be off-guard.

Many people are taking classes in karate and other forms of self-defense to ward off any form of attack. Inquire if there are any classes given in your community.

3. Major Social Developmental Tasks During Adolescence

For Use with Chapter 22

Growth and development occur in adolescence in four ways. Three of them are *physical, mental,* and *emotional* growth. The fourth way, *social* growth, is also very important. In this area, some basic developmental tasks for adolescence have been identified. A developmental task is simply *something that needs to occur during a particular age for a person to continue his or her growth toward becoming a healthy, mature adult.*

Much of this development in adolescence centers around social growth. The major tasks include:

1. forming more mature relationships with peers of both sexes,
2. achieving a masculine or feminine social role,
3. accepting one's physique and using one's body effectively,

4. achieving emotional independence from parents and other adults,
5. preparing for marriage and family life,
6. preparing for a career,
7. acquiring a set of personal standards as a guide to behavior,
8. developing social intelligence,
9. developing conceptual and problem-solving skills.

Development is gradual, as is change. You now know the tasks that are important during adolescence. Use the goal-setting technique to achieve your tasks. Set a goal for each and a time limit. Assess how well you are working toward achieving each task and leading to your goal. Outline certain behaviors that might help you to stay on track. Ask for assistance as you progress. Always remember that other people can help you to reach your goals.

4. Achieving Personal Identity

For Use with Chapter 22

Perhaps one of the more critical social developmental tasks is achieving a personal identity, the *factors you believe make up the unique you.* This task has a great impact on all other factors and centers around one's self-concept. Questions like "Who am I?" and "What do I want to be as a person?" are common in this search for identity. This is closely linked with one's emotional needs (see Chapter 5).

Here are some questions you can ask yourself as you form your personal identity, the unique you:

- Am I carrying out my responsibilities on my own, without needing someone to remind me of them?
- Do I get my schoolwork done as it is due?
- Can I make decisions on what to do, without my peers swaying me?
- Am I thinking of what type of work I am interested in doing after high school?
- Have I examined my beliefs on what types of behaviors are appropriate for males and females?
- Do I know the image I project as a male or a female?
- Does my behavior reflect a personal set of standards by which I live?
- Do I know what people like and do not like about me?
- Do I expect to work for what I get or want, rather than just "having things happen for me"?

5. Dealing with Peer Pressure

For Use with Chapter 22

- When to say "Yes" and when to say "No."
- When to move toward the peer group and when to back away.
- When to go along with others and when to decide for yourself.

These are all important decisions that you have probably been faced with and will continue to face. What do you do if your decision goes against what the group is doing? How do you follow your beliefs and not lose face with peers? You can learn to say "No" by following these simple steps:

- Use your decision-making skills as outlined in Chapter 5 and in this Handbook.
- If your decision is "No," then say "No" without feeling you need to justify yourself.
- You will probably be asked to justify why you have refused. This should alert you to the fact that the person asking you has not really accepted your decision, so any explanation will be challenged. Again, you can repeat "No."

  Here you need to tell yourself that this is a good decision *for you*, that you will feel better when this pressure is over, and that you will not have to worry about selling yourself out because of others.
- Remember, you may need to repeat yourself several times. Do not be talked into something just because your first "No" was not enough.
- If the person persists, *leave*.
- Lastly, avoid compromise if you feel strongly about something. Compromise can be a slow way of saying "Yes."

F. Consumerism and Health

1. Being a Wise Consumer

For Use with Chapter 23

Being a wise consumer involves certain behaviors, or skills. Use the following checklist to see how wise a consumer you are.

1. I know whether I am buying a product because I *need* it or *want* it.
2. Before I buy, I compare products for ingredients, price, packaging, and warranties.
3. I read the label before buying a product.
4. I am aware of factors such as advertising and peers that might influence my purchase.
5. I return products if I am not satisfied or if they are defective.
6. I recognize gimmicks that sellers use to influence my purchase of often fraudulent products.
7. I understand the purpose of advertising and how it is designed to make me want a product or feel that I need a product.
8. I check the material, product, or device before I buy it to be sure that the item is in good working order or is in its original packaging.
9. I read advertisements closely so that I am clear about what they are saying and not saying.
10. I avoid emotional or impulse buying.
11. I do not feel intimidated by a high-powered, pushy salesperson.
12. I do not let myself be talked into things because they are on a special "just this one time" sale.

2. Dealing with Faulty Products

For Use with Chapter 23

Even the most careful shoppers find themselves buying products or securing services that do not work right or serve them well. Sometimes merchants and manufacturers are less than enthusiastic about resolving difficulties. This is why it is necessary for you, as a consumer, to know what to do and where to go for help. Here are some tips to follow:

1. Identify the problem and what you feel would be a fair way to solve it.

2. Have some documentation available to back up your complaint (for example, sales receipt, canceled check, warranty).

3. Go back to the person who sold you the item or performed the service. State the problem and what you would like to have happen to resolve the problem.

4. If this person is not helpful, then ask to see the store manager or supervisor. Repeat your story. Most problems are resolved at this level.

5. If you are not satisfied with the response at this level, do not give up. If the company operates nationally or the product is a national brand, write a letter to the president or the director of consumer affairs of the company. The points that your letter should include are:

   a. Your purchase.
   b. Name of product or serial number or model number or service.
   c. Date and location of purchase or service.
   d. Statement of the problem.
   e. History of the problem.
   f. Request for satisfaction.
   g. Copies of all documents.
   h. Request for action within a reasonable time.
   i. Your address and phone number.

3. Checklist for Choosing a Health Care Professional

For Use with Chapters 23 and 24

Basic Information

Name _____

Address _____

Phone (office) _____

   (24-hour answering service) _____

Hospital affiliation(s) _____

Type of Professional

Family doctor, obstetrician/gynecologist, nurse-practitioner, pediatrician, internist (specialist in internal medicine), physician's assistant or "P.A."

Type of Practice

Solo practice, group practice, single-specialty group, multiple specialty group

Professional Affiliations

Teaching appointment at a university, on hospital medical staff, specialist (three-year internship), member of professional medical group(s)

Use of Paramedical Professionals

Nurse-practitioners, physicians' assistants, nurse midwives

Basic Services

Sees patients by appointment only, allows walk-in visits, practice covered at all times, allows at least 15 minutes per routine visit, thorough health history plus current medical records kept, medical records open to patients concerned, gives advice on the phone, 1- to 5-day wait for routine visits

Accessibility

Bus or nearby public transportation, free parking nearby

Special Services

Babysitting, patient-education classes offered or encouraged

Medical / Laboratory Services

X ray in building or nearby, minor surgery in office, treats fractures, blood tests, cardiograms, casting and minor orthopedic services, urine tests and strep tests without a full office call required

Billing Information

Immediate payment required, new patient prepayment required, accepts Medicare/Medicaid, will discuss fees and charges, will help prepare insurance forms, discount for cash payments

Medical Philosophy

The professional's positions on vitamins and nutrition, medical self-care, tranquilizers, antibiotics, second opinions, other matters that concern you

4. How to Use Unit Pricing

For Use with Chapters 8, 9, and 23

Unit pricing is a method of pricing that shows the cost per ounce of a product, and which also tells how much different sizes of the same product cost per unit.

Shelf and product labeling can help save you money. Unit pricing can identify the most economical brands or sizes of a given product. When shelf labeling is not provided, you can compute the unit price for yourself. For the greatest savings, consider buying generic products.

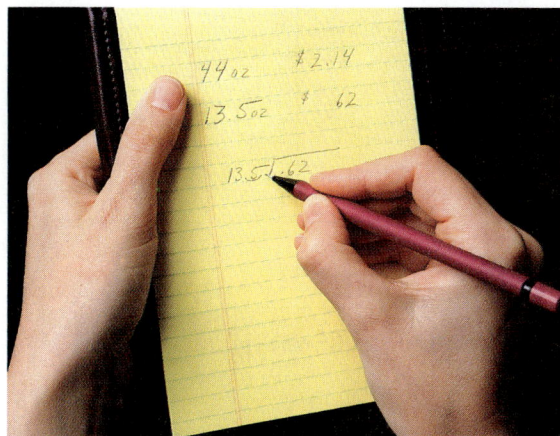

Compute the unit prices for the products and sizes given in the table below.

Product	Net Weight	Price	Unit Price
Brand			
Cornflakes	7 oz.	$ .60	?
Cornflakes	12 oz.	$ .84	?
Brand			
Granola	16 oz.	$1.69	?
Granola	32 oz.	$2.88	?

5. How to Read a Prescription Label

For Use with Chapters 10 and 23

```
J. D. Smith, M.D. ———————————————— Doctor
1022 Pine Avenue
Main Town, Wisconsin
                                   ———————— Patient
Name:  Pam Green
                                   ———————— Patient's Address
Address: 732 Cherry Dr.            ———————— Medicine and Quantity
         Main Town, WI             ———————— Number of Capsules
RX
                                   ———————— Directions
         tetracycline 100 mg
         # 21
         dig: 1 tid               ———————— Refill
Refill ○ Time(s)  J. D. Smith     ———————— Doctor's Signature
Date            5/6/86            ———————— Date of Prescription
```

Good Neighbor Pharmacy

500 Burnett Road
Main Town, WI
Phone 998-602-3478

5/6/86

Pam Green

Tetracycline   100mg

Take one capsule
three times a day
for infection.

No. 39610

Dr. Smith   TRN/0

G. Safety and Emergency Care

1. Medical Supplies for the Home

For Use with Chapters 26 and 27

Home Medicine Cabinet

- Absorbent cotton (a medium-size box)
- Assorted plastic bandage strips (1″, ⅜″, ⅝″, snips and spots)
- Gauze bandage rolls (1″ x 5′)
- Waterproof adhesive tape (10′ roll)
- First-aid anesthetic spray
- Eye wash (boric acid)
- Eye wash cup
- Eye-ear-nose dropper
- Sodium chloride (salt) tablets
- Ointment for rashes, chafed skin, abrasions
- Merthiolate (general antiseptic)
- Foot powder
- Aspirin
- Tweezers
- Thermometer
- First-Aid Manual

Home Emergency Supplies

- Flashlight
- Extra set of batteries
- Candle
- Matches
- Baking soda (to put out grease or flammable liquid fires)
- Portable radio (battery operated)
- Fire extinguisher
- Hammer*
- Pliers*
- Pipe wrench*
- Adjustable wrench*
- Common screwdriver*
- Phillips screwdriver*

First Aid Supplies**

- First-aid dressing pads, 2"x 2", 4"x 4" (a box of 12 each)
- Gauze bandage rolls, 1"x 5', 2"x 5'
- Waterproof adhesive tape (10' roll)
- Large bath towels (2 for cutting up into various sizes)
- Small bath towels (2)
- Bed sheet (1 for cutting up in various sizes)
- Triangular bandage (4 of them, 37"x 37", for a sling or as a covering)
- Mild soap (1 bar)
- Table salt and baking soda (small packages, for shock)
- Paper drinking cups (24)
- Flashlight (1)
- Extra set of batteries
- Safety pins (20 pins, 1½" long)
- Scissors with blunt tips (1 pair)
- Tweezers (1)
- Eyedropper (1)
- Splints (12, ¼" x 3½" x 15")
- Wooden tongue blades (12)
- Measuring spoons
- Tourniquet (2" wide x 20" long strip of cloth, short stick)
- First-Aid Manual

* This tool should have a rubber-insulated handle to prevent electric shock.
** First-aid supplies should be kept in a moisture-proof box. They can be kept on hand or carried on family outings.

2. Using a Thermometer

For Use with Chapters 29 and 31

Types of Common Thermometers

There are many different types of thermometers for home use. The most popular ones are:

- *the standard glass thermometer*, which records temperature through the use of mercury, and which takes 2 to 7 minutes to give a reading;
- *the digital thermometer*, which records temperature in 1 to 3 seconds;
- *the strip thermometer*, a strip of material which, when applied to the forehead or held in the mouth, records a person's temperature within 10 to 15 seconds.

Methods of Taking Temperatures

The methods of finding the temperature with a standard glass thermometer are:

- *oral*, which takes around 4 minutes and which registers 98.6° F when normal;
- *rectal*, which takes around 2 minutes and which registers 99.6° F when normal;
- *axillary* (at the armpit), which takes around 7 minutes and which registers 97.6° F when normal.

The standard glass thermometer usually comes in two varieties: (1) for rectal use and (2) for oral and axillary use. It is recommended by health professionals that the rectal method be used for infants and children. Temperatures can be taken orally when the child can be trusted to hold the thermometer securely in the mouth and not bite down on it.

Reading the Temperature Orally

When using the oral technique, place the thermometer under the tongue at the left or right side of the mouth. After 4 minutes, read it. If it registers 98.6° F, your temperature is normal. If it is between 100° F and 101° F, you have a medium fever. If it is between 101º F and 102° F, you have a high fever. If it goes over 102° F, see a doctor or seek other medical help.

96   100   106
98.6   102

3. First-Aid Procedures

For Use with Chapters 26 and 27

Condition	Symptoms	Treatment
Burns, scalds	Redness and pain; moderate burn will blister; severe burn shows tissue destruction.	Ice for small burn. Cool (not ice) water to big burn. Wash with cool water and soap. Sterile dressing. No ointment. Do not remove clothing stuck to burn. Call doctor if extensive, blistered, or white, dry, painless.
Cuts, bruises	Cuts bleed and hurt; bruises get red, swollen, and hurt.	Elevate the extremity. Clean cuts with soap and water. Stop bleeding by applying pressure. Apply cold cloths or ice packs to bruises to relieve pain and reduce swelling. Call your doctor if cuts do not close.
Dog bite	Skin may be punctured or torn; may show teeth/fang marks.	Wash with soap and water. Cover with sterile dressing and bandage. Capture animal to observe for rabies. (If must kill, preserve head for rabies tests.) Report to doctor or hospital.
Drowning	Unconscious; not breathing; heart may have stopped.	If victim has pulse but no breath, give mouth-to-mouth resuscitation. If heart stopped, give CPR, if trained. Do not move head, neck, or back unnecessarily. Call ambulance.
Drug overdose	Unconsciousness; cold or clammy skin, dilated pupils; no breathing; heart may have stopped.	Call an ambulance. Give CPR, if trained.
Earache	Pain; possible dizziness or discharge from ear; possible fever.	Call your doctor. Relieve pain by applying cool or warm compresses to ear, whichever gives relief.
Electric shock	Unconsciousness; pale, bluish skin that is clammy and mottled in appearance.	Turn off current. Break contact with dry wood or dry cloth. If no breath, give mouth-to-mouth resuscitation. If no pulse, give CPR, if trained. Keep person warm. Call ambulance.
Eyes	Chemical burns	Flood the eye with water, continuously and gently, for at least 15 minutes.
	Specks in the eye	Lift the upper eyelid outward and down over the lower lid. Let tears wash out the foreign body. Do not rub eye.
	Blow to the eye	Apply cold compresses immediately for 15 minutes; again each hour as needed. If the eye becomes discolored ("black eye"), call a doctor to examine for internal damage.
	Cuts and punctures	Bandage lightly and see a doctor at once. Do not wash the eye or try to remove any object stuck in it.
Fainting	Pale, clammy skin; dizziness; shallow breathing; sweating; temporary unconsciousness.	Place lying down, with legs raised higher than body. Loosen clothing. Apply cold cloths to face. Call your doctor if fainting reoccurs.

Condition	Symptoms	Treatment
Fever	Body temperature over 98.6° F (37° C); hot forehead.	Increase fluid intake. Do not cover excessively. Cooling sponges with water only. Call your doctor if fever is over 102° F or persists.
Fractures, dislocations	Severe pain; deformity; loss of motion; possible protruding bones.	Call doctor. Do not move injured part until splinted. If legs, back, neck are injured, keep person lying flat and call ambulance. Cover open wounds with available clean fabric. Keep person warm. Give nothing to drink.
Frostbite	Skin flushed, then changing to white or grayish yellow; blister may appear; cold and numb; pain.	Do not rub the area. Quickly warm by immersing in tepid water (102° F–105° F), if available.
Heart attack	Persistent chest pain, often radiating to left shoulder and arm; difficulty breathing; lips, skin, and fingernails turn blue.	Call an ambulance. Place victim in a comfortable position, sitting up. Use pillows for support. Keep warm and loosen collar. If trained, administer CPR; otherwise give mouth-to-mouth resuscitation if breathing has stopped. Give nothing by mouth.
Heat stroke/ exhaustion	*Heat Exhaustion:* paleness; headache and weakness; possible nausea. *Heat Stroke:* also vomits; is flushed and confused.	Put cold cloths on skin. Give salty fluid such as broth, water and salt. If person vomits or becomes flushed and confused, he has heat stroke. Call ambulance or doctor.
Nosebleed	Bleeding nose	Seat person in a leaning forward position. Apply pressure to the site of bleeding by squeezing the bleeding nostril. Cold compresses to the nose and face are also helpful. If bleeding does not stop, take person to emergency room.
Poisoning	Symptoms vary: throat or stomach pains; mouth burns; vomiting; drowsiness.	Call Poison Center or doctor. If directed, give syrup of ipecac. Do not force liquids or induce vomiting unless so directed.
Shock	Due to injury, illness, poison; pale, mottled face; cold sweat; fast breathing; weak pulse.	Keep warm, lying down, feet raised. Call doctor or ambulance. No fluids or food. Clear airway. If the person has lower face/jaw injuries, or is unconscious, lay on side to drain. Avoid rough or excessive handling.
Stroke	Unconscious; heavy breathing; apparent weakness in face or limbs on one side of body; inability to speak.	Cover person with a light blanket. Turn head of vomiting person to side. Give no stimulants and nothing to eat or drink. Call an ambulance.
Sunburn	Redness; pain 8–12 hours after exposure; blisters, if severe.	If mild, apply soothing ointment. Call doctor if severe and if 15% of body (child, 10%) is burned, or with fever and sickness. Protect burned area from sun. If blisters break, apply sterile dressing.
Toothache	Pain; tooth is sensitive to hot and cold food and fluids.	Give aspirin. Call dentist.

4. First Aid for a Choking Victim

For Use with Chapter 28

Choking in Infants or Small Children

To dislodge an object from a small child's windpipe, turn the child upside down over one arm. Using the heel of the other hand, give quick blows to the child's back between the shoulder blades.

Choking in Older Children and Adults

Ask, "Are you choking?" If the victim cannot respond, begin first aid immediately. Begin **abdominal thrusts**, also known as the *Heimlich Maneuver*.

1. Wrap your arms around the victim's waist, with the thumb side of your wrist against the victim's abdomen. Place your hand just above the waist and just below the tip of the breastbone.
2. Grasp your fist with your other hand and press it into the abdomen with four quick, upward thrusts.
3. If this does not work, repeat the process.

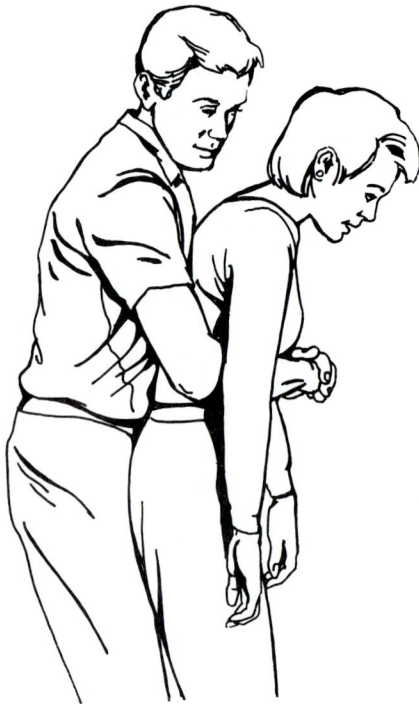

You Can Prevent Choking

Some simple practices can help to prevent choking:

- Take small bites of food.
- Eat slowly, chewing food thoroughly.
- Do not talk or laugh with food in your mouth.
- Do not go to sleep at night with chewing gum or any other matter in your mouth.

5. Mouth-to-Mouth Resuscitation

For Use with Chapter 28

In the event of respiratory failure, someone must give oxygen to the victim immediately. The most practical method in such an emergency situation is *mouth-to-mouth respiration or mouth-to-nose respiration*. **Artificial respiration,** or **resuscitation** (ree-sus-uh-**tah**-shun), has two basic objectives:

1. to maintain an open airway,
2. to restore breathing by maintaining an alternating increase and decrease in chest expansion.

Giving Artificial Respiration to Adults

The steps that a person should follow in giving artificial respiration to adults are:

1. Check to see if the victim is conscious. Shake the person gently and ask, "Are you all right?"
2. If there is no response, place one hand under the neck and one on the forehead and tilt the victim's head back, pointing the chin upward. This moves the jaw and tongue forward, opening the airway.
3. Place your ear and cheek close to the victim's mouth and nose. *Look, listen,* and *feel. Look* at the chest to see if it is rising and falling; *listen* and *feel* for the air that is being exhaled.
4. If there is no breathing, pinch the victim's nostrils shut with your index finger and thumb.
5. Place your mouth over the victim's mouth, forming a seal.

6. Give the person two full breaths.

7. Keep the head tilted. Then *look, listen,* and *feel* again. Check the pulse. If there is a pulse but no breathing, begin giving the victim one breath every five seconds.

8. Watch the chest to see whether it is rising and falling. If it is, you know that air is getting into the lungs.

Giving Artificial Respiration to Children

For children (ages one to eight) and infants (up to one year of age), do not tilt the head as far back. Your mouth will cover and form a seal around the infant's mouth and nose. Use full breaths for the infant, at the rate of one every three seconds. Give a child about one breath every four seconds.

If you check for a pulse, and the victim is not breathing and has no pulse, it means that the victim's heart has stopped. The air is not being pumped to the brain, and the brain can die after about five minutes without oxygen. You must begin *cardiopulmonary resuscitation* (**kard**-ee-oh-**pull**-mah-ner-ee ree-sus-uh-**tah**-shun) immediately, if you are trained to do so.

H. Disease Prevention

1. Your Disease Prevention Efforts

For Use with Chapter 29

Disease prevention on an individual level goes on every day. You have read of most of the following health behaviors in this book. Some of them sound simple—even elementary—yet many people fail to practice them regularly. Be responsible for promoting your own wellness. Keep these behaviors in mind. They will help you to maintain a high level of personal wellness.

1. I keep my immunization records up to date.
2. I have periodic medical and dental checkups.
3. I eat a daily balanced diet.
4. I get at least eight hours of sleep a night.
5. I exercise vigorously at least three times a week.
6. I do not smoke.
7. I avoid using towels that others have used.
8. I avoid using other people's combs and brushes.
9. I take a few minutes each day to relax.
10. I stay home at least the first day that symptoms of illness appear.
11. I listen and respond to my body's messages that it is tired or that something may be wrong.
12. I wash my hands before every meal.
13. I shower or bathe regularly.
14. I do not share eating utensils or glasses with other people.
15. I cover my mouth when I cough or sneeze.
16. I avoid walking barefooted in locker rooms and shower rooms.

2. Recommended Immunization Schedule for Children

For Use with Chapter 29

Age	Vaccinations	
2 months	Diphtheria (1st of 5)[a] Pertussis (1st of 5)[a] Tetanus (1st of 5)[a]	DPT
	Trivalent oral polio[b] (1st of 4)	
4 months	Diphtheria (2nd of 5) Pertussis (2nd of 5) Tetanus (2nd of 5) Polio (2nd of 4)	
6 months	Diphtheria (3rd of 5) Pertussis (3rd of 5) Tetanus (3rd of 5) Polio (optional, but some physicians give this additional dose)	
15 months	Measles[a, c] Mumps[a, d] Rubella[a]	
18 months	Diphtheria (4th of 5) Pertussis (4th of 5) Tetanus (4th of 5) Polio (3rd of 4)	
At school entry (4 through 6 years)	Diphtheria (5th of 5) Pertussis (5th of 5) Tetanus (5th of 5) Polio (4th of 4)	
14 through 16 and every 10 years thereafter[e]	Diphtheria booster Tetanus booster	

[a] Usually combined into one shot.
[b] **Trivalent** means that it *protects against all strains of polio*. A child gets three doses of trivalent oral polio vaccine (at 3, 6, and 8 months), followed by boosters.
[c] A measles injection usually gives lifetime immunity.
[d] Immunity from mumps is known to last for six years.
[e] People in their teens can become quite ill from pertussis vaccine, so they are given a special adult vaccine, called DT vaccine.

I. Conservation and the Environment

1. Your Efforts to Effect Change

For Use with Chapter 33

Are you someone who takes action, who believes an individual's efforts can make a difference? Read the following statements. Indicate *yes* or *no* to each, depending on whether or not they describe you.

1. I sometimes think about conserving energy, but then think, "What's the use, I'm just one person."
2. I write to my legislature to support legislation on environmental quality.
3. I say something to people who are littering.
4. If I pass a piece of litter, I pick it up and put it in a garbage container.
5. I keep informed on environmental issues, especially those in my community.
6. I seldom concern myself with environmental issues because they are out of my control.
7. We will always have land and air, so I really don't worry too much about the environment.
8. If my community were trying to rezone a park area to make a parking lot, I would petition against it.
9. I know what the zoning laws are in my community.
10. I would participate in an Earth Day or Ride Your Bike to School Day.

Scoring. If you answered *yes* to numbers 2 to 5 and 8 to 10, give yourself 4 points each. If you answered *no* to numbers 1, 6, and 7, also give yourself 4 points for each. Add up your score.

28 to 40: *Excellent!* You think you can contribute and act accordingly.

16 to 27: *You are on the right track.* Every little bit helps.

15 or below: *Beware!* You might find you do not have much of an environment left to enjoy.

2. Writing to Elected Officials

For Use with Chapter 33

Most people do not let their elected officials know how they feel about various legislation or proposed legislation but then are quick to complain when a bill is passed that they do not like. This is especially true for state and local officials. Most voters are ignorant of the impact that a letter can have.

Here are some guidelines for writing to an elected official:

1. Keep your letter short.
2. Express your views in a simple, straightforward manner.
3. Limit your letter to one or two key issues.
4. Cite data or arguments to support your position.
5. Be respectful but firm about your position.
6. Ask for a specific response, such as: please let me know your views on this issue, or please tell me if you support this bill.

The important thing is that you take the time to act.

Glossary

Abdominal hernia (ab-**dahm**-uh-nul **her**-nee-uh). A condition in which the upper part of the stomach pushes through the diaphragm. (Ch. 19)

Abdominal thrusts. *See* Heimlich maneuver. (Ch. 28)

Abiotic (ay-bye-**ot**-ick). The nonliving environment of ecosystems, including air, water, and soil. (Ch. 32)

Abrasion (uh-**bray**-shun). A type of wound in which there is damage to the outer layers of skin, with little or no bleeding, and danger of infection. (Ch. 27)

Abscessed tooth. A condition that occurs when a badly decayed tooth progresses to the stage of pus collecting in, and tissue becoming inflamed around, the bone sockets of a tooth. (Ch. 4)

Accident chain. A group of five characteristics that are present in almost all accidents: the situation, the unsafe habit, the unsafe act, the accident, and the injuries. The first three characteristics are the links in the chain and the last two are the result. (Ch. 26)

Acclimatize (uh-**klie**-muh-tize). The ability of the body to adapt to change. (Ch. 2)

Accommodation. The adjustment the eyes make to regulate the light rays passing through to penetrate the lens, which adjusts to focus the light on the retina. (Ch. 4)

Acid agent. An additive used to control the amount of acid in soft drinks, bakery products, and desserts. (Ch. 9)

Acid rain. A situation that occurs when ordinary rain passes through atmosphere polluted with sulfur and nitrogen oxides and picks up these chemicals. (Ch. 32)

Acne (**ak**-knee). A clogging of the pores of the skin. (Ch. 3)

Acquired immunodeficiency syndrome (uh-**kwired** im-you-no-duh-**fish**-un-see **sin**-drum) **(AIDS).** A sexually transmitted condition in which a certain virus attacks one of the key lymphocytes in the body—the T4 lymphocyte cell, which controls and regulates the body's immune system. (Ch. 30)

Acromegaly (ak-row-**meg**-ah-lee). A condition in which the soft tissue over the bones enlarges, making the face look massive and the hands large and awkward. (Ch. 16)

Active immunity. The immunity that the body develops. (Ch. 29)

Addiction. The physical dependence on a certain drug, which the user needs all the time. *See* Physical dependence. (Ch. 10)

Additives (**ad**-uh-tives). Substances added directly to food or substances that come in contact with food sometime before they reach the consumer. (Ch. 9)

Adenosine triphosphate (ah-**dean**-uh-sin try-**fahs**-fate) **(ATP).** An important nonprotein, chemical substance in muscle tissue. (Ch. 15)

Adenoviruses (ad-ee-no-**vie**-rus-ez). Viruses that cause cold symptoms in the early spring and summer. (Ch. 29)

Adipose (**add**-ee-pose) **tissue.** A type of connective tissue in which many of the cells are filled with fat. (Ch. 9)

Adrenal cortex (uh-**dree**-nul **kor**-teks). An adrenal gland that secretes a mixture of hormones, including a group of chemical compounds known as steroids, that affect numerous bodily functions. *See* Steroids. (Ch. 16)

Adrenal (uh-**dree**-nul) **glands.** Glands that consist of the adrenal cortex and the adrenal medulla and produce and secrete a substance called adrenaline, which prepares a person for a "fight or flight" response. *See* Adrenaline. (Ch. 6,16)

Adrenaline (uh-**dren**-uhl-en). A hormone secreted by the adrenal medulla that increases heart action, raises blood pressure, increases respiration, and suppresses the digestive process, also called the emergency hormone. (Ch. 6, 16)

Adrenal medulla. The adrenal gland that secretes the hormone epinephrine, more commonly known as adrenaline. *See* Adrenaline; Epinephrine (Ch. 6, 16)

Adrenocorticotropic (ad-dree-no-**kort**-eh-ko-tro-pik) **hormone (ACTH).** A hormone that triggers the manufacture and secretions of the outer layer of the adrenal glands. (Ch. 16)

Aerobic (uh-**row**-bick). A type of process that requires oxygen and is much more efficient and results in a higher yield of energy than the anaerobic process. (Ch. 15)

Aerobic exercise. A nonstop vigorous exercise, such as brisk walking, jogging, swimming, or cycling, that requires the body to increase its use of oxygen, is rhythmic and sustained, and uses the large muscle groups. (Ch. 2)

Afterbirth. The name given to the placenta after the uterus contracts to expel it. (Ch. 21)

Age pigment. A pigment that is thought to be the result of cells becoming less efficient in processing and ridding themselves of cell wastes. (Ch. 22)

Agglutination (uh-**glute**-en-ay-shun). A process that occurs when the mixing of certain blood types causes blood cells to mass together. (Ch. 18)

Air pollution. The contamination of the atmosphere by waste products. (Ch. 32)

Al-Anon. A group that helps the husbands and wives and other friends and relatives of alcoholics. (Ch. 12)

Alateen. A group that helps children and teenagers whose parents are alcoholics. (Ch. 12)

Alcoholics Anonymous (AA). A worldwide support group of recovered or recovering alcoholics who provide support and help to others trying to achieve sobriety. (Ch. 12)

Alcoholism. The physical and psychological addiction (dependence) to alcohol. (Ch. 12)

Aldosterone (al-doh-ster-rone). The principal, most potent hormone produced by the adrenal cortex; maintains the body's water balance. (Ch. 16)

Alienation (a-lee-en-**na**-shun). A feeling of being cut off from others, whether voluntarily or involuntarily. (Ch. 27)

Alimentary (ah-**luh**-ment-uh-ree) **canal.** *See* Gastrointestinal tract. (Ch. 19)

Alkaline agent. An additive used to control the amount of alkaline in soft drinks, bakery products, and desserts. (Ch. 9)

Alkaloid (al-kuh-loid). A chemical whose structure is closely akin to poisons. (Ch. 13)

Alveoli (al-**vee**-ohl-lee). A cluster of thin-walled air sacs located at the end of the bronchial tubes. (Ch. 18)

Alzheimer (als-high-mer) **disease.** A degenerative disease that attacks the brain, destroying brain cells. (Ch. 14)

Amino (ah-**mee**-no) **acids.** Molecules that contain nitrogen. The body is able to make all but eight of these twenty-two acids. *See* Essential amino acids. (Ch. 8)

Amniocentesis (am-nee-oh-sen-**tee**-sus). A medical procedure that enables a physician to examine the chromosomes and to study the body chemistry of an unborn child. (Ch. 21)

Amotivational syndrome. The effect of marijuana on repeated users who may become apathetic and lethargic, withdrawing from involvement in academic and social activities. (Ch. 13)

Amphetamines (am-**fet**-uh means). Stimulants used in medicine to reduce fatigue and drowsiness or to suppress the appetite. (Ch. 13)

Anaerobic (an-uh-**row**-bick). A type of process that does not require the presence of oxygen. (Ch. 15)

Anaerobic exercise. A type of exercise to improve basic body movement and muscle strength. This exercise does not require the body to increase its use of oxygen but centers on specific groups of muscles. (Ch. 2)

Analgesics (an-al-**jeez**-icks). A group of drugs that are designed to relieve or stop pain and that alter the nervous system. (Ch. 10)

Anemia (uh-**nee**-mee-uh). A condition in which a person has a deficiency in the number of red blood cells or a reduced hemoglobin level, and the body tissues do not receive enough oxygen. (Ch. 18)

Anesthetics (an-us-**thet**-icks). Substances that cause loss of sensation with or without loss of consciousness. (Ch. 21)

Angel dust. *See* Phencyclidine. (Ch. 13)

Anger. The second stage of accepting death, which is a natural reaction and an outlet for resentment at being a victim. (Ch. 22)

Angina pains. Intense attacks of chest pain. *See* Angina pectoris. (Ch. 31)

Angina pectoris (an-**jigh**-nuh **peck**-tah-rus). A condition in which pain and tightness or pressure in the chest occur as a result of the heart's not getting enough oxygen; often experienced by people who have atherosclerosis. (Ch. 31)

Angiocardiography (an-jee-oh-kard-ee-**og**-ruh-fee). A device that provides a picture of the heart, its vessels, and its chambers. (Ch. 31)

Anorexia nervosa (an-uh-**rex**-ee-uh ner-**voh**-suh). A behavior involving the irrational fear of becoming overweight, which results in severe weight loss from self-starvation. (Ch. 9)

Antacids (ant-**ass**-ids). Medicines that reduce or alleviate stomach acidity. (Ch. 10)

Anterior pituitary lobe. A lobe of the pituitary gland that secretes different hormones and has a great effect on other glands. (Ch. 16)

Antiarrhythmics (ant-uh-ah-**rith**-micks). One group of cardiovascular drugs given in cases of arrhythmia, which is any disturbance in the rate, or rhythm, of the heart. (Ch. 10)

Antibiotic (ant-uh-by-**ot**-ik). A drug produced by microscopic living organisms that works to destroy microscopic disease-producing organisms in the body. (Ch. 10)

Antibodies (ant-uh-bod-eez). Proteins released into the blood to neutralize or destroy invading disease-producing germs. (Ch. 10, 29)

Antidepressants (ant-ee-dee-**press**-ents). A group of drugs that are designed to relieve emotional depression and that alter the nervous system. (Ch. 10)

Antidiuretic (ant-ee-die-yur-**ret**-ick) **hormone (ADH).** A hormone produced in the hypothalamus to regulate the balance of water in the body. (Ch. 16)

Antigens (ant-uh-jens). The microbes or foreign bodies that stimulate the production of antibodies. (Ch. 29)

Antihistamines (ant-ee-hiss-tah-mens). Cold remedies. (Ch. 10)

Antisera (ant-e-ser-ah). Blood fluids that contain antibodies and act more quickly than vaccines. (Ch. 10)

Anus (**ay**-nus). The outlet of the digestive tract. (Ch. 19)

Aorta (ay-**ort**-uh). The body's largest artery. (Ch. 18)

Appendicitis (uh-pen-duh-**site**-us). Inflammation of the appendix. (Ch. 19)

Appendicular (ap-en-**dick**-u-lar) **skeleton.** One of two major subdivisions of the skeleton; includes the bones of the shoulders, arms, hips, and legs. *See* Axial skeleton. (Ch. 15)

Aqueous humor (ak-kwee-us **hu-**mer). A watery fluid that fills the cavity between the cornea and the lens of the eye. (Ch. 4)

Arachnoid (uh-**rack**-noid). The middle membrane of the spinal meninges, which is a thin, transparent sheath lying directly under the dura mater. (Ch. 14)

Arches. Supportive bony structures that are shaped like an arc on the inside of the foot. (Ch. 3)

Arteries (art-uh-reez). The body's largest blood vessels, which carry blood away from the heart. (Ch. 18)

Arterioles (are-**tier**-ee-olls). Smaller blood vessels, into which arteries branch, that regulate the flow of blood into the capillaries. (Ch. 18)

Arteriosclerosis (are-tier-ee-oh-skler-**roh**-sis). Hardening of the arteries, a condition that develops when fatty deposits containing cholesterol collect on the inner walls of blood vessels, narrowing the passageway for the blood. (Ch. 8, 31)

Arthritis (are-**thrite**-us). A term referring to at least 100 conditions that cause aching and pain in the joints and connective tissue throughout the body. The two most common types are rheumatoid arthritis and osteoarthritis. (Ch. 31)

Artificial pacemaker. A small unit that is implanted in the chest muscle and wired to the heart and that transmits an electrical impulse to the heart, causing the heart to beat. (Ch. 31)

Artificial respiration. Mouth-to-mouth or mouth-to-nose respiration used in an emergency situation; also called artificial resuscitation. (Ch. 28)

Artificial resuscitation (ree-sus-uh-**tay**-shun). *See* Artificial respiration. (Ch. 28)

Asbestosis (as-bes-**toe**-sus). A potentially fatal disease that blocks the lungs with thick fibrous tissue; also called white lung disease. (Ch. 32)

Aspirin. A nonnarcotic pain reliever that contains salicylic acid and is the most widely used nonprescription drug in the United States. (Ch. 10)

Asthma. *See* Bronchial asthma. (Ch. 18)

Astigmatism (a-**stig**-muh-tiz-um). An eye condition that occurs when the curvature of the lens is uneven and in which light rays focus at different points, causing the image to be uneven. (Ch. 4)

Atherosclerosis (ath-uh-roh-skler-**roh**-sis). A thickening of the arterial wall due to fatty deposits. (Ch. 31)

Athlete's foot. An infection caused by fungi growing in the warm, moist areas of the foot. (Ch. 3, 29)

Atrioventricular (ay-tree-oh-ven-**trik**-you-lar) **bundle (A-V bundle).** A structure that receives an electrical impulse from the A-V node, resulting in the contraction of the ventricles, which forces blood into the arteries. (Ch. 18)

Atrioventricular node (A-V node). A structure located at the base of the right atrium that allows the atria to contract, thereby emptying the blood into the ventricles. (Ch. 18)

Atrium (ay-tree-um). An upper heart chamber. (Ch. 18)

Audiometer (aw-dee-**om**-eh-ter). An instrument used to test for hearing acuteness and pitch discrimination. (Ch. 4)

Auditory (aw-duh-tor-ee) **nerve.** The nerve from which fibers extend to each hair cell in the organ of Corti and to the hair cells of the saccule, utricle, and semicircular canals. (Ch. 4)

Auricle (or-ree-kul). *See* Outer ear. (Ch. 4)

Autonomic (ot-uh-**nom**-ick) **division.** One of two divisions of the peripheral nervous system; maintains the equilibrium of the body's constant temperature, con-trols smooth muscles, and regulates the heartbeat. (Ch. 14)

Autonomic nervous system (ANS). A system that works with the medulla and midbrain to carry out basic body functions; composed of the sympathetic system and the parasympathetic system. (Ch. 14)

Autonomy (aw-**tahn**-un-mee). The confidence that one can control one's body, impulses, and environment. (Ch. 22)

Aversion therapy. A technique in which smokers experience unpleasant feelings each time they smoke, so that they make a negative association. (Ch. 11)

Avulsion (a-**vul**-shun). A type of wound in which tissue is separated from the victim's body, usually occurring in an auto accident or an animal bite. (Ch. 27)

Axial (ak-see-ul) **skeleton.** One of two major subdivisions of the skeleton; includes the head, neck, and trunk of the body. *See* also Appendicular skeleton. (Ch. 15)

Axons (aks-ons). Tubelike fibers that carry impulses away from the cell body. (Ch. 14)

Bacilli (buh-**sil**-eye). Rod-shaped disease-causing bacteria. (Ch. 29)

Bacteria. One-celled organisms that rank among the most widespread of all living things. (Ch. 29)

Barbiturates (bar-**bich**-u-ruts). Depressant drugs that alter and slow down the nervous system and are used to give relief to moderate or mild anxiety or tension, to aid in sleep, and to prevent seizures. *See* Hypnotics. (Ch. 10, 13, 14)

Basal metabolism (bay-sul meh-**tab**-oh-liz-um). The absolute minimum amount of energy required to keep up the life process in the human body. (Ch. 1)

B cells. A type of lymphocyte that is responsible for producing antibodies to destroy or neutralize an invading germ. (Ch. 29)

Behavior. People's actions or

reactions in relation to their environment. (Ch. 26)

Behavioral therapy. The technique of working with patients to help them change their habits, phobias, and fears. (Ch. 7)

Benign (buh-**nine**). Harmless; noncancerous. (Ch. 17, 31)

Beta blockers. Drugs that decrease heart activity and are used to treat high blood pressure. (Ch. 6)

Bile. A digestive juice, produced in the liver and stored in the gallbladder, that helps to break down fats and also promotes absorption. (Ch. 19)

Binaural (by-**naw**-ral) **hearing.** The ability to determine the direction a sound comes from by being able to hear it with both ears. (Ch. 4)

Biofeedback. Biological feedback about one's body. (Ch. 29)

Biological age. How well different parts of the body are functioning. (Ch. 22)

Biopsy (by-**op**-see). A procedure that involves removing a small piece of tissue from a tumor and examining it under a microscope to determine whether the tumor is malignant or benign. (Ch. 31)

Biosphere (**bye**-us-sfear). A thin layer of soil, water, and air near the earth's surface. (Ch. 32)

Biotic (bye-**ot**-ick) **communities.** Plants and animals providing each other with life-sustaining material in the biosphere. (Ch. 32)

Birth defects. Genetic conditions and many other types of diseases and disorders caused by a variety of factors. (Ch. 21)

Blackhead. An acne condition that develops when a plug of oil in a pore is exposed to air and darkens. (Ch. 3)

Blind spot. The point where the optic nerve enters the eye. Vision in this spot is not possible because no rods or cones are in this area. (Ch. 4)

Blister. A baglike point on the skin, usually full of liquid. (Ch. 3)

Blood. A substance made up of a liquid component called plasma and other components such as platelets, red blood cells, and white blood cells. (Ch. 18)

Blood alcohol level (BAL). The measure of the proportional weight of alcohol per 100 units of blood, expressed as a percentage. (Ch. 12)

Blood clot. A blockage that forms in the rough surface of the artery walls and combines with the slower blood flow. *See* Thrombus. (Ch. 31)

Blood pressure. The force of the blood on the walls of the blood vessels that moves blood through the circulatory system. (Ch. 18)

Blood sugar level. The amount of sugar, or glucose, in the body. (Ch. 1)

Blood types. The classification for human red blood cells under types A, B, AB, or O, and as Rh-positive or Rh-negative blood. (Ch. 18)

Body metabolism. The rate at which body cells produce energy. (Ch. 16)

Body system. All of the complex systems of the body that work together and are dependent upon one another. (Ch. 21)

Boils. Skin infections caused by bacteria, resulting in swelling, redness, and the formation of pus. (Ch. 3)

Booster shots. Injections of killed-virus vaccine that are given to add to the antibody strength in guarding against infection. (Ch. 29)

Botulism (**botch**-uh-liz-um). The most serious kind of food poisoning; caused by toxins formed by the growth of botulism organisms common in soil. (Ch. 19)

Brain. The portion of the central nervous system that is the organ of thought and neural coordination and that lies in the cranial cavity. (Ch. 14)

Brain death. An event that occurs when oxygen is cut off from all of the brain cells. (Ch. 22)

Brain stem. Portion of the brain that contains the important organs of the cranial nerves and the mechanisms for coordinating and integrating all incoming information. (Ch. 14)

Breast cancer. Cancer of the breast, which may first appear with signs of a lump, hard knot, or tissue thickening in the area between the armpit and the breast. (Ch. 17)

Breathing. The means by which the body allows air to reach the lungs and to leave the lungs. (Ch. 18)

Bronchi (**bron**-khi). Two lower tubes of the trachea leading to the lungs. (Ch. 18)

Bronchial asthma (**bron**-kee-ohl **az**-muh). A condition that can result from a sensitivity to pollen, dust, certain foods, or animal hair. (Ch. 18)

Bronchial pneumonia. A bacterial infection of the bronchioles. (Ch. 18)

Bronchial tubes. *See* Bronchi. (Ch. 18)

Bronchioles (**bron**-kee-ohls). Divisions of the bronchial tubes. (Ch. 18)

Bronchitis (bron-**kite**-us). An inflammation of the lining of the bronchial tubes. (Ch. 18)

Bruise. An injury to tissues under the skin, also called a contusion. (Ch. 2)

Bulimia (buh-**lim**-ee-uh). An episodic pattern of binge eating that involves rapid consumption of a large quantity of food in a relatively short period of time. (Ch. 9)

Bunion (**bun**-yun). A painful bony swelling in the first joint of the big toe. (Ch. 3)

Bursas (**burr**-suhs). Small sacs of fluid contained in the joints that aid in the movement of muscles over bone. (Ch. 15)

Bursitis (burr-**site**-us). A painful condition occurring when a bursa becomes inflamed. (Ch. 15)

Café coronaries. The name given to choking accidents in restaurants. (Ch. 28)

Caffeine (caf-**feen**). A stimulant that is often an ingredient in cold remedies and is used to counteract the drowsiness effect of anti-histamines. It is also an alkaloid. (Ch. 8, 10)

Calculus. *See* Tartar. (Ch. 4)

Caliper (**kal**-uh-purr). A device about the size and look of a handcuff that measures the thickness of the skin. (Ch. 9)

Callus (**kal**-us). A hard, thickened part of skin on the foot. (Ch. 3)

Cancer. Any abnormal, uncontrolled cell growth; a malignancy. (Ch. 17, 31)

CAPD. A new system for dialysis. (Ch. 19)

Capillaries (**kap**-uh-lehr-eez). The smallest blood vessels in the body, which allow for the passage of food and oxygen from the blood to the body cells and also pick up the cells' waste products. (Ch. 18)

Carbohydrate loading. The practice of increasing the amount of glycogen in the muscles; also called glycogen packing. (Ch. 9)

Carbohydrates (kar-bow-**high**-drates). The starches and sugars that come mainly from plant food and give the body much of the energy it needs each day. (Ch. 8)

Carbon monoxide (**kar**-bun mah-**nock**-side). A colorless, odorless, poisonous gas, mainly released into the air by car exhausts. (Ch. 11, 32)

Carcinogens (kar-**sin**-ah-jins). Cancer-causing agents. (Ch. 11, 31)

Carcinoma (kars-en-**oh**-muh) **cancers.** Cancers that start in the epithelial tissue. (Ch. 31)

Cardiac (**kar**-dee-ak) **arrest.** Complete stoppage of the heart. (Ch. 31)

Cardiac catheterization. A process used to take pictures of the heart, the vessels, and the chambers by means of a catheter inserted into an artery or vein, while a doctor observes with a fluoroscope. (Ch. 31)

Cardiac muscle. A special type of striated cell forming the fibers for the walls of the heart. (Ch. 15)

Cardiopulmonary resuscitation (**kard**-ee-oh-pull-mah-ner-ee ree-sus-uh-**tah**-shun) **(CPR).** A lifesaving technique that requires breathing for the victim, while forcing the heart to pump blood by applying pressure to the victim's chest. (Ch. 22, 28)

Cardiovascular system. The entire circulatory system, including the heart, the blood vessels, and the blood. (Ch. 18)

Carotid (kuh-**rot**-id) **pulse.** The pulse located on each side of the neck, just below the ear. (Ch. 28)

Cartilage (**kart**-uh-ledge). Strong, elastic material that gives form rather than rigidity. (Ch. 15)

Cataract (**kat**-uh-ract). A clouded lens that causes blurred or hazy vision and problems with night vision. (Ch. 4)

Catheter (**kath**-uh-ter). A thin, flexible tube that can be guided into the body organs. (Ch. 18, 31)

Cell. The basic structure of all living things. (Ch. 21)

Cell body. The center for receiving and sending nerve impulses. (Ch. 14)

Cementum. The substance in the root area of a tooth that covers the dentin. (Ch. 4)

Central nervous system (CNS). One of the two divisions of the nervous system; composed of the brain and the spinal cord. (Ch. 14)

Centrifuge (**sen**-truh-fuge) **machine.** A machine that separates plasma from whole blood by whirling it at a high speed, causing the blood cells to settle to the bottom and leaving a layer of plasma on top. (Ch. 18)

Cerebellum (ser-uh-**bell**-um). The second largest portion of the brain; responsible for smooth, coordinated muscle movements. (Ch. 13, 14)

Cerebral cortex (ser-**ree**-bral **kor**-teks). The white matter of the brain that is covered by a thin layer of gray matter, consists mainly of neuron-cell bodies, and governs higher mental activities, such as memory and reasoning. (Ch. 13, 14)

Cerebral embolism. The condition in which a wandering blood clot, called an embolus, is carried in the bloodstream, usually from a heart that is damaged by disease, and becomes wedged in one of the cerebral arteries. (Ch. 31)

Cerebral hemispheres (**hem**-ess-fears). The two identical halves of the cerebrum each of which has four lobes. (Ch. 14)

Cerebral hemorrhage. A condition that occurs when a diseased artery in the brain bursts and floods the surrounding brain tissue with blood. (Ch. 31)

Cerebral palsy (ser-**ree**-bral **pall**-see). A group of nonprogressive neurological disorders that are the result of damage to the cerebrum. (Ch. 14)

Cerebral thrombosis (throm-**boh**-sis). The blocking of a cerebral artery by a thrombus, or blood clot, that forms inside the artery. (Ch. 31)

Cerebrospinal (ser-ree-bro-**spy**-nul) **fluid.** Fluid that acts as a shock absorber and helps to protect the spinal cord from injury. (Ch. 31)

Cerebrum (ser-**ree**-brum). One of the three divisions of the brain and the largest and most complex part of the brain. (Ch. 14)

Cervical cancer. Cancer of the cervix, which is diagnosed by means of a Pap smear. (Ch. 17)

Cervix (**sir**-viks). The neck of the uterus. (Ch. 17, 21)

Chancre (**shang**-kur). The first sign of syphilis; a reddish sore at the place where the germ enters the body, usually on the genitals. (Ch. 30)

Chemical name. The name of a drug of use only to a chemist, who sees the chemical formula as a very precise description of the chemical composition of the drug. (Ch. 10)

Chemotherapy (key-moh-**ther**-uh-pea). The use of chemicals in the treatment of cancer. (Ch. 31)

Chewing tobacco. Tobacco leaf. (Ch. 11)

Child abuse. Physical abuse of a child, which may include sexual abuse and emotional abuse. (Ch. 20)

Chip fractures. Injuries in which a piece of bone is broken off or chipped. (Ch. 15)

Chlamydia (kluh-**mid**-ee-uh). A sexually transmitted infection that attacks the male and female reproductive organs and is caused by several different microorganisms that are similar to bacteria, but closer in size to viruses. (Ch. 30)

Cholesterol (koh-**les**-tuh-rall). A fatty, waxlike substance that is an essential part of the membrane of each cell in the human body. (Ch. 8)

Chorionic villus biopsy (kor-ee-on-ick **vil**-us bi-**op**-sy). A method of investigating the health of a fetus by removing a small piece of membrane from the chorion, a covering for the fetus. This method can be used at about the ninth week of fetal development. (Ch. 21)

Choroid (**kor**-oid). The middle layer of the eyeball wall, containing the iris, the suspensory ligaments, and the ciliary muscles. (Ch. 4)

Chromosomes (**kro**-muh-zohmz). Tiny structures within the nuclei of cells that help to determine and continue the types of living things. (Ch. 21)

Chronic (**kron**-ick). Something that happens repeatedly. (Ch. 20)

Chronic bronchitis (bron-**kite**-iz). Persistent, recurring excessive mucous secretion of the bronchial tree, and a disorder caused by continual irritation, particularly from air pollution and cigarette smoke. (Ch. 18)

Chronic fatigue. Constant fatigue, stiffness, and lack of coordination. (Ch. 1)

Chronic obstructive pulmonary diseases (COPD). Diseases associated with cigarette smoking. The two principal diseases are chronic bronchitis and pulmonary emphysema. (Ch. 11)

Cilia (**sih**-lee-ah). The hairlike projections along the respiratory tract that act as filters for air particles. (Ch. 11)

Circuits. Pathways along which the electrical signals from brain cells are sent from cell to cell. They receive and process information much like a computer. (Ch. 14)

Circuit training courses. Obstacle courses that provide for a variety of exercise, utilizing simple equipment spaced around a designated area. (Ch. 2)

Cirrhosis (suh-**row**-sis). A condition that occurs from heavy alcohol use and destroys tissues in the liver, which are replaced by scar tissue. (Ch. 12)

Cleft (kleft) **lip.** A congenital defect of the lip. (Ch. 21)

Cleft palate (**pal**-ut). A congenital defect of the palate. (Ch. 21)

Clinical death. The event that occurs when a person's body systems stop working. (Ch. 22)

Clostridium botulinum (klah-**strid**-ee-um **botch**-uh-len-um). Any one of various soil or intestinal bacteria that causes this common type of food poisoning. (Ch. 19)

Clostridium perfringens (**purr**-frin-gens). A common type of food poisoning and the bacteria that cause it. These bacteria are found in soil, water, milk, dust, sewage, and in the intestinal areas of humans and animals. (Ch. 19)

Clubfoot. A congenital birth defect that involves a misformed or distorted foot that is out of a normal position. (Ch. 21)

Cobalt (**koh**-balt) **units.** The radiation energy that penetrates a tumor without damaging the skin and destroys the cells by disrupting their chemical actions. (Ch. 31)

Cocaine (**koh**-kane). A stimulant that causes an increased heartbeat and a rise in blood pressure and body temperature and produces a feeling of euphoria and high energy. (Ch. 13)

Cocci (**kock**-eye). Spherical or round bacteria that cause disease. (Ch. 29)

Cochlea (**koh**-klee-ah). A small snail-like structure in the inner

ear that is made up of three fluid-filled ducts and is the seat of the hearing organ. (Ch. 4)

Codeine (**koh**-deen). A narcotic analgesic that is used for very strong pain and for severe coughing. (Ch. 10, 13)

Cold sore. A blister that forms on or around the lips and is caused by a virus. *See* Herpes simplex type I. (Ch. 3)

Colon (**koh**-lun). *See* Large intestine. (Ch. 19)

Color blindness. A condition in which a person has difficulty perceiving certain colors. (Ch. 4)

Communicable (kuh-**mu**-nuh-kuh-bul). A type of situation in which a person can pass on microorganisms to another person. (Ch. 29)

Communication. In the case of a family, an openness among family members. (Ch. 20)

Companions. Workers who take care of the elderly or disabled. (Ch. 27)

Complete protein foods. Foods that contain all eight essential amino acids, including most animal foods, such as fish, meat, eggs, milk, and poultry. *See* Incomplete protein foods. (Ch. 8)

Complex carbohydrates. Starchy foods, such as potatoes, bread, and pasta, that have the same number of calories, ounce for ounce, as protein and fewer calories than fats. (Ch. 8)

Compound fractures. Injuries in which the broken bone protrudes through the skin and much blood can be lost. (Ch. 15)

Cones. Light-sensitive receptors, located in the retina, that are cone-shaped, register light and darkness, are used in bright light, and are able to detect differences in color. (Ch. 4)

Congenital problems. Problems existing at birth. (Ch. 21)

Congenital syphilis. A condition that occurs when a pregnant woman who has syphilis transfers the infection to her unborn child. (Ch. 30)

Conjunctiva (con-junk-**tee**-vah). A protective mucous membrane attached to the inner surface of the eyelids that continues over the outer surface of the eyeball. (Ch. 4)

Conjunctivitis (con-junk-tuh-**vite**-us). Inflammation of the conjunctiva, or membrane that covers the eyeball. (Ch. 4)

Connecting neurons. The neurons that provide the link between sensory input and muscle activity. (Ch. 14)

Constipation (kahn-stuh-**pay**-shun). A condition in which the feces become massed or hard in the small intestine. (Ch. 19)

Constricts. Contracts, or becomes smaller. (Ch. 13)

Consumer. Anyone who uses a product or a service. (Ch. 23)

Consumer safety officer. A person whose responsibilities include the inspection of any facilities for the production, packaging, or storage of any item that the Food and Drug Administration regulates. (Ch. 23)

Contaminated. Germ-laden. (Ch. 19)

Contamination (kun-tam-uh-**nay**-shun). The falling of substances into a wound. (Ch. 27)

Continuum (kon-**tin**-you-um). A chart showing the progress of an activity, movement, or cycle. (Ch. 1)

Contract. To shorten. (Ch. 15)

Contraction. Shrinkage in size. (Ch. 4)

Contusion. *See* Bruise. (Ch. 2)

Cooling down. A decrease of activity in which muscles continue to assist in pumping up the blood until a person's pulse rate slows. (Ch. 2)

Corn. An overgrowth of the skin at some point on the toe. (Ch. 3)

Cornea (**kore**-nee-uh). The colorless, transparent part of the eyeball in front of the eye that is like a round clear dish supplied with many free nerve endings; also called the window of the eye. (Ch. 4)

Coronary bypass surgery. Surgery to create detours around obstructed or narrowed coronary arteries. (Ch. 31)

Coronary embolism (**kar**-uh-nare-ee **em**-buh-liz-um). A traveling clot that blocks a coronary artery in the heart. (Ch. 18)

Corona viruses (kuh-**row**-nuh **vie**-rus-ez). Viruses that cause about 15 to 20% of all colds, mostly in the winter. (Ch. 29)

Corrosivity (kuh-**roh**-siv-uh-tee). A dangerous characteristic of a hazardous waste that poses a requirement that the waste be placed in special containers because of its ability to corrode, or eat away, standard containers. (Ch. 32)

Cortisone (**kort**-uh-zone). A hormone that is produced by the adrenal cortex and works to control the metabolism of carbohydrates, fats, and proteins. (Ch. 16)

Cowper's gland (**cow**-purr's **gland**). A gland that supplies fluids that mix with the sperm to form semen. (Ch. 17)

Coxsackie viruses (**kock**-sak-ee **vie**-rus-ez). Viruses that cause poliomyelitis and meningitis, fevers, and heart disease in infants. (Ch. 29)

CPM. *See* Continuous passive movement. (Ch. 27)

CPR. *See* Cardiopulmonary resusitation. (Ch. 22, 28)

Crack. A very strong, pure form of cocaine. (Ch. 13)

Cranial cavity (**kray**-nee-uhl **kav**-it-tee). The cavity in which the brain lies. (Ch. 14)

Cranial meninges (men-**in**-jez). Membranes that are continuous with the meninges of the spinal cord. (Ch. 14)

Cretinism (**kree**-tin-iz-um). A condition that is caused by a lack of thyroid hormones during the growth years and results in arrested growth, mental retardation, slow heart rate, and dry, yellowish skin. (Ch. 16)

Crista (**kris**-tah). An organ that is located at the end of each semicircular canal and consists of tiny hairs covered by a dome-shaped, jellylike mass called the cupule. (Ch. 4)

Crossed eyes. A condition that can occur when the eye muscles of both eyes do not work together, causing one or both eyes to turn inward or outward; also called strabismus. (Ch. 4)

Crown. The visible part of a tooth. (Ch. 4)

Cupule (**kup**-pule). A dome-shaped, jellylike mass that covers each crista. (Ch. 4)

Cuticle (**cute**-i-kul). The nonliving epidermis that surrounds the edges of a person's fingernails and toenails. (Ch. 3)

Cystic fibrosis (**sis**-tik fie-**bro**-sus). A disorder that affects the mucous-secreting gland and the sweat glands. (Ch. 21)

Cystitis (**sis**-ti-tus). A kidney infection caused by bacteria that usually come from the bladder and may cause a pain in the back or the lower part of the abdomen. (Ch. 19)

Dandruff. A common hair and scalp problem caused by the flaking of the outer layer of dead skin cells that cover the skull. (Ch. 3)

Decayed tooth. *See* Abscessed tooth. (Ch. 4)

Decibels (**des**-uh-belz) (**dB**). The unit of measurement of intensity of sound and its loudness or softness. (Ch. 4, 32)

Defense mechanisms. Strategies that people use to cope with stressful situations. (Ch. 7)

Deflect. To bounce back. (Ch. 3)

Degeneration. A breakdown or deterioration of the structures of nervous tissue. (Ch. 14)

Dehydration (dee-high-**dray**-shun). Excess loss of body fluid. (Ch. 19)

Delayed onset muscle soreness (DOM). Strenuous, unaccustomed exercise causing certain muscles to become painful, with the pain showing up sometime after the exercise. (Ch. 2)

Delirium tremens (de-**leer**-ee-um **trem**-enz) (**DTs**). Withdrawal symptoms that are associated with alcoholism and consist of hot and cold flashes, tremors, nightmares, hallucinations, and fear of people and animals. (Ch. 12)

Dendrites (den-drites). Thread-like extensions of the cell body that receive and conduct impulses toward the cell body. (Ch. 14)

Dentin. The material that surrounds the pulp of a tooth. (Ch. 4)

Dentistry. The art or profession of a person who is skilled in practicing the prevention, diagnosis, and treatment of injuries, diseases, and malformations of the teeth, mouth, and jaws. (Ch. 4)

Deoxyribonucleic acid (dee-och-see-**rye**-bow-new-**clay**-ic **ass**-id) **(DNA).** The special genetic chemical compound that is necessary for the process of heredity. (Ch. 3, 21)

Depressants (dee-press-ents). Drugs that tend to slow down certain body functions and reactions by slowing down the nervous system; also called sedatives. (Ch. 13, 14)

Dermatology (der-muh-**taul**-uh-jee). A branch of medicine dealing with the skin, its structure and function, its diseases and their treatment. (Ch. 3)

Dermis (dur-mis). The inner layer of skin, which is made up of living cells. (Ch. 3)

Designer drugs. Drugs that are made with synthetic substances in such combinations as to produce products that are similar to the illegal drugs. (Ch. 13)

Detached retina. A retina separated from the underlying tissue. (Ch. 4)

Detoxification (de-tox-suh-fah-**kay**-shun). The process by which the poisonous effects of alcohol are lessened in the body. (Ch. 12)

Developmental (de-vel-up-**ment**-tal) **task.** Something that needs to occur during a particular age period for a person to continue his or her growth toward becoming a healthy, maturing adult. (Ch. 22)

Diabetes (die-uh-**bee**-tees). A chronic disease, which can be controlled but as yet cannot be cured, that affects the way the body uses food. The diabetic person does not produce enough insulin or the body cells cannot use effectively what the body produces. (Ch. 31)

Diabetes classifications. Classifications issued by the National Diabetes Data Group: type I, insulin-dependent diabetes, affecting mainly children and adults, and type II, noninsulin-dependent diabetes, affecting adults over 40 years of age. (Ch. 31)

Diabetes mellitus (die-uh-bee-tees **mel**-lite-us). The familial, or family, name for diabetes. (Ch. 16)

Dialysis (die-**al**-uh-sis). An artificial blood-cleansing system that removes the impurities from the blood. (Ch. 19)

Diaphragm (die-uh-fram). A muscle that separates the chest and abdominal cavities. (Ch. 18)

Diarrhea (die-uh-**ree**-uh). A condition in which the feces become liquid and are expelled frequently. (Ch. 19)

Diastolic (die-uh-**stahl**-ick) pressure. The point in heart action when arterial pressure is at its lowest. (Ch. 18)

Dietetics (die-uh-**tet**-icks). The science of nutrition. (Ch. 8)

Dietitian (die-uh-**tish**-un). A professional who works in the field of dietetics. (Ch. 8)

Digitalis (dij-uh-**tah**-lis). One group of cardiovascular drugs that works to increase the force of contractions in the heart. (Ch. 10)

Dilation (die-**lay**-shun). The act of opening, or expanding or enlarging in size. (Ch. 4, 21)

Dipping. The use of small packets of pulverized tobacco, also called snuff. (Ch. 11)

Dislocation (dis-low-**kay**-shun). An injury that occurs when the end of a bone is pushed out of its joint. (Ch. 2)

Diuretics (die-yur-**ret**-icks). One group of cardiovascular drugs that helps to relieve the body of water and sodium. The National Collegiate Athletic Association has banned the use of diuretics by college athletes. (Ch. 10, 13)

Doctor of osteopathy (os-tee-op-uh-thee) **(DO).** A specialist who performs many of the same functions as a medical doctor and has similar training; treats the musculoskeletal system by diagnosis, drug and therapy prescription, surgery, and patient education. (Ch. 15)

Domiciliary (dom-uh-**sil**-uh-er-ee) **care home.** A type of arrangement in which no nursing care is involved and no medicine is administered. It is more of a dormitory arrangement for people who can care for themselves. (Ch. 24)

Dominant gene. The expressed gene in a pair of genes. (Ch. 21)

Dormant. Inactive. (Ch. 30)

Down syndrome. A genetic disorder characterized by mild to serious physical and mental retardation, a result of a chromosome abnormality in which an infant has inherited an extra chromosome. (Ch. 14, 21)

Drownproofing. A prevention technique against drowning, in which the swimmer takes a deep breath, sinks into the water, and breathes the air out slowly. While below the water's surface, the swimmer moves hands up and down and kicks feet up and down, causing him or her to rise above the water's surface. At the surface the swimmer takes another deep breath, and repeats the process. (Ch. 26)

Drug. Any substance, other than food, that when taken into the body alters the structure or function of the body in some way. (Ch. 10)

Drug abuse. The taking of drugs in ways for which they are not medically intended, or the use of substances that are illegal or not intended to be taken into the body. (Ch. 13)

Drug interaction. A reaction that occurs when two or more different drugs are taken at the same time, causing strong side effects. (Ch. 10)

Drug misuse. The use of a drug in a way that it is not intended. (Ch. 13)

Drug therapy. The use of drugs to reduce a mental disorder or to prepare for psychoanalysis or psychotherapy. (Ch. 7)

Drug use. The use of a drug that is taken when needed, as directed, and only for the purpose that it is intended. (Ch. 13)

DTs. *See* Delirium tremens. (Ch. 12)

Duodenal (due-odd-un-ul) ulcers. Ulcers that develop in the duodenum, or widest division of the small intestine. (Ch. 19)

Duodenum (due-uh-dee-num). The first and widest division of the small intestine. (Ch. 19)

Dura mater (do-rah may-ter). The tough, protective outermost membrane of the spinal meninges. (Ch. 14)

Dwarf. A very small person whose arms and legs are quite short. (Ch. 16)

Dysorganization (dis-org-uh-nuh-zay-shun). Dr. Karl Menninger's five levels of progressive mental illness. (Ch. 7)

Echoviruses (eck-oh-vie-rus-ez). Viruses that can cause meningitis and diarrhea. (Ch. 29)

Ecology (ee-kahl-uh-jee). The branch of science that deals with the interrelationships between living organisms and their environment. (Ch. 32)

Ecosystems (ee-koh-sis-tums). Large units that are the living part of the biotic communities and also include the nonliving abiotic environment. (Ch. 32)

EDR. *See* Electrodermal response. (Ch. 29)

EEG. *See* Electroencephalogram. (Ch. 29)

Effective drug. A drug that is approved by the Food and Drug Administration. (Ch. 10)

Ejaculation (ee-jak-yuh-lay-shun). The sudden discharging of semen from the body. (Ch. 17)

Electrocardiogram ee-lek-troh-**kard**-ee-uh-gram) **(EKG or ECG).** A graphic picture of the electric activity of the heart that is traced on graph paper. (Ch. 18, 31)

Electroconvulsive (ee-lek-tro-kun-vul-siv) therapy. Electric shock given to a patient under an anesthetic, usually on a side of the brain. This treatment can sometimes help severely depressed patients. (Ch. 7)

Electrodermal (ee-lek-troh-der-mul) response (EDR). The feedback of changes in skin resistance as a result of skin perspiration. (Ch. 29)

Electroencephalogram (ee-lek-troh-en-sef-uh-luh-gram) (EEG). The feedback of bioelectric information from the brain regarding changes in the brain-wave status. (Ch. 29)

Electromyogram (ee-lek-troh-my-uh-gram) (EMG). The feedback of bioelectric information from the muscles regarding muscle tension. (Ch. 29)

Elimination (ee-lim-uh-nay-shun). The expulsion of undigested food or body wastes. (Ch. 19)

Embolus (em-buh-luss). A moving blood clot that breaks away from the artery wall and is carried in the blood flow. (Ch. 18, 31)

Embryo (em-bree-oh). A cluster of constantly dividing cells in the first stages of development. (Ch. 21)

Emotions. A person's feelings, which affect thinking, relationships with other people, behavior, and success or failure at accomplishing a given task. (Ch. 5)

Emulsifiers (ee-mull-suh-fie-urs). Additives placed in food products to change the volume. (Ch. 9)

Enamel. A hard material that covers the crown of a tooth. (Ch. 4)

Encephalitis (en-sef-uh-lite-us). An infectious disease that is an inflammation of the cells of the brain. (Ch. 14)

Endocardium (en-doe-kard-ee-um). The inner layer of the heart made up of a thin membrane that lines all of the heart and chambers, and covers structures, such as the heart valves, that project into them. (Ch. 18)

Endocrine (en-doe-krin) glands. Glands that do not have ducts but release their secretions directly into the bloodstream. (Ch. 16)

Endocrine hormones. Substances that the endocrine system produces and the blood carries to various parts of the body and that affect these parts in various ways. (Ch. 16)

Endocrine system. A system that works with the nervous system to regulate certain activities of the body. (Ch. 16)

Endometriosis (en-doe-mee-tree-oh-suhs). A condition in which the inner lining of the uterus, the endometrium, is present abnormally in the abdominal cavity. (Ch. 17)

Endometrium (en-doe-mee-tree-um). The inner lining of the uterus. (Ch. 17)

Energy. The ability to do work. (Ch. 33)

Enriched. A food that has nutrients added to it. (Ch. 8).

Enteroviruses (ent-uh-row-vie-rus-ez). Viruses that cause gastrointestinal disorders that are sometimes misnamed stomach or intestinal flu even though they are not types of influenza but diseases in their own right. (Ch. 29)

Environmental Impact Statement. The National Environmental Policy Act of 1969 that recognized the need to give environmental consideration to any federal project. (Ch. 33)

Enzymes (en-zimes). Substances that promote or initiate the chemical reactions in the body. (Ch. 8)

Epicardium (ep-uh-kard-ee-um). The protective outer layer of the heart that adheres to the heart wall. (Ch. 18)

Epidemic conjunctivitis (con-junk-tuh-vite-us). An eye infection that affects the sclera and causes reddening; also called pinkeye. (Ch. 4)

Epidemiology (ep-uh-dee-mee-aul-uh-jee). The study of the causes, spread, and control of disease. (Ch. 25)

Epidermis (ep-uh-**dur**-mis). The outer layer of skin, which is made up of dead cells that are constantly being rubbed off and replaced by new cells. (Ch. 3)

Epididymis (ep-uh-**did**-uh-miss). A large coiled tube that is located at the outer surface of each testicle and stores the sperm after they are produced. (Ch. 17)

Epiglottis (ep-uh-**glot**-us). A flap of tissue covering the opening of the trachea that closes to keep food from entering the respiratory system. (Ch. 18, 19)

Epilepsy (**ep**-uh-lep-see). A disorder of the nervous system caused by a sudden burst of nerve impulses in the brain. (Ch. 14)

Epinephrine (ep-uh-**nef**-rin). *See* Adrenaline. (Ch. 16)

Epiphyses (eh-**pif**-uh-sees). The enlarged ends of long bones that form a joint with another bone. (Ch. 15)

Epstein-Barr virus. The virus that causes infectious mononucleosis. (Ch. 29)

Escape. The running away from a problem through daydreaming, books, even excessive sleep. (Ch. 7)

Esophagus (ee-**sahf**-ah-gus). A tube that extends from the pharnyx to the stomach and through which food enters on its way to the stomach. (Ch. 19)

Essential amino (ah-**mee**-no) **acids.** The eight amino acids that the body cannot make and a diet must supply in order for the body to make the hundreds of different proteins needed. (Ch. 8)

Essential fatty acids. A term used to describe certain fatty acids necessary for growth and maintenance. (Ch. 8)

Essential nutrients. Nutrients that the body cannot make itself or cannot make in sufficient amounts. (Ch. 8)

Estrogen (**es**-tro-jin). A female sex hormone. (Ch. 16, 22)

Ethyl alcohol (**eth**-ull **al**-kuh-hall). The active substance in distilled spirits. (Ch. 12)

Eustachian tube (you-**stay**-she-un **toob**). A tube that connects the nasal cavity in the back of the throat with the middle ear. (Ch. 4)

Exocrine (**ex**-so-krin) **glands.** Glands that have ducts which carry their secretions to specific places in the body. (Ch. 16)

Extended family. Relatives who act as a support system for a nuclear family unit. (Ch. 20)

Extensors (ik-**sten**-sores). Muscles that straighten a limb. (Ch. 15)

External auditory canal. A passageway whose outer part is lined with fine hairs and tiny wax-producing glands, which protect the ear by keeping out foreign substances. (Ch. 4)

Eyeball. A structure in the eye cavity that is made up of three layers: the sclera, the choroid, and the retina. (Ch. 4)

Eyebrow. A growth of hair that protects the eyes from foreign particles, perspiration, and direct rays of light. (Ch. 4)

Eyelashes. Hairs that line the outer edge of the eyelids and help to keep foreign particles out of the eyes. (Ch. 4)

Eyelids. Folds of skin that protect the eye by covering its surface. (Ch. 4)

Fallen arches. *See* Flat feet. (Ch. 3)

Fallopian (fa-**low**-pea-un) **tubes.** A pair of tubes through one of which a mature egg released from the ovary travels to the uterus, or womb. (Ch. 17)

Family cycle. The major events in the life of a family. (Ch. 21)

Farsightedness. An eye condition that occurs when the light rays are focused behind the retina and a person can see clearly at a distance, but sees close-up material as blurred; also called hyperopia. (Ch. 4)

Fats. Nutrients that supply food energy in compact form and provide more than two-thirds as much energy as carbohydrates or proteins; also known as lipids. (Ch. 8)

Fat-soluble vitamins. Vitamins that can accumulate and are stored in the body's fatty tissue, including vitamins A, D, E, and K, which are generally found in meat and oils. (Ch. 8)

Feces (**fee**-sees). Semisolid wastes. (Ch. 19)

Femur. The longest and strongest bone in the body; also called thighbone. (Ch. 15)

Fermentation (fur-men-**tay**-shun). The process that produces alcohol by the action of yeast on sugar and starches. (Ch. 12)

Fertilization (fur-tuh-luh-**zay**-shun). The union of an egg cell from the female and a sperm cell from the male. (Ch. 17, 21)

Fertilized egg cell. The cell that is formed by the union of an egg cell and a sperm cell. (Ch. 21)

Fetal alcohol syndrome (**feet**-ull **al**-kuh-hall **sin**-drum). A syndrome of physical, mental, and behavioral abnormalities and birth defects that affects children born to mothers who drink heavily during pregnancy. (Ch. 12)

Fetus (**feet**-us). Name given to the developing individual after two months in the uterus, by which time all vital organs have started to develop. (Ch. 21)

Fever. The condition that occurs when internal body heat is formed faster than the body can get rid of it, thus raising body temperature. (Ch. 29)

Fiber. The nondigestible part of wheat and roughage found in fruits and vegetables, but not found in animal cells. (Ch. 8)

Fibrillation (fib-ruh-**lay**-shun). A condition occurring when the muscle fibers of the heart work without coordination, having an irregular rhythm and contracting usually at a fast rate. (Ch. 31)

First aid. The immediate temporary care given to a person who has become sick or who has been injured; also called emergency care. (Ch. 27)

First-degree burns. Burns resulting from overexposure to sunlight, contact with hot objects, or scalding. Only the epidermis is involved, and healing is usually rapid. (Ch. 27)

Fitness. Physical and mental soundness. (Ch. 1)

Flat bones. Bones, such as the ribs, that consist of two plates of hard bone with a softer material between them. (Ch. 15)

Flat feet. A condition in which the underside of the foot touches the ground. This condition results when the muscles, ligaments, and connective tissues supporting the arches of the feet weaken. (Ch. 3)

Flatulence (flach-uh-lents). Gas in the stomach or the small intestine. (Ch. 19)

Flavoring agents. Additives that are placed in some foods to make them taste better. (Ch. 9)

Flexibility. The range of movement of the joints. (Ch. 2)

Flexors (flek-sores). Muscles that bend a limb. (Ch. 15)

Flossing. Cleaning between the teeth with a special string. (Ch. 4)

Fluorocarbon (floor-oh-**kar-**bun). A gas used in spray cans to force out their contents. (Ch. 32)

Fluoroscope (flure-uh-scope). A machine similar to a chest X-ray machine, except that it provides a live picture. (Ch. 31)

Follicle (fol-i-kul). A small pocket in the dermis that holds a hair root. (Ch. 3)

Follicle-stimulating hormone (FSH). A gonadotropic hormone. (Ch. 16)

Fossil fuels. Stored energy that people use in the form of coal, petroleum, and natural gas. (Ch. 32)

Fracture (frak-chur). Any type of break in a bone, which may be classified as simple, compound, incomplete, chip, nonunion, and stress. (Ch. 15, 27)

Fraternal twins. Two embryos, each with a different genetic makeup, that develop when a female releases two cells and a

separate sperm cell fertilizes each one. (Ch. 21)

Freebasing. A process of using cocaine by chemically converting it and smoking it; a most potent and addictive form. (Ch. 13)

Frontal lobe. The lobe of the cerebral hemispheres that controls voluntary movements, personality, and some of the neurons involved with speech and memory. (Ch. 14)

Frostbite. A condition that occurs when a body part is exposed to a freezing or near-freezing temperature. The body tissue freezes, as ice crystals begin to form between the cells, and normal activity of the cells slows and even stops, causing the skin to become insensitive to any feeling. (Ch. 2, 27)

Frustration. The feeling that comes when a person is kept from doing or achieving something and negatively affects his or her efforts, hopes, and desires. (Ch. 7)

FSH. *See* Follicle-stimulating hormone. (Ch. 16)

Functional disorder. A disorder that results from one of many psychological causes, but in which no brain damage is involved. (Ch. 7)

Fungi (fun-guy). Simple plants that cannot make their own food and that cause infections of the scalp, such as ringworm, and of the feet, such as athlete's foot. (Ch. 29)

Gallbladder. A small sac, located on the undersurface of the liver, that stores bile. (Ch. 19)

Gallstones. Small crystals formed from bile that can block the bile duct between the gallbladder and the duodenum. (Ch. 19)

Ganglia (gang-lee-uh). Masses of nerve tissue. (Ch. 14)

Gangrene (gan-green). The actual death of tissue in a part of the body. (Ch. 27)

Gastric (gas-trik) **juices.** Juices that are secreted from the stomach during digestion and consist

of hydrochloric acid, digestive enzymes, and mucus. (Ch. 19)

Gastric ulcers. Ulcers that develop in the stomach. (Ch. 19)

Gastritis (geh-**strite-**us). An inflammation of the gastric mucous membrane. (Ch. 19)

Gastrointestinal (gas-tro-in-**tess-**tun-ul) **tract.** A muscular tube about 30 feet long through which food travels and is digested and absorbed; also called the alimentary canal. (Ch. 19)

Generativity (jen-uh-rah-**tive-**uh-tee). An active concern for young people. (Ch. 22)

Generic name. The universal name of a drug, which is simpler than the chemical name. (Ch. 10)

Genes (jeans). Tiny protein molecules that control hereditary characteristics. (Ch. 21)

Genetic (juh-**net-**ick) **code.** The code that regulates what the many body cells are supposed to do. (Ch. 21)

Genetic condition. A term that refers to a genetic disease, disorder, illness, or other condition of malfunction with which an individual is born. (Ch. 21)

Genital (jen-uh-tul). Referring to the organs of the reproductive area, especially the external area. (Ch. 17)

Genital herpes. Another name for the sexually transmitted disease herpes simplex virus type II. (Ch. 30)

Genital itching. Itching in the external reproductive area. (Ch. 17)

Genital warts. A sexually transmitted disease in which pink or reddish warts with cauliflower-like tops appear. (Ch. 30)

Gerontologists (jer-un-**tahl-**uh-jists). People who study and work in the area of aging and often with the elderly. (Ch. 22)

Gigantism (jie-**gan-**tiz-um). A condition in which the bones lengthen abnormally and the person becomes abnormally tall. (Ch. 16)

Gingivitis (jin-juh-**vite-**us). A disorder of the mouth in which the gums become red and swollen and bleed easily; caused by plaque, misaligned teeth, or deposits of decaying food. (Ch. 4)

Gland. A cell, or group of cells, or an organ that secretes a substance. (Ch. 16)

Glaucoma (glaw-**koh**-mah). A condition that occurs when fluid pressure increases in the eyeball, possibly causing damage to the optic nerve and blindness. (Ch. 4)

Glomerulus (glah-**mer**-uh-lus). A twisted knot of small blood vessels. (Ch. 19)

Glucagon (**glue**-kuh-gon). A hormone secreted by the islets of Langerhans that stimulates the liver to convert glycogen into glucose. (Ch. 16)

Glycogen (**gly**-koh-jin). An important organic compound in muscles that can be stored in the cells and used as the body needs energy; also known as starch. (Ch. 8, 15)

Glucose (**glue**-kose). A substance that is produced by the breakdown of carbohydrates and circulates throughout the body, providing a ready source of fuel for cells; also called blood sugar. (Ch. 8, 15, 31)

Glycerol (**gliss**-uh-roll). An alcohol molecule to which fatty acids attach; a sweet, syrupy substance. (Ch. 19)

Goiter (**goit**-er). A disorder of the thyroid gland that is caused by a deficiency of iodine and in which the thyroid gland enlarges in an attempt to make up for the lack of iodine necessary for production of its hormones. (Ch. 16)

Gonadotropic (go-nad-uh-**trop**-ick) **hormones.** Two hormones that are secreted by the pituitary gland and which control the growth, development, and functions of the gonads. (Ch. 16)

Gonads. The organs of reproduction. (Ch. 16)

Gonorrhea (gahn-uh-**ree**-uh). A sexually transmitted disease that is caused by a bacteria germ that lives in the warm, moist areas of the body. (Ch. 30)

Grand mal. An epileptic seizure that usually lasts for two to five minutes, with the victim's losing consciousness. (Ch. 14)

Greenhouse effect. The process by which the earth is warmed by carbon dioxide. (Ch. 32)

Group therapy. A type of therapy in which several people with similar problems meet to pool experiences and learn from one another, with a doctor as a guide. (Ch. 7)

Gynecology (gine-uh-**kaul**-uh-jee) **(GYN).** A branch of medicine that deals with the diseases and hygiene of women. (Ch. 17)

Halitosis (hal-uh-**toe**-sis). A gastrointestinal condition that can result from disorders of the teeth or the gums, eating certain foods, indigestion, and using tobacco; also known as bad breath. (Ch. 4, 19)

Hallucinogens (hal-**loos**-en-oh-jenz). A group of illegal drugs that alter a person's consciousness, thus altering the nervous system and producing imaginary visions and objects in the brain. (Ch. 10, 13, 14)

Hangnail. Slivers of cuticle that separate along the edges of a fingernail or a toenail. (Ch. 3)

Hashish. A dark brown resin collected from the tops of the cannibis plant; also called hash. *See* Marijuana. (Ch. 13)

Head lice. Insects that live in the hair and feed off the scalp. (Ch. 3)

Health. The state of total physical, mental, and social well-being, not just freedom from sickness and ailments. (Ch. 1)

Health-Care Financing Administration. A division of the Department of Health and Human Services that is concerned with the Medicare and Medicaid programs. *See* Medicaid; Medicare. (Ch. 25)

Health education. The providing of health information in such a way that it influences people to

take positive action about their health. (Ch. 1, 24)

Heart. The body's pump. (Ch. 18)

Heart attack. A condition that occurs when a thrombus or an embolus blocks a coronary artery. (Ch. 31)

Heartburn. A gastrointestinal disorder that occurs when the stomach's acid contents back up into the esophagus. (Ch. 19)

Heart and lung endurance. The ability of the heart and lungs to deliver needed oxygen to the body during exercise, without causing undue stress, and then quickly return to a resting rate. (Ch. 2)

Heart murmur. An abnormal sound in the heart, usually because of a defective valve in the heart. (Ch. 18)

Heart muscle. *See* Cardiac muscle. (Ch. 15)

Heart transplant. A procedure in which a heart is completely removed and another one is put in its place. (Ch. 31)

Heat cramps. A problem that occurs when a person loses a large amount of body salt through perspiring and the muscles cramp up. (Ch. 2)

Heat exhaustion. A condition resulting from exercise or overexertion in a hot, humid atmosphere. The body becomes overheated, with the loss of a large amount of water and salt. (Ch. 2)

Heatstroke. A life-threatening condition that follows prolonged exposure to direct sun rays, leading to potassium or salt depletion. (Ch. 2)

Heimlich maneuver. Abdominal thrusts to alleviate choking. (Ch. 28)

Hemoglobin (**hee**-muh-glo-bin). The red, oxygen-carrying pigment in the red blood cells. (Ch. 18)

Hemophilia (he-muh-**fill**-ee-uh). An inherited disease in which the blood of males clots very slowly or not at all. (Ch. 18)

Hemorrhages (**hem**-uh-ruh-jehs). Uncontrollable bleeding. (Ch. 31)

Hepatitis (hep-uh-**tite**-us). A disease involving an inflammation of the liver. There are two main types: toxic hepatitis and viral hepatitis. (Ch. 19, 29)

Hernia (**her**-nee-uh). A protusion of a part of the body through a weakened area in the muscle sheet supporting an organ in the abdomen; also called a rupture. (Ch. 2, 17)

Heroin (**herr**-oh-win). The most addictive narcotic known, which is also illegal in most countries. (Ch. 13)

Herpes (**hur**-peas) **simplex virus type I.** A virus that causes cold sores on or around the mouth. (Ch. 30)

Herpes simplex virus type II. A virus that causes blisterlike sores in the genital area, is transmitted by sexual contact, and is presently an incurable sexually transmitted disease; also called genital herpes. (Ch. 30)

Herpesviruses (hur-peas-**vie**-rus-ez). Viruses such as herpes simplex type I that are responsible for cold sores, and viruses such as herpes simplex type II that cause a sexually transmitted disease. (Ch. 29)

Hiccups (**hick**-ups). A condition that occurs when the diaphragm goes into spasms, or contractions. (Ch. 18)

High blood pressure. A condition that occurs when blood pressure goes up and stays up; also called hypertension. (Ch. 31)

Holistic (ho-**lis**-tik) **health centers.** Centers that examine health in terms of the total person and put together a "wellness" plan for what an individual can do to improve personal health. (Ch. 24)

Hormones (**hor**-mones). Body chemicals that act as chemical regulators by stimulating a reaction in some part of the body, by producing changes in body structures, and by regulating the rate of body metabolism. (Ch. 3, 5, 16)

Hospice (**hoss**-pus). A health-care outlet that offers a way of caring for the dying, not just a place where the dying are cared for. (Ch. 24)

Host. The plant or animal that a parasite or pathogen feeds upon. (Ch. 29)

Human immunodeficiency (im-you-no-duh-**fish**-un-see) **virus.** The name of the virus that causes AIDS. (Ch. 30)

Hydrocarbons. The unburned chemicals in car exhausts. (Ch. 32)

Hydrostatic (high-dro-**stat**-ick) **weighing.** A method of measuring a person's percentage of body fat when the person is submerged in a large water tank. (Ch. 9)

Hypertension (**high**-purr-ten-shun). *See* High blood pressure. (Ch. 31)

Hyperventilation (high-purr-vent-uh-**lay**-shun). Overbreathing. (Ch. 18)

Hypnotics (hip-**naht**-icks). A group of very strong sedative drugs that give relief to moderate or mild anxiety or tension and also aid in sleep, thus altering the nervous system. (Ch. 10, 13)

Hypochondria (high-poh-**kon**-dree-ah). A preoccupation with the body and with fear of presumed illness. (Ch. 7)

Hypoglycemia (high-poh-gly-**see**-ah). An abnormal decrease of sugar in the blood. (Ch. 31)

Hypothalamus (hy-poe-**thal**-uh-hmus). A nerve center in the brain that forms the lower part of the interbrain and is a part of the endocrine system. Neurons from the hypothalamus stimulate the pituitary gland to release hormones to govern appetite, sleep, and emotions. (Ch. 6, 13, 14)

Ideal weight. The weight that is best for a person's height and body size. (Ch. 9)

Identical twins. The result that occurs when a fertilized egg cell divides and two embryos develop, each having the same genetic information. (Ch. 21)

Ileum (**ill**-ee-um). The third and largest division of the small intestine. (Ch. 19)

Illegal drugs. The type of drugs, also called street drugs, that are unlawful to buy. (Ch. 13)

Immune response. The body's production of disease-fighting cells and antibodies. (Ch. 29)

Immunity (im-**you**-nuht-ee). The body's ability to resist harmful substances known as immunogens. *See* Immunogens. (Ch. 29)

Immunization (im-yah-nigh-**zay**-shun). Any medical procedure that enables a person to develop immunity to specific disease-producing organisms. (Ch. 29)

Immunogens (im-**mune**-uh-jens). Disease-producing germs that are harmful, including poisons from certain insects, spiders, and snakes. (Ch. 29)

Incision. A type of wound that usually is a result of the body's being cut by a knife, glass, or sharp rock. Bleeding may be heavy. Deep cuts can damage muscles and nerve tissue. (Ch. 27)

Incomplete fractures. Injuries in which the bone is cracked but not broken. (Ch. 15)

Incomplete protein foods. Plant foods such as grains, seeds, peas, and beans that contain some but not all of the eight essential amino acids. (Ch. 8)

Incus (**ing**-kuz). The middle bone of the middle ear that connects the malleus and the innermost bone, the stapes; also called the anvil. (Ch. 4)

Infection. A condition caused by bacteria that invade and live in the body tissue; a condition caused by the introduction of harmful germs into a wound. (Ch. 3, 27)

Infectious (in-**feck**-shus) **diseases.** Diseases that a person can catch. (Ch. 29)

Infectious hepatitis. A liver infection that is transmitted through direct contact or through contact with germ-laden food, water, or utensils. (Ch. 19)

Ingrown toenail. A condition that results when pressure bearing down on the foot pushes the nail into the skin of the toe and cuts it. (Ch. 3)

Inguinal (**in**-gwan-ul) **hernia.** A common hernia of the male reproductive system caused by a weak spot in the abdominal wall near the top of the scrotum. (Ch. 17)

Inhalants (in-**hay**-lants). Substances whose fumes are sniffed and inhaled to give a hallucinogenic high. (Ch. 13)

Injuries. Body damage that occurs from an accident; the fifth and last link or result of an accident chain. (Ch. 26)

Inner ear. Organ of hearing and equilibrium consisting of the vestibule, semicircular canals, and the cochlea; also called the labyrinth. (Ch. 4)

Inorganic (in-or-**gan**-ick). Type of substance that does not come from a living source, such as minerals and water. (Ch. 8)

Inpatients. People who require prolonged health care and who are admitted to and occupy a bed in a health facility. (Ch. 24)

Insulin (in-suh-linn). A hormone secretion from the islets of Langerhans that stimulates the formation of glycogen from glucose and causes the blood sugar to be transported across cell membranes. (Ch. 16, 31)

Intensity. The loudness or softness of sound, which is measured in decibels. (Ch. 4)

Interbrain. A section of the brain that consists of the thalamus and the hypothalamus; also called the diencephalon. *See* Hypothalamus; Thalamus. (Ch. 14)

Intermediary host. A human, an animal, a plant, food, or soil in which a pathogen lives before it invades a noninfected organism. (Ch. 29)

Interpersonal conflict. A disagreement or an argument between two or more people. (Ch. 7)

Interstitial (int-ur-**stish**-ul) **fluid.** A fluid that nourishes body tissues; also called lymph. (Ch. 29)

Intrapersonal conflict. Conflict within a person. (Ch. 7)

Intravenously (in-trah-**vee**-nus-lee). Taken in the veins. (Ch. 10)

Iris (**eye**-ris). Front portion of the eye that gives the eye its color, is located in front of the lens, and contains the pupil. (Ch. 4)

Islets of Langerhans. Small clusters of cells throughout the pancreas that secrete insulin and glucagon. (Ch. 16)

Isokinetic exercise. A type of exercise involving resistance by muscular effort that moves at a fixed speed, such as pushing and pulling against a hydraulic lever. (Ch. 2)

Isometric exercise. A type of exercise involving muscular contraction, but little or no movement of the body part that is stressed. A person's muscle tension builds strength. (Ch. 2)

Isotonic exercise. A type of strength-developing exercise such as pushups, pullups, and situps. (Ch. 2)

Jaundice (**jaun**-dus). A yellowish coloring of the skin caused by bile. (Ch. 19, 29)

Jejunum (jeh-**joo**-num). The middle division of the small intestine. (Ch. 19)

Jock itch. A skin irritation caused by fungi growing in the warm, moist areas of the body. (Ch. 3)

Joint. The point at which two bones meet. A joint may be freely movable, partially movable, or immovable. (Ch. 15)

Keratin (**kerr**-uh-tin). A transparent, proteinlike substance that makes nails hard. (Ch. 3)

Kidney failure. Stoppage of the kidneys, a situation that occurs as the result of the blockage of urine, a very serious case of nephritis, or loss of blood. (Ch. 19)

Kidneys. The two organs that excrete the waste products of metabolism; each kidney is made up of three sections: renal cortex, renal medulla, and renal pelvis. (Ch. 19)

Kidney stones. Stonelike particles in the kidneys that are sometimes formed from mineral salts and urea. (Ch. 19)

Killed-virus vaccine. A type of vaccine that causes the body to produce antibodies, but that is not as powerful as the live-virus vaccine. (Ch. 29)

Laceration (las-uh-**ray**-shun). A type of wound in which there is a jagged, irregular tearing of the skin. Bleeding may be heavy, and chances of infection and damage to inner tissue are greater than in the case of an incision. (Ch. 27)

Lacrimal gland (**lak**-ree-mul **gland**). A gland that is located above each eye and is responsible for producing tears. (Ch. 4)

Lactic (**lak**-tick) **acid.** A waste product of the anaerobic process. A buildup of this acid causes muscle pain and fatigue and interferes with the ability of the muscle cells to contract. (Ch. 15)

Lactobacilli (lak-toe-buh-**sil**-eye). Resident bacteria, found in the gastrointestinal tract, that produce lactic acid from simple carbohydrates. (Ch. 29)

Large intestine. The lower part of the digestive tract; also called the colon. (Ch. 19)

Larynx (**lair**-inks). The throat; also known as the voice box because it contains the vocal chords. (Ch. 18)

Lazy eye. Reduced or dim vision. (Ch. 4)

Leader nutrients. The key nutrients that a food group supplies. (Ch. 8)

Lead poisoning. A condition that occurs when too much lead enters the body. (Ch. 32)

Lens. A spherical body that is located behind the eye and held by the suspensory ligaments. The lens is curved and forms on the retina an image of what is before it. (Ch. 4)

Leukemia (lew-**kee**-mee-uh). Both a bone and a blood disease. As a bone disease, leukemia is caused by cancer cells that attack the marrow of the bone. As a blood disease, leukemia is caused when an excess of white blood cells begin to crowd out the red blood cells. (Ch. 15, 18)

Leukocytes. *See* White blood cells. (Ch. 18)

Leukoplakia (lew-koh-**plah**-kee-uh). Thickened, white leathery-appearing spots on the inside of a nonsmoking tobacco user's mouth. (Ch. 11)

Licensed practical nurse (LPN). A member of a health-care team who performs much of the patient care that registered nurses formerly performed and works in all specialized areas of a hospital; also called a licensed vocational nurse. (Ch. 33)

Life-style factors. Factors related to the way people live. (Ch. 1)

Lifetime sports. Sports such as tennis, swimming, and softball that can be enjoyed and partici-pated in throughout life. (Ch. 1)

Ligaments (**lig**-uh-ments). Strong bands or cords of tissue that join bones or keep organs in place. (Ch. 15)

Lipase (**lie**-paz). An enzyme that splits fats into fatty acids and glycerol. (Ch. 19)

Lipids. *See* Fats. (Ch. 8)

Lipoproteins (lie-poe-**pro**-teens). Special molecules that carry cholesterol. (Ch. 8)

Liver. The largest and perhaps most versatile gland in the body; produces bile; converts glucose to glycogen; maintains the body's balance of blood sugar; carries out partial metabolism of carbo-hydrates, fats, and proteins; changes toxic wastes; and stores fat-soluble and water-soluble vitamins. (Ch. 19)

Live-virus vaccine. The type of vaccine that is produced by grow-ing a virus over and over until it is a very weak germ that cannot cause a disease but can make the body form antibodies. (Ch. 29)

Lobar (**low**-bar) **pneumonia.** A bacterial infection within the respiratory passages themselves. (Ch. 18)

Lobes. Sections or divisions of a body part or organ. (Ch. 18)

Lockjaw. *See* Tetanus. (Ch. 29)

Long bones. The bones that serve as levers. (Ch. 15)

Look-alike drugs. Drugs deliber-ately designed to look like street drugs. (Ch. 13)

LSD. Standing for lysergic acid diethylamide (lah-sir-**jik ass**-id die-eth-ul-**am**-ide), a hallucino-genic, illegal drug that is reponsi-ble for public awarenesss of hallucinogens and causes unpre-dictable and extreme reactions. (Ch. 13)

Lung capacity. The amount of air that a person can take in with a single breath. (Ch. 1)

Lungs. Breathing organs that contain two sections, or lobes. (Ch. 18)

Luteinizing (loot-in-eyes-**ing**) **hormone (LH).** The gonado-tropic hormones that stimulate cells in the ovaries to produce estrogen and progesterone, and in the testes to produce testosterone. (Ch. 16)

Lymph. The interstitial fluid that nourishes body tissue. (Ch. 29)

Lymphatic system. A circula-tory network that provides a means of returning fluid from the body tissues to the heart. (Ch. 29)

Lymph nodes. Glandlike struc-tures that serve as filters to screen out bacteria. (Ch. 29)

Lymphocyte (**lim**-fuh-site). A type of white blood cell that is manufactured in the bone mar-row and transported through the lymph system and helps to pro-duce immunity. (Ch. 29)

Malaria. A disease caused by a pathogenic protozoan and trans-mitted to humans by the bite of a mosquito. (Ch. 29)

Malignant (muh-**lig**-nunt). Can-cerous. (Ch. 31)

Malleus (**mal**-ee-us). The first and largest bone in the middle ear. It is attached to the eardrum and is also called the hammer. (Ch. 4)

Malocclusion (mal-uh-**klue**-shun). A condition in which the teeth of the upper and lower jaws do not properly align. (Ch. 4)

Marijuana (mar-uh-**wan**-uh). A hallucinogenic drug that comes from the hemp plant; its scientific name is *Cannibis sativa*. (Ch. 13)

Marrow. The blood-forming matter inside the bones. (Ch. 15)

Mastication (mas-tuh-**kay**-shun). The process of chewing. (Ch. 19)

Mastoid (**mass**-toid) **process.** A series of small air-filled spaces in the bones that lie behind the middle ear and connect with the middle ear. (Ch. 4)

Maximum pulse rate. The most that a heart should beat per minute. (Ch. 2)

Medicaid. A government insur-ance program for low-income individuals and families. (Ch. 24, 25)

Medicare. A government insur-ance program for people 65 and older. (Ch. 24, 25)

Medical secretary—medical assistant. A specialist who is trained to perform a wide range of activities to promote office effi-ciency and allow doctors and others the time to attend to their medical practice. (Ch. 29)

Medicine. A kind of drug that is taken into or applied to the body to prevent or cure a disease or disabling condition. (Ch. 10)

Medulla (meh-**dull**-ah). The lowest part of the brain stem; contains control centers that regu-late heartbeat, breathing, and the diameter of the blood vessels. (Ch. 14)

Medullary (meh-**dull**-ah-ree) **canal.** A narrow space through-out the length of a shaft that is linked with tough connective tissue and filled with yellow bone marrow. (Ch. 15)

Melanin (**mell**-lah-nin). A pig-ment that mainly gives the skin its color and also gives color to the hair and the eyes. (Ch. 3)

Meningitis (men-in-**jite**-us). An infectious disease that is an inflammation of the meninges. (Ch. 14)

Menstrual (**men**-stru-uhl) **cycle.** The time from the beginning of one menstrual period to the onset of the next; usually about 28 days. (Ch. 17)

Menstruation (men-stru-**way**-shun). The process of passing off the lining of the uterus. (Ch. 17)

Mental disorders. A term used to describe the broad range of mental health problems. (Ch. 7)

Mental health. The ability to like and accept oneself, to be able to express emotions in an acceptable, healthy way, and to be able to face the problems and stresses of daily living. (Ch. 1, 5)

Mental illness. A mental disorder, disease, or disturbance that prevents a person from leading a happy, healthful life. (Ch. 7)

Metabolic rate. The rate at which the body burns calories. (Ch. 1)

Metabolism (meh-**tab**-oh-liz-um). The process by which cells in the body produce energy. (Ch. 16)

Metastasis (meh-**tass**-tah-sis). The process that occurs when cancer cells break away from a malignant area, travel to other parts of the body, and further invade and destroy the tissues and organs involved. (Ch. 31)

Micronutrients (my-kroh-**new**-tree-ents). Organic substances that are essential in minute amounts in a person's diet, including iron and vitamins A, B₁, B₂, and C. (Ch. 8)

Microorganisms (**my**-kroh-or-guh-niz-ums). Tiny germs that cause many of the most common diseases, the infectious diseases. *See* Infectious diseases. (Ch. 29)

Midbrain. Portion of the brain that connects the brain stem with the cerebrum and the fibers from the cerebellum. Its nerve centers help control movements of the eyes and the size of the pupils. (Ch. 14)

Midget. A very small person. (Ch. 16)

Miscarriage. The expulsion of a human fetus that is not capable of living. (Ch. 30)

Mole. A small, round, slightly thick place on the skin. (Ch. 3)

Monocytes (**mahn**-uh-sites). Large leukocytes produced in the bone marrow that, like neutrophils, carry out phagocytosis. (Ch. 29)

Monoglyceride (mon-oh-**gliss**-uh-ride). A fatty acid attached to a glycerol molecule. (Ch. 8)

Mononucleosis (**mahn**-oh-new-klee-oh-sus). An infectious disease, common among young people, that develops as the result of a large, abnormal increase in the number of lymphocytes in the blood. (Ch. 29)

Monounsaturated (mon-oh-un-**satch**-uh-rate-ed) **fats.** Fats in which the fatty acid molecule has room for two more hydrogen atoms. (Ch. 8)

Morphine. An addictive narcotic analgesic used for intense pain. (Ch. 10, 13)

Motor end plates. Tiny button-like endings by which numerous branch neurons contact muscle fibers.

Motor neurons. Neurons that carry impulses from connecting neurons within the brain or spinal cord to the muscles and glands. (Ch. 14)

Multiple sclerosis (**mul**-tah-puhl skler-**roh**-sis) **(MS).** A degenerative disease that destroys the myelin sheath that surrounds many nerve fibers. (Ch. 14)

Multiplier effect. The result of taking alcohol with other drugs. (Ch. 12)

Muscle cramps. A condition that occurs when a muscle contracts tightly and will not relax. (Ch. 2)

Muscle endurance. How well a group of muscles can keep performing over a period of time without causing undue fatigue. (Ch. 2)

Muscle strength. The great amount of work the muscles can do at a given time. (Ch. 2)

Muscle tone. A certain degree of firmness of the muscles. (Ch. 15)

Muscular dystrophy (**dis**-troh-fee). A muscular disease that is characterized by a progressive

wasting away of skeletal muscles. (Ch. 15)

Myasthenia gravis (my-as-**thee**-nee-uh **grav**-is). A muscular disease that is characterized by weakness and quick fatigue of the voluntary muscles. (Ch. 15)

Myelin (**my**-uh-len). A whitish coating of fatty material that appears in many of the axons in the peripheral nervous system, insulating the nerve fibers and speeding the transmission of impulses. (Ch. 14)

Myocardium (my-oh-**kard**-ee-um). The middle layer of the heart that consists of cardiac muscle tissue. (Ch. 18)

Myopia (my-oh-**pea**-ah). *See* Nearsightedness. (Ch. 4)

Myxedema (mix-eh-**dee**-mah). A condition that results from a lack of growth in adulthood. (Ch. 16)

Narcotics (nar-**kot**-ticks). Very powerful analgesics that stop very strong pain by working on the brain and the nervous system. These drugs bring on sleep or loss of feeling. (Ch. 10, 13)

Nausea (**naw**-zee-uh). An ill feeling in the stomach. (Ch. 19)

Nearsightedness. A condition in which the light rays are focused in front of the retina and a person can see clearly close up, but not see clearly at a distance; also called myopia. (Ch. 4)

Nephritis (**nef**-rite-us). A condition that occurs when the nephrons of the kidney become infected. The acute or chronic illness may take different forms, depending on the type of bacteria causing the infection. (Ch. 19)

Nephrons (**nef**-rons). The filters of the kidneys. (Ch. 19)

Nerve impulse. An electrical charge that races from the point of stimulation to the brain or spinal cord. (Ch. 14)

Neurons (**new**-rons). Nerve cells. (Ch. 14)

Neurosis (new-**row**-sis). A disorder in which anxiety or fear prevents a person from functioning effectively in day-to-day living. (Ch. 7)

Neurotransmitters (new-row-trans-**mitt**-ers). Body chemicals that send tiny electrical impulses throughout the nervous system, controlling involuntary functions, memory, sleep, and motor activities. (Ch. 13)

Neutrophils (**new**-trah-fils). Mainly white blood cells that the tiny blood vessels at the site of infection release to fight germs and that surround and literally eat up the invading germs. (Ch. 29)

Nicotine (**nick**-ah-teen). A poisonous drug stimulant, found in tobacco, that acts on the adrenal glands and heart tissue. (Ch. 11)

Night blindness. The vision problem that occurs when people who do not have enough visual purple in their eyes cannot see well in dim light. (Ch. 4)

Nitrogen dioxide (**nigh**-truh-jun di-**ach**-side). One of the ingredients that contributes to ozone, or photochemical, smog. (Ch. 32)

Nocturnal emission (nock-**turn**-ul ee-**mish**-shun). An ejaculation that takes place in males during puberty, usually during sleep; also called a wet dream. (Ch. 17)

Noncommunicable (nahn-kuh-mu-nuh-kuh-bul) **diseases.** Diseases that are not capable of being transmitted through contact with an infected or afflicted person. (Ch. 29, 31)

Nongonococcal urethritis (non-gon-uh-**kock**-ul yur-ee-**thrite**-us) **(NGU).** A sexually transmitted disease caused by several different kinds of bacteria-like organisms that affect the urethra in men and the cervix in women. It is also a nonspecific sexually transmitted disease. (Ch. 30)

Noninfectious (nahn-in-**feck**-shus) **diseases.** Diseases that occur from sources within the body itself, usually through some malfunction of a body system. These diseases are not contagious, and are also called noncommunicable diseases. (Ch. 29, 31)

Nonsmokers' Bill of Rights. A bill adopted in 1974 by the National Interagency Council on Smoking and Health, declaring the nonsmoker's three basic rights: the right to breathe clean air, the right to speak out, and the right to act. (Ch. 11)

Nonspecific STD. A sexually transmitted disease whose specific cause has not yet been discovered. (Ch. 30)

Nonspecific vaginitis. An infection that is caused by bacteria and has symptoms of itching, an odorless discharge, and a burning sensation during urination. (Ch. 17)

Nonunion fractures. Injuries in which the bone does not heal properly. (Ch. 15)

Nuclear family. A unit made up of a mother, a father, and children, or any combination of the three. (Ch. 20)

Nuclei (**new**-klee-eye). The central structures within cells. (Ch. 21)

Nutrient density. A term that refers to how nutritious food is relative to the number of calories it contains. (Ch. 9)

Nutrients (**new**-tree-ents). Chemical substances that are obtained from food during digestion. (Ch. 8)

Nutrient supplements. Additives that are in the form of vitamins and minerals. (Ch. 9)

Nutrition. Eating the proper food for growth and development. (Ch. 8)

OB. *See* Obstetrics (Ch. 17)

Obese (o-**beece**). An excess of fat, or adipose tissue, in the body. (Ch. 9)

Obesity (o-**bee**-suh-tee). A condition caused by an excessive amount of fat in the body. (Ch. 1)

Obstetrics (ob-**ste**-tricks) **(OB).** The field of medical science that deals with female reproduction. (Ch. 17)

Occupational therapy. The field of study specializing in evaluating a person's abilities in light of the

person's emotional or physical handicap. (Ch. 7)

Office of Human Development Services. A federal office in charge of programs for groups with special needs, such as handicapped people, American Indians, and residents of rural areas. (Ch. 25)

Olfactory cells (ohl-**fack**-te-ree celz). The millions of receptors that detect smell and are embedded in the mucous membrane on the topside of each nasal cavity. (Ch. 4)

Open dating. A food-dating method that provides a date on a product to show the consumer when the product should be removed from the shelves, the deadline on using it, or when it was packaged. (Ch. 8)

Open-heart surgery. Heart surgery in which a heart-lung machine performs the job of the heart and lungs for several hours during the operation so that a surgeon can open the heart for inspection and treatment. (Ch. 31)

Optic nerve. A large nerve cable that connects the eye with the brain. (Ch. 4)

Optometrist (op-**tom**-uh-trist). A person who diagnoses vision defects and signs of disease and prescribes correction lenses and other treatment, when necessary.

Organ of Corti. An organ that contains hearing receptors. (Ch. 4)

Organic (or-**gan**-ick). A substance that comes from a living source, such as carbohydrates, fats, protein, and vitamins. (Ch. 8)

Organic disorder. A disorder that is caused by a physical illness or injury that affects the brain. (Ch. 7)

Organs. Certain body parts that have special structures and do special work. (Ch. 21)

Ossicles (**ah**-see-kulz). The small bones that are linked together and connect the eardrum with the inner ear. (Ch. 4)

Ossification (os-seh-fuh-**kay**-shun). The process by which cartilage cells are replaced by bone cells and minerals and in which calcium deposits form between the bone cells. (Ch. 15)

Osteoarthritis (ahs-tee-oh-are-**thrite**-us). The most common form of arthritis, which results from wear and tear in the mechanical parts of a joint. (Ch. 31)

Osteoblasts (**os**-tee-oh-blasts). Bone-forming cells that are important in bone growth and repair. (Ch. 15)

Osteomyelitis (os-tee-oh-my-uh-**lite**-us). The term given to many kinds of inflammation of the soft inner surface of the bones. (Ch. 15)

Osteopathy (**os**-tee-op-uh-thee). Treatment of the musculoskeletal system. (Ch. 7)

Osteoporosis (**os**-tee-oh-puh-roh-sis). A condition in which a person is not getting enough nourishment to sustain the proper growth of the bones; results from a low-calorie and low-calcium diet. (Ch. 15)

Otosclerosis (ot-**oh**-scluh-row-sis). A hereditary disease that is a common cause of partial deafness and occurs because of an overgrowth of bone, causing the ossicles to lose their ability to move. (Ch. 4)

Outer ear. Fleshy curved part of the ear that is attached to each side of the head and is composed of fatty tissue and cartilage; its cuplike shape collects sound waves and directs them into the ear; also called the auricle. (Ch. 4)

Outpatients. People who receive various medical, dental, or other health services in a health facility and then return home. (Ch. 24)

Ovaries (**oh**-var-eez). The two reproductive organs that contain the egg cells in the female. (Ch. 17)

Over-the-counter (OTC) drug. A drug that the FDA decides is safe to use without a doctor's supervision and can be sold without a prescription—over the counter. (Ch. 10)

Overweight. A condition in which a person weighs more than the desirable weight for his or her age and size. (Ch. 9)

Ovulation (ahv-you-**lay**-shun). The release of a mature egg cell from the ovary. (Ch. 17)

Oxidation (ox-suh-**day**-shun). A process in which the liver changes alcohol to water, carbon dioxide, and energy. Also, the chemical breakdown of sugar in tissues to produce energy. (Ch. 12, 15)

Oxytocin (ox-suh-**tow**-sin). A hormone produced by the hypothalamus that stimulates the smooth muscle in the walls of internal organs. (Ch. 16)

Ozone (**oh**-zone). One component of photochemical smog. (Ch. 32)

Pain. A protective sensation for the body, indicating overstimulation of any sensory nerve and damage or potential damage to body tissue. (Ch. 3)

Pancreas (**pan**-kree-us). A digestive gland that is both an exocrine and endocrine gland and that serves the digestive and endocrine systems. (Ch. 16, 19)

Pancreatic (pan-**kree**-at-ick) **duct.** The duct leading from the pancreas to the duodenum. (Ch. 19)

Papillae (pah-**pil**-lie). Small, velvetlike projections that cover the tongue's surface. (Ch. 19)

Pap smear. A test through which a doctor can check for cervical and uterine cancer in females. (Ch. 17, 31)

Paranoia (par-uh-**noy**-uh). An all-absorbing apprehension that interferes with the carrying on of normal activity. (Ch. 7)

Parasite (**pear**-uh-site). A microorganism that feeds upon a living plant or animal. (Ch. 29)

Parasympathetic (pear-uh-sym-pah-**thet**-ick) **system.** One of two parts of the autonomic nervous system; the system that opposes the actions of the sympathetic system, slowing down the heartbeat, opening blood vessels, and lowering blood pressure. (Ch. 14)

Parathyroid (par-uh-**thy**-roid) **glands.** Four brownish-yellow glands, the smallest in the endocrine system, that regulate the body's calcium and phosphorous balance. (Ch. 16)

Paregoric (par-uh-**gore**-ick). A narcotic that is used to treat teething or to stop diarrhea. (Ch. 13)

Parietal (pah-**rye**-eh-tull) **lobe.** A lobe of the cerebral hemispheres that is involved with a wide variety of sensory information, such as heat, cold, pain, touch, and body position in space. (Ch. 14)

Parkinson disease. A degenerative disease that interferes with the transmission of nerve impulses from the motor areas of the brain. (Ch. 14)

Paratoid (puh-**raht**-id) **glands.** One pair of the three pairs of salivary glands, which are located below and in front of the ears. (Ch. 14, 19)

Particulates (par-**tik**-yuh-luts). Actual particles of soot, ash, and fallout, solid and liquid matter, suspended in the air. (Ch. 32)

Passive immunity. A temporary immunity that an infant acquires from the mother before birth. (Ch. 29)

Pathogens (**path**-uh-jens). Microorganisms that cause infectious diseases. (Ch. 29)

Pathological (path-oh-**lah**-jah-kal) **fatigue.** Fatigue brought on by the overworking of the body's defense mechanisms for fighting disease. (Ch. 6)

Pelvic inflammatory (in-**flam**-uh-torr-ee) **disease (PID).** A painful infection of the Fallopian tubes, ovaries, and pelvic area. (Ch. 30)

Penicillins (pen-uh-**sill**-lens). Antibiotics that kill a wide variety of bacteria. (Ch. 10)

Penis. The external organ of the male reproductive system. (Ch. 17)

Peptic (pep-tik) **ulcers.** Open sores that develop in the digestive system. (Ch. 19)

Pericardium (per-uh-**kard**-ee-um). The loose-fitting sac that encloses the heart. (Ch. 18)

Periodontal (per-ee-oh-**don**-tal) **disease.** A disease that results from the destructive action of bacteria in a person's mouth. (Ch. 4)

Periodontitis (per-ee-oh-**don**-tite-us). *See* Pyorrhea. (Ch. 4)

Periodontium (per-ee-oh-**don**-tee-um). An area located immediately around the teeth that is made up of the gums, periodontal ligament, and jawbone. (Ch. 4)

Periosteum (per-ee-**ahs**-tee-um). A tough membrane that covers the outer surface of bone and contains bone-forming cells called osteoblasts. (Ch. 15)

Peripheral (pur-**rif**-er-rull) **nervous system (PNS).** A main division of the nervous system that carries all of the messages sent between the central nervous system and the rest of the body. (Ch. 14)

Peristalsis (per-uh-**stahl**-sis). A series of involuntary muscular contractions that move food through the esophagus. (Ch. 19)

Peritoneum (per-ut-un-**ee**-um). The semipenetrable membrane that lines the abdominal cavity. (Ch. 19)

Personal identity. The factors that a person believes make up his or her unique self. (Ch. 22)

Personality. All of a person's traits, attitudes, feelings, behaviors, and habits, including his or her strengths, weaknesses, likes, and dislikes. (Ch. 5)

Personality disorder. A condition that causes a person to respond inappropriately in certain situations or interfere with others' interactions. (Ch. 7)

Perspiration. Water and other waste products that are secreted from the sweat glands and help to cool down the body. (Ch. 3)

Petit mal. A very slight epileptic seizure in which the victim goes into a daze or has a blank stare. (Ch. 14)

Phagocytosis (fag-uh-suh-**toe**-sis). The process whereby neutrophils eat up invading bacteria germs at the site of an infection. (Ch. 29)

Pharynx (**fair**-inks). A cavity in the upper part of the throat into which air moves on its way to the trachea. (Ch. 18)

Phencyclidine (feen-**sik**-luh-dine) **(PCP).** A powerful and dangerous hallucinogen that is prepared synthetically from laboratory chemicals; also known as angel dust. (Ch. 13)

Phobia (**foe**-bee-ah). A persistent fear of something. (Ch. 5)

Phonocardiography (**foe**-no-kard-ee-og-ruh-fee). The placing of a microphone on the chest to record heart sound signals. (Ch. 31)

Photochemical pollution. Pollution that is formed by hydrocarbons reacting with sunlight and that restricts the food-processing capabilities of plants. (Ch. 32)

Photosynthesis (foe-toe-**sin**-thuh-sis). The process by which plants use light to make food. (Ch. 32)

Physical dependence. The case in which a drug user's body develops a need for a drug. *See* Withdrawal. (Ch. 10)

Physical fitness. The ability to carry out daily tasks easily and to have enough reserve energy to respond to unexpected demands made upon oneself. (Ch. 2)

Physical health. The care of one's body and its ability to meet the demands of daily living. (Ch. 1)

Pia (**pea**-uh) **mater.** The inner membrane of the spinal meninges that contains many blood vessels and provides nourishment to the cells of the brain and spinal cord. (Ch. 14)

Pimple. An acne condition that develops when bacteria get into a clogged pore and inflame it, causing the pimple to develop a yellowish pus. (Ch. 3)

Pinched nerve. A common injury in which one of the spinal disks moves slightly as a result of a sudden jerking of the body, a blow, a fall, or a jolt in a car accident. (Ch. 14)

Pinch test. An obesity test that involves pinching a fold of skin on the back of the upper arm or at the hipbone, just below the waist. If the fold is more than one inch thick, the person has too much body fat. *See* Caliper. (Ch. 9)

Pineal (pin-**ee**-el) **gland.** A pea-sized gland located in the brain. Although its functions are not fully known, it seems to have a part in a person's sexual development. (Ch. 16)

Pinkeye. *See* Epidemic conjunctivitis. (Ch. 4)

Pitch. The number of sound vibrations per second; also called frequency. (Ch. 4)

Pituitary (puh-**too**-it-err-ee) **gland.** The endocrine gland that secretes a substance that stimulates the adrenal glands and has many regulatory functions. (Ch. 6, 16)

Placebo (plah-**chay**-bow). A substance that has no medical value but is given for its psychological effect. (Ch. 23)

Placebo effect. An effect that occurs when people think they are taking medicine and their symptoms are relieved. (Ch. 23)

Placenta (pluh-**sent**-tuh). A blood-rich tissue that transfers oxygen and nutrients from the mother's blood to the embryo. (Ch. 21)

Plaque (**plack**). A sticky, colorless film that acts on sugar to form acids that destroy tooth enamel and irritate gums. (Ch. 4)

Plasma (**plaz**-mah). A yellow fluid that makes up about 55% of the total volume of the body's blood and is about 92% water and 8% protein; the water carries dissolved nutrients, waste products, and mineral salts. (Ch. 18)

Plateaus. Periods of time when a person does not see himself or herself losing weight. (Ch. 9)

Platelets (**plate**-lits). The smallest solid elements in the blood that prevent the body's loss of blood by initiating a chain of reactions that result in the clotting of blood. (Ch. 18)

Pleurisy (**plure**-uh-see). A bacterial infection or an irritation of the pleural membrane covering the lungs. (Ch. 18)

PMS. *See* Premenstrual syndrome. (Ch. 17)

Pneumonia (new-**moan**-yuh). A lung infection. (Ch. 18)

Poison. Any substance—solid, liquid, or gas—that tends to impair health or cause death when introduced into the body or onto the skin surface. (Ch. 27)

Poison-control centers. A nationwide network of centers that have been set up in and around large cities to provide assistance about poison and where to go for help. (Ch. 27)

Poisonous. The characteristic of a chemical substance that can cause poor health, permanent injury, or death. (Ch. 27)

Poliomyelitis (poe-lee-oh-my-uh-**lite**-us). An infectious disease caused by viruses that enter the body through the mouth, reach the bloodstream through the stomach or lungs, and then attack the central nervous system; also known as polio. (Ch. 14)

Polyunsaturated (paul-ee-un-**satch**-uh-rate-ed) **fat.** A fat in which the fatty acid has room for four or more additional hydrogen atoms. (Ch. 8)

Pons (**pahnz**). A mass of nerve fibers that serves primarily as a pathway for nerve traits passing to and from the cerebrum. (Ch. 14)

Pooling. A condition that can occur during exercise if the leg muscles suddenly relax and the blood collects in the extremities instead of going back to the heart; this condition can cause lightheadedness, even fainting. (Ch. 2)

Pores. Tiny holes in the skin that open to release perspiration. (Ch. 3)

Posterior pituitary lobe. A lobe of the pituitary gland that secretes the antidiuretic hormone and the oxytocin hormone. (Ch. 16)

Prematurely. Before its time. (Ch. 3)

Premenstrual syndrome (PMS). A variety of symptoms that some females experience before their menstrual periods, including nervous tension, anxiety, irritability, bloating, depression, mood swings, and fatigue. (Ch. 17)

Prescription (pre-**scrip**-shun). A physician's written order to a pharmacist to give a certain medicine to a patient. (Ch. 10)

Prescription drugs. Drugs that are given by a physician's order. (Ch. 10)

Pressure-point technique. The technique of applying pressure to the main artery supplying blood to the affected limb. (Ch. 27)

Preventive agents. A group of cardiovascular drugs that works to prevent such conditions as high blood pressure, blood clots, and the development of fatty deposits in the blood vessels. (Ch. 10)

Primary care. Care that a patient seeks on his or her own. (Ch. 24)

Priorities. What is important to a person. (Ch. 6)

Problem solving. Making decisions. (Ch. 5)

Process. The procedures or steps involved in developing a skill. (Ch. 5)

Progesterone (pro-**jes**-ter-rone). A female sex hormone. (Ch. 16, 22)

Prostate cancer. Cancer of the prostate gland. (Ch. 7)

Prostate gland (**pros**-tate **gland**). The gland that secretes a fluid to mix with the sperm to form ejaculatory fluid, or semen. *See* Semen. (Ch. 17)

Protein (**pro**-teen). A nutrient that helps build and maintain all body tissues. (Ch. 8)

Protozoans (**prote**-uh-zoe-uns). Single-celled organisms that are larger and have a more complex cellular structure than bacteria and cause malaria, African sleeping sickness, and amebic dysentery; also called protozoas. (Ch. 29)

Psoriasis (suh-**rye**-uh-sis). An ailment in which red patches appear on the skin, followed by the skin's turning white and flaking off. (Ch. 3)

Psychiatrist (sigh-**ki**-ah-trist). A specialist who deals with mental, emotional, and behavioral disorders of the mind. (Ch. 7, 24)

Psychoactive drugs. Drugs that affect the nervous system. *See* Depressants; Hallucinogens; Narcotics; Stimulants. (Ch. 13)

Psychoanalysis (sigh-koh-uh-**nal**-uh-sis). A therapy that a psychiatrist uses with a patient for a one-to-one analysis of the patient's life, particularly his or her early life, to ascertain the early roots of a mental problem. (Ch. 7)

Psychological fatigue. The most common type of fatigue, which is brought on by mental reactions. (Ch. 6)

Psychological dependence. A condition in which a drug user becomes mentally dependent on a drug. (Ch. 10)

Psychosomatic (sigh-koh-so-**mat**-tick). A type of illness that can occur from social or personal situations causing anxiety, frustration, or tension, and triggering the stress response, which may lead to the development of physical ailments; literally mind–body. (Ch. 6)

Psychotherapy (sigh-koh-**ther**-uh-pea). Discussion by a patient and psychiatrist aimed at bringing out the problem, understanding it, and deriving a possible solution. (Ch. 7)

Psychotic (sigh-**kah**-tick). A condition in which a person's perception of reality is so distorted that he or she is unable to function properly in the environment. (Ch. 7)

Puberty (pew-burt-ee). The period of time when physical development, specifically the development of secondary sex characteristics, begins. (Ch. 22)

Pubic lice. Parasites that feed on tiny human blood vessels, usually around the body hair; often classified as a sexually transmitted disease. (Ch. 30)

Pulled muscle. A condition that occurs when the large muscle or tendon that connects the muscle to the bone is separated or torn from its point of attachment. *See* Torn muscle. (Ch. 2)

Pulmonary (pull-mah-ner-ee) artery. An artery that carries the oxygenated blood from the heart to the lungs. (Ch. 18)

Pulmonary edema (pull-mah-ner-ee eh-dee-muh). A condition that occurs when fluid builds up in the air sacs of the lungs. (Ch. 32)

Pulmonary embolism. A clot blocking the pulmonary vein that carries blood from the lungs to the heart. (Ch. 18)

Pulmonary emphysema (pull-mah-ner-ee em-fah-zee-muh). A disorder of the air sacs of the lungs through which oxygen is absorbed into the body. (Ch. 11)

Pulmonary vein. A vein that carries blood back to the heart from the lungs. (Ch. 18)

Pulp. A very sensitive, living tissue inside the tooth. (Ch. 4)

Pulse recovery rate. The rate at which the heart beats following activity. (Ch. 2)

Puncture (punk-sher). A type of wound produced by an object's piercing the skin (bullets, pins, nail, splinters), with limited external bleeding; may involve potential internal damage to organs, with an increased possibility of infection, such as tetanus. *See* Tetanus. (Ch. 27)

Pupil. The black circle in the center of the iris of the eye; actually, a round hole through which light passes. (Ch. 4)

Pyorrhea (pie-or-ree-uh). An inflammation of the membrane that covers the bony sockets of the teeth; also known as periodontitis. (Ch. 4)

Pyrogens (pie-ruh-jens). Poisons that invading bacteria manufacture and that cause fever by affecting the body's temperature-control centers. (Ch. 29)

Quackery. The practices of a dishonest medicine promoter. (Ch. 23)

Rabies (ray-beez). A virus disease of the nervous system that eventually causes madness and death. Dogs, squirrels, and rats are the common carriers of this disease. (Ch. 27)

Radiation. An X-ray treatment often used in the treatment of cancer by means of cobalt units. *See* Cobalt units. (Ch. 31)

Radioactive. The type of waste products produced in nuclear fission, which changes the nuclei of atoms and causes them to give off radiation, posing serious health and environmental problems. (Ch. 33)

Rape. Sexual intercourse without a person's consent, brought on through threats, force, or sometimes, violence. (Ch. 21)

Rapid eye movements (REM). Fast movement of the closed eyes during sleep. (Ch. 14)

Rationalization. An attempt to justify one's actions with an excuse rather than admitting to one's failure or mistake. (Ch. 7)

RDA. *See* Recommended Dietary Allowances. (Ch. 8)

Reaction time. A person's response to stimuli. (Ch. 1)

Reactivity (ree-ack-tiv-uh-tee). A dangerous characteristic of a hazardous waste that causes the waste to react in some way when exposed to air or water or to shock or heat. (Ch. 32)

Receptors. Special sensory neurons. (Ch. 14)

Recessive gene. The unexpressed gene in a pair of genes. (Ch. 21)

Recommended Dietary Allowances (RDA). A guide that reflects the latest information about food and the body's need for certain nutrients. (Ch. 8)

Recuperation (ree-koo-pur-ray-shun). The act of restoring; recovering strength or health. (Ch. 1)

Recycled. Used again; often applied to solid wastes that can be re-formed in some way. (Ch. 32)

Red blood cells. Cells that are manufactured by red bone marrow and carry hemoglobin; also called red corpuscles. (Ch. 18)

Red bone marrow. An agent that produces red corpuscles and most of the white corpuscles of the blood. (Ch. 15)

Red corpuscles. *See* Red blood cells. (Ch. 18)

Reflex (ree-fleks). A spontaneous response of the body to a stimulus. (Ch. 14)

Reflex arc. The nerve chain of sensory and motor neurons involved in a reflex action. (Ch. 14)

Regression. The act of retreating to an earlier time that seems less threatening and requires less responsibility. (Ch. 7)

Reproductive system. The body systems in the male and female that are responsible for the reproduction of offspring. (Ch. 17)

Rescue breathing. See *artificial* respiration. (Ch. 28)

Resident bacteria. Bacteria that live in the mouth and intestines and on the skin and help to protect a person from harmful bacteria. (Ch. 29)

Respiration (res-pur-ray-shun). The process by which gases, oxygen, and carbon dioxide are exchanged in the lungs. (Ch. 18)

Resting rate. The metabolic rate when one is in a resting state. (Ch. 1)

Retina (reh-tin-uh). The third layer of the wall of the eyeball. (Ch. 4)

Rheumatoid (rue-muh-toid) arthritis. The most serious type of arthritis, in which a disabling inflammation of the joints occurs. (Ch. 31)

Rh factors. Certain protein factors present in the blood of about 85% of the population. (Ch. 18)

Rhinoviruses (rye-no-vie-rus-ez). Viruses that cause about 50%

of all colds by attacking the cells in the nasal passages; they tend to cause colds in the summer and fall. (Ch. 29)

Rickettsias (rik-**et**-see-uhs). Organisms that are considered intermediate between a virus and a bacterium. (Ch. 29)

Ringworm. An infection of the scalp caused by a fungus that lives off dead skin. (Ch. 3, 29)

Risk. A chance of encountering danger or harm. (Ch. 26)

Risk factor. A characteristic that has been shown to increase the chances of getting heart disease. (Ch. 31)

Rods. Light-sensitive receptors located in the retina that are cylindrical, register light and darkness, and are used in dim light. They contain a chemical called visual purple, which makes seeing in dim light possible. (Ch. 4)

Role confusion. Difficulty in attaining a clear sense of one's own identity. (Ch. 22)

Root. A major part of a tooth that is located inside the gum. (Ch. 4)

Root canal. The part of the pulp cavity that lies in the root of a tooth. (Ch. 4)

Rubella (rue-**bell**-uh). German measles. (Ch. 21)

Rupture. *See* Hernia. (Ch. 2, 17)

Safe drug. An FDA-approved drug. (Ch. 10)

Safety-conscious attitude. An attitude in which a person believes that he or she can prevent accidents by putting into action the rules that he or she knows. (Ch. 26)

Safety consciousness. Being aware of safety. (Ch. 26)

Saliva (suh-**lie**-vuh). A mixture of water and various chemicals formed in the mouth. (Ch. 19)

Salivary (**sal**-uh-ver-ee) **glands.** The glands that secrete saliva. *See* Saliva. (Ch. 19)

Salmonella (sal-mah-**nell**-uh). Bacteria that are mainly present in the meat of sick animals, raw or improperly pasteurized milk,

infected egg products, fertilizer, and foods contaminated by rats or flies. (Ch. 19)

S-A node. *See* Sinoatrial node. (Ch. 18)

Saprophytes (**sap**-ruh-fites). Bacteria that digest nonliving food materials such as milk and meat. (Ch. 29)

Sarcoma (sar-**koh**-muh) **cancers.** Cancers that begin in the tissue that forms the body's supporting structures. (Ch. 31)

Saturated (**satch**-uh-rate-ed) **fatty acid.** A fatty acid that has as many hydrogen atoms as possible attached to its carbon chain. (Ch. 8)

Scabies (**skay**-bees). A condition in which tiny parasitic mites burrow under the skin. Although classified as a sexually transmitted disease, scabies is not always acquired through sexual contact. (Ch. 30)

Schizophrenia (skit-zoe-**free**-nee-uh). A mental disorder and the most common type of psychosis; literally, split mind. (Ch. 7)

Sclera (**sklay**-ruh). The white, tough membrane that helps the eye keep its spherical shape and helps to protect the eye's delicate inner structure. (Ch. 4)

Sclerosis (skler-**roh**-sis). A hardening. (Ch. 31)

Scrotum (**skro**-tum). The sac that encloses the testicles. (Ch. 17)

Sebum (**see**-bum). An oil secreted by oil glands that makes the skin soft and pliable. Excess sebum can cause acne. (Ch. 3)

Secondary sex characteristics. The characteristics that develop during puberty, including body hair and the development of breasts in the female and muscles in the male. (Ch. 22)

Second-degree burns. Burns that result from very deep sunburn and contact with hot liquid and destroy the epidermis and part of the dermis. (Ch. 27)

Sedative (**sed**-uh-tive). A substance that depresses or quiets the central nervous system. (Ch. 12)

Sedentary (**sed**-en-ter-ee). Inactive living or a way of life that is mostly spent sitting down. (Ch. 1) (Ch. 1)

Seizure. A physical reaction to a sudden burst of nerve impulses in the brain. (Ch. 14)

Self-concept. The sum total of how a person views himself or herself. (Ch. 5)

Semen (**see**-mun). Seminal fluid. (Ch. 17)

Semicircular canals. Three canals located in the inner ear and set at right angles to one another that are responsible for a person's sense of balance. (Ch. 4)

Seminal vesicles (**sem**-uh-nul **ves**-uh-kuls). The two pouches that secrete a fluid which mixes with the sperm to make them mobile and to provide nourishment. (Ch. 17)

Senile (**seen**-ile). Exhibiting a loss of mental abilities; usually characteristic of old age. (Ch. 30)

Sense organ functions. Functions that allow one to use the senses to their optimal, or fullest, levels. (Ch. 1)

Sensitized. Made receptive. (Ch. 3)

Sensory deafness. A hearing loss that occurs in the inner ear because of damage to the cochlea, auditory nerve, and/or part of the brain or because of continued exposure to high-intensity noise or because of tumors. (Ch. 4, 32)

Sensory neurons. The nerve cells that send impulses from special sensory nerve cells, called receptors, toward the central nervous system. (Ch. 14)

Serum hepatitis. A form of liver infection that results from a transfusion of contaminated human blood, from unclean needles used to administer drugs, from saliva, and from sexual activity. (Ch. 19)

Sexually transmitted disease (STD). A communicable disease that is spread from person to person through sexual contact; more commonly called a venereal disease, or VD. (Ch. 30)

Shaft. A thin area where bones narrow between the joint ends. (Ch. 15)

Shelf life. The length of time a drug can be kept before it becomes ineffective or dangerous. (Ch. 10)

Shock. A condition that results from a serious depression of the major vital functions. (Ch. 27)

Short bones. Bones such as those in the wrists and ankles that are made of soft material covered with a thin layer of harder bone. (Ch. 15)

Sickle-cell (sick-ul-sell) anemia. An inherited blood condition or disorder, resulting from a defect in the hemoglobin with red blood cells, which clump together and obstruct the flow of blood and oxygen to the tissues. (Ch. 18, 21)

Sidestream smoke. Second-hand smoke, or smoke inhaled by non-smokers. (Ch. 11, 21, 31)

Simmond's disease. A rare disease that causes premature aging, muscle weakness, and a wasting away of the body. (Ch. 16)

Simple carbohydrates. Foods, such as sugars, that provide energy but are high in calories. (Ch. 8)

Simple fractures. Injuries in which the broken bone does not protrude through the skin. (Ch. 15)

Sinoatrial (sigh-no-ay-tree-uhl) node (S-A node). A mass of specialized heart tissue in the right atrium that initiates each heartbeat, setting the pace for the heart; also called the pacemaker. (Ch. 18)

Sinuses (sigh-nus-ez). Air-filled spaces in the skull that open into the nasal cavity. (Ch. 18)

Situation. A certain position or set of circumstances at a given moment, and the first link in an accident chain. (Ch. 26)

Skull. A bony structure consisting of eight cranial bones that protects the brain. (Ch. 14)

Small intestine. A digestive organ that consists of the duodenum, the jejunum, and the ileum. The majority of the chemical breakdown of food takes place in the small intestine. (Ch. 19)

Smoke detector. A device that is placed on a ceiling and that sounds an alarm if smoke passes into it. (Ch. 26)

Smog. A blend of smoke and fog. (Ch. 32)

Smooth muscle. A muscle located in the gastrointestinal tract and blood vessels; sometimes called an unstriated muscle. (Ch. 15)

Snuff. *See* Dipping. (Ch. 11)

Socialization (sohsh-uh-luh-zay-shun). Participation in the processes particular to a cultural group. (Ch. 21)

Social worker. A person who provides a link between the medical service center and the client and his or her family. (Ch. 7)

Solar energy. Heat energy that sunlight produces as it strikes a surface. (Ch. 33)

Somatic (soh-mat-ick) division. One of the two divisions of the peripheral nervous system that includes sensory neurons and motor neurons. (Ch. 14)

Somatotropic (soh-mat-toe-tro-pik) hormone. A hormone that has a marked influence on muscles, kidneys, fat tissue, and the liver, and especially influences skeletal growth and height. (Ch. 16)

Sound waves. Vibrations in the air that are caused by anything that moves and that must reach the organ of Corti before a person can hear. (Ch. 4)

Spasms (spaz-ums). Contractions. (Ch. 18)

Specialty cigarettes. Cigarettes that are prepared with tobacco and other ingredients, such as cloves. (Ch. 11)

Sperm cell. The male cell that unites with a female egg cell to form a fertilized egg cell. (Ch. 17)

Sphincter (sfink-ter) muscle. A muscle that consists of rings of muscular fiber. (Ch. 19)

Sphygmomanometer (sfig-moh-mah-nom-uh-ter). An instrument used to measure blood pressure. (Ch. 18)

Spinal cord. A nerve cable that goes from the brain down to the spinal column. (Ch. 14)

Spinal meninges (spy-nul men-in-jez). Three membranes that cover and protect the spinal cord. (Ch. 14)

Spirilla (spy-ril-uh). Disease-causing bacteria that are spiral, or twisted, like a corkscrew. (Ch. 29)

Spirochete (spy-roh-keet). A small bacterium that causes syphilis. (Ch. 30)

Sprain. A condition caused by a violent, sudden stretching of a joint or ligament. (Ch. 2)

Stabilizers. Additives placed in food products to change the texture of some food. (Ch. 9)

Stapes (stay-peez). A stirrup-shaped bone that attaches to the inner ear and is the smallest bone in the human body; also called stirrup. (Ch. 4)

Staphylococcus (staf-uh-low-kock-us). A disease-causing bacterium that may be clustered like grapes and is the number one food poisoner in the United States. (Ch. 19, 29)

Starchy foods. *See* Complex carbohydrates. (Ch. 8)

STD. *See* Sexually transmitted disease. (Ch. 30)

Sterility (stuh-rill-uh-tee). The inability to reproduce. In the male, a condition wherein the sperm is weak or malformed or is unable to join an egg cell. In the female, a condition that occurs because of failure to ovulate, the blocking of Fallopian tubes, or endometriosis. (Ch. 17, 30)

Steroids (stir-oids). A group of chemical compounds secreted by the adrenal cortex that affect numerous bodily functions. (Ch. 16)

Stethoscope (steth-uh-skope). An instrument designed for hearing sounds produced by the body. (Ch. 18)

Sties (steyes). Eye infections caused by bacteria that lodge in the glands of the eyelids. (Ch. 4)

Stigma (**stig**-mah). A blot on a person's good name. (Ch. 7)

Stimulants (**stim**-you-lunts). A group of drugs that alter and speed up the nervous system by making a person feel more alert and active, reducing distractibility in hyperactive children, and suppressing appetite. (Ch. 10, 13, 14)

Stimulated tactily. Touched. (Ch. 3)

Stomach. A digestive organ that stores food until it is ready to enter the small intestine, mixes the food and gastric juices to form chyme, and controls the rate at which food enters the small intestine. (Ch. 19)

Strabismus (struh-**biz**-mus). *See* Crossed eyes. (Ch. 4)

Strain. A condition occurring in the muscles when they are overworked. (Ch. 2)

Streptococcus (strep-tuh-**kock**-us). A disease-causing bacterium that may appear in long chains of bacteria. (Ch. 29)

Stress. The body's general response to any situation. (Ch. 6)

Stress fractures. Injuries in which a bone is strained in some way, causing a weakness in it. Such fractures occur through the repeated use of some part of the body. (Ch. 15)

Stressor. Something that initiates a stress response. (Ch. 6)

Striated (**strye**-ate-ed) **muscle.** Skeletal muscle. (Ch. 15)

Stroke. A condition that occurs when a thrombus or an embolus blocks an artery leading to the brain, thus blocking the brain's supply of oxygen and damaging brain cells. (Ch. 31)

Stroke volume. The amount of blood pumped out of the heart with each beat. (Ch. 15)

Subcutaneous (sub-kew-**tain**-nee-us) **layer.** The deepest layer of skin, which is made up of fatty tissue and serves as the body's natural insulation against heat and cold. (Ch. 3)

Sublingual (sub-**lin**-gue-wul) **glands.** A pair of salivary glands located under the tongue. (Ch. 19)

Submandibular (sub-man-**dib**-you-lur) **glands.** A pair of salivary glands located below the jaw. (Ch. 19)

Suicide. The taking of one's own life. (Ch. 7)

Sulfa (**sull**-fah) **drugs.** A large family of germ killers that are made from certain chemical substances. (Ch. 10)

Sulfur dioxide (**sul**-fur die-**ach**-side). A poisonous gas that is a product of the burning of fossil fuels such as oil or coal. (Ch. 32)

Sun-blocking agents. Opaque substances that deflect ultraviolet rays. (Ch. 3)

Sunscreens. Products that absorb the stronger, midday rays of the sun that are the cause of sunburn. (Ch. 3)

Support system. A group of people with whom another person can find support, such as family, friends, a church person, teachers, employers, or other relatives. (Ch. 6)

Suspensory ligaments (suh-**spen**-suh-ree **lig**-uh-mints). Ligaments that hold the lens of the eyes and are connected to the ciliary muscles. (Ch. 4)

Sympathetic (sym-pah-**thet**-ick) **system.** One of two parts of the autonomic nervous system; the part that responds to the body's needs during increased activities and in emergencies. (Ch. 14)

Synapse (**sin**-aps). The junction between the axon end of one neuron and the dendrite of another neuron. (Ch. 14)

Synovial (cy-**no**-vee-ul) **fluid.** A fluid secreted by the synovial membrane that lubricates the ends of the bones within the joints. (Ch. 15)

Synovial membrane. The inner lining of the cavities of joint capsules that secretes synovial fluid. (Ch. 15, 31)

Synthetically (sin-**thet**-ick-uh-lee). Composed from laboratory chemicals. (Ch. 13)

Syphilis (**sif**-uh-lus). A sexually transmitted disease that attacks many parts of the body and is caused by a small bacterium called a spirochete. (Ch. 30)

Systems. Collections of organs that work together to perform one overall function. (Ch. 21)

Systolic (**sis**-tahl-ik) **pressure.** The point in heart action when arterial pressure is greatest. (Ch. 18)

Tampon. Sanitary protection worn inside the vagina. (Ch. 17)

Tar. A thick, dark liquid obtained from burning tobacco. (Ch. 11)

Target pulse rate. The rate at which the heart must work for exercise to be aerobic. (Ch. 2)

Tartar. A very hard substance that irritates the underlying bones of the mouth, as well as the surrounding gums of the teeth; also called calculus. (Ch. 4)

Taste buds. Sensitive areas on the tongue that consist of about 9,000 nerve endings that are most heavily concentrated around the papillae. (Ch. 4, 19)

T cells. A type of lymphocyte, produced in the bone marrow that travels to the thymus gland, and then ends up with the B cells in the bloodstream, where the T cells attack an invading substance or organism directly by the process of phagocytosis. (Ch. 29)

Temporal bone. The hardest bone in the human body, which lines the inner two-thirds of the auditory canal. (Ch. 4)

Temporal lobe. A lobe of the cerebral hemispheres that contains the sense of hearing and possibly the senses of taste and smell. (Ch. 14)

Tendinitis (ten-**duh**-nite-us). An injury that occurs when a tendon is stretched or torn. (Ch. 2)

Tendons (**ten**-dons). Strong parallel fibers massed tightly together that join muscle to bone, or muscle to muscle. (Ch. 15)

Tertiary (**ter**-she-err-ee). A type of health care that is needed when the patient's condition requires advanced equipment or treatment. (Ch. 24)

Testes (**tes**-teez). *See* Testicles. (Ch. 16, 17)

Testicles (**tes**-ti-kuls). Two small glands that are a major part of the male reproductive system because sperm are produced in them; also called testes. (Ch. 17)

Testicular (tes-**tick**-you-lar) **cancer.** A common cancer in males; hard lumps, or nodules, on the testes may be a sign. (Ch. 17)

Testimonial (tes-tuh-**mow**-nee-ul). A person's enthusiastic recommendation of a product. (Ch. 23)

Testosterone (tes-**tos**-ter-rone). The male sex hormone. (Ch. 16, 22)

Tetanus (**tet**-un-us). A serious, infectious disease caused by bacteria, normally living in the soil, that enter the body through a wound and produce a poison that affects muscles and nerves in the body; also called lockjaw. (Ch. 27, 29)

Tetany (**tet**-un-ee). Muscle spasms that can be quite painful. (Ch. 16)

Tetracyclines (tet-rah-**sigh**-kleens). Antibiotics, less effective than penicillins, that are used to treat infection. (Ch. 10)

Thalamus (**thal**-uh-mus). One of the two parts of the midbrain; a large mass of gray matter containing many nuclei that function as relay stations for incoming sensory impulses. (Ch. 14)

Therapies (**ther**-uh-peas). Treatment techniques. (Ch. 7)

Thermal (**thur**-mul) **pollution.** A situation that occurs when nuclear-power plants return the water they use to the rivers and streams before cooling it down; also called heat pollution. (Ch. 33)

Thermal trainer. An instrument used to record the feedback of changes in skin temperature as a result of blood flow. (Ch. 29)

Thickeners. Additives placed in some food products to change their texture. (Ch. 9)

Third-degree burns. Burns caused by flames, burning clothing, immersion in hot water, and electricity. Both the epidermis and the dermis are destroyed. (Ch. 27)

Thrombosis (throm-**boh**-sis). The presence or formation of a blood clot within a blood vessel. (Ch. 18)

Thrombus (**throm**-bus). A blood clot. (Ch. 18, 31)

Thymus (**thie**-mus) **gland.** A gland that is located behind the breastbone, near the heart, and whose functions are not fully known but may play an important part in the body's immune system. (Ch. 16)

Thyroid (**thy**-roid) **gland.** The largest gland of the endocrine system; it produces the hormone thyroxine. (Ch. 16)

Thyroid-stimulating hormone (TSH). A hormone that regulates both the size and activity of the thyroid gland. (Ch. 16)

Thyroxine (thy-**rok**-sin). A hormone produced by the thyroid gland that affects all tissues in the body by causing certain chemical reactions. (Ch. 16)

Time-management skills. A person's effective ways of arranging his or her time. (Ch. 6)

Tissues. Cells that do similar work together. (Ch. 21)

Tolerance. In the case of drugs, a condition in which the body becomes used to a drug's effects. (Ch. 10)

Toothache. A painful condition that occurs when a tooth becomes inflamed because of cavities or a disease. (Ch. 4)

Tooth decay. The most common noncommunicable disease of the digestive system. (Ch. 19)

Torn cartilage (**kart**-uh-ledge). An injury in which the strong connective tissue has been pulled out from the bone. (Ch. 2)

Torn muscle. A condition that occurs when the large muscle or tendon that connects the muscle to the bone is separated or torn from its point of attachment. (Ch. 2)

Toxic. Poisonous. (Ch. 10)

Toxic hepatitis. A condition that results from exposure to certain chemicals as they enter the body by being swallowed, inhaled, injected, or absorbed through the skin. (Ch. 29)

Toxicity (tahk-**sis**-ut-ee). A dangerous characteristic of a hazardous waste that causes the waste to release poisonous substances into the air. (Ch. 32)

Toxins (**tahk**-suns). Poisons that some bacteria produce to cause a disease. (Ch. 29)

Toxoids (**tahk**-soids). Treated toxins that stimulate the production of antibodies and establish active immunity against diphtheria and tetanus. (Ch. 29)

Trachea (**tray**-key-uh). The windpipe, which extends into the chest and divides into two branches called bronchi, or bronchial tubes. (Ch. 18)

Traction. A procedure for treating an injury in which weights are used to balance out parts of the spinal cord and to give relief from pain. (Ch. 14)

Trade name. The name that a manufacturer assigns to a drug or product. (Ch. 10)

Tranquilizers (**tran**-quill-lize-ers). A group of drugs that alter the nervous system and are used to relieve anxiety or tension, and to relieve insomnia due to anxiety and tension. These sedatives calm the emotions without changing the users ability to stay alert or think clearly. (Ch. 10, 13)

Transmission deafness. A hearing problem in which sound waves are prevented from reaching the eardrum or in which sound waves are not being transmitted to the cochlea. (Ch. 4)

Trichinosis (trik-uh-no-sus). A disease caused by an intestinal roundworm and transmitted primarily from eating improperly cooked meat—specifically, pork. (Ch. 29)

Trichomoniasis (trik-uh-mah-**nigh**-uh-sus). A sexually transmitted vaginal infection that is caused by a protozoan. It usually occurs at the end of a menstrual period, with symptoms of an odorous discharge, genital itching, and a burning sensation during urination from urethra and bladder infections. (Ch. 17, 30)

Triglyceride (try-**gliss**-uh-ride). Three fatty acids attached to one glycerol molecule. (Ch. 8)

Trihalomethanes (try-hal-uh-**meth**-anes) **(THMS).** Cancer-producing substances that are widely found in drinking water. (Ch. 25)

Trypsin (**trip**-sin). An enzyme that breaks down partially digested proteins during digestion. (Ch. 19)

Tuberculosis (too-ber-kue-**low**-sis). An infectious bacterial disease of the lungs characterized by the growth of tubercules, or sores, on the lungs. (Ch. 18)

Tumor. A mass of tissue that can be benign or malignant. (Ch. 31)

Turbidity (ter-**bid**-ut-ee). The tiny particles suspended in most water that comes from surface sources. (Ch. 32)

Ulcer (**ul**-sir). An open sore in the skin or in the mucous membrane; also, an open sore in the stomach lining caused by the increased flow of gastric juices. (Ch. 12, 19)

Ultra Imager. A machine that translates high-frequency sound waves, called ultrasound, reflected from heart tissues into an image that appears on a video screen. (Ch. 18)

Ultrasonography (ul-tra-**son**-og-ruh-fee). A method of investigating the health of a fetus by using sound waves to project light images on a screen. (Ch. 21)

Ultraviolet rays. Light rays that come from the sun. (Ch. 3)

Umbilical (um-**bill**-uh-kuhl) **cord.** A cord that connects an embryo with the placenta. (Ch. 21)

Underweight. Below normal or average weight. (Ch. 9)

Unit pricing. A method of pricing that shows the cost per ounce or per count of a product, and also tells how much different sizes of the same product cost per unit. (Ch. 8, 23)

Universal donor. A person who has type O blood and can give blood to any other person with any type of blood. (Ch. 18)

Universal recipient. A person who has type AB-positive blood and can receive any type of blood. (Ch. 18)

Unsafe act. An act stemming from a person's being so preoccupied that he or she does not take safety precautions; also the third link in the accident chain. (Ch. 26)

Unsafe habit. Putting oneself in danger by taking careless risks; also the second link in the accident chain. (Ch. 26)

Unsaturated (un-**satch**-uh-rate-ed) **fats.** Fats with carbon molecules that each hold only one hydrogen atom. (Ch. 8)

Unstriated (un-**strye**-ate-ed) **muscle.** *See* Smooth muscle. (Ch. 15)

Urea (you-**ree**-uh). The less toxic and chief solid substance in urine. (Ch. 19)

Uremia (you-**ree**-me-uh). A severe disease that occurs when the kidneys slow down in their function of filtering wastes from the blood and urea and other wastes then build up in the body and poison it. (Ch. 19)

Ureter (**you**-ree-tur). A tube that leads from each kidney to the bladder. (Ch. 19)

Urethra (you-**ree**-thruh). A tube-like organ that connects with the bladder. In the male, it also connects with the vas deferens. (Ch. 17, 19)

Uric (**you**-rik) **acid.** An acid found in urine. (Ch. 19)

Urine. The body's liquid waste material. (Ch. 19)

Uterine cancer. The cancer, or malignancy, of the uterus, diagnosed by a Pap smear. (Ch. 17)

Uterus (**you**-tur-us). A small, muscular pear-shaped organ,

about the size of a fist, where a fertilized egg will grow in the female. (Ch. 17)

Uvula (**you**-vuh-luh). A small, muscular flap of tissue suspended at the back of the mouth that closes the opening to the nasal passages. (Ch. 19)

Vaccination (vak-suh-**nay**-shun). The process of injecting vaccine into the body. (Ch. 29)

Vaccines (vak-**seens**). Disease-prevention drugs that cause the body to develop antibodies to fight disease-causing germs, thus making the body immune to a disease. These preparations are composed of dead or weakened viruses. (Ch. 10, 29)

Vagina (vuh-**jine**-uh). A muscular, very elastic tube in the female that serves as a passageway to the uterus; also called the birth canal. (Ch. 17)

Vaginitis (vaj-uh-**nite**-us). A sexually transmitted common vaginal infection in females. (Ch. 17, 30)

Valium. A trademark for the tranquilizer diazepam; the most widely prescribed medicine in the world. (Ch. 10)

Values. Guides for how a person lives—what is important to a person. (Ch. 5)

Valves. Flaplike structures that are designed to keep blood flowing in the proper direction. (Ch. 18)

Varicose (**var**-uh-kose) **veins.** Swollen and enlarged veins. (Ch. 18)

Vascular system. The system of vessels that transports the blood. (Ch. 18)

Vas deferens (vahs **def**-ur-enz). A tube that connects the epididymis at one end and the urethra at the other. (Ch. 17)

Vasodilators (**vah**-so-die-**late**-ors). One group of cardiovascular drugs that dilate the veins and arteries to increase blood and oxygen flow. (Ch. 10)

Veins. The vessels that carry the blood back to the heart. (Ch. 18)

Venereal (vuh-**neer**-ee-ul) **disease (VD).** A communicable disease that is spread from person to person through sexual contact; also called sexually transmitted disease. (Ch. 30)

Ventricle (**ven**-truh-kuhl). A lower chamber of the heart. (Ch. 18)

Ventricular (ven-**trik**-cue-lur) **fibrillation.** A usually fatal condition that occurs when fibrillation takes place in the ventricles, prohibiting the ventricles from pumping blood out of the heart. *See* Fibrillation. (Ch. 31)

Venules (**ven**-yules). Tiny branches of veins into which the capillaries lead. (Ch. 18)

Vestibule (**ves**-tuh-bule). The central part of the inner ear that contains tiny, baglike structures lined with hair cells that are called the utricle and the saccule. (Ch. 4)

Villi (**vil**-lie). Millions of finger-like projections that line the small intestine. (Ch. 19)

Virus (**vie**-rus). A germ that is the smallest known, simplest form of life. It has no nucleus, no cytoplasm, and no cell membrane, but does consist of nucleic acid, a complex chemical. (Ch. 29)

Vitamins. Substances containing compounds necessary for growth and the maintenance of life; classified into fat-soluble vitamins and water-soluble vitamins. (Ch. 8)

Vitiligo (vit-uh-**lee**-go). A skin condition caused by an absence of melanin in certain patches of skin. (Ch. 3)

Vitreous humor (**vit**-ree-us **hu**-mer). A glasslike, thick fluid found behind the lens that keeps the eyeball firm. (Ch. 4)

Vocal chords. Folds of stretched tissue that produce sound as air passes over them, causing a vibration. (Ch. 18)

Warming up. Stretching the muscles, preparing them for the exertion that is to come. (Ch. 2)

Wart. A small skin growth caused by a virus. (Ch. 3)

Water. Next to air, the most important substance for maintaining life. (Ch. 8)

Water pollution. The condition in which wastes accumulate to a point at which water's natural purification processes are unable to break down the wastes into harmless forms. (Ch. 32)

Water-soluble vitamins. Vitamins that dissolve in water; mainly vitamins C and B complex, which are found in fruits and vegetables. (Ch. 8)

Weight control. A person's attaining as near to his or her ideal weight as possible, and then staying at it. (Ch. 9)

Wellness. A way of living each day that includes choices and decisions based on healthy attitudes. (Ch. 1)

White blood cells. Cells that destroy invading disease bacteria; also called leukocytes. (Ch. 18)

Whitehead. An acne condition resulting from oil getting trapped in a pore. (Ch. 3)

Withdrawal. A condition that occurs when a drug user is addicted to a certain drug but does not take it; symptoms include negative, unpleasant physical or mental reactions. (Ch. 10)

Withdrawal symptoms. Negative, unpleasant physical or mental reactions caused by withdrawing from the use of an additive substance. *See* Delirium tremens. (Ch. 12)

Xiphoid (**zigh**-foid) **process.** The bony structure where the ribs come together to meet the breastbone. (Ch. 28)

Yeast infection. A vaginal infection caused by a fungus; signs include a thick, white discharge and genital itching. (Ch. 17)

Index

Genes, 376, 378–380
Geneticists, 377
Genetics, 377–381
  code, 379
  condition, 382
  disease, 274
  and disorders, 259, 263–266,
    382–385
Genital herpes, 540
Genital itching, 303–304
Genital sores/warts, 544
Germ, vitamin-rich, in flour, 140
Germ-laden food, 344
Germs, 38, 520–521. *See also* Bacteria;
    Viruses
Gerontologists, 398
Gigantism, 289
Gingivitis, 58
Glands
  adrenal, 101
  digestive, 335–336
  in the ears, 67
  and endocrine system, 286–293
  oil, 39–40
  pituitary, 102
  salivary, 331
  sweat, 40
Glaucoma, 64
Globulins, 180
Glomerulus, 338
Glucagon, 292, 336
Glucose, 141, 292, 336, 569
Glycogen, 139, 172, 177, 292
Glycerol, 143, 144
Goal setting, 94
Goiter, 290
Gonadotropic hormone, 288
Gonads, 288
Gonorrhea, 515, 535–537
Good Samaritan law, 507
Gout, 273
Government
  and environmentalists, 613
  insurance programs, 436
  and nuclear energy, 604
  role of, in conservation, 608
  regulatory bodies in, 604
  services for consumers, 422–426
Government, federal
  agencies, 615–616
  and health care, 448–450
  and health facilities, 430–433
Grand mal, 264
Granulocytes, 522
Gray matter, 252, 253
Greenhouse effect, 585
Grief, stages of, 403
Grooming, 38
Group practice, 436
Group therapy, 126, 127–129
Growth. *See also* Development
  emotional, 394–395
  physical, 395
  social, 395
  and teenage marriages, 368–369
  theories of, 389–391

Gums, 55, 56, 58
Gynecologist, 434
Gynecology, 304, 434

Habits, health, 85, 86
Hair, 37–38, 40, 45–46
  in ears, 67–69
Halitosis, 57, 59, 339
Hallucinogens, 225, 231, 239, 259
Handicap, 110
Hangnails, 46
Hashish, 232
Hazardous waste, 593–594
Hazards, 465
Headache, 101
Head injuries, 259
Head lice, 45
Headphones, 462
Healing, 34
Health
  careers in, *See* Careers
  and cigarettes, 197
  definition of, 3–5
  education, 3–4
  facilities, 429–431
  habits, 8–9, 81–82, 394
  insurance, 436–437, 439
  organizations, 444–452
  products, purchasing, 411–413
  promotion, 429
  resources, 429
  triangle, 5, 8
Health-care
  delivery, 429
  professional (choosing a), 435
  services, 125–129
  stages of, 432–433
Health and Human Services, Department of, 448–450
Health-Maintenance Organizations, 436–437
Health Resources Administration (HRA), 449
Health Services Administration, 449
Hearing, binaural, 70
  and noise pollution, 597, 600
Heart
  action, and adrenal glands, 291
  attack, definition of, 551–552
  chamber, 5, 309
  defibrillator, 555
  disease, 161
  disease, preventing, 559
  disease, treating, 556–560
  drugs that affect the, 180–181
  and exercise, 21, 26, 28
  heartburn, 339–340
Heartbeat, 26
Heart-lung machine, 558
Heart-valve surgery, 558–560
Heat
  cramps, 32–33, 492
  exhaustion, 33
  and fire, 467
  in home, 606, 609. *See also* Solar
    heating

  for muscle relaxation, 31, 32
  pollution, 603–604
Heaters, space, 468
Heatstroke, 33
Helping Hand Services, Inc., 496
Hemoglobins, 198, 314
Hemophilia, 316–317
Hemorrhage, cerebral, 554
Hemp plant, 232
Hepatitis, 342, 517, 531, 591
Hereditary diseases. *See also* Genetics
Heredity, 85, 376–386
Hernias, 32, 298–299
Heroin, 229–231
Herpes simplex, 44, 516, 540–541
Hertz, 72
Hiccups, 322
High blood pressure, 157, 161
High-density lipoproteins, 143
High-risk behaviors, 230
High-risk group, 230
Highway Action Coalition, 614
Hippocrates, 124
Histamine, 189
Holistic health center, 439
Home, safety in the, 465–471
Home health aide, 496
Homes, nursing, 431–433
Hope, 402, 415
Hopelessness, 125
Hormones
  and acne, 43
  and cholesterol, 143
  and emotional changes, 87
  function of, 286–293
  and marijuana, 236
  in reproductive system, 392
Hospice, 440
Hospitals, 430–433
Host, 514
  intermediary, 519, 520
Hotline services, consumer, 419
Houston Ship Channel, 613
Human Development Services, Office of, 449
Human immunodeficiency virus, 542
Humidity, 585
Hunger, 82–83, 135–136
Hurricanes, 493
Hydrocarbons, 580–581
Hydrochloric acid (HCl), 189, 333, 341
Hydrogen, 139, 144–145
Hydrophobia, 89
Hydrostatic weighing, 161–162
Hyperactive, 182
Hyperaroused, 227
Hyperopia, 64
Hypertension, 157, 549–550. *See also*
    Blood pressure
Hyperventilation, 322
Hypnotics, 182, 229
Hypochondria, 114, 125

Photosynthesis, 585
Physical appearance, 38
Physical dependence, on drugs, 183
Physical fatigue, 103
Physical fitness, 19. *See also* Exercise
Physical growth, in adolescence, 393
Physical health, 4–5, 91–92
Physical needs, 82–84
Physical therapy, 31, 34
Physician, 126–127, 183, 433–434
Pia mater, 252
Pimple, 43
Pinched nerve, 259
Pinch test, 162
Pineal gland, 287–288
Pinkeye, 65
Pipe smokers, 199
Pitch, 72
Pituitary gland, 101, 255, 287–290, 293, 392
Placebo, 415–416
Placenta, 374
Planning, stress management, 108
Plant foods, 148–149
Plant life
  and acid rain, 587
  and air pollution, 581–582
  and carbon dioxide, 584–585
  and thermal pollution, 603–604
  and water pollution, 590
Plaque, 56, 59, 550
Plasma, 313–314
Plastic surgeon, 435
Plateau, 166
Platelets, 313, 315
Pleurisy, 325
PMS (premenstrual syndrome), 303
Pneumonia, 323, 515
Podiatrist, 50
Podiatry, 50
Poison-control centers, 484–485
Poisoning, 483–487
  first aid for, 484–485
  food, 343–345
  lead, 583–584
Poisonous gas, 197
Poisonous snakes, 486
Poisonous substances, and the liver, 182
Poisons
  and bacteria, 515
  and caffeine, 226, 234
  food, 343–346
  and home safety, 465–466
  and immunogens, 522
  and marijuana, 233
  toxic substances as, 595–596
Polio, 260–263, 451, 525
Pollutant Standards Index (PSI), 580–581
Pollutants, air, control of, 613
Pollution
  air, 580–587, 613
  automobile, 582–583

control of, 611–616
  noise, 597–598, 600
  photochemical, 581, 582
  thermal, 603–604
  water, 611–614
Polyunsaturated fat, 144–145
Pons, 254–255
Pooling, of blood, 24
Pores, 40
Posterior lobe, 288, 289
Posture, 38, 47–51, 320
Potassium, 33, 171, 291
Poultry, 153, 425
Practical Nurse Education and Service, 441
Pregnancy, 198, 304, 385. *See also* Reproductive system; Genetics
Premenstrual syndrome (PMS), 303
Prenatal care, 373–374
Prescription drugs, 185, 190–193, 544. *See also* Medicines
Preservatives, 173
President's Council on Physical Fitness and Sports, 28–29
Pressure-point technique, 481, 482
Preventive agents, 181
Price, of health products, 411
Primary care, 432, 434
Priorities, establishing, 107–108
Private insurance programs, 436–437
Private practice, 433
Problems, facing, 119–122
Problems, mental health, 125–129
Problem solving, 92–96
Product safety, 422–423
Professions, helping, and mental health, 125–129
Progesterone, 289, 293, 392
Projection, 119
Proprietary health facilities, 430
Prostate cancer, 298–299
Prostate gland, 297
Protein
  and athletics, 173
  in blood, 314–315
  and diet, 169
  and digestion, 333, 335, 336
  in foods, 137, 140, 147–149, 153
  and genes (DNA bases), 379, 522
  and lipoproteins, 143
  molecules, in chromosomes, 376
  in muscle, 277
Protozoans, 304, 514, 518, 544
Psilocybin, 231
Psoriasis, 44
Psychiatric social workers, 125, 128–129
Psychiatrists, 125, 126, 435
Psychiatry, 124–126, 434
Psychiatry, and Neurology, Board of, 126
Psychoactive drugs, 225–237
Psychoanalysis, 126
Psychological dependence, on drugs, 183
Psychological fatigue, 103–104

Psychological reactions, to marijuana, 233–235
Psychologist, 95, 125, 127
Psychology, 95
Psychosis, 114, 116–117
Psychosomatic, 104
Psychotherapy, 124, 126, 127
Psychotic, 116
Puberty, 296, 298, 392
Pubic lice, 544
Public health nurse, 545
Public Health Service 424, 448, 449–450
Pulmonary edema, 582
Pulmonary embolism, 319
Pulmonary emphysema, 198, 326–327
Pulp, 55
Pulse
  carotid, 505
  checking for, 505
  rate, 26–27
  recovery rate, 21, 26
Puncture wounds, 479, 486
Pupil, of eye, 62
Purging, 170–171
Pyorrhea, 58
Pyrogens, 521
Pyrophobia, 89

Quaaludes, 229
Quack, 414
Quackery, 414–416, 568
Quality, product, 412

Rabies, 261, 263, 485, 516, 519
Radiation, 385, 563–565
Radioactive, 604
Radiologist, 435
Ralph Nader's Public Citizen, 422
Rape, 360–361, HB22
Rapid eye movement (REM), 258
Rattlesnake, 485, 486
Reactions
  bodily, chemical, 183
  drug, 183
  time, 12
Reactivity, 593
Reasoning, and adolescence, 394
Recall, 422
Receptors, 54, 63, 69, 249
Recessive gene, 378, 379–380, 384
Recognition, need for, 83
Recommended Dietary Allowances (RDA), 155
Recreation, and safety, 472–474
Recuperation, 14
Recycling, solid waste, 592
Red blood cells, 313–314, 317
Red bone marrow, 271–272, 314, 315
Red corpuscles, 271–272
Reflex (action), 257
Reflex arc, 257
Reflexes, and brain, 253
Refreezing, 346
Refrigeration, 344–345
Refusal skills, 238

Sphincter muscle, 332, 339–340
Sphygmomanometer, 313
Spinal column, 259, 308
Spinal cord, 250–255, 259, 262–266
Spinal meninges, 251
Spinal nerves, 256
Spirochete, 537
Sports, 15, 32, 234, 472–474
Sprains, 30–31, 489. *See also* Injuries
Stabilizers, 173
Stages, of development, 389–391
Stapes, 67
Staphylococcus, 343, 344
Starches, 139, 154, 333, 336
State boards, licensing, 420
State Fish and Game Commission, 612
Sterility, 298–299, 303, 536
Sternum, 308
Steroids, 234, 291
Stethoscope, 313
Stiffness, 12
Stigma, 114
Stillbirth, 537, 539
Stimulants, 182, 225–228, 234, 258
Stomach
    and acidity, 188
    and alcohol, 208
    digestion in the, 333
    disorders of the, 341–342
    and drugs, 182–183, 187, 208
Strabismus, 64
Strain, muscle, 31
Strategies, coping, 119–121
Street drugs, 234, 238
Strength, muscle, 19
Strep throat, 515
Stress
    colds and, 189
    description of, 98–103
    defense mechanisms and, 119–121
    fatigue and, 103–104
    heart disease and, 559
    hypertension and, 550
    managing, 105–106, 108–110,
        119–121
    types of, 99
Stress fracture, 273
Stressor, 99–100, 102
Striated muscle, 275
Stroke, 319, 551–554
Stroke volume, 280
Structure, and family, 356
Strychnine, 230, 234
Sty, 60
Subcutaneous (skin), 39
Sublimation, 120
Sucrose, 141
Sugar
    in American diet, 156–157
    calories and, 170
    in carbohydrates, 139
    diabetes and, 569, 570
    fermentation of, 207
    muscle energy and, 277–279
    names for, 141

reactions to, 173
    tooth decay and, 56
Suicide, 115–117
Sulfa drugs, 180
Sulfur, 605
Sulfur dioxide, 583
Sun
    -blocking agents, 41
    exposure, 33
    protection factor (SPF), 41
    and skin, 40–42
    sunburn, 41–42
    sunscreen, 41
    tanning, 40–41
Supplements, nutrient, 173
Support group, 109–110
Support system, 109
Surgeon, 265, 435
Surgery
    cancer, 564
    cartilage, 31
    coronary bypass, 558
    and health care, 434
    and related careers in, 265
Surgical technologist, certified, 265
Suspensory ligaments, 62
Swallowing, 331, 483–485
Sweat glands, 40
Swimming, 472–473
Sympathetic nervous system, 291
Sympathetic system, 256
Sympathomimetic amines, 234
Synapses, 144, 250
Synovial fluid, 272
Synovial membrane, 272, 573
Synthetic (drugs), 239
Syphilis, 515, 537–539
Systems
    circulatory, 13, 307–319
    digestive, 329–346
    endocrine, 285–293
    excretory, 336–337
    muscular, 275–283
    nervous, 12, 246–266
    respiratory, 13, 320–327
    skeletal, 268–274
Systolic pressure, 312

T cells, 523
T 4 lymphocyte cells, 542–543
Talking, guidelines, for expressing
    feelings, 91
Tapeworms, 518
Tar, 197
Target pulse rate, 26–27
Tartar, 56
Taste buds, 54, 330
Tay-Sachs, 382–383, 386
Tear ducts, 60
Tears, 60
Teenagers, and alcohol, 214–220
Teenagers, and marriage, 368–369
Teeth, 53–59, 73, 197
Tel-Med Corporation, 423

Temperature
    body, and fever, 33, 521
    and food poisoning, 345
    and frostbite, 495
    inversion, 584
Temporal lobe, 70, 253, 255
Tendinitis, 31
Tendons, 277
Tennis elbow, 31
Tension, 101
Tertiary care, 433
Testes, 287, 289, 293, 296–297
Testicles, 296
Testicular cancer, 298, 299
Testimonials, for products, 413
Testosterone, 236, 289, 293, 296, 392
Tetanus, 451, 479, 525
Tetany, 290–291
Tetracycline, 180, 536, 541
Tetrahydrocannabinol (THC), 232–234
Thalamus, 255
Therapies, 34, 125–129
Therapist, 128
Therapy programs, 34, 202, 429
Thermal pollution, 603
Thermal trainer, 529
Thiamine, 153
Thinking skills, in adolescence, 393
Third-degree burns, 489–491
Thirst, 82–83
Thoracic surgeon, 435
Thrombosis, 317, 319, 553
Thrombus, 319, 551
Thymus gland, 287, 291, 542
    and lymphocytes, 522
Thyroid gland, 287, 289
Thyroid-stimulating hormone, (TSH),
    289
Thyroxine, 290
Time, and stress, 106
Time-management skills, 106–108
Tinnitus, 72
Tissue
    connective, 31
    definition of, 372
    fatty, 39
    muscle, 277–279
    and frostbite, 33
Titanium dioxide, 41
Tobacco, 195–202
Toeing out, 48
Toenail, ingrown, 47
Tolerance, to drugs, 183
Tongue, 54, 331–332
Toothache, 55
Tooth decay, 342–343
Topical antibiotics, 180
Tornado, 493
Toxic chemicals, in body, 182
Toxic hepatitis, 531
Toxicity, 593
Toxicology, 238
Toxic Substances Control Act, 594, 608
Toxic substances, 594–596
Toxic wastes, 336

Toxins, 343, 515, 525
Toxoids, 525
Trachea, 290, 320–321, 332
Traction, 259
Trade name, of drug, 186
Tradition, 412
Traits, 85
Tranquilizers, 182, 228
Transmission, of pathogen, 519–520
Transplant, kidney, 339
Transportation, and consumer complaints, 425–426
Tree People, 614
Trichinosis, 518
Trichomoniasis, 303–304, 544
Triglycerides, 143
Trihalomethanes (THMS), 447
Trypsin, 335
Tuberculosis, 325, 451, 515, 521
Tubule, 338
Tumor, 561, 562
Turbidity, 591
Twins, 381
Type A and B personalities, 106
Typhoid fever, 528, 591
Typhus fever, 517

Ulcers, 197, 208, 341
Ultrasonography, 384
Ultraviolet rays, 41–42
Umbilical cord, 374
Underweight, 161, 166–167
United Nations, 450
Unit pricing, 155, 411
Universal donor, 315
Universal medical emergency identification, 492
Universal name, 186
Universal recipient, 315
Unsafe act/habit, 460
Unsaturated fat, 144–145
Unstriated muscle, 275
Urea, 336, 338
Uremia, 338
Ureter, 337
Urethra, 297–298, 337, 541
Uric acid, 273, 336
Urination, and infection, 535, 540, 541
Urine, 297–298, 338
Urologist, 435
U.S. Forest Service (USFS), 616
U.S. Department of Agriculture, National Dietary Guidelines, 174
U.S. Postal Service, 421
U.S. Senate Select Committee on Nutrition and Human Needs, 140, 156
U.S. Steel Corporation, 613
Uterine cancer, 305
Uterus, 300–301, 303
Utricle, 68
Uvula, 332
Vaccination, 451–452
Vaccines, 180, 524–526, 531

Vagina, 300–301
Vaginitis, 303, 544
Values, 86
Valves, 309, 311, 558–560
Varicose veins, 317–319
Vascular surgeon, 435
Vascular system, 319
Vas deferens, 297
Vasodilators, 181
Vegetables, 152–154
Veins, 311–312
Venereal disease (VD), 535–544
Venereal Disease Research Laboratory (VDRL), 538
Ventricle, 309–310, 312
Ventricular fibrillation, 553, 555
Venules, 311
Vestibule, 68–69
Veterans Administration, 430
Vibrations, 69, 72
Villi, 334
Violence, 123
Viral hepatitis, 531
Viruses
    and colds, 530
    and digestion, 342
    osteomyelitis, 273
    and STD, 539–543, 544
    types of, 514, 516–517, 521
    and vaccines, 524–525
Vision, 64–65
Visual purple, 63
Vitamins, 137, 149–151, 172
    in carbohydrates, 140
    fat-soluble,
        A, 149, 154, 169, 336
        D, 143, 149, 336
        E, 149, 336
        K, 149–151, 335–336
    water-soluble,
        B complex, 149–151, 169, 335, 336
        C, 149–151, 154, 169
Vitiligo, 44
Vitreous humor, 62
Voice box, 321
Volume (of sound, and deafness), 71
Voluntary muscles, 281
Voluntary response, 100
Vomiting, 170–171, 340, 344–345, 484
Von Beneden, Edouard, 378
Von Nageli, Karl Wilhelm, 378
Voters, and environmental decisions, 608–611

Walking, 26
Warming up, 24–25, 32
Warts, 44, 544
Waste products, from cells, 103, 311
Wastes, and pollution, 590–596
Water
    and nutrients, 137, 147, 152
    in body, 33, 277, 291, 313–314, 336
    and burns, 489

conservation, 606, 611–614
and digestion, 331, 340
filters, 447
for frostbite, 497
government regulations for, 608
pollution, 589–591
power, 603
purity of, 591
as resource, 588
-soluble vitamins, 149
Water moccasin (snake), 485, 486
Water Pollution Control Act, 608
Weather
    and air pollution, 582–587
    -related risks, 32–33
Weber test, 72
Weight, *See also* Eating disorders
    control, 13–14, 26, 161–174, 303
    problems, 415, 416
    training, 25
Wellness. *See also* Health; Fitness
    definition of, 4, 6–8
    and parenthood, 370–372, 385
    and stress, 104–105
Wet dream, 298
Wheat, 152
White blood cells, 313, 315, 317, 522
White corpuscles, 271
Whitehead (acne), 43
White matter, 252, 253
Whole blood, 316
Whooping cough, 451
Willamette River (Oregon), 612
Windchill, 495
Windpipe, 321, 332
Withdrawal (from drugs) 183–184, 218, 228
Womb, 301, 374–375
Wonder drug, 180
Work, and family, 354–355
Workout, 24, 25
World Health Organization (WHO), 450–452, 526
Worry, and fatigue, 103–104
Wounds, 479–483, 486, 487. *See also* Injuries

Xiphoid process, 505
X-linked conditions, 385
X ray, 325, 562–565

Yeast, 207
Yeast infection, 303
Yellow bone marrow, 272
Yellow fever, 528

Zinc oxide, 41
Zoophobia, 89